ENGLISH LEGAL SYSTEM

ENGLISH LEGAL SYSTEM

English Legal System—The Fundamentals

SIXTH EDITION

by
MICHAEL BROMBY
Senior Lecturer in Law,
Truman Bodden Law School of the Cayman Islands; and
Honorary Lecturer in Law,
University of Liverpool

Sweet & Maxwell

Thomson Reuters™

Published in 2025 by Thomson Reuters, trading as Sweet & Maxwell.
(Thomson Reuters is registered in England & Wales, Company No 1679046.
Registered Office and address for service:
5 Canada Square, Canary Wharf, London E14 5AQ.)

For further information on our products and services,
visit *www.sweetandmaxwell.co.uk*

Typeset by Cheshire Typesetting Ltd, Cuddington, Cheshire
Printed and bound by CPI Group (UK) Ltd, Croydon, CR0 4YY

Print ISBN: 978-0-414-12742-5
ProView ISBN: 978-0-414-12747-0
eBook ISBN: 978-0-414-12744-9
Print and ProView ISBN: 978-0-414-12743-2

MIX
Paper | Supporting responsible forestry
FSC® C013604

A CIP catalogue record for this book is available from the British Library

Acknowledgements

Grateful acknowledgement is made for permission to reproduce data/extracts from:

The Incorporated Council of Law Reporting for England and Wales: Law Reports and Weekly Law Reports

Penny Darbyshire, "The lamp that shows that freedom lives—is it worth the candle?" [1991] Crim. L.R. 740–752

Solicitors Regulation Authority: Figure 16 "Qualifying as a solicitor through the SQE" on p.125

TSO: under the Open Government Licence. *See http://www.nationalarchives.gov.uk/doc/open-government-licence/version/3/*

Dedication

For my students, past and present, who have shown interest and enthusiasm (of various levels), and continue to inspire me to teach.

Preface

If the law section of any good bookshop is perused there can be found a number of textbooks that are dedicated to explaining the intricacies of the English legal system. Some are large heavy tomes that take forever and a day to read but provide the reader with an in-depth and highly intellectual view of the system; others aim to explain the basic law but provide little insight into the issues that have arisen or can arise. This textbook aims to be slightly different to those other textbooks as it aims to do "what it says on the tin" (so to speak) and explain the "fundamentals" of the English legal system, whilst also highlighting and addressing the issues that can and do occur. The text is primarily focused towards undergraduate law students but would be of equal interest to those studying A-level law, CILEX, a law module in another discipline, or simply to those who are interested in learning about the English legal system for personal reasons. To aid understanding there is found within each chapter a number of visual aids (flowcharts, graphs and grids, etc.) so that that complex or important information is broken down into a user-friendly format. At the end of each chapter a number of Self Test Questions will be found so that understanding and retention of information can be evaluated.

The law is stated as I believe it to be on 1 May 2025; if there are any errors or omissions then I apologise.

Michael Bromby

Contents

List of Figures

Abbreviations

AJA 1999	Access to Justice Act 1999
AJA 1969	Administration of Justice Act 1969
BA 1976	Bail Act 1976
BPTC	Bar Professional Training Course
CA 2003	Courts Act 2003
CAA 1968	Criminal Appeal Act 1968
CAA 1995	Criminal Appeal Act 1995
CCA 1981	Contempt of Court Act 1981
CCRC	Criminal Complaints Review Commission
CDA 1998	Crime and Disorder Act 1998
CFA	Conditional Fee Agreement (NOT Contingency Fee Agreement)
CILEx	Chartered Institute of Legal Executives
CJA 1988	Criminal Justice Act 1988
CJA 2003	Criminal Justice Act 2003
CJA 2009	Coroners and Justice Act 2009
CJPOA 1991	Criminal Justice and Public Order Act 1991
CLSA 1990	Courts and Legal Services Act 1990
CPIA 1996	Criminal Procedure and Investigations Act 1996
CPQ	CILEX Professional Qualification
CPR	Civil Procedure Rules
CPS	Crown Prosecution Service
CRA 2005	Constitutional Reform Act 2005
CrimPR	Criminal Procedure Rules
ECHR	European Convention on Human Rights and Fundamental Freedoms
ECJ	European Court of Justice (now Court of Justice of the European Communities)
ECtHR	European Court of Human Rights
HCCCJ(A)O 2014	High Court and County Courts Jurisdiction (Amendment) Order 2014
HMSO	Her Majesty's Stationery Office
HRA 1998	Human Rights Act 1998
IA 1978	Interpretation Act 1978
ICLR	Incorporated Council of Law Reporting
IPS	ILEX Professional Standards

JA 1974	Juries Act 1974
JAC	Judicial Appointments Commission
JCPC	Judicial Committee of the Privy Council
JSB	Judicial Studies Board
LASPO 2012	Legal Aid, Sentencing and Punishment of Offenders Act 2012
LPC	Legal Practice Course
LSB	Legal Services Board
LSC	Legal Services Commission
MCA 1980	Magistrates' Court Act 1980
MCSG	Magistrates' Court Sentencing Guidelines
OAPA 1861	Offences against the Person Act 1861
OPSI	Office of Public Sector Information
PACE 1984	Police and Criminal Evidence Act 1984
PCC(S)A 2000	Powers of Criminal Courts (Sentencing) Act 2000
PCD	Professional Conduct Department
PCSC	Police, Crime, Sentencing and Courts
PGDL	Post-Graduate Diploma in Law
POA 1985	Prosecution of Offences Act 1985
POM	Personal Offender Mitigation
PSR	Pre-Sentence Report
QWE	Qualifying Work Experience
SCA 1981	Senior Courts Act 1981
SDT	Solicitors Disciplinary Tribunal
SGC	Sentencing Guidelines Council (now the Sentencing Council)
SQE	Solicitors Qualifying Examination
TA 1968	Theft Act 1968
TCEA 2007	Tribunals, Courts and Enforcement Act 2007
TIC	[Offences] Taken into Consideration
VPS	Victim Personal Statement

Guided Tour

Chapter Overview

Each chapter opens with a bulleted outline of the main concepts and ideas to be covered.

> **Introduction to the English Legal System** **1**
>
> CHAPTER OVERVIEW
>
> In this chapter we will:
>
> - **Consider why the legal system is known as the "English" legal system.**
> - **Identify the main sources of law.**
> - **Discuss the historical development and the differences between common law, equity and legislation.**

Key Extracts

Key extracts are boxed throughout to make them easily identifiable.

> **The principle, therefore, of parliamentary sovereignty means neither more nor less than this, namely that 'Parliament' has the right to make or unmake any law whatever; and further, that no person or body is recognised by the law of England as having a right to override or set aside the legislation of Parliament.**
> **A.V. Dicey, *An Introduction to the Study of the Law of the Constitution* (MacMillan 1885)**
>
> Effectively this means that Parliament has the right to make any law that it so chooses (even if it were completely absurd) and that if Parliament creates a law (no matter how absurd)

Key Cases

All cases are highlighted making your research of the subject easier.

> A further example of an advertisement construed as an offer is the case of Lefkowitz v Great Minneapolis Surplus Stores Inc (1957) 86 N.W. 2d 689. In this case the defendant placed the following advertisement in a newspaper: "Saturday 9 A.M. Sharp 3 Brand New Fur Worth to $100.00. First Come First Served. $1 Each". The claimant saw the advertisement and was the first person to enter the store on the Saturday morning. The store refused to sell him a fur coat, relying on the argument that it only intended to sell the coats to women (although no such restriction appeared in the advertisement).
>
> The Supreme Court of Minnesota held that an advertisement was in fact an *offer*, stating that the advertisement was "clear, definite, and explicit, and left nothing open for negotiation". The words "First Come First Served" are interesting here, as the use of such words reduces the

Over to you boxes

A tool to help you develop your critical thinking abilities, Over to you boxes challenge you to engage with and question the subject.

> **Over to you**
>
> **What role do you think the Inns of Court originally played in the professional life of a barrister and do you think the modern-day role of the Inns has changed much from this?**

Diagrams, charts, etc.

Included throughout, diagrams, charts and grids enable you to grasp complex legal principles with ease.

FIGURE 18 **Route to becoming a barrister**

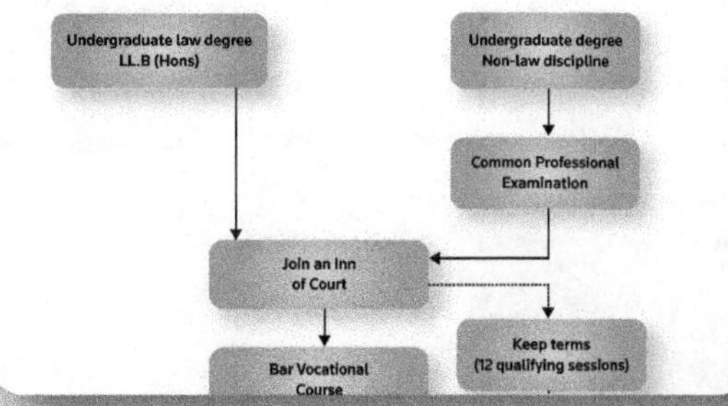

Summary

1. Paralegals are individuals who are either not legally qualified or who are legally qualified but who are working in a non-fee-earning capacity within a legal firm. They are essential to the running of a firm as they undertake a large majority of the work that it would not be cost-effective to require a fee-paid member of staff to do.
2. Legal executives are described as the third limb to the legal profession. They are qualified under, and regulated by, the Chartered Institute of Legal Executives, and

Summary

Each chapter closes with a summary to recap the main points and ensure you haven't missed anything crucial.

Key Cases

Case	Court	Salient point
Earl of Oxford's Case (1616)	Court of Chancery	Where the common law and equity came into conflict then equity is to prevail.
D&C Builders Ltd v Rees [1966]	Court of Appeal	A party who is relying on equitable principles must themselves come to equity with 'clean hands'.
R. (on the application of Jackson) v Att Gen [2005]	House of Lords	The House held the Parliament Act 1949 to be lawful as it only made an administrative change to the Parliament Act 1911 and therefore no major constitutional reform had taken place.

Key cases grids

To help with revision of key cases, here's a handy grid with salient points to remember.

Further Reading

C. Barnett, "Justices' clerks" [2006] 62(5) *Magistrate* 135.
Considers the role of justices' clerks and expresses concern at the dramatic decline in their numbers.

I. Dennis, "Judging magistrates" [2001] Crim. L.R. 71–72.
Home Office and LCD report on Judiciary in the Magistrates' Courts including workload of lay and stipendiary magistrates, working methods, surveys of public and professional opinion, costs and comparison with other jurisdictions.

Further Reading

To help you broaden your perspective we provide selected further reading at the end of each chapter.

Self Test Questions

1. The "English legal system" encompasses:
   (a) England
   (b) England and Scotland
   (c) England and Wales
   (d) England, Scotland and Wales
2. Parliamentary sovereignty means that Parliament is:
   (a) supreme to any other law-making body in the UK
   (b) supreme to any other law-making body in Europe
   (c) supreme to any other law-making body in the world
   (d) supreme to any other law-making body in the universe
3. Equity developed due to failings in:

Self Test Questions

Test your knowledge of the topics covered with Self Test Questions at the end of each chapter. You'll find the correct answers in the Appendix.

Table of Cases

Ghaidan v Godin-Mendoza; sub nom. Mendoza v Ghaidan; Ghaidan v Mendoza; Godin-Mendoza v Ghaidan [2004] UKHL 30; [2004] 2 A.C. 557; [2004] 3 W.L.R. 113 2–030, 2–067

Godin-Mendoza v Ghaidan. *See* Ghaidan v Godin-Mendoza

Goode v Martin [2001] EWCA Civ 1899; [2002] 1 W.L.R. 1828; [2002] 1 All E.R. 620 8–018

Hanif v United Kingdom (52999/08); Khan v United Kingdom (61779/08) [2012] 3 Costs L.O. 355; (2012) 55 E.H.R.R. 16 ECtHR 7–011

Heydon's Case, 76 E.R. 637; (1584) 3 Co. Rep. 7 KB 2–053

Hutchinson v United Kingdom (57592/08) (2015) 61 E.H.R.R. 13; 38 B.H.R.C. 67 ECtHR 11–026

Hutton v Esher Urban DC [1974] Ch. 167; [1973] 2 W.L.R. 917; [1973] 2 All E.R. 1123 CA (Civ Div) 2–046

Lane v London Electricity Board [1955] 1 W.L.R. 106; [1955] 1 All E.R. 324 (Note) QBD 2–058

London & North Eastern Railway Co (LNER) v Berriman; sub nom. Berriman v London & North Eastern Railway Co (LNER) [1946] A.C. 278; [1946] 1 All E.R. 255 HL 2–050

London Street Tramways Co Ltd v London CC [1898] A.C. 375 HL 2–009

Marshall v Southampton and South West Hampshire AHA (152/84) EU:C:1986:84; [1986] Q.B. 401; [1986] 2 W.L.R. 780; [1986] 2 All E.R. 584 1–030

Mattison v Hart, 139 E.R. 147; (1854) 14 C.B. 357 CCP 2–051

Maunsell v Olins [1975] A.C. 373; [1974] 3 W.L.R. 835 HL 2–048

Morelle v Wakeling [1955] 2 Q.B. 379; [1955] 2 W.L.R. 672 CA 2–015, 2–016

Moy v Pettman Smith (A Firm) [2005] UKHL 7; [2005] 1 W.L.R. 581; [2005] 1 All E.R. 903 4–036

Muir v Keay (1874–75) L.R. 10 Q.B. 594 QBD 2–060

Murphy v Brentwood DC [1991] 1 A.C. 398; [1990] 3 W.L.R. 414 HL 2–010

OB v Director of the Serious Fraud Office [2012] EWCA Crim 901; [2012] 1 W.L.R. 3188; [2012] 3 All E.R. 1017 2–041

Pepper (Inspector of Taxes) v Hart; sub nom. Pepper v Hart [1993] A.C. 593; [1992] 3 W.L.R. 1032 HL 2–065

Petrovic v Austria (20458/92) (2001) 33 E.H.R.R. 14; 4 B.H.R.C. 232 ECtHR 2–030

Practice Direction (Crown Ct: Guidance to Jurors); sub nom. Consolidated Criminal Practice Direction (Amendment No.4) (Guidance to Jurors) [2004] 1 W.L.R. 665; [2004] 2 Cr. App. R. 1 CA (Crim Div) 7–027, 7–028

Practice Direction (QBD: Justices: Clerk to Court) [2000] 1 W.L.R. 1886; [2000] 4 All E.R. 895 QBD 5–030, 5–031

Practice Direction (Sup Ct: Judgments: Form and Citation); sub nom. Practice Direction (Sup Ct: Form of Judgments, Paragraph Marking and Neutral Citation); Practice Note (Sup Ct: Judgments: Neutral Citation) [2001] 1 W.L.R. 194; [2001] 1 All E.R. 193 Sup Ct 3–017

Table of Statutes

1981 **Senior Courts Act (c.54)** 6–012, 6–032
s.10 6–012
s.28 12–016
s.31(3) 12–037
s.81 9–070
1984 **County Courts Act (c.28)** 8–021
1984 **Police and Criminal Evidence Act (c.60)**
s.37 9–012
s.47 9–061
s.79 9–085
1984 **Public Health (Control of Disease) Act (c.22)** 1–026
1985 **Prosecution of Offences Act (c.23)** 9–013
s.3(2)(a) 9–013
s.10 9–013
1985 **Administration of Justice Act (c.61)** 4–023
1988 **Merchant Shipping Act (c.12)** 1–029
1988 **Criminal Justice Act (c.33)** 9–030, 12–026
s.35 12–005
s.36 12–005
1988 **Legal Aid Act (c.34)** 10–004
1989 **Official Secrets Act (c.6)** 7–016
1989 **Football Spectators Act (c.37)** 1–022
s.1(2) 1–022
(7) 1–022
1989 **Children Act (c.41)** 5–009
1990 **Courts and Legal Services Act (c.41)** 4–007, 4–024, 6–020, 8–006, 10–018
s.1 8–021
(3) 8–021
s.27 4–024
s.58 10–017
(2) 10–017
s.58A 10–018
s.71 6–012
1991 **War Crimes Act (c.13)** 1–020, 2–061
1993 **Judicial Pensions and Retirement Act (c.8)** 6–031
1994 **Criminal Justice and Public Order Act (c.33)**
s.25 9–063
s.35 9–084
s.51 7–033
1995 **Criminal Appeal Act (c.35)**
Pt 2 12–030
1996 **Police Act (c.16)**
s.89 9–049, 11–011
1996 **Arbitration Act (c.23)** 8–060
s.1 8–060, 8–061
s.33 8–060
s.69 8–061
1996 **Criminal Procedure and Investigations Act (c.25)**
s.54 7–033, 12–012
1998 **Crime and Disorder Act (c.37)** 9–025
s.51 9–040, 9–041, 9–042
s.65 9–025
1998 **Human Rights Act (c.42)** 1–006, 1–034, 2–011, 2–027, 2–028, 2–029, 2–030, 2–067, 6–001, 6–024, 8–018
s.2 1–034, 2–027, 2–028, 2–030
(1) 5–030
s.3 2–027, 2–067, 2–068
(1) 1–006, 8–018
s.4 1–006
s.6 12–036
s.19 1–006
Sch.1 1–033
1998 **Scotland Act (c.46)** 1–003
1998 **Northern Ireland Act (c.47)** 1–003
1999 **European Parliamentary Elections Act (c.1)** 1–020
1999 **Access to Justice Act (c.22)** 4–007, 10–006, 10–007, 10–018, 12–032, 12–035
s.1(1) 10–007
Sch.3 para.5 10–015

Table of Statutory Instruments

Table of International and European Conventions and Legislation

Introduction to the English Legal System

1

CHAPTER OVERVIEW

In this chapter we will:

- **Consider why the legal system is known as the "English" legal system.**
- **Identify the main sources of law.**
- **Discuss the historical development and the differences between common law, equity and legislation.**
- **Explain how primary and secondary legislation differs.**
- **Explain the process that is undertaken in the enactment of legislation.**
- **Consider the relationship between European sources of law and domestic law.**

Summary

Key Cases

Further Reading

Self Test Questions

Introduction

1-001 The English legal system is a wide and varied topic that covers everything from how the courts work through to how to use and interpret the law. The aim of this text is to explain the main principles of this system so that a basic understanding of the fundamentals can be gained. There is little to no black letter-law found between the covers of this book as the substantive law is left to other more suitable topics (such as criminal law and contract law). What will be covered is a consideration of the main driving doctrines and the common procedures found within the justice system as a whole.

A comprehensive understanding of the legal system is vital for everyone coming to the law; be they law students, students studying other disciplines (such as architecture or medicine), or even laypeople who simply have a personal interest in the law. Students often wonder why they have to study the English legal system and it is sometimes perceived as a "non-topic", or not "proper law". However, this perception is dangerously flawed as the law does not occur in a vacuum and therefore it is essential for a comprehensive understanding of the system to be developed at an early stage so that an overall perspective can be gained. It is all well and good learning the academic legal rules as to what constitutes the offence of assault, but it is also necessary to know how an allegation of assault would be dealt with by the justice system; for example, who would prosecute, what court would hear the case, and what would happen if the defendant were convicted. A basic appreciation of the English legal system will provide a student with the necessary foundations so that a clear understanding of the objective and workings of the substantive law can then be achieved.

This text will follow a logical pathway through the main elements of the justice system. It will explain and analyse the processes, and will consider the impact of recent changes to the system, as well as any potential changes that may yet occur. The law is never static but always changing depending on the societal needs of the time.

In this first chapter we will consider the different *sources* of law that can be found within the English legal system.

The Constitution

1-002 The UK, unlike the majority of the civilised world, does not have a written constitution but, rather, it has an unwritten one. A constitution is most commonly described as a system of governance, which details the structure, powers, and duties of the Government and the rights that are to be conferred on the citizens living within the state. The Oxford Concise Dictionary defines the term "constitution" as meaning:

A body of fundamental principles or established precedents according to which a state or organisation is governed.

Essentially, a constitution is constructed of the customs, institutions and laws which have been combined to create the Government and to which all of those who live within the community are required to accede. However, the term "constitution" does not just apply to the Government as any political entity can have a constitution that sets out its fundamental principles, amongst other things.

A constitution is normally a written document that sets out the structure of the Government and the institutions within it. It is a codification of the laws of the land that can be turned to and relied upon by any person who falls under its reach. A codified constitution provides a range of benefits, in that it can be simple to identify and access, as well as being easy to understand by all of those who come to it. The problem, however, with a codified constitution is that it is a rigid and generally inflexible source. If the law needs to be modified to reflect the changes in society then this can be quite difficult to achieve as it would involve amending the original constitution and to do this it means that special procedures must be undertaken, such as the calling of a referendum.

As stated above, the UK does not have a written constitution but, rather, an unwritten one, which is constructed from the wealth of rules that regulate the state. These rules can be found within statute law, case law, custom and conventions. Whilst statute law and case law are indeed in a written format, the content is ever changing and not consolidated in one single place. The UK's constitution is entrenched in the fabric of the country's historical development and, although it cannot be identified easily, it is an accepted form of governance. A problem that comes with an unwritten constitution is that it can often be difficult to find the principle that is being relied upon as the legal and democratic make-up of the country has developed in a rather piecemeal fashion over a prolonged period of time. The benefits, however, are that the rules of law are flexible and can be remoulded so as to develop in a way that matches the development of society. If a problem occurs that cannot be dealt with by the law as it is at that time then new legislation can be drafted so as to quickly combat the problem. This flexibility is generally heralded as a positive benefit; however, this positive can easily be turned into a negative due to the fact that the law can be changed rapidly and therefore often without due consideration as to the ramifications of the amendments.

Why the "English" Legal System?

The "British Isles", the "United Kingdom", or "Great Britain"; all of these names are used to **1–003** refer to the territory of which England is a part, so why, therefore, is the legal system referred to as the "English" legal system and not the "United Kingdom" legal system or the legal system of "Great Britain"? Each of these jurisdiction titles (which are used interchangeably and often not very accurately) actually denote a different composition of the variety of countries and islands that could potentially be included as part of that jurisdiction.

Over to you

Make a list of the countries/islands that you would include under the following headings:

- **British Isles**
- **UK**
- **Great Britain**

It is suggested that the main countries and islands contained within each list would be England, Wales, Scotland and Ireland (with the latter possibly being split down further into Northern Ireland and the Republic of Ireland). The above nomenclatures do generally involve these listed countries, but each one also has its own individual membership of a myriad of other islands found within the "British" state.

For instance, the term "Great Britain" is taken to include England, Wales, Scotland and the outlying islands of Orkney, Shetland and the Hebrides. The title "United Kingdom" covers Great Britain (so England, Wales, Scotland, Orkney, Shetland and the Hebrides) *and* Northern Ireland. The "British Isles" is a composition of the UK, the Channel Islands (Jersey, Guernsey, Alderney, Sark) and the Isle of Man. Ireland, or, more correctly, the Republic of Ireland, is a separate jurisdiction all together, yet within the British Isles.

As there are so many different combinations of these geographical locations it would be difficult (if not next to impossible) to bring all of the individual territories together underneath one single umbrella of a legal system. As a result, the British Isles is split into a number of separate legal jurisdictions: England and Wales, Scotland, Northern Ireland, and the Channel Islands. Originally England, Wales, Scotland and Northern Ireland had their own individual legal systems but in the 15th century, under the rule of Henry VII, the legal jurisdiction of Wales was absorbed into that of England's so that one unified jurisdiction was created (and this is to what the term the "English legal system" relates). Scotland and Northern Ireland were viewed as having separate jurisdictions and remained largely independent but could not create primary legislation and were subject to the laws made by the English Parliament.

In 1998 both Scotland and Northern Ireland were granted powers (under the Scotland Act 1998 and the Northern Ireland Act 1998, respectively) to create legislation that was applicable only in those distinct jurisdictions. The Scotland Act 2012 and 2016 has made a number of further adjustments to the boundary of devolved responsibilities and provides Scotland with an even greater level of fiscal autonomy. Wales is also becoming more independent due to the devolution of powers and the creation of the Welsh Government and Welsh Parliament, which has, since 2007, been permitted to enact a degree of primary legislation. However, it is likely to be a long time before Wales is viewed as a legal jurisdiction in its own right and so, for the foreseeable future, the term the "English legal system" will be taken to cover both England and Wales.

Beyond the British Isles, the English Legal System and common law principles are applied to the British Overseas Territories, of which there are 14 albeit some are uninhabited. These territories do not form part of the UK, but the UK Government does have various responsibilities to oversee good governance, defence and maintains foreign relations on behalf of the territories. They are indeed separate legal jurisdictions, but operate in a very similar way to England and Wales. To a lesser extent, the Commonwealth Realms, of which there are now 15 since Barbados gained independence in 2021, are also derived from English common law, but their legal systems have now diverged from English law in various ways.

Who Makes the Law?

There are three predominant sources (or makers) of the law within the English legal system, which are: **1-004**

- Parliament;
- the Courts; and
- the Council of Europe.

Prior to the UK's exit from the European Union (EU) (Brexit), there was a fourth source or maker of law which was the legislative, executive and judicial branches of the EU.

Parliament

Parliament is the English legal system's principal law-making body. It consists of the House of Commons, the House of Lords and the monarch. It is responsible for passing the laws that will then govern the lives of everyone who comes within its jurisdiction. One fundamental doctrine of the English legal system is that of Parliamentary sovereignty, which means that Parliament is viewed as supreme (the highest source) in respect of the creation of laws. In 1885 the British jurist and constitutional theorist Albert Dicey stated that: **1-005**

> **The principle, therefore, of parliamentary sovereignty means neither more nor less than this, namely that 'Parliament' has the right to make or unmake any law whatever; and further, that no person or body is recognised by the law of England as having a right to override or set aside the legislation of Parliament.**
>
> **A.V. Dicey, *An Introduction to the Study of the Law of the Constitution* (MacMillan 1885)**

Effectively this means that Parliament has the right to make any law that it so chooses (even if it were completely absurd) and that if Parliament creates a law (no matter how absurd) then those who live within the jurisdiction must abide by it, whether they agree with it or not. Even the courts are not permitted to go against legislation enacted by Parliament and are required to apply and enforce it regardless of individual opinion. The reason it is accepted that Parliament holds this supremacy is because of the fact that Parliament is democratically elected. Every person who lives within the jurisdiction (and who is eligible to vote) has the right to have a say in the constitution of Parliament and, as a result, this allows Parliament to be taken as the superior law-making body in respect of regulating the lives of the citizens who live under its powers. Although Parliament is the principal law-making body there is a degree of limitation to, and regulation of, these powers. If Parliament was to make a law that was wholly unacceptable to the society it served then the individuals responsible could be removed from the position of power through the democratic process. When the composition of Parliament changes, the successors are not bound to retain the laws previously enacted by their predecessors and so the new incumbents could repeal or amend the offending legislation.

1-006 The true extent of the supremacy of Parliament has been challenged over recent decades ever since UK joined the EU in 1973, which culminated in the UK EU membership referendum in 2016 where 51.9% of the voters voted for the UK to leave the EU. The EU has the power to make law that is applicable to all of its Member States and each Member State is then duty bound to follow and apply this law under the terms of its membership of the EU. Therefore, if a law enacted by the EU was considered to be incompatible with UK domestic law then the law made by the EU took priority, but this is no longer the case since Brexit was completed in 2020. The influence of EU law in the future is yet to be seen, so whilst the UK may find it convenient to follow EU law, there is no duty to do so beyond the terms of the Brexit agreement.

Another perceived "blow" to the status of Parliamentary sovereignty has come about due to the enactment of the Human Rights Act 1998 (HRA 1998). The HRA 1998 requires the UK to ensure that its legislation is compatible with the European Convention on Human Rights and Fundamental Freedoms (1950) (ECHR) and if there is an alleged breach of the ECHR then under the HRA 1998 the matter can be dealt with by the domestic courts as opposed to having to resort to the jurisdiction of the European Court of Human Rights (ECtHR) in Strasbourg, which is not to be confused with the Court of Justice of the EU. Britain was one of the initial signatories to the ECHR in 1950 but, at first, being a signatory did not require Britain to set aside any of its domestic laws in preference of the ECHR. Rather, if a citizen of the UK wished to rely upon a Convention right then he was required to take the case to the ECtHR in Strasbourg. In such cases the UK attempted to abide by the ECHR as best it could but if any issues of incompatibility arose (between the ECHR and domestic law) then the matter was resolved outside of the domestic jurisdiction and consequently it did not impinge upon the domestic rule of law.

The implementation of the HRA 1998 changed the way in which the ECHR impacted upon the domestic law. Section 3(1) of the HRA 1998 sets out that:

So far as it is possible to do so, primary legislation and subordinate legislation must be read and given effect in a way which is compatible with the Convention rights.

It can be argued that the requirement to try and interpret domestic legislation in a way that is compatible with the ECHR has further eroded the principle of Parliamentary supremacy as, by attempting to ensure compatibility, the courts may effectively go against the original intentions of Parliament in enacting the legislation, thereby inadvertently proclaiming that the ECHR is in essence superior to domestic law. Even when new legislation is under formulation, Parliament is required (under s.19 of the HRA 1998) to consider whether the legislation is to be compatible with the ECHR and to make a declaration to this effect. However, the HRA 1998 does not declare the ECHR to be supreme and there are a number of safeguards found within it that allow domestic law to take precedence (even if only for a limited time) over Convention rights. Under s.4 of the HRA 1998 the courts are not permitted to overrule domestic law in favour of the ECHR. If an issue of incompatibility does arise the courts are required to apply the domestic law in question and then make a "declaration of incompatibility", from which it is envisaged that Parliament will review the incompatible legislation and make suitable amendments to the law. In respect of the requirement to consider proposed legislation in line with the ECHR, it is not mandatory for new legislation to actually be compatible with the ECHR, rather the requirement is for such considerations to be undertaken (and if it then is deemed as incompatible a declaration must be made to this effect), but it is highly unlikely that new legislation would be enacted if considered incompatible as it would simply be challenged through the courts at a later point in time. The current Government has announced plans to reform the HRA, but this is currently in very early stages and legislation is yet to be introduced.

The Courts

The courts do, after a fashion, make law; not in the way that Parliament does, but rather they can change the ways in which the law is applied (due to their interpretation of the legislation) and they can further develop the law by way of the common law (see "Common Law", below). They are entirely independent of Parliament and the Government, and in some ways they act as a control mechanism to these other powers. **1-007**

THE SEPARATION OF POWERS

In the 18th century the great political philosopher Montesquieu, to describe the method employed by democratic states to govern their affairs, coined the phrase the "separation of powers". Montesquieu's philosophy was that "government should be set up so that no man need be afraid of another", and he considered that the arrangement of a state's administrative system by way of the separation of powers was a method that would help to ensure that this philosophy was achieved on a practical level. **1-008**

The separation of powers model is tripartite in form and it involves the separating of the state into three individual elements: the executive, the legislature, and the judiciary. The executive is comprised of the Government and governmental servants, such as local authorities and the police. The legislature is Parliament (as described above), and the judiciary involves the authority

FIGURE 1 **The separation of power**

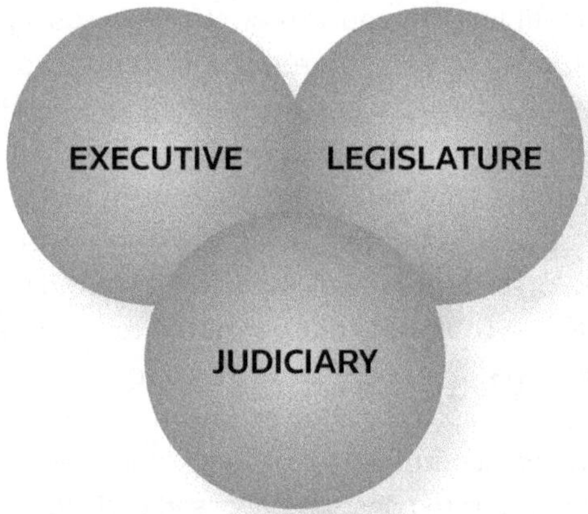

exercised by the judges. Each individual element must work together to ensure that the state functions properly but, as they are all independent of each other, it means that no single part can become too powerful or dominant. The English system is heralded a great success in maintaining a separation of powers but, realistically, there can never be a complete separation as each limb must work closely with each other and there will inevitably be overlap in the responsibilities and duties.

THE RULE OF LAW

1–009 Another fundamental doctrine of the English legal system is that which is known as the rule of law. The principle behind this rule is that no person is above the law. Paine, an 18th-century British revolutionary, summarised this concept when he commented:

> **For as in absolute governments the king is law, so in free countries the law ought to be king; and there ought to be no other.**
>
> **Thomas Paine, *Common Sense* (Philadelphia: W. & T. Bradford, 1776)**

A.V. Dicey also set out three principles, which he felt encompassed this doctrine. These being:

1. the absolute supremacy or predominance of regular law as opposed to the influence of arbitrary power;

2. equality before the law or the equal subjection of all classes to the ordinary law of the land administered by the ordinary courts; and
3. the law of the constitution is a consequence of the rights of individuals as defined and enforced by the courts.

A.V. Dicey, *The Law of the Constitution* (Oxford: OUP, 2013)

Lord Bingham has written extensively, extra curial (this means writings that are not legal judgments but academic writing), on the topic of the rule of law. He identifies eight sub-rules that help to define the scope of principle of the rule of law: **1–010**

1. the law must be accessible and so far as possible intelligible, clear and predictable;
2. questions of legal right and liability should ordinarily be resolved by application of the law and not the exercise of discretion;
3. the laws of the land should apply equally to all;
4. the law must afford adequate protection of fundamental human rights;
5. means must be provided for resolving, without prohibitive cost or inordinate delay, bona fide civil disputes which the parties themselves are unable to resolve;
6. ministers and public officers at all levels must exercise the powers conferred on them reasonably, in good faith, for the purpose of which the powers were conferred and without exceeding the limits of such powers;
7. adjudicative procedures provided by the state should be fair;
8. compliance by the state with its obligations in international law, the law which whether deriving from treaty or international custom and practice governs the conduct of nations.

Lord Bingham, "The Rule of Law" (2007) 66 C.L.J. 67–85.

These principles essentially set out that persons should only be regulated by the settled law; that they should only be punished according to the law; and that everyone, no matter who they are, is subject to the law. No person should be punished or tried arbitrarily, or be punished or tried due to arbitrary laws. The extent to which the modern day English legal system holds true to these principles can be said to be under some doubt, as in recent times (especially in relation to the "war on terror") the law has permitted the authorities to detain individuals for significantly long periods of time without charge (although this has been successfully challenged in **A v Secretary of State for the Home Department** [2004] UKHL 56). The UK has also been forced to apologise for being complicit with America in the practice of extraordinary rendition. Extraordinary rendition occurs when an individual is kidnapped by state representatives and transferred between states, with the aim of his detention being without recourse to the legal system. A number of detainees in Guantanamo Bay are believed to have arrived at that location by way of this procedure and it is often associated with the use of torture and inhuman treatment. Britain has always vehemently denied having any involvement with the practice of extraordinary rendition but on 21 February 2008 the Government had to formally apologise after it was discovered that a number of rendition flights had stopped on UK territory to refuel in 2002.

Sources of Law

FIGURE 2 **Sources of law**

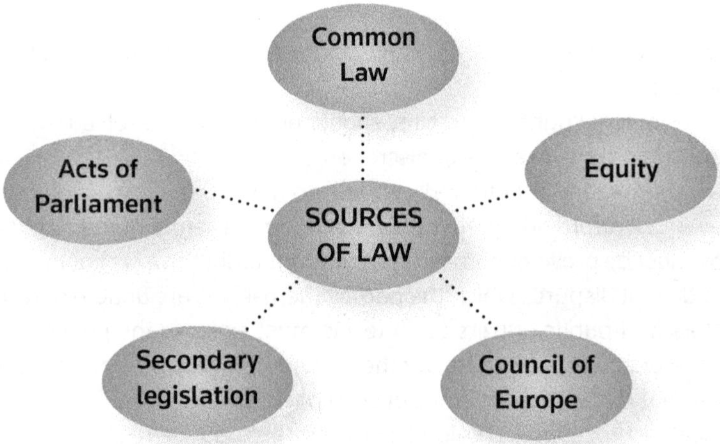

Common Law

1–011 Prior to the Norman Conquest of 1066 there were many different rules of law found all over the country. The law being applied at this point was custom law which varied depending on local customs, for example, in the Midlands area Mercian law was used, whilst in the north Dane law was predominant. William the Conqueror realised that these different systems were difficult to manage and would be a bar to obtaining effective rule over the country as a whole. So as to bring uniformity to the land, William decided to set up a central system of government that would include the justice system. Initially, the King and his representatives travelled the length and breadth of the country to discover the local customs and listen to and resolve the disputes of his subjects. This system of justice became known as the *Curia Regis* (King's Court) and it was the very beginning of the common law system. From the workings of the *Curia Regis* evolved a uniform law that applied to everyone within its jurisdiction; the law was common to everyone and it became known colloquially as the "common law".

Today the common law is still a fundamental principle of the English legal system working alongside the law of equity (see "Equity", below) and legislation created by Parliament. An example of the common law can be seen in the fact that killing someone is a criminal offence. The offence of murder is not found within any statute, but the fact that it a crime is entrenched within the common law by way of the legal treatises "Institutes of the Lawes of England", written by Sir Edward Coke and published between 1628 and 1644, as here it was stated that:

> **Murder is when a [person] . . . unlawfully killeth . . . any reasonable creature *in rerum natura* under the Queen's peace, with malice aforethought . . .**
>
> ***Coke's Institutes* 3 Co Inst 47**

As a result of the development of a uniform justice system the principle of stare decisis arose. This Latin term means that courts must "stand by their decision" and so follow the principles laid down in previous cases. It is from this that the doctrine of binding precedent has developed. This doctrine is where a court may be required to follow a previous decision of another court depending on which court heard the case (see Ch.2, "The Court Hierarchy and Judicial Precedent"). Although this doctrine of binding precedent has many benefits to it (such as consistency in the law) it was originally developed in such a way that the courts could not go against it even if they believed the previous decision to be wrong or that the application of it would end in an unjust result in the case they were dealing with. This meant that the law could not develop in a satisfactory manner and any errors were simply compounded instead of being rectified. This system of inflexibility has been softened over the years and now, in certain circumstances (see Ch.2, "The Court Hierarchy and Judicial Precedent"), a previous decision of the court can be departed from.

Originally, any claim brought under the common law had to be begun by way of a writ **1-012** (a document detailing the basis of the action) and the principle of *ubi remedium ibi ius* applied, meaning that a right only existed if there was the procedure to enforce it. This resulted in cases being dismissed on procedural grounds as if the party bringing the case had failed to fill in the writ correctly or, if the substantive law did not provide for the action, then the matter would be thrown out of court and the party would have to begin the process all over again. This very rigid system has been eroded over time and now the substance of the claim, as opposed to the procedure, is taken to be the most important factor by the court.

Despite there being certain flaws within the common law system it was heralded as an overall success and transported to all the countries within the British Empire, which latterly became known as the Commonwealth of Nations, frequently shortened to the Commonwealth. Even though the British Empire has since been disbanded, these Commonwealth countries (for example Australia, Canada and Hong Kong) still have a common law system in place and largely follow the same principles as the UK (even though the individual laws may be different).

This system can be contrasted with the civil law system found throughout the majority of Europe and associated countries.

Equity

1-013 There is a well-known maxim that is often recited in relation to the concept of equity and that is:

"He who comes to equity must come with clean hands".

Equity is all about the idea of fairness and natural justice. It is often viewed as plugging the gaps and loopholes of the common law so that the strictness of the substantive law does not stand in the way of achieving what is essentially right and just. Equity developed alongside the principles of the common law as a result of the common law's failings and equity originally helped to achieve a suitable outcome where the one provided by the common law was viewed as inappropriate. Initially, the only remedy that was available to an aggrieved party under the common law was damages. Damages could be highly satisfactory in certain cases, for example where the claimant's property had been destroyed or he had been swindled out of some goods or money, but where a claimant had a situation such as the defendant running a brothel next to his house or the defendant's animals constantly eating all of his crops (we are going back many, many years here) a financial remedy would not help to rectify the situation. What the claimant would want in these examples is for the nuisance to stop and not just to be compensated and then have to continue living with the problem.

The state of the law and the limited possibilities of redress resulted in a large volume of claimants being unhappy with the remedy granted. As a result, these disheartened litigants began to petition the King in the hope that he would provide them with a remedy. Initially the King took a personal interest in the plight of his subjects, but as time went on and the volume of petitions increased (at some point during the 15th century) he handed the responsibility of assessing the petitions over to the Lord High Chancellor (whose role later evolved into that of the Lord Chancellor). Due to the high number of referrals, the Lord High Chancellor created a specialist court to deal with such matters and the court was named the Court of Chancery (now the Chancery Division of the High Court). The court was run by the Lord High Chancellor and he would make judgment based on his opinion of the merits of the case put forward by the parties; the participants were truly at the Lord High Chancellor's mercy as there was no hierarchy of case precedence established for this court.

1-014 As the Court of Chancery developed the common law judges became increasingly dissatisfied with the state of affairs, as they viewed the court to be a method of overriding and usurping their authority; if a litigant was unhappy with the remedy provided for by the common law court then he could turn to the Court of Chancery for a more favourable one. This rivalry between the two courts came to a climax in the **Earl of Oxford's Case** (1616) 1 Rep. Ch. 1, where the two courts came into direct conflict. The common law court held that the law dictated one outcome, whilst equity dictated the exact opposite (and the Court of Chancery judges threatened to imprison those concerned unless they acted as directed). The case was referred to the King to rule upon the matter. He held that where there was a conflict between the common law and equity then equity would prevail. Logically this decision was correct as if equity could not prevail over the common law then it would not be able to fulfil its purpose of providing justice where the common law could not.

Although the matter was settled as a principle of law there could still be found a degree of contention between the two court structures and this persisted until equity evolved into a more formalised set of rules and the doctrine of precedent began to have a noticeable impact upon decisions. The Judicature Acts of 1873–1875 succeeded in alleviating the remaining antagonism between the two systems by restructuring the entire court system so that the common law and equity were working together (and could be administered by all courts), as opposed to against each other. Under these Acts all courts are now able to turn to both common law and equitable remedies depending on which is deemed to be the most appropriate in respect of the individual case, although equity will still always prevail where there is a conflict between the two remedies.

EQUITABLE REMEDIES

Over to you

What types of remedies would you class as equitable? Write a list and then consider why you thought each remedy to be equitable.

Equity provides an increased selection of remedies that the court can turn to so as to satisfactorily resolve the specific issues at hand. The remedies that can be found under the rules of equity are: 1–015

- **Injunction**—this requires the defendant to either cease a certain action or, in certain cases, it can require the defendant to *undertake* a certain action (e.g. cease making noise after 11pm, or undertake necessary repairs to a dangerous building).
- **Specific performance**—this requires the defendant to fulfil an obligation that he had agreed to undertake (e.g. completing the building of a new house after there has been a dispute as to payment).
- **Rescission**—this returns the parties to the position they were in prior to a contract being made (e.g. if the contract was to supply goods in return for payment and the payment was withheld, rescission can ensure that the goods (or their value) are returned to the supplier).

The granting of an equitable remedy is a matter of discretion for the courts. A successful claimant will always receive the common law remedy of damages (if appropriate) but the court is required to take into consideration the justness of its actions when considering equitable remedies. For example, even if an equitable remedy would be of great benefit to one party (take the granting of an injunction so as to abate a noise nuisance) but it were to disproportionately disadvantage the other party (so the injunction to stop the noise would detrimentally affect the other party's business) then the court would be unlikely to grant such a remedy. Equity is always about fairness and natural justice and this is in respect of all parties to the matter, not just the party bringing the claim.

MODERN DAY EQUITY

1–016 The court's current approach to equitable matters can be seen in the case of ***D&C Builders Ltd v Rees*** [1966] 2 Q.B. 617. D&C Builders Ltd (a small building firm) had been contracted to undertake building work at the defendant's (the Rees') house. The Rees had already paid D&C Builders part of the monies for the work (£250 out of a £732 total) but then refused to pay the remaining balance due to their decision that the standard and quality of the work was not acceptable. D&C Builders were in serious financial difficulties at this time and were near the point of bankruptcy; the Rees were aware of this fact. The Rees approached D&C Builders and offered £300 in full and final settlement of their bill for the building works. D&C Builders reluctantly accepted this offer. Under contract law the decision to accept such an offer would be held to be the end of the matter but D&C Builders brought proceedings against the Rees to recover the outstanding amount. The Court of Appeal held that the Rees were liable to pay D&C Builders the remainder of the money owed as they had not "come to equity with clean hands"; they were aware of D&C Builders' financial situation and had attempted to take advantage of it. To hold in the Rees' favour would have resulted in an injustice being performed and it was a potential injustice that equity could remedy.

The equitable maxim of "He who comes to equity must come with clean hands" is not the only maxim. There are a number of others such as, "equity is equality", "equity will not suffer a wrong without a remedy" and "he who seeks equity must do equity", etc. Each is an accepted principle of equity and has associated cases that can be used to illustrate its workings.

Legislation

1–017 Legislation is created by Parliament (as discussed above), which consists of the Houses of Parliament (the House of Lords and the House of Commons) and the monarch (currently the King). Legislation is the formal enactment of rules into a document containing the law. Legislation is commonly referred to in one of three ways: legislation, statute or Acts of Parliament. It does not matter which name is used as they all mean the same thing. For legislation to be created it must undergo a lengthy process which aims to ensure its suitability, appropriateness and robustness. Often there will be an identifiable catalyst behind the desire to legislate on a specific issue (e.g. the Coronavirus Act 2020 was enacted in response to the Covid-19 global health pandemic).

Often (but not always) legislation starts out as a consultation paper known as a Green Paper where the initial proposals are set out by government with the purpose of the paper being commented upon by interested parties. After the initial consultation process has taken place the Green Paper will then be formally drafted into a more detailed document called a White Paper, which sets out the clear basis of the intended legislation. This again will be put out for consultation for a set period of time (generally three months) so as to gather further views and recommendations on the proposals.

BILLS

All legislation (whether it went through the consultation process or not) will begin life as a Bill. **1–018**
A Bill can arise from one of three sources, these being:

- public Bills;
- private members' Bills; or
- private Bills.

A public Bill is one that is drafted by Parliament and the intention will be for the proposals to become part of the law of the country and be applicable to society as a whole. Parliamentary legislative draftsmen, whose main occupation is to draft the laws of the country, will draft a public Bill.

A private member's Bill is a draft Bill prepared by a backbench MP and the member will often have a personal reason for proposing the legislation. The member does not have to produce a full version of the draft Bill but rather must provide its short title (what it will be called) and long title (which provides a brief description of what it involves) (see Ch.3, "Referring to Legislation" for a fuller explanation of these terms). A private member's Bill can be introduced into the House of Commons in one of three ways. The first is the ballot, where the member has to enter a ballot and the first seven private member's Bills drawn will then be afforded one day of debating time in the House. A private member's Bill selected by ballot will stand the best chance of becoming law as it will receive a substantial amount of debating time. The second method is known as the 10-minute rule where the member is provided with 10 minutes to outline the idea of the Bill to the House and, although it is unlikely that a Bill will go on to become law through this process, it allows the member to raise awareness of the issues it contains. The final method is by way of a presentation. The member will be allowed briefly to present on the Bill, but the presentation actually involves doing little more than introducing the name of the Bill into the House and, as such, very little else generally results from such a presentation.

A private Bill is one brought by an individual or public body, such as a local authority, with the aim of conferring a specific benefit upon the party, or affording them relief from another law or wrongdoing. If the Bill is enacted into legislation then only the party who has made the application will be subject to its powers. For example, University of London Act 2018 was a private Bill brought before Parliament to modernise the governance arrangements for the university. The provisions of the Act will only cover the University of London and no other university or institution.

Over to you

For a Bill to become legislation it has to pass through a long and quite complicated process. Try to draw a flowchart detailing all of the specific stages you imagine a Bill would need to pass through before successfully being enacted.

THE ENACTMENT OF LEGISLATION

1–019 The process of enacting legislation is anything but straightforward. A Bill will normally be first considered in the House of Commons before potentially being passed through to the House of Lords (although certain legislation can be introduced directly into the House of Lords, as was the Arbitration Act 2025). The House of Lords can then either accept the proposed Bill and pass it on for Royal Assent (a rubber-stamping exercise by the monarch) or reject it and send it back to the House of Commons where the whole process will start all over again. If the House of Lords reject the legislation for a second time then there is the possibility for the Bill to essentially leapfrog the House of Lords and go straight to receiving Royal Assent. More frequently, the upper house may propose amendments which then go back and forth between the two until accepted, in a process known as "ping pong" as recently seen in the passage of the Police, Crime, Sentencing and Courts Act 2022.

The first reading

Calling this first stage a "reading" is really a bit of a deception as the Bill is not actually read in full by the House of Commons at this point but rather the Speaker of the House reads out the short title of the Bill and will set a date for the second reading of the Bill. This stage is simply to alert the members' attention to the existence of the Bill so that they can consider it before the second formal reading.

The second reading

The second reading of a Bill is a very important stage in relation to its viability. It is at this point that the House debates the principles of the Bill and, following the debate, the House will be asked to vote on the Bill. If the Bill receives a favourable vote then there is a good chance that it will eventually make it on to the statute books. The Hansard transcript of the second reading can be interesting, if not lengthy, reading to gain more insights into the contentious issues and policy debates for any Bill. More concise information that supports the

Government's position for its own Bills can be found in the Explanatory Notes that accompany each Government Bill online.

The committee stage

As the House of Commons only has a limited period of time in which to consider the Bill the finer details cannot be given the attention that they require. To address this problem a specific committee will be convened with the purpose of perusing the Bill in minute detail and ensuring that the wording and structure is satisfactory. It is at this point that any issues that came to light during the debate stage (the second reading) can be considered and appropriate amendments can be made.

The report stage

After an in-depth review of the Bill has been conducted by the committee it will then report back to the House of Commons and outline any amendments that it has made. These amendments will then be debated upon and a vote will be taken in respect of each amendment.

The third reading

This is the final stage for a Bill to be considered by the House of Commons on its first (and possibly only) passage through it. The third reading will involve the amended Bill being presented to the House and then it will be opened up for a short debate. By this point all the relevant amendments have been made and so the debate is generally only concerned with the principles of the Bill. The House will then vote upon the acceptance or rejection of the Bill.

The House of Lords

If the House of Commons rejects the Bill then the matter goes no further. If, however, it accepts the Bill then it will be passed up to the House of Lords for further debate and scrutiny. The House of Lords will follow the same three-stage reading process as the House of Commons did. If the House of Lords accepts the Bill then it will be approved and passed to the monarch for Royal Assent. If the House of Lords rejects the Bill then it will be returned to the House of Commons for the whole process to start all over again.

If the House of Lords rejects a Bill on its second consideration then it does not necessarily mean that is the end of the matter as there are certain instances provided for by legislation that mean the House of Lords' approval is not required and the Bill can move straight to receiving Royal Assent.

Prior to the Parliament Acts of 1911 and 1949 proposed legislation required the approval of **1-020** both Houses of Parliament. This requirement of double approval led to a number of Bills being rejected by the House of Lords and never being enacted as the House had the ultimate power to block any legislation with which it disagreed. The 1911 Act removed some of the House of Lords' powers to restrict the development of the law by only permitting it to delay the enactment of legislation for a two-year period before it would automatically receive Royal Assent on the condition that the House of Commons had approved it in three successive sessions.

Where the Bill was a "money bill" (meaning that it concerned matters of taxation) the maximum delay that could be caused by House of Lords was a period of one month before it proceeded on to gain Royal Assent. The 1949 Act further reduced the delay that could be enforced by the House of Lords in respect of general Bills down to one year (as long as it was passed by the House of Commons in two successive sessions).

The Parliament Act 1911 was only used on three occasions and one of those was for the passing of the 1949 Act (which further eroded the House of Lords' powers), and the 1949 Act has since only been used four times to pass the:

- War Crimes Act 1991;
- European Parliamentary Elections Act 1999;
- Sexual Offences (Amendment) Act 2000; and the
- Hunting Act 2004.

After the passing of the controversial Sexual Offences (Amendment) Act 2000 (which lowered the age of consent for male homosexual activity to 16) and the Hunting Act 2004 (which prohibits the hunting of wild mammals with dogs) the validity of the Parliament Act 1949 was challenged by the Countryside Alliance in the case of **R. (on the application of Jackson) v Att Gen** [2005] UKHL 56. The submissions were that as the Parliament Act 1911 was used to amend the law and pass the 1949 Act without the Lords' approval then the later Act was unlawful (or at the very least secondary legislation) as the 1911 Act did not contain the provisions for such an action. The House of Lords (sitting in its judicial capacity) held that the 1949 Act was lawful as although the 1911 Act did not provide for making any major constitutional changes the amendment enacted by the 1949 Act (reducing the delay time down from two years to one year) was effectively only an administrative change and, as there was no major constitutional reform, the law and the decision (the Hunting Act 2004) could stand.

Royal Assent

As stated above the process of receiving Royal Assent is in practical terms only an administrative one. Traditionally the monarch was required to give his or her considered consent to any new legislation before it would come into force. Nowadays, the King must still give his consent to the legislation but this will not be "considered" consent (he may not necessarily sit down and read every proposed Act of Parliament). Consent will never be refused by the monarch and it has been mooted on many an occasion that if the monarch were presented with his or her own death warrant he or she would still be obliged to sign it (although this theory has yet to be tested!). Once legislation receives Royal Assent it is viewed as being immediately in force (and therefore law) unless a later date has been specified for its enactment.

FIGURE 3 **Enactment of legislation**

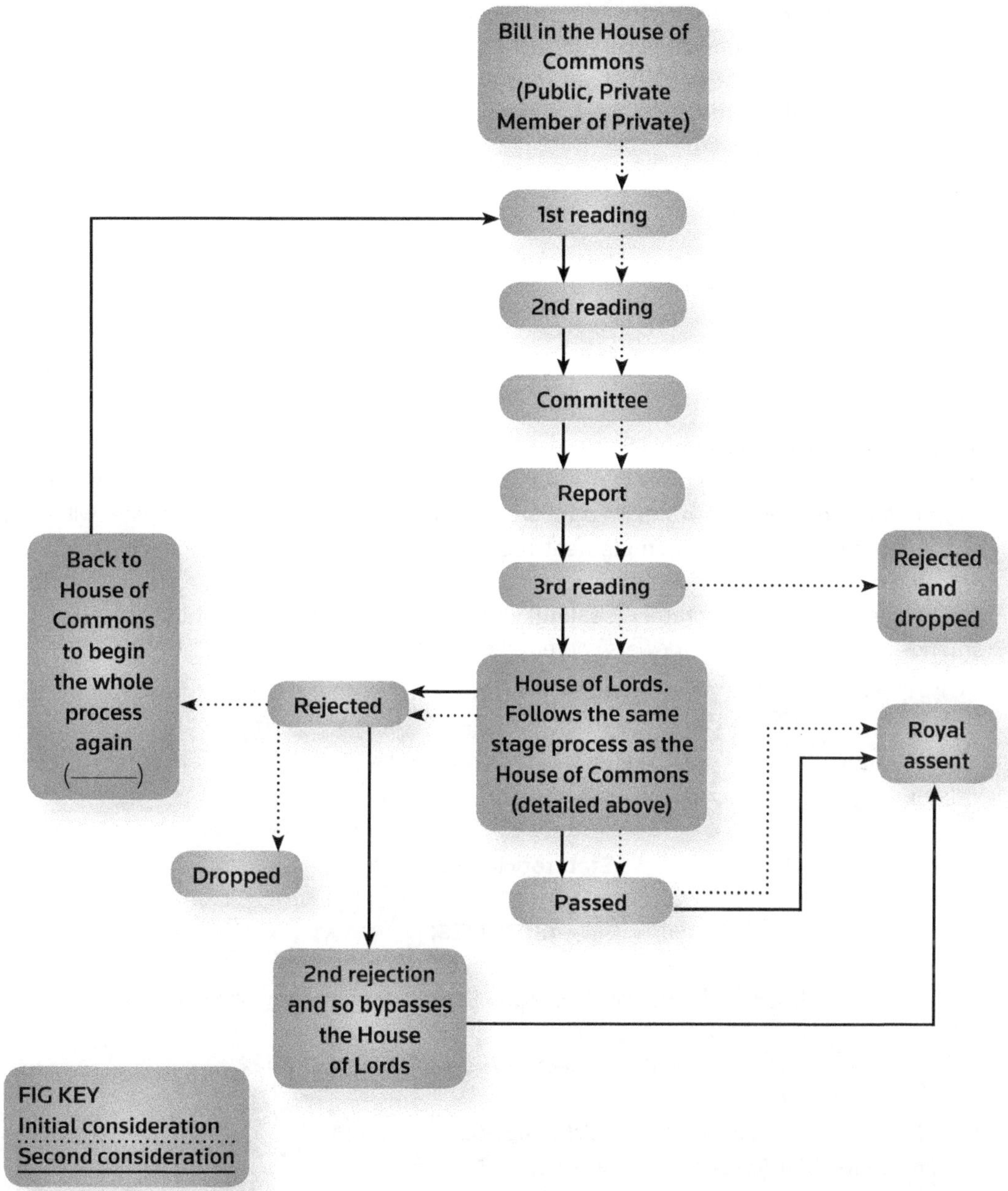

The flow chart at Figure 3 should provide a useful aid in understanding this process (begin by following the dotted line to its logical conclusion before considering the route of the solid line).

Delegated legislation

1-021 Delegated or secondary legislation occurs when Parliament provides a certain body (normally a local authority/government) with the ability to make law. Parliament will pass an Act (described as the "parent Act") that sets out the basis and scope for the particular law and then it will permit the nominated body to flesh out the necessary detail to the framework of the parent Act by producing appropriate delegated legislation.

Delegated legislation can be made in one of three ways:

- statutory instruments;
- byelaws; and
- orders in Council.

STATUTORY INSTRUMENTS

1-022 Parliament can confer the power to make a statutory instrument upon a government department or Minister. Parliament will pass a parent/enabling Act and then the Minister will draft a statutory instrument (SI) to implement the requirements of the enabling Act. The SI will have the same status as an Act and will not be viewed as inferior legislation. An example of an SI is the Footballer Spectators (Seating) Order 2022 (SI 2022/728) (set out below), which amended the exercise of the powers conferred by the Football Spectators Act 1989.

Over to you

What does SI 2022/728 provide? What is its effect?

Statutory Instruments

(2022/728)

Sports Grounds and Sporting Events, England and Wales

The Football Spectators (Seating) Order 2022

Made	***29th June 2022***
Laid before Parliament	***4th July 2022***
Coming into force	***25th July 2022***

The Secretary of State makes the following Order in exercise of the powers conferred by section 11 of the Football Spectators Act 1989(a), having consulted the Sports Grounds Safety Authority in accordance with section 11(4) of that Act.

Citation, commencement and interpretation

1.—(1) This Order may be cited as the Football Spectators (Seating) Order 2022 and shall come into force on 25th July 2022.

(2) This Order extends to England and Wales.

(3) In this Order—

(a) a "seat incorporating a barrier" is a seat that incorporates a barrier into its construction which limits the forward movement of spectators while allowing their lateral movement;

(b) a "seat with an independent barrier" is a seat located directly behind a barrier which does not form part of the seat and which limits the forward movement of spectators while allowing their lateral movement.

Direction

2. The Secretary of State directs the Sports Grounds Safety Authority to include a condition imposing the requirements as respects the seating of spectators at designated football matches specified in Schedule 1 in any licence to admit spectators to the premises specified in Schedule 2.

[...]

Nigel Huddleston
Parliamentary Under Secretary of State

29th June 2022 Department for Digital, Culture, Media and Sport

Schedule 1

Requirements to be Imposed

1. Only seated accommodation is to be provided for spectators at a designated football match, except in areas of the premises where there are seats incorporating a barrier or seats with an independent barrier.

2. Spectators are only to be admitted to watch a designated football match from seated accommodation, except where they are admitted to watch the designated

football match from areas of the premises where there are seats incorporating a barrier or seats with an independent barrier.

Schedule 2

Premises in respect of which a condition imposing requirements as respects the seating of spectators at football matches must be imposed

A. F. C. Bournemouth

Arsenal Football Club

Aston Villa Football Club

Barnsley Football Club

[...]

EXPLANATORY NOTE

(This note is not part of the Order)

This Order directs the Sports Grounds Safety Authority to include in any licence to admit spectators (as defined in section 1(7) of the Football Spectators Act 1989 (c. 37)) to the premises listed in Schedule 2, a condition imposing the requirements specified in Schedule 1 as respects the seating of spectators at designated football matches at those premises. "Designated football matches" are those association football matches designated by the Secretary of State, under powers conferred by section 1(2) of that Act.

This Order replaces conditions as respects the seating of spectators at designated football matches previously imposed in relation to those premises and revokes the Orders listed in Schedule 3. A full impact assessment has not been produced for this instrument as no, or no significant, impact on the private, voluntary or public sectors is foreseen.

This particular SI relates to a requirement for all-seated accommodation in a total of 68 football stadia across England. This is a significant increase from the five listed stadia in the previous SI 2021/1239. The Football Spectators Act 1989, which is the 'parent' Act, confers a power on a government minister to issue such Orders, and indeed many have been made over the years. Historically, the driver for such legislative provisions goes back to the Hillsborough stadium disaster during the 1989 semi-final of the FA Cup in which 97 people died and many more were injured.

BYELAWS

A byelaw is passed by a body such as a local authority, or a public or nationalised body (e.g. British Rail) to regulate certain behaviour under its area or control. For example, section 77 of the Public Health Act 1961 allows a local authority to make byelaws in relation to the cleanliness of premises and the cleanliness of barbers and hairdressers in that local authority area. **1–023**

ORDERS IN COUNCIL

An Order in Council is more formally known as an Order of the Legislative Committee of the Privy Council and, essentially, it is another form of a SI. This method of legislating tends to be reserved for passing the most important pieces of secondary legislation, or it is used as a method to pass legislation in times of emergency. For example, on 14 March 2018 an Order was made by the Privy Council under the Succession to the Crown Act 2013 to allow Prince Henry of Wales (who is better-known as Prince Harry and currently fifth in line for the throne) to marry Rachel Meghan Markle. **1–024**

WHY THE NEED FOR DELEGATED LEGISLATION?

There are a number of benefits for allowing the creation of legislation to be drafted by parties other than Parliament. **1–025**

Speed

It can take a long period of time for a Bill to pass through Parliament and become law (months or even years) and so, if the legislation is required urgently, the Parliamentary process is unable to facilitate this. Other bodies (such as the Privy Council or local authorities) have more time available to deal with such matters so that the legislation can be brought into force at the time that it is needed. Allowing other bodies to pass law also alleviates some of the burden on Parliament, which then permits Parliament to spend more time debating the most important or complex laws.

Knowledge

As byelaws can be passed by the local authority concerned then the relevant authority will have the necessary local knowledge to determine whether such a byelaw is required, and what should be contained within it. The same can be said of the byelaws passed by an organisation such as British Rail. As British Rail's work is primarily concerned with the railway network it is best placed to appreciate what legislation is required to ensure a satisfactory service to the public. Parliament is often too far removed from the situation to determine what is and what is not appropriate.

Flexibility

Appropriate legislation can be created and amended as required depending on the circumstances at the time. Not every possible scenario can be envisaged by Parliament and this allows for the law to change with the unforeseen.

CONTROL IN THE MAKING OF DELEGATED LEGISLATION

1–026 Obviously it would not be ideal if local authorities or MPs were given free rein to create any law they chose as this could result in a small area of the country or a small group of people being subject to draconian laws. Therefore there are procedures in place to stop the power to make legislation being abused.

Parliamentary supervision

Parliament will often require (by way of the parent Act) that any delegated legislation be laid before it for approval before it is brought into force. There are two ways that this can be done; one is by way of affirmative resolution and the other is by way of negative resolution. Affirmative resolution requires the proposed secondary legislation to be put before Parliament so that it can then be voted upon. Negative resolution again requires the draft legislation to be put before Parliament but this time if no opposition to the proposed legislation is raised within a specified period of time (normally 40 days) then the draft legislation becomes law. A "super-affirmative" procedure involves an additional stage of scrutiny, usually for statutory instruments that amend or repeal an Act of Parliament. For an example of an enabling power with a required super-affirmative procedure, see Local Government Act 2000 (c.22), s.9. This provides for greater parliamentary scrutiny and formal statements to be made on the proposed changes. Finally, secondary legislation that would usually be made under the affirmative procedure may need to come into force more quickly in emergency situations. The "made affirmative" or "urgent" procedure allows for secondary legislation to come into force immediately upon signature of the Minister. They must, however, be approved by Parliament within a statutory period of 28 or 40 days. Coronavirus lockdown regulations made under the Public Health (Control of Disease) Act 1984 were made using this procedure.

Committee supervision

There are a number of Parliamentary committees that are charged with scrutinising secondary legislation (i.e. the Joint Committee on Statutory Instruments (reports to both the Commons and the Lords) and the various Delegated Legislation Committees set up for each SI or group of SIs). The committees are primarily there to act as a safeguard and have no independent powers to legislate. The Joint Committee on Statutory Instruments, for example, considers proposed statutory instruments (although it is concerned with the technicalities of the legislation, not its merits) and it will then report back to both Houses as to the practicalities and viability of the proposals.

Judicial control

The judiciary cannot ignore or overrule secondary legislation (as it equally cannot with primary legislation) but a court can undergo a process known as judicial review (see Ch.12, "Judicial Review") to ensure that it is appropriate. If a court concludes that the legislation is not appropriate for its purpose then the court can declare it void by way of finding it to be ultra vires (beyond the powers of the body who enacted it). There are two forms of ultra vires, procedural and substantive. Procedural ultra vires is where it is held that the procedures, as laid out under the parent Act, have not been complied with. Substantive ultra vires is where the secondary legislation goes beyond what was intended by Parliament via enabling Act.

The European Union

The EU and European law as a topic is discussed in detail by numerous textbooks so only a brief overview will be provided here, so that the links between the EU and the English legal system can be identified. The position set out below is reflective of the situation following the cessation of UK membership on 31 January 2020. **1-027**

In 1951, the ECSC Treaty, signed by France, West Germany, the Netherlands, Belgium, Luxembourg and Italy, created the European Coal and Steel Community (ECSC). In the aftermath of the Second World War it was recognised by those nations that such a war should never happen again and, to try and establish a political alliance and help with the regeneration of the countries, the ECSC was born. The ECSC was an agreement to encourage greater co-operation and freedom in the areas of trade and energy. In 1957 the EEC Treaty, which created the European Economic Community (the EEC), was signed by the same six founding states. This body later became the European Community (EC), following the EU Treaty in 1993; this Treaty was also responsible for the creation of the EU. The EC no longer exists after the eventual ratification of the Treaty of Lisbon in 2009 and its member countries are now simply members of the EU. Over the years many countries have joined the EU but the UK is the only country to have left the bloc. It is important to understand some of the basic principles of the EU legal system in order to appreciate the logic behind some UK case law and statutes as these rules remain in force domestically, unless repealed by Parliament or overturned by the courts.

EU LEGISLATION

There is both primary and secondary EU legislation. Primary EU legislation is found within Treaties (as discussed below) and there are four types of secondary legislation, these being: **1-028**

- **Regulations**—similar to UK Acts of Parliament and come into force in all Member States upon enactment.
- **Directives**—set out the objectives intended to be achieved but each Member State then has to enact *specific* legislation to achieve these objectives.

- **Decisions**—addressed to a particular Member State, company or person upon whom they are binding. They do not have wider application.
- **Recommendations (and Opinions)**—strictly not legislation but, although not binding, a recommendation should not be ignored by to whom it is addressed.

THE EFFECT OF THE EU ON DOMESTIC LAW

1–029 The European Communities Act 1972 provided for the law of the EU to be absorbed into domestic law. Section 2(1) of the Act stated:

> **All such rights, powers, liabilities, obligations and restrictions from time to time created or arising by or under the Treaties, and all such remedies and procedures from time to time provided for by or under the Treaties, as in accordance with the Treaties are without further enactment to be given legal effect or used in the United Kingdom shall be recognised and available in law, and be enforced, allowed and followed accordingly.**

Upon being ratified, EU Treaties automatically become part of domestic law and neither the Government nor Parliament need do anything to achieve this. Where domestic law is held to be incompatible with European law the domestic law must be suspended until the matter is remedied. A leading case on this point is the case of **R. v Secretary for Transport Ex p. Factortame Ltd (No.3) (C-221/89)** [1991] 3 All E.R. 769, ECJ, which involved the granting of shipping licences under the Merchant Shipping Act 1988. The European Court of Justice (ECJ) held that the Divisional Court had decided correctly in that a domestic court was entitled to set aside domestic law where it conflicted with European law. It also held that the Merchant Shipping Act 1988 could not stand as it was in breach of the relevant European law. UK domestic law no longer requires to conform to European law, but the decisions made during EU membership will still stand.

1–030 Secondary EU legislation can also have direct effect in that a Member State can be found to be in breach even if the state has failed to take any *positive* action in respect of its implementation. An example of the effect of this automatic application of EU law can be seen in the case of **Marshall v Southampton and South West Hampshire AHA** [1986] 2 All E.R. 584, ECJ. In Marshall, the 62-year-old female appellant was informed by her employers (Southampton Health Authority) that she was required to retire. The domestic law at that time set out that a woman should retire at 60 and a man at 65 and the issue of retirement age did not fall under the remit of the Sex Discrimination Act 1975. However, European law had been passed, namely Directive 1976/207, the Equal Opportunities Directive [1976] OJ L39/40, which addressed the issue of retirement age, and so the appellant took her case to the ECJ alleging a breach of this Directive. The ECJ held that Mrs Marshall should succeed in her case as the UK had not implemented the Directive correctly and she was entitled to use the provision against her employer to stop them forcibly retiring her. Even though the Directive had not been properly transposed into domestic law it was still regarded as being part of the law.

FIGURE 4 **Member States of the European Union**

Austria	Germany	Poland
Belgium	Greece	Portugal
Bulgaria	Hungary	Romania
Croatia	Ireland	Slovakia
Cyprus	Italy	Slovenia
Czech Republic	Latvia	Spain
Denmark	Lithuania	Sweden
Estonia	Luxembourg	
Finland	Malta	
France	Netherlands	

Over to you

What, if any, problems can you envisage following the UK's withdrawal from the EU? What rules do you think the UK may choose to adopt for convenient trade or economic purposes, and what areas of domestic law do you think the UK's legislature and or judiciary will change the most?

THE COURT OF JUSTICE OF THE EUROPEAN COMMUNITIES

As the EU has a large number of Member States who each speak different languages and have different systems of law, confusion can occur as to how the legislation from the EU should be interpreted in a particular Member State. To remedy any such issue a Member State can make a reference to the Court of Justice of the European Communities (CJEU), known as the European Court of Justice (ECJ) prior to the Treaty of Lisbon, under Art.267 of the Treaty on Functioning of the European Union (ex Art.234). 1–031

The CJEU acts in a supervisory capacity in relation to the enactment and interpretation of EU legislation so that the law is interpreted consistently by all Member States. It is mandatory to make such a reference where there can be no further appeal from within the domestic courts, and the lower courts have the discretion to make a reference in certain situations. Once a reference has been made on a certain point no other reference on the same point can be made by any Member State and the decision of the CJEU becomes binding on all Member States.

The Council of Europe

1–032 The effect of the ECHR on domestic law has been described above (see **1–006**) but the organisation that is responsible for the ECHR and why it is so important will now be considered. The Council of Europe introduced the ECHR in 1953. The Council of Europe is a separate entity to that of the EU (even though it is also based in Strasbourg where the EU Parliament is also situated) and it is mainly concerned with the concept of basic human rights, as opposed to political matters. The UK has permitted its citizens to rely upon the rights set out in the Convention since 1966 but, initially, if they wished to do so, they were required to travel to the ECtHR in Strasbourg, as the domestic courts were originally unable to deal with such matters. To become a member of the Council of Europe a state has to ratify (sign) the ECHR and, at present, 46 states (far more than belong to the EU) have done just that and only one state, Russia, has been expelled. There are also a number of states waiting to be permitted to sign the ECHR and be granted membership to the Council of Europe; becoming an ECHR signatory is often seen as a precursor to becoming an EU Member State. However, these waiting countries tend to have human rights issues that need resolving before they will be permitted to sign. There are also six countries that have "observer status" with the Council of Europe. This means that these observers are not signatories to the ECHR, nor are they members of the Council of Europe, but that they have an interest in the work undertaken by the Council and are keen to maintain close links and open lines of communication. The current observer states are: Canada, the Holy See, Israel, the United States, Mexico and Japan.

Over to you

Try and list the 46 Member States of the Council of Europe. Which countries do you think might be waiting for membership, and why?

THE EUROPEAN CONVENTION ON HUMAN RIGHTS

1–033 The ECHR contains a number of basic human rights, each set out in a protocol. They are not absolute and can be qualified in certain circumstances. The brief overview of the main rights is set out in the table below and full details can either be found in the ECHR or in Sch.1 to the HRA 1998.

British Bill of Rights

1–034 Repeal or reform of the current human rights regime has often been debated, frequently with the aim to remove the jurisdiction of the ECtHR in Strasbourg. A Consultation Paper, published in December 2021, Human Rights Act Reform: A Modern Bill of Rights CP588, set out proposals to reform the HRA and establish a British Bill of Rights. The Bill of Rights Bill introduced in June 2022 would have repealed and replaced the Human Rights Act 1998 with sweeping changes that some argued would have lowered the level of protection given to human rights and significantly weakened the ability to enforce these rights through the courts to hold the state accountable for human rights violations. This Bill was scrapped in June 2023 and any imminent change is now seen as unlikely, although future debates will almost certainly take place.

Over to you

What impact, if any, do you think a new British Bill of Rights would have on the level of future litigation, even in settled areas of human rights law? The extent to which human rights law will change and the potential for conflict with the ECHR will only become clear once there is draft legislation published and debates in both Houses of Parliament further refine any proposals before coming into effect.

Law Review and Reform

The law is always changing and often it evolves in reaction to the needs of society. To ensure that the law develops appropriately and remains fit for its purpose there are a number of bodies that review the laws of the land and make recommendations as to how they could be improved and reformed. **1–035**

- **Parliament**—the members of Parliament will review and introduce new legislation (by the methods discussed above) so that the needs of society are met. Changes in legislation will be dependent on the political stance of the government at that time.
- **Judiciary**—the judiciary can, to a certain degree, reform the law through the doctrine of precedent but this is rarely a quick process.
- **Law reform agencies**—such as the Law Commission, which is charged with the objectives of simplifying and codifying the law. The Law Commission writes consultation papers that the Government may then act upon by way of drafting proposed legislation in line with the Law Commission's recommendations.
- **The media**—public outcry can have a significant effect on the direction the development of legislation may take and if there is enough reporting by the media (which allegedly reflects the feelings of the nation) then Parliament (as a democratically elected body) may listen and implement appropriate changes. The enactment of Police, Crime, Sentencing and Courts Act 2022 (which includes mandatory life sentences for the killers of emergency services workers) is evidence of the influence of the media (who refer to this legislation as "Harper's Law" after the death of PC Harper in 2019) upon the law-making process.
- **Academics**—legal academics who specialise in a certain area of law can provide insightful and authoritative commentary on the law. Increasingly, academic writings are being cited in court as authority and are having a perceptible impact upon the development of the law.

FIGURE 5 **Articles of the ECHR**

Article	Title	Details
Art. 2	Right to life	Protects the right of every person to his or her life. Contains exceptions for the cases of lawful executions, and deaths as a result of acting in self-defence.
Art. 3	Prohibition of torture	Prohibits torture, and "inhuman or degrading treatment or punishment". There are no exceptions or limitations on this right.
Art. 4	Prohibition of slavery	Prohibits slavery and forced labour.
Art. 5	Right to liberty and security	Everyone has the right to liberty and security of person. Should only be subject to lawful arrest and detention and should be informed of arrest in a language that is understood and should have access to the judicial system.
Art. 6	Right to a fair trial	Everyone charged with an offence or in determining civil matters has the right to a public hearing before an independent and impartial tribunal within reasonable time. Everyone is presumed innocent until proven guilty.
Art. 7	No punishment without law	Prohibits the retrospective criminalisation of acts and omissions so no person may be punished for an act that was not a criminal offence at the time of its commission.
Art. 8	Right to respect for private and family life	Everyone has a right to respect for one's "private and family life, his home and his correspondence". This is a broad Article in the situations it can cover.
Art. 9	Freedom of thought, religion and conscience	The freedom to change a religion or belief, and to manifest a religion or belief in worship, teaching, practice and observance.
Art. 10	Right to freedom of expression	The freedom to hold opinions, and to receive and impart information and ideas.
Art. 11	Freedom of assembly and association	Protects the right to freedom of assembly and association, including the right to form trade unions.
Art. 12	Right to marry	Provides the right for men and women of marriageable age to marry and establish a family in accordance with domestic laws.
Art. 14	Prohibition of discrimination	Protects against discrimination based on grounds such as sex, race, colour, language, religion, etc. The right is limited in scope only to discrimination with respect to other rights under the Convention.

- **Europe**—at present only the ECtHR has an impact upon law reform in the UK due to the fact that domestic laws need to be compatible with this source. However, following Brexit the EU may continue to have an indirect influence upon the development of UK law.
- **Royal Commissions**—created by the Government to investigate matters of general public concern. Examples of Royal Commission reviews include the Woolf Report (Department of Constitutional Affairs, *Access to Justice Final Report to the Lord Chancellor* (1996) (Woolf Report)—see Ch.8 on the Civil Justice System) and the Auld Review (Lord Chancellor's Department, *A review of the Criminal Courts of England & Wales* (2001) (Auld Review)—see Ch.9 on the Criminal Justice System).
- **Pressure groups**—groups such as the National Society for the Prevention of Cruelty to Children (NSPCC) and Fathers for Justice can also have an impact upon the way in which the Government and Parliament reform the law.

Summary

1. The British constitution is an unwritten one made up from case law, legislation, conventions and custom. This is diametrically opposed to the majority of the civilised world where there are written constitutions that codify laws. An unwritten constitution brings with it certain benefits, such as flexibility.
2. The English legal system holds jurisdiction over both England and Wales. Scotland, Northern Ireland, the Republic of Ireland and the Channel Isles have their own independent legal jurisdictions, as do the Overseas Territories.
3. Parliament is the English legal system's principal law-making body and the law that it enacts is applicable to every person within that jurisdiction. Parliamentary sovereignty means that Parliament's will is supreme, and the sole law-making body for the UK.
4. The courts develop the law through case law and act as a control mechanism to the other limbs of the state administration system; these being the executive and the legislature.
5. The rule of law doctrine ensures that persons should only be regulated by the settled law; that they should only be punished according to the law; and that everyone, no matter who they are, is subject to the law.
6. The common law has developed over time through the system of case law. The principle of stare decisis means that previous decisions of the court have to be followed, helping to ensure that there is consistency in the law.

7. Equity was developed to fill the loopholes in the common law and provide appropriate and effective remedy where the common law could not. The remedies provided under equity can now be utilised by all courts.

8. Legislation is the codification of rules and regulations. The creation of legislation involves a long and complex process, first through the House of Commons and then through the House of Lords. Originally the House of Lords could block any proposed legislation that it opposed but now House of Lords approval can be circumnavigated in certain circumstances. For legislation to be deemed as in force it must first receive Royal Assent.

9. Delegated legislation is statutory law created by a body other than Parliament. Secondary legislation can be created by way of a statutory instrument, byelaw or Order of Council.

10. UK membership of the EU has, historically, impacted upon the supremacy of Parliament. If there was a conflict between European and domestic law, European law took precedence. From 31 January 2020 onwards EU law no longer has any direct impact on UK law.

11. The Council of Europe is responsible for the ECHR. The ECHR sets out the basic rights that are afforded to any citizen of a signatory state. The UK permitted the right to rely on the ECHR in the domestic courts via the introduction of the HRA 1998.

12. Different agencies continuously review the law so as to ensure that appropriate amendments are made and so that the law does not become stagnant and lacking in suitability.

Key Cases

Case	Court	Salient point
Earl of Oxford's Case (1616)	**Court of Chancery**	**Where the common law and equity came into conflict then equity is to prevail.**
D&C Builders Ltd v Rees [1966]	**Court of Appeal**	**A party who is relying on equitable principles must themselves come to equity with 'clean hands'.**
R. (on the application of Jackson) v Att Gen [2005]	**House of Lords**	**The House held the Parliament Act 1949 to be lawful as it only made an administrative change to the Parliament Act 1911 and therefore no major constitutional reform had taken place.**

Further Reading

N.W. Barber, "Against a written constitution" [2008] P.L. Spr, 11–18.

Assesses the implications of the adoption of a written constitution and questions whether such a document would do no more than simply codifying the existing rules.

Lord Bingham, "The rule of law" [2007] 66(1) C.L.J. 67–85.

Discusses the rule of the and the role of the Lord Chancellor.

R. Craig, "Could the Government Advise the Queen to Refuse Royal Assent to a Backbench Bill?" (UK Constitutional Law Association, 2019) *UK Constitutional Law Blog, https://ukconstitutionallaw.org/2019/01/22/robert-craig-could-the-government-advise-the-queen-to-refuse-royal-assent-to-a-backbench-bill/* [Accessed 1 May 2025].

Considers the ceremonial role of the monarch in relation to granting royal assent, specifically in relation to the Brexit legislation.

The Law Society, "Human Rights Act reforms and the Bill of Rights Bill" *https://www.lawsociety.org.uk/topics/human-rights/human-rights-act-reforms* [Accessed 1 May 2025].

Explains the proposals for human rights reform and the responses that were made by the Law Society.

H. Wildbore and F. Klug, "Follow or lead? The Human Rights Act and the European Court of Human Rights" [2010] 6 E.H.R.L.R. 621–630.

Discusses the scope of the duty under the Human Rights Act 1998 s.2 for domestic courts to "take into account" Strasbourg jurisprudence when considering a right under the European Convention on Human Rights 1950.

Self Test Questions

1. The "English legal system" geographically encompasses:
   (a) England
   (b) England and Scotland
   (c) England and Wales
   (d) England, Scotland and Wales
2. Parliamentary sovereignty means that Parliament is:
   (a) supreme to any other law-making body in the UK
   (b) supreme to any other law-making body in Europe
   (c) supreme to any other law-making body in the world
   (d) supreme to any other law-making body in the universe
3. Equity developed due to failings in:
   (a) the civil law system
   (b) legislation

(c) the European Union
(d) the common law

4. If the House of Lords reject a Bill on two successive occasions then:
   (a) the Bill is dropped
   (b) the Bill returns for a third passing through the House of Commons
   (c) the Bill bypasses the need for House of Lords' approval and receives Royal Assent
   (d) the Bill has to be redrafted entirely
5. Delegated legislation is:
   (a) superior to primary legislation
   (b) inferior to primary legislation
   (c) equal to primary legislation
   (d) subordinate to primary legislation

Judicial Reasoning

2

CHAPTER OVERVIEW

In this chapter we will:

- **Explain the concept of precedent.**
- **Discover how precedent works in different courts and how the court hierarchy can affect it.**
- **Consider methods the judiciary use to avoid precedent.**
- **Introduce the concept of statutory interpretation and discuss why interpretation of the law may become an issue.**
- **Explain the different methods of statutory interpretation.**
- **Explain the different aids to statutory interpretation.**

Introduction

2-001 Although Parliament is responsible for the creation of the majority of laws within the English legal system it is the courts and the judiciary who are charged with the interpretation and application of these laws. This interpretation and application needs to be consistent so as to ensure that fairness and justness is achieved for everyone who comes to the law. In this chapter consideration will be given to the methods, such as the principle of precedent, that the courts employ to ensure that this consistency is achieved, and we will also consider the issues that the use of such methods also raise.

The latter part of the chapter will then discuss the different methods of statutory interpretation that can be utilised by the judiciary. The law under consideration in the court may have been drafted over 100 years ago when the draftsmen had no foresight of the way that society would develop (for example, how could a draftsman drafting legislation relating to computer use in the 1960s have ever envisaged the same laws being applied to the use of an iPhone?), or the law may be badly drafted and not clear in its meaning. It is up to the judiciary to interpret these laws in the most appropriate way possible in the existing circumstances and, in doing so, there are a number of techniques and aids they may turn to for assistance.

Do Judges Make Law?

> **[The judge] being sworn to determine, not according to his private sentiments ... not according to his own private judgment, but according to the known laws and customs of the land: not delegated to pronounce a new law, but to maintain and expound the old one.**
>
> **William Blackstone, *Commentaries on the Law of England*, Vol. I (Clarendon Press, 1769) (*Blackstone's Commentaries*)**

2-002 The English jurist and professor, Sir William Blackstone, authored (between 1765–1769) what became known as one of the most authoritative guides to English law. As part of his thoughts on the legal system and the role of the judiciary within the law-making process, he developed the declaratory theory, the basis of which being that the role of the judge is to discover and declare the law, but not to make the law. It could be argued that Blackstone had a very two-dimensional view of the role of the judge and the law, and his theory has been criticised by a number of academic writers (such Ronald Dworkin in *Law's Empire* (Cambridge MA: Harvard University Press, 1986) and David Kairys in *The Politics of Law*, 3rd edn (Basic Books, 1998)) who have submitted that the role of the judge (to declare the law) is not as simplistic as that proposed by Blackstone. If a judge's role were only to state the law as it is written then there would be little need for the judiciary or lawyers, as any layperson could come to the law, read what was there and apply it. The role of judges, it appears, is to *apply* the laws as set out by Parliament, but in doing so they also have the responsibility of moulding and developing the laws of the country, creating legal principles along the way that work together with the statutory provisions of Parliament and which, ultimately, try to follow the ebb and flow of the needs of the society at that specific point in time.

The judiciary are not the primary lawmakers but they do have a significant effect on the law through the methods and doctrines they employ whilst interpreting these laws. There are two key ways in which the judiciary can influence the evolution of the law; these are by the doctrine of precedent and the practice of statutory interpretation.

Precedent

There is a highly entrenched and fundamental doctrine within the English legal system that helps to develop and mould the direction that the law takes. This doctrine is known as judicial precedent and it stems from the principle of stare decisis, which comes from the Latin phrase *stare decisis et non quieta mover*, meaning "stand by decisions and do not move that which is quiet" (stare decisis therefore meaning "stand by the decision"). The doctrine works by requiring judges to follow the decisions that have been made in previous cases, thus ensuring that there is a consistency in the law and that people coming to the law (or their lawyers) will be able to make an educated guess as to the potential success and likely outcome of their case. By being able to refer back to previously decided cases the courts are able to ensure that the law develops in a fair and just manner, and it also means that a great deal of time can be saved as judges do not have to start from scratch but can make reference to what is already there and then use this in their own decision-making processes. **2-003**

One point to note is that the principle of stare decisis differs from that of the principle known as res judicata. Res judicata translates as "the thing has been judged", meaning that the court has already decided the issue between the parties and that the decision should not be changed. For example, if, in a case of disputed paternity arising out of a claim for child maintenance, a court in London has already determined that the man in question is the father of a child and consequently liable to pay maintenance then that man is prevented from reopening the case in another court (e.g. in Bristol) to try and achieve a different and possibly more favourable decision, such as a finding that he is not the child's father and therefore not liable to pay child maintenance. The matter is deemed to have been settled by the London court and, subject to the usual appeal routes, cannot be reheard – it is res judicata. This doctrine is in place to prevent disgruntled litigants attempting to re-litigate on the same point as to allow this would prove unfair and costly to the other party to the case, and would result in the legal system being overwhelmed by already decided cases.

The working effect of the concept of stare decisis is that there are two types of precedent found within the English legal system: one is binding precedent, meaning that it *must* be followed (subject to certain narrow exceptions); and the other is persuasive precedent, which means that the court *may* follow it, depending on whether the previous decision is found to be persuasive in relation to the matter under consideration.

Binding Precedent

2-004 Binding precedent can be found in the ratio decidendi of the case. This Latin term translates as the "reason for the decision" and is often just shortened to ratio. The plural, rationes decidendi, is used where there is more than one ratio in a case. Essentially, the ratio is the reasoning behind why the judge came to the conclusion that they did (see Ch.3, "Identifying the Ratio Deciendi"). The ratio is the binding element of the case and it is the principle of law (based on the facts of the case) that can then be applied in future cases.

The ratio, however, is not just the overall decision in the case. The decision in a case is specific to that individual case and need not be followed in future cases (even if the facts seem identical). The decision is the judgment as to who is successful or as to whether the defendant (in a criminal case) is guilty or innocent. The decision in the case will be of vital importance to the parties involved but will be of little or no interest to the lawyers. Conversely, the ratio of the case will probably be of little or no interest to the parties to the case (they will just care vehemently about the result and how it affects them), but it will be of great interest to the lawyers who acted in the case as well as any lawyer who considers the case at a later date, as it will inform them as to *why* the court made the decision it did and how that decision will then impact upon future cases.

The ratio of a case and its effects can be illustrated by reference to the case of **Donoghue v Stephenson** [1932] A.C. 562, the ratio of which has proved to be highly influential upon the development of the law of torts. In **Donoghue** the plaintiff's friend brought the plantiff a drink of ginger beer, which was in an opaque glass bottle; she poured out half of the drink into a glass and drank it. She then poured out the remainder of the contents of the bottle and, in doing so, out fell a decomposed snail. The plaintiff then claimed to have suffered a stomach upset and emotional trauma as a result. As the plaintiff had not bought the drink herself there was no contractual relationship between her and the vendor so, instead, she brought a claim in tort against the manufacturer of the ginger beer, alleging that it owed her a duty of care. At first instance the case was dismissed but the plaintiff appealed to the House of Lords and Lord Atkin delivered the infamous judgment that contained the now legendary "neighbour principle". Lord Atkin (at page 580) stated:

> **There must be, and is, some general conception of relations giving rise to a duty of care, of which the particular cases found in the books are but instances . . . The rule that you are to love your neighbour becomes in law you must not injure your neighbour; and the lawyer's question: Who is my neighbour? receives a restricted reply. You must take reasonable care to avoid acts or omissions which you can reasonably foresee would be likely to injure your neighbour. Who, then, in law, is my neighbour? The answer seems to be—persons who are so closely and directly affected by my act that I ought reasonably to have them in contemplation as being so affected when I am directing my mind to the acts or omissions that are called in question.**

The overall decision in the case was that the manufacturers were liable to pay the plaintiff damages in respect of the injuries suffered. This is the point that the plaintiff and the defendant (the manufacturer) were primarily concerned with. The ratio of the case however produced a legal principle that dramatically changed the direction of tort law. The ratio propounded by the case of **Donoghue** is that, where an established duty of care does not already exist, a person will owe a duty of care not to injure those who it can reasonably be foreseen would be affected by their acts or omissions. This decision had far-reaching implications; a car driver now owes a duty of care to everyone on the road and all pedestrians; a manufacturer is responsible for ensuring that no harm comes from its goods, and an individual must ensure that he does nothing which could result in the harm of another. **2–005**

Not every case heard by the courts is reported and only those which are published can be relied upon as precedent (Ch.3 explores how cases are reported) as it is impossible to rely upon a case as authority if the material facts and the precise ratio cannot be identified. Further, not every statement of law is to be deemed to be authoritative ratio and there may be principles created by a case that are superfluous to the actual decision but nevertheless become persuasive (but not binding) precedent in their own right.

Persuasive Precedent

Persuasive precedent can come from many sources and it can be just as valuable to the courts as that of binding precedent. The most persuasive precedent is that which is known as obiter dicta. **2–006**

OBITER DICTA

The Latin term obiter dicta (or obiter for short) translates as "things said by the way" and it can be found within the part of the judgment in a case that does not go directly to the ratio. Strictly speaking, there are two types of types of obiter. The first is where a judge in a case makes a statement of law that is not linked to the material facts of the case (thereby not being part of the ratio). Examples of this type of obiter can be found in the discussions of the judiciary when they are considering hypothetical cases or facts whilst bearing in mind the decision in a case. It may be that they state what they would have decided if the facts of the case had been different (so if the facts were X they would have decided Y, but, as the facts are actually A, they must therefore decide B). This type of precedent is not binding but it can be highly persuasive, especially where the hypothetical scenario given is similar to the factual basis of a later case under consideration. **2–007**

The second type of obiter is where a judge discusses the facts of the case and makes a statement as to the law based on those facts but that statement does not become part of the ratio. An example of when this can occur is where there is a dissenting judgment in a case (where a judge does not agree with the decision of the majority in the case and gives his reasons for doing so).

OTHER SOURCES OF PERSUASIVE PRECEDENT

2–008 Persuasive precedent does not have to just come from the judges and there are other sources that can be cited as persuasive that are important to be aware of. The most common sources of persuasive precedent are listed below.

- Obiter dicta.
- A dissenting judgment.
- A minority judgment (where the judge agrees with the overall majority decision but has different reasons for doing so).
- The Privy Council.
- Lower courts.
- Courts from other jurisdictions.
- Academic commentary.
- Law reform agencies.

The Court Hierarchy and Judicial Precedent

Over to you

The court hierarchy determines how much attention should be paid to previous court decisions as the courts higher in the hierarchy are binding upon the lower courts whilst the decisions of lower courts will only be persuasive upon the higher courts.

Draw a chart of where you believe each court sits in the hierarchy in order to ascertain which binds which court. You can check how accurate you were by comparison of your chart to the one found later in this chapter.

The Supreme Court

2–009 The Supreme Court (formerly known as the House of Lords) is the final appellate court in England and Wales. The Supreme Court replaced the Appellate Committee of the House of Lords on 1 October 2009 when judicial authority was transferred to it and away from the House of Lords. The purpose of the Supreme Court's creation was to ensure that the separation of powers (see Ch.1) was effective, as the inception of this final appellate court further ensures that the judicial function of the Appellate Committee is now explicitly separate from both the Government and Parliament. When considering matters of precedent, however, previous House of Lords decisions may still be relevant and applicable. The principles governing how the House of Lords, and now the Supreme Court, decisions should be approached in relation to issues of precedent are explained in detail below; the overarching principle is that the Supreme Court is bound by itself and previous by House of Lords decisions unless the below principles apply. In relation to the lower domestic courts, a Supreme Court or House of Lords decision will bind inferior courts unless the decision has since been overruled or reversed by the European Court of Human Rights.

Until 1966, as established under the principle in **London Street Tramways Co Ltd v London CC** [1898] A.C 375, the House of Lords was strictly bound by its own previous decisions. The rationale behind being so bound was that there had to be a final point where there could be no further litigation brought in a matter. This approach, however, obviously meant that the law could not develop with the changing times as a decision made by the House in the 1800s could still be binding upon it in 2010, even if the reasoning and decision in the case was no longer appropriate; nor could mistakes in the law be rectified. So as to remedy this defect, the House of Lords, in 1966, issued a **Practice Statement** [1966] 1 W.L.R. 1234, which set out that the House of Lords could, in certain circumstances, could depart from a previous decision.

Their Lordships regard the use of precedent as an indispensable foundation upon which to decide what is the law and its application to individual cases. It provides at least some degree of certainty upon which individuals can rely in the conduct of their affairs, as well as a basis for orderly development of legal rules.

Their Lordships nevertheless recognise that too rigid adherence to precedent may lead to injustice in a particular case and also unduly restrict the proper development of the law. They propose, therefore, to modify their present practice and, while treating former decisions of this House as normally binding, to depart from a previous decision when it appears right to do so.

In this connection they will bear in mind the danger of disturbing retrospectively the basis on which contracts, settlements of property, and fiscal arrangements have been entered into and also the special need for certainty as to the criminal law.

This announcement is not intended to affect the use of precedent elsewhere than in this House.

This **Practice Statement** gave the Lords the power to depart from previous decisions where it was deemed "right to do so" and this was to be decided by the Lords on a case-by-case basis. The House did not employ this power until two years after the release of the **Practice Statement** and the first case where it was used was that of **Conway v Rimmer** [1968] A.C. 910, which overruled the earlier House of Lords decision of **Duncan v Cammell Laird & Co Ltd (Discovery)** [1942] A.C. 624. In **Duncan v Cammell Laird & Co** the House had held that the Crown did not need to disclose certain information under the principle of "public interest immunity" due to the fact that the country was at war. The later case of **Conway v Rimmer** occurred in a time of peace and so the reasoning behind the decision in the earlier case of **Duncan v Cammell Laird & Co** was no longer relevant. As a result the House of Lords determined that it was therefore right to depart from the decision in deciding **Conway v Rimmer** and invoked the powers to do so as set out in the Practice Statement.

2–010 The power to depart from a previous decision was used infrequently by the House and there are only a handful of cases where it was been employed. In **Murphy v Brentwood DC** [1991] 1 A.C. 398 the House overruled the previous case of **Anns v Merton LBC** [1978] A.C. 728, holding that a local authority could be liable for not remedying known defects in property before any damage occurred. In the criminal case of **R. v Shivpuri (Pyare)** [1987] A.C. 1 the previous House of Lords decision in the case of **Anderton v Ryan** [1985] 2 All E.R. 355 was departed from, despite it only being made a year earlier. In **Shivpuri**, Lord Bridge, in relation to the use of the **Practice Statement**, stated at [23]:

> **Is it permissible to depart from precedent under the *Practice Statement (Judicial Precedent)* [1966] 1 W.L.R. 1234 notwithstanding the especial need for certainty in the criminal law? The following considerations lead me to answer that question affirmatively. First, I am undeterred by the consideration that the decision in *Anderton v Ryan* was so recent. The *Practice Statement* is an effective abandonment of our pretention to infallibility. If a serious error embodied in a decision of this House has distorted the law, the sooner it is corrected the better. Secondly, I cannot see how, in the very nature of the case, anyone could have acted in reliance on the law as propounded in *Anderton v Ryan* in the belief that he was acting innocently and now find that, after all, he is to be held to have committed a criminal offence.**

In this case the House of Lords set out its reluctance to depart from previous decisions concerning criminal cases due to the need for certainty within the criminal law. However, only a year after the case of **Shivpuri** the Lords were once again faced with the dilemma of whether or not to overrule another criminal case. In the case of **R. v Howe (Michael Anthony)** [1987] A.C. 417 the House was required to consider its previous decision in the case of **DPP for Northern Ireland v Lynch** [1975] 2 W.L.R. 641, which set out that duress could be a defence for murder. The House in **Howe** determined that the case of **Lynch** had been wrongly decided and that, consequently, the development of the law had taken a wrong turn. The House overruled **Lynch** and asserted in **Howe** that duress could never be a defence to murder.

In fact, of the handful of cases where the power to depart from previous decisions was invoked by the House, the majority have been criminal cases. For example, in the case of **R. v G** [2003] UKHL 50 the House held that the longstanding decision in **R. v Caldwell** [1982] A.C. 341 should be departed from due to the unjust results that its principle created. In **Caldwell** it was held that where a person caused criminal damage he would be liable if a reasonable person could have foreseen that such damage would have resulted, even if the defendant did not or could not have seen that possibility themselves. This principle was applied by the courts in criminal damage cases for over 23 years, resulting in decisions such as that of **Elliott v C (A Minor)** [1983] 1 W.L.R. 939. In **Elliott v C** the House, applying the case of **Caldwell**, held that a young girl of 14 years with learning difficulties was liable for criminal damage through burning down a shed, despite her lack of understanding or foresight of the consequences of her actions, because a reasonable person would have foreseen such a result. Obviously, this was not a satisfactory state of affairs as liability was being imposed where the defendant was not morally culpable. When the case of **R. v G** came before the House the opportunity to rectify the situation was seized. **R. v G** involved the conviction and subsequent appeals of two young boys (aged 11 and 12) for the offence of causing criminal damage. The boys had lit a fire in a wheelie bin and, thinking that it would burn itself out, left whilst it was still alight. Unfortunately the fire took hold and caused damage to the surrounding properties that equated to almost a million pounds. The boys were convicted and their initial appeal refused as the court was bound by the case of **Caldwell**. Upon reflection, the House, whilst quashing the boys' convictions, determined that the **Caldwell** principle was wrong and that a person should only be liable if he personally foresaw the possibility of the harm being caused. The House used the powers proscribed by the **Practice Statement** to depart from the earlier binding decision and, in doing so, was able to remedy a longstanding defect in the law.

Despite the use of the Practice Statement in the cases described above (and there are also other examples not considered here), the House was still cautious in respect of using this power, and its reluctance to apply it unless absolutely appropriate was evident in the case of **R. v Kansal (Yash Pal) (No.2)** [2002] 2 A.C. 69. In **Kansal** the House concluded that it had probably got the law wrong in the earlier case of **R. v Lambert** [2002] 2 A.C. 545 but nevertheless applied the law in **Lambert** as the House was of the opinion that the issue under discussion in both cases, and the decision taken in the earlier case (this being that the HRA 1998 would not have retrospective effect on appeals where the original decision in the case had been made before the Act had come into force), would have little long-term effect on the development and application of the law. Overruling the earlier case would simply not have achieved anything in terms of creating worthwhile legal principle, as the matter was one that was likely to not come before the courts again. **2-011**

Overall the House would only depart from previous decision where it was felt it was right to do so and, as there were other methods available to the House to avoid previous precedent, such as distinguishing a case, or rejecting a case due to it being made per incuriam (see **2-015**), or having to depart to ensure compatibility with the HRA 1998, then there was often no need to invoke the **Practice Statement** powers.

Upon inception the Supreme Court did not issue a new Practice Statement but continued to follow the same principles and Practice Statement as the previous House of Lords had done. The adoption of this practice was formalised in the decision of **Austin v Southwark London Borough Council** [2011] 1 A.C. 355, where Lord Hope explained at [25] that:

> **The Supreme Court has not thought it necessary to reissue the Practice Statement as a fresh statement of practice in the court's own name. This is because it has as much effect in this court as it did before the Appellate Committee in the House of Lords. It was part of the established jurisprudence relating to the conduct of appeals in the House of Lords which was transferred to this court. . . .**

Therefore, the Supreme Court is technically bound by its own previous decisions, as well as the decisions of the previous House of Lords, and is only to depart from them where it is right to do so. It is also important to note that despite the House of Lords, as an appellate court, being consigned to the history books its judicial decisions remain perfectly valid and, consequently, the Supreme Court and all the lower courts must ensure that these decisions are still given appropriate weight and consideration.

The Privy Council

2-012 The Judicial Committee of the Privy Council (JCPC) is frequently referred to as simply the Privy Council, which technically is the name of a larger body of several hundred members who formally advise the sovereign on the exercise of the royal prerogative and issues executive instruments, a form of legislation known as Orders in Council. The Judicial Committee, however, is a smaller body of judges with very few domestic responsibilities within the English legal system. They act as the appellate court for the Church of England and hear appeals from the Disciplinary Committee of the Royal College of Veterinary Surgeons, the High Court of Chivalry and other rarely invoked domestic matters.

Predominantly, the Privy Council sits as the final court of appeal for the British Overseas Territories and for some, but not all, Commonwealth countries. Although the judicial composition is primarily the same as the Supreme Court (the same judges sit both in the Supreme Court and in the Privy Council, but the composition may also include senior judges from other commonwealth countries) the Privy Council is not binding upon the domestic courts. It is, however, extremely persuasive upon the courts of England and Wales and the decisions will generally be followed by the Supreme Court and the lower courts (if there is not a binding Supreme Court/House of Lords authority already on that point of law). Obviously if the judiciary were to make a certain decision upon a point of law whilst sitting in the Privy Council it would then be very unlikely for them not to follow it when they later sat in the Supreme Court and heard a case on the same point of law.

The sheer persuasiveness of a decision of the Privy Council can be illustrated by reference to the effect of the Court's decision in the case of **Att Gen for Jersey v Holley** [2005] UKPC 23. Under English law, the House of Lords in **R. v Smith (Morgan)** [2001] 1 A.C. 146 had held that whilst considering the defence to murder of provocation as set out under s.3 of the Homicide

Act 1957 (a defence now repealed by the Coroners and Justice Act 2009 and replaced with a defence of loss of control), it was entitled to take into account the specific personal characteristics of the defendant when determining whether the provocation was such that it would have made the reasonable man lose his self-control and act in the way that the defendant had done. This opened up the possibility of the defence being used in cases where the defendant was suffering from depression or another mental illness (a situation which had already been legislated for under s.2 of the Homicide Act 1957 by way of the defence of diminished responsibility). The same issue then arose again in the case of **Holley** where the defendant was a chronic alcoholic and had killed his girlfriend whilst under the influence of drink. The defendant submitted evidence to the Court that his alcoholism was a disease and so should be taken into account when assessing his level of self-control in relation to the provocation suffered. At first instance the Court disregarded the evidence of his alcoholism, but on appeal it was accepted that the evidence was such that the jury could have taken it into account and consequently his murder conviction was reduced to one of manslaughter. The Att Gen appealed to the Privy Council (on an undertaking that he would not seek to restore the defendant's original conviction), which held, on allowing the appeal, that characteristics such as alcoholism (those which would affect the defendant's level of self-control) should not be attributed to the reasonable man (who the defendant was to be judged by) as Parliament had not legislated for this under the defence of provocation but, rather, the defence of diminished responsibility had been enacted to cover such circumstances. This decision was obviously contrary to that decided by the House of Lords in **Smith** and the Privy Council had refused to follow that decision as it thought it to be wrong in law (the Privy Council is not bound by domestic law).

The question then arose as to whether the Privy Council case was to be binding upon the English courts due the unusual composition of the Court that heard the appeal (nine Law Lords sat on the panel). Professor Ashworth commented on the matter in Ashworth, "Appeal: precedent—Privy Council decision overruling decision of House of Lords" [2005] Crim. L.R. 966: **2-013**

> **Is *Holley* binding on English courts? There may be a purist strain of argument to the effect that it is not, since it concerns another legal system (that of Jersey). However, the reality is that nine Lords of Appeal in Ordinary sat in this case, and that for practical purposes it was intended to be equivalent of a sitting of the House of Lords. It is likely that anyone attempting to argue that *Morgan Smith* is still good law in England and Wales would receive short shrift, and the Court of Appeal in *van Dongen* [2005] 2 Cr. App. R. 632, para.61 assumed, without deciding, that *Holley* now represents English law.**

The Court of Appeal then addressed the issue in the case of **R. v James** [2006] EWCA Crim 14.

Over to you

Read the decision of R. v James [2006] EWCA Crim 14.

What decision did the Court come to in respect of the issue of precedent and why?

2-014 The rules of precedent dictated that the Court of Appeal was bound to follow the decision of the House of Lords in **Smith** but in this particular case it went against the decision of the House and followed the preferred decision of the Privy Council in **Holley**. Lord Phillips of Matravers CJ gave judgment, and, on the point of precedent, he stated (at [42]):

> **The rule that this court must always follow a decision of the House of Lords and, indeed, one of its own decisions rather than a decision of the Privy Council is one that was established at a time when no tribunal other than the House of Lords itself could rule that a previous decision of the House of Lords was no longer good law. Once one postulates that there are circumstances in which a decision of the Judicial Committee of the Privy Council can take precedence over a decision of the House of Lords, it seems to us that this court must be bound in those circumstances to prefer the decision of the Privy Council to the prior decision of the House of Lords. That, so it seems to us, is the position that has been reached in the case of these appeals.**

In essence what the Court of Appeal did in the case of **James** was overrule the House of Lords' decision in **Smith** and state that the Privy Council's judgment in **Holley** should be followed as authority instead. Lord Phillips explained the reasoning behind the Court's decision, stating (at [43]) that:

> (i) All nine of the Lords of Appeal in Ordinary sitting in **Holley's** case agreed in the course of their judgments that the result reached by the majority clarified definitively English law on the issue in question.
> (ii) The majority in **Holley's** case constituted half the Appellate Committee of the House of Lords. We do not know whether there would have been agreement that the result was definitive had the members of the Board divided five/four.
> (iii) In the circumstances, the result of any appeal on the issue to the House of Lords is a foregone conclusion.

It appears that the Court of Appeal took the decision that it did so as to avoid further unnecessary litigation; if the matter could be finalised in the Court of Appeal due to highly persuasive authority then what was the point of the matter progressing to the House where the Law Lords would simply come to the same decision. The Court of Appeal, however, did acknowledge that the circumstances in the case were extremely unusual due to the comprehensive composition of the Court in **Holley** and it appreciated that such a situation would be very unlikely to arise again.

The Court of Appeal—Civil Division

Despite the anomaly discussed above in relation to the cases of **Holley** and **Smith** the Court of Appeal is bound by the Supreme Court (and previous House of Lords decisions) as the Supreme Court is a superior court (as was the House of Lords when it was in existence). The Court of Appeal (both civil and criminal divisions) binds the courts below it in the court hierarchy, and it is normally bound by its own previous decisions, this principle being known as the self-binding rule. **2-015**

There are, however, exceptions to the self-binding rule where the Court of Appeal can depart from a previous decision and these exceptions are set out by Lord Green MR in the case of **Young v Bristol Aeroplane Co Ltd** [1944] K.B. 718. There are three exceptions to the rule.

1. Where there are previous conflicting decisions of the Court of Appeal. In such circumstances the Court may choose to follow whichever authority it deems to be most appropriate. In practice the Court will often follow the latest decision although it is not obliged to. The case that is not followed is then taken to be overruled. It may seem strange that the same Court can create conflicting decisions but it is entirely possible. There are often differently constituted Court of Appeal hearings occurring on the same day and they may end up dealing with the same issue of law but come to differing conclusions.
2. Where a previous Court of Appeal decision conflicts with a later decision of the Supreme Court or House of Lords but that decision has not expressly overruled the Court of Appeal decision. When this occurs the Court of Appeal is obliged to follow the Supreme Court or House of Lords decision under the normal rules of precedent, even if it is not in agreement with the decision.
3. Where the previous decision of the Court of Appeal has been made per incuriam. The Latin term per incuriam translates as "made through lack of care" but this does not just mean that the Court can ignore the decision because it is of the opinion that it was wrongly decided. The term per incuriam has a far more specific meaning than this and how this principle should be approached was set out in the case of **Morelle v Wakeling** [1955] 2 Q.B. 379 (see **2-016**).

In **Morelle v Wakeling** the Court was charged with determining what was meant by the term per incuriam and the conclusion of the Court as to this question was (Per Evershed MR at 406) that: **2-016**

> **As a general rule the only cases in which decisions should be held to have been given per incuriam are those of decisions given in ignorance or forgetfulness of some inconsistent statutory provision or of some authority binding on the court concerned: so that in such cases some part of the decision or some step in the reasoning on which it is based is found, on that account, to be demonstrably wrong.**
>
> **Per Evershed MR at 406**

This principle was extended slightly in later cases, such as **Williams v Fawcett** [1986] Q.B. 604, to cover a situation where there has been a "manifest slip or error" which has had an effect on the liberty of the subject and that the case is unlikely to reach the House of Lords (now the Supreme Court) for the error to be corrected.

Lord Denning MR, as a long-serving Court of Appeal judge, was not enamoured with the self-binding rule imposed on the Court and, in a number of cases (for example, **Gallie v Lee** [1969] 2 Ch. 217, **Broome v Cassell & Co Ltd** [1971] 2 W.L.R. 853 and **Rookes v Barnard** [1964] 1 All E.R. 367), he championed the propositions that the Court of Appeal should be subject to the same **Practice Statement** as the then House of Lords and so be able to depart from its own previous decisions, and that the Court of Appeal should not be strictly bound by the House of Lords, and consequently should be able to declare the House's decisions as per incuriam where appropriate. This debate as to the extent of the self-binding rule continued until the case of **Davis v Johnson** [1979] A.C. 264, where the House of Lords clarified the matter and asserted its authority over the Court of Appeal.

2–017 In the Court of Appeal hearing of **Davis v Johnson** Lord Denning MR directly questioned the appropriateness of the Court of Appeal being strictly bound by the House of Lords and he put forward a voracious argument as to why, in his opinion, this state of affairs was wrong (at 278).

> **On principle, it seems to me that, while this court should regard itself as normally bound by a previous decision of the court, nevertheless it should be at liberty to depart from it if it is convinced that the previous decision was wrong. What is the argument to the contrary? It is said that if an error has been made, this court has no option but to continue the error and leave it to be corrected by the House of Lords. The answer is this: the House of Lords may never have an opportunity to correct the error: and thus it may be perpetuated indefinitely, perhaps for ever. . . . an erroneous decision on a point of law can again be perpetuated for ever. Even if all those objections are put on one side and there is an appeal to the House of Lords, it usually takes 12 months or more for the House of Lords to reach its decision. What then is the position of the lower courts meanwhile? They are in a dilemma. Either they have to apply the erroneous decision of the Court of Appeal, or they have to adjourn all fresh cases to await the decision of the House of Lords. That has often happened. So justice is delayed—and often denied—by the lapse of time before the error is corrected.**

The arguments put forward by Lord Denning MR as to why the Court of Appeal should be allowed to depart from a previous House of Lords decision seem to contain both logic and substance. Lord Denning MR concluded (at 282) that:

> **So I suggest that we are entitled to lay down new guidelines. To my mind, this court should apply similar guidelines to those adopted by the House of Lords in 1966. Whenever it appears to this court that a previous decision was wrong, we should be at liberty to depart from it if we think it right to do so. Normally—in nearly every case of course—we would adhere to it. But in an exceptional case we are at liberty to depart from it.**

When the case was then heard on appeal in the House of Lords, Lord Diplock addressed the issues raised by Lord Denning MR in the lower court and provided a firm answer to the suggestions made. **2–018**

> **[T]he rule as it had been laid down in the *Bristol Aeroplane* case [1944] K.B. 718 had never been questioned thereafter until, following upon the announcement by Lord Gardiner L.C. in 1966 [*Practice Statement (Judicial Precedent)* [1966] 1 W.L.R. 1234] that the House of Lords would feel free in exceptional cases to depart from a previous decision of its own, Lord Denning MR conducted what may be described, I hope without offence, as a one-man crusade with the object of freeing the Court of Appeal from the shackles which the doctrine of stare decisis imposed upon its liberty of decision by the application of the rule laid down in the *Bristol Aeroplane* case to its own previous decisions; or, for that matter, by any decisions of this House itself of which the Court of Appeal disapproved. . . .**
>
> **In my opinion, this House should take this occasion to re-affirm expressly, unequivocably and unanimously that the rule laid down in the *Bristol Aeroplane* case [1944] K.B. 718 as to stare decisis is still binding on the Court of Appeal.**

Lord Diplock effectively shot down in flames the campaign that Lord Denning MR had mounted against the hierarchical nature of precedent within the courts. As the House of Lords could itself rectify any previous error made in law it was of the opinion that the Court of Appeal need not concern itself with correcting such errors, it was an intermediate court and its role was not to correct its superiors but to concentrate on applying the law as it was.

The status of the Court of Appeal in the precedent stakes has not since been queried and the rule that the Court is bound by the Supreme Court or House of Lords and that it is binding on itself stands firm. One does, however, have to wonder whether Lord Denning MR was on to something with his suggestions, as if a case could be dealt with satisfactorily at a lower court level than the House of Lords then surely this could only be of benefit to the justice system as a whole.

The Court of Appeal—Criminal Division

2-019 The Criminal Division of the Court of Appeal is subject to the same rules of precedent as the Civil Division (**Young v Bristol Aeroplane**). However, as the Court is dealing with matters of liberty as opposed to simply civil remedies (which are often financial in nature) the Criminal Division of the Court of Appeal has been slightly more flexible in its interpretation of these rules. In the case of **R. v Taylor** [1950] 2 K.B. 368 at 371, Lord Goddard CJ set out the approach to be taken by the criminal court:

> **This court, however, has to deal with questions involving the liberty of the subject, and if it finds, on reconsideration, that, in the opinion of a full court assembled for that purpose, the law has been either misapplied or misunderstood in a decision which it has previously given, and that, on the strength of that decision, an accused person has been sentenced and imprisoned it is the bounden duty of the court to reconsider the earlier decision with a view to seeing whether that person had been properly convicted.**

The Criminal Division of the Court of Appeal court was not willing to be ruled so strictly due to nature of the cases it heard. This principle of flexibility was reaffirmed in the case of **R. v Simpson (Ian McDonald)** [2004] Q.B. 118, where the Court held that that the rules as to precedent reflected the practice of the courts and were of considerable importance in achieving the appropriate degree of certainty as to the law, but that the rules should not be regarded as so rigid that they could not develop in order to meet contemporary needs. In **Simpson** the Court held that a five-judge constituted court could determine that a previous Court of Appeal (Criminal Division) decision was incorrect and therefore not binding upon it.

The degree of flexibility to be exercised has since been tempered by the Criminal Division of the Court of Appeal decision in **R. v Magro** [2011] Q.B. 398, where the Court held that the discretion extended in Simpson does not entitle the court to disregard a previous decision where it is authority on a distinct and clearly identified point of law reached after full argument and close analysis of the relevant legal provisions. Such a decision is to remain as binding precedent and only the Supreme Court possesses the authority to reconsider the decision upon appeal.

The High Court

2-020 The High Court can be split into two distinct sections, the Divisional Court/Administrative Courts of the High Court, and the High Court Divisions. Within both tiers there are three distinct divisions, each division dealing with a different area of expertise. These divisions are the King's Bench Division, the Family Division and the Chancery Division.

THE ADMINISTRATIVE/DIVISIONAL COURTS OF THE HIGH COURT

The Administrative/Divisional Courts of the High Court are appellate courts that work in a very similar capacity to that of the Court of Appeal but the cases heard stem from the work of the High Court Divisions. As a result, the Administrative/Divisional Courts are bound in the same way as the Court of Appeal; they are bound by all superior courts, they are self-binding and follow the principles established in **Young v Bristol Aeroplane**, and they bind all inferior courts. 2–021

THE HIGH COURT DIVISIONS

The High Court Divisions are predominately first instance courts. All courts superior to it bind each High Court Division and its decisions are binding to all courts below it in the hierarchy. It is not, however, bound by itself. A Chancery Division judge will not be bound by a decision made by a Family Division judge (although it would be a rare occasion for them to be considering the same issue anyway), and a Family Division judge will not be bound by the decision of another Family Division judge. That being said, previous decisions by other High Court judges will be viewed as extremely persuasive due to the concept of judicial comity, which is that a judge will follow previous decisions made by other judges in the Division as a sign of respect and for consistency in the law. 2–022

FIGURE 6 **The High Court**

Administrative Court (appellate court)	**Family Divisional Court (appellate court)**	**Chancery Divisional Court (appellate court)**
King's Bench Division (first instance)	**Family Division (first instance)**	**Chancery Division (first instance)**

Crown Court

As a court of first instance, and one that is towards the bottom of the court hierarchy, the Crown Court is bound by all of the courts above it and it has no binding effect upon itself or on other courts (although the decision of a High Court judge sitting in the Crown will certainly be quite persuasive). The Crown Court is not self-binding and there are three main reasons for this (which also applies equally to the High Court, above). The first being that the Court deals primarily with matters of fact, as opposed to points of law, and therefore each case will be different in respect of its facts. The second being that the court is concerned with the consideration 2–023 of a person's liberty and it would be unjust to apply strict precedent in such circumstances. The third being that the majority of Crown Court cases are not recorded and so it would be nigh on impossible to be bound by a decision that could not be referenced and referred to. However, the limited number of Crown Court cases that are reported can sometimes have a persuasive effect on other courts, depending, of course, on the individual facts of the cases.

Magistrates' Courts and County Courts

2–024 All other courts are superior to these two courts and these courts are viewed as being equally the most inferior courts in the hierarchy. The relevant courts above them bind them and they are not binding on themselves or other courts.

Tribunals

FIGURE 7 **The hierarchy of precedent within the court system**

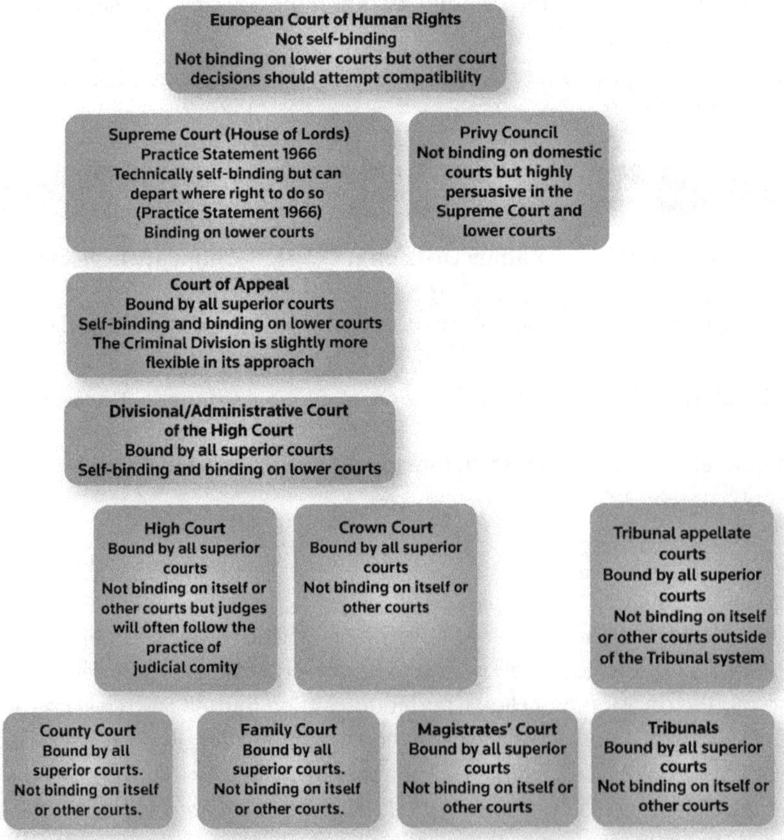

Tribunals are structured in a similar manner to the High Court and follow similar principles on precedent. The upper-tier of the tribunal will bind the lower-tier of the tribunal. There are a variety of different tribunals that specialise in distinct areas of law; for example, there are distinct tribunals to deal with matters of immigration law, of employment law, and of social security law. The upper-tier of a tribunal will only bind its relevant lower-tier counterpart (so the upper-tier of the Immigration and Asylum Tribunal will only bind the lower-tier of the Immigration and Asylum Tribunal and will not bind the lower-tier of the Employment Tribunal). Tribunals are bound by superior court decisions (i.e. the Court of Appeal and the Supreme Court/House of Lords). 2–025

The Court of Justice of the European Communities

The Court of Justice of the European Communities (CJEU) is more commonly referred to as the European Court of Justice, or the ECJ for short. The CJEU is the court responsible for the interpretation of EU law and it is tasked with ensuring that the interpretation of the law is consistent throughout the member EU countries. It is also responsible for settling legal disputes between EU governments and institutions. Within the European Union, the CJEU is supreme; the principles created by the Court in relation to the interpretations of treaties and other EU legislation must be followed by the courts within the legal systems of EU member countries. Prior to Brexit, this was also the case for courts within the English legal system; now, CJEU precedent is merely persuasive on the English courts, rather than binding. The CJEU, however, is not self-binding and can depart from earlier decisions where appropriate. See the discussion in Ch.1 as to the impact of the UK referendum on EU membership in respect of the future reach of the CJEU in respect of domestic courts. 2–026

Precedent and Jurisprudence of the ECtHR

The European Court of Human Rights

As the European Court of Human Rights (ECtHR) is concerned with matters involving an individual's basic human rights it has been, and to a certain degree still is, difficult to instil a set rule of precedent in relation to how the decisions of this European court should be approached by the domestic courts. The introduction of the HRA 1998 had a significant impact upon the doctrine of precedent in this area. 2–027

Section 2 of the HRA 1998 provides that:

> A court or tribunal determining a question which has arisen in connection with a Convention right must take into account any—

(a) judgment, decision, declaration or advisory opinion of the European Court of Human Rights,
(b) opinion of the Commission given in a report adopted under Article 31 of the Convention,
(c) decision of the Commission in connection with Article 26 or 27(2) of the Convention, or
(d) decision of the Committee of Ministers taken under Article 46 of the Convention,

whenever made or given, so far as, in the opinion of the court or tribunal, it is relevant to the proceedings in which that question has arisen.

The UK Parliament is required to try and ensure that domestic legislation is compatible with the provisions of the European Convention on Human Rights (ECHR) so far as is possible (s.3 HRA 1998); if, from the outset, all domestic legislation was compatible with the Convention then the need to bring a case citing a breach would be greatly reduced. However, compatibility is not a mandatory requirement imposed upon all Member States; rather it is a goal to be achieved wherever possible.

Over to you

Read s.2 of the HRA 1998 (above). Does it make the authorities set out in the provision binding upon the domestic courts?

2–028 In understanding how s.2 should be approached by the domestic courts in respect of matters of precedent there are two key points that need to be considered. The first is to contemplate what the phrase "take into account" means; and the second is to determine how the word "must" should be interpreted. Section 2 imposes an obligation upon the courts to take notice of the jurisprudence of the ECtHR; a domestic court cannot simply ignore an authority specified within the section. Does this, therefore, then mean that the domestic courts are bound by those authorities set out in s.2; are they compelled to apply it even where it may not be appropriate to do so?

When the HRA 1998 was being scrutinised by Parliament the incumbent Lord Chancellor, Lord Irvine, opined that insisting the domestic courts were bound by the ECtHR would produce results that would be inconsistent with the very spirit of the ECHR. Lord Irvine stated that:

> **The United Kingdom is not bound in international law to follow that Court's judgments in cases to which the United Kingdom had not been a party, and it would be strange to require courts in the United Kingdom to be bound by such cases.**
> **House of Lords, 583 HL Official Report, 5th Series, col.511 (18 November 1997)**

However, the House of Lords in **R. (on the application of Alconbury) v Secretary of State for the Environment, Transport and the Regions** [2001] UKHL 23 considered the matter and concluded that, although not bound, domestic courts should try to ensure that ECtHR decisions were followed whenever possible. The primary reasoning being so as to prevent a case being unnecessarily referred on the ECtHR for judgment if the matter could have been satisfactorily dealt with by the domestic courts.

The domestic courts have been unable to definitively agree whether or not this means that they are bound by ECtHR decisions. In the case of **R. v (on the application of Ullah) v Secretary of State for the Home Department** [2004] 2 A.C. 323 the House of Lords determined that, although the decisions of the ECtHR were not strictly binding, the courts, in the absence of special circumstances, should not depart from clear and consistent jurisprudence from the European court. In **R. v Horncastle** [2010] 2 A.C. 373 Lord Phillips, in giving the unanimous decision of the court, stated [at 11]:

> **The requirement to "take into account" the Strasbourg jurisprudence will normally result in the domestic court applying principles that are clearly established by the Strasbourg court. There will, however, be rare occasions where the domestic court has concerns as to whether a decision of the Strasbourg court sufficiently appreciates or accommodates particular aspects of our domestic process. In such circumstances it is open to the domestic court to decline to follow the Strasbourg decision. . .**

In **R. (Chester) v Secretary of State for Justice** [2013] 3 W.L.R. 1076, Lord Mance, whilst **2-029**
delivering the unanimous judgment of the Supreme Court, appeared to limit the ability of the domestic courts to depart from a previous decision of the ECtHR, stating, at [27], that:

> **But there are limits to this process, ... It would have then to involve some truly fundamental principle of our law or some most egregious oversight or misunderstanding before it could be appropriate for this court to contemplate an outright refusal to follow Strasbourg authority at the Grand Chamber level.**

In respect of the general doctrine of precedent and the implications of s.2 of the HRA 1998 upon the domestic courts, Lord Mance continued, at [121], to state:

> **In the ordinary use of language, to "take into account" a decision of the European Court of Human Rights means no more than to consider it, which is consistent with rejecting it as wrong. However, this is not an approach that a United Kingdom court can adopt, save in altogether exceptional cases. The courts have for many years interpreted statutes and developed the common law**

so as to achieve consistency between the domestic law of the United Kingdom and its international obligations, so far as they are free to do so. In enacting the Human Rights Act 1998, Parliament must be taken to have been aware that effect would be given to the Act in accordance with this long-standing principle. A decision of the European Court of Human Rights is more than an opinion about the meaning of the Convention. It is an adjudication by the tribunal which the United Kingdom has by Treaty agreed should give definitive rulings on the subject. The courts are therefore bound to treat them as the authoritative expositions of the Convention which the Convention intends them to be, unless it is apparent that it has misunderstood or overlooked some significant feature of English law or practice which may, when properly explained, lead to the decision being reviewed by the Strasbourg court.

This Supreme Court decision can be taken to curtail the discretion of the domestic courts to disregard an ECtHR decision unless that decision is viewed as being fundamentally flawed and open to review due it being made in error in reference to the relevant principles of English law. Although not technically bound it appears that the accepted effect of s.2 of the HRA 1998 is for all English courts, even the Supreme Court, to treat the jurisprudence of the ECtHR as definitive, binding authority.

2–030 This principle of precedent applies to both superior and inferior domestic courts alike. So, for example, if the Court of Appeal is bound by a prior precedent of the Supreme Court (or House of Lords) but deems the decision to be incompatible with the ECHR then the Court of Appeal must follow the Convention provisions and declare the superior domestic court's decision to be bad law.

This is exactly what happened in the leading case of **Ghaidan v Godin-Mendoza** [2002] EWCA Civ 1533. In **Ghaidan v Godin-Mendoza** Mr Mendoza had, from 1972, lived in a flat with his homosexual partner, over which his partner had a protected tenancy. Mr Mendoza's partner died in 2001 and the landlord tried to repossess the flat. The court at first instance granted Mr Mendoza an assured tenancy, which was not as secure as the protected tenancy, as initially Mr Mendoza was not taken to come under the term "surviving spouse" as set out in the Rent Act 1977. Mr Mendoza appealed to the Court of Appeal on the grounds that since he and the original tenant were partners in a longstanding homosexual relationship, the Court was obliged to read the 1977 Act in a way which was compatible with his Convention rights (namely art.8 and art.14), and so he should be treated as the spouse of the original tenant and therefore be granted statutory tenancy. There was ECtHR jurisprudence on this matter (**Petrovic v Austria** (2001) 33 E.H.R.R. 14) stating that such an action amounted to discrimination under the Convention.

The Court of Appeal was bound by the earlier, pre-HRA 1998, House of Lords decision of **Fitzpatrick v Sterling** [2001] A.C. 27, which set out that a homosexual partner cannot be viewed as a surviving spouse but would, rather, be viewed as a member of the deceased person's family. The Court acknowledged that Mr Mendoza would be discriminated against and his Convention rights would be breached if the decision in **Fitzpatrick v Sterling** were applied and so it granted Mr Mendoza statutory tenancy, and held that the words "as his or her wife or husband" in the Rent Act 1977 should be read as meaning "as if they were his or her wife or husband". By doing so the Court of Appeal essentially overruled the House of Lords decision in **Fitzpatrick v Sterling** by invoking the powers provided under s.2 of the HRA 1998, although the Court did not directly state this. The House of Lords then confirmed that the approach adopted by the Court of Appeal was the correct one to take when it approved the Court of Appeal decision in the case (**Godin-Mendoza v Ghaidan** [2004] UKHL 30).

The effect of this is that the lower courts can now overrule the superior court's decisions if the decision is incompatible with Convention rights. This does not however, mean that the hierarchy of precedent has been destroyed but rather that the rule of Parliamentary Supremacy is to be obeyed. The HRA 1998 is domestic legislation and, as such, it will always take precedence over case law (as does any legislation passed by Parliament) and therefore in such a case the lower court will only be enforcing the will of Parliament.

Precedent in Practice

Although the rules of precedent described above may seem to be rigid and inflexible (despite the exceptions and the introduction of the 1966 Practice Statement) there are certain ways in which a court might avoid having to follow a binding precedent. 2-031

Distinguishing

One of the easiest ways to avoid following precedent is to distinguish on its facts the instant case from the binding case. The binding principle of a case is found within the ratio decidendi and this in itself stems from the material facts of the case. If the court can find a distinction between the material facts of the instant case and the material facts of the precedent case then it can distinguish between them and consequently not have to follow the decision that would have otherwise been binding. Every case is unique on its own facts so it may be said that this should be a simple task to achieve, but the court will only employ this method of avoiding precedent when the fact patterns of the two cases are different enough to justify departure from what would normally be binding. 2-032

Overruling

A previous binding decision can be overruled on a point of law by a higher court, which will then remove the precedence of the overruled case. So, if the Court of Appeal decides a point of law (e.g. that it is illegal to wear underwear on a Tuesday) then this will be binding upon all lower courts. However, if the Supreme Court were then to hear a different case but on a similar point 2-033 (that it is illegal to wear underwear at all) and come to the opposite decision (that it is not illegal to wear underwear) then this new decision will overrule the earlier decision of the Court of Appeal (as, if it is not illegal to wear underwear at any time, then, logically, it cannot be illegal to wear it on a Tuesday) and the Court of Appeal decision on the matter will no longer be good law and should not be applied in future cases.

A classic example of this principle at work can be seen in the case of **R. v R** [1992] 1 A.C. 599. In **R. v R** a husband had been charged and convicted of the attempted rape of his wife. He appealed on the basis that the law set out that a husband could not be liable for raping his wife (or attempting to do so). The House of Lords recognised that there was, entrenched in the law since the 1700s, the common law principle that a husband could not be guilty of such an offence, the authority for this stemming from the writings of Sir Matthew Hale in the text *History of the Pleas of the Crown*, 1st edn (1736), vol.1, Ch. 58, p.629 who stated that:

> **. . . [T]he husband cannot be guilty of a rape committed by himself upon his lawful wife, for by their mutual matrimonial consent and contract the wife hath given up herself in this kind unto her husband which she cannot retract.**

It could be argued that this was not the most politically correct or acceptable statement ever to be made but nevertheless it was settled law that a husband had the right to rape his wife without facing criminal liability. The Lords appreciated that this view did not sit well with modern societal views (remember this was only 1992—not that long ago) and therefore they took the decision to overrule the common law and hold that a husband could be held liable for the rape, or attempted rape, of his wife.

Over to you

So what then happens to those people convicted or held liable under the old law when that law is deemed to no longer be good?

2–034 An overruled case, therefore, has what is known as retrospective effect. This means that it is deemed to have never have been law in the first place and that any person who was convicted under that principle should then be able to appeal his conviction. For example, in 1980 Mr X was convicted of manslaughter due to him supplying the victim with a drug, which the victim then self-injected and fatally overdosed on. In 1988 Mr Y was convicted of the same offence and his appeal was rejected, with the case of Mr X being cited as binding precedent. In 2000 Mr Z was then tried and convicted of exactly the same offence but, on appeal, the House of Lords decided that a person cannot be guilty of manslaughter for simply supplying the drug, as the victim decided to take the drug autonomously and was not forced to do so by the defendant. The Court quashed Mr Z's conviction and stated that the principle of law from Mr X's case was overruled and was now to be considered as bad law. What does this then mean for Mr Y? As the effect of the overruling is retrospective it means that Mr Y can now appeal his conviction on the basis that it was decided on an incorrect principle of law.

The English law does not allow, at present, the doctrine of *prospective* overruling (as is favoured in America). Prospective overruling occurs whereby the court will decide to overrule a principle of law in respect of all future cases but that it will still apply the (soon to be bad) principle of law to all cases or transactions that have already commenced by the date of the judgment in question. With the principle of prospective overruling the overruling cannot be relied upon by any settled cases. This may seem very unfair to the defendants in those cases but the principle seems to be mainly applied in money cases, or where there is a business transaction that would result in unjustness occurring in respect of the parties involved if the law were to be changed at that point in time (for example, if the terms of a contract were to be invalidated due to a subsequent change in the law it could be very disadvantageous for a party to that contract). The use of prospective overruling in English law has been mooted as a possibility but it is unlikely that it will ever become an accepted principle of the English legal system.

Precedent can also be overruled by statute law. If Parliament were to enact a new piece of legislation that was at odds with a principle found within the common law then the legislation would take precedence due to the doctrine of Parliamentary supremacy and the case law would therefore become obsolete.

Reversing

As an individual case passes through the appeal process the appellate court may do one of two things; it may either dismiss the appeal, whereby the original decision of the lower court stands, or it can allow the appeal and reverse the decision of the lower court. Reversing means that the decision of the lower court is changed, and this will be done in circumstances where the higher court believes that the lower court interpreted the law incorrectly. By reversing a decision the higher court effectively overrules the lower court's decision and thereby any principle established by the lower court is then to be viewed as bad law. **2-035**

Arguments for and against the Doctrine of Judicial Precedent

FIGURE 8 **Arguments for and against the doctrine of judicial precedent**

Arguments for	Arguments against
Time saving The judge does not have to start from scratch but can consider past precedents to help with the decision.	**Promotes laziness** As a judge only has to refer to previous decisions he does not have to fully consider the matter.
Certainty The law is settled so that a person coming to the law or a lawyer advising on the law can assess the likely outcome of the case based on past decisions.	**Stagnation** The law stagnates as the judiciary can refer to past precedent and need not consider new and innovative ways of dealing with a case.
Justice It would be unfair and unjust for a decision to be taken in one case and then the same set of facts arise again and the opposite decision be taken instead.	**Difficult to remedy mistakes** Any errors in the application of the law can only be remedied if the same issues arise again in a later case that is heard by a higher court.
Consistency Links into certainty and justice. By providing consistency then different courts throughout the jurisdiction will apply the same law.	**Backwards looking** Links into stagnation. Precedent involves looking back at how the law was decided as opposed to looking forward as to how the law should be decided.
Flexibility Precedent allows the courts to develop the law with the changing times and so reliance on Parliament changing the law is not required.	**Unconstitutional** Parliament should be the only law-makers in the country and by being involved in the development of case law in this manner the courts are infringing on the functions of from Parliament.

Statutory Interpretation

As discussed in the previous chapter, Parliament makes legislation. However, once legislation has been passed by Parliament that is not the end of the matter, in fact, it could almost be said to be the beginning as laws are not just made to keep Parliament busy, but are rather designed to be used and relied upon by members of society and the courts, and this is where the real problems start. Historically, Parliament has passed a phenomenal amount of legislation per year, for example, in 2007 it passed 31 Acts of Parliament, in 2006 55 Acts were passed, and in 2013 50 new Acts received Royal Assent; these figures do not include the thousands of statutory instruments that were also created. As so many new laws enter the statute books and because there are statutes that date back so many years it is inevitable that problems will arise as to the meaning of a particular statutory provision and how the law is to be applied. Uncertainty as to the law is a very unsatisfactory state of affairs (in fact, art.7 of the ECHR requires there to be certainty within the law) and uncertainty in law and how to deal with this appropriately is an issue that the courts are continuously required to face. In the remainder of this chapter consideration will be given as to why such uncertainty can arise and the methods the courts use to deal with this, which are known as techniques of statutory interpretation. A quick point to note before considering this matter in detail is the difference between the terms "statutory interpretation" and "statutory construction". Statutory interpretation involves the consideration of what is meant by the word in question; what does it mean? Whereas statutory construction involves the application of the word once it has been defined. Essentially, statutory construction means how should the courts then apply and use that word. **2–036**

Why is there Uncertainty in the Law?

There are a number of reasons as to why uncertainty as to the meaning of the law may arise. **2–037**

AUTOMATIC IMPLICATIONS

Human beings, not robots, draft legislation and therefore legislation has the potential to be as fallible as the draftsman who drafted it. A draft Bill is normally passed through both the House of Commons and the House of Lords, where it is repeatedly scrutinised and any major errors or omissions are usually spotted. However, there may be situations where a specific word is omitted from the statute, as everyone who considered it came to the conclusion that the meaning was implicit. For example, if a statute sets out that "it is illegal for a person with a child or a dog to enter a restaurant" then how would this apply to a person who had with them both a child *and* a dog? The legislation does not expressly say that a person with a child *and* a dog would be committing an offence if he entered the restaurant but it would be implied from its meaning. Where a situation arises that is not expressly legislated for then complications and uncertainty may arise. **2–038**

A BROAD TERM

2-039 Where the word in a statute can be said to have a broad meaning then problems may occur. A draftsman may try and capture a number of possibilities within one statutory provision so that it is all-encompassing, but, by doing so, create uncertainty. Take, for example, a statute that states: "it is an offence to keep any domestic animal within a residential house". What does the term "domestic" mean here? Does it mean any animal that is a common household pet, such as a cat or dog? But, if so, does it then cover animals such as a pig or a llama? Some people keep both of these animals as pets. Or does it mean animals domestic to the UK? What, then, about tropical fish, an iguana or a tarantula? All of these animals are regularly kept as pets within residential homes in the UK, but they are certainly not domestic to the UK. A broad meaning may not provide the level of specific detail actually required.

AMBIGUITY

2-040 A word within the English language can have more than one meaning and it may be difficult to determine which meaning was intended. For example, the word "bear" can mean:

- an animal (a big, grizzly, brown one);
- to carry (a weight either physically or emotionally);
- to support something (the chair could bear her weight);
- to accept or tolerate (you must bear the responsibility);
- to wait or be patient (bear with me);
- to produce (a mother can bear a child, or a tree can bear fruit); or
- to change direction (bear north-east at the big tree).

The meaning given to a word can have a dramatic effect on the overall meaning of a sentence and sometimes it is difficult to identify which meaning was intended by Parliament. In the case of **R. v Allen** (1872) L.R. 1 C.C.R. 367 the word "marry", as found in s.57 of the Offences against the Person Act 1861 (OAPA 1861), was under consideration. An offence under s.57 is committed if a person were "to marry while one's original spouse was still alive" (and they had not divorced). The question in **R. v Allen** was whether the term meant that a legally binding marriage ceremony must have been undertaken or whether it could just mean going through a ceremony of marriage. If it were the former interpretation then that would mean that the offence of bigamy could never be committed, as any subsequent marriage where the person is already legally married is not held to be valid. If it meant the second option, that only a marriage ceremony had to be performed, then this would mean that the offence of bigamy could be committed. The court held that the word "marry" in s.57 was to be given the latter meaning so as to give effect to the aim of the statute.

ERROR

2-041 Errors do occur, even in important legal documents such as an Act of Parliament. It is easy for a person to make a mistake that others then do not notice until it is too late to rectify the problem. Acts of Parliament go through several stages of scrutiny in which most errors are identified along the way. Subordinate legislation is more error-prone and so a correction slip can be published alongside the original to rectify small or obvious mistakes that could still give rise to confusion. Errors of substance would require the parliamentary process to engage in a formal amendment, or the courts could rectify the mistake by applying common law principles of statutory construction (for example see **OB v Director of the Serious Fraud Office** [2012] EWCA Crim 901) where Parliament had inadvertently removed a right of appeal.

UNFORESEEN EVENTS

Even the most forward-thinking and imaginative person cannot foresee every development in society. For example, 50 years ago the concept of email would have been hard to grasp by the majority of the public. The issue of unforeseen events occurred in the case of **R. v Ireland** [1998] A.C. 147, where the defendant was tried under s.47 of the OAPA 1861 for causing psychiatric harm to the victim (he had made a number of silent phone calls to her and as a result she suffered from a psychiatric illness). The problem that arose was due to the fact that s.47 is the offence of "assault occasioning actual bodily harm" and this then left a question as to whether or not "bodily harm" also included "psychiatric harm", as when the statute was drafted in 1861, psychiatric harm was not contemplated. The Lords held that psychiatric harm was to come under the term "bodily harm" and that the Act should be construed in light of the scientific knowledge current at the time of the offence as opposed to the knowledge at the time of drafting. The statute was to be viewed as a living one that could be adapted to keep up with the changing times and new medical and scientific developments. **2-042**

CHANGING LANGUAGE

The English language is not static. Words become redundant or their meaning change over time. The language used in the times of some of the literary greats, such as Geoffrey Chaucer, would make little sense to most people in the 21st century, but it was at one time the accepted form of the English language. Nowadays, txt speak (sorry, text speak) is becoming more common and (quite worryingly) more accepted as a version of the English language. A good illustration of the ways that the meaning of words can change over time is by considering the word "gay". It now has very different connotations as to what it did 40 years ago; the word is now more closely associated with homosexuality than with the feeling of being happy. Language, therefore, can change and this can leave the judiciary with a degree of confusion when the word that has changed is found within a statute. In the case of **Cheeseman v DPP**, The Times, 2 November 1990 the word "passengers", as meant in s.28 of the Town and Country Planning Act 1847, was under consideration. The meaning of the word "passengers" was of critical importance to the case as the offence the defendant had been charged with under s.28 was that of "wilfully and indecently exposing his person in a street to the annoyance of passengers". Two policemen had apprehended the defendant for masturbating in a public toilet, and it was under dispute as to whether or not the policemen were passengers under the Act. The Court investigated the meaning of the word as in 1847, when the legislation was drafted, **2-043** and discovered that it then meant "a passer-by", whereas under the modern interpretation it meant someone who is carried in a vehicle (so in a car or a bus). It was the same word but with two completely different meanings, all due to the development of language. (Whether Mr Cheeseman was found guilty or not is considered in "Literal Rule" at **2–049**.)

FIGURE 9 **Common causes of statutory uncertainty**

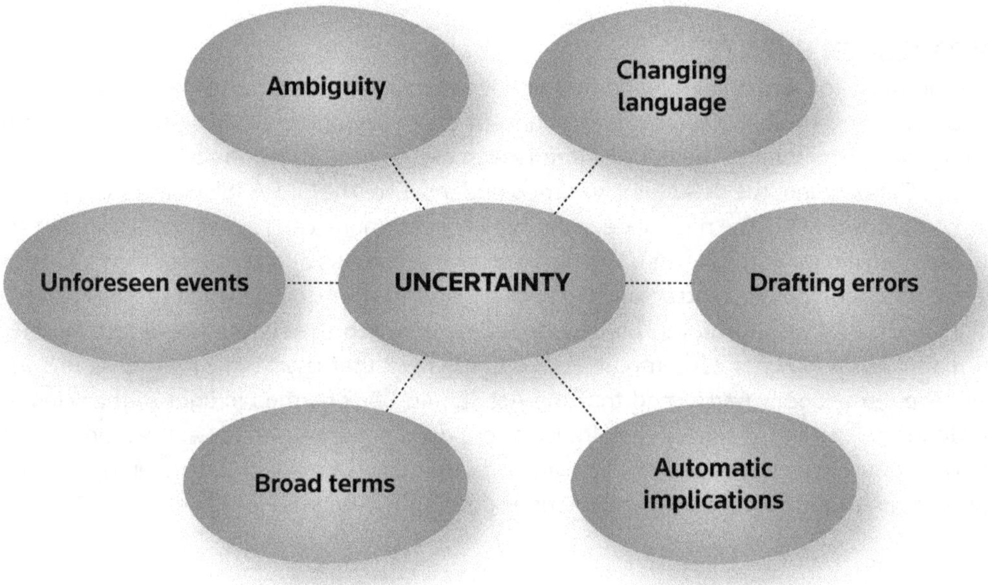

Applying the (Uncertain) Law

2–044 It is the role of judges to apply the law as enacted by Parliament to the case in front of them. In a straightforward case this is quite simple. If the statute states that X would be guilty of theft if he stole some money and X then steals some money, it would be an easy task for the court to come to conclusion that X is therefore guilty of theft. However, if X had stolen some bars of gold, that were technically not money, what is the court to do? He has obviously committed an offence as he has stolen something (and it has quite a high financial value to it) but the item is not money. Should the court interpret the law by giving precise meaning to the words that Parliament has used, so that "money" would mean legal tender (coins and notes), or should it interpret the law in such a way that it seeks to follow Parliament's *intention*, so "money" could then mean anything that has a financial value? The way in which the court chooses to interpret the meaning could have a significant effect on the case (here, whether X is guilty or innocent of the offence) and so the court has to be careful as to which interpretation it chooses to employ.

To help in the task of applying often-uncertain law, the judiciary have developed a number of techniques to aid interpretation, which are considered below.

The Act

Many Acts of Parliament have a specific definitional section contained within them so that those using the statute can make reference to it to determine the intentions of Parliament in respect of the meaning of a specific word. The section will only include a certain number of words (often those where it was anticipated that problems might arise as to the meaning) and it is really luck that dictates whether the word in issue is one that is defined in the definitional section. Judges may also turn to other sections within the same Act to see how the word is dealt with elsewhere and to see whether this gives guidance to the way in which it should be interpreted in respect of the section under scrutiny. Similarly, the preamble or long title of the statute may provide clues as to meaning of the word in question (see Ch.3, "Referring to Legislation"). 2–045

The Interpretation Act 1978

The Interpretation Act 1978 provides a number of standard definitions that can be found throughout the different Acts of Parliament. So, for example, the Interpretation Act 1978 sets out that where the word "he" is used it should also mean "she" where applicable. 2–046

In the case of **Hutton v Esher Urban DC** [1973] 2 All E.R. 1123 the Court was faced with the problem of interpreting the phrase "in, on or over any land". The council wished to build a new sewer to drain surface water from the houses and roads and also to take floodwater from the river. The most economic line was for the sewer to go straight through Mr Hutton's bungalow, which would mean that it would have to be demolished. Mr Hutton argued that his bungalow was not "land," however, the Court held, after referring to the Interpretation Act 1978, that the word "land" was to include buildings. Mr Hutton's bungalow was duly demolished.

Explanatory Notes

Since 1999 explanatory notes that explain both the general purpose of the Act and the individual sections, have accompanied all new Acts of Parliament. The preparation of these explanatory notes is required to aid the passage of the Bill through Parliament and now these notes are occasionally cited in court as an aid to statutory interpretation (see Ch.3, "Explanatory Notes" for further details). They are also extremely useful documents to explain the policy background which can be valuable background reading for law school tutorials or essays. 2–047

Rules of Interpretation

2-048 Where judges have considered the sources discussed but still not found a resolution to the interpretation of the word they may then look to one of the rules of interpretation that have been developed by the judiciary over time. There are four mains rules of interpretation:

- literal rule;
- golden rule;
- mischief rule; and
- purposive approach.

Each one considers the word and its meaning in a different way and each can produce a very different result when applied to the same word. The individual judge in a case will decide which, if any, rule he wishes to employ and many judges will have a preferred rule that they return to time and time again. Obviously as the choice of rule to be used is left to the discretion of the individual judge it means that one judge may interpret the word (by the use of a certain rule) in a different way to how another judge would have done so (by employing a different rule). However, once the meaning of a word is defined, and it does not matter by which technique this occurs, then that will be taken to be the meaning of the word in later cases by way of the doctrine of precedent. The way in which the judiciary view the use of the rules on statutory interpretation was commented upon by Lord Reid in the case of **Maunsell v Olins** [1975] A.C. 373, when he stated:

> **They are not rules in the ordinary sense of having some binding force. They are our servants, not our masters. They are aids to construction, presumptions or pointers. Not infrequently one "rule" points in one direction, another in a different direction. In each case we must look at all relevant circumstances and decide as a matter of judgment what weight to attach to any particular "rule".**

Literal Rule

2-049 The literal rule is often the first rule that a judge will employ when attempting to interpret a statute, and it works by way of the judge construing the words to their ordinary and grammatical meaning, whatever the end result. The fact that a completely ridiculous result could come from using the literal rule should not deter a judge from employing it as can be evidenced from Lord Esher's statement in **R. v City of London Court Judge** [1892] 1 Q.B. 273.

> **If the words of an Act are clear, you must follow them, even though they lead to a manifest absurdity. The Court has nothing to do with the question whether the legislature has committed an absurdity.**

It is often quite easy to identify whether judges are using the literal rule or not as they tend to use words and phrases such as "natural", "ordinary" and "literal", and they may look to what the dictionary definition of the word is so as to identify the common everyday meaning of the word. The literal rule can work very well in some cases and can result in some ridiculous conclusions in others. An example of the literal rule ending in the absurd is seen in the case of **Whiteley v Chappell** (1868) L.R. 4 Q.B. 147.

In **Whiteley v Chappell** the defendant had been convicted of the offence of impersonating a person entitled to vote. The defendant had impersonated a person who had been entitled to vote at the time of registration but who had subsequently died before the election. On appeal the question for the Court was whether the legislation covered the situation where the defendant was impersonating a dead person. The Court held that he could not be guilty of such an offence as the person whom he had impersonated was dead at the point of impersonation for the purposes of voting and therefore he was not a person who was entitled to vote—due to being dead. Hannen J, acknowledging the result, stated that:

> **I regret that we are obliged to come to the conclusion that the offence charged was not proved; but it would be wrong to strain words to meet the justice of the present case, because it might make a precedent, and lead to dangerous consequences in other cases.**

Another case where the use of the literal rule ended in a result that could not have been intended by Parliament when it enacted the legislation in question was that of **Fisher v Bell** [1960] 3 All E.R. 731. In this case a shopkeeper had placed for sale in his shop window a flick knife. He was charged with the offence under s.1 of the Restriction of Offensive Weapons Act 1959 of offering a knife for sale. An issue arose as to whether the defendant was making an offer to sell or whether it in fact was merely an invitation to treat (where a person comes and makes an offer which the seller can then accept or reject but the seller makes no offer himself). Under the law of contract the displaying of goods in a shop window (or offering them) is taken to only be an invitation to treat and so the Court of Appeal held that the defendant could not be guilty of the offence charged. **2–050**

Despite the Court recognising that such a situation could not have been outside of the intentions and minds of Parliament when it enacted the legislation, the judge in the case, Lord Parker CJ, refused to fill in any of the "gaps" left by Parliament in the drafting of the legislation, stating that to do so would "[A]ppear to me to be a naked usurpation of the legislative function under the thin disguise of interpretation."

If we return now to the case of **Cheeseman v DPP** (discussed at **2–043**) the Court was left with a dilemma as to whether the term "passengers" should apply to the policemen who had arrested Mr Cheeseman in the public toilets. Taking the 1847 meaning of the word to be a passer-by, the Court decided that it would not have any difficulty with stretching that to a member of the public who had wandered into the public toilets, but because the policemen had stationed themselves in the public toilets waiting for Mr Cheeseman (a number of complaints had been made by the public alerting them to Mr Cheeseman's activities) then they could not be strictly described as "passers-by" or "passengers" and therefore his conviction was quashed.

The use of the literal rule can be a very straightforward no-nonsense way in which to resolve an issue concerning interpretation and its application does respect the supremacy of Parliament in regards to it being the primary lawmaker. However, its application can also result in some ridiculous and often very harsh decisions being made. In **London & North Eastern Railway Co v Berriman** [1946] 1 All E.R. 255 a widow failed in her claim for compensation after her husband had been killed whilst maintaining a train track. The legislation only covered situations where the death occurred whilst the victim had been relaying or repairing the train tracks, not maintaining them, so the Court, when applying the literal rule to the wording of the legislation, dismissed the widow's claim.

Golden Rule

2-051 The golden rule can be explained best as an extension of the literal rule that is to be applied where the literal rule results in absurdity, as in some of the case examples above. The literal rule should be applied initially and the words be construed according to their ordinary plain meaning wherever possible, the golden rule then only being turned to as and when necessary. One of the first examples of the golden rule can be seen in the case of **Mattison v Hart** (1854) 14 C.B. 357, where it was stated that:

> **We must, therefore, in this case have recourse to what is called the golden rule of construction, as applied to Acts of Parliament, viz, to give the words used by the legislature their plain meaning unless it is manifest from the general scope and intention of the statute, injustice and absurdity would result ... .**

A judge is not obliged to employ the golden rule if he believes that to do so would be to move away from the intention of Parliament. An example of a case where the golden rule was used was in **R. v Allen** (1872) L.R. 1 C.C.R. 367 (see "Ambiguity" at **2–040**) where the literal interpretation of the word "marriage" (in s.57 of the OAPA 1861) would have required there to be a legally binding marriage undertaken, but this could not occur due to the offence in question being bigamy (which already required the offender to be legally married before he could commit the offence and so any subsequent marriage would be automatically void). To avoid absurdity the Court applied the golden rule instead, which resulted in the defendant being found guilty of the offence in question.

2-052 The golden rule can also be applied by the courts where the application of the literal rule would result in a completely unacceptable decision, as occurred in the case of **Re Sigsworth** [1935] Ch. 89. Here, a son who had murdered his mother would have inherited his mother's estate had the Court not decided to apply the golden rule to stop him benefiting from his ill-gotten gains.

In **Adler v George** [1964] 2 Q.B. 7 the golden rule was used to halt a rather ingenious but also rather ridiculous submission from the appellant. The appellant had been convicted of obstructing a member of Her Majesty's armed forces whilst in a prohibited vicinity. The statute that he was charged and convicted under set out that it was an offence to obstruct someone "in the vicinity of a prohibited place". The appellant submitted that as he had actually been in the prohibited place then, as "in" could not be construed to mean the same as "in the vicinity", which it was argued denoted being outside but near to the prohibited area, there was consequently no evidence against him. The Court applied the golden rule so as to avoid the appellant being acquitted and held that the term "in the vicinity of" was to be interpreted as meaning "in or in the vicinity of".

The golden rule is often described as being similar to the purposive approach (discussed at **2-055**) and it can be quite difficult to identify at times, especially when the judge does not specifically state that he is employing the golden rule or that he does not clearly identify what he views as being the potentially absurd result. What is an absurd result is also open to wide interpretation in itself and it can mean different things to different people, for example, in **R. v Allen** the absurd result was that the statutory offence (bigamy) would have been unworkable if the rule had not been applied, whereas in **Re Sigsworth** the golden rule was used to stop what the Court viewed as a completely unacceptable result (benefiting from the murder he perpetrated) due to the moral behaviour of the defendant.

Mischief Rule

The very old case known as **Heydon's Case** (1584) 3 Co. Rep. 7a sets out the principles of this rule of statutory interpretation. The four key elements are: **2-053**

- What was the law prior to the Act?
- What was the mischief (problem) that needed to be remedied?
- What was the remedy that Parliament wanted to impose?
- What was the purpose behind the remedy?

The mischief rule requires judges to perform an element of detective work in respect of determining what the Act is actually all about. It is very different to the literal rule, which is only interested in applying what is written in the statute, as the mischief rule looks to the will and intention of Parliament and then interprets the law in a way that is compatible with this.

For example, in **Smith v Hughes** [1960] 1 W.L.R. 830 two women had been convicted under s.1 of the Street Offences Act 1959, which made it an offence, "for a common prostitute to loiter or solicit in a street or public place for the purposes of prostitution". The women were aware of the offence and so they carried out their profession from upon a balcony and through a first-floor window, banging on the window or calling from the balcony to attract the attention of the passing men. They were convicted under s.1 but appealed on the grounds that they were not "in the street or public" when they had been calling out to the men. Lord Parker CJ, whilst dismissing their appeal stated:

> **The sole question here is whether in those circumstances each defendant was soliciting in a street or public place. The words of section 1(1) of the Act of 1959 are in this form: "It shall be an offence for a common prostitute to loiter or solicit in a street or public place for the purpose of prostitution." Observe that it does not say there specifically that the person who is doing the soliciting must be in the street. Equally, it does not say that it is enough if the person who receives the solicitation or to whom it is addressed is in the street. For my part, I approach the matter by considering what is the mischief aimed at by this Act. Everybody knows that this was an Act intended to clean up the streets, to enable people to walk along the streets without being molested or solicited by common prostitutes. Viewed in that way, it can matter little whether the prostitute is soliciting while in the street or is standing in a doorway or on a balcony, or at a window, or whether the window is shut or open or half open; in each case her solicitation is projected to and addressed to somebody walking in the street.**

2–054 The Court considered the purpose of the legislation and what mischief it intended to remedy (prostitutes plying their wares on the streets) and, although the statute itself did not expressly cover the situation before the Court, the judges in the case were of the opinion that the use of the mischief rule so as to ensure the liability of the women was appropriate.

The mischief rule was again employed in the later case of **Royal College of Nursing of the UK v DHSS** [1981] A.C. 800. Here, the issue involved the interpretation of s.1(1) of the Abortion Act 1967, which provides that, ". . . a person shall not be guilty of an offence under the law relating to abortion when a pregnancy is terminated by a registered medical practitioner. . ." When the Act was initially passed all terminations were carried out surgically by a qualified doctor but, as medicine had advanced, it had become possible for an abortion to be conducted non-invasively by the taking of certain drugs. This non-invasive procedure could be carried out by a registered nurse and did not require a doctor to be present. The Government Department of Health and Social Security sent out a circular specifying that a nurse could lawfully carry out such a procedure so long as it was conducted under the supervision of qualified medical practitioner (a doctor). The Royal College of Nursing sought a declaration that the information contained in the circular relating to the legality of a nurse's action was incorrect. Upon consideration the House of Lords held that the directions set out in the circular were lawful and therefore a nurse could carry out such a drug-induced abortion provided it was carried out under appropriate supervision. The decision was a rather controversial one and only achieved by a narrow majority. The Lords considered the mischief rule when interpreting the section and they came to the conclusion that the mischief considered by Parliament when enacting the legislation was to prevent the practice of back-street abortions. Therefore, allowing the abortion to be carried out in an appropriate medical setting under the care of a nurse was, in respect of the purpose of the legislation, an achievement. Lord Wilberforce and Lord Edmund-Davies preferred the literal rule approach to interpretation and voiced their opinion that by deciding as the House did it was effectively rewriting legislation, which was the role of Parliament and not the judiciary.

Purposive Approach

Not so much a true "rule", but rather more like a philosophical approach (as its name suggests), the purposive approach is at the opposite end of the statutory interpretation spectrum to that of the literal rule. Instead of a judge simply saying what he sees (as he would with the literal rule) the purposive approach involves the judge considering what the intentions of Parliament were when it enacted the legislation. It is often confused with the mischief rule as both methods do consider the will of Parliament, but the mischief rule could be described as looking back at the problem that needed remedying, whereas the purposive approach looks forward to discover what Parliament was trying to achieve (there may not even have been a mischief present but Parliament simply wanted to legislate for something new). A good example of the purposive approach in action can be seen in the case of **R. v Registrar General Ex p. Smith (Ex p. Smith)** [1991] 2 W.L.R. 782. 2–055

In **Ex p. Smith** the appellant had been adopted as a young baby and as he grew up he began to show signs of severe mental disturbance, which resulted in him expressing hatred towards his adoptive parents. He was then convicted of murder and whilst in prison he committed a further murder, as a result of which he was subsequently moved to the secure Broadmoor hospital. The appellant then applied under s.51 of the Adoption Act 1976 for a copy of his birth certificate. Section 51 provided that:

> **Subject to subsections (4) and (6), the Registrar General shall on an application made in the prescribed manner by an adopted person a record of whose birth is kept by the Registrar General and who has attained the age of 18 years supply to that person on payment of the prescribed fee (if any) such information as is necessary to enable that person to obtain a certified copy of the record of his birth.**

The application was denied on the grounds that the psychiatrist had reported that he believed that the appellant might well have hostile feelings for his birth mother and could present a realistic danger to her. The Court held that s.51 should be interpreted in a purposive way and that if it was thought that the appellant would use the information to commit a crime in the future then there should be no discretion to allow the appellant access to this information. Lord Justice Staughton, when handing down the judgment of the Court commented that: 2–056

> **If it be the law that Parliament, even when enacting statutory duties in apparently absolute terms, is presumed not to have intended that they should apply so as to reward serious crime in the past, it seems to me that Parliament must likewise be presumed not to have intended to promote serious crime in the future. That is consistent with the growing tendency, perhaps encouraged by Europe, towards a purposive construction of statutes. . .**

The purposive approach can be quite difficult to differentiate from the mischief rule (and many commentators will say that they are one and the same thing) but over recent times this approach has become one of the more favoured ones in respect of statutory interpretation, especially in consideration of human rights issues, and can be frequently identified within case law when the judges have been considering the meaning of the legislation in question.

Rules of Language

2-057 There are also certain rules of language that can be used to aid statutory interpretation. The interpretation rules considered above ("Rules of Interpretation") have generally focused on a specific word within the statute, but it must be remembered that the word is not in a vacuum as it sits within a sentence, and the meaning of that sentence can only be understood if it is read in full. The rules of language encourage the consideration of the words surrounding the word in question so as to try and glean an idea as to its true meaning. They all have (rather hard to pronounce) Latin names but their concepts are actually quite easy to understand.

THE EJUSDEM GENERIS RULE

2-058 This means that when general words follow particular words then the general words are limited to the thing considered by the particular words. For example, if the Act contained the words "chocolate, candy, butterscotch and other confectionery" then the "other confectionery" would be taken to mean other sweets, and would not include items like crisps or fruit.

In the case of **Lane v London Electricity Board** [1955] 1 All E.R. 324 the ejusdem generis rule was applied. The plaintiff was an electrician who had been instructed by his employers to install extra lighting at a substation. Whilst checking the already installed lighting prior to starting the installation of the new lights, the plaintiff slipped and fell, injuring his knee. He brought a claim under The Electricity Regulations 1908 (reg.26), which provided that:

> **All those parts of premises in which apparatus is placed shall be adequately lighted to prevent danger.**
>
> **"Danger" is defined by the regulations as meaning danger to health or danger to life or limb from shock, burn, or other injury to persons employed, or from fire attendant upon the generation, transformation, distribution, or use of electrical energy.**

The question before the Court was whether the words, "or other injury" could include the fact that the claimant's foot had slipped and the harm was caused whilst he was inspecting the lighting. The Court held that in this context the regulation must be read ejusdem generis with "shock" or "burn". In other words, it is to be taken to mean "or other injury due to electrical energy" and therefore could not be extended to a fall.

EXPRESSIO UNIUS EST EXCLUSIO ALTERIUS

This rule of language is simple to understand and apply. It effectively means that the expression of one thing implies the exclusion of another, so where specific words are used and are not followed by general words, the Act only applies to the specific words mentioned. **2-059**

If an Act set out that it was an offence to keep "guinea pigs, gerbils and rabbits" it would mean that keeping a hamster is perfectly legal as a hamster is not specifically named in the Act.

NOSCITUR A SOCIIS

This is where the meaning of a word can be gathered from its context. In **Muir v Keay** (1875) L.R. 10 Q.B. 594 the defendant had been convicted of keeping a refreshment house without a licence under s.6 of 23 & 24 Vict c.27 (Refreshment Houses Act 1860), which provided that: **2-060**

> **. . . [A]ll houses, rooms, shops, or buildings, kept open for public refreshment, resort, and entertainment, during certain hours of the night, are to be deemed refreshment houses and require a licence.**

The defendant owned premises known as The Café. It opened during the night and on the night in question there were present 17 females and 20 males, all of whom were supplied with cigars, coffee, and ginger beer. The defendant appealed his conviction contending that the words "and entertainment" required there to be musical or other form of public performance on the premises for the offence to have been committed. The Court dismissed the appeal and held, applying the *noscitur a sociis* rule, that other entertainment did not have to involve music or a public performance, but rather it could include simply providing a reception for customers to congregate in, as was the case at The Café. The meaning of the term "and entertainment" was to be taken from the other words within the section so "public refreshment" and "resort" did not imply any form of musical entertainment and therefore the word "entertainment" within that section did not either.

Presumptions

Another intrinsic aid to statutory interpretation is that of presumptions. A judge in certain circumstances can make presumptions as to the law. If there is nothing to say that the presumption should not stand then it will be accepted by the judge, however, if the statute states **2-061** something that goes against the presumption then it will be rebutted and cannot stand. The most common presumptions are listed below:

Statute does not change the common law

This means that unless a statute expressly states that the common law has been changed then the common law will remain as it is. For the avoidance of doubt, some statutes will state that the common law position remains unchanged.

There is a presumption in favour of mens rea in a criminal case

This presumption means that a person will not be convicted of a criminal offence unless it can be proved beyond reasonable doubt that they meant to commit the offence. If an Act is silent on the mens rea (the mental element of the offence) then the court should read into the Act an appropriate mens rea for the offence in question. There are certain offences where this presumption can be rebutted and these are known as strict liability offences. This means that a person will be guilty of the offence for simply carrying out the prohibited act, he did not have to mean to do so. An example of an offence where the presumption of mens rea is rebutted is that of speeding. A person does not have to intend to speed to be guilty of the offence; he simply has to go over the speed limit. Even if the driver did not realise he was speeding he will still have committed the offence.

The monarch is not subject to the provisions of any statute

Meaning that the King could go around breaking any law that he wished as there is a presumption that he is not bound by any statute unless it expressly states that he is.

Legislation does not apply retrospectively

Legislation will normally only apply from the date it is brought into force. It will not apply to events that occurred before the legislation was enacted unless this is clearly stated.

Over to you

Jim likes kicking dogs and cats, every dog or cat he sees he kicks (or at least tries to). On Monday it was not an offence to kick animals and Jim had a great day as he kicked 20 cats and three dogs. On Wednesday Parliament enacted a law that stated that kicking any animal would result in a criminal conviction.

Can Jim now be prosecuted for his actions on Monday?

Jim cannot be prosecuted under the law for his actions on Monday, as the law does not apply retrospectively. However if Jim then went and kicked a dog on Thursday he would be guilty of the offence, even if he were unaware that this behaviour had now been criminalised. Only the Act of Parliament in question can rebut the presumption that the law does not apply retrospectively by expressly stating this fact. There are a few exceptions to this rule, for example, in respect of certain revenue laws for tax avoidance, the War Crimes Act 1991 which allowed for anyone to be prosecuted war crimes in Germany and the Mental Health (Approval Functions) Act 2012 which is entirely retrospective for approvals given before the Act.

Aids to Interpretation

As well as using the statutory interpretation techniques described above, a judge can also turn to a number of "aids" to interpretation to help him in his quest to understand what the statute means. Aids to interpretation can be split down into two types: "intrinsic" aids and "extrinsic" aids. 2-062

Intrinsic Aids

Intrinsic aids are aids found within the Act itself and the most commonly used intrinsic aids are the ones described in "The Act" (other sections within the Act) and "Explanatory Notes", above. Also, if referring to older pieces of legislation the "long title" or "preamble" (see Ch.3, "Referring to Legislation") may give guidance as to the intentions of Parliament. The Act itself may provide guidance, as help in interpretation may be derived from the headings given to the different parts of the Act and/or the individual section headings; there may also be found an "Interpretation" section within the Act, which sets out the definition of the more commonly used terms within that statute. One thing to note here is that an intrinsic aid is one which can only be found within the specific Act that is being dealt with. If, for example, the judge is dealing with the interpretation of a word contained within the Highways Act 1980, and in determining the interpretation he turns to the Highways Act 1835 for reference, then, despite it having the same title, the 1835 Act will be an extrinsic aid to interpretation as it is not contained within the 1980 Act. 2-063

Extrinsic Aids

Extrinsic aids are aids that a judge refers to for help with interpretation but which are outside of the Act. Some common extrinsic aids to interpretation are: 2-064

- the historical setting;
- other Acts of Parliament;
- case law;
- dictionaries;
- textbooks/academic commentary;
- *Hansard*;
- reports; and
- treaties and international conventions.

Many of these extrinsic aids are quite self-explanatory but one does warrant further consideration.

HANSARD

2-065 *Hansard* is a documentary record of the daily ministerial debates that take place in Parliament. Originally the courts prohibited the use of *Hansard* as an aid to statutory interpretation, as reference to it was thought to promote confusion, not clarity, and that it was an unreliable source. Lord Denning, however, was very much of the opinion that *Hansard* could be a valuable aid to interpretation and in the case of **Davis v Johnson** [1979] A.C. 264 he admitted to having referred to it before delivering his judgment (although this action was swiftly condemned in the House of Lords).

The rule against referring to *Hansard* was overturned in the landmark case of **Pepper (Inspector of Taxes) v Hart** [1993] A.C. 593 where the House of Lords set out that it could be referred to as an aid to statutory interpretation, but only in certain circumstances. These circumstances being when:

- the legislation is ambiguous or obscure or leads to an absurdity;
- the material relied upon from *Hansard* consists of one or more statements by a minister or other promoter of the Bill, together, if necessary, with such other Parliamentary material as is necessary to understand such statements and their effect;
- the statements relied upon are clear.

If the statutory provision is not ambiguous, or the statements that are to be relied upon are not clear then *Hansard* will not be permitted as an aid to statutory interpretation. The use of *Hansard* was confirmed, and even extended slightly, in the later case of **Three Rivers DC v Bank of England (No.2)** [1996] 2 All E.R. 363. This case was concerned with the introduction of a European Directive into English law and the Court held that *Hansard* could be relied upon where the provision concerned was not ambiguous but that it was important to interpret the statute so as to give effect to its obligations, therefore *Hansard* could be referred to so as to discover the purpose of the legislation.

2-066 The use of *Hansard* is now an accepted aid to statutory interpretation and it has been used effectively in many cases. It seems that Lord Denning was right to champion its use and his comment in **Davis v Johnson** appears to have been an innovative and logical view of such a potentially valuable source.

Some may say—and indeed have said—that judges should not pay any attention what is said in Parliament. They should grope about in the dark for the meaning of an Act without switching on the light. I do not accede to this view.

Human Rights Act 1998

The HRA 1998 (as discussed at "Precedents and Jurisprudence of the ECtHR", above) also allows the ECHR to be used as an extrinsic aid to statutory interpretation. The courts are required to ensure that domestic legislation is interpreted in a way that is compatible with Convention rights (s.3 of the HRA 1998) and, in doing so, they are permitted to consult the individual rights of the Convention as an aid to discover how to interpret domestic law (see above discussion of **Ghaidan v Godin-Mendoza** [2002] EWCA Civ 1533). 2-067

The case of **R. v A** [2001] UKHL 25 is another example of where the law was interpreted in such a way so as to be compatible with Convention rights. In **R. v A** it was alleged that the defendant had raped the complainant. The defendant's case was that sexual intercourse had taken place but that the complainant had consented. The defendant made an application to the trial judge to cross-examine the complainant about her previous sexual behaviour.

Section 41 of the Youth Justice and Criminal Evidence Act 1999 provides for an embargo on the cross-examination of the complainant's previous sexual history without the leave of the court. Leave (permission) to cross-examine on this topic will only be given in limited circumstances (s.41(3) and (5)). The defendant was denied leave to conduct the cross-examination. Upon an interlocutory (interim) appeal to the House of Lords the defendant contended that the embargo on undertaking such questioning was a breach of his right to a fair trial under art.6 of the ECHR. Article 6(3) sets out that:

> **Everyone charged with a criminal offence has the following minimum rights . . .**
>
> **(d) to examine or have examined witnesses against him. . . .**

The House was required to consider whether s.41 should be read in accordance with s.3 of the HRA 1998, so as to make it compatible with the defendant's art.6 rights, meaning, if accepted, that cross-examination of the complainant should have been allowed. 2-068

Lord Steyn, when delivering his opinion on the matter stated that:

> **In my view section 3 requires the court to subordinate the niceties of the language of section 41(3)(c), and in particular the touchstone of coincidence, to broader considerations of relevance judged by logical and common sense criteria of time and circumstances . . . [the] test of admissibility is whether the evidence (and so the questioning in relation to it) is nevertheless so relevant to the issue of consent that to exclude it would endanger the fairness of the trial under article 6 of the Convention. If this test is satisfied the evidence should not be excluded.**

Essentially, what Lord Steyn was saying (and what the House held) was that s.41 should be read in a way that is compatible with Convention rights and that the embargo on questioning a complainant about his previous sexual history should only be lifted where the questioning is relevant to a fact in issue in the case and such questioning is necessary to ensure that the defendant receives a fair trial.

Summary

1. The doctrine of judicial precedent stems from the principle of stare decisis, which means that previous decisions of the court should be stood by and followed in later cases. This doctrine helps to ensure that there is consistency and fairness in the law and it also aids a judge in the decision-making process as the judge does not have to start from scratch but can, rather, refer back to past cases for assistance.
2. Precedent can either be binding (that which *must* be followed) or persuasive (that which *can* be followed) depending on which court decided the case. The general rules of precedent are that the higher courts bind the lower courts, a court on the same level of the hierarchy (e.g. the Court of Appeal) will be self-binding and the lower courts do not bind any other court.
3. Binding precedent is found within the ratio decidendi of a case. The ratio is the reason for the decision and it is the principle of law based on the facts of the case that can then be applied in future cases. Persuasive precedent can be found in a variety of sources such, as obiter dicta, this being the part of the judgment in a case that does not go directly to the ratio. Dissenting judgments, points made that are not directly related to the material facts of a case and Privy Council opinions, are other examples of persuasive precedent.
4. The doctrine of precedent follows the hierarchy of the court system. The Supreme Court is binding upon all lower courts.
5. The Supreme Court, following the 1966 Practice Statement, as issued by the House of Lords, can depart from previous decisions if it is of the opinion that it is right to do so. The Supreme Court will normally be quite reluctant to depart from settled law but will do so where it is appropriate and necessary, such as to rectify a mistake in the law or to develop the law in line with the development of society.
6. The Privy Council is not binding on the domestic courts. However, Privy Council decisions will be highly persuasive precedent and will most likely be followed by the Supreme Court.
7. The Court of Appeal is self-binding and is not permitted to depart from its own previous decisions unless one of the exceptions, as set out in **Young v Bristol**

Aeroplane Co Ltd [1944] K.B. 718, is satisfied. These conditions are that there are two conflicting Court of Appeal decisions, or there is a conflicting Supreme Court/ House of Lords decision, or that the decision was made per incuriam. The Court of Appeal Criminal Division has slightly more flexibility in respect of departing from previous decisions due to the fact that it is concerned with a person's liberty, but it still must apply the same rules as the Civil Division.

8. The Divisional/Administrative Courts of the High Court are bound in the same way as the Court of Appeal. The High Court (first instance court) is bound by all superior courts but is not self-binding.

9. The lower courts (Crown, magistrates and tribunals) are not self-binding nor are they binding on any other court. They can, however, be persuasive.

10. To avoid a binding precedent the court may seek to distinguish the case on its facts, overrule it (if it is a higher court) or reverse it (which means that no other court will be bound by any precedent created by the part that was overruled).

11. The HRA 1998 must be taken into account when considering the precedent of cases as the court, under s.2, is required to ensure that ECHR decisions and principles are taken into account when considering domestic law.

12. If the court is uncertain as the meaning of a word or phrase in a statutory provision then it will be obliged to interpret the word so as to give application to the law. There are a number of different rules developed by the judiciary so as to aid them in this task.

13. The literal rule is where the word in question is given its ordinary, natural and plain meaning no matter what the end result is. Often a dictionary will be used to discover the everyday meaning of the word in question.

14. The golden rule is where the literal rule is applied but the end result by way of its application is absurd. If this is the case then the judge can interpret the word in a way to avoid such absurdity.

15. The mischief rule is where the judge will look to the mischief (or wrong) that Parliament was trying to remedy when it enacted the statute. The words will then be interpreted in a way that is consistent with that aim. The mischief rule is very close to the purposive approach.

16. The purposive approach is where the judge will look to the purpose of the legislation, essentially identifying what Parliament was trying to achieve.

17. The judiciary can also turn to interpretation aids to help them. Aids can either be intrinsic or extrinsic. Intrinsic aids will be those found within the statute itself, whereas extrinsic aids will be those from outside of the case, i.e. case law, law reports, academic commentary and *Hansard*, etc.

Key Cases Grid

Case	Court	Salient point
London Street Tramways Co Ltd v London CC [1898]	House of Lords	The case confirmed that the judicial capacity of the House of Lords was bound by its own previous decisions.
Practice Statement [1966]	House of Lords	The Practice Statement set out that the House of Lords had the power to depart from previous decisions where it was deemed "right to do so."
Conway v Rimmer [1968]	House of Lords	The first case in which the House of Lords utilised its powers to depart under the Practice Statement of 1966, departing from the earlier decision of Duncan v Cammell Laird & Co Ltd.
Austin v Southwark London Borough Council [2011]	Supreme Court	The Supreme Court expressly recognised that the Practice Statement of 1966 applied to matters of precedent in the Supreme Court in the same way that it had applied in the House of Lords.
R. v James [2006]	Court of Appeal	In the R. v James the Court of Appeal favoured the decision of the Privy Council in the case of Att Gen for Jersey v Holley [2005] over the binding House of Lords decision in R. v Smith (Morgan) [2001], illustrating the possible persuasiveness of decisions of the Privy Council.
Young v Bristol Aeroplane [1944]	Court of Appeal	The exception to the self-binding rule in the Court of Appeal are set out in this case and are as follows: 1. Where there are previous conflicting decisions of the Court of Appeal 2. Where a previous decision of the Court of Appeal conflicts with a later decision of the House of Lords 3. Where the previous decision of the Court of Appeal has been made per incuriam.
Ghaidan v Godin-Mendoza [2002]	Court of Appeal	Due to the enactment of the Human Rights Act 1998 the Court of Appeal were able to overrule the House of Lords decision of Fitzpatrick v Sterling [2001] because it was deemed to be incompatible with Convention rights.

Case	Court	Salient point
Heydon's Case (1584)	Court of King's Bench	**Sets out the principles of the method of statutory interpretation known as the Mischief Rule. The four key questions to ask are:** • **What was the law prior to the Act?** • **What was the mischief that needed to be remedied?** • **What was the remedy that Parliament wanted to impose?** • **What was the purpose behind the remedy?**

Further Reading

E. Bell, "Judicial perspectives on statutory interpretation" [2013] 39(2) C.L.B. 245–281.

Reviews how judges in common law jurisdictions approach the task of statutory interpretation.

R. Clayton, "The Government's New Proposals for the Human Rights Act: An Assessment" [2022] 2 E.H.R.L.R. 81–96.

This opinion piece assesses the UK Government's proposals to reform the Human Rights Act 1998.

P. Joseph, "Parliament's attenuated privilege of freedom of speech" [2010] 126(Oct) L.Q.R. 568–592.

Examines the scope of Parliamentary privilege with focus on the impact of the case of *Pepper v Hart*.

C. O'Cinneide, "Human rights law in the UK – is there a need for fundamental reform?" [2012] 6 E.H.R.L.R. 595–607.

Considers the current state of the human rights law in response to the criticisms levied against it by politicians and the public; also considers the impact of the proposed UK Bill of Rights.

Lord Sales, "Statutory Interpretation in Theory and Practice" Talk to the Office of Parliamentary Counsel 20 March 2025 *https://supremecourt.uk/uploads/speech_lord_sales_200325_3e4c4980d6.pdf* [Accessed 1 May 2025].

Lord Sales provides a reflection on his role as a judge in statutory interpretation.

Self Test Questions

1. Persuasive precedent can come from:
   (a) the Privy Council
   (b) academic commentary
   (c) lower courts
   (d) all of the above
2. The Court of Appeal can depart from one of its own previous decisions when:
   (a) it does not agree with the decision
   (b) the decision is made per incuriam
   (c) the decision is res judicata
   (d) it wants to develop the law
3. The term "reversing" means:
   (a) the facts of the case are different
   (b) the court declares a previous case as bad law
   (c) the court changes the outcome of the instant case
   (d) the court changes its own mind
4. To avoid an absurd result a judge will employ which technique of statutory interpretation:
   (a) the literal rule
   (b) the golden rule
   (c) the mischief rule
   (d) the purposive approach
5. Which source below is not an extrinsic aid to interpretation?
   (a) case law
   (b) *Hansard*
   (c) another Act of Parliament
   (d) the *Noscitur a Sociis* rule

How to Find the Law and Use It

3

CHAPTER OVERVIEW

In this chapter we will:

- **Describe how to find cases and legislation in both hard copy and online.**
- **Explain what a citation is and how to use it.**
- **Explain how to read a case and distil relevant information such as the material facts, legal issue and ratio decidendi.**
- **Provide a worked example of a case analysis.**
- **Explain how to read legislation.**

Introduction

3-001 The focus of this text is not really on skills, the primary purpose being to explain the English legal system as it is at the time of writing. However, there are certain skills that it would be beneficial to consider. These skills include the art of being able to find the law and then use it effectively once it has been found, which is what will be the focus of this chapter.

It is surprising how many undergraduate law students can explain the theoretical basis of the law, such as what a legal issue is or what is meant by a ratio decidendi, but, on being asked to identify them in a law report, they have no idea of how to actually find these principles, or even where to start looking. This chapter will aim to explain how to find the law, be it case law or statute, and then how to go ahead and use it once found. Case law and statutes are the tools of the trade for a lawyer, just as a hammer and a blowtorch are for a plumber, and a screwdriver and electrical tape are for an electrician. It would be a very worrying moment if a supposedly qualified plumber picked up a blowtorch and then asked what it did; the same could be said if a lawyer stood up in court and asked the judge what the law was.

Finding Case Law

Online

3-002 A necessary thing to know is where to find the law. On being asked to find either a case or a statutory provision, most law students will immediately refer to one of the online databases, such as Westlaw UK and LexisNexis. These legal databases are a veritable treasure trove of legal materials; they stock the majority of cases, legislation, journals and other legal sources, and are relatively easy to use. It is not an objective of this chapter to explain in detail how to use these databases as there are other textbooks available that are more directed towards developing these skills (see "Further Reading" at the end of the chapter), so only a brief explanation will be given here. To illustrate how a case can be found by way of an online resource, reference will be made to the Westlaw UK online database. The case that will be searched for is a very famous criminal law case known as **R. v Ireland; Burstow.** At present, it is assumed that we only know the case name.

On entering the Westlaw UK site, if searching for a case, it is advisable to go to the link entitled "Cases" (found on the top of the page next to the Westlaw UK logo) as, in doing so, the scope of the electronic search will be limited to judicial decisions only. On clicking upon the link for Cases the following screen will appear.

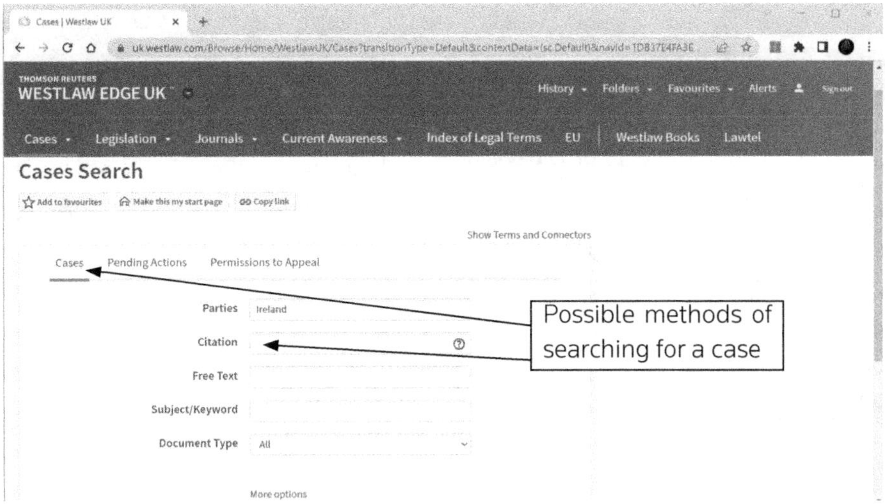

The search box allows the input of either "Free Text", which can be used when the general area of law is known (e.g. assault or police powers and judicial review) but no further details are available or known. The "Party Names" search box should be completed where the name(s) of those involved in the case are known, and the "Citation" search box can be used when the exact citation of the case is known. A case citation is the numbers and letters found after the case name, i.e. "[2006] 2 All E.R. 66", (see "Citations", below, for further details). As the case being searched for is that of **R. v Ireland; Burstow**, the name "Ireland" has been typed into the "Party Names" box. Clicking on the "Search" button will result in the following being shown. 3–003

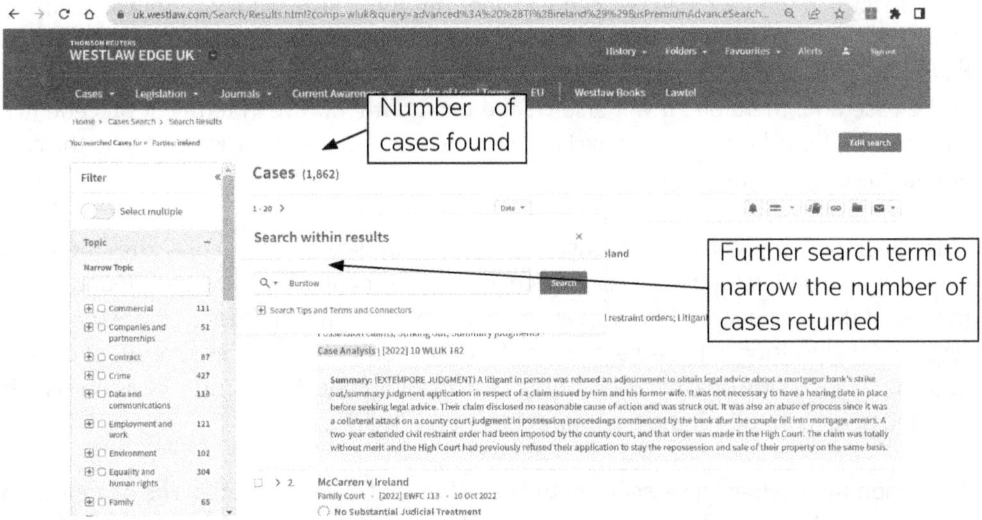

The search term "Ireland" has returned over 2,000 potential matches, which is a large volume of cases and therefore needs to be pared down further so that the specific case we are looking for can be identified. To do this, the legal database provides for a further search to be conducted 3–004

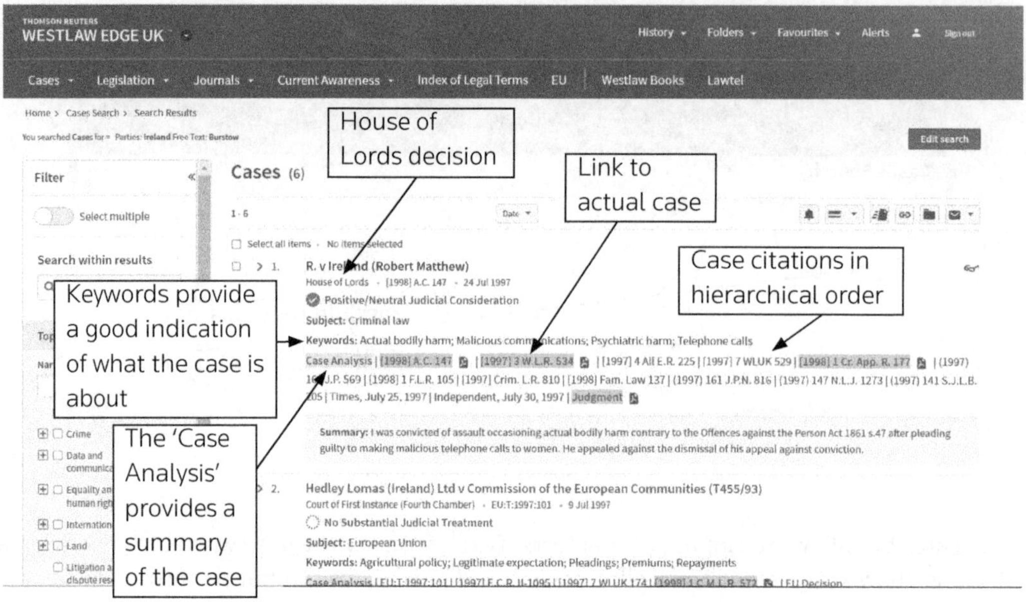

within the limits of the first search results, and it is here that the term "Burstow" (the other party name in the case) can be entered. The results that this returns can be seen in the box below.

3–005 There are now only six results left (with four of these six results relating to the same case). Setting aside the **Hedley Lomas** case and by only focusing on the results with either "Ireland" or "Burstow" in the case name it can be seen that the first result showing was heard by the House of Lords. As the House of Lords was then the highest court within the domestic court hierarchy (refer to Ch.2 for further discussion on this point) then this will be the latest decision in the case and, therefore, it will also be the most authoritative in terms of precedent. If the case citation [1998] A.C. 147 is then clicked on then the House of Lords' opinion in the case will appear (as shown in the next box).

This screen now shows the actual case decision. It is imperative to not only know how to find a case, but also understand what is included in the document once it has been found. Set out at the top of the case is what is known as the headnote. The headnote is a summary of the case facts and the decision in the case; the case facts are normally set out in a couple of paragraphs and it provides a very brief overview of the case. A summary of the court's decision will also be detailed here (normally under a paragraph entitled "Held").

The headnote provides the essence of the case, but that is all it provides. The headnote should never be relied upon as the definitive guide to the case as it is only a signpost as to what can be found within the actual judgment. Headnotes are good to use for determining whether or not a particular case may be of use; they are a quick reference point. They should not, however, be used or relied upon as authority. The authority comes only from the decision of the court (as set

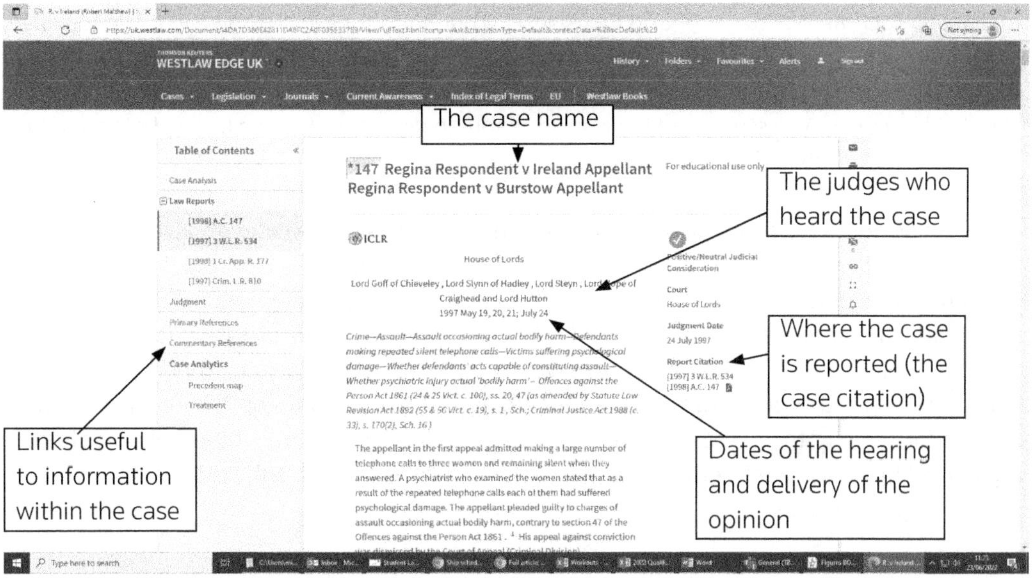

out in the judge's speech/judgment) and this judgment can normally be located in the document after the headnote and the summary of the counsels' arguments in the case.

The Library

There is another place that the law can be found, and this is, unfortunately, a place that stu- **3–006**
dents are frequenting less and less. This place is the library. The law libraries in most institutions are well stocked and easy to navigate and are therefore well worth a visit. Over recent years, possibly due to the development of the Internet and online resources, it seems that many students have lost (or simply not developed) the vital skills that using a library provides. By physically going into a library and walking around, picking up the books and law reports from the shelves etc., a student will become more aware of what the law actually involves, as it becomes more tangible and real than words on a computer screen could ever be. Being able to visualise what the different law report series' look like and what the citation [2002] 3 All E.R. 456, or [1975] 1 A.C. 186 relates to will have a significantly positive impact on an individual's understanding of the law as a whole.

Many students are not aware of the vast array of resources available to them as they do not get to see all the different sources whilst working online; generally, students will only be aware of the resources that they regularly use and this can result in them being cheated out of a wealth of other sources that will aid them in their studies and help develop their understanding to a more in-depth level. Being able effectively to use the hard copies of the law reports is an important skill to learn because when in practice if lawyers are required to find a certain case or journal to help in the preparation of a case they will normally not have access to the online resources, such as Westlaw UK and LexisNexis. They will be required to search the local law library, either in their firm or set of chambers, or at the court; and it will often be imperative that the lawyer knows precisely where to look so that the relevant report can be found quickly as the court will not wait. As a student of law it is advisable to discover what the library holds and how to use the hard copies of the sources located there.

By not utilising the library students are often unaware of valuable sources such as *Halsbury's Statutes of England and Wales*, and the *Halsbury's Laws of England and Wales*. *Halsbury's Statutes* contains up-to-date versions of all the statutes in England and Wales, and *Halsbury's Laws* is, essentially, a comprehensive encyclopedia of the law with details of relevant authority and statutes. LexisNexis publishes the *Halsbury's* series and so it can also be found online, but it cannot be stressed enough that students should aim to use the hard-copy sources in the library at least for some of their research during their time studying law; even if this only entails finding in the library one case per week (or even per month) as this will still help the development of these essential skills.

Understanding cases

Case names

3–007 The name of a case is a good initial indicator of whether the case is a criminal case or a civil one, and who the parties to the case are. However, the name alone can be confusing when there are multiple appeals, retrials or other parties with the same or very similar names.

CRIMINAL CASE NAMES

3–008 Criminal cases are quite easy to identify, as the most common criminal case heading format is (for example) **R. v Brown**, *or* **Regina v Brown**. The **R.** or **Rex** (or **Regina** if the monarch at that time is a Queen) stands for the Crown (the King), and the monarch is named first as he or she is the party who is bringing the proceedings (prosecuting). The defendant (in this example, **Brown**) is then named second as he is the party whom the proceedings are brought against.

A quick note needs to be made in respect of both the **R.** and the **v** in the case name. The **R.**, as noted above, stands for "the Crown" and this is how it should be orated (simply saying the letter "R" should be avoided at all costs). The terms "King" or "Queen" should only ever be used in the Privy Council and no other forum. Similarly the *v* is not to be said out loud as "versus", this is the American style and should not be used within the English courts. The **v** should be said as either "and", or "against". So the case name of **R. v Brown** would be said orally as either, "the Crown and Brown", or "the Crown against Brown", with the latter being the preferred option.

Another style of criminal case name that can be found within the law reports is (for example) **Green v DPP**. Here the case name indicates that Green is appealing by way of case stated (see Ch.12, "Appeal by way of case stated") against the Director of Public Prosecutions (the DPP) who is the head of the Crown Prosecution Service (see Ch.9, "The Crown Prosecution Service"). Green is the party bringing the proceedings and the DPP is the defendant in the matter. The name of the case would therefore be orated as "Green against the Director of Public Prosecutions".

A further criminal case name is, for example, that of the **Attorney-General's Reference (No.1 of 2008)**. This case name indicates that the Attorney-General has made a reference to the court to clarify a point of law (a form of appeal, see Ch.12, "Attorney General's References" for further details) following either the acquittal of the defendant or the imposition of an unduly lenient sentence.

CIVIL CASE NAMES

In civil matters the case name will include the names of those involved in the dispute and their named order will indicate what their roles in the dispute are. So, for example, the case name of **Green v Brown** would indicate that Green was bringing a cause of action against Brown (e.g. suing him for damages for personal injuries caused by a car crash). If, in the same case, the names were later switched so that the case name became **Brown v Green**, this would then show that at first instance Green was successful and that Brown has subsequently appealed the decision. Brown has therefore become the person bringing the proceedings (by way of appealing) and Green (now second named) has to defend the appeal. These case names would be orated as "Green and/against Brown" or "Brown and/against Green". This procedure of first naming the party bringing the particular proceedings may well change in the near future as it has been mooted that the party names should remain consistent throughout so as to avoid any confusion or doubt as to the roles of the parties and stage of proceedings. If this practice were removed then people coming to the law would need to refer to the case chronology (it is always good practice to do this anyway) to determine the stage that proceedings had reached. **3-009**

Judicial review claims, brought against public authorities alleging a breach of public law, are civil proceedings but brought in the name of the Crown, acting "on the application of" the name of the applicant. For example, **R. (on the application of Miller and another) v Secretary of State for Exiting the European Union** [2017] UKSC 5. Prior to 2001, cases were styled using "ex parte", for example **R. v Bow Street Metropolitan Stipendiary Magistrate Ex p. Pinochet Ugarte (No.2)** [2000] 1 A.C. 119.

Some civil matters involving children or wills and estates use *Re*, a Latin term meaning "in the matter of", for example **In re A (Children) (Conjoined Twins: Surgical Separation)** [2001] Fam 147.

Case Chronologies

Each case report will set out the case history in what is known as the case chronology. The chronology of a case can be found by reading past the headnote of a case to the part where **3-010** the court hearings and decisions are listed. This is sometimes entitled "Case history" and sometimes it is not bestowed with any particular title. Case chronologies provide invaluable information to any person reading a case (especially when new to the law) as they set out what has happened so far, which then makes understanding what is going on in the case easier. It is often assumed that if a case is being heard on appeal then the defendant must have been convicted (if a criminal matter) or been found liable (if a civil matter) and therefore must be the party bringing the appeal. This, however, is not always the case. It may be that the prosecution or claimant are lodging an appeal to clarify a point of law or are asserting that the decision was erroneous due to a failure by the court. Or the circumstances may be that a defendant (or the prosecution) has had one appeal already refused and are appealing further on that point, or that the lower court has already allowed an appeal and a further appeal to that decision is being sought. Who is appealing and against what are vital facts to know and the case chronology is the source via which to identify this information. The importance of a case chronology will increase dramatically if the proposals to keep the case name the same throughout the duration of the case become the norm. To illustrate what information is included in a typical case chronology, consider the case chronology of the case of **Ireland; Burstow** below.

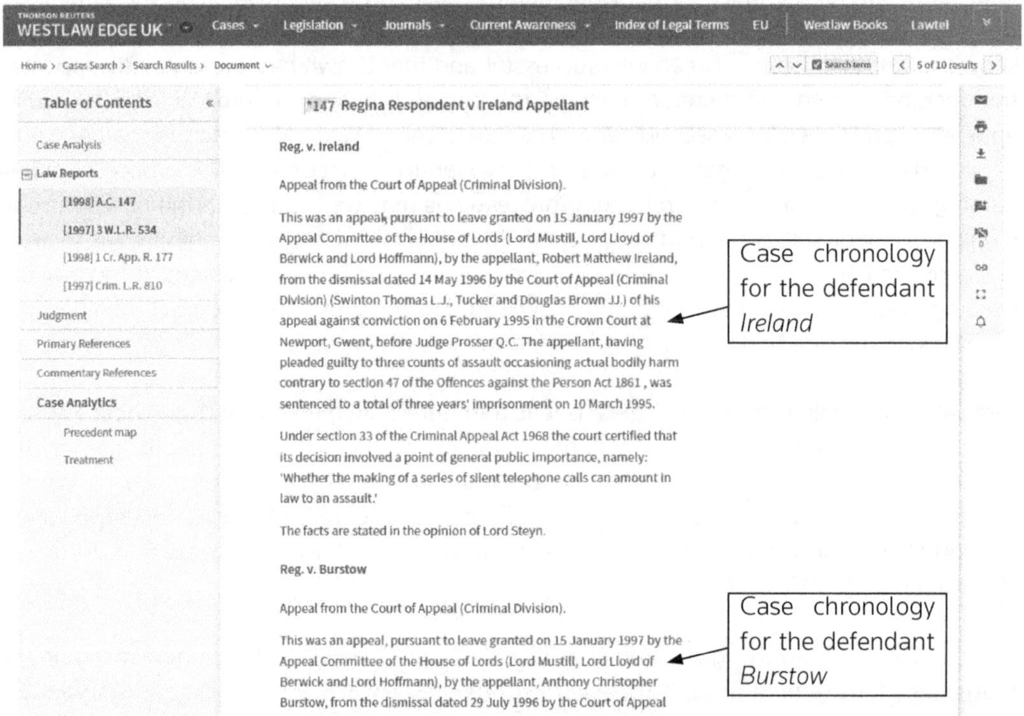

Over to you

Write out in a concise list the case chronology for *Ireland* and the case chronology for *Burstow*.

Citations

Students are often baffled about the meaning of the letters and numbers that follow a case name. These alphabetical and numerical characters are known as the case citation and getting to grips with the meaning of these case citations is an imperative skill to acquire. If a lawyer is required to refer to a case in court (or if a student is required to refer to a case during a moot or mock trial) then the full correct case citation needs to be given. Judicial reasoning is reported in a number of different sources and these sources have a hierarchical structure of their own. If a case is to be cited in a court, in a moot or even in a written document then it is important that the most appropriate citation is given. **3–011**

Case citations contain all the necessary information for the individual case to be located. The citations can be easily broken down into four component parts, these are:

1. the year the case was reported in (although this is not required if the case citation has round brackets);
2. the volume number (if appropriate) of the law series;
3. the standard abbreviation of the law series; and
4. the page number upon which the case starts or the case number of that year (when a neutral citation (see "Neutral Citations", below)).

So, for example, the citation of [1978] 2 W.L.R. 2002 means:

FIGURE 10 **Citation explanation**

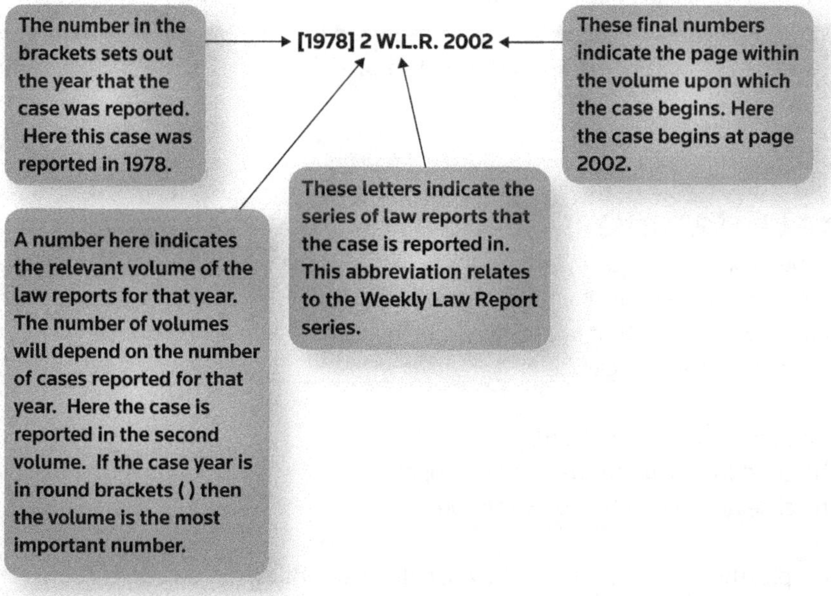

3–012 Listed below are some examples of the most commonly found case citations and law series abbreviations, coupled with an explanation of what these citations mean:

FIGURE 11 **Citations and abbreviations**

Citation	Meaning
[2003] A.C. 556	Reported in the Appeal Cases for 2003 at page 556
[2001] 3 W.L.R. 93	Reported in the 3rd volume of the Weekly Law Reports for 2001 at page 93
[1997] 1 Q.B. 1039	Reported in the 1st volume of the Queen's Bench Reports for 1997 at page 1039
[2008] F.L.R. 56	Reported in the Family Law Report for 2008 at page 56
(1978) 67 Cr. App. R. 14	Reported in the 67th volume of the Criminal Appeal Reports at page 14. The Criminal Appeal reports were identified by the volume number until the completion of the 99th volume when the series adopted the more traditional way of reporting cases, with the focus on the year as opposed to the volume number
[2006] 2 Cr. App. R. 274	Reported in the 2nd volume of the Criminal Appeal Reports for 2006 at page 274 (The new style Criminal Appeal Report citation (note the square [ ] brackets))
[2004] 1 All E.R. 879	Reported in the 1st volume of the All England Reports for 2004 at page 879
(1997) 24 E.H.R.R. 39	The 39th case reported in the 24th volume of the European Human Rights Reports.

Neutral Citations

3–013 Due to the increased use of electronic reporting of cases, the courts have further devised a form of citation known as the neutral citation (introduced 11 January 2001). These citations contain the information of the case that relates to the actual court hearing (as opposed to a law reporting series). Neutral citations can be broken down into:

1. the year the case was heard;
2. the court in which the case was heard; and
3. the case number as heard by the court.

So, for example, the neutral citation [2007] UKHL 13 stands for:

FIGURE 12 **Citation explanation**

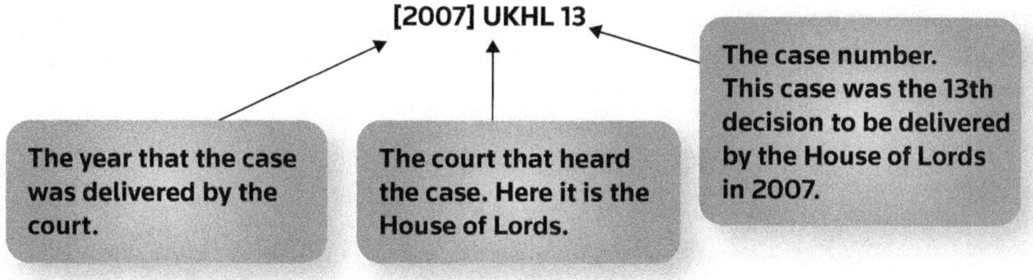

The common abbreviations of the neutral citations are as follows: 3–014

FIGURE 13 **Neutral citations**

Abbreviation	Court
UKSC	United Kingdom Supreme Court
UKHL	United Kingdom House of Lords
UKPC	United Kingdom Privy Council
EWCA	England and Wales Court of Appeal (the abbreviation will normally be followed by either "Crim" or "Civ" so as to indicate whether is was heard under the Court of Appeals criminal or civil jurisdiction)
EWHC	England and Wales High Court

Case Reporting Hierarchy

Not every case that is heard within the justice system is reported; only those that are deemed to be of sufficient legal interest will make it into the casebooks. Those cases heard in the superior courts (so the Supreme Court or Court of Appeal) will often be reported as they will set out some important rule of law or principle, etc. that will be of use to future cases (by way of precedent). Often a single case can be found reported in a number of different law series and it is important to know which report of the case in which series is the most appropriate report to cite. There is a hierarchy of law reports, just as there is a court hierarchy and a hierarchy of precedent, and both judges and lawyers alike adhere to the use of this hierarchy. 3–015

The hierarchy of the law reports is as set out in the table below, with the most authoritative series being at the top of the table graduating down to the least authoritative.

FIGURE 14 **Law Reports**

Series Title	Abbreviation	Publisher
The Law Reports	AC (Appeal Cases) Ch (Chancery Division) Fam (Family Division) KB (King's Bench Division)	ICLR
The Weekly Law Reports	W.L.R.	ICLR
All England Law Reports	All E.R.	LexisNexis (Commercial)
Individual Law Reports	Abbreviation dependent on the specific series	Series dependent (Commercial)

Incorporated Council of Law Reporting

3–016 The Incorporated Council of Law Reporting (ICLR) was established in 1865 with the object of:

> **Preparation and publication, in a convenient form, at a moderate price, and under gratuitous Professional control, of [The Law] Reports of Judicial Decisions of the Superior and Appellate Courts in England.**
>
> **ICLR Memorandum and Articles of Association, 1870**

The ICLR is currently registered as a charity and it is a non-profit-making organisation. It aims to report all cases that:

- introduce, or appear to introduce, a new principle or a new rule;
- materially modify an existing principle or rule;
- settle, or materially tend to settle, a question upon which the law is doubtful; and
- are for any reason peculiarly instructive.

The ICLR guidelines set out that a law report should be accurate, contain everything material and useful, and should be as concise as possible whilst still remaining consistent with these objectives. In particular, the report should show the parties the nature of the pleadings, the essential facts, the points contended by counsel and the grounds on which the judgment was based, as well as the judgment, decree, or order actually pronounced. The ICLR states that there is a universal view amongst the judiciary that there are too many cases published per year and that therefore the ICLR are determined to only publish those cases that really matter and which create binding precedent.

Lord Woolf CJ, in the **Practice Direction (Judgments: Form and Citation) (Supreme Court)** [2001] 1 W.L.R. 194, stated, in relation to the citation of judgments in court, that: 3–017

> **For avoidance of doubt, it should be emphasised that both the High Court and the Court of Appeal require that where a case has been reported in the official Law Reports published by the Incorporated Council of Law Reporting for England and Wales it must be cited from that source. Other series may only be used when a case is not reported in the Law Reports.**

Therefore, the law report series published by the ICLR, and especially the Law Reports, is the preferable source to be cited wherever possible. The rationale behind this is that the judge and counsel in the case check the cases for accuracy before they are published in the Law Reports. This ensures that the Law Reports provide accurate and accepted versions of the case. The Weekly Law Reports (or the "Weeklies" as they are informally called) are also published by the ICLR but these are not double-checked by the judge involved in the case before publication. This means that the Weeklies are often quicker to be published but that their accuracy cannot be guaranteed. Those cases published in the Weeklies will normally make it into the Law Reports after a while.

Commercial Reports

The remainder of the law reports series are published for commercial purposes. The most commonly used commercially available law reporting series is the All England Law Reports, published by LexisNexis and this is readily found on the online legal databases, as well as in the law libraries up and down the country. The commercial law reports can be an excellent source to turn to, especially where the case under consideration is on a principle of law not yet discussed by the higher courts (for example, cases which are reported in the Road Traffic Reports (R.T.R.), or a case that was heard in the Technology and Construction Court (T.C.C.)). Caution should be heeded when considering the commercial reports simply due to the possibility of issues of accuracy and if a case is reported both in Law Reports and a commercial report the Law Report version should always be used, as this will be viewed as the most authoritative source. 3–018

How to Use the Law

Case Analysis

Once the relevant law has been identified it is not always easy to then know what to do with it. A reported case will have some important element to it (decision and principle) as otherwise it would not have been reported. Being able to analyse a case so that the specific importance of an individual case can be identified is an essential skill to develop. To be able to assess whether a case is relevant and useful it is necessary to be able to extract three essential pieces 3–019 of information from it (and what is meant by relevant and useful will wholly depend on the reasons for the case being referred to). These three elements are the material facts, the legal issues and the ratio decidendi.

MATERIAL FACTS

3–020 When analysing a case it is important to be able to identify which facts in the case are material (important) and which facts are immaterial. There is often set out in the judgment a number of facts that were important to the specific case (maybe even a few pages' worth) but all of these facts will not necessarily be described as "material facts". Material facts are generally described as those facts that were vital to deciding the outcome of the case and they may include both matters of fact and matters of law. The material facts will link in directly with the issue and the ratio of the case and if any material fact were omitted or changed then the outcome of the case (the ratio) or the legal issue would be different.

What the material facts of a case are will depend on what the case is about and which facts are pertinent to the issue in question. Often it can be said that certain details, such as names of the parties, the date that the incident happened and the exact location of the event are not relevant to the issue. For example, on 5 September at 4:02pm Bill and Georgina had a road traffic accident at the traffic lights on Stamford Street. Bill's black Volvo XC90 crashed into the rear end of Georgina's powder-blue Fiat 500. Georgina suffered whiplash and successfully sued Bill for damages for her injuries. Bill then appealed against the amount of damages awarded by the court on the basis that Georgina was negligent due to the fact that she was not wearing a seatbelt at the time of the accident and therefore contributed to her injuries.

The material facts here would be that the appellant's vehicle crashed into respondent's vehicle, causing her personal injury. The respondent was successful in her claim for damages in respect of the personal injury suffered. The appellant is alleging that at the time of the accident the respondent was not wearing a seatbelt and therefore could be said to have been contributorily negligent.

3–021 What would not be material to the issue (was there contributory negligence or not) are facts such as the parties' names; it would not matter if they were called Bill and Georgina, or Frank and Sue. The time that the accident occurred would also not be relevant; it would not matter if the accident had happened at 4:02pm, 4:04pm or even 4:10pm. Nor would the road name be of any importance, it wouldn't impact upon the legal issue if the road was called Stamford Street, Main Road or Holly Crescent. The make, model and colour of the vehicles would not be material, as it would not matter if Bill had been driving a pink Mini Cooper as opposed to a black Volvo XC90; he still crashed into her vehicle. Finally, the date would not be relevant to the issue as the accident could have happened in September, May or June, it would not change the issue as to whether or not the respondent contributed to the extent of her injuries due to her negligence in not wearing a seatbelt.

However, it must be appreciated that what is and what is not a material fact (i.e. a date or a party's age) will be dependent on the particular issue in question. For example, on 1 July, James had sex with Felicity, believing her to be over the age of legal consent (i.e. 16 years old) but Felicity was actually 15 years old on 1 July, her 16th birthday being on 25 July. If James were then charged with the offence of having sexual intercourse with a minor then both the date the sexual intercourse took place and Felicity's date of birth (both being matters of fact) will be material facts in establishing whether the offence has been committed or not. The legal age of consent will also be a material fact (and is a matter of law) as James can only be found guilty of the offence of having sexual intercourse with a minor if the legal age of consent is over the age of 16.

LEGAL ISSUE

A legal issue can be described as the question that the court has been asked to resolve. The legal issue will be termed as a question and it goes to the crux of the case. Often the legal issue is relatively easy to identify as the court will make a statement such as "The question in this appeal is. . .", or "We have been asked to consider whether. . .". Frequently the court will set out the legal issue clearly in the terms of the "certified question" (so it may state "The certified question in this case is as to whether. . ."). A point to note here is that there can also be more than one legal issue in a case, there can often be found two or three legal issues that all need to be resolved by the court, and, although they may be interrelated, each individual issue will have its own specific focus. **3–022**

An example of the court setting out a legal issue clearly and concisely (and quite helpfully) can be found in the House of Lords decision of **R. v Kennedy (Simon)** [2007] UKHL 38. In *Kennedy* the appellant had been convicted of manslaughter. The facts of the case are that the appellant prepared a syringe of heroin and handed it to the victim, who immediately injected himself and returned the syringe to the appellant. The appellant then left the room. The victim died shortly thereafter as a result of the injection and the appellant was charged with the offence of supplying a Class A drug and the offence of manslaughter. He was convicted on both counts. The appellant appealed to the Court of Appeal on the manslaughter conviction but his appeal was dismissed as the Court held that even though he had not physically injected the victim with the drug he had been acting jointly with the victim in the administering of the drug by preparing and supplying him with the syringe. The appellant then appealed to the House of Lords contending that the victim was an autonomous individual who had injected the heroin of his own free will and therefore the appellant had not caused the victim to administer the drug to himself, and therefore should be acquitted. The legal issue in the case is found in the speech of Lord Bingham (at para.2), where he stated:

The question certified by the Court of Appeal (Criminal Division) for the opinion of the House neatly encapsulates the question raised by this appeal:

"When is it appropriate to find someone guilty of manslaughter where that person has been involved in the supply of a class A controlled drug which is then freely and voluntarily self-administered by the person to whom it was supplied and the administration of the drug then causes his death?"

The issue to be determined in the case of **Kennedy** is easy to identify. The legal issue is the question that the court needs to decide and in answering this question it will determine the overall decision as to whether the appellant's appeal will succeed or fail. The legal issue also provides a good pointer when considering whether a decision in a case is binding upon a future case or not. If the issue concerns the same matters then it may well have to be taken into account in later cases on that point. However, not every legal issue will be so concisely and succinctly stated as it was in **Kennedy** and this often means that the legal issue in the case has to be determined by a process of elimination and deduction, as with a little perseverance and the use of logical and considered reasoning it is possible to discover what the question was that the court was trying to resolve. If the issue is not immediately apparent it is worth considering the questions of "what is the case concerned with?" and "what is the court trying to decide?" so as to try and pinpoint what the specific legal issue is. After determining the legal issue it is always prudent to go back and check the material facts identified so as to ensure that they are actually material to the legal issue.

IDENTIFYING THE RATIO DECIDENDI

3–023 What is meant by the term ratio decidendi (ratio) has been discussed in detail in Ch.2. What will now be considered is how a ratio can be identified. A common misconception is that the ratio is considered to be the overall decision in the case, so whether the appeal was allowed or dismissed or whether the conviction was quashed or upheld, but although the overall decision is certainly important (especially to the parties involved) it does not form part of the legal ratio. The ratio is essentially the court's reasoning behind its decision (why it came to the conclusion that it did) and the detailed answer to the question (the legal issue) before it.

Unfortunately there is no clear part in the case where the judge sets out the ratio, there is no heading of "Ratio" to be found within a case report, nor will the judge show consideration to those who will later read his speech and try to distil the principles from within it by saying something as direct and helpful as, "and the ratio of this case is. . .". Finding the ratio can often feel like trying to find a needle in a haystack, especially when new to the law, but it does become easier over time with practice and experience. The ratio is the opinion of the judge as to the answer to the legal issue. If there is more than one judge handing down a decision then there may well be more than one ratio in the case (each judge may have his own different opinion as to the reasoning to the overall conclusion); in fact even a decision from a single judge can provide for more than one ratio. Take, for example, the question of whether a school is good or not. One parent whose child goes to the school may say that the school is good because his child is happy there, another parent may say that the school is good because the teachers are all engaged in teaching the pupils. A person who has no connection with the school may determine that the school is good because it performs well in the league tables or a pupil who attends the school may conclude that the school is good because he studies subjects that he likes and because all his friends go there. The overall collective answer to the question (is the school good?) is that, "yes, the school is good", but each person asked has his own individual opinion(s) as to what actually makes the school good (they each provide their own ratio).

If we return to the decision of the House of Lords in **Kennedy**, the Court answered the legal issue by stating: **3–024**

The answer to the certified question is: "In the case of a fully-informed and responsible adult, never." The appeal must be allowed and the appellant's conviction for manslaughter quashed.

In **Kennedy** the House of Lords held that to establish the crime of unlawful act manslaughter, it had to be shown that the defendant had committed an unlawful act, which was criminal in nature, and that it was a significant cause of the death (the elements of the offence). The Court concluded that the criminal law generally assumed the existence of free will and that informed adults of sound mind were to be treated as autonomous beings, able to make their own decisions on how to act. Therefore a defendant could not to be treated as having caused the victim to act in a certain way if the victim made a voluntary and informed decision to act in that manner. In **Kennedy** the Court concluded that the victim had freely and voluntarily administered the injection to himself and that the appellant had not helped in the administration of the injection, nor had the appellant and the victim acted together as the heroin had been self-administered by the victim. The overall decision of the case was that the appeal should be allowed but the reasoning behind why it should (the ratio) is far more complex than just a simple yes or no answer.

A way in which the accuracy of the ratio can be determined is to consider it alongside the legal issue to see if they match. Does the ratio answer the legal issue? Does it set out the reasons for the answer? If the answer is "yes", then it is likely that the ratio has been correctly identified; if the answer is "no" then it is time to return to the case, check the material facts and the legal issue, and then reconsider the case to see how the question raised was ultimately answered.

Case Analysis—a Worked Example

3-025 Below is an extract from the case of **R. v Cockburn** [2008] EWCA Crim 316. The worked example will illustrate how to distil the key points, the material facts, legal issue and ratio, from the case.

Regina v Cockburn

Case No: 2007/03792-C4

Court of Appeal (Criminal Division)

28 February 2008

[2008] EWCA Crim 316

2008 WL 546399

Before: The President of the Queen's Bench Division
Mr Justice Davis and Mr Justice David Clarke

Date: 28/02/2008, Hearing dates: 12th February 2008

On Appeal from the Crown Court at Maidstone Mr Recorder Wilson

Representation

- Mr M. Magarian for the Appellant.
- Mr J. Higgs for the Crown.

Judgment

President of the Queen's Bench Division:

1. These are our reasons for dismissing the appeal by Nigel Cockburn against his conviction in the Crown Court at Maidstone. The statement of offence alleged setting a mantrap with intent, contrary to section 31 of the Offences against the Person Act 1861. The particulars were that between 1 January 2006 and 11 July 2006, the appellant set or placed, or caused to be set or placed, a mantrap or other engine calculated to destroy human life or inflict grievous bodily harm, with intent that the same or whereby the same may destroy or inflict grievous bodily harm on a trespasser or other person coming into contact therewith.

2. This offence is rarely charged. The question in this appeal was whether, having heard evidence from a defence expert, the Recorder was right to reject the submission that, as a matter of statutory construction, an undoubtedly dangerous contraption positioned by the appellant on top of some farm equipment in a shed on his land was capable or not of falling within the ambit of section 31. The Recorder decided that it was so capable. He directed the jury accordingly. The jury concluded that the contraption was indeed an engine for the purposes of section 31 and that the necessary intent had been proved: hence this appeal.
3. Section 31 of the 1861 Act provides:

> 'Whosoever shall set or place, or cause to be set or placed, any spring-gun, man-trap, or other engine calculated to destroy human life or inflict grievous bodily harm, with intent that the same or whereby the same may destroy or inflict grievous bodily harm upon a trespasser or other person coming in contact therewith, shall be guilty . . . Provided that nothing in this section contained shall extend to make it illegal to set or place any gin or trap such as may have been or may be usually set or placed with the intent of destroying vermin: Provided also, that nothing in this section shall be deemed to make it unlawful to set or place, or cause to be set or placed, or to be continued set or placed, from sunset to sunrise, any spring-gun, man-trap, or other engine which shall be set or placed, or caused or continued to be set or placed in a dwelling house for the protection thereof."

4. The contraption set by the appellant was neither a spring-gun nor a man-trap. The conviction could only have been sustained if it was an 'other engine calculated to destroy human life or inflict grievous bodily harm'. Briefly, it is a spiked metal object made from two pieces of heavy steel plate into which some 20 4-inch long nails, protruding at different angles, are welded. It was connected by a metal rod or wire to the roof frame of a shed on the appellant's land. Another wire connected it to the shed door. When the shed door was opened it was activated and the force of gravity caused it to swing downwards and catch the person entering through the door.
5. On 11 July 2006, in the course of a lawful investigation of the appellant's property, an army officer pushed open the shed door. As he did so, with good sense, he took the precaution of holding his arm across his face. The spiked object struck his forearm rather than his face. Two nails entered into his clothing, and a third punctured his forearm. His injuries could well have been very much more serious than they were.
6. It was submitted on behalf of the appellant that this object was not and could not be treated as an engine. The power needed to work it was applied exclusively by nature, gravity. No other form of stored energy or force was involved. This therefore was not a mechanical contrivance at all, and the decision of this court in **R v Munks**

[1964] 1 Q.B. 304 provides clear authority for the proposition that if the object was not such a contrivance it could not be an "other engine" for the purposes of section 31.

7. In **Munks** the appellant connected a wire from an electric light in the kitchen, through into the living room, and fastened it to the handle of the French window. He fixed another wire leading from the kitchen so that it would hang down inside the window in such a way that anyone opening the window from the outside, and coming into contact with the hanging wire, would suffer a severe electric shock. The electric wires were deliberately arranged so as to create the risk of electric shock if an electric light switch happened to be switched on at the time. It was deliberately fixed by the appellant to prevent his wife getting into the house. The point at issue was whether the two wires fastened and draped at the window, bringing electricity to it when the kitchen switch was on, amounted to an "engine" calculated to inflict grievous bodily harm. The appellant was convicted on the basis that it was, and he appealed arguing that the word "engine" had two distinct meanings, one broader than the other. The court accepted the analysis that the broader meaning included a contrivance or device, and would extend to what was described as the electrical contrivance in the case. The narrower meaning however was equally recognised, and was limited to a mechanical contrivance or machine. By contrast with the broad approach taken by the court in **Allen v Thompson** [1970] L.R. 5 Q.B. 336, where section 3 of the Game Act 1831 was under consideration, the court adopted the narrower rather than the broader of the two possible meanings. In argument it was in effect conceded by the Crown that the word spring-gun and man-trap both referred to mechanical contrivances. Given that concession it was virtually inevitable that the court would conclude that the words "or other engine" must mean "other mechanical contrivance". It was decided that although the arrangements of these wires amounted to an electrical contrivance, it did not constitute a mechanical contrivance, and was therefore not an "other engine" for the purposes of section 31.

8. On the face of it any engine calculated to kill or inflict grievous bodily harm falls within the ambit of section 31. The Oxford English Dictionary, among other descriptions, describes an engine as a "mechanical contrivance, machine, implement, tool". Something of the breadth of its meaning at the time when the Act came into force is identified in the Dictionary itself where, among other references, we find a pair of scissors described as a "little engine" in the *Rape of the Lock* (1712–1714) and a description of "engines of restraint and pain" at the victim's feet in *Death Slavery* (1866). None of these references dilutes or could dilute the authority of **Munks**, although they suggest that the Crown's argument in that case was more constrained than it perhaps should have been.

9. In these circumstances, there is no reason for giving (and every reason, given the evident purpose behind the legislation, for not giving) the words "spring-gun" or "man-trap" or "other engine" an unduly narrow meaning. In **Munks**, it is true that

a very wide definition of the word "engine" was rejected, and in the context of the electrical device with which it was concerned the word "engine" was said to connote a mechanical contrivance. However we reject the argument implicit in the submissions that **Munks** was intended to or could redefine the statutory language of section 31 by replacing the words "other engine" with "other mechanical contrivance". The court cannot re-write statutory language which has been unamended for nearly 200 years. In any event the words "mechanical contrivance", as used in **Munks**, are not to be applied restrictively so as to lead to the exclusion of a contraption, which falls within the ambit of the statute. On the rare occasions when this question arises for decision, the object itself as well as the manner, if any, in which it may be activated should be examined pragmatically to see whether, looked at overall, it falls within the statutory language. In **Munks**, the placing of cables on or by a door through which an electric current could pass was held not to be sufficient of a mechanical contrivance to be an "engine". In the present case, using ordinary language, the contraption was certainly a contrivance. It was mechanical, since as a mechanism, it was triggered into dangerous movement by inadvertent pressure on a wire or string. In short therefore it is properly described as a mechanical contrivance or machine, and it unquestionably is an "other engine" for the purposes of section 31 of the 1861 Act. For these reasons the main ground of appeal failed.

Over to you

Consider the list of facts below. These facts have all been taken from the case of Cockburn but not every fact is material. Select from the list those facts that you believe are material.

- **The appellant was convicted at Maidstone Crown Court.**
- **The appellant's name was Nigel Cockburn.**
- **The appellant was convicted of an offence under s.31 of the OAPA 1861, which states: "Whosoever shall set or place, or cause to be set or placed, any spring-gun, man-trap, or other engine calculated to destroy human life or inflict grievous bodily harm, with intent that the same or whereby the same may destroy or inflict grievous bodily harm upon a trespasser or other person coming in contact therewith, shall be guilty [of an offence]".**
- **The offence is rarely charged.**
- **The appellant had set a contraption, which was neither a spring-gun nor a man-trap, which was calculated to destroy life or inflict grievous bodily harm.**
- **The contraption was a spiked metal object from which some nails protruded.**
- **The nails were four inches long.**
- **The contraption was connected by a metal rod or wire to the roof frame of a shed on the appellant's land.**

- **The contraption was connected to the door of a shed on the appellant's land.**
- **The contraption was set as such that when the shed door was open the contraption was activated and the contraption would swing down towards to the door, striking any person who was entering the shed at that time.**
- **The appellant submitted that this object was not and could not be treated as an engine. The power needed to work it was applied exclusively by nature, gravity.**
- **The victim was an army officer who had lawfully attended the appellant's property on 11 July 2006.**
- **The victim had opened the shed door and had been hit by the contraption, but had managed to shield their body and face so that the injuries were only inflicted upon the victim's arm.**
- **Two nails entered into his clothing, and a third punctured his forearm. His injuries could easily have been more serious than they were.**

MATERIAL FACTS

3–026 The facts that are material to the case of **Cockburn** are as follows and the reasons as to why these particular facts are material will become clear once the legal issue has been identified.

- The appellant was convicted of an offence under s.31 OAPA 1861, which states:

  "Whosoever shall set or place, or cause to be set or placed, any spring-gun, man-trap, or other engine calculated to destroy human life or inflict grievous bodily harm, with intent that the same or whereby the same may destroy or inflict grievous bodily harm upon a trespasser or other person coming in contact therewith, shall be guilty [of an offence]".

- The appellant had set a contraption, which was neither a spring-gun nor a man-trap, which was calculated to destroy life or inflict grievous bodily harm.
- The contraption was made from a spiked metal object, from which nails protruded.
- The contraption was connected to the door of a shed on the appellant's land.
- The contraption was set as such that when the shed door was open the contraption was activated and the contraption would swing down towards to the door, striking any person who was entering the shed at that time.
- The victim had opened the shed door and had been hit by the contraption, but had managed to shield his body and face so that the injuries were only inflicted upon the victim's arm.

As can be seen, many of the facts identified above in the "Over to you" box are not material to the case decision. It does not matter whether the victim was an army officer or a local vet;

his profession is not relevant to the legal issue. It is not important to identify whether the incident occurred on 11 July 2006, it could have easily have occurred on 5 November 2007, or 24 December 1988. The court is not concerned with the fact that the nails entered his clothing, or that his forearm was punctured, it is only concerned with the fact that he had been injured. There would have been no fundamental change in the case if the appellant been convicted at Leicester Crown Court instead of Maidstone Crown Court, and the appellant's name is not relevant, as if he had been called Chris Cringle this would not have changed the outcome and principles of the case. As stated above the material facts are directly linked to the legal issue and the ratio.

Over to you

What is the legal issue in the case of *Cockburn*?

LEGAL ISSUE

In **Cockburn** there is no specific part of the judgment that clearly sets out the legal issue. At no point does judge say "the legal issue in this case is. . .". This means that an educated guess must be taken as to what the legal issue was. **3–027**

From reading the judgment we can deduce that the case is not about what constitutes grievous bodily harm. Although the case is based on the OAPA 1861 it does not consider whether the injuries suffered by the victim amount to grievous bodily harm (this is why the fact that the victim's clothes and forearm were punctured was not a material one). Further, it can be assumed upon reading the case, that the issue was not as to whether a person is allowed to set up a booby trap to protect his land from trespassers. If that were the issue then more would have been made about the fact that the victim had attended the appellant's property to *lawfully* search the premises.

The issue in the case revolves around the statutory provision that the appellant was convicted under, namely s.31. Section 31 sets out that:

> **Whosoever shall set or place, or cause to be set or placed, any spring-gun, man-trap, or other engine calculated to destroy human life or inflict grievous bodily harm, with intent that the same or whereby the same may destroy or inflict grievous bodily harm upon a trespasser or other person coming in contact therewith, shall be guilty [of an offence].**

The Court concluded that the contraption set by the appellant was not a spring-gun or a man-trap. The only other factor that could therefore be under consideration by the Court was as to whether the contraption was an "engine" as defined under the Act. If consideration is given to para.6 of the case it can be seen that the appellant submitted that the contraption could not be an engine as it was not a mechanical contrivance and worked purely by the forces of gravity. The submission was based upon the authority of the case of **Munks** [1964] 1 Q.B. 304, which provided for the proposition that if the object was not such a contrivance it could not be an "other engine" for the purposes of s.31.

Therefore, the logical conclusion to come to, after analysing the case, would be that the legal issue was whether an "engine" under s.31 of the OAPA 1861 had to be a mechanical contrivance.

Over to you

What is the ratio decidendi of *Cockburn*?

RATIO DECIDENDI

3–028 The ratio of the case (in the author's opinion) is as follows: that an "engine" under s.31 of the OAPA 1861 did not have to be a mechanical contrivance as, if this is had been what Parliament intended, then it would have stated so in the legislation. (This is the answer to the general question together with the reasoning for the answer.) However, the contraption in the instant case did amount to a mechanical contrivance as the mechanism was triggered by the opening of the shed door, upon which gravity then took over, and therefore it fell firmly within the meaning of "engine" under the statute. (This is a more case-specific ratio, which relates directly to the material facts of the case.)

Finding and Using Legislation

3–029 All legislation passed by Parliament is catalogued by the Office of Public Sector Information (OPSI) and copies of legislation are freely available online through His Majesty's Stationery Office (HMSO) at *http://www.legislation.gov.uk* [accessed 1 May 2025], which is now part of the OPSI.

Statute law (or Acts of Parliament) can also be found in hard copy in most law libraries. There are many texts that are solely concerned with providing the relevant statutory provisions for a specific area of law. For example, the Blackstone's series of statute books (published by OUP) comprehensively cover all topic areas from criminal law and family law through to medical law and public law. Each statute book contains all the pertinent and necessary statutes for that area of law (so in a family law statute book there will be reproduced the relevant statutory provisions on divorce, financial matters, childcare law and adoption, etc.). As well as the individual statute books, there is also the Halsbury's series, which sets out all the laws of England and Wales within one chronological series.

Online sources will generally hold all the relevant statutory provisions in the databases and this is where the online sources come into their own as it is possible to search for the exact section and/or subsection that is required without having to trawl through pages and pages of irrelevant sections (although do not forget the comments made above about the usefulness of hard copy sources).

To illustrate how to find a specific statutory provision online we will once again return to the Westlaw UK database. The focus of the search will be on the statutory defence to murder of diminished responsibility.

To search specifically for legislation it is advisable to go to the link entitled "Legislation" at the top of the page (see the screen below), although simply un-ticking all of the boxes on the left hand side of the screen except for "Legislation", will allow you to perform a general search by way of the search box on the Westlaw UK main home page.

If the exact title of the legislation is not known then the "Free Text" box can be used to input related words so that a general search is performed. For example if the required legislation concerned the defence to murder of diminished responsibility then the term "diminished responsibility" in quote marks could be typed in here. This would then bring up a list of related provisions and each would have to be searched through manually to find the specific section required. For example, with the term "diminished responsibility" 39 results are returned and each one would have to be looked at individually so as to identify the relevant provision.

If the title of the relevant legislation were known then this could be typed into the "Act/SI Title" box (for example, here, the Homicide Act 1957). If the search were conducted with the term the "Homicide Act 1957" then only that specific Act would be returned by the search engine. The box below shows an example of the different methods that can be used to search for one particular source. Note that the title box yields a predictive text result as you type, thus reducing the need to type out in full any lengthy names of the much longer titled statutes. 3-030

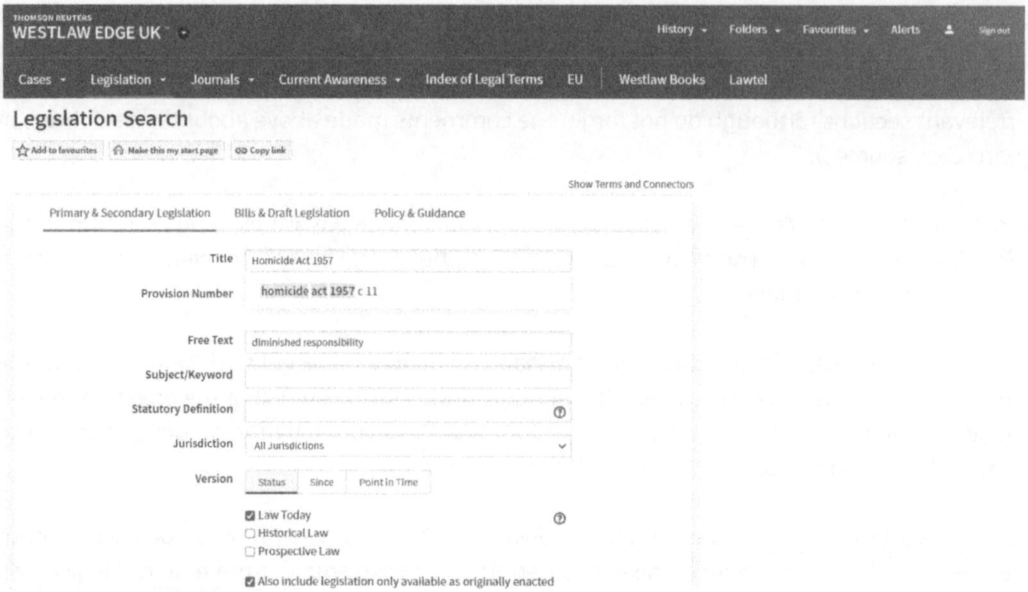

Clicking "Search" will then return any results. For the above search five results are returned (Arrangement of Act, Arrangement of Provisions and, s.2 Persons suffering from diminished responsibility etc). Clicking on the link to s.2 will take you straight to the relevant statutory provision. Note also that there are two versions to this section: an older version that ran from enactment until 3 October 2010 and then the current version that is in force today. Both contain different and important provisions that are typically addressed in any criminal law module.

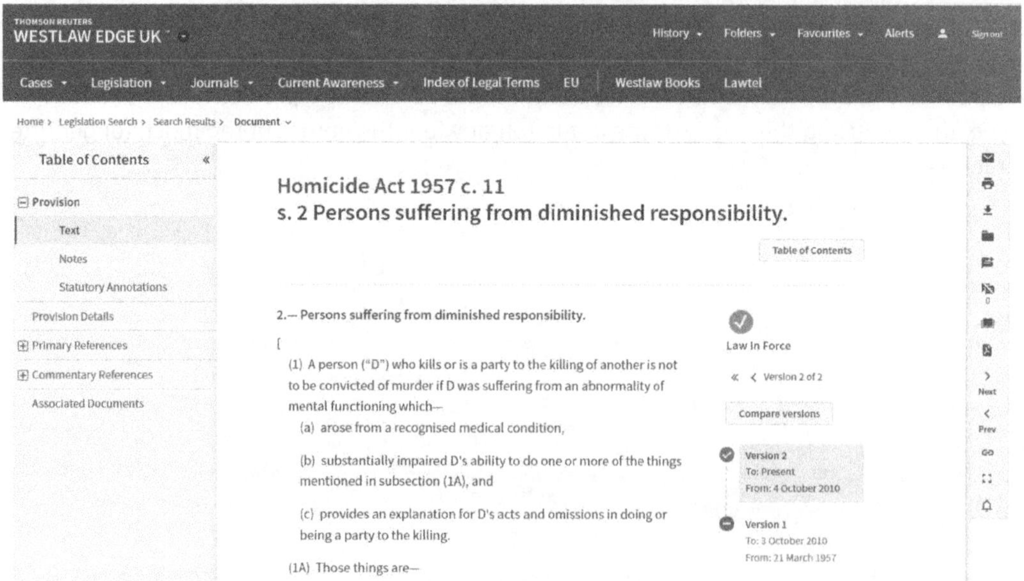

Westlaw UK is a relatively helpful online database. If you were to click on the link in the search results entitled "Arrangement of Act" (instead of going straight to the specific section number) this would lead to what is, effectively, the contents page of the Act. The different sections will be set out in a list (s.1, s.2, s.3, etc.) each with a link that can be clicked upon to access that specific individual section.

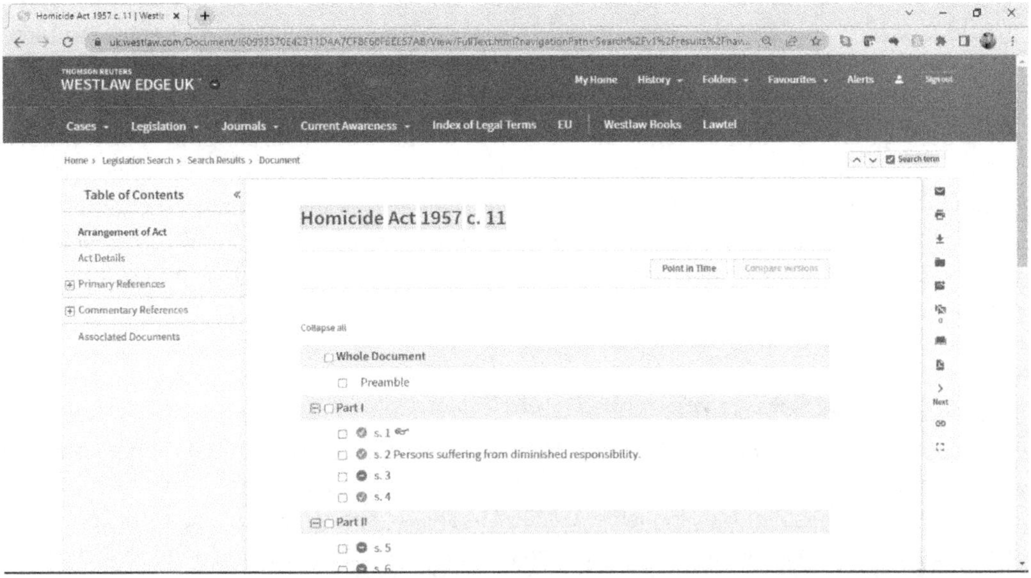

Over to you

Looking at the screen above, what do you think the circle next to ss.3 and 5–9 indicates?

If a certain section has been repealed (removed from the statute books) or if there are amendments pending to a certain section or sections then these will be highlighted on the contents page (Arrangement of Act), which will provide an indication as to the legislation's status. A red "no entry sign" means that the section has been repealed and an "!" means that amendments are pending. This helps to ensure that only up-to-date legislation is used.

Referring to Legislation

There are a number of different ways that legislation can be referred to. The usual way of referring to an Act is by what is known as its short title. The short title of the Act currently under discussion is the Homicide Act 1957. However, an Act can also be referred to by its "long title" or "preamble", as well as its "Chapter number". The long title or preamble sets out the purpose of the Act (in the case of the Homicide Act 1957 this was to make amendments to the law relating to homicide). Long titles used to be far more complex and informative, some running 3–031 to a number of paragraphs, whereas now, the method of referencing to the long title has been reduced dramatically and, as a result, although they are still used, they no longer contain such a large amount of information.

The Chapter number is an interesting historical remnant as to how the law was traditionally referred to. Originally Acts of Parliament were bound into a single book for each year; so all the laws passed in a specific year (say 1957) would be bound together to create one large volume containing the law for that year. Each Act added to the book over the course of the year would be assigned a Chapter number and this related to the order in which the laws were made during that year. So the Homicide Act 1957 would have been the eleventh statute passed in 1957. Originally, Acts of Parliament were only referred to by the Chapter number and so it would have been said that a defendant had contravened s.1 of the eleventh Chapter for 1957, rather than s.1 of the Homicide Act. This tradition has largely fallen by the wayside and now only the short title is really referred to (although in other jurisdictions such as the USA, laws are still referred to by the Chapter number).

Reading a Statute

3–032 It is relatively easy to read a statutory provision that only has one section but matters become more complex where a single section then has a number of subsections, each dealing with a different point (e.g. s.2 of the Homicide Act 1957 as shown above). When a statutory provision has a number of subsections it is crucial to ensure that the correct section and subsection are cited when referring to them. It may be that one subsection is not applicable to the circumstances whilst another is highly relevant; citing the incorrect section and subsection in court could have dramatic consequences (although it is more likely that the judge or another lawyer would point out the mistake so it may only result in embarrassment, which is still bad enough).

For example, consider the provisions found within s.116 of the Criminal Justice Act 2003 (CJA 2003) (shown in the box below). The CJA 2003, as a complete statute, is notorious among legal practitioners for being badly drafted, and the sections can at times seem convoluted and difficult to understand as they tend to include a lot of unnecessary detail. Section 116 concerns the admissibility (allowing) of evidence into a criminal court when the witness (whose evidence it is) is not available.

Over to you

Read s.116 of the CJA 2003 below and then consider the following scenario.

Brenda witnessed Diane murder John. At the time Brenda gave a statement to the police stating what she saw but she has since died. At Diane's trial the prosecution want to adduce Brenda's statement.

What does s.116 say about this?

116 Cases where a witness is unavailable

(1) In criminal proceedings a statement not made in oral evidence in the proceedings is admissible as evidence of any matter stated if—
   (a) oral evidence given in the proceedings by the person who made the statement would be admissible as evidence of that matter,
   (b) the person who made the statement (the relevant person) is identified to the court's satisfaction, and
   (c) any of the five conditions mentioned in subsection (2) is satisfied.

(2) The conditions are—
   (a) that the relevant person is dead;
   (b) that the relevant person is unfit to be a witness because of his bodily or mental condition;
   (c) that the relevant person is outside the United Kingdom and it is not reasonably practicable to secure his attendance;
   (d) that the relevant person cannot be found although such steps as it is reasonably practicable to take to find him have been taken;
   (e) that through fear the relevant person does not give (or does not continue to give) oral evidence in the proceedings, either at all or in connection with the subject matter of the statement, and the court gives leave for the statement to be given in evidence.

(3) For the purposes of subsection (2)(e) "fear" is to be widely construed and (for example) includes fear of the death or injury of another person or of financial loss.

(4) Leave may be given under subsection (2)(e) only if the court considers that the statement ought to be admitted in the interests of justice, having regard—
   (a) to the statement's contents,
   (b) to any risk that its admission or exclusion will result in unfairness to any party to the proceedings (and in particular to how difficult it will be to challenge the statement if the relevant person does not give oral evidence),
   (c) in appropriate cases, to the fact that a direction under section 19 of the Youth Justice and Criminal Evidence Act 1999 (c. 23) (special measures for the giving of evidence by fearful witnesses etc.) could be made in relation to the relevant person, and
   (d) to any other relevant circumstances.

(5) A condition set out in any paragraph of subsection (2) which is in fact satisfied is to be treated as not satisfied if it is shown that the circumstances described in that paragraph are caused—
   (a) by the person in support of whose case it is sought to give the statement in evidence, or
   (b) by a person acting on his behalf,

   in order to prevent the relevant person giving oral evidence in the proceedings (whether at all or in connection with the subject matter of the statement).

3–033 Section 116(1) sets out that such a statement as described above can be admitted as evidence so long as the person could have given the evidence personally in court (subject to the usual rules of evidence), that he has been identified to the court's satisfaction (subs. (b)) and that one of the conditions in subs. (2) has been satisfied. Brenda has died and so the relevant condition can be found under s.116(2)(a). If this specific subsection is cited then there should be no issue with respect to allowing the evidence into court, but, if by accident s.116(2)(c) was cited instead (the relevant person is outside of the UK and cannot attend court), then there would be questions raised as to why she could not attend; this could be slightly awkward and sensitive considering the fact that Brenda is dead. The exact provision to be relied upon has to be identified. Also, simply stating that the evidence could be admitted under s.116 would not be sufficient, as this would not satisfactorily identify the reason behind why Brenda is not able to give evidence in person. When considering statutory provisions, exactness is the key.

Explanatory notes

3–034 To accompany the enactment of new legislation Parliament now produces explanatory notes to help explain the new provisions and the intentions behind their creation. For example the summary of the explanatory notes for the CJA 2003 states that:

> **In July 2002 the Government published a White Paper outlining its plans for the criminal justice system, from crime prevention through to the punishment and rehabilitation of offenders. *Justice for All* (Cm 5563) focused particularly on reforms to court procedure and sentencing, to make trials faster and to deliver clear, consistent and appropriate sentencing. On these issues the White Paper built on the proposals in two consultation documents: *Review of the Criminal Courts of England and Wales by Sir Robin Auld* (2001) and *Making Punishment Work: report of a review of the sentencing framework of England and Wales (2001)* by John Halliday.**
>
> **This Act is intended to introduce reforms in these two areas. With regard to court procedure, the Act aims to improve the management of cases through the courts by involving the Crown Prosecution Service in charging decisions, by reforming the system for allocating cases to court, and by increasing magistrates' sentencing powers so that fewer cases have to go to the Crown Court. It will enable action to be taken to reduce breaches of bail by introducing a new presumption against bail in certain circumstances.**
>
> **The Act is designed to ensure that criminal trials are run more efficiently and to reduce the scope for abuse of the system. It will reform the rules on advance disclosure of evidence and will allow for judge-alone trial in cases involving threats and intimidation of juries, and paves the way for judge-alone trial in exceptionally long, complex serious fraud cases. It will ensure the wider**

involvement of the community as a whole by reforming rules on jury service. Rules on evidence will be changed to allow the use of previous convictions where relevant, and to allow the use of reported (hearsay) evidence where there is good reason why the original source cannot be present, or where the judge otherwise considers it would be appropriate. It will enable any witness to give evidence using live links. A right of appeal for the prosecution against judicial decisions to direct or order an acquittal before the jury has been asked to consider the evidence will be introduced to balance the defendant's right of appeal against both conviction and sentence. The Act will also make it possible in certain very serious cases for a retrial to take place despite an earlier acquittal if there is new and compelling evidence of an accused's guilt.

The notes help to give a clear indication as to the driving force behind the Act and they can **3–035**
be invaluable to those attempting to understand and interpret it. When considering the detail provided regarding the admissibility of absent witnesses (which are applicable to the example concerning Brenda above), the notes state that:

The provisions in [. . .] are intended, so far as necessary, to codify the law relating to the admissibility of out of court statements in criminal proceedings. They aim to simplify the law and to provide greater certainty as to the circumstances when such evidence will be admitted. The main provisions [. . .] remove the old common law rule against the admission of [such] evidence and provide that such evidence will be admissible (on behalf of the prosecution and defence) provided certain safeguards are met.

The explanatory notes can be useful tools, the judiciary is increasingly relying upon them in an effort to interpret legislation and it is not uncommon to come across a case where the judge has turned to the explanatory notes to a statute as an aid to statutory interpretation (see Ch.2, "Explanatory Notes").

Summary

1. The law (statutes, cases and other sources) can be found both online and in the library. Most educational institutions will have a well-stocked law library and will subscribe to a number of online legal databases, such as Westlaw UK and LexisNexis.

2. Students are advised to make the most of the online databases but it is stressed that the hard copies found within the libraries should not be forgotten about

and should be used on a regular basis so that valuable research skills can be developed.

3. The case names are helpful to identify the type of proceedings, the parties in the case and their respective roles.
4. Citations indicate where a reported case can be located. The citations set out the year, volume, law reports series and page number where the case is reported. Neutral citations are used to identify the case by its court hearing. There is a hierarchy of law report series, with the Law Reports (published by the ICLR) being the most authoritative, going down to the commercial individual law reports.
5. The material facts of a case are those facts that are vital to the outcome and the reasoning behind the case. Details such as party names and dates are not generally material and the material facts often need to be identified by a process of elimination, which can involve taking into consideration the legal issues and ratio decidendi of the case.
6. The legal issue is the question being posed to the court that it is required to resolve. This can often be identified by the use of the phrase "the certified question", or by the fact that it is set out clearly as a specific question. However, there are many cases where the legal issue is not readily identifiable and the case will require careful scrutiny to deduce it.
7. The ratio decidendi is the legal reasoning behind the decision in a case. There may be more than one ratio per case and even per judge. The ratio is the judge's opinion as to why they have come to the conclusion that they have. The ratio should match up with both the legal issue and the material facts.
8. Legislation can be referred to by a number of different methods, such as the short title (the most common reference), the long title/preamble and the Chapter number. When using a statute it is important to be very specific when referencing it.
9. Many statutes are supplemented by explanatory notes that are published by Parliament to aid the understanding and interpretation of a statute. Reference to explanatory notes is becoming more commonplace in respect of statutory interpretation by the judiciary.

Further Reading

J. Holland and J. Webb, *Learning Legal Rules*, 11th edn (Oxford University Press, 2022).
This book considers the legal theory, structure, practice and techniques of legal analysis.

A. Neal, A. Bradney, F. Cownie and J. Masson, *How to Study Law*, 9th edn (Sweet & Maxwell, 2021).
This book demonstrates how to find, read and analyse a variety of legal materials.

C. Turner and J. Boylan-Kemp, *Unlocking Legal Learning*, 3rd edn (Routledge, 2012), Chs 4 and 5.

Chapters 4 and 5 explain how to identify, obtain and then use primary and secondary sources of law.

G. Williams, *Learning the Law*, 17th edn (Sweet & Maxwell, 2020).

This book introduces students to the basic legal materials such as statutes and case law, and explains how these are to be read and interpreted in the light of common law doctrines of precedent.

Self Test Questions

1. Authoritative case law can be found:
- **(a)** online
- **(b)** in the library
- **(c)** in a journal
- **(d)** all of the above

2. The case name **Charleston v DPP** means that:
- **(a)** Charleston is appealing and the DPP is the defendant
- **(b)** the DPP is appealing and Charleston is the defendant
- **(c)** Charleston is being prosecuted by the DPP
- **(d)** the Attorney-General is clarifying a point of law upon Charleston's conviction

3. The citation [2000] 5 Q.B. 202 means:
- **(a)** the case was the fifth case reported for the Queen's Bench Division for 2000
- **(b)** the case was the 202nd case reported for the Queen's Bench Division for 2000
- **(c)** the case was reported in the fifth volume of the Queen's Bench Reports for 2000 at page 202
- **(d)** the case was the 202nd case reported in the fifth volume of the Queen's Bench Reports for 2000

4. The All E.R. reports are:
- **(a)** the most authoritative law reporting series
- **(b)** the least authoritative law reporting series
- **(c)** published by the ICLR
- **(d)** commercially published

5. The most commonly used reference title for legislation is the:
- **(a)** Chapter number
- **(b)** short title
- **(c)** long title
- **(d)** preamble

The Legal Profession

4

CHAPTER OVERVIEW

In this chapter we will:

- **Explain about the different legal personnel who work within the justice system.**
- **Discuss how to become a qualified lawyer (barrister, solicitor or legal executive).**
- **Analyse the changes that have occurred, and are currently occurring, within the legal profession and the likely future of the profession as a result of these changes.**
- **Consider the various regulatory bodies associated with the legal profession.**

Summary

Key Cases

Further Reading

Self Test Questions

Introduction

4-001 The landscape in respect of the legal profession is undergoing a monumental change at present. This change is affecting the way in which legal services are provided, it is impacting upon the roles and responsibilities of the legal personnel working within the system, and it is beginning to affect the way that legal education is both provided and taught.

This chapter will discuss the state of the legal profession as it is today; consideration will be given to the legal personnel who work within the legal services sector, the changes that have occurred to date and the way that the future of the profession is being shaped.

Legal Personnel

4-002 The term "legal personnel" encompasses all of those people who work within the legal system. A large number of these people work in an administrative capacity (i.e. court clerks and listing officers) or within one of the peripheral agencies involved in the maintaining of justice (i.e. the Probation Service and the Prison Service). However, a large number of people included in this figure are those who are known colloquially as "legal professionals". This title encompasses those who are viewed as the traditional "lawyers" of the profession (solicitors and barristers), as well as those individuals who work within the system, such as paralegals and legal executives, who are present in high numbers, but are less well known by lay people outside of the legal world; these different legal roles will be the focus of this chapter.

Paralegals

4-003 Within the plethora of law firms up and down the country there will be commonly found employees who hold the title of "paralegal". Paralegals are the people who carry out a lot of the basic work for a law firm. They generally undertake the type of work that does not require a highly qualified (and therefore expensive) solicitor to do. Paralegals may or may not be legally qualified, as there is no specific requirement that they have to be so qualified, but most of them will hold some form of legal qualification. Quite often both undergraduate and postgraduate law students will work as a paralegal either during their study vacations whilst undertaking their course or, on a full-time basis, after they have completed their course and are considering what their next career step will be.

The exact nature of the work they undertake will depend entirely on the focus of the firm that they are employed by. If the firm are criminal defence solicitors then paralegals may find themselves regularly visiting prisons to take statements from clients, or they may often be found sitting behind a barrister in court taking down notes for the case file. If the firm in question deals with matters of personal injury then paralegals may be responsible for meeting clients and taking down details of their claims, they may be required to fill out the necessary forms required for arranging funding for the litigation, or they may be charged with instructing counsel or expert witnesses. If conveyancing (buying and selling houses) is the main staple of the firm's work then paralegals may be responsible for taking instructions from the clients, conducting the relevant searches on the property and making an application for the title deeds, etc. As can be seen, the work covered by paralegals is not particularly complex and, as the issues are generally straightforward, it is more appropriate that it is carried out by a paralegal rather than a highly paid fee-earner.

Legal Executives

Another employee that is regularly found within law firms is a legal executive. Legal executives are fellows and/or members of the Chartered Institution of Legal Executives, which is otherwise known as CILEX. CILEX was established in 1963, with the support of the Law Society, and it describes itself as being recognised as "the third branch of the legal profession". It provides training and regulation for non-solicitor staff employed in fee-earning work so that these staff can be recognised for their skills and knowledge and so that the standards within the profession can be improved. CILEX lawyers are regulated by the Legal Services Act 2007 and are "authorised persons" for the purposes of undertaking one of the six "reserved legal activities" under the 2007 Act. These reserved activities are: the exercise of rights of audience; the conducting of litigation; specified instrument activities; probate activities; and notarial activities. A CILEX lawyer specialises in a particular area of law and is trained to the same standard as a solicitor in that area. 4-004

CILEX currently has over 18,000 members (legal executives) and a legal executive is a qualified lawyer (although not a solicitor or a barrister) who specialises in a particular area of law. In 2021, CILEX introduced a new qualification framework. This includes a non-graduate route to qualification as a lawyer as well as providing apprenticeships.

Once the individual has successfully completed these educational and vocational requirements he will become a Fellow of CILEX and will be issued with an annual practising certificate. A range of non-practising, dual qualified, associate or affiliate memberships is also available. 4-005

The legal executive route is simply a different way of becoming professionally qualified. It takes approximately four years to become a member of CILEX and this is achieved by a combination of studying and working in practice. The advantages of becoming qualified via CILEX are that a student can work and earn a wage at the same time as studying, thereby reducing the potential for accruing debt whilst also gaining valuable work le. Also, if an individual becomes a full Fellow of CILEX, then they do not have to undergo a training contract (see "Qualifying as a solicitor", below) on completion of the CILEX Professional Qualification (CPQ) examinations, as they will have already satisfied the work placement requirement whilst becoming a Fellow of CILEX.

Qualifying as a legal professional by way of CILEX is not to be considered as a second-rate option. Graduate members and Fellows of CILEX are often responsible for the mainstay of a solicitor firm's work, and the Law Society, who supported its initial establishment and supports its ongoing work, recognises the quality of the training provided by CILEX and describes the process as "lengthy, demanding and challenging". Chartered Legal Executive lawyers with five years' post-qualification experience are also now eligible to be appointed into certain judicial roles.

FIGURE 15 **CILEX career routes**

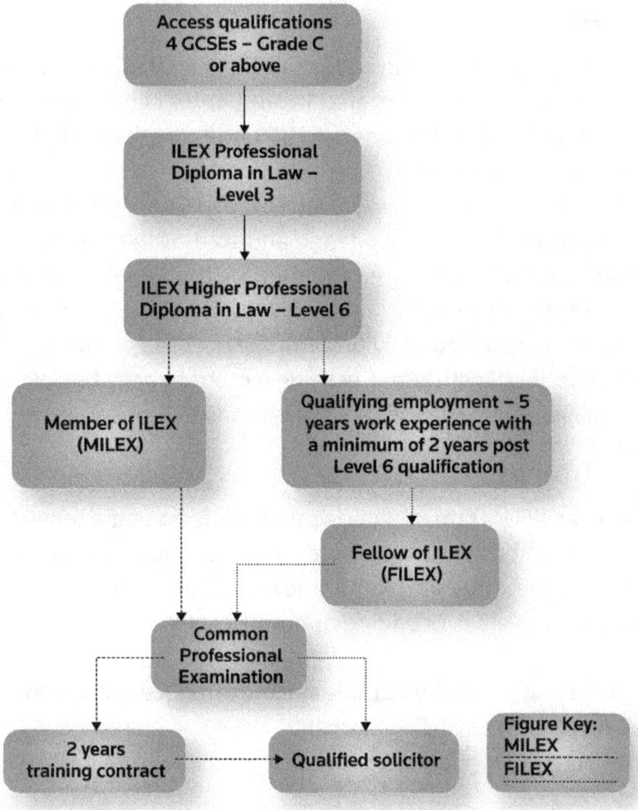

Solicitors

Over to you

What type of work is a solicitor involved in on a day-to-day basis? Does this change depending on the area of law the individual solicitor or the solicitors' firm practises? What different areas of law could a solicitor practise in?

Solicitors are often perceived by the public to be the front line of the legal profession. This is generally because solicitors are the first port of call for anyone considering undertaking any form of legal action, or by those who are being prosecuted or litigated against. The public can directly access solicitors and, as such, the majority of their work involves face-to-face contact with their clients or contact via the telephone or by way of email and fax. The nature and place of the client contact will generally be dependent upon the focus of the work undertaken by the particular solicitor. For example, a criminal solicitor may be required to see clients at a prison or in a police station (even in the middle of the night if he is on call); a commercial solicitor may be required to meet clients in his own office or at the company premises; and a solicitor who specialises in environmental law may have to meet clients out in the field (e.g. at a sewage treatment plant or at the side of a river bank). **4–006**

Solicitors tend to specialise and practice in one area (or possibly two closely related areas) of law, such as criminal law, family law, commercial law or personal injury law. Solicitors are employed by businesses known as firms and a firm of solicitors may also specialise in only one area of law, or, more often, they may be more of a general firm and have a number of different departments each specialising in a specific area of law. Firms can vary tremendously in both size and financial turnover, for example, the firms described as being members of the illustrious "Magic Circle" of the legal world (i.e. Allen & Overy, Clifford Chance, Slaughter & May, Freshfields Bruckhaus Deringer and Linklaters) are multi-million-pound, highly-prestigious and highly-staffed law firms. However, a high street law firm may only be a small outfit with a limited turnover and a handful of staff. Neither is superior to the other, they are both law firms but with a different focus.

Solicitors can form partnerships with each other; in fact, this is usual practice, as most firms will be comprised of a number of "equity partners" who have a financial interest in the business and are entitled to a proportion of profits made by the company. Also, there are "salaried partners" who are paid a salary by the firm but have no ownership interest in the business and are not eligible to any share of the profits. The development of limited liability partnerships (LLP) is also on the increase within solicitors' firms as under a normal partnership arrangement the partners are personally liable for any claim made against the company (even after the point of retirement) but, under the LLP business structure, liability is restricted to only the cases that the partner had personal responsibility for. A recent development in the provision of legal services has been the creation of Alternative Business Structures (ABS). Under the Legal Services Act 2007 provisions, which came into force in October 2011, legal services can now be offered by multi-disciplinary partnerships, meaning that a legal business can now be owned and managed by a non-legal organisation, such as Tesco, the AA or the Co-op (see "The Changing Professions", below, for further discussion on this point). **4–007**

Traditionally, the work of solicitors was a rather paper-based affair, as they only had rights of audience (the right to advocate in a court) in the lower courts of the magistrates' courts and the county courts; the right to advocate in the higher courts being retained solely by the barrister side of the legal profession. However, under the Courts and Legal Services Act 1990 and the Access to Justice Act 1999 this division of work and responsibility between the professions has been diluted and now solicitors can gain higher rights of audience and become solicitor-advocates, meaning that they can advocate in any domestic court within England and Wales (see "The Changing Professions", below, for a fuller discussion on this point). This has opened up the professional remit of solicitors and they are now eligible to become King's Counsel (see "King's Counsel", at **4–017**) and members of the judiciary.

COMPOSITION

4–008 According to the Law Society's *Annual Statistical Report 2023 (Executive Summary)* published in January 2025 there were 197,378 solicitors on the Roll as at 31 July 2023. This represents a 9% decrease on the previous year, the first decline in numbers for the first time in nine years, as The Solicitors Regulation Authority (SRA) reintroduced the keeping of the roll exercise in April 2023, meaning solicitors without a practising certificate must apply to remain on the roll. Out of this figure, 162,120 held practising certificates (a certificate is required by any person holding themselves out to provide legal work under s.1A of the Solicitors Act 1974), with the remainder working mainly in commerce and industry, the public sector, or abroad. The report figures show that the profession is relatively equally split in terms of gender, with over half of all solicitors holding practising certificates being female, outnumbering men by 8,289. A significant number either did not share their sex (19,018) or preferred not to say (229). The number of practising certificate holders from Black, Asian and minority ethnic groups is reported as 13%, but 28% did not share data on this metric, which, according to the Law Society represents an increasingly unreliable dataset that potentially skews their understanding of diversity in the profession. The median age of practising certificate holders is 44, meaning that half the population is above this age and the other half are below 44.

QUALIFYING AS A SOLICITOR

4–009 Traditionally, qualifying as a solicitor was viewed as the less competitive route of entry into the legal profession (as compared to that of a barrister) but over recent years the allure of becoming a legal practitioner has become an increasingly attractive prospect, with a higher number of students undertaking a relevant undergraduate and/or postgraduate course so as to enter the profession. As a result of these increased numbers of students vying to become a solicitor, the competition for entry into the profession has also dramatically increased. The decision to become a solicitor now involves almost the same level of risk that the decision to become a barrister does (see "Qualifying as a barrister", below).

The Law Society set out that there are seven potential routes to becoming a solicitor and these are as:

- a law graduate;
- a non-law graduate;
- an overseas lawyer (transfer);

- a barrister (transfer) (see "Barristers", below);
- a Scottish/Northern Irish lawyer (transfer);
- a Fellow of the Chartered Institute of Legal Executives (FCILEX) (see "Legal Executives", at **4–004**); or as
- a justices' clerk (see Ch.5, "Legal Advisers").

This text will consider the common current route taken to become a solicitor: by way of a law degree or a non-law degree, following the changes implemented on 1 September 2021 by the introduction of the Solicitors Qualifying Examination (SQE) route.

The current initial starting point is for a potential solicitor to undertake an undergraduate degree and achieve at least a 2:2 (lower second class degree), although, realistically, to stand any chance of success, this really needs to be a 2:1 degree classification. The degree does not have to be a law degree (LL.B. (Hons)) and can be in any discipline that the student finds interesting, or it could be any other level 6 qualification such as an approved degree apprenticeship. The main requirement is that reasonable grades are achieved in all assessments from the very start of the degree (even in the first year) as individual assessment grades will be considered by firms when deciding whether or not to offer work experience and/or a training contract. **4–010**

Previously, if a student undertook a degree in a non-law discipline then he was required to complete a further year of study known as the Common Professional Examination or Post-Graduate Diploma in Law (PGDL). This qualification is, like the Legal Practice Course (LPC), now largely unavailable to school-leavers embarking on a legal career. Whilst a law degree will most likely prepare a candidate for the SQE1 examinations below, a non-law graduate cannot reasonably expect to pass the SQE1 examinations without undertaking a comprehensive preparation course. **4–011**

SOLICITORS QUALIFYING EXAMINATION (SQE)

The SQE1 stage comprises two in-person assessments that can be taken at one of a number of venues in the UK, or available internationally, of 180 single best answer multiple choice questions. Single best answer questions require a candidate to select the single, most accurate option based on the specific question being asked. However, the incorrect options are plausible as they can be partially or wholly incorrect or based on common misconceptions. SQE1 covers the following subject areas in the first 180 questions: Business Law and Practice; Dispute Resolution; Contract; Tort; Legal System of England and Wales; Constitutional and Administrative Law and EU Law and Legal Services; and in the second 180 questions: Property Practice; Wills and the Administration of Estates; Solicitors Accounts; Land Law; Trusts; Criminal Law and Practice. Examined pervasively across the two assessments is the topic Ethics and Professional Conduct. Sample questions and answers can be found on the Solicitors Regulation Authority website *https://sqe.sra.org.uk/exam-arrangements/assessment-information/sqe1-sample-questions* [accessed 1 May 2025]. **4–012**

SQE2 is also divided into two parts. Firstly, SQE2 Oral assesses advocacy skills in a dispute resolution and a criminal litigation context along with interview and attendance note/legal analysis skills in a property and probate context. These oral assessments take place over two half-days. SQE2 comprises a total of 12 written legal skills assessments and takes place over three half-days. Successful candidates must be able to demonstrate that they have reached the standard of competency of a Day One Solicitor, that they can apply fundamental legal principles in the skills-based situations covered by SQE2 in a way that addresses the client's needs and concerns. They will need sufficient knowledge to make them competent to practise on the basis that they can look up detail later.

Finally, a period of two years' full-time (or equivalent) Qualifying Work Experience (QWE) is required. This is more flexible than the previous training contract requirements as QWE can be gained before, during or after the SQE assessments. In fact, it can be gained in up to four different organisations, in paid or volunteer work, and could include time spent on placement during a law degree or working in a law clinic. It must, however, involve providing "legal services". The Legal Services Act 2007 (s.12) defines legal activity and can help candidates decide whether their role involves delivering legal services.

Below is an example of how a graduate could qualify.

FIGURE 16 Qualifying as a solicitor through the SQE

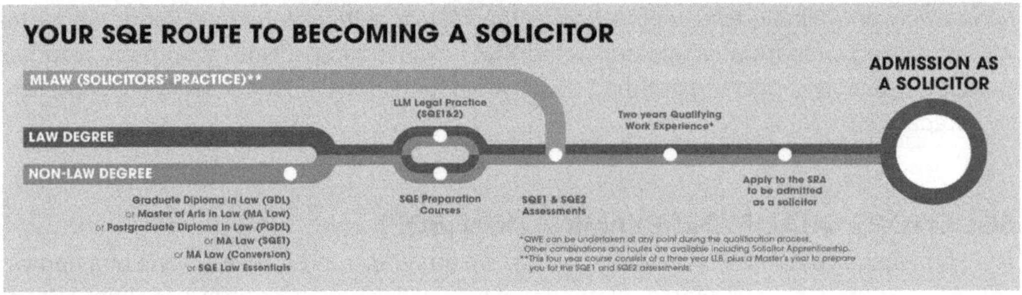

Barristers

Over to you

What type of work is a barrister involved in on a day-to-day basis? Does this change depending on the area of law the individual barrister practises? What different areas of law could a barrister practise in?

4–013 When most people think of a barrister, the image of an individual embodying the spirit of Rumpole of the Bailey or Kavanagh QC tends to spring to mind (younger readers may need to ask their parents or indeed grandparents about these characters), meaning that the general view of a barrister is a person who wears a wig and gown and is responsible for presenting a case in the courtroom (and, in respect of *Silk* and *North Square*, also having a great social life). This general image is not incorrect (even regarding the social life when the time is available) but it is not a complete picture of the work that a barrister undertakes professionally. Barristers do present (advocate) cases in the courtroom but they also undertake a lot of research to be able to do so (they do not have assistants to help them with this but must do all the work themselves): they draft opinions, give advice, act as negotiators and mediators, and a whole lot more. In fact, barristers who specialise in certain areas of the law, such as banking and maritime law, may spend very little time advocating in court and the majority of their time negotiating on behalf of and advising clients instead. The Bar Council (see "The General Council of the Bar", below, for further information on this organisation) describes barristers as:

> **[s]pecialist legal advisers and court room advocates. They are independent and objective and trained to advise clients on the strengths as well as the weaknesses of their case. They have specialist knowledge and experience in and out of court which can make a substantial difference to the outcome of a case.**

The main difference between solicitors and barristers is that a barrister is prevented from "conducting litigation" on behalf of a client and can only act *upon* the client's instructions, whereas a solicitor can act *in place* of a client and conduct the litigation *for him* (so solicitors can write letters, make applications to the court and even sign documents in place of the client).

Barristers are generally self-employed professionals, working out of shared offices known as chambers alongside other self-employed barristers. Chambers can vary in size from those where there are only a handful of barristers; to ones known, informally, as super-chambers, where there can be well over 100 barristers working from the premises. A set of chambers may be specialised and only focus on one specific area of the law, for example, criminal law or family law and all the barristers who work out of that chambers will practise only in that area, or it may be a common law chambers and offer expertise in a range of different areas of law (e.g. civil law, personal injury, criminal and family law)—the law that it covers will depend on the specialisms of the individual barristers who work from the chambers. The unique structure of a chambers allows a number of barristers to pool together and share facilities (such as office space, office equipment and administrative support, etc.) and the costs that those resources incur, as normally each barrister is required to pay rent or fees towards the upkeep and day-to-day running of the chambers. Administrative support for the barristers is provided by an employee of the chambers (or employees depending on the size of the chambers), known as a clerk. A barristers' clerk is responsible for allocating the work that comes into chambers from solicitors to the individual barristers, he keeps the barristers' diaries, chases outstanding bills, and ensures that all the work is adequately covered by an appropriately experienced practitioner 4–014 (for example, in a common law chambers, he would ensure that a criminal case is allocated to a barrister who has relevant criminal law experience and not a barrister who practises solely in medical negligence law).

Not every barrister is self-employed though and many work in an employed capacity within industry and commerce, government departments and as members of in-house legal teams. The benefits to being an employed barrister are the security of a regular wage, holiday entitlement, sick pay and pensions, etc. whereas a self-employed barrister who is responsible for, and only accountable to, himself does not benefit from the perks and allowances gained from an employed status. If a self-employed barrister does not work then he simply does not earn. According to the statistics compiled by the Bar Standards Board, there were 13,622 practising self-employed barristers in England and Wales in 2021 and there were 3,076 practising barristers working in an employed capacity. A small number were reported as practising in a dual capacity (565) or sole practitioners (634).

Barristers have recently been granted even more flexibility in their working structure following an amendment to the profession's Code of Conduct due to the introduction of new business models under the Legal Services Act 2007 (see below, under "The Changing Professions"). Barristers can now become managers of Legal Disciplinary Practices (LDPs), which would allow them to work in both a self-employed and employed capacity simultaneously. Barristers can now become shareholders in LDPs, they can share offices and premises with others, they are permitted to investigate and collect evidence, and they can take witness statements, attend police stations and conduct correspondence, all which were previously prohibited under the old rules.

INNS OF COURT

4–015 The profession of a barrister has existed since the 13th century and, as a result, the modern-day profession is steeped in tradition. For a barrister to be able to practise he must first be "called to the Bar". This does not mean that he has been invited down to the pub by his friends or fellow barristers, but rather that he has been inaugurated into the profession by becoming an accepted member of one of the four Inns of Court. The Inns of Court are almost as old as the profession itself and they have played an integral role in the development and regulation of the profession since about the 17th century. The four Inns of Court are:

- Lincoln's Inn;
- Inner Temple;
- Middle Temple; and
- Gray's Inn.

Over to you

What role do you think the Inns of Court originally played in the professional life of a barrister and do you think the modern-day role of the Inns has changed much from this?

Lincoln's Inn appears to be the oldest Inn of Court, with records detailing its activities dating back to 1422 in the Black Books, and it currently has the highest number of members of any Inn of Court. Each Inn is equal in its status but is individual in its own history and traditions. The Inns of Court seem to have originated as the living quarters for apprentices at law during the 14th and 15th centuries, and the word "Inn" appears to be derived from the term "hospitium", meaning a townhouse or mansion that was used to house students. The Inns used to provide (and still do to a large degree) everything that was then required by the students of law; they provided the students with a place to sleep, a hall to eat and drink in, a chapel to pray in and a library to conduct their research and learning within. By the 17th century it was a requirement for any person who wished to advocate in the courts to be a member of one of the Inns.

The Inns of Court still play a vital role in the development of an individual's career as a Barrister-at-law and they are heavily involved in the provision of educational activities, bursaries and scholarships, and dining facilities, as well as calling members to the Bar and disciplining barristers. As barristers are no longer all based within the confines of London and there are many who now work in the provinces (outside of London) the Inns do not offer the level of accommodation that they once did but they still provide all of the other functions (the chapel, library and dining facilities, etc.) that have been available to their members since their establishment over 500 years ago.

It does not matter which Inn of Court a budding barrister decides to join, it is simply a matter of personal choice. Some will join Lincoln's Inn because of the grandeur of the buildings, others because of the educational activities it offers; some will prefer to join Gray's Inn or one of the two Temples because of the smaller and more exclusive feel that these Inns offer, or perhaps because of the previous famous members and associations. The author Bram Stoker (*Dracula*) was a member of Inner Temple and the Inn is reputed to have links with Geoffrey Chaucer (*The Canterbury Tales*); Middle Temple had members such as Sir Walter Raleigh and Charles Dickens; and Gray's Inn is where William Shakespeare's play, *A Comedy of Errors*, was first performed in 1594. Lincoln's Inn boasts Lord Denning as a past member and its alumni include many previous Prime Ministers such as Baroness Thatcher and Tony Blair. The decision to apply for membership to a particular Inn is an individual decision but once an Inn of Court has been decided upon, and admittance has been granted, the individual barrister will belong to that Inn for life (unless they are later disbarred). **4–016**

A prospective student barrister is required to choose and join an Inn of Court before the commencement of his vocational studies on the Bar Professional Training Course (BPTC) (discussed below). Upon being accepted into the chosen Inn as a student barrister (or "inner" barrister if the traditional terminology is to be used; a barrister becomes an "outer" barrister upon call) the student is then required to undertake a tradition known as "keeping terms" before he can be formally called to the Bar as a barrister-at-law. "Keeping terms" means that a student is required to attend 10 qualifying sessions at the Inn before he can be called and admitted fully to the Inn. These qualifying sessions are normally achieved by the individual dining at his Inn of Court (each dining session counts as one qualifying unit). Dining takes place during one of the four dining terms (each term lasts for between nine and 14 days) spread over the year: the dining periods are split into Hilary, Easter, Trinity and Michaelmas. Originally, the idea of keeping terms revolved around the fact that the student barristers all resided in or near their Inn of Court and the requirement for them to keep terms meant that they were heavily involved in the day-to-day life of their chosen Inn (students were originally expected to complete 48 qualifying sessions). Nowadays, the number of sessions required to be completed has been reduced down to 12 due to the fact that many students do not live and work in London (the BPTC can be studied at institutes up and down the country and there are now barristers' chambers found in nearly every major town and city) and therefore the requirement to dine 48 times would be too onerous. By requiring potential barristers to still satisfy the keeping terms requirement the Inns are helping to ensure that the traditions of the Inns are continued and that the student barristers who do live and work at the other end of the country are afforded the opportunity to become, and feel part of, the very fabric of the Inn. Often individual Inns will now provide an educational day or weekend where students can gain more than one qualifying unit in a short space of time.

The highest rank of membership that an individual can achieve in an Inn is that of a Master of the Bench (informally known as a Bencher). The Benchers of an Inn preside over the Inn and form its governing body, and they are responsible for student admissions to the Inn, calling to the Bar and member (especially student member) discipline. On average, each Inn of Court has approximately 200 Benchers and they are generally selected from those members of the Inn who hold judicial office or have been appointed as King's Counsel (see below), although Honorary Benchers may also be appointed (often from the Royal family) and they do not need to be a member of the Inn or even a lawyer (although they are not permitted to vote or hold office within the Inn).

KING'S COUNSEL

4-017 The title of King's Counsel (post-nominal KC) is bestowed on those barristers and solicitor-advocates deemed to be professionally excellent and successful in their chosen field of law. The five competencies that must be demonstrated during the application process are:

- understanding and using the law;
- written and oral advocacy;

- working (productively) with others;
- showing an understanding of diversity and cultural issues; and
- integrity.

When a lawyer becomes a KC he is permitted to wear a gown made of silk to identify his status, as opposed to the traditional heavier cloth gown worn by the other members of the Bar. As a result of wearing this silk gown, KCs are informally referred to as "silks", other barristers who have not achieved this status are called "junior barristers" (regardless of their age or time at the Bar). The title of KC is a mark of distinction against the individual lawyer's name and it is often viewed as a "kite mark" or "gold star" depicting the individual's high legal ability, intellect and competence.

When a KC is involved in a case he will sit on the very front bench of the courtroom directly in front of the judge and will be the first to speak on behalf of the client. A KC is also permitted to take into court a lectern upon which to rest notes if they so wish (junior barristers are not permitted this luxury). KCs will be called to undertake the most complex and lengthy cases and those that have a high public profile, and are often accompanied in a case by a junior barrister who will assist by undertaking a lot of the less complex work (assisting a KC in such a way has been said to be the making of more than one junior barrister's career).

The selection of KCs from the ranks of the junior Bar (solicitors were originally unable to become KCs until the introduction of higher rights of audience) used to be conducted by way of a secret sounding in the same way that judges were selected (see Ch.6, "Old Style Appointments" for a detailed explanation of this process). In 2003 the process of selecting QCs by this method was suspended for consultation and it was at this point believed by most of the legal profession that the post of QC would ultimately be abolished. However, the consultation process uncovered a large amount of support for the position of QCs, in that the title allowed the excellence of those individuals who had gained it to be recognised by persons outside of the immediate legal circle. The idea of abolition was replaced by one of reform and that reform was to focus on the appointment method as opposed to the actual position of QCs.

The reform that followed involved the establishment of an independent selection panel with the aim of providing a fair and transparent means of identifying excellence in advocacy in the higher courts. The panel is charged with being rigorous and objective in its selection, whilst promoting diversity, equality and fairness. The panel is comprised of nine individuals who are a mix of retired members of the judiciary, senior barristers and solicitors and lay members, and is chaired by a lay member. To determine whether a candidate should be appointed as a KC the panel assesses the applications against a Competency Framework, which includes criteria such as: **4-018**

- understanding and using of the law;
- oral and written advocacy;

- working with others;
- diversity; and
- integrity.

Interviews of those applicants shortlisted are then conducted and references taken, as is the normal process for a job or promotion, with appointments then being formally made by the Secretary of State. In 2021 the open competition included the appointment of 101 KCs, of which 45 were women, 15 were of an ethnic origin other than white, and five were solicitor-advocates.

It could appear, on first consideration of the above figures, that the establishment of the selection panel has not addressed issues of equality and diversity in the selection process. However, upon closer inspection of the data it seems that the composition of the candidates actually applying to become KCs is still at this moment rather reflective of the stereotypical view of the Bar (that it is dominated by white middle-class males). Out of the total 274 applicants only 73 were female and only 39 of all applicants declared an ethnic origin other than white. However, a significant proportion of those women who applied (62%) were successful when compared to the number of men who applied and were successful (28%).

ACCESS TO BARRISTERS

4-019 Traditionally barristers were only allowed to take instructions from "professional clients", in other words, from solicitors, so members of the public could not gain direct access to a barrister. This resulted in barristers being perceived as unapproachable and set above the other members of the legal profession. In 1999 the Bar Council set up a pilot study, known as BarDIRECT, to assess the effects of certain professionals and organisations, such as the police force and trade unions, etc. being allowed to have direct access to a barrister without the need to instruct a solicitor; effectively cutting out the middleman. The pilot study was heralded to be a success, despite the reservations of the Law Society, which was of the opinion that allowing direct access to barristers was a further erosion of the professional remit of a solicitor, and in 2004 the Bar Council rolled out a nationwide scheme which permitted an individual to access a barrister directly, by way of the Public Access Rules.

There are now three ways in which a barrister can be instructed. These are:

- Professional Client Access;
- Public Access; and
- Licensed Access.

Professional Client Access is the traditional method of instructing a barrister and this can be done either via a solicitor, designated legal advice centres, other authorised litigators and employed barristers, etc. A barrister can be instructed by this method to act in any matter and in relation to all types of work. The majority of work undertaken by barristers is a result of them being instructed in this manner.

Public Access (by way of the 2004 Public Access Rules) allows members of the public and commercial and non-commercial organisations to instruct barristers directly. For barristers to undertake Public Access work they must be qualified post-pupillage (see below) for a period of at least three years; they must also have undertaken a one-day training course; and they must have registered their intentions to accept work in this way. Public Access is now permitted as a method to instruct a barrister in all areas of law, including criminal law, family law and immigration law (previously these areas of law were expressly prohibited under the Public Access scheme). A barrister must be careful not to undertake any work that amounts to conducting litigation (issuing proceedings, instructing experts or paying court fees, etc.) as these courses of action are still prohibited under the Public Access Rules. In such cases the barrister would again be obliged to refer the client to an appropriate professional organisation. The Bar Council website (*http://www.barcouncil.org.uk* [accessed 1 May 2025]) provides a searchable database for barristers who participate in the Public Access scheme.

Licensed Access is the modern interpretation of the old BarDIRECT (or Direct Professional Access scheme). This method of access involves certain organisations becoming licensed by the Bar Council to instruct barristers directly, although responsibility for licensing has been passed to the Bar Standards Board since 1 January 2008. An organisation will be deemed to be suitable to receive such a licence if it is felt that it has sufficient experience in a particular area of law. Examples of those organisations currently licensed include the Institute of Chartered Accountants, the Royal Institute of British Architects, the Asylum Support Appeals Project, the Devon Fire Authority, the British Transport Police and the Kennel Club. **4–020**

Despite the concerns of the Law Society that the work of solicitors would be further diminished due to the increased accessibility of barristers it appears that the main recourse of the individual client to a barrister is still conducted in the traditional method by way of a solicitor and that the new Licensed Access scheme has not had too detrimental an impact on the quantity of work available to either profession.

Over to you

Should the public be allowed direct access to barristers? If so, why? If not, why not?

QUALIFYING AS A BARRISTER

Becoming a barrister is not an easy task and is certainly not one that should be approached lightly as the profession is highly competitive and difficult to get a foothold in. It is a career that involves considerable determination, dedication, a large financial investment and very thick skin. The initial starting point is for a potential barrister to undertake an undergraduate degree and achieve at least a 2:1 (upper second class degree), the degree does not have to be a law degree (LL.B. (Hons)) and can be in any discipline that the student finds interesting. **4–021**

The main requirement is that a high grade is achieved in all assessments from the very start of the degree (even in the first year) as individual assessment grades will be considered by a Chambers when deciding whether to offer work experience and/or pupillage. There are many potential candidates out there who an individual will be competing against, and, as such, an individual must attain a mark and other achievements (such as mooting, debating, work experience and a placement year) that will set them apart from those other candidates. There are barristers in practice who only attained a third or 2:2 at degree level and who have carved themselves out a very successful career, but, due to the increased volume of students who now wish to pursue a career at the Bar, this lower level of academic achievement is simply no longer acceptable; there is anecdotal evidence that chambers, when considering potential pupils, will simply discard without further consideration all applications detailing anything less than a 2:1.

If a student undertakes a non-law discipline then he will be required to complete a further year of study known as the Common Professional Examination (or Postgraduate Diploma in Law). This qualification allows the student to gain the legal knowledge of the seven foundations of law (see "Qualifying as a solicitor", at **4–009**) as required by the Bar Council (or the Law Society if the individual wishes to become a solicitor). Upon successful completion of this undergraduate study the student must then obtain a place on the BPTC, which is a year-long postgraduate course that covers the theoretical aspect of being a barrister. On the BPTC a student will learn the necessary skills to enable them to become an effective advocate, to draft complex legal documents and opinions, undertake negotiation, prepare cases and develop conference skills (such as interviewing a client). The core modules that are taught include civil litigation and remedies, criminal litigation and sentencing, professional ethics and evidence. A student will also be given the choice to undertake a number of elective modules, such as advanced criminal litigation or immigration, depending on individual interests. Securing a place on the BPTC is a difficult task in itself as there are a limited number of institutions that offer the course nationwide and these providers are restricted as to the number of places that they can offer. Invariably there are more applicants than there are places and each year a large number of hopeful barristers are disappointed when their applications to undertake the BPTC are rejected. If an individual is successful on gaining a place on a BPTC course then it is important that they achieve a good mark at the end of it. There is, again, further anecdotal evidence that applications for pupillage made by individuals who have not attained either a Very Competent or Outstanding on the BPTC are also discarded without further consideration.

4–022 Upon completion of the BPTC, providing that the student has kept the requisite number of terms as prescribed by the Inns of Court (see **4–016**), he will be called to the Bar as a barrister-at-law. However, the bestowing of this title does not allow a newly called barrister to begin immediate professional practice as a barrister. All barristers must undergo a year-long period of work experience, known as pupillage, to be able to gain a practising certificate. This is where the competition in the profession is further amplified, as there are simply not enough pupillages available to accommodate the yearly supply of BPTC graduates (often over 250 applications will often be received for just one pupillage). Pupillage must be undertaken in chambers under the supervision of a recognised pupil master or mistress. These supervisors are barristers of at least seven years call who are willing to undertake the supervision of a pupil for the length of the pupillage. A pupil barrister must be paid a wage by their chambers (the minimum that must be paid is £12,000 per annum, although the larger sets of chambers can often pay considerably more than this). The requirement that chambers pay a pupil a minimum wage was a condition brought in by the Bar Council in an effort to address the severe financial difficulties that many pupil barristers were faced with due to a number of chambers offering unpaid pupillages. Unfortunately, the imposition of a minimum wage has had the effect of curtailing the number of pupillages on offer as the wage must be paid directly by chambers. As each barrister in chambers is self-employed this has meant that the number of pupillages offered by an individual chambers has been reduced, and in the cases of the smaller chambers, they are often not able to offer any pupillages at all. Competition to attain a pupillage is intensely fierce with the rejection rate (even to get an interview let alone a pupillage) being extremely high. When the fact that a similar number are called to the Bar each year is coupled with the fact that the number of pupillages on offer very rarely increases then the high level of competitiveness can be appreciated as those who did not attain a pupillage the previous year will still be applying for one the following year along with the newly graduated BPTC cohort for that year.

If an individual perseveres until they obtain a pupillage (or if they are simply gifted or lucky and gets one almost immediately) then the year-long pupillage is split down into two parts. The "first six" (essentially, the first six months) will be spent following the pupil master or mistress to and from court and conferences and helping to conduct research and draft documents, etc. During this first six months the pupil is prevented from undertaking any paid work (except some agency work) and they simply learn from watching. The "second six" then involves the pupil being allowed to take on their own caseload and conduct cases under the watchful eye of their supervisor. Throughout the pupillage a pupil is required to undergo further training on advocacy and other practical skills, as organised by the Bar Council or the Inns of Court, so as to further their professional development. Upon completion of a pupillage it is then necessary for the pupil barrister to find a permanent tenancy in a set of chambers. This can often be quite a difficult task to achieve in itself, as many chambers do not have the space or the work to accommodate another tenant (remember all barristers are self-employed and are effectively in competition with one another for work). Many chambers will not take on a pupil if they do not have the ability to offer tenancy at the end of the year, however, there are a number of chambers that will offer pupillage to a number of pupils but will then only have the space for one (or even no) tenants at the end of it. Those pupils who are unable to secure tenancy are often allowed to "squat" within chambers for a number of months (often called a "third six") until they manage to secure a tenancy at another set of chambers.

FIGURE 17 **Route to becoming a barrister**

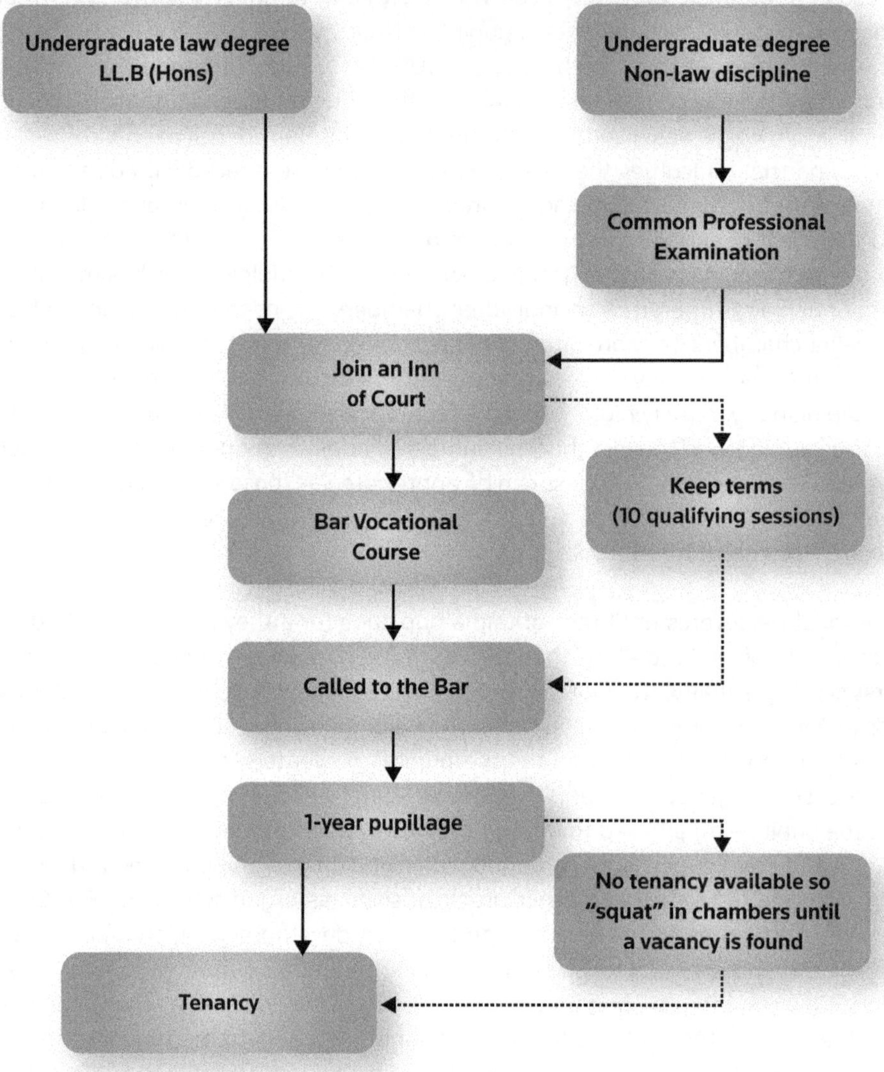

It is only after successful completion of these different stages that an individual will become a practising barrister and can then begin to build up their own client base and start their professional career. Barristers are required to undertake continuing profession development (CPD) throughout their practising life so that they remain competent and up-to-date practitioners. Becoming a barrister is a very long process and at the end of it all an individual can be left with debts that, on average, exceed £50,000.

The Changing Professions

40 years ago the demarcation between the two main limbs of the legal profession (solicitors and barristers) was clear, with each profession having defined separate roles and responsibilities; however, over recent years, these professions have begun to merge and the line between them has become blurred to the point of there being now almost only one profession—that of a "lawyer". 4–023

The change in the services provided by the professions, and in effect the beginning of the merging of the professions, started with the 1979 report conducted by the Royal Commission on Legal Services (otherwise known as the Benson Commission). The Benson Commission was charged with assessing the state of exclusivity that existed between the two professions to determine whether it provided a fair and workable system. At this point in time an individual who wished or needed to bring litigation was forced to employ two lawyers (a barrister and a solicitor); whereas the Commission thought that there was the possibility that only one "lawyer" might actually be needed. The Commission also considered the issue of reserved work, which was work that could only be carried out by a certain body as specified by statute (i.e. appearing as an advocate in court). Overall, the Commission reported that the legal profession was functioning as well as could be expected and it did not recommend any immediate or radical changes to the provision of legal services. The Law Society was not satisfied with the findings of the report and began to mount a challenge to the fact that solicitors were prevented from being able to advocate in the higher courts. It was felt that often it was inappropriate and unnecessary for a case to be handed over to the care of a barrister for presentation in court, especially as there were many solicitors who were capable and willing to advocate in court if given the opportunity.

The Administration of Justice Act 1985 brought about the first significant change to the work conducted by solicitors and marked the beginning of the dissolution of barriers between the legal professions. The monopoly enjoyed by solicitors in the previously reserved area of conveyancing (the buying and selling of properties) was removed by the 1985 Act, as it provided for a system of licensed conveyancers who could also provide this service. The Act set out that the service of conveyancing could be conducted by any person who was suitably qualified (although this did not mean that a qualification as a solicitor was required) so long as they were insured and accountable for the work undertaken. The enactment of this change appears to have stemmed from the fact that a large number of solicitors had, to an extent, been abusing their hold over this area of the market. Criticisms had been levied against the fact that the fees charged for conveyancing work were astronomical and the level of service received and quality of work was often inadequate. Other interested bodies, such as estate agents and banks, had voiced a strong opinion that they should be allowed to provide conveyancing services and, if permitted, it would be more beneficial for the customers who required these services as they would only have to access one professional as opposed to two or three (e.g. Halifax now encompasses an estate agent, a mortgage advisory department, and conveyancing services). The Administration of Justice Act 1985 allowed this extended provision of services to occur, despite the lamenting of the Law Society as to the encroachment upon the work of solicitors.

4–024 The enactment of the Courts and Legal Services Act 1990 (CLSA 1990) five years later had the next major impact upon the provision of legal services. This time, however, the change was more favourably weighted in respect of the solicitors' branch of the profession. The CLSA 1990 provided what the Law Society had been campaigning for—higher rights of audience for solicitors. Under the Act, the provision of advocacy was to be determined by assessment of an individual's qualifications and membership of a regulated profession. Section 27 allowed the Law Society to grant a Certificate of Advocacy to a solicitor who had undergone the requisite training. Solicitors who have been successful in achieving the higher rights of advocacy are called solicitor-advocates and, as a result of these higher rights, they are eligible to be promoted to the rank of a KC and can become a member of the judiciary. The Bar Council was not overly enthused with the prospect of solicitors being allowed the right to advocate in the courts as it had concerns about the possibility of the quality of the advocacy being diminished as a result. The Bar was also concerned that the introduction of such a right would lead to unfavourable competition in respect of the amount of work available at the Bar. These concerns have not been realised as, to date, just over 2,000 solicitors have taken the step to become a solicitor-advocate; the quality of advocacy provided is accepted as being equal in quality to that provided by barristers and, in respect of the concerns over the availability of work, the Legal Services Commission were forced to ask solicitor-advocates to undertake work refused by the members of the Bar when it went on strike over issues of pay.

The movement towards a further merging of the professions was again discussed in the report *Competition in Professions*, (OFT, March 2001). The report focused on considering the future of the professions and the effect that the distinct division between the two limbs (solicitors and barristers) was having on the provision of legal services to the public. The conclusion of the report was that the restrictions upon direct access to barristers constrained healthy competition between the two professions, that such competition was essential for the development and continuation of the high standards of both of the professions and that the role of KCs should be abolished (the result of this recommendation has already been discussed above). The Bar Council responded to the recommendation of direct access to barristers by the introduction of the BarDIRECT and Public Access schemes (see "Access to barristers", at **4–019**).

4–025 In 2003 the Government conducted a further review into the regulation and provision of legal services (*Review of the regulatory framework for legal services in England and Wales* (Department for Constitutional Affairs, March 2004)), which was headed by Sir David Clementi. The review had two main terms of reference, these being:

- to consider what regulatory framework would be best to promote competition, innovation and the public and consumer interest in the legal sector; and
- to recommend a framework which will be independent in representing the public and consumer interest.

In essence, the Clementi Report recommended a reduction in the self-governance of the professions, that a new Legal Services Board should be set up in respect of overseeing the professions, and that a new Office of Legal Complaints should be established in respect of the providers of legal services. The report and its recommendations were warmly accepted by the Government with the result being the Legal Services Act 2007, which received Royal Assent on 30 October 2007 and which provides for a number of key changes to the profession.

The new measures provided for by the Legal Services Act 2007 were:

- a single and fully independent Office for Legal Complaints (OLC) to remove complaints-handling from the legal professions and restore consumer confidence;
- Alternative Business Structures (ABSs) that will enable consumers to obtain services from one business entity that brings together lawyers and non-lawyers, increasing competitiveness and improving services;
- a new Legal Services Board (LSB) to act as a single, independent and publicly-accountable regulator with the power to enforce high standards in the legal sector, replacing the maze of regulators with overlapping powers; and
- a clear set of regulatory objectives for the regulation of legal services which all parts of the system will need to work together to deliver, including promoting and maintaining adherence to professional principles.

The ethos behind the Legal Services Act 2007 was to provide a legal profession that works together as opposed to against each other, and is more accessible and user-friendly for the consumer.

The new Alternative Business Structure (ABS) provision of legal services to the public proved to **4–026** be one of the most controversial elements of the Act. The Ministry of Justice stated that ABSs will allow for "increased flexibility" in the legal market and "increased access to finance". Non-legal firms, such as banks, insurance companies and estate agents are now able to form ABSs and provide both legal and non-legal services under one roof. This new concept has become known colloquially as "Tesco Law" as it is now possible for a large company, such as Tesco, to set up an ABS under the new regulations. Each potential ABS provider will need to satisfy the relevant licensing authority (i.e. the SRA and BSB) that it is competent to provide such services and, if a non-lawyer is to own more than a 10 per cent share of the body, then he will have to undergo a "fitness-to-own" test. ABS firms started operating from 6 October 2011 and Premier Property Lawyers (approved by the Council of Licensed Conveyancers) was the first ABS to be established. It was quickly followed by the Halifax, Co-op and the AA, who are all now offering the provision of legal services. The introduction of ABSs will inevitably have far-reaching consequences for those now entering the legal profession and it may be that the solicitors and barristers of the future are more likely to be all-round lawyers working in an ABS, as opposed to belonging exclusively to one camp or the other of the "old style" legal system.

Regulation of the Professions

LEGAL SERVICES BOARD

4–027 As a result of the Legal Services Act 2007 the Legal Services Board (LSB) came into existence on 1 January 2009 and became fully operational one year later in January 2010. The LSB sets out that its overriding mandate is:

to ensure that regulation in the legal services sector is carried out in the public interest; and that the interests of consumers are placed at the heart of the system.

The LSB is an independent body which is accountable to Parliament through the Lord Chancellor and it is sponsored by the Ministry of Justice. Its overall aim is:

to contribute to the reform and modernisation of the legal services market in the interests of consumers, enhancing quality, ensuring value for money and improving access to justice across England and Wales.

Its primary function, and method of achieving the above aim, is to act as an overseer to the legal regulators—it is a regulator for the regulators—and in doing so it is responsible for ensuring that the eight regulatory objectives stipulated in the 2007 Act are achieved. These eight objectives are:

- protecting and promoting the public interest;
- supporting the constitutional principle of the rule of law;
- improving access to justice;
- protecting and promoting the interests of consumers;
- promoting competition in the provision of services in the legal sector;
- encouraging an independent, strong, diverse and effective legal profession;
- increasing public understanding of citizens legal rights and duties; and
- promoting and maintaining adherence to the professional principles of independence and integrity, proper standards of work, observing the best interests of the client and the duty to the court, and maintaining client confidentiality.

The LSB oversees the Approved Regulators in respect of the different branches of the legal profession, and the Office for Legal Complaints (OLC) to ensure that they all carry out their own independent regulatory functions to the required standards. 4–028

FIGURE 18 **Branches of the legal profession and related Approved Regulators overseen by the LSB**

Profession	Representative Body	Independent Regulatory Body
Legal Executives	Charted Institute of Legal Executives	ILEX Professional Standards Limited
Solicitors	Law Society	Solicitors Regulation Authority
Barristers	Bar Council	Bar Standards Board
Licensed Conveyancers	Society for Licensed Conveyancers	Council for Licensed Conveyancers
Patent Attorneys	Chartered Institute of Patent Attorneys	Intellectual Property Regulation Board
Trade Mark Attorneys	Institute of Trade Mark Attorneys	Intellectual Property Regulation Board
Costs Lawyers	Association of Costs Lawyers	Costs Lawyers Standards Board
Notaries	The Notaries Society; Society of Scrivener Notaries	The Master of Faculties

REGULATION OF CILEX

CILEX is regulated by ILEX Professional Standards (IPS), which is an organisation established in 2008. IPS is part of the CILEX group but has its own Board of Directors to ensure independence. It is responsible for all regulatory matters relating to CILEX and CILEX members and it states its aim as being: 4–029

> **[t]o define, promote and secure, in the public interest, proper standards of professional conduct and behaviour.**

IPS are concerned with ensuring that the public are educated as to the work of CILEX members, making sure that its members are aware of the standards and conduct expected from them, and helping practitioners achieve, and where possible, exceed, the required standards.

REGULATION OF SOLICITORS

4–030 The regulation of the solicitors' profession has been the focus of unreserved criticism over recent years with the result that the bodies providing regulation have undergone numerous changes, although often these changes only amounted to what was essentially a change of name as opposed to any direct action to address the criticisms raised. To discover how the profession is now regulated it is necessary to consider the historical development and functions of the bodies involved.

The Law Society

4–031 The Law Society was founded on 2 June 1825, although originally its title was "The Society of Attorneys, Solicitors, Proctors and others not being Barristers, practising in the Courts of Law and Equity of the United Kingdom"; by 1903 the Society had reduced this title to that of simply "The Law Society". The Law Society was originally the only organisation charged with both representing solicitors' rights and regulating their behaviour and it was as early as 1834 when the Society first brought proceedings against practitioners who were acting dishonestly.

Over to you

Can you think of any criticisms that could be made of the Law Society in respect of its regulatory role at this time?

Criticisms were then voiced about the fact that the Society tended to side with the solicitors when an allegation was made (obviously a Society that had both the function of representation and regulation of the same professionals was faced with rather a large conflict of interest), and in 1983 the Solicitors Complaints Bureau was established as an independent limb of the Law Society in an effort to tackle these criticisms. The Bureau was not the success that it was hoped it would be as it was not truly independent of the Law Society and it could only work under the powers delegated to it by the Society. As such, the Bureau's powers were limited and it could only impose the maximum compensation payable by a solicitor at a meagre £1,000 and, as a result, it was viewed to be inefficient to the point of near-incompetence when dealing with the claims made. To address these new criticisms levied at the Law Society, in 1996 the Bureau was changed to the Office for Supervision of Solicitors, but the issues were still not directly tackled and the problems identified with the original Bureau remained. As a final effort to tackle the concerns the Office for Supervision of Solicitors became the Consumer Complaints Service in 2004, though this again appeared to be more of a name change than an effective address of any of the problems identified. In 2007, widespread change occurred in respect of the organisations charged with regulating the profession and dealing with consumer complaints. These regulatory responsibilities were removed entirely from the Law Society by the establishment of the Solicitors Regulation Authority and the Legal Complaints Service (both discussed at, **4–032** and **4–040**). The Law Society is now only responsible for the representation of solicitors by way of negotiating with and lobbying the newly created regulatory bodies and the Government, and providing training, advice and support to all solicitors within its jurisdiction.

Solicitors Regulation Authority

The Solicitors Regulation Authority (SRA) was established in January 2007 (although it had previously existed under the guise of the Law Society Regulation Board). The SRA is the independent regulatory body of the Law Society and it sets out its aim as being: 4–032

To set, promote and secure in the public interest standards of behaviour and professional performance necessary to ensure that clients receive a good service and that the rule of law is upheld.

The organisation's key objectives are: to set the standards for the profession; to provide support and monitoring to the profession in respect of compliance with the required standards; to ensure that consumers are protected; to ensure that any disciplinary action taken and enforcement of such is appropriate for the circumstances; and to help provide access to justice and consumer information and ensure transparency across the profession. The SRA produces the Code of Conduct that members of the profession must abide by and it is charged with the responsibility of issuing practising certificates to all practising solicitors.

Solicitors Disciplinary Tribunal

The Solicitors Disciplinary Tribunal (SDT) is a statutory tribunal enacted under s.46 of the Solicitors Act 1974. The SDT adjudicates alleged breaches of the rules of professional conduct that are designed to maintain the reputation of the solicitors' profession in respect of honesty, probity, trustworthiness, independence and integrity. The SDT has the power to strike solicitors from the Roll, suspend them from practice, or fine or reprimand them. Any fines imposed are payable to HM Treasury and the Tribunal can award costs but not compensation. The SDT is currently comprised of 43 members, all of whom are appointed by the Master of the Rolls (see Ch.6, "The Master of the Rolls"); two-thirds of the Tribunal are solicitors and one-third are laypeople. The Annual Report for 2013 shows that the SDT struck off 75 solicitors, suspended nine indefinitely from practice, suspended 34 for a fixed period, imposed fines upon 81, and reprimanded 18. 4–033

REGULATION OF BARRISTERS

The General Council of the Bar

The General Council of the Bar, otherwise known as the Bar Council, was established in 1894 as the primary body charged with governing and representing the interests of all barristers called to the Bar. The Bar Council sets out its primary objectives as being: 4–034

- to represent the Bar as a modern and forward-looking profession which seeks to maintain and improve the quality and standard of service to all clients;
- to maintain and enhance professional standards;
- to maintain effective complaints and disciplinary procedures;
- to develop an effective, fair and affordable system for recruiting, and of regulating entry, to the profession;
- to regulate education and training for the profession;
- to combat discrimination and disadvantage at the Bar;
- to develop and promote the work of the Bar;
- to conduct research and promote the Bar's views on matters affecting the administration of justice, including substantive law reform;
- to provide services for members of the Bar, e.g. fee collection, publications, conferences, guidance on practice management and development; and
- to promote the Bar's interests with Government, the EU, the Law Society, international Bars and other organisations with common interests.

Originally, the Bar Council was responsible for both the representation and regulation of barristers. It produces, maintains and enforces the Bar Code of Conduct, which sets out how all barristers should conduct themselves and, if a client wished to make a complaint against an individual barrister regarding their behaviour or conduct, then they would do so to the Bar Council. The Bar Council was only able to discipline a barrister by way of either suspending them from practice, forcing them to apologise to the client, imposing a fine or, in very serious cases, disbarring them (which meant that they were stripped of their title as barrister and no longer allowed to practise). However, although the barrister would be appropriately dealt with in respect of the complaint, the client making the complaint received no form of redress (except for the occasional apology). As a result of the limited regulatory capacity of the Bar Council, and the fact that the general perception of the public was that the Bar Council closed ranks around its barristers when any complaint was made, the complaints procedure was reformed in 1997. This reform brought the introduction of an independent Complaints Commissioner (who was charged with assessing the seriousness of a complaint made) and the Professional Conduct and Complaints Committee (PCC) (which would consider any complaint referred to them by the Complaints Commissioner and determine what, if any, action should be taken in respect of the complaint). The PCC was able to enforce sanctions, such as the barrister being required to pay the complainant up to £5,000 in compensation, and it was able to suspend, fine or disbar a barrister. The PCC is now known as the Professional Conduct Department of the Bar Standards Board (see below).

The Bar Standards Board

4–035 Historically, the Bar Council was the sole organisation responsible for performing both a representative and regulatory function in respect of barristers. As this dual role of both representation and regulation resulted in conflicting interests the Bar Council established the Bar Standards Board (BSB) in January 2006 so as to act as an independent regulatory body for barristers. The BSB sets out its functions as:

- setting the education and training requirements for becoming a barrister;
- setting continuing training requirements to ensure that barristers' skills are maintained throughout their careers;
- setting standards of conduct for barristers;
- monitoring the service provided by barristers to assure quality; and
- handling complaints against barristers and taking disciplinary or other action where appropriate.

As a result, the BSB now deals with any complaints made against a barrister. The Professional Conduct Department (PCD) is responsible for the initial assessment of the merits of any complaint made against a barrister. The PCD deals with complaints that concern matters of professional misconduct (such as misleading the court, not adhering to rules of client confidentiality or acting against a client's instructions), or matters of inadequate professional service (such as poor or inadequate work on a case or being rude to a client), but it is limited in its powers to deal with professional negligence and it will not consider a complaint which focuses on a barrister's conduct in their personal life. All complaints must be made within six months of the event complained of occurring. Upon receipt of a complaint, the PCD will assess the validity of the complaint and dismiss the matter if it does not contain any evidence of professional misconduct or inadequate professional service, or if it is received out of time. If the complaint shows valid grounds then the PCD will investigate the matter further and, upon conclusion of the investigation, may either dismiss the complaint (if there is found to be insufficient evidence) or refer the complaint to the Bar Tribunals and Adjudication Service for an appropriate panel hearing of the matter.

If the client is unhappy with the manner in which a complaint was dealt with by the BSB then they may still refer the matter to the Office of Legal Complaints, which is the body responsible for overseeing the complaints system in respect of the legal profession (see "Legal Ombudsman", at **4-040**, for more detail on this body).

Professional negligence

The BSB considers complaints that involve matters of professional misconduct or matters of inadequate professional service and it consequently has very limited powers when the issue being complained about involves professional negligence. The reason for this is that traditionally barristers were immune to complaints and actions brought against them in respect of claims for professional negligence, as set out in the case of **Rondel v Worsley** [1969] 1 A.C. 191. In **Rondel v Worsley** the House of Lords held: that a barrister was to be immune from being sued for negligent work in court and that this decision was based on matters of public policy due to the facts that the administration of justice required that a barrister should be able to carry out his duty to the court fearlessly and independently; that actions for negligence against barristers would make the retrying of the original actions inevitable and so prolong litigation that would be contrary to the public interest; and that a barrister was obliged to accept any client, however difficult, who sought his services and so consequently it would be unjust if the **4-036** barrister could then be sued by a client simply because that client was unsatisfied with the result obtained.

This immunity was then abolished by the House of Lords in the landmark case of **Arthur JS Hall & Co v Simons** [2002] 1 A.C. 615. **Arthur JS Hall & Co v Simons** involved three cases of negligence brought against solicitors. The solicitors relied on the immunity of advocates from negligence suits and, at first instance, this argument succeeded and the claims were struck out as being unsustainable. On appeal the Court of Appeal reversed this decision finding that the cases had been wrongly struck out and that there was no public policy reason for allowing immunity. The Court held that there were no longer any valid justifications for the exemption of legal representatives from litigation founded on allegations of professional negligence as to allow immunity would deprive a client, injured by the professional negligence of legal representatives, of an appropriate remedy. On appeal the House of Lords in dismissing the appeal, held that the Court of Appeal was correct in its conclusion that the public policy arguments in favour of exemption were no longer appropriate. It concluded that the effect of the wasted costs order (a method of sanctioning advocates for improper case conduct) was empirical evidence that the standards of advocacy had not declined with such a liability being imposed and, as the courts were able to judge between errors of judgement which were inevitable in the art of advocacy, and true negligence, the floodgates would not be opened to negligence claims. Lord Hope, Lord Hutton and Lord Hobhouse dissented by holding that immunity was still required in criminal proceedings, but the majority determined that, although there was a different and broader remit for reinvestigation in criminal proceedings, the immunity should be removed in both spheres of legal work.

The courts have since interpreted this principle quite narrowly, as can been seen in the case of **Moy v Pettman Smith (A Firm)** [2005] UKHL 7. Here the House declined to impose liability on a barrister in a claim for negligence, holding that the purpose of the removal of immunity was not to stifle an advocate's independence of mind and that the advice given by the barrister in question fell within the range of that to be expected of reasonably competent counsel of the barrister's seniority and purported experience. This approach to the application of the principle and the reluctance to find liability against members of the legal profession differs to the approach taken by other professions (i.e. the medical profession) where the competence of an individual is to be judged by the standards of a reasonably competent practioner (regardless of the individual's seniority or purported experience).

Over to you

Should legal professionals be held liable for their negligence?

Professional ethics

The profession is regulated by the Code of Conduct set out in the Bar Standards Board Handbook (currently version 4.6, December 2020), which is a comprehensive handbook setting out the standards that are required of those who fall under the regulation of the BSB. If a barrister breaches his or her professional ethics then it may well be a disciplinary matter. **4–037**

The Handbook contains the Core Duties that must be adhered to. These Core Duties are as follows:

- You must observe your duty to the court in the administration of justice.
- You must act in the best interests of each client.
- You must act with honesty and integrity.
- You must maintain your independence.
- You must not behave in a way which is likely to diminish the trust and confidence which the public places in you or in the profession.
- You must keep the affairs of each client confidential.
- You must provide a competent standard of work and service to each client.
- You must not discriminate unlawfully against any person.
- You must be open and co-operative with your regulators.
- You must take reasonable steps to manage your practice, or carry out your role within your practice, competently and in such a way as to achieve compliance with your legal and regulatory obligations.

These Core Duties apply to all barristers whether they are self-employed, employed or even non-practising and they not only apply in their professional lives but also cross over into their private lives, meaning that any barrister who acts in a manner contrary to these principles (e.g. by moonlighting as a loan shark, or a lap-dancer) could face disciplinary actions for this behaviour.

In Part 2 – C. The Conduct Rules, Rule C3 sets out that: **4–038**

You owe a duty to the *court* to act with independence in the interests of justice. This duty overrides any inconsistent obligations which you may have (other than obligations under the criminal law). It includes the following specific obligations which apply whether you are acting as an advocate or are otherwise involved in the conduct of litigation in whatever role (with the exception of Rule C3.1 below, which applies when acting as an advocate):

1. – you must not knowingly or recklessly mislead or attempt to mislead the *court*;

> **2. – you must not abuse your role as an advocate;**
> **3. – you must take reasonable steps to avoid wasting the *court's* time;**
> **4. – you must take reasonable steps to ensure that the *court* has before it all relevant decisions and legislative provisions;**
> **5. – you must ensure that your ability to act independently is not compromised.**

It is of the utmost importance that these rules are strictly adhered to. For example, if a client in a criminal case told his barrister that he had committed the offence that he was being tried for then the barrister could not continue representing the client as an innocent person to the court. To continue to do so would be to deceive the court and would breach the barrister's overriding duty to the court. In such a case the barrister could only put the prosecution evidence to proof (try and show that the prosecution evidence was weak), or he could withdraw from the case due to being professionally embarrassed.

4–039 The Handbook is a lengthy document that provides guidance and regulation on almost every facet of a barrister's professional (and personal) conduct and it is not intended to recount here every provision set out in it as this is something that is studied in great detail on the BPTC. However, attention will be drawn to one final rule and that is the provision found in r.C29, which is known as the cab-rank rule.

Rule C29 provides that:

> **If you receive *instructions* from a *professional client*, and you are:**
>
> **1. a *self-employed barrister* instructed by a *professional client* [...] and the *instructions* are appropriate taking into account the experience, seniority and/or field of practice of yourself or (as appropriate) of the *named authorised individual* you must, [. . .] accept the *instructions* addressed specifically to you, irrespective of:**
> **a. the identity of the *client*;**
> **b. the nature of the case to which the *instructions* relate;**
> **c. whether the *client* is paying privately or is publicly funded; and**
> **d. any belief or opinion which you may have formed as to the character, reputation, cause, conduct, guilt or innocence of the *client*.**

The cab-rank rule essentially requires a barrister to accept any case presented to them regardless of the identity of client, the facts of the case or the barrister's own opinion as to the salubriousness of the client. The rule takes its name from the principle employed at taxi ranks. If a person goes to catch a taxi at a taxi rank then they cannot pick and choose which taxi they will take, they must take the first taxi in the queue at the rank and cannot opt for the fifth one along just because the driver looks nicer or the vehicle looks safer. The same principle applies to a barrister's acceptance of work. A barrister could not refuse a case simply because the client was a drug dealer and they had strong views against drug pushers; they could not refuse to defend a client even if they were a paedophile or a child murderer or a serial killer; no matter how unpleasant or personally offensive a barrister finds a case or a client they are obliged to accept it so long as he has the expertise to conduct the case. Further, upon acceptance of the case, the barrister is obliged to promote and protect fearlessly the client's interests as (set out under r.C15) and so cannot purposefully do a bad job.

Legal Ombudsman

Discussed above are the methods that an individual can take to make a complaint against a solicitor or a barrister. If, however, after completing the procedures provided by the relevant agencies (the LSC or the BSB) the complainant is still not satisfied with the outcome of his complaint then he has the further option of complaining to the Legal Ombudsman. 4–040

The Legal Ombudsman was established by the Office for Legal Complaints under the Legal Services Act 2007 as Parliament was of the opinion that the complaints system needed to be simplified. The Legal Ombudsman opened for business on 6 October 2010 and it provides a free service to all members of the public, very small businesses, charities, clubs and trusts. It is an impartial body and its remit is to resolve legal complaints in a fair and independent way and for everyone to have access to legal services in which they have confidence. It states its mission statement to be:

Our task is to run an independent ombudsman scheme that will resolve complaints about lawyers in a fair and effective way, where we are shrewd and decisive when tackling complex issues and that is open so we can give focused feedback to help drive improvements to legal services.

The Legal Ombudsman can deal with complaints concerning all of the varying legal positions such as barristers, solicitors, law costs draftsmen, notaries, legal executives, etc. Any complaint must be made within 12 months of the matter complained of occurring, and the matter must have been first raised directly with the legal party being complained about. The Legal Ombudsman will hear complaints that concern matters such as a lawyer not following client instructions, unreasonable delays, failure to provide accurate information, failure to provide adequate information as to costs, disclosure of confidential information to other parties, etc. If the Ombudsman concludes that there was an issue with the service provided by the lawyer then it can require the lawyer to apologise, return any outstanding documents, rectify the situation (if possible), and pay back any losses suffered up to the total of £30,000 or pay compensation.

Summary

1. Paralegals are individuals who are either not legally qualified or who are legally qualified but who are working in a non-fee-earning capacity within a legal firm. They are essential to the running of a firm as they undertake a large majority of the work that it would not be cost-effective to require a fee-paid member of staff to do.

2. Legal executives are described as the third limb to the legal profession. They are qualified under, and regulated by, the Chartered Institute of Legal Executives, and they work in a fee-paid capacity. Becoming a legal executive can provide an individual with a non-traditional, but increasingly popular, route to becoming a qualified lawyer.

3. Solicitors are at the front line of the legal profession, dealing with their clients on a face-to-face basis. They are allowed to conduct litigation on behalf of their clients and the majority of their work is paper-based, although they are now also able to achieve higher rights of audience and advocate in the higher courts.

4. To qualify as a solicitor an individual must first undertake a law degree or a non-law discipline degree followed then by the Common Profession Examination. Upon successful completion of this he must then register with the Law Society as a student solicitor before continuing on to take the one-year Legal Practice Course (LPC). Finally, upon completion of the LPC the individual must secure a two-year training contract before being fully qualified to practise as a solicitor in his or her own right.

5. The Law Society provides representation for all solicitors within England and Wales, whereas the Solicitors Regulation Authority acts in a regulatory capacity over the profession. The Legal Services Board investigates complaints made against members of the profession, and the Solicitors Disciplinary Tribunal is a statutory body that disciplines solicitors who are found to have breached the rules of professional conduct.

6. Barristers traditionally act as advocates within the courtroom. They are generally prevented from conducting litigation on behalf of their lay clients and can only act upon the instructions of a professional client: a solicitor. They are generally self-employed and work out of shared facilities with other barristers, known as chambers.

7. A barrister must belong to one of the four Inns of Court, which are the bodies responsible for the calling of barristers to the Bar (inaugurating them into the profession).

8. Barristers and solicitor-advocates who can demonstrate all competencies to a standard of excellence are eligible to become King's Counsel (KCs). KCs are those advocates who are viewed as being professionally excellent and successful in their chosen field of law.

9. Originally, access to barristers could only be obtained through a solicitor but now a barrister can be instructed in one of three ways: Professional Client Access (through a solicitor or other authorised litigator); Public Access in respect of civil matters; and Licensed Access through a licensed body.

10. To qualify as a barrister an individual must undertake either a law degree or a non-law discipline followed by the Common Professional Examination. This is followed by the completion of the Bar Professional Training Course (BPTC), and then the individual must try and secure a one-year work placement known as pupillage. Pupillage can be very difficult to achieve due to the high number of BPTC graduates and the limited number of pupillages available.

11. The Bar Council is the representative body for the barrister's profession, whereas the Bar Standards Board deals with any complaints made against a member of the profession. Barristers can now also be personally sued for professional negligence.

12. Barristers are governed by the Bar Code of Conduct, which sets out that their primary duty lies to the court. Barristers are bound by the "cab-rank" rule, which provides that they cannot refuse a case based on their personal opinions and prejudices.

13. The Legal Ombudsman is an independent body that reviews and investigates complaints made where an individual is not satisfied with the conduct of the complaints procedure provided by the professions.

14. The individual professions of solicitors and barristers have begun to merge together over the last quarter of a century and their individual roles are no longer clearly defined. The enactment of the Legal Services Act 2007 and the introduction of ABS firms are expected to eventually erode the remaining distinction between the two limbs of the legal profession.

Key Cases

Case	Court	Salient point
Rondel v Worsley [1969]	**House of Lords**	**The House held that a barrister was immune to being sued for negligence in relation to his professional work. This decision was based on matters of public policy and the administration of justice.**
Arthur JS Hall & Co v Simons [2002]	**House of Lords**	**The House overruled the previous decision of Rondel v Worsley [1969] on the grounds that there were no longer valid public policy grounds for exempting legal professionals (both solicitors and barristers) from liability for negligence arising out of their professional work; immunity from litigation for negligence was abolished.**

Further Reading

M. Davies, "The demise of professional self-regulation? Evidence from the 'ideal type' professions of medicine and law" (2010) 26(1) P.N. 3–38.

Considers the concept of self-regulation in both the legal and medical professions, with reference to the Legal Services Act 2007.

C. Harrison, *From Student to Solicitor: The Complete Guide to Securing a Training Contract*, 2nd edn (Sweet & Maxwell, 2015).

A practical book written for those who wish to become a solicitor.

K. Underwood, "The Legal Services Bill—death by regulation?" [2007] 26 C.J.Q. 124–133.

Discusses the history of the Legal Services Bill and the proposals relating to ABSs.

Self Test Questions

1. The body that represents solicitors in England and Wales is the:
   (a) Legal Services Commission
   (b) Law Society
   (c) Solicitors Regulation Authority
   (d) Legal Complaints Service
2. Barristers are called to the:
   (a) Bar
   (b) Bench
   (c) Cloth
   (d) Inn
3. King's Counsel are otherwise known as:
   (a) satins
   (b) velvets
   (c) silks
   (d) God
4. Barristers can refuse to take a case because:
   (a) they do not like the client
   (b) they are disgusted by the nature of the case
   (c) they suspect the defendant to be guilty
   (d) they are inexperienced in the area of law involved
5. The higher rights of audience for solicitors were introduced by the:
   (a) Administration of Justice Act 1985
   (b) Courts and Legal Services Act 1990
   (c) Access to Justice Act 1999
   (d) Legal Services Act 2007

Magistrates

5

CHAPTER OVERVIEW

In this chapter we will:

- Discover the historical role of the magistrates' court.
- Explain who is eligible to become a magistrate.
- Consider the role of a magistrate.
- Evaluate the composition of the magistrates' bench.
- Consider how magistrates are recruited and trained.
- Discuss the sentencing powers of the magistrates' court.

Introduction

5–001 The magistrates' court is one of the busiest courts within the justice system. Unlike the Crown Court, it is always written in lower case and uses the plural possessive apostrophe. They are found in every major town and city, as well as in a number of the smaller market towns throughout the country. The magistrates' court is a court with primarily criminal jurisdiction, but it also has limited jurisdiction in relation to a number of civil matters, such as liquor licensing appeals and gaming issues, as well as family law jurisdiction.

The magistrates' court is a part of His Majesty's Courts and Tribunal Service (HMCTS), which is, in turn, an executive agency of the government department now known as the Ministry of Justice. The HMCTS was created on 1 April 2011, when it brought together the existing separate court and tribunal services to form one integrated agency. HMCTS sets out its aim as being:

> **[t]o ensure that all citizens receive timely access to justice according to their different needs, whether as victims or witnesses of crime, defendants accused of crimes, consumers in debt, children at risk of harm, businesses involved in commercial disputes or as individuals asserting their employment rights or challenging the decisions of government bodies.**

Every criminal case will pass through the doors of the magistrates' court at some point in time, even if very briefly on its way to being sent to the Crown Court. In fact, the volume of work considered in the magistrates' court could be illustrated by the fact that the court deals with over 95 per cent of all criminal cases from start to finish. To aid the working of such a busy court there are approximately 13,000 magistrates, (this number is down by more than half in the last decade) who are more formally known as Justices of the Peace, employed by the court, as well as district judges and deputy district judges (see Ch.6, "District judges", for further details). When the magistrates hear a case they will normally sit in a panel of three, known as the Bench, and they will be divided into two "wingers" and one "chair". The chair will announce the decision of the magistrates to the court and deliver the reasoning for the decision, whilst the two wingers will remain silent when in the courtroom. All three magistrates, however, take the decision in the case equally and this can be done by way of a majority vote (two to one), hence the need for a panel of three so as to avoid any stalemate positions.

History

Over to you

Where do you think the role of the magistrate came from?

The first mention of a magistrate dates back well into the 12th century, as in 1195 the then king, Richard I, appointed a number of his knights to be charged with the position of keeping law and order. These knights became known as the Keepers of the Peace and were effectively the first magistrates of the land, although at this point they did not have a judicial role and were probably more akin to an early form of a police force. 5-002

In 1361 the title of the Keepers of the Peace changed to its modern-day name of justices of the peace by way of the enactment of the Justices of the Peace Act 1361. This Act is quite unusual in the fact that it only contains one section (statutory provision), which states:

> **Who shall be Justices of the Peace. First, that in every County of England shall be assigned for the keeping of the Peace, one Lord, and with him three or four of the most worthy in the County, with some learned in the Law, and they shall have Power to restrain the Offenders, Rioters, and all other Barators, and to pursue, arrest, take, and chastise them according to their Trespass or Offence; and to cause them to be imprisoned and duly punished according to the Law and Customs of the Realm, and according to that which to them shall seem best to do by their Discretions and good Advisement; [. . .]; and to take and arrest all those that they may find by Indictment, or by Suspicion, and to put them in Prison; and to take of all them that be [not] of good Fame, where they shall be found, sufficient Surety and Mainprise of their good Behaviour towards the King and his People, and the other duly to punish; to the Intent that the People be not by such Rioters or Rebels troubled nor endamaged, nor the Peace blemished, nor Merchants nor other passing by the Highways of the Realm disturbed, nor put in the Peril which may happen of such Offenders.**

Following the enactment of this statute the justices of the peace now had the ability and powers to be able to arrest alleged offenders, investigate offences and punish offenders appropriately. At around the same time as the enactment of this statute, Parliament also passed a statute that required the justices of the peace to meet four times a year so as to conduct matters of local business; these sessions became known as the Quarter Sessions. 5-003

The magistrates' role continued to expand over the years and, responsible not only for conducting criminal matters, they also began to develop a large administrative role. In the 14th century they became responsible for the regulation of wages; in 1576 they were required to provide "houses of correction" (early prisons) where those who had committed criminal acts could be detained; in 1597 they assumed responsibility over the Poor Laws; and in 1652 they were granted the powers to be able to conduct marriages. The remit of the magistrates became massive, almost to an unworkable point and, consequently, from about 1829 onwards, the magistrates began to be relieved of the large share of their administrative duties. By the latter end of the 19th century, local councils had assumed the large majority of these functions, leaving the magistrates to deal with mainly criminal matters and the occasional administrative role in relation to issues such as liquor licensing laws.

FIGURE 19 **Historical development of the magistracy**

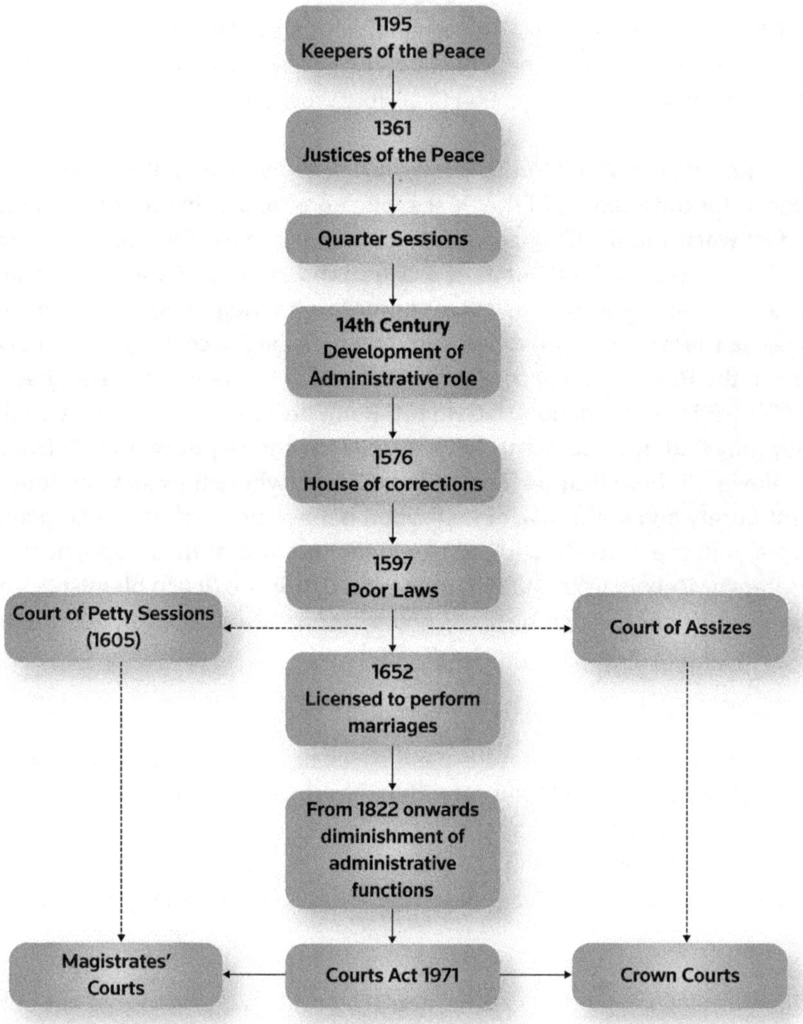

The criminal side of the magistrates' work also expanded rapidly over the years, so much so that the Quarter Sessions were quickly found not to provide a sufficient amount of time in which to appropriately deal with the large volume of cases. Consequently, in 1605, the Privy Council set out that the magistrates should meet at more regular intervals (many local magistrates had been meeting on an informal basis in-between the Quarter Sessions by this point anyway). These more frequent meetings became known as the Petty Sessions and, at around the same time, the Court of Assizes was also developed, with its function being to deal with the more serious criminal cases where a jury was required. The Quarter (and now Petty) Sessions continued for 600 years until, under the Courts Act 1971, the Petty Sessions became formally known as the magistrates' court, and the Court of Assizes became the Crown Court.

Eligibility

The first point to note in respect of magistrates is that they are not required to have any legal or professional qualifications; they do not need to know the law, they must simply be interested in and dedicated to serving the community in which they live. In fact, the eligibility criteria are generally quite wide and therefore this leaves the possibility of becoming a magistrate open to a broad sector of society. This has not always been the case though, as, prior to 1906, there was a property qualification restriction upon becoming a magistrate, meaning that any person who wished to stand as a magistrate had to own their own land. Women were also originally prevented from becoming magistrates until the law changed In 1919. **5-004**

Nowadays, a prospective magistrate simply has to be aged between 18 and 74, although even this eligibility criterion has been the subject of recent change as, prior to 2004, the minimum age that a magistrate could be appointed at was 27. In 2003, approximately 4 per cent of all magistrates were aged under 40, resulting in an unrepresentative view of the composition of society. To redress this imbalance in the magistracy, the Government initiated a £4 million, three-year recruitment drive to try and attract younger people to sit on the bench. The recruitment drive has appeared to have a degree of limited success with a number of younger candidates being accepted into the judicial ranks of the magistrates' court. For example, in 2004, the appointment of two magistrates aged 21 and 24 occurred, and, in 2006, the country's youngest ever magistrate, at the age of 19, was appointed to sit on the Pontefract Bench. However, although lowering the age of eligibility is in line with the age of majority and is aimed at producing a more diverse and varied judicial Bench, the changes have also attracted widespread criticism; it has been commonly opined by members of the legal profession and the public alike, that a person under the age of 27 is not possessed with the maturity or life skills necessary to hear and judge something so serious as a criminal case.

As well as being within the requisite age boundaries, a potential magistrate must also be of good standing within the community. Those who have been subject to serious criminal convictions, or a number of minor convictions, are automatically disqualified from sitting as a magistrate, as are those who have been declared bankrupt. There are a number of professions that will also preclude a person from sitting on the Bench, as those who are members, or whose spouse or partner is a member, of a law enforcement agency (such as the police force, traffic wardens or the armed forces) or who work within the criminal justice system (as court staff, for the probation service, Crown Prosecution Service or prison service, etc.) cannot be appointed as a magistrate. The reasoning behind this exclusion is that such a person's professional role would not be seen as being compatible with the role of a magistrate. Obviously, if a person **5-005** worked for the police force or for the Crown Prosecution Service then he may be viewed as being biased or prejudiced in favour of the prosecution, thereby not affording the defendant a fair trial. Even if the individual involved would not actually be biased, the public image put forward by the courts must be considered so as to avoid any perceived impartiality; as the old adage states "justice must not only be done, but it must also be seen to be done".

The Role of a Magistrate

Over to you

What do you think the role of a magistrate is? Do you know anyone who is a magistrate? If so, talk to them and find out what it's really like to sit in court and the types of issues they have to deal with.

5–006 Being a magistrate is not a financially rewarding occupation as all magistrates sit as unpaid volunteers; they are individuals who are willing to give up their spare time and help to deliver justice within their own community. Becoming a magistrate is certainly not a way for a person to find fame and fortune, but it is a method for allowing individuals to give something back to society, and a desire to sit as a magistrate can often be said to come from an individual's having a strong sense of civic duty and responsibility. Although magistrates are unpaid, they are allowed to claim back any expenses that they incur in the course of carrying out their judicial functions. This means that they can recoup any monies spent on travel or subsistence but these losses must have actually been incurred and they must also be reasonable; putting in a claim for a £200 lunch would certainly be viewed as excessive.

The level of dedication and commitment required to become a magistrate can also be viewed as quite onerous, as the minimum time that they must agree to "sit" is a least 26 half-days per year. A half-day is classed as either 10am to 2pm, or 2pm to 5pm, with arrival to be half an hour prior to the commencement of court so that the magistrates can prepare in advance of sitting. Some magistrates' courts are organised on a full-day basis and in such situations the magistrates must be able to sit for full days, as and when required by the court. Even though the minimum required time to sit is 26 half-days per year it is envisaged that a magistrate will sit more frequently than this; in fact, the average sitting time is between 35 and 45 half-days per year. If an individual magistrate sits more regularly than this then there becomes the danger that the Bench will not be representative of the local community. The Magistrates' Courts Association sets out that a magistrate should not spend more than 70 half-days sitting per year, unless the sittings are spread out within different courts (youth courts, family courts, etc), and the absolute maximum that a magistrate is permitted to sit is 100 half-days per year.

Arrangements for sittings are worked out well in advance on a rota basis and it is usually possible to make changes in an emergency. Obviously, sitting as a magistrate requires a great deal of considered commitment, as the requirements can have an impact on both the magistrate's work and home life. It is preferred that individual magistrate sittings are scheduled at regular intervals throughout the year so that the necessary level of competence required for court can be maintained, but it is also accepted that certain individuals may need to have their sitting times scheduled during specific periods, for example, during term-time for those with school-age children, or during school holidays for school teachers. However, employers are legally obliged to allow their employees time off to undertake lay magistracy duties. **5–007**

As well as the regular required sitting days, magistrates are also expected to attend extra-curricular meetings and training sessions. This is to ensure that they are kept up to date with any new developments in the law, as well as to ensure that they receive continuous professional development so that they remain competent in their roles. These extra sessions are generally held outside of normal working hours (often at weekends) so that all magistrates should be able to attend these additional commitments. If a magistrate has more time to spare, then he may volunteer, when sufficiently experienced, for extra sittings or he may undertake further training so that he can sit on the Family or Youth Panels, or the Betting and Gaming or Licensing Appeals (see below for further details on the work of these courts).

As stated above, the majority of a magistrate's work will involve sitting in the criminal court. A magistrate's role includes, amongst other things: **5–008**

- presiding over a trial, determining whether a defendant is guilty or not, and passing the appropriate sentence;
- deciding on requests for remand in custody;
- deciding on applications for bail; and
- committing more serious cases to the Crown Court.

Deciding to sit as a magistrate is a decision that carries with it a large amount of responsibility as the role involves deliberating upon a person's guilt and innocence and, ultimately, determining issues concerning his welfare and liberty. Magistrates consider the evidence in each case and reach a verdict. If a defendant is found guilty, or pleads guilty, they decide on the most appropriate sentence. Magistrates deal with the less serious criminal cases, such as minor theft, criminal damage, public disorder and motoring offences.

As stated above, magistrates normally sit in a panel of three members, but they do have the legislative powers to carry out some judicial work whilst sitting as a single justice of the peace, such as deciding whether to vary or extend bail conditions, make pre-hearing directions, and dealing with summary, non-imprisonable matters on the papers as opposed to at a hearing.

Furthermore, magistrates are not just limited to presiding over the adult criminal courts; after receiving appropriate training, an individual magistrate may extend his judicial jurisdiction to both the family and youth courts.

The Family Court

5-009 Magistrates can undertake a large degree of family court work. Magistrates who sit in the family courts are specially selected and trained and they will deal with issues such as those relating to the breakdown of a marriage, child contact and residence orders under the Children Act 1989, adoption orders, protection orders in relation to cases of domestic violence, and public law matters relating to the care and control of children.

The Youth Court

5-010 As young persons under the age of 18 cannot normally be tried in the adult criminal courts (the magistrates' or the Crown Court) then there is a court system in place so that they may be tried effectively and fairly. The youth court will hear cases involving offenders aged between 10 and 17 years. The magistrates who sit in the youth court are again specially trained and they sit on what is known as a youth panel. Youth courts are courts that are heard *in camera*; this means that they are not open to the public and only those involved in the case will attend the hearing. The court hearings are far more informal than the traditional adult courts and there is much more interaction between the defendant, their family and the court than is usually found in other courts. Magistrates in the youth court have extended sentencing powers as they can sentence for up to 24 months (as opposed to the standard six months in the adult courts).

Civil Courts

5-011 Despite losing the vast majority of their administrative powers, magistrates still carry out certain judicial functions within the civil justice system as they deal with matters such as appeals relating to the refusal to grant a liquor licence (local authorities are responsible initially for deciding whether or not to grant such a licence), and issues relating to betting and gaming. They also hear cases involving debt recovery on behalf of utility companies and local authorities (i.e. non-payment of council tax, etc.).

Crown Court

5-012 Magistrates may also occasionally appear in the Crown Court when hearing appeals from the magistrates' court (see Ch.12, "Appeals" for further details) where they sit with a Crown Court judge.

Appointment

Magistrates are appointed by the Lord Chief Justice, after consultation with the Lord Chancellor, by instrument on behalf and in the name of His Majesty. The Lord Chancellor's decision as to which individuals are suitable for appointment to the magistracy is guided by the involvement of the advisory committees. These committees will assess the potential candidates and make recommendations regarding the individual candidates. **5–013**

Prior to the enactment of the Courts Act 2003, the areas of Lancashire, Greater Manchester and Merseyside were unique in the appointment of magistrates, insomuch as a magistrate would not be appointed by the Lord Chancellor, but rather by the Chancellor of the Duchy of Lancaster. The reasons for the difference in the appointment system was one that was steeped in history but now, due to the introduction of s.10 of the Courts Act, this rather quaint British tradition has been eroded and the appointment of magistrates is now a unified system countrywide.

The Advisory Committees

There are a number of advisory committees throughout the length and breadth of the country, forming a network of committees, each one serving its local geographical area. The committee's role is to determine the number of magistrates that should be appointed per year for its local area and it will consider the individual applications made by any potential magistrates. The committees are also responsible for monitoring and ensuring that appointed magistrates fulfil their allotted sitting duties and they may be called to investigate and advise if any issues regarding the competency of a magistrate are raised. The committees are responsible directly to the Lord Chancellor. **5–014**

The committees are comprised of people who live within the local area. At least one-third of the committee must consist of persons who do not hold a judicial role (so they must not be magistrates themselves), whereas the remaining two-thirds of the committee must consist of serving magistrates. The purpose of involving laypeople in the appointment of magistrates is to ensure a diverse perspective on the needs and requirements of the local area, thereby making sure that a representative Bench is maintained.

Personal Qualities of Magistrates

To determine whether a candidate will make a suitable magistrate the relevant advisory committee will initially consider the application in line with reference to the six key personal qualities set out by the Lord Chancellor. These six key qualities are: **5–015**

- good character;
- understanding and communication;

- social awareness;
- maturity and sound temperament;
- sound judgement; and
- commitment and reliability.

These qualities go towards assessing the candidate's judicial qualities and determining whether or not they will make a good magistrate. First, a magistrate must be of good character, as he must command the confidence, respect and trust of the public and have personal integrity. If a candidate possessed a number of criminal convictions or were bankrupt themselves, there would be a concern over whether they would be able to make unbiased decisions as to the culpability of the defendant in a case; they may not be able to view the case objectively and this could result in unfair and unjust decisions being taken. The necessity for a magistrate to possess understanding and the ability to communicate effectively is of high importance for obvious reasons; if a magistrate had poor language skills or a very limited level of intelligence then he would not be able to effectively assess the evidence presented in a case. This lack of understanding could have severely detrimental consequences upon the fairness of a case and could result in perverse decisions being made. The same reasoning can be applied to the necessity for a magistrate to be able to communicate effectively. Magistrates must work together in their deliberations and, if one member of the Bench cannot put forward his views on the case in a comprehensive manner, then this may also result in an unjust decision being made. Magistrates also need to possess the ability to convey their reasoning and decision to the court in an understandable manner and this would be severely impeded if the magistrate in question lacked competent communication skills.

5-016 Social awareness is also a required quality of a magistrate; this awareness is to include an appreciation and acceptance of the rule of law, as well as the ability to respect people from different ethnic, cultural or social backgrounds. By being socially aware the magistrate will be able to assess the evidence and the manner of the case being presented and be able to use such inherent information to assist in the making of the appropriate decision. One of the principles behind the role of a magistrate is that he is aware of the social issues that directly affect the local area in which he sits, as well as any wider societal values and issues. For example, if a local area has a large drug and gun crime problem then the magistrates' social awareness may allow them to consider imposing a heavier sentence so as to act as a deterrent to others in the locality who continue to partake in such criminal activity. What is a social issue in one geographical area may not be in another and, as such, the magistrates will need to possess such information so as to be able to serve their community effectively.

Maturity, sound judgement and temperament are all a prerequisite of being appointed to a judicial position. These skills encompass the willingness to listen, to be decisive, and to be firm but fair where necessary, but always with a high degree of courtesy and humanity. If magistrates do not hold these qualities then there is the danger that there will be no consistency or logic in their decision-making processes. The requirement of these judicial qualities, especially in relation to maturity, has been raised as a concern in relation to the appointment of young magistrates. As stated above, it can be argued that a person who is only 19 or 20 years old has not "lived enough" to gain sufficient life experience to then enable him to make rational and sound decisions as regards the fate of another human being. Magistrates must also possess the ability to think logically, to be able to weigh up both sides of the argument and balance them to reach a considered conclusion and, in doing so, they must also work with an open and objective mind and not be influenced by prejudices of any kind.

Finally, there is a direct need for potential magistrates to be able to commit to the role and be reliable in their judicial functions. If a candidate's personal circumstances allude to the fact that they will not be able to fully dedicate themselves to the requirements of the role (maybe due to work or family commitments) then the committee assessing them may come to the conclusion that the candidate does not satisfy this element of the six key qualities. The committee will look to see if the candidate has the help and support of their family, friends and employer as all of these could have a bearing on the level of reliability. The candidate must also be of good health. The court system would become inefficient and slow if magistrates did not turn up to court when required as cases would be delayed, and the longer there is a delay in a criminal case then the higher the chance the defendant will not be afforded a fair trial. **5–017**

Overall, aspiring magistrates need to be well-rounded, balanced people. They must be able to assimilate factual information as they will be presented with a wealth of evidence to work their way through, they must be able to make reasoned decisions with care, thought and impartiality; they must also be able to work together as a team and take account of the reasoning and views of others.

Selection Process

Appointments to the magistracy are not conducted by way of a set competition, where an advert for vacancies is published with a closing date for applications to be made, but rather the application process is an open one where an interested candidate can make an application at any time during the year. The application is made by way of a set application form to the local magistrates' advisory committee, which reviews and sifts the applications in preparation of calling those potential candidates who appear to possess the necessary skills and criteria on paper to interview. **5–018**

The interview stage of selection is normally a two-stage process whereby the potential candidates will be asked to attend a first interview, which will be concerned with assessing whether they do in fact possess the personal qualities and attributes necessary to become a magistrate. Either a subcommittee of the advisory committee or a specially convened interview panel comprising members of the advisory committee will conduct this initial interview. The panel will normally interview a number of potential magistrates on the same day and the interview will take the form of a standard job interview, with the candidates being asked general questions about themselves.

5-019 If, after the initial interview, the panel is convinced that an individual does possess the necessary qualities required to become a magistrate then the candidate may, depending on local advisory committee policy, be requested to return at a later date for a second interview. This second interview will predominately focus on determining the candidate's judicial aptitude and ability to cope with such a role. To assess these skills the candidate will be given a number of case studies to consider. These case studies will involve common scenarios that occur regularly within the magistrates' court, and the candidate will be questioned about them so that the panel can ascertain their views on issues such as crime and punishment. The candidate may be asked to identify the relevant issues in a case, or to suggest an appropriate sentence, and may also be asked about responses to certain ethical and moral issues. The case studies and the candidate's reactions to them will then allow the panel to judge whether the candidate would be suitable to become a magistrate. Obviously, a person who indicates that they would acquit all defendants who come before them due to a high level of sympathy would not be an appropriate person to sit as a magistrate. Conversely, nor would a person be thought to be suitable if they were insistent on handing out six-month sentences for all offenders, regardless of the offence or its circumstances.

Once the advisory committee has identified those candidates who it believes are suitable for selection as magistrates then it will notify the Lord Chancellor (by way of his office) so that they may then appoint them officially. The process to be selected and appointed as a magistrate is a rather long one that can, on average, take somewhere between six and twelve months to achieve.

A Reflective Bench

5-020 As the Bench in the magistrates' court effectively replaces the role of the jury in the Crown Court, the advisory committee must try to ensure that the Bench is reflective of the community that it serves. To ensure that a defendant has a fair trial, the composition of the Bench that hears the case should be diverse; one of the functions of the advisory committee is to encourage applications to the magistracy, and indeed the advisory committee membership itself, from underrepresented groups. The Lord Chancellor's Directions to Advisory Committees (*https://www.judiciary.uk/guidance-and-resources/advisory-committees-justices-peace/* [accessed 1 May 2025]) sets out the five key attributes that must be demonstrated in successful applications to the magistracy:

- Understand and appreciate different perspectives;
- Make fair, impartial and transparent decisions;
- Communicate with sensitivity and respect;
- Show self-awareness and be open to learning; and
- Work and engage with people professionally.

Candidates must permanently reside in the jurisdiction of England and Wales at the time of application and, to maintain the principle of local justice, candidates should apply to an area close to where they live or work. Prior to the enactment of the Courts Act 2003, it was a necessary requirement for magistrates to live within 15 miles of the local court where they were to serve. This requirement has now been made obsolete. Where an Advisory Committee receives an application from a person who does not live or work within a reasonable distance of the area they are applying to, candidates should be encouraged to apply to the area in which they live or work. Applications may be transferred to a different area with the candidate's agreement, if there is an open recruitment campaign.

The ethnic origins and diversity of the Bench must also be considered, and this should **5-021** be assessed in relation to the general ethnic composition of the local area of the specific magistrates' court. The number of persons from ethnic minorities is a more telling figure as to the true diversity of the Bench as, in 2013, only 8.4 per cent of all magistrates were from a black and minority ethnic (BME) group. This figure is a slight increase from previous years where the figure had been around 8 per cent. 16% of all new appointments made in 2023/24 were from an ethnic minority background. Whilst there is no specific requirement or target for ethnic minority membership, an advisory committee may consider age, gender and ethnic origins to be important in relation to the five factors listed above. Indeed, the Lord Chancellor's Directions specifically state "candidates must be assessed on merit against the five key attributes and the requirements in the role description. No other factors may be considered".

The occupation of a candidate is, however, a relevant factor, as a range of occupations are incompatible with being a magistrate. CPS prosecutors and employees, police or community support officers, prison and probation staff, store detectives and private investigators are all ineligible occupations or activities. However, there are some professions that are surprisingly eligible for appointment as lay magistrates: solicitors, social workers, members of Parliament and members of the armed forces are typically eligible but may depend on the exact circumstances or have conditions attached.

Despite these directions and guidance factors for advisory committees and the more general drive to achieve a diverse and fully reflective magistracy, the absence of any actual requirements to achieve gender and ethnic minority representations means that diversity of the bench may not necessarily be achieved.

Recruitment

The Strategy for the Magistracy 2019–22 (Magistrates' Association, "Strategy for the Magistracy **5-022** for 2019–22" *https://www.magistrates-association.org.uk/publication/strategy-for-the-magistracy/)* (accessed 1 May 2025) stated that there is at present a shortage of magistrates. It stated that over 50% of serving magistrates will reach retirement within the next 10 years. The more recent increase to 75 in the general age of retirement brought in by the Public Service Pensions and Judicial Offices Act 2022 for most judicial office holders, including magistrates, may alleviate some of that pressure. An effective judicial deployment protocol will be developed to provide a clear prediction of the next three years.

In the foreword to the 2003 the National Strategy for the Recruitment of Lay Magistrates, Lord Falconer, then Lord Chancellor, set out that it would:

> **[e]xamine not only how to raise the profile of the magistracy generally, but also to develop a framework to target the recruitment and retention of magistrates from under-represented groups, whilst continuing to draw on the support of those who have traditionally provided the backbone of local recruitment. The strategy will aim to highlight the importance of the work of magistrates, particularly to employers, who must be persuaded that, by allowing staff who are magistrates time off to carry out their duties, they are contributing enormously to the maintenance of local justice and the values of good citizenship. This approach will also be designed to encourage the self-employed that they, too, have a role to play in serving their community by directing their individual talents towards furthering the cause of justice in the community.**

The idea behind the Strategy was to combine best practice and ensure that recruitment was carried out in a targeted, professional and co-ordinated manner. The three main strategic objectives were:

- to recruit and retain magistrates from a diverse spectrum of the population;
- to raise the profile of the magistracy and dispel generally held misconceptions about its make-up and the entry requirements; and
- to support the appointments process.

5–023 In relation to the recruitment and retaining of magistrates, the Strategy highlighted two areas of high importance; the first was in relation to targeting and encouraging employers to release staff so that they could fulfil their magistrates' duties, and the second related to the revision of existing methods of recruitment with the consideration of alternative methods. The proposed action for tackling the first high priority issue was to develop a campaign specifically directed towards employers so that they became aware of the benefits that can be gained from having an employee who also sits as a magistrate. The Strategy set out that these benefits could include the employee gaining a number of marketable skills that are transferable to the workplace at no added cost to the employer. The examples given in the Strategy of the types of transferable skills acquired were the moral authority to make difficult decisions, self-confidence, teamwork, appraisal, and mentoring and communication skills. As a result of the action taken to tackle this part of the Strategy, the employers of potential magistrates are now provided with an information pack on the role and the functions of the magistracy and how it may benefit them.

The proposed action for the second high priority point was for a well-directed recruitment campaign to be conducted through a variety of media outlets, such as local newspapers and radio, as well as specialist publications that targeted specific groups, e.g. Asian community newsletters, local community groups and community centres, etc. A large part of the recruitment problem appeared to stem from the fact that people were simply not aware that they could apply to become magistrates without any formal qualifications or experience. Adverts now go out across a range of media outlets that reach a far wider and more diverse sector of society than ever occurred previously.

The Strategy also highlighted the need, amongst other things, to:

- provide an online application system;
- develop a simple leaflet setting out the role, responsibilities and duties of a magistrate and the training that is provided so that candidates can achieve the necessary competencies;
- undertake research into the possible barriers that exist to stop people coming forward, such as age or self-employment, and take appropriate steps to break down those barriers;
- create networks to support and encourage magistrates from ethnic minorities and those with disabilities; and
- build in more flexibility in relation to court sitting requirements.

The objectives highlighted by the Recruitment Strategy were to ensure that there was a **5–024** continued improvement in the recruitment of magistrates from a socially wide and diverse background so that the Bench could move towards fully reflecting the society that it serves. However, there will always be issues with achieving such a reflective composition of the magistracy due to everyday practicalities of life. Those who put themselves forward to sit as a magistrate are generally those who have the time, resources and inclination to do so. This invariably means that they are people who have already established their careers and they do not need to impress their employers with complete job commitment, or they have developed the confidence in themselves to approach their managers to request the time off to fulfil their magistrates' duties. It would be very unusual to find a person in his early twenties who would feel comfortable enough to approach his employer to discuss such matters. As a result, the magistracy consists of a larger number of middle-aged persons than younger ones (although do note the earlier comments on this point). Additionally, the occupation or the class of an individual can have an effect on his abilities and desires to become a magistrate. Many magistrates are individuals who hold middle management and professional roles, where the idea of serving a civic duty is quite readily accepted, or they are semi-retired individuals who are looking for something to occupy their time. People from every walk of life (bar the previously discussed exceptions) can apply to sit as a magistrate, but again it is difficult to envisage a single mum of four children having any spare time, or being willing to give up any spare time that she does have, to sit as a magistrate. Due to circumstances of life, and despite the recruitment drive initiated by the Government, the magistracy is still heavily weighted in favour of middle-aged, middle-class white people, which, unfortunately, falls short of being a truly reflective representation of our society as it is today.

The Oath

5-025 Upon appointment, all new magistrates must swear the judicial oath in a confirmation that they will carry out their judicial duties in an appropriate and responsible manner. The judicial oath is:

> **I, ..., swear that I will well and truly serve our Sovereign Lord King Charles the Third, in the office of Justice of the Peace and I will do right to all manner of people after the laws and usages of the Realm without fear or favour, affection or ill will.**

By pledging their allegiance to the Crown it is envisaged that magistrates will uphold the oath and commit to carrying out their duties and functions in an appropriate manner.

Training

5-026 As magistrates generally have little knowledge of the law and the court system it is important that they are sufficiently trained so that they can carry out their role effectively. This does not mean that they need to be taught the laws of the country in detail, as they have a legal adviser in the courtroom to aid and assist them with such intricacies (see "Legal Advisers", at **5-030**), but they do need to be aware of issues such as the relevant court procedures and their powers of sentencing, etc. The Judicial College supervises the training of magistrates; however, the majority of the training is actually undertaken and delivered by the local legal advisers via the Magistrate Area Training Committees (MATCs). The training is mandatory for all new magistrates, and, even once initially trained, all magistrates are expected to continue on with their professional development and attend further training so that they can maintain their competencies within the courtroom. Details of the training are now found in the framework laid down by the National Training Programme for Magistrates which sets out the three basic competencies magistrates are required to demonstrate:

1. managing yourself;
2. working as a member of the team; and
3. making judicial decisions.

Each competency involves a number of different skills that magistrates are required to master, but every competency (and skill) is equally as important as the others. Examples of the skills required under the first competency of "managing yourself" would include obtaining and reading the relevant paperwork, ensuring that each person is aware of their role in court that day, being aware of the documentation that may provide guidance whilst in court and checking to identify any potential conflicts of interest. The second competency of "working as a member of the team" includes skills such as being able to express views clearly and concisely, being able to listen to and give consideration to colleagues' contributions and being able to challenge discriminatory comments made by colleagues. The final competency of "making judicial decisions" sets out skills such as having a knowledge of the legal framework and principles that apply to the magistrates' court, being able to identify, analyse and assess the relevant information and evidence and having an understanding of the court system and the doctrine of precedent.

All magistrates should receive their own copy of the competence framework, as well as details as to the level and sequence of training that they need to undertake. The Judicial College oversees the training that must be taken by a newly appointed magistrate before they are allowed to sit in the court so that they can achieve the three competencies as detailed above.

The first training that new magistrates will receive is known as Initial Introductory Training and this is where the new magistrates will be introduced to the magistracy and the life of the Bench. This initial training period will be for at least a three-hour period. After the new magistrates have completed the initial training, they will then go on to undertake what is known as the Initial Core Training. The requirement of this core training involves the completion of 12 separate modules, and each one must be completed before the magistrate may sit in the court. The 12 separate modules follow the syllabus set by the Judicial College and they cover: **5–027**

- a magistrate's training and development;
- judicial decision-making;
- the jurisdiction of magistrates;
- case management and preliminary decisions;
- pleas before venue and mode of trial;
- summary trial, evidence and determining guilt or innocence;
- sentencing;
- road traffic cases, disqualification and endorsement;
- enforcement of court orders;
- out-of-court business, applications and other hearings;
- magistrates in context; and
- review and planning for ongoing training and development.

This core training will take place over an absolute minimum of three days (18 hours), although feasibly this may take longer due to individual magistrates' commitments. The training will also be supplemented by a number of activities so that a well-rounded view of the role of a magistrate is gained. These activities will include a number of court observations, visits to other institutions (i.e. prisons), and there will also be a degree of mentoring provided by an experienced magistrate. After magistrates have successfully completed the initial training they **5–028** will be ready to sit in court. At first, this will be by way of mentored sittings, and then they will eventually progress to sitting as (winger) magistrates in their own right on the Bench.

Approximately 12 months after starting to sit, a magistrate is required to undergo 12 hours of Consolidation Training so as to consolidate and examine all that they have learned so far. After a magistrate has sat for approximately two years they will then be appraised so as to check that they are meeting the required competencies and it is at this point that any issues can be identified and addressed as necessary. If a magistrate is found to not be meeting the competencies then the appraiser will recommend that they receive further training so that they are able to improve and meet the necessary criteria. If, after further training and appraisals, the magistrate is unable to evidence that they can satisfy the competencies then the matter will be referred to the Bench Training and Development Committee, which, upon review, may decide to recommend to the Lord Chancellor that the magistrate be relieved of his position.

5–029 Even after a magistrate has undertaken the consolidation training and appraisal they are still expected to attend further training so as to continue on with their professional and personal development. The further training consists of six hours' worth of First Continuation Training, which prepares the magistrate for their second appraisal and introduces the possibility of becoming a chair of the Bench. After this they will then undergo Winger Continuation Training. This continuation training is scheduled to take place every three years and it has the purpose of providing the magistrates with an opportunity to review their current practices and competencies.

If a magistrate decides that they want to become a chair, or that they wish to work within the family or youth courts, then they must undergo the relevant training for that role, as each one carries with it its own competencies and framework that must be achieved.

The structure and training of magistrates has become far more focused over the past two decades due to Lord Justice Auld's comments in his 2001 review of the criminal courts. Lord Auld identified that the then training programme was overly complicated and, in parts, unachievable (for example, it had 104 core competencies) and that there was a lack of consistency and standard of training provided by different magistracy areas. The Government and those involved in the administration of the magistracy listened to those criticisms and took them on board, resulting in a generally fit for purpose training programme, although these training provisions are still continuously under review by the Judicial College so that at least the level currently being attained in terms of quality is sustained, if not bettered.

Legal Advisers

5–030 As magistrates are not legally qualified it is imperative that someone who is well versed in the law advises them. So that the magistrates can be advised appropriately and carry out their judicial functions there is, in every magistrates' court, a person who is known as a legal adviser (formerly known as justices' clerks). Since 2010 all newly appointed legal advisers must be either a qualified solicitor or barrister. There are currently approximately 2,000 legal advisers working within magistrates' courts over the length and breadth of the country.

The **Practice Direction (QBD: Justices: Clerk to the Court)** [2000] 1 W.L.R. 1886 sets out that a legal adviser is responsible for:

- the legal advice tendered to the justices within the area;
- the performance of any of the functions set out below by any member of their staff acting as legal adviser;
- ensuring that competent advice is available to justices when the justice's clerk is not personally present in court; and
- the effective delivery of case management and the reduction of unnecessary delay.

Legal advisers must provide the justices with any advice required to properly perform their judicial functions. Advice may be given on matters such as:

- questions of law (including ECtHR jurisprudence and those matters set out in s.2(1) of the HRA 1998);
- questions of mixed law and fact;
- matters of practice and procedure;
- the range of penalties available;
- any relevant decisions of the superior courts or other guidelines;
- other issues relevant to the matter before the court; and
- the appropriate decision-making structure to be applied in any given case.

A legal adviser is required to provide the magistrates with this help and advice even in situations where they do not directly request such help and, in addition to advising the court, the legal adviser further holds a responsibility to assist the court, where appropriate, as to the formulation of reasons and the recording of those reasons. The **Practice Direction** further places an onus on the magistrates to refer to the legal adviser at any point where they feel it necessary, as it states:

> **At any time, justices are entitled to receive advice to assist them in discharging their responsibilities. If they are in any doubt as to the evidence which has been given, they should seek the aid of their legal adviser.**

There are a number of procedural issues that must be taken into account when considering **5-031**
the role of a legal adviser within the magistrates' court, especially in relation to ensuring that the defendant receives a fair trial. The main one of these is that the magistrates, and

not the legal adviser, are to be the triers of fact in the courtroom and it is of vital importance that the legal adviser does not exert any undue pressure or influence upon the magistrates in their decision-making processes; there is an inherent danger that this could occur simply due to the legal adviser's knowledge and the magistrates' reliance upon it for guidance. To ensure that the defendant's rights are not breached, the **Practice Direction** sets out that any advice sought or received from the legal adviser should be done in open court so that all parties to the proceedings are privy to the advice. The magistrates can request that the legal adviser joins them in the retiring room whilst they are deliberating, but this must only be for a reasonable length of time for the purposes of delivering the requested advice. In the case of **R. v Eccles Justices Ex p. Fitzpatrick** (1989) 89 Cr. App. R. 324 it was held that it was not acceptable for a legal adviser to retire with the justices for 25 minutes out of the 30 minutes that it took for the justices to make their decision. To decide otherwise would have been to allow ostensible bias, and even if there were no actual bias, then the appearance of such bias would have been overwhelming to the point of denying the defendant a fair trial.

If the magistrates wish their legal adviser to join them in the retiring room then this request must be made in open court and in the presence of all parties. If the legal adviser does provide them with legal advice whilst they are retired from the court then the legal adviser must repeat this to all parties when the court reconvenes, and, upon this occurring, all parties will be permitted to make representations on this advice, if they so wish.

Sentencing Powers

5–032 As the magistrates' court deals with summary and less serious offences it has limited sentencing powers. Currently, the maximum custodial sentence that a magistrates' court can impose for a single offence has increased from six to 12 months' imprisonment (see "Summary Offences", 9–031). The majority of summary only offences (save for a few exceptions) will have a maximum term of imprisonment of six months and so the recent change will be confined mostly to either-way offences.

As well as being able to impose custodial sentences the magistrates can also impose a variety of non-custodial sentences (see Ch.11, "Non-custodial Sentences", for further details on available sentences), and they can also impose a fine.

There has been an element of impending reform in recent years in relation to the sentencing powers of the magistrates' court. So as to enlarge the potential number of cases that could be heard by the magistrates' court, the Government felt that it would be appropriate to increase the magistrates' maximum sentencing powers for a single offence to 12 months (and 24 months with consecutive sentences for two or more offences) and that the level of fine that could be imposed could be increased to £15,000. The idea of increasing the fine quickly fell by the wayside, but the magistrates' court sentencing powers were increased by way of statute to a maximum of 12 months for a single offence under s.154 of the Criminal Justice Act 2003. Magistrates received comprehensive training on the extent of their new powers in anticipation of them coming into force but, this section was repealed by the Sentencing Act 2020 and the increase in sentencing powers did not happen until 2024.

However, the Legal Aid, Sentencing and Punishment of Offenders Act 2012 reignited the issue of increasing the fining power of the magistrates' court as ss.85 and 86 provided for magistrates being given the power to impose unlimited fines for some offences. On 10 June 2014 the government published a draft statutory instrument: The Legal Aid, Sentencing and Punishment of Offenders Act 2012 (Disapplication of Section 85(1), Fines Expressed as Proportions and Consequential Amendments) Regulations 2014, which set out the proposed fine increases in detail following removal of the £5,000 cap. This was then implemented by way of The Legal Aid, Sentencing and Punishment of Offenders Act 2012 (Disapplication of Section 85(1), Fines Expressed as Proportions and Consequential Amendments) Regulations 2015 and the £5,000 was removed for offences committed after 3 March 2015. **5-033**

The level of fine imposed by a magistrates' court is dependent on the particular offence committed, and there are five fine levels that increase in amount in correlation to perceived severity of the offence. As can been seen from the table below, the four-fold increase in magistrates' fining power is a significant development in the delivery of justice in this court, and it is envisaged that these changes will mean that the magistrates' court is able to become more effective in passing appropriate sentences and hearing more serious cases. However, magistrates will still have to pay reference to the Magistrates' Court Sentencing Guidelines and the level of fine it imposes will still have to be proportionate to both the offence charged and the financial circumstances of the offender; there will be little justice done by imposing a £9,000 fine upon an individual who is on benefits, has no savings to their name, and who simply could not pay such a high tariff within any reasonable timescale.

The table below sets out the current maximum level of fine and an example offence for each level.

FIGURE 20 **Increases in maximum levels of fine**

Level	Maximum fine	Offence examples
1	£200	Unauthorised cycle racing on public ways
2	£500	Driving a motor cycle without a protective helmet
3	£1,500	Sale of alcohol to a drunk person, or being drunk and disorderly in a public place
4	£2,500	Speeding on the motorway
5	Unlimited	Defective brakes on a goods vehicle

Over to you

Do you think magistrates' court sentencing powers should have been increased to allow the imposition of an unlimited fine? If you were to reform the law in this area what maximum sentence (custodial and financial) would you set for this court? Would you go further than the CJA 2003 and LASPO 2012 provisions?

FIGURE 21 **Magistrates' court sentencing powers**

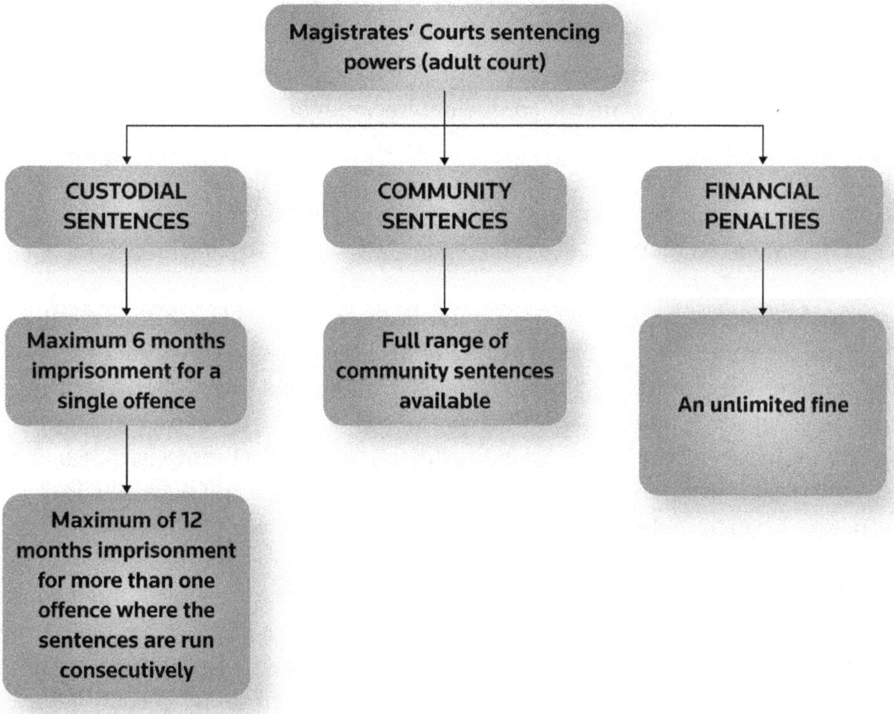

Resignation and Removal

The resignation or removal of a magistrate is governed by s.11 of the Courts Act 2003 (CA 2003). Section 11 states that: **5–034**

> (1) A lay justice may resign his office at any time.
> (2) The Lord Chancellor may, with the concurrence of the Lord Chief Justice, remove a lay justice from his office by an instrument on behalf and in the name of Her Majesty—
>   (a) on the ground of incapacity or misbehaviour,
>   (b) on the ground of a persistent failure to meet such standards of competence as are prescribed by a direction given by the Lord Chancellor with the concurrence of the Lord Chief Justice, or
>   (c) if he is satisfied that the lay justice is declining or neglecting to take a proper part in the exercise of his functions as a justice of the peace.

Please note: section 10 of the Interpretation Act 1978 states that "[I]n any Act a reference to the Sovereign reigning at the time of the passing of the Act is to be construed, unless the contrary intention appears, as a reference to the Sovereign for the time being".

Section 11(1) sets out that a magistrate can at any time resign from the Bench, but it is hoped that, once appointed, a magistrate will continue to serve for at least five years before deciding to resign from their duties. If a magistrate decides to serve for as long as they are allowed then they will be retired from service at the age of 76. Upon retirement or resignation, a magistrate is allowed to keep the official title of "Justice of the Peace" as a sign of recognition for services to the court and their community.

Every year there is a very small number of magistrates who do not wish to leave the Bench when it is thought appropriate for them to do so and, as a result, the Lord Chancellor has been granted the powers to remove such persons under s.11(2) of the CA 2003. Under subs.(2)(a), the Lord Chancellor can require a person to be removed from the list of magistrates if it is felt that they are incapable of continuing on with and conducting their responsibilities. A magistrate will generally be removed under this process where they are too ill to be able to sit in court but have not resigned from the post.

5–035 The alleged misbehaviour of the magistrate is another ground for removal under subs.(1)(a), and the reasons for such a removal will generally be where a magistrate has been convicted of a criminal offence. However, a criminal conviction is not always a necessary prerequisite for a removal from post and, in 2008, a magistrate was barred from sitting in court following his dismissal from his employed work due to allegations of gross misconduct. Where there is a persistent failure by a magistrate to meet the standards of competence the Lord Chancellor has the power to remove such a magistrate under s.11(2)(b). This power of removal is there to help reinforce the training initiative and to ensure that all magistrates comply fully with the training requirements.

The final reason for removal is found under s.11(2)(c), and this can be used by the Lord Chancellor where a magistrate refuses to, or neglects to, fulfil their judicial obligations. Examples of when this power may be used are where a magistrate continuously fails to sit for the required minimum number of sittings, or if they repeatedly fail to turn up for court when they are obliged to do so. A magistrate can also be removed under this provision if they refuse to operate a law enacted by the Government. In 2007, a magistrate refused to hear cases in the family court on the basis of religious grounds; stating that he could not deliberate on cases that involved issues of gay adoption as such matters offended his religious beliefs. The magistrate formally resigned from his post, but had he not done so, then the Lord Chancellor could have requested his removal from post under s.11(2) due to his refusal to implement the law.

FIGURE 22 **Advantages/disadvantages**

Advantages	Disadvantages
Lay participation The average cost of employing lay magistrates is £52.10 per hour. If all the lay magistrates were removed from the system and replaced with professional judges then the cost would increase by several million pounds.	**Low acquittal rate** There is an approximately 90% conviction rate in the magistrates' court. Concerns have been raised as to whether there is an element of prosecution bias as the magistrates will often see the same prosecutor, which may possibly affect their judgement.
Gender balance Approximately 56% of magistrates are women. In comparison only 28% of the judiciary (fee paid and legally qualified persons) are female.	**Inconsistent** Differing sentences for very similar offences. For example, in 2001 for the offence of burglary in Teeside only 20% of offenders received immediate custody, whilst in Birmingham 41% received custody for the same offence.
Reflective of society Ethnic minorities are better represented at approximately 8%, as opposed to the 5% in the judiciary. Magistrates can come from all sectors of society so they can be (for example) dinner ladies, bus drivers, plumbers, accountants, teachers, housewives and doctors.	**Not truly diverse** The composition of the magistrates' bench is perceived as being middle-class and middle-aged. Despite recruitment drives and initiatives there is still only a minority of magistrates who are under the age of 40.

Summary

1. There are approximately 13,000 lay magistrates working in the courts across England and Wales. They deal with over 95 per cent of all the criminal cases brought to court and also have limited jurisdiction in other courts, such as the family, youth and civil courts.

2. The Bench in the magistrates' court will usually consist of three lay magistrates (a chair and two wingers) or a single district judge. Where there are three lay magistrates on the Bench then the decision will be made by way of majority. Magistrates do not have to be legally or professionally qualified to sit in such a capacity.

3. The role of a magistrate has existed since about the 12th century. Originally, magistrates were appointed as keepers of the peace, and could almost be described as an early police force. The powers and responsibilities have developed and changed dramatically over the years to arrive at the modern-day magistrates' role.

4. To be eligible to sit as a magistrate, a person must be between the ages of 18 and 76, although a person close to the retirement age may not normally be selected to sit as a magistrate. The person must not be disqualified from sitting or work within the criminal justice system or associated agencies.

5. Lay magistrates sit in a voluntary capacity and only receive payment of any reasonable expenses incurred. They must be able to commit to sitting for at least 26 half-days per year.

6. Applications to become a magistrate are reviewed by the advisory committee for the local area, which will consider the applicant in line with the six key qualities. These are: good character, understanding and communication, social awareness, maturity and sound temperament, sound judgement, and commitment and reliability.

7. The advisory committee will select candidates who meet the six key qualities and who will ensure that the local Bench is one reflective of the society in which it is based. To achieve a balanced representation on the local magistracy, factors such as a candidate's gender, age, occupation, geographical location, ethnic origin, social background and political affiliation will be taken into account. Even if a candidate is viewed as being highly suitable for appointment, they may still not be selected as a magistrate if their appointment would unbalance the Bench in one of the above key areas.

8. Magistrates undergo a structured training process upon appointment so that they are able to become fully competent in the skills that they require to sit on the Bench. Training and appraisal continues throughout their career as magistrates, and magistrates are required to be able to evidence the three key competencies, which are: managing yourself, working as a member of the team, and making judicial decisions.

9. Magistrates, as laypeople, are aided and advised on the law in court by a legal adviser, known previously as a justices' clerk. The legal adviser is there to direct them on the appropriate law but is not permitted to direct the magistrates as to what their decision should be. Any advice given by a legal adviser should be done in open court and, if the legal adviser does give the magistrates any advice out of court, they must explain the advice given to the court once the court reconvenes.

10. Magistrates have the powers to impose a maximum custodial sentence of six months (rising to 12 months for more than one offence with consecutive sentences), community sentences, or an unlimited fine.

11. A magistrate is required to retire at the age of 76 but may resign at any point prior to this. The Lord Chancellor has the power to remove a magistrate from office when he is either incapable of carrying out their judicial functions, have misbehaved, are deemed to be incompetent, or are neglecting or refusing to carry out their responsibilities.

Further Reading

C. Barnett, "Justices' clerks" [2006] 62(5) *Magistrate* 135.

Considers the role of justices' clerks and expresses concern at the dramatic decline in their numbers.

I. Dennis, "Judging magistrates" [2001] Crim. L.R. 71–72.

Home Office and LCD report on Judiciary in the magistrates' courts including workload of lay and stipendiary magistrates, working methods, surveys of public and professional opinion, costs and comparison with other jurisdictions.

A. Mimmack, "The legal adviser and the retiring room—where is the boundary?" [2007] 63(3) *Magistrate* 91.

Sets out the functions of the legal adviser or justices' clerk and the situations in which the legal adviser is permitted to join the bench in the retiring room.

P.G. Norton, "650 years of the magistracy" (2010) 18(4) Com. Jud. J. 3–7.

Outlines the history of the magistrates' court system in England and Wales, and reviews its current operation.

Self Test Questions

1. The maximum length of time that a magistrates' court can impose a custodial sentence for a single offence is:
   (a) 6 months
   (b) 12 months
   (c) 24 months
   (d) A magistrates' court cannot impose custodial sentences
2. Magistrates can sit in the:
   (a) youth court
   (b) family court
   (c) Crown Court
   (d) all of the above

3. Magistrates are appointed on their:
   (a) political views
   (b) sentencing policies
   (c) personal qualities
   (d) physical appearance
4. Once trained, magistrates are appraised:
   (a) annually
   (b) every three years
   (c) every five years
   (d) never
5. Magistrates are expected to sit in court for a minimum of:
   (a) 10 days per year
   (b) 26 half-days per year
   (c) 52 half-days per year
   (d) 100 days per year

The Judiciary

6

CHAPTER OVERVIEW

In this chapter we will:

- **Discover what the different judicial roles are.**
- **Explain the judicial appointments process.**
- **Consider how the judiciary are trained.**
- **Discover how a judge can be removed from office.**
- **Consider the composition of the judiciary.**

Introduction

6-001 The judiciary is a fundamental element of the English legal system. It helps to ensure that the rule of law (see Ch.1, "The rule of law", at **1-009**) is upheld and that all of those people who come to the law are dealt with fairly and justly. In their everyday capacity judges sit in the courts and tribunals of England and Wales and hear disputes between the different parties who refer to the jurisdiction of courts. As a collective, they cover every individual area of law that can be brought before the courts, from criminal cases to family matters, through to civil claims and more. Their role is to govern the proceedings, make decisions and deliver judgment on the matters before them and, in the case of a criminal trial with a jury, judges are required to explain the law and direct the jury on how to apply it to the facts. Judges are, in the majority of the courts, the primary triers and deciders of fact and they are expected to carry out this function in an impartial and objective manner (otherwise known as the rule of law). They must keep all of their personal views and prejudices away from the courtroom and must only apply the laws of the country as they are at that time.

The judiciary, as one of the limbs of the State's administrative system, is also charged with ensuring that the other limbs (the executive and the legislature (see Ch.1, "The separation of powers", at **1-008**)) do not become too powerful or abuse their positions. The introduction of the HRA 1998 has provided the judiciary with more scope to be able to undertake this function and the case of **A v Secretary of State for the Home Department** [2004] UKHL 56 (as discussed in Ch.1, "The rule of law", at **1-009**) is an example of how the judiciary can use their powers to this avail. The decision by the House of Lords in the case of **A v Secretary of State for the Home Department** resulted in the legislation under which the appellants were detained (the Anti-Terrorism, Crime and Security Act 2001) being declared unlawful and so, consequently, Parliament was forced to repeal the legislation. The judiciary had challenged the extent of Parliament's law-making abilities and won.

The Judicial Hierarchy

6-002 Just as the court system is based on a hierarchy, so too is the judiciary. There are superior (or senior) judges who sit within the superior courts and there are inferior judges who sit within inferior courts. The use of the terms "inferior" and "superior" should not be allowed to cloud the perception of the equal importance of all judges within the legal system, as an individual magistrate, it could be argued, is just as important as a Supreme Court Justice, because if magistrates were removed from the judicial system then the whole legal system would be liable to collapse. The inferior judges keep the legal system ticking over on an everyday basis whereas the superior judges are there to deliberate and decide upon certain principles of law that can have far-reaching implications for society.

Over to you

Before reading the rest of the section below, write a list of the different judges and judicial positions you might encounter in the judicial system. Put them in hierarchical order from most senior to least senior.

The Lord/Lady Chief Justice

Following the introduction of the Constitutional Reform Act 2005 (CRA 2005), the Lord Chief Justice became the head of the judiciary of England and Wales and the President of the Courts of England and Wales. These roles were traditionally the responsibility of the Lord Chancellor until the implementation of the CRA 2005 (see "The Lord Chancellor", below, at **6–017**), which removed the judicial functions from the post of Lord Chancellor. Before the introduction of the 2005 Act the Lord Chief Justice was historically the second highest judge in the English legal system. The Lord Chief Justice has now been granted powers to appoint certain ranks of judges under the Crime and Courts Act 2013 Sch.13; a power that traditionally lay with the Lord Chancellor (see "Judicial Appointments", below, at **6–020**). **6–003**

The incumbent Lady Chief Justice is the first woman to hold this post and as such assumed the title "Lady Chief Justice". The officeholder has over 400 statutory duties, but their key responsibilities are:

- representing the views of the judiciary of England and Wales to Parliament and the Government;
- the welfare, training and guidance of the judiciary in England and Wales within resources made available by the Lord Chancellor (the Lord Chief Justice discusses with government the provision of resources for the judiciary); and
- the deployment of judges and allocation of work in courts in England and Wales.

The Lady Chief Justice is also involved in sitting on the most important criminal, civil and family cases, and giving judgments and laying down Practice Directions in the most important appeal cases. She shares, with the Lord Chancellor, responsibility for the Judicial Conduct Investigation Office (JCIO) (formerly the Office for Judicial Complaints), which is the body responsible for maintaining judicial discipline by investigating and determining upon complaints made against judicial officeholders. She is also President of the Sentencing Council (a public body designed to support the decision-making process and encourage consistency in sentencing throughout the court system). Further, she is the President of the Courts of England and Wales and she may sit and hear cases in any English or Welsh court, including the magistrates' courts.

The Lord/Lady Chief Justice is selected by a specially appointed panel from within the Judicial Appointments Commission (JAC) (see below for further details on the JAC) and the position is normally appointed from within the ranks of appeal court judges (the Lord and Lady Justices). However, the JAC are not prevented from selecting the Lord Chief Justice from within the ranks of the Supreme Court.

Heads of Division

6–004 As the scope of the courts of England and Wales is so vast there are also the Heads of Division who work underneath the Lady Chief Justice to ensure that the courts run smoothly. At present, there are five Heads of Division, each with a different area of responsibility. These Heads are as follows:

THE LORD/LADY CHIEF JUSTICE

6–005 Although the Lady Chief Justice is the head of the judiciary, part of that role is to also preside over the Court of Appeal (Criminal Division) as the head of that division. However, as she is already the President of the Courts and therefore in a position of substantial authority, she is entitled to appoint another Court of Appeal judge to sit in this position in his place.

THE MASTER OF THE ROLLS

6–006 The Master of the Rolls (MR) is the Head of Civil Justice, President of the Court of Appeal (Civil Division) and a judge of the Court of Appeal. Traditionally, the Master was charged with the safekeeping of charters, patents and records of important court judgments written on parchment rolls. He still has responsibility for documents of national importance, and is the person responsible for authorising the practice of solicitors (professional rules and regulations), although his main work is involved with the organisation of the civil justice system.

The role is viewed as being the second most important judicial role (under that of the Lord Chief Justice) and the Master is responsible for the deployment and organisation of the work of the judges of the civil division, as well as presiding over the court (he will often hear the most difficult and sensitive cases). Appointed by the King on the recommendation of a selection panel convened by the JAC, he is normally appointed from among the ranks of the ranks of the Lord Justices of Appeal. The Master of the Rolls is given the prefix "Right Honourable" upon appointment.

THE PRESIDENT OF THE FAMILY DIVISION

6–007 The President of the Family Division and Head of Family Justice presides over panels hearing family law matters in the Court of Appeal, and is also the administrative head of the Family Division of the High Court. The President is a Court of Appeal judge and presides over the 19 High Court Family Division judges.

The President of the Family Division is appointed by the King on the recommendation of a selection panel convened by the JAC. The head of this division is normally selected from within the ranks of the Lord Justices of Appeal.

THE CHANCELLOR OF THE HIGH COURT

The Chancellor of the High Court (previously known as the Vice-Chancellor prior to the CRA 2005) is the vice-president of the Chancery Division of the Supreme Court (the Lord Chancellor is the President). The role of Vice-Chancellor was created in 1813 and the Vice-Chancellor's duties were to help the Lord Chancellor in the administration of justice. The role disappeared in 1873 but was then reinstated in 1970. The modern-day role of the Vice-Chancellor is to organise and manage business of the Chancery Division on a day-to-day basis. The Lord Chancellor, from the ranks of the High Court Chancery Division judges, appoints the Vice-Chancellor. **6-008**

THE PRESIDENT OF THE KING'S BENCH DIVISION

The President of the King's Bench Division is responsible for the everyday work of the King's Bench Division. **6-009**

The President of the King's Bench Division is appointed by the King on the recommendation of a selection panel convened by the JAC. The head of this division is normally selected from within the ranks of the Lord Justices of Appeal.

Superior Judges

JUSTICES OF THE SUPREME COURT

The Justices of the Supreme Court are the 12 most senior judges within the jurisdiction of England and Wales. They sit in the Supreme Court, which is the final domestic court of appeal, and the Privy Council. The Supreme Court was established in October 2009 in order to achieve a greater separation of powers between the most senior judges and the Upper House of Parliament (the House of Lords), and to enhance the transparency between the courts and the State. Prior to August 2009, the Justices of the Supreme Court sat as Lords of Appeal in Ordinary in the judicial capacity of the House of Lords and were more commonly known as the Law Lords (irrespective of whether they were male or female). Upon the inception of the Supreme Court, the Lords of Appeal became the Justices of the Supreme Court. **6-010**

The Justices remain members of the House of Lords (Parliamentary division) but are no longer permitted to sit or vote in the House (previously, the Law Lords could carry out all of these functions and also became life peers on appointment). They also occasionally chair major public inquiries, such as the one conducted into the death of the Ministry of Defence scientist Dr David Kelly.

6-011 When in business, the House of Lords heard between 80 and 90 appeals per year and sat from Monday to Thursday throughout the law terms (the times of the year when the Court sits) and the Supreme Court hears a slightly lower caseload, deciding between 53–67 cases per annum over the past few years. The composition of the Court is normally five justices, although this may increase to a panel of seven, nine, or even a full panel, depending on the nature and interest of the case. A full bench of 11 Justices (a vacancy existed at the time) sat for **R. (on the application of Miller) v Secretary of State for Exiting the European Union** [2017] UKSC 5, decided by a majority of 8:3; and again in **R. (on the application of Miller) v The Prime Minister** [2019] UKSC 41 during which Lord Briggs did not sit to ensure an odd number of judges, although this judgment was in the end a unanimous decision.

A hearing by the Supreme Court is rather an informal affair as the justices sit around a horseshoe table and do not wear robes. The hearing is almost conversational in style, with counsel for the parties presenting their cases and the justices frequently asking questions and challenging them on points. Judgment by the Court is normally reserved, meaning that the justices do not deliver an immediate decision but, rather, take time to consider and discuss the issues and submissions made before making their opinions public. It takes the Court an average of three months to return a judgment in a case, but a decision will be expedited in cases involving children or whenever else it is appropriate to do so. The judgment is known as an opinion and they do not read them out in Court in full but, rather, give a brief summary setting out details of how they are to dispose of the appeal. A full written copy of the prepared speeches is then posted on the Supreme Court website immediately after the judgment is pronounced. Previously, it was prohibited to record proceedings in any court in the English legal system but now all hearings in the Supreme Court are recorded and any person can request a copy; the hearings are now also streamed live daily.

Justices of the Supreme Court are appointed by the King on the advice of the Prime Minister, following nomination by a specially convened selection committee consisting of the President and Deputy President of the Supreme Court and other members of the JAC.

LORD/LADY JUSTICES OF APPEAL

6-012 There is a statutory maximum number of 39 Lord or Lady Justices of Appeal who, along with the ex-officio Heads of Division, preside over the Court of Appeal as defined by the Senior Courts Act 1981 (though originally, under the Supreme Court of Judicature Act 1881, the number of Lord Justices was fixed at only five). Lord Justices of Appeal are normally selected from the ranks of the High Court judges and they will be appointed by the King on the recommendation of the Prime Minister, who receives advice from the Lord Chancellor after they have consulted with the senior members of the judiciary (the statutory requirements for becoming a Lord Justice of Appeal are set out in s.10 of the Senior Courts Act 1981 (as amended by s.71 of the CLSA 1990)).

Originally, a judge appointed to sit in the Court of Appeal was required to be called Lord, regardless of gender, as it was not envisaged that a female would ever hold such a position. Elizabeth Butler-Sloss, who was the first woman to be appointed to the position of a Lord Justice of Appeal in 1988, was called Lord until the law was changed under the CA 2003. Section 63 of the 2003 Act now permits a female Court of Appeal Judge to be called Lady Justice of Appeal. In 2025 there were nine such Lady Justices, approximately one-quarter of the bench. Upon appointment, men are knighted and women are made a Dame by tradition.

JUSTICES OF HIS MAJESTY'S HIGH COURT OF JUSTICE

His Majesty's High Court of Justice, or High Court judges, otherwise known as puisne judges (derived from a French term for junior, or later-born and pronounced as "puny"), work within the jurisdiction of England and Wales. Theoretically, these judges along with the Heads of Division can sit in any of the three High Court divisions, though in practice they are generally assigned to a specific one (King's Bench, Chancery or Family). Their work also consists of trying the most serious criminal cases in the Crown Court, hearing important civil cases and assisting the Lord Justices of Appeal to hear criminal appeals. **6–013**

There is a statutory maximum of 108 puisne High Court judges, who are appointed by the King on the recommendation of the Lord Chancellor after an open competition, administered by the JAC. This means that the vacancy will be advertised in the national press and applications are made in the same way as with any other type of job, although there is no job interview but rather a system of consultation. To be suitably qualified for selection as a High Court judge an individual must have had a right of audience (the right of a lawyer to appear and speak as an advocate in court) for all proceedings in the High Court for at least seven years, or have been a circuit judge for at least two years. High Court judges are generally selected from the ranks of King's Counsel (see Ch.4) and, although solicitor-advocates are eligible to be appointed as a High Court judge, only seven have, at present, been appointed from this background.

The High Court is found in the Royal Courts of Justice on the Strand in London and this is where the High Court judges are based, however, there are several High Court circuits and district registries in major cities across England and Wales.

Inferior Judges

CIRCUIT JUDGES

Circuit judges are at the top of the inferior judicial hierarchy and they carry out the majority of Crown Court work. As well as sitting in the Crown Court, circuit judges have the jurisdiction to sit in the Court of Appeal (Criminal Division) when requested to do so. **6–014**

Circuit judges take their name from the fact that they are assigned to a particular legal area (circuit) in the country. There are six legal circuits or regions throughout England and Wales and each has a number of senior circuit judges who are responsible for the judicial business within that area. The six regions of England and Wales are:

- Midland;
- Northern;
- North Eastern;
- South Eastern;
- Western; and
- Wales & Chester.

The King on the recommendation of the Lord Chief Justice, appoints circuit judges after an open competition, as administered by the JAC. The statutory qualifications required are the same as for a High Court judge, or the individual in question must have already been a recorder (see **6–015**) or have held another full-time judicial office for at least three years previously. Vacancies are advertised through the national press and interested candidates must make an application to the JAC for consideration.

RECORDERS

6–015 A recorder is essentially a part-time judge, expected to sit for 30 days per annum, who has mainly criminal jurisdiction but can sit in the county courts as and when required. Serving as a recorder is sometimes seen as being like an apprenticeship to becoming a circuit judge.

The King on the recommendation of the Lord Chief Justice, appoints recorders after an open competition, as administered by the JAC. They are appointed on a five-year basis that can be automatically renewed.

DISTRICT JUDGES

6–016 District judges are at the bottom of the judicial hierarchy in terms of employed judges. They can appear in the criminal and civil magistrates' courts (although the vast majority of district judges sit within the civil jurisdiction). Originally, criminal jurisdiction district judges were called stipendiaries, and civil jurisdiction district judges were known as registrars. To become a district judge most will have already served as a deputy (part-time) district judge for at least a two-year period. The King on the recommendation of the Lord Chief Justice, appoints them after an open competition as administered by the JAC.

The Lord Chancellor

6–017 The role of the Lord Chancellor has existed since at least the 14th century, although it has been mooted that the role has actually been around in some form or other since as far back as 605 AD. Historically, the role has been the highest judicial office that could be held within

England and Wales, and it is a role that has been central to the development of the English legal system. The Lord Chancellor originally wielded a great deal of power over each of the different arms of the State, and their (the first female Lord Chancellor Elizabeth Truss (2016–17) was not styled as "Lady Chancellor") modern-day role during the last century has included him being a both Cabinet Minister, Speaker in the House of Lords and the head of both the judiciary and the Lord Chancellor's Department. As a result of the Lord Chancellor's wide remit, the position came under a great deal of criticism due to the fact that it spanned all three limbs of State administration, and indeed ecclesiastical appointments in the Church of England, which directly contradicted the separation of powers doctrine as propounded by Montesquieu (Ch.1, "The separation of powers", at **1–008**). By being involved in every limb there were concerns raised regarding the independence of the judiciary. It was argued that this was being compromised, and that full transparency could not be achieved due to the fact that the legal system was presided over by a politician.

In June 2003 the Prime Minister undertook a Cabinet reshuffle and Lord Irvine, who was the then Lord Chancellor, was removed from his role (this was easily achieved as the Lord Chancellor is appointed by the Prime Minister and so can be removed from office as simply as any other Cabinet Minister can be). An announcement was made that the role of the Lord Chancellor was to be abolished, and the Lord Chancellor's Department was to be disbanded and replaced with the Department for Constitutional Affairs. The intention of the reshuffle was to transfer the Lord Chancellor's ministerial powers to a newly created position of Secretary of State for Constitutional Affairs, and to transfer the judicial powers held by the Lord Chancellor to the newly created position of Lord Chief Justice. Lord Falconer was then duly appointed to the dual role of Secretary of State for Constitutional Affairs and Lord Chancellor. Under the first half of his title he was given the responsibility of abolishing the second half. However, this change in role meant that Lord Falconer had no right to sit as a member of the judiciary or be heavily involved in the appointment process of new judges (as could the old Lord Chancellor), nor could he be Speaker in the House of Lords. The legislation responsible for these monumental changes was the proposed Constitutional Reform Bill 2004.

Upon these changes being implemented there was widespread outcry against them. There **6–018** was much criticism levied against the fact that the changes had been carried out in great haste, that the Bill had passed through Parliament too quickly and that little consideration had been given to its implications. The judiciary were concerned that the removal of the role of Lord Chancellor would actually impede their independence as opposed to entrench it, and Lord Woolf (who at that time was the Lord Chief Justice) stated in "The rule of law and a change in the constitution" [2004] 63(2) C.L.J. 317–330 that the announcement made as to the abolition of the role of the Lord Chancellor:

> **clearly indicated an extraordinary lack of appreciation of the significance of what was being proposed.**

So as to address the concerns that were voiced from the highest reaches of the judiciary, and due to the fact that the House of Lords was opposing the Bill, the Government drafted a consultation paper (Department for Constitutional Affairs, *Constitutional Reforms: Reforming the Office of the Lord Chancellor* (2003) CP 13/03) and the result of this was that the judiciary and the Government were able to reach a consensus under what is now known as the Concordat (Department for Constitutional Affairs, *The Lord Chancellor's Judiciary-Related Functions: Proposals* (2004)), which was made by way of an oral statement to the House of Lords on 26 January 2004, and which focused on the future role of the Lord Chancellor. The Concordat set out that:

- the Lord Chief Justice, as head of the Judiciary of England and Wales, would take on a new role in relation to judicial appointments, judicial wellbeing, and complaints and discipline;
- the Lord Chancellor would no longer be a judge but would be responsible for the administration of the courts and ensuring that the judiciary was able to fulfil its role;
- a new administrative support office for the Lord Chief Justice and the senior judiciary would be set up in April 2006—this new office would reaffirm the policy separation between the judiciary and the executive, ensuring that the Lord Chief Justice and the senior judiciary would be able to discharge all their statutory functions in relation to the judiciary, magistrates and the delivery of justice effectively and efficiently;
- a Judicial Complaints Office would also be launched in April 2006, and would improve the service provided to court users; it would be jointly responsible to both the Lord Chief Justice and the Lord Chancellor for the operation of the judicial complaints and discipline system; and
- the roles and responsibilities of the Lord Chancellor and Lord Chief Justice in relation to the JAC and the appointment of judges were set out here (and in the Constitutional Reform Act).

6–019 The Constitutional Reform Bill was duly amended so as to not abolish the role of the Lord Chancellor but rather to modify the role as set out under the Concordat. The Bill was then passed by the House of Lords and became the CRA 2005. As a result of this process, the Lord Chancellor now no longer sits as a member of the judiciary, they are no longer the head of the judiciary, nor do they have any significant powers over the judicial appointments process, further, they are also no longer Speaker in the House of Lords. They do, however, remain the head of the government department the Ministry for Justice (formerly called the Ministry for Constitutional Affairs). The current responsibilities of the Secretary of State include:

- overall strategy;
- resourcing;
- judicial appointments;
- ensuring judicial diversity;

- Lords reform;
- party funding; and
- constitutional renewal.

The focus of the Lord Chancellor is now far more political than legislative or judicial, and there has been a degree of separation of powers achieved as per the original aim. However, whether the separation has gone too far or not far enough remains to be seen. One other change to come from the CRA 2005 is that the Lord Chancellor no longer needs to be legally qualified (obviously, if they no longer head the judiciary or sit as a judge then legal qualifications are not a necessity) and now, by way of s.2 of the CRA 2005, the only qualification requirement is for the person appointed to be qualified by "experience". Consequently, this has opened up the door for a government minister, an MP or even a university law lecturer to become Lord Chancellor and, in 2012, Chris Grayling MP was appointed as the first ever non-lawyer to hold this position. The subsequent three holders of this office were also non-lawyers, marking a significant trend towards political appointments.

Over to you

Do you think the reduction in the Lord Chancellor's powers and responsibilities has achieved the intended aim? Do you think the role of the Lord Chancellor should be maintained or abolished? What is the reasoning for your answer?

Judicial Appointments

Old Style Appointments

The method by which judges were appointed prior to 2006 received much condemnation **6–020** as it was seen as a secretive and discriminatory process that was dominated by politicians. Originally, the pool of potential judicial candidates was quite limited as only those with higher rights of audience (so essentially barristers) could be appointed. In 1990 this limited source of candidates was expanded when solicitors were permitted to gain higher rights under the CLSA 1990 (see Ch.4, "The Changing Professions" at **4–023**).

As can probably be gathered from the discussion above, the Lord Chancellor used to play a major role in the selection and appointment of the judiciary. Judges were to be appointed by the monarch who was advised by the Lord Chancellor, and, in the case of the Law Lords and Lord Justices of Appeal, the Lord Chancellor would advise the Prime Minister who would then go on to make recommendations to the monarch. The normal way of applying for a job is that an advertisement is placed, interested candidates put in their applications and then those who make it through the short-listing process are called for interview. However, senior judicial positions (from the High Court and upwards) were never advertised in this open and transparent way, rather it was done more by way of a tap on the shoulder, or a whisper in the ear in the robing room during a court recess. This meant that the individuals put forward for High Court judicial appointments were not really representative of the judiciary as a whole as they were essentially handpicked on the back of the personal opinion of the Lord Chancellor and senior members of the judiciary.

6–021 Traditionally, once an individual had expressed interest in a judicial vacancy then suitability for the position would be determined by way of an informal inquiry known as a secret sounding. Here, the Department of Constitutional Affairs, under its Legal and Judicial Services Group, would gather together a wealth of information about the potential candidate which would be intensely scrutinised before a decision as to whether or not to appoint would be made. The information gathered on a potential candidate varied widely in quality and relevance to the individual's abilities to become a judge. Leading barristers and judges would be approached to offer their views on the individual and much personal opinion as to the candidate's character was included. This could be highly positive or highly negative, depending on whether the person offering the opinion liked the candidate or not, and there is anecdotal evidence that information, such as what the candidate got up to socially and who they were friends with, was taken into account.

As a result of the criticisms voiced in respect of this method of recruitment, the Government set up an inquiry into the judicial appointments process. The inquiry was carried out by Sir Leonard Peachy, and his findings were published by the Department of Constitutional Affairs in *The Independent Scrutiny of the Appointment Process of Judges and Queen's Counsel* in December 1999 (this report is commonly known as the Peachy Report). The findings of the Peachy Report were that the judicial appointments process was mainly satisfactory, but there were three main criticisms, these being that the process was secretive, discriminatory and dominated by politicians (as stated above).

6–022 In respect of the first criticism of it being secretive, it was found that the judicial appointments system often favoured those with a good network of contacts over those who had the potential to become an excellent judge. It seemed that the old adage "it's not what you know but who you know" was very much in effect. The Law Society mounted a campaign against the process of secret soundings and refused to take part in any recruitment conducted by that method, equating it to the "old boys' network", and stating that it did not allow fair competition as it was controlled by barristers looking to appoint other barristers into the higher ranks of the judiciary, and consequently that solicitors were therefore never considered. It also argued that it did not allow those who had been put forward for a judicial vacancy to know what was being said about them and therefore they were unable to bring any defence or make refutations to any allegations made against them. The Association of Personal Injury Lawyers and the Equal Opportunities Commission, amongst other bodies, also expressed their support for the Law Society and their disappointment in the way that the judiciary were selected.

The second criticism focused on the fact that the appointments process could be seen as discriminatory. Research undertaken by the Association of Women Barristers showed that most judges recommended barristers from within their own set of chambers and that approximately 50 per cent of all judicial appointments came from within only seven sets of chambers. This research emphasised the fact that there was a monopoly on the market held by a small niche of the legal world and that this had the effect of ethnic minorities and women being bypassed. The secretiveness of the secret sounding process allowed for discrimination to take place, as often those who proposed the candidates would look to colleagues who they were close to and respected by. It was mainly, therefore, white middle-class males putting forward other white middle-class males. **6–023**

The fact that the Lord Chancellor and the Prime Minister oversaw the process was the main focus of the final criticism; that politicians dominated the selection process. At that time, the Lord Chancellor was a member of the judiciary, the legislature and the executive and, as such, there was the possibility that the position within the executive could potentially be seen to have an impact on the candidates chosen for judicial office (even if, in practice, it did not). The fact that the Prime Minister had to approve all appointments into higher judicial offices could also be viewed as an interference with the independence of the judiciary (i.e. Lady Thatcher once selected the Lord Chancellor's second choice of candidate over his first choice). The enactment of the HRA 1998 also brought this issue into consideration as, under it, the Government is obliged to ensure that everyone has the right to be tried by a fair and impartial tribunal (art.6) and the fact that the executive was involved in the appointments process could be argued to undermine this obligation.

Although the Peachy Report did not recommend any radical changes to the appointments process (it advocated the retention of the secret soundings), it did recommend that a Commissioner for Judicial Appointments be appointed to oversee the recruitment process. The Government accepted this proposal and the first Commissioner was appointed into post in 2001. However, the main flaw with the newly created role was that the Commissioner had no power over the appointments process; he was simply there to supervise and audit. After being in post for two years and reviewing the appointments process, the Commissioner undertook a full-scale audit of the High Court judge appointment process and concluded that it was in urgent need of reform and that no further appointments of High Court judges should take place under the system as it lacked both accountability and transparency. In response, the Government drafted a consultation paper (DCA, *Constitutional Reform: A New Way of Appointing Judges*, July 2003), which set out in its foreword that: **6–024**

> **In a modern democratic society it is no longer acceptable for judicial appointments to be entirely in the hands of a Government Minister. For example the judiciary is often involved in adjudicating on the lawfulness of actions of the Executive. And so the appointments system must be, and must be seen to be, independent of Government. It must be transparent. It must be accountable. And it must inspire public confidence.**

> **There is a second point. As the existing Commission for Judicial Appointments pointed out in its first annual report, the current judiciary is overwhelmingly white, male, and from a narrow social and educational background. To an extent, this reflects the pool of qualified candidates from which judicial appointments are made: intake to the legal professions has, until recently, been dominated by precisely these social groups.**
>
> **Of course the fundamental principle in appointing Judges is and must remain selection on merit. However the Government is committed to opening up the system of appointments, to attract suitably qualified candidates both from a wider range of social backgrounds and from a wider range of legal practice. To do so, and, to create a system which commands the confidence of professionals and the public, and is seen as affording equal opportunities to all suitably qualified applicants, will require fresh approaches and a major re-engineering of the processes for appointment. Those processes must be resourced with the appropriate professional skills and expertise and underpinned by modern human resource best practice.**

6-025 This reflected many of the criticisms raised earlier by the Peachy Report and, so as to combat these criticisms and ensure that the appointments process was fair and transparent, the Government announced that it intended

> **[t]o establish an independent Judicial Appointments Commission to recommend candidates for appointment as Judges on a more transparent basis. There is already such an independent commission in place for selecting Judges in Scotland and one forms part of the agreed settlement in Northern Ireland. There will now be one for England and Wales.**

The proposal to create an independent body charged with overseeing the appointments process was greeted with much enthusiasm and, under the CRA 2005, the Judicial Appointments Commission (JAC) was established.

New Style Appointments

6-026 The JAC took over the recruitment process of the lower ranks of the judiciary (up to and including High Court judges) on 3 April 2006. It set out that its remit was to:

> **[s]elect candidates for judicial office. We do so on merit, through fair and open competition, from the widest range of eligible candidates.**

Its statutory responsibilities under the CRA 2005 are:

- to select candidates solely on merit;
- to select only people of good character; and
- to have regard to the need to encourage applications from a wider range of candidates.

The JAC is comprised of 15 commissioners who are drawn from the judiciary, the legal profession, the tribunals, the lay magistracy and the lay public. The Chairman of the JAC must be a layperson and the composition of the remaining 14 members must be five judicial members, two professional members (maximum of one barrister, one solicitor and one CILEX fellow), five lay members, one tribunal member and one lay justice member.

The appointments process under the JAC now begins with a request from His Majesty's Courts and Tribunals Service to appoint a new judge. The position is then widely advertised in the national press, in legal publications and online. On receipt of the applications, the JAC will check the candidates' eligibility for the post and make an initial good character assessment of the applicants; references may also be taken at this point. The applications will then be shortlisted and the selected candidates invited to take the qualifying test. The candidates who are successful in the test are then invited to attend a selection day, where they may be asked to partake in a role play depicting a judicial exercise, and a formal interview—references will be taken at this point if not obtained already. Following the selection day, the Commission will prepare a report on its findings as to the candidates' suitability, and these reports will then be passed to the Lord Chief Justice and another suitably qualified person for statutory consultation as required under ss.88(3) and 94(3) of the CRA 2005. Finally, any outstanding good character checks on the proposed candidates will be performed by way of consulting with the police, His Majesty's Revenue and Customs and any other relevant professional bodies before the final recommendations are made to the Lord Chancellor or the Lord Chief Justice depending on the seniority of judicial role. The JAC will only recommend one candidate per vacancy and the Lord Chancellor or Lord Chief Justice can reject that recommendation, but only if they provide reasoning for doing so, and they cannot select another candidate as a replacement (this is to prevent any personal preferences coming into the process). **6–027**

In making its selection, the JAC will consider the five core qualities and abilities which are required to hold judicial office. These are cited as follows. **6–028**

- **Exercising judgment**—demonstrates integrity and applies independence of mind to make incisive, fair and legally sound decisions.
- **Possessing and building knowledge**—possesses a detailed knowledge of a relevant jurisdiction, law and practice. Demonstrates an ability and willingness to learn and develop professionally.

- **Assimilating and clarifying information**—quickly assimilates information to identify essential issues, develops a clear understanding and clarifies uncertainty through eliciting and exploring information.
- **Working and communicating with others**—conducts proceedings appropriately, recognises diversity and shows an appreciation of the wider impact of communications. Builds rapport, demonstrating good communication skills and empathy.
- **Managing work efficiently**—works and plans effectively to make the best use of available resources.

The Tribunal, Courts and Enforcement Act 2007 has also had an impact on the people who could apply to be a judge. Prior to the 2007 Act, those eligible to be appointed to the judiciary had to have held a lower court right of audience (essentially, barristers and solicitors) for at least seven years, but the Act has relaxed this qualification requirement to five years, dependent on the post. The aim behind this relaxation is to widen the diversity of the judicial Bench and to make the career route of becoming a judge accessible to a greater number and wider pool of people. This means that individuals with alternative legal qualifications, such as through CILEx or alternative legal experience (i.e. legal academics), are now eligible to apply to sit as a judge.

Training

6–029 Although members of the judiciary are generally viewed as being amongst some of the finest brains in the country, they are still required to undergo periodic training so as to ensure that they are kept up to date with the law. Judicial training is predominantly overseen by the Judicial College (formerly the Judicial Studies Board), though occasionally outside agencies, such as social workers or doctors, may be involved in imparting certain specialist knowledge to the judiciary.

In April 2011 the Judicial College took over responsibility to provide training for all full- and part-time judges in England and Wales, for overseeing the training of lay magistrates and chairmen, as well training the non-legal members of the tribunals. The Judicial College Strategy 2021–2025 sets out six objectives:

- Playing our part in ensuring the judiciary has the right skills and knowledge;
- Meeting the future needs of the magistracy;
- Preparing for innovation and change;
- Effective leadership;
- Contributing to a transparent and outward facing judiciary; and
- High quality support for modern training.

The vision of the College is to become and be recognised as a world leader in judicial education.

The Judicial College is very proactive in providing suitable training for the judiciary so that the high standards of the profession are maintained, and it often offers refresher and intensive courses to all members of the judiciary. However, this was not always the case. Prior to the creation of Judicial College's predecessor, the Judicial Studies Board (JSB) (and also whilst the JSB was still in its infancy), there was little training available in relation to the undertaking of judicial duties. Thankfully though, the situation has changed for the better and the Judicial College now offers excellent training, which it then further supplements with the production of useful guidance books for judges. There is now no reason for a judge to be uninformed as to the developments in the law or as to any topics of current social importance relevant to their area of jurisdiction.

Judicial Robes

The judiciary began to wear robes in medieval times and then, from around 1400, a colour-coding system began to emerge, with violet robes being worn during the winter, green robes in the summer and red robes for full dress occasions. In 1635, Westminster produced the "Judge's Rules" which set out the definitive guide to what robes should be worn by the judiciary on what occasion. A judge's status could be identified by the gown worn, so, for example, High Court judges were often called the red judges due to the fact that their robes were predominantly red in colour. Then in the 17th century, under the reign of Charles II, the judiciary began to wear the horsehair wigs that have now become synonymous with the position of a judge. The tradition of the judiciary wearing wigs and gowns stems from the concept of what was thought to be decent attire for a person holding such office, and it has also been thought that the wearing of such garments would help to protect judges' anonymity from the criminals with whom they were dealing. 6–030

Very recently there has been a break in tradition in respect of the judiciary and legal counsel wearing wigs and these garments are no longer required to be worn in family cases or civil courts (although their use remains for the moment in the criminal courtroom). The traditional gowns that were worn by the judiciary have also undergone a radical change as the fashion designer Betty Jackson designed a whole range of more modern judicial robes to replace the traditional wig, wing collar and bands, and black gowns. Now, the gowns are made in a dark navy fabric with a velvet trim on the cuffs. As a nod to tradition, and to denote the seniority of the judge, the gowns are trimmed with coloured bands. These are gold for the Court of Appeal judges and the heads of the High Court divisions, red for High Court judges, lilac for circuit judges when they sit as a deputy High Court judge, and blue for district judges. The Justices of the Supreme Court sit in lounge suits but do possess traditional style robes for ceremonial occasions. The new robes incurred a one-off cost of £450,000 and so, once the judges have their new robes, they must ensure that they take care of them, as a spokesman for Lord Phillips stated:

They will be replaced after ten years. At present they get one set of robes and they have to keep them for life—like a RSPCA dog—however flea-ridden.
"Model Judge and his funky new gown",
***The Times*, Tuesday 13 May 2008**

Termination of Appointment

Retirement

6–031 Under the Public Service Pensions and Judicial Offices Act 2022 all judges must retire on their 75th birthday. This marks an increase from the previous retirement of 70 under the Judicial Pensions and Retirement Act 1993.

Dismissal

6–032 Generally, judges are safeguarded from dismissal under the principle of "security of tenure during good behaviour" as set out under the Senior Courts Act 1981 (formerly, this principle was provided for by the Act of Settlement 1701). This means that judges will only be removed from office if they misbehave badly. This principle provides security in a judicial position and ensures judicial independence, as the Government cannot simply remove judges if they make a ruling that the establishment does not agree with. It would be a sorry state of affairs if judges refused to make rulings on the basis they may be sacked. The principle of security of tenure follows on from the doctrine of the separation of powers in respect of the different limbs of State administration (as discussed in Ch.1, "The separation of powers", at **1–008**).

Heads of Divisions, Justices of the Supreme Court, Justices of Appeal and High Court judges are extremely well protected in their tenure as they can only be formally removed by the King, *after* the removal has received approval by way of an affirmative vote on the resolution in both Houses of Parliament. No judge in either the 20th century, or so far in the 21st century, has ever been removed from office by this method.

The Lord Chancellor can, under the Courts Act 1971, dismiss inferior judges on the grounds of incapacity or misbehaviour. This power has only been invoked once in modern times and that was on 5 December 1983 in relation to Judge Bruce Campbell, who was dismissed after being caught smuggling 125 litres of whisky and 9,000 cigarettes into Britain on his private yacht. He pleaded guilty to the offence of evading duty and was given the option to resign (as is normally the case, and this is the likely reason as to why there is only one reported precedent of a judge being dismissed in such a manner) but he refused to accept it and opted for dismissal instead because, due to a small quirk in the law, being removed from office by this method meant he was still able to keep his judicial pension.

The option to dismiss a judge on the grounds of incapacity also exists but is rarely exercised. There is anecdotal evidence ("His honour is gone. His Honour must go", The Daily Telegraph, 1 October 2006) that the inability of even a senior judge to perform his duties fully will be given the blind eye. 6–033

Even Judges who have developed Alzheimer's disease while still on the job have not been forced out. In 1979, when Lord Widgery was Lord Chief Justice, he was, according to more than one observer, "visibly and distressingly half-senile". But his fellow Judges covered up for him and wrote his judgments. He was not dismissed: he continued to fall asleep on the bench for another nine months before he retired.

Even though a senior judge, as mentioned in the extract above, would have to have been removed by Parliament, the rumours continue that this culture still exists within the lower judiciary and that a judge will only be removed if there is no other option available.

Discipline

Judges can, to a certain degree, be disciplined in relation to their actions. Judges may be suspended from sitting in a judicial capacity if they are the subject of ongoing criminal enquiries, or if it is felt by the Lord Chancellor to be a necessary precaution to take in the face of preserving public confidence. The higher courts can also have a sanctioning effect on judges by giving dressing-downs in the courtroom, and the media can have a far-reaching and quite dramatic impact by publicly humiliating judges whose decisions or behaviour it does not agree with. An example of this can be seen in the media reaction to the 2006 case of an immigration judge who allegedly employed an illegal immigrant as a cleaner, and was allegedly also involved in blackmail and drugs. He was investigated and suspended from his judicial duties, but still received full pay whilst the investigation was ongoing. The media, especially the tabloids, had a field day with this and certainly provided some impromptu disciplining in respect of shattering his reputation. 6–034

Criticisms of the Composition of the Judiciary

The main criticism that has been levied at the composition of the judiciary is that it is dominated by white, middle-class, middle-aged men. The introduction of the JAC was one method of trying to resolve this lack of diversity on the Bench, but this resolution can only happen slowly as current members of the judiciary resign or retire and new vacancies are created. The figures provided by the Judiciary of England and Wales in the Courts Diversity Statistics (as at 1 April 2024) show that the judiciary is still heavily weighted in favour of the stereotypical judge 6–035 (white and male), with the figures showing that female judges make up 38 per cent of all full-time judges in the traditional court system, and that this percentage is reduced as the seniority of the judge (and court) increases. However, the Tribunals Diversity Statistics (again, as at 1 April 2024) demonstrate a much more even split in terms of gender appointment, with more than half (53%) of all the Tribunal judges being women. The number of judges sitting from an ethnic minority background is also less than representative of society as, in the traditional court system, this amounts to 11 per cent of the total judiciary (as at 1 April 2024). The Tribunal system is no more representative of society than the traditional court system, with 13 per cent of the appointed judges coming from a BME group.

The issue of lack of diversity within the judiciary was one that was recognised as needing rectification, and so in an effort to tackle the issue, the Crime and Courts Act 2013 Sch.13 was enacted containing provisions that allow for positive discrimination in the employment process; where two candidates for judicial office are of equal merit then the JAC can prefer one of them over the other for the purpose of increasing diversity within that particular group of the judiciary. It appears from the statistics available that although the aims of increasing diversity within the judiciary, both in relation to gender and ethnicity, were realised to some extent initially post the introduction of Sch.13, any ongoing increase in diversity then stalled as the figures following enactment in 2014 were very much in the same ballpark as the more recent statistics released in 2024 (as discussed above), meaning that the desired continuing growth of a diverse judiciary has perhaps not been achieved as well as had been hoped and anticipated.

Summary

1. There is a judicial hierarchy, just as there is for the court system. The judiciary can be split into two groups, the superior (or senior) judges and the inferior judges. The category of superior judges includes High Court judges, Lord Justices of Appeal, the Justices of the Supreme Court and the Heads of Divisions. The category of inferior judges includes circuit judges, recorders and district judges.
2. Originally, the Lord Chancellor was a member of the executive, legislature and judiciary as he was the head of the judiciary, Head of the Lord Chancellor's Office, Speaker in the House of Lords and a Cabinet Minister. To try to achieve a clearer separation of powers it was declared in 2003 that the role of the Lord Chancellor was to be abolished. This received a strong negative reaction and so the CRA 2005 created a modified role of Lord Chancellor. The Lord Chancellor is now mainly a Cabinet Minister and their judicial responsibilities have been passed to the newly created post of Lord Chief Justice.
3. Traditionally, judges were appointed by way of secret soundings. These involved the Lord Chancellor gathering information about the candidate from a variety

of sources and then making a personal judgment on the candidate's suitability. The process was criticised as being dominated by politicians, secretive and discriminatory.

4. The JAC was established in April 2006 to appoint all judges up to and including High Court judges. It now considers the merits, judicial qualities and potential of the individual. The Commission consists of a panel of 15 people who are a mix of the judiciary, legal profession and laypeople, etc. and after the recruitment process it recommends a candidate to the Lord Chancellor or Lord Chief Justice for appointment. The Lord Chancellor or Lord Chief Justice can reject the Commission's selection but must give reasons and cannot appoint anyone else in that place.
5. The judiciary undergo continuous training via the Judicial College and other relevant agencies.
6. The tradition of wearing horsehair wigs and different coloured robes has almost come to an end. Wigs are now only worn in the Crown Court, and the traditional robes have been replaced with ones that are of a more modern design.
7. All judges must retire at age 75. They can resign before this date if they so wish. The judiciary work under the principle of security of tenure, meaning that they cannot be easily removed from post if they make a decision that the Government does not agree with. This principle is to help maintain the separation of powers.
8. Judges who are High Court judges or above can only be removed from office by the King upon a resolution of both Houses of Parliament. This has not been done in living memory.
9. Inferior judges can be removed due to either misbehaviour or incapacity and only one judge has been removed from office in this way in recent years.
10. The Supreme Court opened its doors in October 2009. It replaced the jurisdiction of the House of Lords and the Privy Council. The Law Lords became the first Justices of the Supreme Court.
11. The composition of the judiciary can still be criticised as it is currently dominated by white, middle-class, middle-aged men although the Tribunal, Courts and Enforcement Act 2007 has opened up the eligibility criteria so it is hoped that in the future the judiciary will be more reflective of society, and the Crime and Courts Act 2013 has provided for positive discrimination to be permitted in the appointment process where there are two candidates of equal merit.

Further Reading

P. Darbyshire, "Where do English and Welsh Judges come from?" [2007] 66(2) C.L.J. 365–388.

Presents the findings of a survey of English and Welsh judges, examining their social and educational backgrounds, the reasons why they studied law, and their legal career histories. Reports on the views of the participants about their experiences of being female, homosexual or formerly a solicitor, and thus minorities in the judicial profession.

B. Hale, "Equality and the judiciary: why should we want more women Judges?" [2001] Aut, P.L. 489–504.

Whether it is important to make judiciary more representative of society, and whether appointment of more women would change style and substance of administration of justice process and democratic legitimacy of judiciary.

P. O'Brien, "Changes to judicial appointments in the Crime and Courts Act 2013" [2014] Apr, P.L. 179–188.

Comments on the amendments made by the Crime and Courts Act 2013 s.20 and Sch.13 to the judicial appointments system introduced by the Constitutional Reform Act 2005 by removing the role of the Lord Chancellor with regard to appointments below High Court level but granting the office new powers with respect to senior appointments.

S. Wilson, "Judicial diversity: where do we go from here?" (2013) 2(1) C.J.I.C.L. 7–15.

Reviews the progress achieved by the efforts to increase the diversity of the judiciary.

Self Test Questions

1. The most superior type of judge in England and Wales is:
- **(a)** the Lord Chancellor
- **(b)** a circuit judge
- **(c)** a Lord Justice of Appeal
- **(d)** a justice of the Supreme Court

2. The Lord Chancellor is now:
- **(a)** the head of the judiciary
- **(b)** the head of the Ministry for Justice
- **(c)** Speaker in the House of Lords
- **(d)** a member of the judiciary

3. Judges used to be appointed by way of:
- **(a)** secret soundings
- **(b)** secret ballots
- **(c)** open competition
- **(d)** automatic promotion

4. Judges are now appointed by:
   (a) the Commissioner for Judicial Appointments
   (b) the Judicial Appointments Commission
   (c) an election process
   (d) the Judicial Appointments Committee
5. The Supreme Court incorporates the:
   (a) Court of Appeal and House of Lords
   (b) Court of Appeal and Privy Council
   (c) House of Lords and Privy Council
   (d) House of Lords

Juries

7

CHAPTER OVERVIEW

In this chapter we will:

- Discover how the role of the jury has developed.
- Consider the role of the jury in the modern-day trial system.
- Explain who is eligible to sit on a jury.
- Evaluate how individual jurors are selected.
- Discuss the concept of jury room secrecy.
- Explain the alternative to jury trial.

Summary

Key Cases

Further Reading

Self Test Questions

Introduction

7-001 **The jury is often described as "the jewel in the Crown" or "the corner-stone" of the British criminal justice system. It is a hallowed institution, which, because of its ancient origin and involvement of 12 randomly selected lay people in the criminal process, commands much public confidence. At the forefront of such confidence is the judges and legal practitioners who, when asked, invariably say that, in general, juries "get it right". For most it is also an important incident of citizenship; De Tocqueville memorably described it as "a peerless teacher of citizenship". However, support for it is not universal, not least among those who have been jurors. And there are many, in particular leading academic lawyers, who express reservations because the public are not permitted by law to know how individual juries reach their verdicts. It is also important to keep in mind how rarely juries are actually used in the trial process given the enormous importance which they are invested with by the public, politicians and legal professions. In fact only about one per cent of criminal cases in England and Wales culminate in trial by jury.**

per Lord Justice Auld, *Criminal Courts Review* (2001) at Ch.5, para.1.

History

7-002 The English jury system, as we know it now, appears to have its roots steeped in the Norman Conquest, during which a very early concept of it was brought to Britain. In 1166 King Henry II began to develop the idea of a more evidentiary form of settling disputes by the issuing of the Assize of Clarendon (an Act of the King). This Assize was to replace the earlier case settlement methods of "trial by battle" (where the parties duelled to determine the successful party) or "trial by ordeal" where an accused person would have to undergo a rather gruesome and painful task on the premise that, if they completed it without injury, or if their injuries healed quickly, they would then be taken to be innocent of whatever charge lay against them. When the Assize was first introduced though, it was nothing like the modern-day "jury" as the jurors were then mainly used for providing local knowledge, acting as witnesses and gathering information, rather than making decisions. In 1215 the concept of an accused person's right to be "tried by their peers" was formalised further in the Magna Carta. The role of the jury continued to change over hundreds of years and by about the 15th century it had begun to assume the role of the independent assessor of fact in a case, and it is from this that its modern-day role has developed.

The fundamental principle behind a jury in more recent times is that an alleged offender is provided with the opportunity to be tried by 12 peers in an effort to ensure that justice is done. A jury should be free from judicial and other pressures and its final decision in the case as to the defendant's guilt or innocence cannot be challenged (except under the allowed routes of appeal). This principle was established in the case known as **Bushell's Case** (1670) Vaugh. 135. Prior to this case, the judge would wield a lot of power over a jury's decision and could effectively coerce it into making the decision that he felt was appropriate in the circumstances, regardless of whether this was the verdict that the jury wanted to return or not. In **Bushell's Case** the defendants were Quakers who had been charged with unlawful assembly. At the end of the trial it became apparent that a number of the jurors were refusing to convict the defendants and the jury returned a not guilty verdict. The trial judge refused to accept this verdict as he was of the opinion that the defendants were guilty and therefore should be convicted as such. In an effort to persuade the jury to officially return a guilty verdict, the judge ordered that the jurors be detained to reconsider their verdict, but without any food or water. The jury again refused to reach a guilty verdict, at which point the judge then fined each of the jurors and committed them to prison until they could pay their fines. The jurors appealed the judge's decision and the Court of Common Pleas (the then appeal court) ordered that the jurors be immediately released, holding that jurors cannot be punished for their verdicts. Following this case it was widely accepted that jurors are independent of the judge, they are charged with the role of deliberating and deciding upon the defendant's guilt or innocence and as such they are the sole arbiters of fact. The judge is there simply to direct on the law but cannot intervene in the jury's decision no matter how much he disagrees with it. If a judge (or other party) attempts to place unacceptable pressure upon the jury to reach a decision then the conviction will be quashed.

Bushell's Case is obviously very old (over 350 years) but this principle is still as applicable to the modern-day jury system, if not more so, as can be demonstrated by the more recent case of **R. v McKenna** [1960] 1 Q.B. 411. In this case the defendants were convicted of charges arising out of the theft of a van containing radio sets. After the jurors had retired for more than two hours, the judge told them that if they did not reach a verdict within 10 minutes they would be kept all night. The jury then, after just a further six minutes, returned a verdict of guilty. On allowing the appeal against conviction the Court held that: 7-003

> **It is a cardinal principle of our criminal law that in considering their verdict, concerning, as it does, the liberty of the subject, a jury shall deliberate in complete freedom, uninfluenced by any promise, unintimidated by any threat. They will stand between the Crown and the subject, and they are still one of the main defences of personal liberty.**

By allowing the appeal, the Court confirmed that, as binding authority indicated, a judge had no power to pre-empt the jury's verdict by directing it to convict and that there was no good reason to depart from that authority.

7–004 The fact that a judge in a case cannot interfere with the jury's decision-making does, however, mean that the jury can acquit a person even if technically guilty under the law, as was confirmed by the House of Lords in the case of **R. v Wang** [2005] UKHL 9. In **Wang** the appellant had been waiting for a train when his bag was stolen. A search was made and the bag found in the possession of a thief who tried to deter the appellant from calling the police by suggesting that the bag contained items the appellant should not be carrying. From the bag the appellant produced a curved martial arts sword, in its sheath. The police were called and, on a search of the bag, a small Gurkha-style knife was also found. The appellant was charged and tried for the possession of the weapons. At trial the appellant testified that he was a Buddhist and practised Shaolin, a traditional martial art. He gave evidence that he had the articles in question, a sword and a knife, with him because he had not liked to leave them in his place of residence and because he liked to stop at remote and uninhabited places to practise Shaolin. At the end of the defence case, the trial judge directed the jury to return guilty verdicts on the ground that the appellant had failed to advance a lawful defence. The appellant appealed, contending that there were no circumstances in which a judge was entitled to direct a jury to return a verdict of guilty. The House of Lords, allowing the appeal and quashing the convictions, stated that the decision of all the factual questions in a case, including the application of the law, was a matter for the jury alone and it was for it to decide whether the defendant was guilty or not.

The Role of the Jury

7–005 The jury system is predominantly used within the Crown Court, although juries do regularly sit in the coroner's court and, on very rare occasion, in the High Court and the County Court. It is an extremely important part of the criminal justice system in ensuring that justice is done and, although it is not failsafe, it is one of the most effective and fair methods of trying those accused of more serious crimes.

The jury's role in a criminal case is to listen to the evidence presented in court and then decide on the defendant's guilt on the basis of that evidence. The judge in the case will direct the jury as to what the law is; it is then for the jury to apply the law to the facts of the case. The jury should have no prior knowledge of the case prior to entering the court (although if the case has been of a high profile in the media this is difficult to control) so that it can hear the evidence in an unbiased way. The jury will return the verdict of guilt or innocence in the case and, if the verdict is one of guilty, the judge will then pass sentence upon the defendant. Once a case has begun the defendant is placed in the charge of the jury and only the jury can discharge them. If the defendant changes the plea to one of guilty after the start of the trial then the jury must still formally return a verdict of guilty (this will be done on the court's direction, which is allowed in these instances) before the court can deal with them in respect of sentencing.

Eligibility

Prior to 1972, there was a property qualification required for an individual to be able to sit as a juror. This meant that a prospective juror had to either own a property or be a tenant. This requirement automatically disqualified a large number of people from being able to partake in jury service. Before the 1970s, it was extremely unusual for women to own a house as property was generally viewed as the right of the males in society. Where women lived in a property with a husband or partner, then only the male name would be on the title deeds to the house, or, if rented, on the tenancy agreement, thereby women were not eligible to sit on a jury. The other sector of society that was automatically discounted from sitting on the jury due to the property qualification was young persons over the age of 18 who were unable or unwilling to move from the family home to a property of their own. Remember that, in these times, women would rarely leave the family home until married and moving to the matrimonial home; thankfully, times have changed since then. **7-006**

The Morris Committee in 1965 undertook a review (Morris Committee, Report of the Royal Commission on Criminal Justice (1965), Ch.1, para.8) of the jury service system and concluded that, as the law stood then, over 95 per cent of women were ineligible for jury service. They concluded that this state of affairs was unfair on both the defendants in a case and to those precluded from jury service due to the property qualification. Juries were supposed to be representative of the society in which they served, and as the vast majority of women and young persons were prevented from sitting upon a jury, this could not be a fair representation of society. As a result of the Morris Committee Report, the law was completely overhauled in 1974 by the enactment of the Juries Act 1974 (JA 1974), which became the governing statute in respect of jury composition.

Section 1 of the JA 1974 (as amended by the CJA 2003 and Criminal Justice and Courts Act 2015 (CJCA 2015)) sets out the qualifications required for a person to be eligible to sit as a juror. Under s.1 every person shall be qualified to be a juror if: **7-007**

- they are aged over 18 and under 76;
- they are registered on the electoral roll;
- they have lived in the UK for at least five years since attaining the age of 13; and
- they are not disqualified or a mentally disordered person.

Schedule 1 to the JA 1974 states that a person will be classified as mentally disordered if they suffer, or have suffered from a mental illness, psychopathic disorder, or mental handicap; or are a resident in a hospital or similar institution; or regularly attend treatment by a medical practitioner. Unfortunately, the Schedule does not seem to distinguish between those who suffer from psychotic behaviour (whom it is assumed the Schedule is intending to prevent from sitting as a juror) and those people who suffer from a mild depressive illness and attend their local GP practice occasionally. If a person is deemed to have a mental disorder under the 1974 Act then they are not just disqualified from sitting as a juror but rather are ineligible to sit as a juror (as is anyone who is under 18 or over 76, or who has lived abroad for the past 15 years, etc.).

The term "disqualification" is also used within the Act and for the purposes of the Act an individual can also be disqualified from jury service following the imposition of a criminal conviction. If a proposed juror has been sentenced to life imprisonment, detention at His Majesty's pleasure, a period of imprisonment for public protection, or been imprisoned for five years or more then the individual in question will be disqualified for life from serving as a juror. Further, if the proposed juror has served a prison term in the last 10 years, or received a suspended sentence or community order then there is a disqualification period of 10 years. These are now the only ways by which persons will be disqualified from jury service. If a person who is disqualified attends for jury service and fails to declare the disqualification, then, if subsequently discovered, a fine of up to £5,000 can be imposed. This imposition of a fine as a sanction for failing to declare an inability to sit as a juror has been put in place as a deterrent. If previously subject to a criminal conviction, as detailed above, then it is thought that a person will not be able to undertake jury responsibilities in an impartial and unbiased way. If a person has spent a number of years within the prison system, it is unlikely that they will wish to send another person into the system, no matter how damning the evidence is. This could then have the result of perverting the justice system and producing unfair acquittals. Further, if it came to light at a later date that a defendant had been convicted by an unconstitutional jury then the appeal process would be opened, which could result in an acquittal and/or a retrial. This would then take up further time and resources of the criminal justice system, which is already overstretched, and could result in the public losing confidence of the workings of the justice system.

Impact of the Criminal Justice Act 2003

7–008 The initial revision of the jury eligibility criteria, under the JA 1974, went a long way to remedying the potential for having an unrepresentative jury. However, prior to 2004 there were still a few categories of people who were viewed as being automatically ineligible for jury service (these were persons who were involved in the administration of justice, so judges, lawyers or the police, or those who were members of the clergy), and some who held a right to be excused from jury service upon request (doctors, members of the armed forces, and those aged between 65 and 70). The rationale behind these excusals was so as to ensure that those who worked within the justice system did not influence a jury, and to ensure that the requirements for jury service did not impact negatively on society in general.

In June and July of 1999 a Home Office research project (Home Office Research Development and Statistics Directorate, *Jury Excusal and Deferral, Research Findings No.102*, 1999) was undertaken to consider the composition of the jury and the numbers of people excused from jury service under the law at that time. The key points of the review were that:

- about 50,000 of those summoned were included in the sample—one-third was available for jury service, half of whom were given deferral to a later date;
- of the remaining two-thirds, 13 per cent were ineligible, disqualified or excused as of right, 15 per cent either failed to attend on the day or had their summonses returned as "undelivered" and 38 per cent were excused;
- the most common reasons for granting excusal were medical (40 per cent of all excusals) and care of young children or the elderly (20 per cent of all excusals); and
- three-quarters of all deferrals were given for either work (39 per cent) or holidays (35 per cent).

From the quarter-of-a-million people summoned for jury service every year the research project set out that only a third of them were actually available to undertake jury service. So the representational jury that was envisaged by the increasing of the potential pool of jurors under the JA 1974 still did not seem to have come to fruition. **7-009**

Lord Justice Auld, commenting on the Home Office research in his *Review of the Criminal Courts* (2001) considered the composition of the jury and concluded that:

The variety of mechanisms and broad scope for avoidance of jury service illustrated by these figures suggest that public perception of it as a civic duty is far from universal. And it is unfair to those who do their jury service, not least because, as a result of others' avoidance of it, they may be required to serve more frequently and for longer than would otherwise be necessary. Most of the exclusions or scope for excusal from jury service deprive juries of the experience and skills of a wide range of professional and otherwise successful and busy people. They create the impression, voiced by many contributors to the Review, that jury service is only for those not important or clever enough to get out of it.

In my view, no-one should be automatically ineligible or excusable from jury service simply because he or she is a member of a certain profession or holds a particular office or job. Where the demands of the office or job are such as to make jury service difficult for him over the period covered by the jury summons, he should be subject to the same regime as the self-employed or ordinary wage earners or others for whom jury service is also costly and burdensome, that is, discretionary excusal or deferral.

The result of the recommendations by Lord Justice Auld, that all persons should be eligible for jury service with the exception of the mentally disordered, caused a lot of controversy, but the recommendations were accepted by the Government and enacted by way of the CJA 2003 (amending s.1 of the JA 1974). This now means that every person, as long as they are not mentally disordered and they satisfy the criteria set out in s.1, will be eligible for jury service.

7-010 When the first judge, Dyson LJ, was summoned in June 2004 for jury service under the new rules, the Lord Chief Justice issued observations, by way of a letter dated 15 June 2004, for judges who were called for jury service. His guidance to the judiciary set out that:

- when a judge serves on a jury he does so as part of his duty as a private citizen;
- if judges are called for jury service they should undertake this duty, unless they can demonstrate good reason as to why they should not serve as summoned;
- a judge should make an application for deferral where he has significant judicial commitments which would make it particularly inconvenient for him to do jury service at the time he was called to do so—judicial commitments should only be a reason for deferral where, if there was no deferral, there could be a significant interference with the administration of justice;
- where a judge attends a court for jury service and finds that he is a member of a jury panel where he is familiar with the judge presiding, a legal representative, the defendant or a potential witness he should raise the matter with the judge presiding;
- it is a matter of discretion for an individual judge sitting on a jury whether he should disclose the fact of his judicial office to fellow members of the jury; and
- judges should avoid the temptation to correct guidance they perceive to be inaccurate as this is outside the scope of their role as jurors.

Since the recent amendments to the JA 1974, numerous barristers, solicitors, KCs and judges have sat on juries without consequence, although there have been a few reported cases where the lawyer in question has not been able to sit on the jury due to knowing somebody involved in the case. It is submitted that this will occasionally continue to occur as the legal world is a small one and jurors are selected to sit on the jury in the area where they reside, which is generally the area in which a lawyer will also work.

7-011 The right for a person involved in the administration of justice to sit on a jury was challenged in the case of **R. v Abdroikov** [2007] UKHL 37. The appeal was a conjoined appeal of three appellants, each of whom had been convicted by a jury that contained either a police officer or a member of the Crown Prosecution Service. The grounds of appeal were that, whilst individuals concerned with the administration of justice were now eligible for jury service, the presence of the police officer and the prosecuting solicitor on the jury had deprived the appellants of a fair trial, contrary to the common law and art.6 of the ECHR. The Court of Appeal dismissed all three appeals holding that a fair-minded and informed observer would not conclude that there was a real possibility that a juror was biased merely because of involvement in some capacity in the administration of justice. The appeal was then taken to the House of Lords, which allowed the appeals in part, due to the fact that, although lawyers and serving police officers were no longer ineligible for jury service, the common law rule that justice should not only be done, but should manifestly be seen to be done, still applied. The Lords held that there was no difference between the common law test and the requirement under art.6 that a person should be tried by an independent and impartial tribunal and that justice was not seen to be done if, on the particular facts of a case, a fair-minded and informed observer would conclude that there was a real possibility of jury bias, whether conscious or unconscious. The House of Lords was not saying that a CPS solicitor or a police officer could never sit on a jury, just that it had to be considered whether there would be an element of bias present, due to the individual facts of the case, if they were to sit on the jury. The decision in **Abdroikov** was then confirmed in the Court of Appeal (Criminal Division) case of **R. v Khan** [2008] Cr. App. R. 13. The European Court of Human Rights considered the matter further in the case of **Hanif and Khan v the United Kingdom** (2012) 55 E.H.R.R. 16, where it was of the opinion that it was of fundamental importance for the courts to inspire confidence in both the public and the accused, and that in doing so there was a need to ensure that juries are both free from bias and from perceived bias. In **Hanif** one of the jurors was a serving police officer and he indicated to the judge that he knew one of the police officers giving evidence; the defence made an application to discharge the juror, which the trial judge refused. The Court held that where a police officer giving evidence is known to the police officer serving as a juror, or where there is police evidence in dispute in the trial, then the police officer should not sit on the jury; for the court to allow otherwise would mean that the tribunal could not be considered to be impartial and consequently there would be a violation of the defendant's art.6 rights.

FIGURE 23 **Who can sit as a juror?**

Eligible	Ineligible	Disqualified
Aged over 18 and under 76; and	**Mentally disordered (as defined under Sch.1, JA 1974)**	**PERMANENTLY Imprisonment for life, at HM's pleasure, for public protection, or for more than 5 years**
Registered on the electoral roll; and		**FOR 10 YEARS Served a term of imprisonment, had a suspended sentence or a community sentence**
Have lived in the UK for the past 5 years		

Excusal from Jury Service

Just because a greater number of people are now eligible to sit on a jury does not mean that they will be forced to serve under any circumstances. The court still has available to it a discretion to excuse a person from jury service where it seems appropriate to do so. For instance, it would be ridiculous to make the mother of a new-born baby serve on a jury as this would be detrimental to both the mother and the child, as well as the defendant in the case; the mother 7–012 would probably be thinking so much about her child that she would not give the evidence in the case her full attention and therefore the defendant could be said to be deprived of a fair trial. Other situations where the court may feel it is appropriate to excuse a person from jury service is where there is a prearranged holiday or business meeting, or a student has scheduled exams to take in that period, or the person is ill at that time. The court will only excuse someone who has a genuine reason that prevents attendance at court at that time, and the person will normally only be granted a deferral from jury service (meaning that the person will still have to attend jury service at a more convenient time in the future).

The court guidance (HMCS, *Jury Summoning Guidance: Guidance for summoning officers when considering deferral and excusal applications*, December 2009) as to excusal and deferral clearly sets out the court's view regarding excusal, as it states:

> **The normal expectation is that everyone summoned for jury service will serve at the time for which they are summoned. It is recognised that there will be occasions where it is not reasonable for a person summoned to serve at the time for which they are summoned. In such circumstances the summoning officer should use his/her discretion to defer the individual to a time more appropriate. Only in extreme circumstances should a person be excused from jury service.**

If, however, a person simply refuses to attend jury service and there is no reasonable excuse for doing so then an offence will be committed under s.20 of the JA 1974. This means that the person will be punished by way of a fine of up to £1,000.

Selection

7–013 Jurors are initially requested to attend court by way of a jury summons; a computer at the Central Summoning Bureau determines exactly who receives a jury summons. Generally, 20 jurors are summoned for each courtroom so as to ensure that there will be 12 suitable jurors to hear the case. If the court in question is a large centre (has a high number of courtrooms) then there may be sent out well over 100 jury summons per fortnight, just for that one court. Jurors are normally expected to attend the court for a two-week period, although this may be extended depending on the length of the trial—some criminal cases have been known to run into months. Once the 20 jurors are at court, each of the names will be put on to a card and the court clerk will then randomly select 12 of the cards, so as to decide who will be empanelled (formally sworn into court) as jurors in the case.

Even once jurors have been summoned and are eligible to sit as jurors, they may still be discharged due to "lack of capacity" (s.10 of the JA 1974). Jurors will be viewed as having a lack of capacity if, for some reason, they are unable to cope with the demands of the trial, such as not understanding English, being deaf or blind. Having a disability will not automatically exclude a person from sitting as a juror (s.9B(2) of the JA 1974), but if a juror is not able to understand what is being said, or is unable to see or hear the evidence then the juror will not be deemed capable of judging the trial and carrying out the functions of a juror fully. This principle, that judges have a residual discretion to discharge a particular juror who ought not to be serving on the jury, has existed at common law for many years and it is considered part of the judge's duty to ensure that there is a fair trial. The origins of this principle can be traced back to the case of **R. v Mansell** (1857) 8 E. & B. 54, where Lord Campbell CJ stated that judges had the discretion and duty to discharge such jurors in order to "prevent scandal and the perversion of justice". However, this discretion should never be used to discharge competent jurors in an attempt to secure a jury drawn from particular sections of the community, or to otherwise influence the overall composition of the jury.

Jury Vetting

Once the panel of jurors has made it through this process they can still be vetted by the lawyers for both the prosecution and the defence. This vetting means that lawyers are allowed to check the jurors for suitability to ensure that they are appropriate members of society to hear and try the case. There are two forms that jury vetting can take; a routine check or an authorised jury check. **7–014**

A routine check involves either a random criminal records office (CRO) check (Home Office Circular 43/1988) or a specific check (Annex to the Attorney-General's Guidelines on Jury Checks *Juries: Right to Stand By: Jury Checks* (1989) 88 Cr. App. R. 123 at 125). In respect of the random check, at regular intervals throughout the year, Crown Court officials submit to their local police a predetermined number of names from those called for jury service in each Crown Court centre for a CRO check. This system of checks is really to keep an eye on those who are sitting for jury service and to make sure that people who are disqualified are not regularly sitting, or attempting to sit, on juries. A specific jury check involves either a Chief Constable or the Director of Public Prosecutions (DPP) running a CRO check on the names of potential jurors in a case. Such a specific check will be undertaken where the Chief Constable or the DPP considers that it would be in the interests of justice so to do. If it is discovered by either of these procedures that persons are disqualified from jury service but have presented themselves as being capable of serving on a jury then the police will consider whether an offence has been committed under s.20(5)(c) of the JA 1974, and will seek advice from the CPS where appropriate.

The second type of check that may be made for the purposes of jury vetting is an "authorised jury check". This is a far more in-depth check on an individual juror and it may involve a CRO check, a Special Branch records check and, occasionally, a Security Services check. An "authorised jury check" can only be authorised by the Attorney-General in accordance with the Attorney-General's Guidelines on Jury Checks. The Attorney-General's justifications for this in-depth check on a specific individual are set out in the Guidelines: **7–015**

There are, however, certain exceptional types of case of public importance for which the provisions as to majority verdicts and the disqualification of jurors may not be sufficient to ensure the proper administration of justice. In such cases it is in the interests of both justice and the public that there should be further safeguards against the possibility of bias and in such cases checks which go beyond the investigation of criminal records may be necessary. The particular aspects of these cases which may make it desirable to seek extra precautions are (a) in security cases a danger that a juror, either voluntarily or under pressure, may make an improper use of evidence which, because of its sensitivity, has been given in camera, (b) in both security and terrorist cases the danger that a juror's political beliefs are so biased as to go beyond normally reflecting the broad spectrum of views and interests in the community to reflect the extreme views of a sectarian interest or pressure group to a degree which might interfere with his fair assessment of the facts of the case or lead him to exert improper pressure on his fellow jurors.

Therefore, this type of vetting should only be used in a limited instance of cases that involve either:

- cases in which national security is involved and part of the evidence is likely to be heard *in camera*; or
- terrorist cases.

7–016 The issue of vetting has been a rather controversial one over the years. The practice first came to public knowledge during the course of the "ABC" trial in 1978. The trial involved allegations of the Official Secrets Act being breached and it was discovered during the course of the trial that the jurors had been vetted for their suitability and "loyalty". This led to the trial being stopped, the jury being discharged, and a fresh trial with a new jury being ordered. There was public outcry on the discovery of this practice of jury vetting, as it called into question the extent to which a jury was actually randomly selected. The resulting media and public attention from the trial forced the Attorney-General to increase transparency with regard to this practice and this resulted in the general publication of the guidelines on jury vetting which, it was acknowledged, had gone on behind the scenes for many years beforehand.

The in-depth jury checks under the second method can only be authorised by the Attorney-General upon the advice of the DPP, and they can only be carried out in extreme cases (as listed above). However, under the present-day state of modern society, especially after 9/11 terrorist attacks in America and the subsequent successful and attempted terror attacks around Britain, it must be considered whether these extended jury checks will become a more regular feature of the jury selection process, and if they do whether they will result in the creation of a hand-picked jury who will, ultimately, do the bidding of the Government in response to the political climate at that time.

The legality of jury vetting has been challenged on a number of occasions in the courts. In the case of **R. v Sheffield Crown Court Ex p. Brownlow** [1980] 2 W.L.R. 892 the Court of Appeal was required to consider this very issue. Two police officers had been charged with assault occasioning actual bodily harm. Prior to the hearing of the trial the officers applied to the judge for the criminal history of all the potential jurors to be supplied to the defence solicitors, so that they could be vetted. The judge in the case ordered that the Chief Constable should supply both the defence and prosecution solicitors with the information requested, which the Chief Constable then appealed. The Court of Appeal, dismissing the appeal, held that although it had no power to intervene in the decision it felt that the practice of jury vetting was, in principle, wrong. Lord Denning MR gave a damning condemnation of the practice stating (at 542): **7–017**

> **To my mind it is unconstitutional for the police authorities to engage in "jury vetting". So long as a person is eligible for jury service, and is not disqualified, I cannot think it right that, behind his back, the police should go through his record so as to enable him to be asked to "stand by for the Crown", or to be challenged by the defence. If this sort of thing is to be allowed, what comes of a man's right of privacy? He is bound to serve on a jury when summoned. Is he thereby liable to have his past record raked up against him—and presented on a plate to prosecuting and defending lawyers—who may use it to keep him out of the jury—and, who knows, it may become known to his neighbours and those about him? Furthermore, as a matter of practical politics, even if jury vetting were allowed, the chances are 1,000 to one against any juror being found unsuitable: and, if he should be, the chances of him being on any particular jury of 12—so as to influence the result—are minimal—especially in these days of majority verdicts.**

However, there has not been consistency in the condemnation of the practice of jury vetting in the courts. In the same year as hearing **Brownlow**, a differently constituted Court of Appeal heard the same issue raised again in the case of **R. v Mason** [1980] 3 W.L.R. 617. Here, before the trial, the police had checked the local criminal records and had supplied the prosecution with the names of those called for jury service who had been convicted of criminal offences. Consequently, four members of the jury were asked to step down as three of them had criminal convictions, although at least one of them was not disqualified by the conviction. The defendant was convicted of two offences of burglary and two offences of handling stolen goods and, upon conviction; he applied for leave to appeal. The Court of Appeal then approved of the jury vetting (even though it was unauthorised) with Lawton LJ setting out that both the Crown and the defence had a right to challenge a member of the jury panel and the random selection of jurors had always been subject to the qualification that the judge and the parties were to decide which members of the jury panel were suitable to serve on a jury in a particular case. The rationale of the Court appears to be that the checking of the potential jurors' criminal records is a method of preventing a crime being committed as it will stop a disqualified juror sitting when **7–018** they ought not to. The case of **R. v Mason** has since been overruled on another point of law but on this principle it still remains good law.

Challenging the Jury

7–019 Once the 12 jurors have been selected, but before they are empanelled by way of taking the oath, the prosecution and defence have the opportunity to challenge the composition of the jury. There are two forms of challenge that can be made towards a juror and these are known as:

- a challenge to the array; and
- a challenge for cause.

Challenge to the Array

7–020 The right to challenge the array is provided for under s.5 of the JA 1974 and the challenge is made towards the entire jury on the basis that it is not representational of society or is biased in some way. Although a challenge to the array is not often made, a classic example of such a challenge can be found in the case of **R. v Danvers** [1982] Crim. L.R. 680. The defendant, who was charged with the offences of rape and indecent assault, was of an ethnic minority but the jury that was empanelled to hear his case consisted entirely of jurors who were Caucasian in origin. The defendant challenged the entire composition of the jury (challenged the array), stating that the jury panel did not reflect the ethnic composition of the community, and on the further ground that an all-white jury could not understand the mental and emotional atmosphere in which black families live, so that a black defendant could not have unreserved confidence in an all-white jury. Essentially the argument was that the jury did not provide a full representation of a cross-section of society and therefore the defendant could not be afforded a fair trial. The Court held, dismissing the challenge to the array, that where the defendant was black there was no requirement in law that there should also be a black jury panel member.

As the jury was selected randomly it was taken by the Court to be the best representation of society that could be achieved by the current method of jury selection; just because the defendant was from an ethnic minority did not mean that at least one member of the jury should be from that origin as well. Imagine if there was the requirement that the jury must always be composed of at least one person who shared the same ethnic origin as the defendant; if the defendant came from Mongolia or was Inuit by origin then it could become extremely difficult to always find a juror from the same ethnic background. If this was a requirement, or even a right by the defendant to request this, then selecting a jury for a trial could become nigh on impossible; the law would move towards a positive selection system, as opposed to a random one, which would bring with it its own inherent problems and allegations of bias or positive discrimination. Couple this fact with the points considered above regarding the problems that can be faced with even compiling a full jury for a case under the current system, even with the amendments under the CJA 2003 to extend the pool of potential candidates, and it would seem that the Court made the correct decision on the basis that the selection system, even if potentially flawed at times, is the best method that we have available to us at present. The Court further confirmed this point in the case of **R. v Ford** [1989] 3 W.L.R. 762, where Lord Lane CJ stated that:

> **The racial composition of a particular panel or part panel would not be grounds for challenge to the array. A challenge to the array is a challenge to the whole panel on the ground of some irregularity in their summoning by the officer responsible. ... [i]n the absence of evidence of specific bias, ethnic origins could not found a valid ground for challenge to an individual juror. The alleged discretion of the judge to intervene in the selection of the jury does not therefore fall within any acknowledged category of judicial power or discretion. ... The conclusion is that, however well-intentioned the judge's motive might be, the judge has no power to influence the composition of the jury, and that it is wrong for him to attempt to do so. If it should ever become desirable that the principle of random selection should be altered, that will have to be done by way of statute and cannot be done by any judicial decision.**

Challenge for Cause

A challenge for cause is a more specific challenge to an individual's right to sit on the jury. Such a challenge is likely to arise where the defendant, or witness, knows or is related to a juror, or knows that a juror is disqualified from jury service. 7–021

In the case of **R. v Wilson** (1996) 8 Admin. L.R. 1 the wife of a prison officer was called to attend jury service. She asked to be excused from service on the basis that her husband worked within the criminal justice system (as could be allowed prior to 2004). Her request was refused and she was required to serve on the jury. The two defendants in the case had been charged with, and were subsequently convicted of, robbery. It later transpired that both of the defendants had been on remand in the same prison in which the juror's husband worked. An appeal was brought on this basis, and the Court of Appeal stated that although there appeared to be no actual bias in the case the justice system required that not only must justice be done but that it also must be seen to be done. The presence of the prison officer's wife on the jury prevented justice being *seen* to be done and therefore the defendants' convictions were quashed and the appeal allowed. This concept of justice being seen to be done, as well as actually being done, is a fundamental principle of the English legal system as it helps to instil public confidence in the whole process. It is not only the lower courts who must adhere to this principle, as even the highest court in the land, the House of Lords (now the Supreme Court), has been found to be subject to it, as evidenced by the case of **R. v Bow Street Metropolitan Stipendiary Magistrate Ex p. Pinochet Ugarte (No.2)** [2000] 1 A.C. 119.

In both challenges, the party making the challenge (either the prosecution or the defence) must give valid reasons as to why the juror(s) should not be allowed to sit on the jury in the case in question.

Stand By

7–022 The prosecution alone has the right to request that an individual is made to stand by. This means that the individual juror selected to stand by will be put to the bottom of the list of potential jurors and only used to try the case if no other suitable jurors are available. If the prosecution wishes to request that a certain juror is made to stand by it is not required to provide any reasoning for its decision. However, this method of challenging a juror is not the same as the American system, where the prosecution and defence are allowed to question the jurors prior to the trial to determine whether (in their eyes) they would make a good or bad juror in the case.

The issue of questioning the jury to discover whether there is any potential bias was raised in the case of **R. v Andrews (Tracey)** [1999] Crim. L.R. 156. The appellant in the case had been convicted of murdering her boyfriend by stabbing him, but her defence throughout the case was that another motorist had killed him in a fit of road rage. The case received a lot of media coverage and the defence was concerned with whether an unbiased jury could be selected due to the amount of publicity surrounding the case. The defence made a submission to the Court that all potential jurors should answer a questionnaire, but the judge rejected this. The appellant appealed but the appeal was dismissed on the ground that only in exceptional circumstances should jurors be questioned, as it was against the principle of random selection. The prosecution, therefore, when wanting to use stand by, only has the information available by way of jury vetting (if this has taken place) and its instincts.

It may seem a little unfair that only the prosecution has the right of stand by, but until 1988 the defence also had a right to challenge individual jurors without particular cause; this was known as peremptory challenge. Under a peremptory challenge the defence could select up to three jurors who it would stand by. This meant that the defence could effectively attempt to try and tailor the jury to one that it felt would be more likely to acquit. For example, in rape trials it is a commonly accepted fact that men are more likely to acquit a defendant than women are, so being able to use a peremptory challenge to remove three women would mean that the defence could try and balance the jury so that it was more male-orientated, and therefore more likely to acquit. This right of challenge was removed from the defence after Lord Roskill's 1986 Fraud Trials Committee highlighted the potential for abuse by the defence, and recommended its abolition. A number of Commonwealth jurisdictions still retain a peremptory challenge for the defence. The number of available challenges vary, for example the New Zealand Juries Act 1981 allows 4 challenges for each party, yet Queensland, Australia allows up to 8 per side under the Jury Act 1995.

Shortly after the abolition of this right of peremptory challenge a number of defendants, in the case of **R. v Thomas** (1989) 88 Cr. App. R. 370, made an invitation to the Court for the judge to stand by some jurors on their behalf. The defendants in the case were four black men who were charged with murder. The jury empanelled in the case consisted of 12 white jurors. Worried about the potential for bias in the case, the defendants made the invitation to the Court in an attempt to ensure some level of black representation on the jury (they could not challenge the array for the reasons discussed above). The Court, whilst acknowledging that the Court did have its own power to stand by a juror and that it could theoretically use this power to secure a proportion of black representation upon the jury, held that the power should only be used sparingly and in very exceptional circumstances. It dismissed the appeal, stating that in the case before it there were no apparent racist undertones, and therefore there was no risk that the defendants would not get a fair trial from an all-white jury. **7–023**

A question could be raised regarding whether the removal of the defendant's right to challenge a juror without cause, whilst the prosecution right is retained, is compatible with art.6 of the ECHR. Surely this difference in power goes firmly against the defendant's right to a fair trial and the doctrine of equality of arms (where both sides should be on a level playing field, and neither one being more disadvantaged than the other). If the prosecution can pick and choose those who it accepts onto the jury then why should the defence also not be able to do so? Gillespie (*The English Legal System*, 1st edn (OUP, 2007) at p.354) briefly addresses this argument but concludes that the practice may be acceptable by way of the right to derogation from art.6 on issues of national security. It cannot be envisaged, though, that issues of national security will be overly dominant in the normal daily life of the Crown Court where this practice regularly occurs. Further, surely, if the rationale behind it is that of being able to protect the interests of the State, then simply providing the judiciary with the power of stand down (which they already possess) is sufficient to deal with such a situation upon the application of the prosecution; there is no real need for the prosecution to have this "right" as a right.

FIGURE 24 The trials and tribulations of becoming a juror

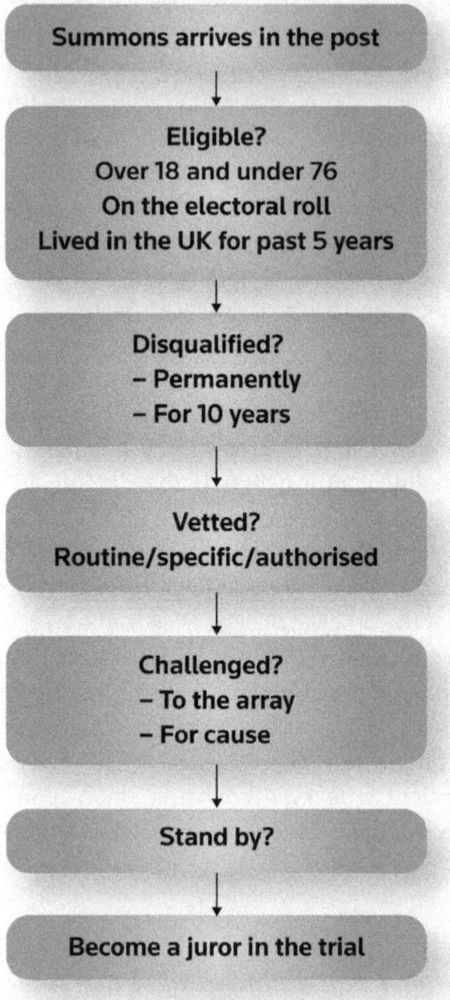

Jury Room Secrecy

7–024 One of the very distinct and special things about a jury is that nobody outside of the jury room will ever (or at least should never) know the reasons for a jury's verdict or how it reached that decision. This principle of jury room secrecy is one that is held very dear in the justice system and, to ensure that it was complied with it was initially legislated for under s.8 of the Contempt of Court Act 1981 (CCA 1981) so as to make disclosure of jury room deliberations a criminal offence. Section 8 set out that:

> (1) Subject to subsection (2) below, it is a contempt of court to obtain, disclose or solicit any particulars of statements made, opinions expressed, arguments advanced or votes cast by members of a jury in the course of their deliberations in any legal proceedings.
> (2) This section does not apply to any disclosure of any particulars—
> (a) in the proceedings in question for the purpose of enabling the jury to arrive at their verdict, or in connection with the delivery of that verdict, or
> (b) in evidence in any subsequent proceedings for an offence alleged to have been committed in relation to the jury in the first mentioned proceedings, or to the publication of any particulars so disclosed.

Essentially, s.8 stated that any deliberations that took place in the jury room were to be kept secret and no enquiries as to how the jury members reached their decision in a case may be made. There are a number of reasons as to why jury room deliberations should remain secret. By making the divulgence of jury room deliberations a criminal offence it is hoped that jurors will be thoroughly dissuaded from selling their stories to the media after the conclusion of the trial; the ban on discussing the conversations within the jury room also helps to protect an individual juror from potential recriminations following an unpopular verdict, as if no one person can speak out and say who was for or against the conviction or acquittal then no single juror can be targeted in the case of any reprisals.

To stop the publication of jury deliberations, the case of **Attorney-General Respondent v Associated Newspapers Ltd** [1994] 2 W.L.R. 277 held that the scope of s.8 was wide enough to catch not just jurors who divulged the jury room deliberations, but also any person who then publicised the *content* of the deliberations after being told them by a juror. 7–025

In **Associated Newspapers Ltd** an article was published in *The Mail on Sunday* revealing the deliberations of a jury in the course of reaching its verdict in a criminal trial. The article referred to how three jurors in the case had allegedly reached their decisions. The journalist who wrote the article had been passed the information by way of a third party that had been in direct contact with the jury members. On publication of the article, the Attorney-General applied for the journalist and the newspaper's editor and publisher to be held in contempt of court under s.8(1) of the CCA 1981. The judge held that s.8(1) did extend to include the newspaper's publisher, editor and journalist and they were all subsequently held in contempt of court. On dismissing the appeal, the House of Lords held that the wording in s.8(1) did include the publication by the journalist as it amounted to a disclosure, as opposed to a recounting of known facts and that s.8 had been enacted by Parliament as a remedy against the publication of jury deliberations as well as their disclosure by individual jurors.

The courts are also extremely reluctant to investigate any allegations surrounding jury room deliberations, even where there are allegations relating to irregularities as to the way in which 7–026 the jury reached its decision. In the case of **R. v Thompson** (1962) 46 Cr. App. R. 72 the Court of Appeal refused to hear evidence pertaining to the fact that the jurors had been shown a list of the defendant's previous convictions before returning a guilty verdict, even though it was alleged that the majority of the jury had come to the conclusion, prior to being aware of the defendant's criminal history, that the defendant was innocent of the offence alleged. The Court of Appeal (Criminal Division) held that the Court had no power to enquire, by taking evidence from jurors, about what had occurred either in the jury box or in the jury room.

If, however, the discrepancy occurs outside of the realm of the jury room, the court will be more minded to intervene and investigate allegations of irregularity, even if this investigation may affect the process of the jury deliberations, as was shown in the case of **R. v Young** [1995] 2 Cr. App. R. 379. In the case of **Young** the jury had retired to a hotel overnight and the allegations related to the ways in which a number of the jurors had conducted themselves during this period. The case was one involving an alleged murder and, on retirement to the hotel, four members of the jury met up and attempted to contact the deceased by way of an Ouija board (usually used at a séance to seek messages from the spirits of absent or deceased persons). They apparently achieved contact with the victim and they asked questions which went directly to the heart of the case, such as who had committed the murder, and the board then allegedly spelt out the defendant's name in response. On return to court the following day the jury delivered a unanimous verdict of guilty. Later, one of the jurors approached the solicitor in the case and provided a written statement of what occurred at the hotel, on the basis of which the appellant lodged an appeal. The Court of Appeal allowed the appeal and held that the instances at the hotel were conducted during a hiatus in the jury sessions and therefore investigation of the jurors' actions within this time was not to be viewed as a breach of s.8. The Court also held that the investigations could only focus on this specific period of time and could not continue on to the point at which the jury officially reconvened the following morning.

7-027 The fact that there is a common law rule against the investigation of jury misconduct has led to a number of cases challenging the validity and lawfulness of this rule under the art.6 right to a fair trial provisions. The leading authority in this matter is, at present, found within the conjoined appeals of **R. v Mirza; R. v Connor** [2004] 2 Cr. App. R. 8. In **Mirza**, after the defendant's conviction, a juror had written to defendant's counsel suggesting that there had been a racial element in the jury's verdict. In **Connor**, there had been a letter from a juror raising concerns about the deliberations of the jury and alleging that the defendants had been found guilty in order to teach them a lesson. Both of the defendants appealed against conviction. The issues before the Court were whether evidence which revealed a lack of impartiality about the deliberations of a jury was always inadmissible under the common law secrecy rule, and whether s.8 of the CCA 1981, if prohibiting the admission of such a statement, was incompatible with art.6 of the ECHR.

The Court held that art.6 was not infringed by the common law rule of secrecy. The role of the jury was that of a collective decision-maker, and during the decision-making process the jurors were to be free from outside interference. The common law rule worked by ensuring that the jurors, following their decision, were protected from external ridicule, criticism and harassment, and it was this that gave the system its strength. The Court recognised that the risk of perversity could not be entirely eliminated but that the balance of advantage lay firmly in favour of preserving the common law rule as a proportionate response to the needs of the jury system. The role of the secrecy rule was recognised in the European jurisprudence as essential to the operation of the jury system so that the rule was compatible, without modification, with a defendant's right to a fair trial under art.6(1).

Following the cases of **Mirza; Connor** the House of Lords issued the **Practice Direction Crown Court: Guidance to Juror** [2004] 1 W.L.R. 665 which stated that:

> **Trial judges should ensure that the jury is alerted to the need to bring any concerns about fellow jurors to the attention of the judge at the time and not wait until the case is concluded. At the same time, it is undesirable to encourage inappropriate criticism of fellow jurors, or to threaten jurors with contempt of court.**

A year after the issuing of this **Practice Direction** the House of Lords was again faced with the issue of a juror divulging details of the jury deliberations in the case of **Attorney-General v Scotcher** [2005] UKHL 36. Following a trial in which the defendants had been convicted by a majority vote of 10:1, the dissenting juror had written to the defendant's mother to urge her to consider an appeal. He deliberately disclosed statements, opinions, arguments and votes of the members of the jury in the course of its deliberations, and did so with the intention of proving that there had been a miscarriage of justice. The juror based his defence on the submission that his art.10 rights (freedom of expression) would be breached if he were to be held in contempt of court for disclosing the deliberations, when his main aim and purpose had been to prevent a miscarriage of justice. **7-028**

The House, on dismissal of the appeal, held that it was not disputed that the juror in question genuinely believed that there had been a miscarriage of justice. Had he written to the Crown Court or to the Court of Appeal with his disclosures then he would not have been in contempt of court. However, by writing to the defendant's mother, he had made disclosures to a third party who had no authority to receive disclosures on behalf of the Court. He had created the risks to the confidentiality of the jurors' deliberations that s.8 was designed to prevent, and he was in contempt of court. Further, the Court held that s.8 of the Act was not incompatible with the right to freedom of expression enshrined in art.10 of the Convention since a juror could draw his concerns to the attention of the trial judge before the jury returned its verdict.

Therefore, both the timing of the alleged irregularities and the party to whom the allegations are made are critical to the question of to whether they can be investigated by the court or not. If the irregularities occur outside of the jury room (as in **Young)** then they can be investigated by the court, as can irregularities that occur during the course of the trial, or irregularities raised *directly* with the court as opposed to a third party.

THE IMPACT OF MODERN MEDIA ON JURY ROOM SECRECY

7–029 The impact of modern media on the workings of the jury room has been keenly felt over the past few years. Due to the integration and acceptance of the internet into daily life the courts have been faced with a number of cases of jurors researching a defendant, or of jurors posting inappropriate comments on social media sites during the course of a trial. In 2011, after the first trial of its kind, a juror (Joanne Fraill) was jailed for contempt of court after she admitted contacting a defendant via Facebook and discussing the case and the ongoing jury deliberations with her. Although the defendant in question had been cleared of all charges at the time of Fraill's contact there was still a live trial in respect of other defendants in the case; as a result of the contact the trial judge was required to discharge the jury, causing a £6 million drug trial to collapse. In sentencing her to eight months in jail (**Attorney General v Fraill** [2011] 2 Cr. App R. 21) the Lord Chief Justice, Lord Judge, stated [at 54]:

> **Her conduct in visiting the internet repeatedly was directly contrary to her oath as a juror, and her contact with the acquitted defendant, as well as her repeated searches on the internet, constituted flagrant breaches of the orders made by the judge for the proper conduct of the trial.**

Only a few months later in January 2012, former university lecturer, Theodora Dallas, was found guilty of contempt of court by three high court judges after she had researched the defendant, who was being tried for causing grievous bodily harm, on the internet. Dallas discovered that the defendant had previously been acquitted of rape and reported this fact to her fellow jurors. Her actions were reported by other jury members to the trial judge, who halted the trial as a result. In sentencing Dallas to six months in custody for the offence of contempt of court (**Attorney General v Dallas** [2012] 1 W.L.R. 991) the Lord Chief Justice, Lord Judge stated [para 43]:

> **Misuse of the internet by a juror is always a most serious irregularity and an effective custodial sentence is virtually inevitable.**

7–030 This issue of jurors making recourse to modern media was recognised and reported upon by the Law Commission in its report Contempt of Court (1): Juror Misconduct and Internet Publications (Law Com No. 304, 9 December 2013). The Law Commission stated that there was a need to ensure that the laws and procedures struck a balance between the public interest in the administration of justice, the defendant's right to a fair trial, and the rights of the jurors concerned. The Commission made the following recommendations:

The introduction of a new statutory offence of sworn jurors in a case deliberately searching for extraneous information related to the case. We recommend that this offence should be triable on indictment, with a jury, in the usual manner. The maximum penalty for the offence should be 2 years' imprisonment and/or an unlimited fine, with the usual sentencing powers available following trial on indictment

The introduction of a specific, statutory, defence to a breach of section 8 of the Contempt of Court Act 1981, where, after the conclusion of the trial, a juror, in genuine belief that they are exposing a miscarriage of justice, discloses the content of jury deliberations to a court official, the police or the Criminal Cases Review Commission. We also recommend the introduction of an exception to the section 8 prohibition on jury research. This would allow for authorised academic research into jury deliberations, with a range of rigorous safeguards in place in order to protect the integrity of the jury's decision and the anonymity of jurors and parties to the trials.

The Law Commission's recommendations were taken on board and in February 2014 the Secretary of State revealed plans to enact a specific criminal offence to deal with jury misconduct in the proposed Criminal Justice and Courts Bill. The result was the creation of four new criminal offences inserted into the Juries Act 1974 by the Criminal Justice and Courts Act 2015 (CJCA 2015), and which replaced the offence under s.8 of the CCA 1981. The four new offences are:

- **Research of the case by jurors during the trial period** (s.20A JA 1974 as inserted by s.71 CJCA 2015). This can include research by asking a question, searching an electronic database or the internet, visiting or inspecting a place or object, conducting an experiment, or asking another person to seek the information. The information sought can be relevant to the persons involved with the case, the judge, the law, the evidence, or court procedure.
- **Sharing research with other jurors** (s.20B JA 1974 as inserted by s.72 CJCA 2015). It is an offence for a juror intentionally to disclose to another jury member information gained in contravention of section 20A.
- **Jurors engaging in other prohibited conduct** (s.20C JA 1974 as inserted by s.73 CJCA 2015). It is an offence for a juror to engage intentionally in prohibited conduct during the trial period. Prohibited conduct means conduct from which it may reasonably be concluded that the person intends to try the issue otherwise than on the basis of the evidence presented (s.20C(1)).
- **Disclosing jury deliberations** (s.20D of JA 1974 as inserted by s.74 CJCA 2015). It is an offence for any person to disclose information about statements made, opinions expressed, arguments advanced, or votes cast by members of the jury during

their deliberations. There are a number of exceptions to this offence, such as where the jury need to deliver the verdict, or where an individual reasonably believes that an offence or contempt of court has been committed in connection with the trial.

If found guilty of any of these offences then a person is liable to imprisonment for a term not exceeding two years or a fine.

RESEARCH INTO JURY ROOM DELIBERATIONS

7–031 A further problem that the rule of secrecy carries with it is the fact that there is never any certainty as to how and why a jury has reached a certain decision (was it by way of careful consideration of all the evidence, or by the toss of a coin?), nor can comprehensive research be carried out into how juries reach decisions. Over recent years, studies into how juries deliberate have been carried out via the use of mock juries; this is where a second jury will sit alongside a real jury in a case but the second jury's deliberations will be free for the researchers to film and scrutinise as it will not be the determining jury in the trial. The practice of using a mock jury as a method of research and study has even made it into the mainstream media in the past few years by way of programmes such as *Consent* (Channel 4, 21 January 2007) and *The Verdict* (BBC 2, 11–15 February 2007). But, as compelling as these programmes were, and as access-all-areas as the research is, it is doubted that these mock juries will ever truly replicate the deliberations that go on behind the closed jury room door. The jurors in the mock trials know that they are being watched, they may even see the cameras filming them, and it is questioned whether a person under these circumstances will act in the same way if in a real jury situation, where no one could be held publicly to account for comments or decisions.

The Government published a consultation paper in 2005 (*Jury research and impropriety* (2005)) where it considered the appropriateness of extending the ability to research into the jury decision-making process. The consultation paper received 41 responses from a wide range of people such as judges, lawyers, academics, the police and the CPS. Overall, the respondents were in favour of allowing some degree of research into the jury decision-making process. The main reason given for this was that:

> **research would permit a better understanding of how juries operate and would allow trial procedures to be improved, thereby assisting jurors in the performance of their duties.**

7–032 Despite apparent reservations about jury research becoming too invasive, effectively meaning that the continuation of research into jury decisions should, for the time being, continue to be conducted by way of mock juries, some real jury studies have been granted permission. In 2010, Prof Cheryl Thomas reported on a number of real and mock jury trials (Ministry of Justice Research Series 1/10: *Are Juries Fair?* The study found little evidence that juries are not fair.

However, it identified several areas where the criminal justice system could assist jurors better to perform their role. The study also demonstrated that section 8 of the Contempt of Court Act 1981 does not prevent comprehensive research about how juries reach their verdicts and that research from other jurisdictions should not be relied upon to understand juries in England and Wales.

FIGURE 25 **Summary of arguments for and against jury room secrecy**

Arguments for jury room secrecy	Arguments against jury room secrecy
Helps to maintain public confidence in the jury system	**Research into how jurors reach their decisions could be undertaken**
Helps to preserve the finality of the verdict	**Miscarriages of justice could be avoided**
Helps to ensure the jury can speak frankly	**It would ensure that the jurors are accountable for their decisions**
Helps to protect jurors from threats and intimidation	**Would enable the public to become more educated in the ways of the justice system**
Protects the privacy of jurors	**It would remove the possibility of bias**

Verdicts

After all the evidence has been heard in the case and the judge has summed up the evidence for the jury and directed on the relevant law the jury will retire to consider its verdict (the decision as to whether the defendant is innocent or guilty of the offence charged. Initially it is hoped that a jury will return a unanimous verdict (a verdict upon which all the members of the jury agree). If, however, after at least two hours of deliberation, it appears to the court that the jurors are not able to agree unanimously then the court may direct the jury to return a majority verdict instead. The courts are given the power to make such a direction under s.17 of the JA 1974. Section 17(1) states that: **7–033**

> (1) [T]he verdict of a jury in proceedings in the Crown Court or the High Court need not be unanimous if—
> (a) in a case where there are not less than eleven jurors, ten of them agree on the verdict; and
> (b) in a case where there are ten jurors, nine of them agree on the verdict.

The court can make such a direction if it appears to the court that the jury has had a reasonable period of time for deliberation when having regard to the nature and complexity of the case. Majority verdicts were originally introduced in 1967 to try and reduce the number of cases where there was the possibility of "jury nobbling" as, when only a unanimous verdict was acceptable, there would be instances where a jury member would be bribed or intimidated (or "nobbled") into giving a certain verdict (generally, not guilty). As the court required unanimity then a stalemate situation could arise and, if the stalemate continued unbroken, then the court would be forced to discharge the jury and order a retrial. The introduction of the majority verdict was a way of avoiding this stalemate, as even if one juror has been "nobbled", it would not matter as the court could accept a guilty verdict from the other 11 members of the jury. The problem of jury nobbling escalated during the 1980s in relation to a number of IRA terrorist trials that occurred at this time and in 1994 it became an offence, under s.51 of the Criminal Justice and Public Order Act 1994 (CJPOA 1994), to threaten or intimidate any person involved in a criminal trial. More recently, s.54 of the Criminal Procedure and Investigations Act 1996 (CPIA 1996) allows for an acquitted person to be retried if a person is subsequently convicted of intimidating or threatening anyone involved in the trial (witnesses or juror). This is a major step forward by the law to ensure that juries are unbiased by outside influences as it goes against the principle of finality (that once a person is acquitted of a crime that is the end of the matter).

7-034 Where a jury does give a majority verdict it is vitally important that the foreman of the jury (the person who stands up in court and pronounces the jury's verdict) provides details of the majority that the decision was made by, so 11:1, 10:2, etc. This is to ensure that a lawful majority verdict has been given. If the foreman only had to say that the defendant was guilty by majority then all those involved in the case would be left forever wondering if the defendant was found guilty by 11:1, or 7:5, etc. It is acceptable to the court (under **R. v Pigg** [1983] 1 All E.R. 56) for the foreman to simply state how many members of the jury agreed with the verdict.

If, for any reason, the jury has diminished in size since the start of the trial (so perhaps a juror has become ill or has died) then there must only be one person who dissents from the majority verdict for it to be lawful. Where the jury number has dropped to nine, the decision must be unanimous, and if for some reason the jury number has fallen below nine then the trial must be stopped and a new trial begun with a fresh jury.

If a defendant is acquitted by way of a majority verdict then it is not necessary for the court to be informed about the jury split on who voted one way or the other; in these instances the simple fact that a majority has decided that the defendant is innocent is sufficient enough detail for the court.

Advantages and Disadvantages of the Jury

The English jury system is held in high esteem by a large part of the westernised world, but it is not without its foibles and problems. As Penny Darbyshire stated in her article "The lamp that shows that freedom lives—is it worth the candle?" ([1991] Crim. L.R. 740–752): 7–035

Too often, eulogies are heaped upon the jury by its defenders who blindly follow their predecessors' mistakes (on Magna Carta) or atheoretical assertions (on jury trial as a constitutional right). They confuse randomness with representativeness and justify the jury as a democratic guardian of civil liberties re-writing the law on our behalf.

In heaping unquestioning praise on the jury, the commentators deceive themselves and the public into thinking jury trial is the 'centrepiece' of the criminal justice system. A mass of research on pre-trial decision-making and plea-bargaining has taught us that this is simply not the case. As Ashworth reminded us in 1988: 'There are few who would now propound the view that the centrepiece of the English criminal process is the trial,' but the jury defenders are still doing just this.

Below, is a table setting out the main advantages and disadvantages of the jury trial. The points included do not identify every plus or minus of the jury system but they set out the main headings, that of course can be expanded upon.

JURY SIZE

The number of jurors has been set at 12 since time immemorial. Scotland, notably, has a jury composed of 15 individuals and many of the Overseas Territories employ a smaller jury of 7 due to the relatively small population of persons who qualify to serve as jurors. Reducing the size of the English jury may be an attractive cost-saving exercise but the consequences are unknown. During the Second World War, the Administration of Justice (Emergency Provisions) Act 1939 provided for the use of 7-person juries to deal with a severe shortage of available jurors. The more recent Covid-19 restrictions on movement not only affected trials, but calls were made and debate took place on reducing the number of jurors returned in the 21st century, despite no reduction in jury size actually taking place (see "Guest blog: How will restricting jury trial and reducing jury numbers affect the delivery of justice?" (10 July 2020) *barcouncil.org.uk, https://www.barcouncil.org.uk/resource/guest-blog-how-will-restricting-jury-trial-and-reducing-jury-numbers-affect-the-delivery-of-justice.html* [Accessed 1 May 2025]). 7–036

FIGURE 26 **Advantages and disadvantages of the jury**

Advantages	Disadvantage
Public confidence	**Lack of competence**
The right to be tried by one's peers is a fundamental right under the English legal system. It is a system that is seen as an effective one and, as famously quoted by Lord Devlin, juries are viewed as "the lamp that shows that freedom lives".	The jury is not legally trained or experienced in any way and is required to deal with complex matters of law, upon its understanding of which often depends a person's liberty. The average randomly selected jury is often not intelligent enough to cope with complicated legal matters.
Public participation	**Attendance**
This links into public confidence. The public becomes involved in the legal system and consequently the courtroom is not viewed as a closed world wholly dominated by lawyers.	Despite the recent reforms in the law it is difficult to find people willing to undertake jury service and many will make excuses and request a deferral. Those people who can attend are often of the same social and economic background, which does not result in a representative jury.
Jury equity	**Perverse verdicts**
Juries are not bound by precedent and can make decisions on the facts of each individual case, nor are they required to give reasoning for their decisions. This means that a jury can make its decisions based on "fairness" as opposed to the law.	The jury will occasionally come to a decision (normally an acquittal) which is difficult to reconcile with the evidence and the law—this is known as a perverse verdict. However, due to the rule on finality the appeal courts will not generally interfere with such a verdict.
A representative panel	**Bias/racial composition**
As there are 12 people on a jury, all of whom have been randomly selected, it should therefore represent a cross-section of society. Due to the number of people on a jury it is envisaged it will be able to make decisions without the influence of bias.	The jury may be biased for a number of reasons (media influence, personal views) and this bias may affect the verdict. There is no requirement for the jury to reflect the ethnic origin of the defendant, and this has been held in a number of cases not to breach a defendant's art.6 rights.
Certainty	**Nobbling**
The jury's verdict provides finality of answer in that the case is finished upon the verdict and is not open to dispute. The verdict cannot be misinterpreted in any way.	Juror/jurors may be intimidated or threatened into returning a verdict, which they would otherwise not have done. The jury system is not impenetrable from outside influences.

Alternatives to Jury Trial

The final point to note in relation to juries is that, although they are predominantly the main way in which an indictable offence will be tried by the Crown, they are not the only way as, over recent years, other alternatives to jury trial have been developed. 7–037

Trial by Judge Alone

The total abolition of juries in all criminal cases has been considered by the Government on a number of occasions, although this consideration has not been taken forward yet. The arguments for the abandonment of the jury are that it would remove the possibilities of jury bias, perverse verdicts and jury nobbling and the "Diplock courts" in Northern Ireland are viewed as a prime example of how well trial by judge alone can work. The Diplock courts were set up in 1972, on the recommendations of Lord Diplock, to hear cases involving serious terrorist threats where a fair hearing by a jury (due to instances of jury nobbling) could not be expected. Lord Justice Auld in his *Review of the Criminal Courts* (2001) also supported the notion of trial by judge alone, stating that: 7–038

> **In short, trial by judge alone, if defendants wish it, has a potential for providing a simpler, more efficient, fairer and more open form of procedure than is now available in many jury trials, with the added advantage of a fully reasoned judgment.**

There are also many arguments against the abandonment of the jury trial, these mainly being that the judge will often not be of the same social class as the defendant and therefore will not have the social awareness that is brought by a jury; that the judge will be biased in favour of the prosecution; and that the judge will be case hardened which will be projected onto the defendant.

The Government have provided for trial by judge alone in certain specified cases, namely, serious or complex fraud trials, under s.43 of the CJA 2003 (although this is not yet in force), and for cases where they may be a danger of jury tampering (s.44 of the CJA 2003).

The first case to tried by a judge alone under the provisions of s.44 of the CJA 2003 is **R. v Twomey** [2010] 1 W.L.R. 630. In **R. v Twomey** the defendants were tried for serious offences resulting from an armed robbery, two previous trials in the matter had collapsed due to jury tampering and an interim application was made for the third trial to be tried by judge alone. This application was initially refused as the judge was of the belief that sufficient measures could be taken to reduce the risk of jury tampering to an acceptable level (albeit that these measures would cost £1.5 million and involve 32 police officers' time for a period of six months). The Crown appealed to the Court of Appeal. In allowing the appeal the Court of Appeal held 7–039 that the right to trial by jury was so deeply entrenched in the constitution that, unless statutory language indicated otherwise, the highest standard of proof (namely, beyond reasonable doubt) as to why a trial by jury should not be allowed was required. Section 44 did not give a discretion; the judge was *required* to make an order of trial without jury if there was evidence of a real and present danger of jury tampering related to the whole trial process and, that even after making due allowance for any reasonable steps that might address and minimise the danger, the judge should be sure that there would be a sufficient likelihood of jury tampering to make trial by judge alone necessary. This would require consideration of the feasibility of the proposed steps and their cost, and also whether such steps might lead to an incurable compromise of the jury's objectivity. The defendants were convicted and appealed their convictions, partly on the basis of the trial by judge alone (**R. v Twomey** [2011] EWCA Crim 8). The Court of Appeal, in dismissing the appeals, held that if trial by judge alone were not permitted then a defendant would be entitled to trial by jury even where the court was satisfied that there was a real and present and unavoidable danger of jury tampering; that would produce an unfair trial and emasculate provisions designed to avoid jury tampering.

Trial by a Panel of Judges

7-040 Although trial by a panel of judges may remove the possibility that a single judge is biased towards the defendant in some way, it would require a complete restructuring of the criminal justice system that can simply not be afforded. To have a panel of three or five judges sat in each case triable on indictment would push the criminal justice bill up massively (by hundreds of thousands of pounds). The reason that magistrates are employed in the majority of criminal cases is to avoid such cost implications.

Trial by Judge and Laypeople

7-041 This method would effectively be a consolidation of the two systems that we have at present (magistrates and Crown Court judges). Here, judges would sit alongside two laypeople (most likely magistrates but they could also be randomly selected members of the public) to decide the case. This system does seem to have a lot of advantages in that there would be reduced potential for bias and there would be a certain element of cross-society representation. However, one of the drawbacks could be that the laypeople acquiesce to the judge in their decisions due to his standing in the court.

Summary

1. Juries have existed in one form or another since their introduction into the English legal system by King Henry II in the 1100s. The modern-day role of the jury is to be the trier of fact responsible for determining the guilt or innocence of the defendant who stands before them as the accused.

2. Jury independence is a sacred principle of the jury system and so a jury should be free from judicial and other pressures and its final decision in the case as to the defendant's guilt or innocence cannot be challenged. Neither a judge, nor any other party, is allowed to intervene or interfere with the jury's decision-making process.
3. To be eligible to be selected as a juror, an individual must be between the ages of 18 and 75, be registered on the electoral roll, have lived in the UK for at least five years and not be either disqualified or mentally disordered. A person will be classed as disqualified for life if they have been sentenced to life imprisonment, detained at His Majesty's pleasure, been imprisoned for public protection or for a period of five years or more. Disqualification from jury service for 10 years will occur where a person has served a prison term in the last 10 years, or received a community sentence or a suspended sentence.
4. The CJA 2003 opened up the potential number of jury candidates by removing the restriction on persons such as judges, lawyers and those employed within the criminal justice system from sitting on a jury.
5. An individual may be excused from jury service where there are exceptional circumstances that would make it inappropriate for the potential juror to sit on a jury at that time. Most persons excused from jury service receive a deferral and therefore must sit as a juror at some point in the near future.
6. A jury will consist of 12 individuals who have been randomly selected by a computer at the Central Summoning Bureau to serve on the jury. There will, on average, be 20 people summoned to sit on each jury so as to ensure that there are at least 12 appropriate individuals who can hear the case.
7. Even once selected, it is not definite that any individual will be on the final jury panel as jurors may be dismissed due to lack of capacity, or because they have been deemed unsuitable following jury vetting checks. Jury vetting checks are investigations into the potential jurors' criminal records or, in certain cases, the jurors' wider background.
8. The whole jury can be challenged (under a challenge to the array) where it is submitted that the jury is not representational. If this challenge is successful then a fresh jury will be empanelled into the case. The right of an individual to sit on the jury can also be challenged (by way of a challenge for cause) where the defendant knows a juror, or it is known that the juror is disqualified or ineligible for jury service. The prosecution also has the right to request a juror to stand by.
9. The discussions that occur within the confines of the jury room are privileged and, after the verdict, they cannot be discussed or investigated by any person. If a person does divulge deliberations that occurred within the jury room then an offence may have been committed.

10. Initially, the jury should attempt to reach a consensus and return a unanimous verdict. If jurors are unable to agree then they are permitted to return a majority verdict after a period of at least two hours' discussion and on the direction of the judge.

Key Cases

Case	Court	Salient point
Bushell's Case (1670)	Court of Common Pleas	Jurors are to be independent of the judge; they are charged with the role of determining the guilt or innocence of the accused and are the sole arbitrators of fact. The judge in the case cannot interfere with the decision of the jury.
R. v Abdroikov [2007]	House of Lords	A defendant should be tried by an impartial and independent tribunal. If a fair-minded and informed observer would conclude that there was a real possibility of jury bias then there would be a violation of the defendant's fair trial rights. Having a police officer or CPS lawyer on the jury would not automatically deem the jury impartial but it would raise the question that would need to be carefully considered by the judge.
Hanif and Khan v the UK (2012)	European Court of Human Rights	Agreed with the decision in R. v Abdroikov and set out that if the police officer on the jury is an acquaintance with an officer involved in the trial, or if there is disputed police evidence, then the inclusion of the said police officer on the jury would mean that it would not be impartial and that there would be a violation of the defendant's art.6 rights.

Case	Court	Salient point
R. v Sheffield Crown Court Ex p. Brownlow [1980]	Court of Appeal	The legality of the practice of jury vetting was questioned; the court held that it was unconstitutional and condemned the practice.
R. v Mason [1980]	Court of Appeal	The court approved the unauthorised jury vetting that had occurred; it held that jury vetting was a valid method of preventing a criminal offence being committed.
R. v Danvers [1982]	Crown Court	There was no requirement in law that the jury should contain a member of the defendant's ethnic or racial background; the jury members were randomly selected and consequently provided a representation of a cross-section of society.
Attorney-General v Associated Newspapers Ltd [1994]	House of Lords	The scope of s.8 Contempt of Court Act 1981 is wide enough to cover any person, be they a juror or not, who publicises the content of jury deliberations.
R. v Mirza [2004]	House of Lords	The common law rule relating to jury secrecy did not contravene art.6 of the ECHR and was necessary to ensure that the jury decision making process is unfettered by concerns over potential retribution or ridicule.

Further Reading

G. Daly and R. Pattenden, "Racial bias and the English criminal trial" [2005] 64(3) C.L.J. 678–710.

Considers the issues with racial bias on juries following the decision in **R. v Mirza**. Discusses whether the principles in **R. v Mirza** breaches a defendant's fair trial rights.

P. Darbyshire, "The lamp that shows that freedom lives—is it worth the candle?" [1991] Crim. L.R. 740–752.

Considers the role of the jury in criminal trials and discusses whether they are still appropriate in the courtroom.

P. Darbyshire, "What can we learn from published jury research? Findings for the Criminal Courts Review" [2001] Crim. L.R. 970–979.

Research into individual accounts of jury service, with recommendations as how to restructure the jury trial process.

P.R. Ferguson, "The criminal jury in England and Scotland: the confidentiality principle and the investigation of impropriety" [2006] 10(3) E. & p. 180–211.

Considers the fact that impropriety in jury deliberations are only exceptionally investigated, which risks the fact that serious impropriety is therefore overlooked, and provides recommendations as how this could be remedied.

S. Lloyd-Bostock, "The Jubilee Line Jurors: does their experience strengthen the argument for judge-only trial in long and complex fraud cases?" [2007] Crim. L.R. 255–273.

Discusses the findings of interviews with jury members on a fraud trial, including understanding of judicial directions and the evidence, and considers whether judge only trials would be better placed in such cases.

K. Quinn, "Jury bias and the European Convention on Human Rights: a well-kept secret?" [2004] Crim. L.R. 998–1014.

Discusses how well jury trial sits with the art.6 Convention right and how jury bias is dealt with. Also considers the secrecy rules and the case of **R. v Mirza**.

J.N. Taylor, "Juries: bias—presence of police officer or employee of Crown Prosecution Service on jury" [2008] Crim. L.R. 134–138.

Analyses the case of *R. v Abdroikov* and the impact on the fairness of a trial by having a serving police officer or CPS officer on the jury.

P. Thornton, "Trial by jury: 50 years of change" [2004] Crim. L.R. 683–701; [2004] Crim. L.R. Supp (50th Anniversary Edition), 119–137.

Reviews the changing nature of the jury between 1954–2004.

Law Commission Report, *Contempt of Court (1): Juror Misconduct and Internet Publications* (Law Com No.304, 9 December 2013).

Self Test Questions

1. To be eligible to sit as a juror a person must be:
- **(a)** registered on the electoral roll
- **(b)** between the ages of 18 and 65
- **(c)** have lived in the UK for at least three years
- **(d)** own their own property

2. A person is disqualified from serving as a juror for 10 years if they have:
- **(a)** been cautioned by the police
- **(b)** received a speeding ticket
- **(c)** received a community sentence
- **(d)** been declared bankrupt

3. Routine jury vetting involves checking a juror's:
   (a) credit score
   (b) employment history
   (c) professional qualifications
   (d) criminal record
4. An individual's right to sit on a jury can be challenged on the grounds that:
   (a) he looks like he will convict the defendant
   (b) a witness in the case knows him
   (c) the defendant lives in the same town as him
   (d) the jury is unrepresentative
5. Section 20D of the Juries Act 1974 applies to:
   (a) the court
   (b) the defendant
   (c) the prosecutor
   (d) any person who discloses details of the jury room deliberations

The Civil Justice System

8

CHAPTER OVERVIEW

In this chapter we will:

- **Explain who the parties to a claim may be.**
- **Consider the evolution of the civil justice system.**
- **Discuss the Civil Procedure Rules 1998.**
- **Explain the civil law jurisdiction.**
- **Consider the ways in which a claim can be settled and enforced.**
- **Look at the alternatives to commencing litigation.**

Summary

Further Reading

Self Test Questions

Introduction

8-001 The civil law silently regulates everyone's lives, although most individuals do not become aware of its existence until a certain matter dictates that they need to become involved with a specific aspect of it. Civil law as a whole governs issues between private individuals (as opposed to criminal law which is the State regulating society's behaviour). It deals with matters concerning rights, obligations, and duties, and it covers a variety of different aspects such as personal injury claims, matters of family law, the buying and selling of houses, and employment law, through to wills, trusts and issues of inheritance, and contract law disputes, etc. For example, if a person has a slip, trip or fall at work (remember those adverts?!), or a car crash which causes an injury, then they will turn to the civil law to try and achieve a remedy for their injuries; they can sue for compensation. Or, if an individual employs a builder to build an extension on their house and the builder refuses to complete the work as agreed, the aggrieved party can bring a claim in civil law against the builder for breach of contract. The civil law, therefore, is involved in many aspects of a person's life and it is virtually impossible for an individual to go through life without encountering at least one limb of the civil law. This is especially as the reach of the civil law extends to the everyday mundane matters in which we all partake, such as buying a ticket to travel on a train or bus or purchasing a chocolate bar from a shop; in these instances we are using the law of contract, often without even being aware of doing so.

The Parties to a Claim

8-002 The parties to a civil claim will be given a particular title depending on what their involvement in a case is and what the action is concerned with. The party bringing the claim is known as the claimant, and the person against whom the claim is being brought is known as the defendant. Prior to the coming into force of the Civil Procedure Rules 1998 (CPR) in April 1999 (see "The Civil Procedure Rules 1998", at **8-007**), the now "claimant" was known as the plaintiff. This change in party title was born out of the principle that the civil system needed to be simplified so that it was understandable, for the most part, by a layperson coming to the proceedings. The term "plaintiff" was thought to be antiquated; the meaning could not easily be identified on first sight, whereas the term "claimant" is more understandable in its meaning and application. As this change in UK terminology (plaintiff to claimant) is still relatively new, the title of plaintiff can still be found in the older law reports.

However, different jurisdictions can use different terminology for the person bringing the cause of action and it is worth being aware of these to avoid confusion. In Scotland, the term "pursuer" is used to describe the party bringing a claim, whereas Hong Kong and America still refer to the party bringing the claim as the plaintiff. The term "defendant" has remained consistent throughout the changes, and most other jurisdictions also describe the person against whom the claim is being brought as the defendant, although in Scotland the word is changed slightly to "defender".

These party titles (claimant and defendant) are the most commonly used within civil law, however, a party may be known by a different title depending on the type of action being brought. If an application (such as an interim application for an injunction) is being made to the court, then the party making the application will be known as the applicant and the person responding to the application will be known as the respondent. Likewise, if the proceedings involve a petition to the court (such as in the case of divorce), then the person bringing the petition will be called the petitioner and the party responding to the petition will be known as the respondent. If the proceedings involve the enforcement of a money order, then the party issuing the proceedings will be the judgment creditor and the opposing party the judgment debtor, and, finally, if the matter is one involving an appeal, then the party appealing will be known as the appellant and the party against whom the appeal is being brought will be the respondent.

Standard of Proof

As the civil law deals with disputes between individuals, and as the remedies are often monetary in nature (as opposed to loss of liberty as in criminal matters), the standard of proof that needs to be shown by a party bringing the claim is of a lesser standard than that in criminal law. To prove a claim within the criminal law system, the party bringing the case (prosecuting) needs to prove the case "beyond reasonable doubt" (see Ch.9), whereas in the civil justice system the party bringing a claim need only prove the case "on the balance of probabilities" to be successful. The term "on the balance of probabilities" basically means that it has been shown that there is more than a 50/50 chance that the facts of the case are as the claimant asserts. The burden of satisfying the standard of proof rests on the party bringing the claim (the claimant). 8-003

History of the Civil Justice System

The civil justice system has developed slowly and quite sporadically. To begin with there were two distinct systems of law—these being common law and civilian law (civil law is still used by many European countries such as France and the Netherlands). The use of these different systems caused a great deal of confusion, which then resulted in delay and inefficiency. As time moved on, the English system moved away from the concept of civil law and common law, and equity elements were developed and transformed into the systems found within the modern English courts. 8-004

Another factor that limited the effectiveness and usefulness of the earlier court system was that the majority of the civil courts were only found in London. This meant that a large number of people who would have benefited from accessing the court system to resolve their disputes were excluded from doing so. Litigation in the courts was highly complex, overly convoluted by the lawyers and the judges and, as a result, very expensive. The system was neither accessible nor user-friendly (only the very rich could really access and benefit from it), and it was, essentially, not fit for purpose. To redress the balance and to open up the possibility of litigation to the masses, a restructuring and expansion of the civil courts began in the mid-1800s. County courts were introduced across the country so that people were not geographically barred from using the court system, and this initiative was swiftly followed by the introduction of the Superior Courts (consisting of the Court of Appeal, High Court, and Crown Court), and then, slightly later, the High Court was split into the three separate divisions (Family, Chancery and King's Bench) that still exist today.

8–005 Despite the reform and expansion of the civil court jurisdiction, the whole civil system was still under-performing and struggling under antiquated and elaborate procedures in place. Delay in the hearing of cases was rife, with the average waiting time for a case to be heard being at least two years for the county court and up to five years for the High Court; and the costs accrued were often astronomical. The system was obviously unsatisfactory and in need of urgent reform.

In 1953 the Evershed Committee carried out one of the first of many reviews of the civil justice system (Lord Chancellor's Department, *Final Report of the Committee on Supreme Court Practice and Procedure* (1953), Cmnd 8878). This review was swiftly followed by the Winn Committee review (Lord Chancellor's Department, *Report of the Committee on Personal Injuries Litigation* (1968), Cmnd 369) and the Cantley Committee review (Lord Chancellor's Department, *Report of the Personal Injuries Litigation Procedure Working Party* (1979), Cmnd 7476). Each of these individual reviews recognised that the main problem with the civil justice system as it was then (see below for further discussion) was that the delays experienced and the costs accrued were disproportionate with the majority of the claims being brought. However, despite highlighting the failings of the system, it provided few suggestions to remedy the situation. As a result, the first major review that had any impact on the *culture* of the system was the Civil Justice Review 1988.

8–006 The Civil Justice Review 1988 undertook a full examination of the system and concluded that the delay experienced by litigants was a fundamental issue of the justice system that needed redressing. The Review appreciated that delay had a negative impact on all those involved in litigation (the defendant, the claimant and any witnesses, etc.), that a lengthy delay could cause valuable evidence to be less reliable or even unavailable, and that such problems would, and did, inevitably result in the erosion of public confidence in the whole civil justice system. To address the issues identified by the Review, it recommended that the county court's jurisdiction be widened so that it could cope with more complex and demanding cases, thereby relieving some of the burden from the High Court (this recommendation was later enacted by the CLSA 1990). However, the extension of the county courts' powers did not directly deal with the issue of delay as, simply shifting the bulk of work from the High Court to the county court did not miraculously reduce the delay in waiting for a case to be heard but simply shifted the emphasis away from the High Court towards the county court, which was already facing delays in excess of two years due to the backlog of cases waiting to be heard.

The Helibron-Hodge Committee 1993 followed the Civil Justice Review 1988. This committee was set up by the Law Society in conjunction with the Bar Council and in its review of the system it concluded that the courts should be charged with taking over the management of the cases and that the majority of potential litigants were discouraged from commencing court proceedings due to the complexity and cost involved. These findings were not ground-breaking, as they mainly echoed the conclusions from prior reports. Again, little action resulted from the report and the unsatisfactory status quo was maintained until the conclusion of the Woolf Report in 1995.

The Civil Procedure Rules 1998

In 1994, Lord Woolf undertook an in-depth and all-encompassing review of the civil justice system as it was then. This review, published in 1996, was called *Access to Justice* and it was charged with exploring all aspects of the civil justice system. Lord Woolf commented in his interim report (before the publication of the final report) that the need to undertake such a review stemmed from the fact that: 8-007

> **Throughout the common law world there is acute concern over the many problems which exist in the resolution of disputes by the civil courts. The problems are basically the same. They concern the processes leading to the decisions made by the courts, rather than the decisions themselves. The process is too expensive, too slow and too complex. It places many litigants at a considerable disadvantage when compared to their opponents. The result is inadequate access to justice and an inefficient and ineffective system.**

While reviewing the area of civil litigation in England and Wales, Lord Woolf identified a number of specific problems with the procedure. These problems included the facts that:

- the environment in which litigation was conducted was an adversarial one;
- litigation was expensive and unaffordable;
- the costs incurred were disproportionate to the cases brought;
- there was no certainty as to the cost in a case;
- the costs incurred were not competitive;
- the time taken to progress a case from the initial claim to a final hearing was too long;
- the time taken to reach settlement was excessive;
- there were delays in obtaining a hearing date;
- the time taken by the hearing itself was too long;
- the procedures in place were too complex;
- legal assistance and advice was often unavailable; and
- civil justice carried a low priority status.

8-008 This is a rather a long list of flaws and problems in the civil justice system, obviously not a satisfactory state of affairs. So as to make the main issues clear, Lord Woolf succinctly (and helpfully) summarised this long list in identifying three main problem areas, these being cost, delay, and complexity (all three being interrelated and stemming from the uncontrolled nature of the litigation process). One of the main flaws that Lord Woolf voiced in relation to the civil justice system was that there was no clear judicial responsibility for managing individual cases or for the overall administration of the civil courts, which, in turn, resulted in the excessive cost implications, the long delays, and the needless complexity of the cases as identified above.

To combat these problems, Lord Woolf's review made numerous suggestions and recommendations on how to improve the civil justice system. The main drive behind the recommendations was for the legal system to accept that there was no alternative but to undertake a fundamental shift in the responsibility for the management of civil litigation. This shift was to involve the responsibility, which then lay on litigants and their legal advisers, moving away from the individual and being assumed by the courts. It was acknowledged by Lord Woolf that such a shift in emphasis would require a radical change in culture for all. It would place a greater responsibility on the judges and the courts in respect of the way a case progressed through the system to a final hearing, and also for the form that the final hearing would take. The system and the procedures therefore needed to be dramatically changed to provide a framework that would allow judicial control to be exercised effectively.

8-009 Following this in-depth review, the Civil Procedure Rules 1998 (CPR) were implemented and brought into force on 26 April 1999. Since this date all civil litigation has been conducted under the provisions found within the CPR (the most recent update of the CPR came into effect on 31 December 2020, following Brexit). The CPR is a vast document and so, to be accessible to legal representatives and laypeople alike, it is split into 82 separate Parts—each Part dealing with a different aspect of civil procedure. Each Part is then split down further into a number of individual rules and, to provide further detail on how each rule and Part should be interpreted, the Parts are then supplemented by a Practice Direction (PD), which provides the necessary information regarding the practical application of the rules. Essentially, the rules set out the substance, and the practice directions add the detail.

The CPR provides guidance and rules for all the different situations that may occur during a civil claim, so, for example, Pt 1 sets out the Overriding Objective of the CPR, Pt 3 contains the rules on Case Management Powers, Pt 6 deals with the Service of Documents, Pt 7 provides details on How to Start Proceedings, and Pt 32 lists how Evidence should be dealt with in civil cases.

Over to you

Imagine that you have been charged with drafting the overriding objective for the civil courts of England and Wales. What would you include in it? What do you think the most fundamentally important principle of the courts should be?

THE OVERRIDING OBJECTIVE

As indicated above, Part 1 of the CPR sets out the Overriding Objective of the whole procedural code. Part 1 provides: 8–010

(1) These Rules are a new procedural code with the overriding objective of enabling the court to deal with cases justly.
(2) Dealing with a case justly includes, so far as is practicable:
  (a) ensuring that the parties are on an equal footing;
  (b) saving expense;
  (c) dealing with the case in ways which are proportionate:
    (i) to the amount of money involved;
    (ii) to the importance of the case;
    (iii) to the complexity of the issues; and
    (iv) to the financial position of each party.
  (d) ensuring that it is dealt with expeditiously and fairly; and
  (e) allotting to it an appropriate share of the court's resources, while taking into account the need to allot resources to other cases.

The main purpose of the CPR is to enable the court to deal with cases justly. So as to achieve this aim, the application of the Overriding Objective is not an optional or discretionary one, but one that must be applied rigorously and properly in any case that requires the court to exercise any power given to it by the rules or when it interprets the rules in any way.

The duty to abide by the Overriding Objective is not just imposed upon the courts but also upon all parties to the litigation. One of the reasons for this imposition on the individual parties to a case is to stop parties employing underhand tactics in an attempt to avoid adverse decisions in a case. For example, if one party to litigation (for illustrative purpose, let us say the defendant) can afford the most expensive lawyers in the country, but the opponent (the claimant) has very limited means, then the requirement to abide by the Overriding Objective should prevent the financial difference between the two parties impacting negatively on the case. For example, the wealthier of the two parties, the defendant, would be banned from running up large costs as a tactic to deter the less wealthy party, the claimant, from continuing with the case. 8–011

Part 1 of the CPR also sets out the court's duty to manage cases actively so as to further the Overriding Objective—this is done by the provision of a very clear and concise list of case management duties. Rule 1.4 states that active case management includes:

> (a) encouraging the parties to co-operate with each other in the conduct of the proceedings;
> (b) identifying the issues at an early stage;
> (c) deciding promptly which issues need full investigation and trial and accordingly disposing summarily of the others;
> (d) deciding the order in which issues are to be resolved;
> (e) encouraging the parties to use an alternative dispute resolution procedure if the court considers that appropriate, and facilitating the use of such procedure;
> (f) helping the parties to settle the whole or part of the case;
> (g) fixing timetables or otherwise controlling the progress of the case;
> (h) considering whether the likely benefits of taking a particular step justify the cost of taking it;
> (i) dealing with as many aspects of the case as it can on the same occasion;
> (j) dealing with the case without the parties needing to attend at court;
> (k) making use of technology; and
> (l) giving directions to ensure that the trial of a case proceeds quickly and efficiently.

8–012 Many of the points are simple common sense, such as encouraging the parties to co-operate with each other; obviously, if the parties can co-operate with each other then issues could potentially be resolved more quickly. By ensuring co-operation, the case could be dealt with expeditiously, thereby saving expense and ultimately fulfilling the aim of the Overriding Objective. In the same manner, the courts are required to make use of technology in relation to their case management duties. By using modern technology, such as computers, the courts will again satisfy the Overriding Objective; for example, requiring the parties to use computers will mean that information can be passed quickly between them (instantaneously via email compared with approximately three days by way of the traditional postal system), and so the case will be dealt with expeditiously. Also, demanding that the parties use resources such as standard word-processed forms will help to avoid potential problems with court documents (such as illegible handwriting) and will decrease the need for precious court resources to be spent on an individual case.

CASE MANAGEMENT POWERS

8–013 To enable the court to ensure that the Overriding Objective is adhered to in all cases, and to give effect to Lord Woolf's recommendations, the courts have been granted extensive case management powers under Pt 3 of the CPR. This Part now requires the courts to take on the main responsibilities as to the management and progression of an individual case, and in doing so relieves the litigants and their legal advisers of the high level of responsibility that they once bore.

Rule 3.1 sets out a list of the ways in which a court can actively manage a case under the CPR. Each of these individual powers relates back to the courts' duty under r.1.4 and, ultimately, to the Overriding Objective. For instance, one of the case management powers found at r.3.1(2)(b) is that the court has the power to adjourn or bring forward a hearing; this power links into the duty found at r.1.4(2)(g) to fix an appropriate timetable for the case and to control the overall progression of the case, thereby furthering the Overriding Objective to deal with cases expeditiously and justly. The court has all these options available to it to use, but of course it will only use those powers that are appropriate in each individual case so as to achieve the Overriding Objective.

The court, under r.3.3, does not have to wait for a party to a case to raise a specific issue before making an order, but can make such an order on its own initiative.

Over to you

To illustrate how and why this power may be invoked, consider the following example:

> **Jim is currently suing Bob for damages for personal injury following a car accident. Their trial is due to begin on Friday. On the Wednesday morning before the trial, the judge in the case decides to review the case file to check that all procedures have been complied with so far. The judge notices that the expert report commissioned by Jim as to his injuries was only received by the defendant the day before (Tuesday) instead of three weeks before the trial date, as required by the case timetable. This report has the potential to impact the outcome of the case greatly, and the defendant will need sufficient time to assimilate the information from the report.**

You are the judge in the case. What should you do?

In such a case the judge may be of the opinion that the defence will request an adjournment at the start of the trial so that it can deal properly with the contents of the report. Instead of waiting until the day of the trial for an adjournment application to be made, the judge, by way of the case management powers, can order an adjournment immediately. This will then allow the defendant to be able to prepare fully for trial (so that both parties are on an equal footing and so that the case is dealt with justly) and will avoid wasting court resources and increasing the case costs as none of the parties, nor their legal teams, will need to attend court on the original first day of trial. 8–014

The court will always be mindful of its case management powers and duties whilst a case progresses, and there are various specific points over the course of a case at which the court will generally conduct a formal review of case progression and assess the needs of the case with regards to its powers. The formal introduction of case management powers to the court does appear, anecdotally, to have helped alleviate a number of problems in the civil justice system as identified by Lord Woolf in his interim report.

INTERPRETATION OF THE CPR

8-015 When the CPR was drafted, it was decided that the style of language used for the rules should be plain, ordinary English, and that complicated legalese should be left behind. The reasoning behind the decision to abandon the complicated and often antiquated legal terminology normally associated with the English legal system was that the use of such language alienated the layperson coming to the law; as, predominantly, users of the legal system were (and still are) people without legal education or experience it was thought that many people were put off commencing and/or continuing with a claim due to the fact they simply could not understand a lot of the procedures involved in cases due to the complicated terminology used. Lord Woolf, in his Final Report, commented on the rationale behind introducing simpler and clearer language by stating that:

> **I said in the interim report that one of my aims was to modernise terminology. I have not approached this dogmatically but on the basis that terminology should be changed where it is useful to do so. I have sought to remove expressions which are meaningless or confusing to non-lawyers (such as "relief" when used to mean a remedy) or where a different expression would more adequately convey what is involved (such as "disclosure" of documents instead of the archaic "discovery"). The various terms for methods of starting a case, such as writ, summons, originating application, will all be replaced by a "claim". The word "plaintiff" will be replaced by "claimant".**
>
> **I have suggested that the word "pleading" should be replaced by "statement of case". Although it is a very familiar expression to lawyers and in some respects a convenient one, the word has become too much identified with a process which the legal profession itself readily acknowledges has to change. This is an instance where a change of language will, I believe, help to underpin a change of attitude and a real change of practice to a more open and straightforward method of stating a claim or defence.**
>
> **I recognise that changes of terminology are discomforting and temporarily inconvenient for those who are very familiar with the existing expressions. But, as I made clear in the interim report, the system of civil justice and the rules which govern it must be broadly comprehensible not only to an inner circle of initiates but to non-professional advisers and, so far as possible, to ordinary people of average ability who are unlikely to have more than a single encounter with the system.**

The Home Office, which was the department responsible for the CPR at the time of their inception, was so committed to the use of plain English as a way to demystify the legal profession that it was awarded the gold level "Crystal Mark" for the use of plain English by the Plain English Campaign; the CPR being one of the documents awarded the Crystal Mark. 8–016

Even though plain English is used throughout the CPR, problems as to the interpretation of a rule can and still do occur. It is commonly accepted that if there is an ambiguity or query over a word's meaning then, initially, the natural meaning of the word should be employed wherever possible (think back to Ch.2, "Judicial Reasoning", on statutory interpretation and the use of the literal rule). Lord Woolf (again in his *Final Report*) anticipated that there would occasionally be problems and questions as to the meaning of some of the words used and suggested that where this did occur the courts should look to the Overriding Objective as a compass to guide them on the right course. He stated that:

> **Every word in the rules should have a purpose, but every word cannot sensibly be given a minutely exact meaning. Civil procedure involves more judgment and knowledge than the rules can directly express. In this respect, rules of court are not like an instruction manual for operating a piece of machinery. Ultimately their purpose is to guide the court and the litigants towards the just resolution of the case. Although the rules can offer detailed directions for the technical steps to be taken, the effectiveness of those steps depends upon the spirit in which they are carried out. That in turn depends on an understanding of the fundamental purpose of the rules and of the underlying system of procedure.**

Over time, the Court of Appeal has added further guidance as to the way in which the CPR should be interpreted and has set limits upon how the Overriding Objective should be used, holding that the courts should refer to the Overriding Objective whenever the rules are unclear as to their meaning but, when the rules are clear as to their meaning, then the courts should not resort to the Overriding Objective in an attempt to assist a deserving case when the plain meaning of the rules unfortunately prevents justice being done. This principle of interpretation is set out in the case of **Vinos v Marks & Spencer** [2001] C.P. Rep. 12 where Lord Justice Gibbson stated that: 8–017

> **The construction of the Civil Procedure Rules, like the construction of any legislation, primary or delegated, requires the application of ordinary canons of construction, though the Civil Procedure Rules, unlike their predecessors, spell out in Part 1 the overriding objective of the new procedural code. The court must seek to give effect to that objective when it exercises any power given to it by the rules or interprets any rule. But the use in rule 1.1(2) of the word "seek" acknowledges that the court can only do what is possible. The language of the rule to be interpreted may be so clear and jussive that the court may not be able**

to give effect to what it may otherwise consider to be the just way of dealing with the case, though in that context it should not be forgotten that the principal mischiefs which the Civil Procedure Rules were intended to counter were excessive costs and delays. Justice to the defendant and to the interests of other litigants may require that a claimant who ignores [procedures] prescribed by the rules forfeits the right to have his claim tried.

Effectively, the Overriding Objective does not allow the court the luxury of discretion, even if the end result is unjust and in essence goes against the spirit of the Overriding Objective.

8-018 The courts must also take into account the HRA 1998 when considering the interpretation of the CPR. Section 3(1) of the HRA 1998 requires the court to read primary and subordinate legislation in a way that is compatible with the Convention rights whenever it is possible to do so. Consequently, problems may occur when the application of the plain meaning of a rule results in a decision that is incompatible with Convention rights, as occurred in the case of **Goode v Martin** [2002] 1 W.L.R. 1828.

In **Goode v Martin** the appellant (who was the claimant in the original proceedings) applied to amend her statement of claim out of time due to reliance upon details raised by the defendant. The trial judge refused the application and the claimant appealed contending that the refusal amounted to a breach of her right to a fair trial under art.6. Her appeal was allowed and the Court held that that both the requirement under CPR r.1.2(b) to give effect to the Overriding Objective of dealing with cases justly and the requirement in s.3(1) of the HRA 1998 to give effect to subordinate legislation in a way which was compatible with the Convention rights, enabled the Court to interpret the language of a rule of court so as to produce a just result and avoid unjustifiable infringement of a litigant's right of access to the Court. Not to allow the claimant to do so would prevent her from putting her amended claim before the Court and would therefore restrict her access to the Court in a way which could not be justified by any sound policy reason and that such a restriction could not be justified. In effect, the Court laid down the principle that the CPR must be interpreted in a way that is compatible with the HRA 1998 wherever possible, even if this interpretation goes directly against the plain meaning of the rule in question, effectively providing the Court with a degree of discretion in certain circumstances.

Overall, the introduction of the CPR has had a major and unprecedented impact upon the conduct of civil litigation, and it can be described as a massive overhaul of this area of law. No matter how small or large a claim is, if it is based within the civil law system, then the CPR will be applicable to it. It appears, nearly 25 years after enactment, that the CPR is an unmitigated success. Of course, civil law has its problems and issues, as all areas of the law do, but, on the whole, Lord Woolf's vision of a streamlined civil justice system seems to have mainly come to fruition.

Jurisdiction

The civil justice system has its own separate court and judicial hierarchy from that of the criminal justice system, although there is a degree of overlap between them, especially in relation to the appellate courts. In addition to the traditional civil court structure there are also a number of specialised tribunals (e.g. the Employment Tribunal and the Immigration Tribunal) that also are part of the collective civil justice system. 8–019

Magistrates' Courts

The first court, which is also generally considered to be the lowest court in the civil court hierarchy, is the magistrates' court. As considered in Ch.5, the magistrates' court is not just charged with considering criminal matters but its jurisdiction also extends a certain amount into the civil realm of the law. When the magistrates' court hears civil cases, the subject matter will normally be family law matters, regulatory law (such as liquor licensing appeals) or payment default matters (these are often local government matters and the claimant will be attempting to obtain missed payments for duties such as council tax from the defendant). The composition of the magistrates' court is the same as for the criminal justice system (see Ch.5). 8–020

County Court

The County Court is one of the busiest courts in the civil justice system, with its origins in the County Courts Act 1846. Back then, 491 County Courts existed as the Lord Chancellor wanted everyone to live within seven miles of a court. Under s.17 of the Crime and Courts Act 2013 (CCA 2013) there is now one single County Court that sits in 173 different locations due to budget constraints and efficiencies. The County Court is governed by the County Courts Act 1984 (as amended), and this statute provides the court with details of its jurisdiction, powers and types of cases it may hear. The types of cases that the County Court will hear include: 8–021

- contract disputes (no upper financial limit);
- tortious matters (no upper financial limit);
- claims for personal injury damages (up to a limit of £50,000);
- claims for debt; and
- landlord and tenant matters.

As the County Court is allowed to hear contract and tort claims (except for personal injury claims) with any financial value, this means that it shares jurisdiction with the High Court for a large number of cases. How cases are then allocated to either the County Court or High Court is set out in s.1 of the CLSA 1990 and the High Court and County Court Jurisdiction Order 1991 (SI 1991/724) (HCCCJO 1991), as amended by the High Court and County Courts Jurisdiction (Amendment) Order 2009 (SI 2009/577) and the High Court and County Court Jurisdiction (Amendment) Order 2014 (SI 2014/821) (HCCCJ(A)O 2014).

To determine which is the most appropriate venue for the case, the court will look to the criteria found in s.1(3) of the CLSA 1990, which focuses on the value of an action, the nature of the proceedings, the parties to the proceedings, the degree of complexity likely to be involved in any aspect of the proceedings, and the importance of any question likely to be raised by, or in the course of, the proceedings. The County Court is essentially the forum in which all but the most complicated civil law proceedings are handled. The HCCCJ(A)O 2014, which came into force on 22 April 2014, increased the financial limit for allowing non-personal injury claims in the High Court from £25,000 to £100,000, meaning that all non-personal injury claims under £100,000 must now be commenced in the County Court.

8–022 The different judges that may sit and hear cases in the county court are district judges, circuit judges and recorders (see Ch.6 for further detail on the judiciary). District judges in the civil courts are very similar to district judges in the criminal courts in respect of their qualifications and powers. In the County Court, district judges have the power to hear any undefended claim brought before them, to conduct trials in any case where the total claimed does not exceed £25,000, and to grant interim and final injunctions. The correct mode of address for a district judge in a county court is "Sir" or "Madam".

Circuit judges sitting in the county court will hear the multi-track cases (see below) that district judges are not permitted to preside over, as well as the more complex lower-value cases. Recorders can often be found sitting in county courts, and again their composition is the same as that of the recorders found in the criminal courts. Recorders are part-time members of the judiciary, and are normally practising lawyers as well; they possess the same powers as circuit judges. The correct mode of address for a circuit judge or a recorder in county court is "Your Honour".

An unusual and unique aspect of the county court is that it employs a specific individual to deal with the paperwork (i.e. service of documents) and enforcement of judgments. This individual is called the Court Bailiff. The High Court has no such employee and is reliant upon the general enforcement officers if it needs to enforce any judgment.

High Court

8–023 The High Court is part of the Superior Court system of England and Wales (along with the Crown Court and the Court of Appeal) and is made up of the Central Offices (based in the Royal Courts of Justice in London) and District Registries (which are spread throughout the country). The High Court is split into three separate divisions, and each division then specialises in different aspects of the civil law and has its own judiciary and administration. The three current divisions of the High Court are the:

- King's Bench Division (KBD);
- Family Division; and
- Chancery Division.

The Family Division deals with cases involving matters of family and matrimonial law; under the CCA 2013 there was the establishment of a new Family Court that took over the work of the Family Division and the family work both the County Court and Magistrates' Court. The Chancery Division deals with cases involving matters of trusts, probate, bankruptcy, intellectual property and land, etc. The KBD has a far larger remit than the other two divisions in the subject matter of the cases it hears, and it generally shares jurisdiction with the County Court. All the cases that do not fall into the Family or Chancery Division specialities will fall under the more general jurisdiction of the KBD. The KBD therefore deals with cases including:

- contract disputes;
- tortious matters;
- personal injury claims for over £50,000;
- judicial review; and
- defamation (these matters must only be dealt with by the High Court).

As well as the three divisions in the High Court, there are also a number of specialist courts within the divisions. These courts include the: **8–024**

- **Technology and Construction Court (KBD and Chancery Division)**—this court hears cases which involve technical or scientific details—common parties will be architects, accountants, IT suppliers, engineers, etc;
- **Administrative Court (KBD)**—this court reviews decisions of public bodies;
- **Admiralty Court (KBD)**—this court hears cases which involve shipping matters;
- **Commercial Court (KBD)**—this court hears cases which involve commercial matters;
- **Company Court (Chancery Division)**—this court deals with claims under a number of specialised company related statutes;
- **Patents Court (Chancery Division)**—this court hears cases involving patent and trademark issues.

Finally, just like the county courts, the High Court also has a number of different classifications of judges who sit within the three divisions; these are Masters of the KBD, district judges, and High Court judges. Masters will only be found within the Central Offices of the KBD in London. They have jurisdiction to deal with most matters that come before the court, and there is only one function that they do not have the jurisdiction to perform, this being that they cannot grant injunctions. The correct term of address is to call the judge "Master", whether they are male or female.

District judges are the district registry equivalent of the London-based Master (London has a Master, whereas Nottingham and Sheffield have district judges). Generally speaking, the county court district judge will be the same person as the High Court district judge (especially in small registry areas). A High Court district judge does not have the power to grant injunctions in the High Court, even though the same person may have the power to grant an injunction in **8–025** the county court. High Court judges hear the most complex and complicated cases in the High Court, as well as cases that involve a high financial value or are of public importance. High Court judges can grant injunctions and also act in an appellate capacity for the High Court.

Beyond these courts lie the higher appeal courts of the Court of Appeal (Civil Division) and the Supreme Court and further discussion of these courts can be found in Chs 2 and 9.

FIGURE 27 **The civil court hierarchy**

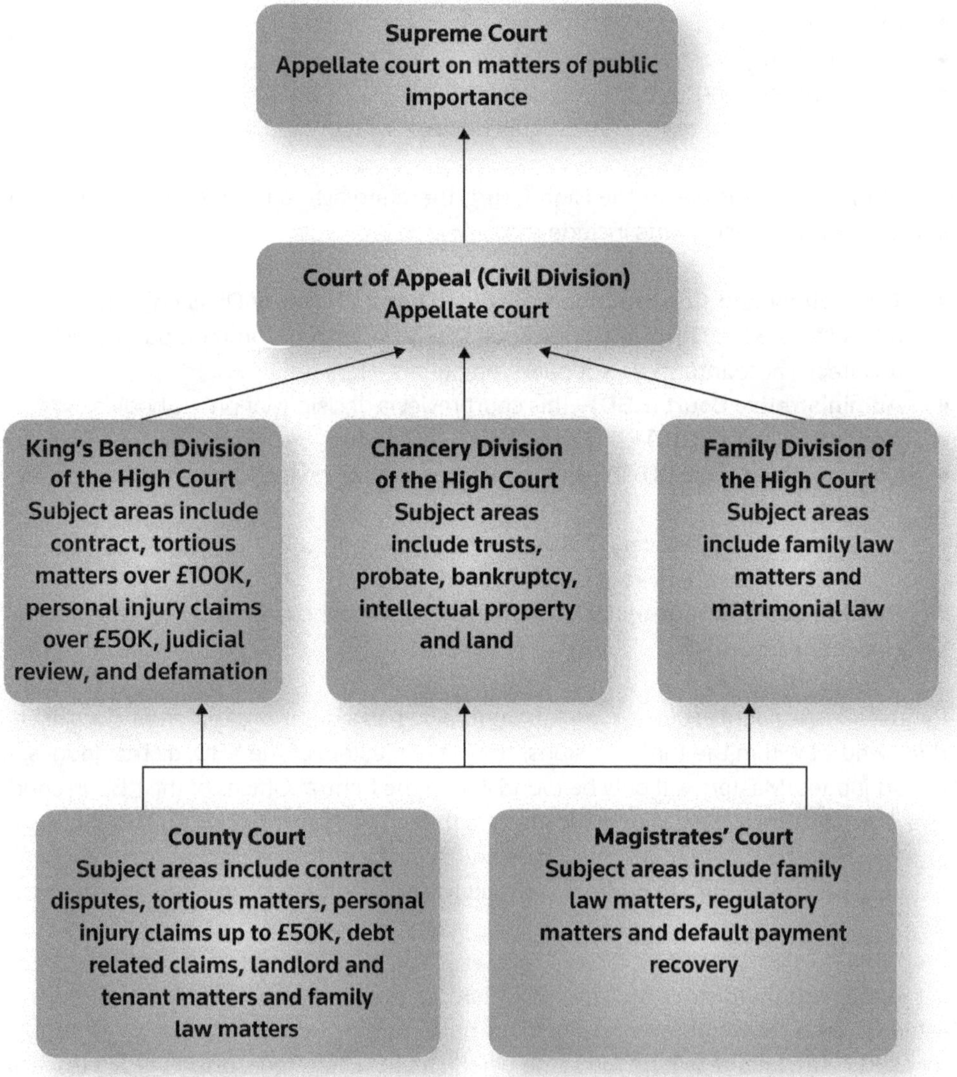

Court Tracks

As a result of the major review of the civil justice system, Lord Woolf devised a new system of allocating cases to the most appropriate court and judge at the commencement of the claim. The reason behind this is that often cases would begin in an inappropriate forum for their content (e.g. before a High Court judge when a district judge in the county court would have been more appropriate). This could then mean that a number of needless hearings would occur before the actual substantive hearing took place, thereby wasting valuable court time and resources, and increasing the case costs considerably. To combat this problem, Lord Woolf created three new civil court tracks, each one having clearly defined parameters as to the types of cases it would deal with and its own individual rules and procedures. These tracks are known as: **8–026**

- the small claims track;
- the fast-track; and
- the multi-track.

As a general rule, the small claims track hears cases where the value of the claim does not exceed £10,000 (or the claim is a personal injury one with the sum not exceeding £1,000); the fast-track deals with claims with a value of between £10,000 and £25,000 (with the exception that it can hear personal injury cases with a value not exceeding £50,000); and the multi-track, which hears claims with a value over £25,000 (or over £50,000 in personal injury matters).

SMALL CLAIMS TRACK

The small claims track is the most informal and simplest track in the civil system. It was created so that laypeople could easily access the justice system and resolve fairly minor issues between themselves without the need to consult a legal representative. The track is set up in such a way that it is accessible by individuals who have never had any experience of legal proceedings before. **8–027**

The types of cases generally suitable for the small claims track include consumer disputes, accident claims, disputes about the ownership of goods and disputes between a landlord and tenant. Cases involving a disputed allegation of dishonesty will not usually be suitable for the small claims track, and the court is not allowed to allocate to the small claims track certain claims in respect of harassment or unlawful eviction.

The small claims track is unique in that the parties to a case are permitted to present their own cases and do not need to seek legal representation (as is the norm with most other court proceedings). A lay representative (a person other than a party to a case) may exercise a right of audience under the Lay Representatives (Rights of Audience) Order 1999 (SI 1999/1225), so long as the client is present at the hearing. Also, employees of a corporate party are permitted to represent their employer in proceedings on this track. These rules are particularly helpful to parties to a claim who are nervous or shy about speaking in the proceedings as, it is hoped they will still be able to present their cases effectively by way of their chosen representatives without being forced to instruct costly legal counsel. Cases are usually held in public, but, to help ensure that the proceedings are not intimidating to any of the parties involved; this public forum is normally held within the confines of the judge's chambers. Judges' chambers are open to the public, but they are usually very small rooms, with just enough seating for the parties and their representatives, and maybe one or two chairs for members of the public. Due to their small confines it is very unusual for members of the public who are not involved in the case to sit in on such proceedings.

8–028 As small claims cases are informal in manner, the rules on evidence and conduct are also more relaxed than is usual in legal proceedings, and the court can adopt any method of proceeding that it believes is fair in the circumstances. The main aim of the court in such claims is to ensure that justice is done (remember the Overriding Objective) and to achieve this it is free to move away from the more traditional procedural rules. Laypersons bringing their claims are unlikely to be aware of the usual strict rules of evidence and so enforcing these strict rules would be likely to result in delays and unnecessary complications. This would then run counter to the Overriding Objective of ensuring that the case is dealt with expeditiously and proportionally.

The other rules that differ in the small claims court from those in other courts are that the parties are not required to give evidence on oath, cross-examination can be limited by the judge, the judge can question witnesses before any other person, and the judge can change the order of the proceedings by requiring all the evidence-in-chief to be given before cross-examination is commenced (see Ch.9). All of these changes are permitted to ensure that the Overriding Objective is adhered to and ultimately achieved.

FAST-TRACK

8–029 The fast-track was created to deal with cases where the financial value of the claim ranged between £10,000 and £25,000, or, in cases of personal injury claims, between £1,000 and £50,000. The normal trial length of a case on the fast-track should be one day or less (this will generally equate to five hours or less of the court's time). There is a standard rule that cases which exceed the financial limits of the fast-track, even by a few hundred pounds (so say £25,750) will be automatically allocated to the multi-track and will only be heard on the fast-track if all parties to the case agree to the case being heard in this forum.

Once the court has decided that the fast-track is the most appropriate track for a case, the court will then commence the detailed procedure required for such cases. The rules governing cases heard on the fast-track are provided for in Pt 28 of the CPR. The first step that the court will take in relation to a fast-track case is to set out the case timetable and consider an appropriate trial date. The trial date will either be a specific date (if the court deems there to be satisfactory information provided so far to do this) or the case will be given a three-week window in which the case must be heard (so as to provide the parties with a date to work towards), and which will be refined to a specific date later in the proceedings.

A typical timetable for a case that is to be heard on the fast-track is as set out below in Figure 28.

FIGURE 28 **A typical fast-track timetable**

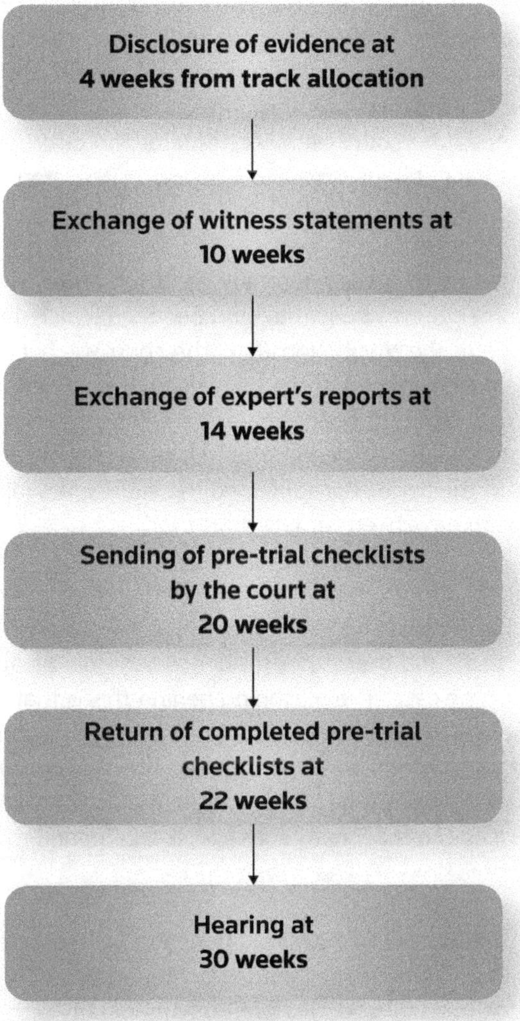

This timetable may look daunting as 30 weeks is basically a seven-month period, but when **8–030**
involved in litigation this time will pass very quickly and there are many things that need to

be done during this time. Instructing experts and obtaining an experts' report can take many months to achieve, there may be a number of witnesses to the incident that need interviewing and their evidence assessing, plus it is never known what the other side will disclose until they actually disclose it and therefore it is difficult to prepare swiftly. In fact, many parties to litigation find that the 30 weeks passes too quickly and that they are not fully prepared (or as prepared as they would like to be) when the trial date does eventually come around. It is also significantly shorter than the average 80 weeks for a claim prior to 1999.

To ensure that all parties are ready for trial when the trial date does come around, the court provides detailed directions in the form of a timetable (see Fig.28). The idea is that if the court can provide sufficient directions on any of the issues that might arise in the case then the case should be ready for trial by the time of its allotted court date. Although the directions are standard ones the court will seek to tailor the directions it gives to the specific requirements of the case, taking into account any of the steps that the parties have already taken.

The first direction that parties to a case normally need to comply with is the disclosure of a statement of the documents on which they propose to rely. Disclosure will generally be required within four weeks of the track allocation. The court will set out a specific date and time that the documents need to be disclosed by (e.g. by 4pm on 3 February 2014). The next stage is the exchange of witness statements; again, this will be a requirement to provide to the other party the statements of all the witnesses upon which a party proposes to rely. This should be done within 10 weeks of the track allocation, and the court will again set a specific date by which this direction needs to have been complied with.

8–031 By 14 weeks from the date of allocation the parties are required to have exchanged any expert reports being used within the case. The CPR limits the use of experts to one expert per party in relation to any expert field, and that expert evidence can only be adduced to a maximum of two expert fields in any one case. The reasoning behind this is that cases on the fast-track are expected to only last one working day and, if more than two experts were called to give evidence (or even to just produce written reports), then there is a distinct possibility that the case will extend beyond the one-day time limit and turn into a case that is, in reality, not suited to the fast-track; at the absolute maximum a fast-track trial period must not be longer than three weeks.

Once all the above direction dates have expired, the court will send to all parties a pre-trial checklist (otherwise known as a listing questionnaire). All parties to the case are then required to complete and return the pre-trial checklist promptly (generally within 14 days). The idea of this checklist is for the parties to a case to set out the actions that they have taken so far in their preparation. It should highlight any issues or incidents of non-compliance with the directions that could jeopardise the trial going ahead at the expected time. The return of the checklist to the court is a mandatory requirement, and if a party fails to comply with the direction they face the possibility of the claim or defence being thrown out. If a party does not return the completed form on time, then the court will issue an order stating that the above will happen without further notice unless a completed checklist is returned within seven days.

Once the court receives the completed forms, the trial date will be assessed for suitability. If no further issues have arisen, the court will either confirm the trial date (if a specific date has been already set), or, if a three-week window has been previously allocated, list the case for trial on a specific date.

The court should give directions as to the evidence, a trial timetable, and a trial time estimate. Here, the judge has the discretion to set directions as to how long different stages of the trial should take, for example how long the claimant's case should take, or how much time will be permitted for closing speeches, etc. Directions will also be given as to the preparation of a trial bundle, and a trial bundle must be prepared by and agreed by every party to a case. It should contain all the documents relied upon in a case and should be presented to the court in indexed and paginated folder format. The claimant is tasked with the responsibility of preparing the trial bundle, and must supply the court, the other parties and all the witnesses to the case with a copy of the bundle at least seven days prior to the trial. The purpose of this bundle being agreed and provided to the judge in advance of the trial is to allow the judge to become familiar with the case and the issues before the trial commences. 8–032

The directions in any given case can be normally provided for in a written format so that the parties do not need to attend court prior to the trial date. However, if it becomes apparent during the course of the trial preparation that a pre-trial hearing will be advantageous, possibly so as to provide special directions or to explain the standard directions, the court can request that a case management conference (CMC) be called so that the issues can be discussed in person. CMCs are dealt with in more detail in relation to the multi-track below.

MULTI-TRACK

The multi-track is the final track in the civil justice system and is the track that deals with all the cases that are not suitable for hearing on the small claims track or fast-track. The variety of cases that may be heard on the multi-track is wide, and therefore this is a track that needs to be flexible in its approach so that each case can be dealt with appropriately. Cases can range from a contract dispute where the sum involved amounts to just over the fast-track threshold (remember that even if the financial value of a claim just exceeds £25,000, or £50,000 in personal injury cases, then the case will be automatically allocated to the multi-track unless all parties consent to it being heard on the fast-track, even if it is apparent that the case is better suited to the fast-track), to cases that are highly complex or involve multi-million pound claims. 8–033

The venue of a multi-track case will be dependent on where the claim originates. If the claim is issued in the London region then the case will normally be heard at the Royal Courts of Justice, unless the claim is for less than £100,000 in which case it can then be transferred to the relevant County Court. If the claim originates outside of the London district then it will normally be allocated to the nearest Civil Trial Centre (there being large trial centres in many major cities across the country). However, if the claim is not overly complex or does not involve a substantial sum of money, then the claim may simply remain at the nearest district court.

Once a case has been assigned to the multi-track one of two things may occur. The first is that the court may already have sufficient information to be able to issue standard directions without the need for a preliminary court hearing. The court's primary concern will be to ensure that the issues between the parties are identified and that the necessary evidence is prepared and disclosed. If the court believes that it can set standard directions upon its own initiative then it will do so, but the parties to the case are encouraged to agree suitable directions between themselves wherever possible.

8–034 If the parties to a case can agree the directions then the court may well approve the suggested directions and give an order in those terms. To be able to agree directions without the need for a formal hearing is advantageous for the purposes of time and costs. Often the legal representatives will be aware of the majority of the issues in a case at this stage and therefore they should be able to suggest a timetable that can be realistically achieved. If the court is required to impose a timetable, then it will not be so knowledgeable about the case and may set a shorter time period for preparation before trial than is actually required. If this does happen and subsequently more time for preparation is needed, then the parties can return to the court to request that the timetable be varied, but this will increase the court costs and will effectively work against the Overriding Objective. It is always preferable to attempt to agree the directions and timetable without the need for court intervention. A point to note with multi-track cases, and one that separates these cases from fast-track cases, is that there is no set timetable (i.e. the 30-week case progression timetable as for fast-track cases) but, rather, the case will progress at a speed appropriate for the case in question.

When the court does not agree the proposed directions (which it is not obliged to do), or the parties cannot agree as to the directions, then the court will call a case management conference (CMC). A CMC will be organised for as soon as is practicable after the identification of its need to ensure that there are no unnecessary delays in the progress of the case. The purpose of the CMC is to identify and deal with the issues that have arisen so far and those that may potentially arise in the near future. The court will set a case timetable at the CMC and make directions on any relevant point that the court deems to be necessary for the progression of the case. The trial date will be set, or a three-week trial window will be allocated as, due to the complex nature of many multi-track claims, the setting of a potential trial date may not be immediately possible, and this may need to be delayed until a point later in the trial preparation.

Pre-Action Protocols

One of the aims of the reformed civil justice system is to attempt to deal with cases without the need for recourse to a formal court hearing, or, if it is determined that a formal court hearing is required to deal with the matter expeditiously, with all issues that can be resolved pre-trial being resolved at this time. One method of resolving disputes and issues at an early stage in proceedings is by way of "pre-action protocols". **8–035**

Lord Woolf, in his review of the civil justice system (the Woolf Report), developed the concept of pre-action protocols as an aid to ensuring that the Overriding Objective was achieved. He stated in his *Final Report* that the introduction of pre-action protocols would help to:

> **Build on and increase the benefits of early but well-informed settlements which genuinely satisfy both parties to a dispute.**

To date, there are 17 pre-action protocols, each dealing with a different cause of action:

- personal injury;
- low value personal injury (employer's and public liability);
- low value personal injury claims in road traffic accidents;
- personal injury claims below the small claims limit in road traffic accidents;
- debt;
- clinical disputes;
- construction and engineering disputes;
- defamation;
- professional negligence;
- judicial review;
- disease and illness;
- housing conditions (England only), or housing disrepair (Wales only);
- possession claims by social landlords;
- possession claims based on mortgage or Home Purchase Plan arrears in respect of residential property;
- dilapidations (commercial property);
- resolution of package travel claims; and
- media and communications.

The objectives of these pre-action protocols are set out in the accompanying Practice Direction and are to:

(1) enable parties to settle the issue between them without the need to start proceedings (that is, a court claim); and
(2) support the efficient management by the court and the parties of proceedings that cannot be avoided.

8–036 In essence, the idea behind the protocols is to try and help the parties to negotiate and settle their claims without the need for recourse to more formal claim procedures. By adhering to the protocols, it is envisaged that the claimant will set out their case to the defendant and, in doing so, allow the defendant a proper chance to respond to the allegations before court proceedings are issued.

There are certain causes of action (e.g. breach of contract) that are not covered by the scope of the protocols but in these types of cases it is envisaged that the parties will follow a similar form of pre-action behaviour, such as considering negotiation pre-claim, etc. so as to further the Overriding Objective and achieve a quick and fair resolution.

The protocols set out a sequence of events that should be undertaken prior to a claim. For example, a claimant's initial step may be to send an informal letter to the defendant (and their insurer if known), which sets out their intention to initiate proceedings against them and includes the brief facts of the claim. The purpose of this informal letter would be to open up the lines of communication between the potential parties and to offer the defendant an opportunity to make admissions and resolve the matter amicably before the more formal process is commenced. If the defendant denies the claim then this informal letter will at least alert them to the issue of pending litigation so that they can instruct a legal representative if necessary and inform their insurers. The letter should contain a clear summary of the facts on which the claim is based and should include an indication of the nature of any injuries suffered, as well as any financial loss incurred and details of any documents that the claimant requires the defendant to disclose.

8–037 Once the defendant has received a pre-action protocol letter they should then reply within a reasonable amount of time—this being 14 days in a straightforward case and no more than three months in a very complex one. In their reply they should identify or confirm the identity of their insurer (if any) and, if necessary, identify any significant omissions from the letter of claim. If there has been no reply by the defendant or insurer then the claimant will be entitled to issue proceedings without continuing with any further pre-action protocol requirements. Once the defendant has acknowledged the claim they will be allowed a maximum period of three months to investigate. After the expiry of this three-month period the defendant is required to reply to the claimant setting out whether they admit to the whole claim, part of the claim, or if they deny any liability. If they deny liability then they will need to supply their reasoning for doing so, as well as their version of events. It is at this point that the defendant will need to disclose any relevant documents and set out if they are arguing contributory negligence.

If a party fails to comply with the pre-action protocols, a Practice Direction sets out the sanctions that may be imposed. If it is felt that the non-compliance has led to the commencement of proceedings which might otherwise have not been commenced, or has led to costs being incurred in the proceedings that might otherwise not have been incurred, the court may make an order so as to put the innocent party in no worse a position than they would have been had the protocol been complied with.

Part 36 Offers

The driving principle behind the civil court system is to ensure that cases are dealt with justly and expeditiously; this often means that the art of negotiation and compromise is viewed as the most preferable way in which to conclude a claim. In fact, this principle is so strong that if the claim could have been concluded at an earlier point but the parties press on through the process of formal litigation, then they may find themselves being punished by the courts (normally by way of the division of the costs in the case). One of the methods available to the parties to encourage and achieve early settlement can be found under Pt 36 of the CPR and is called an "offer to settle", which is more commonly known as a Part 36 offer. 8–038

Part 36 offers tend to come into play when informal negotiations have broken down and one of the parties to the claim (normally the defendant) wishes to try and conclude the claim on a more formal basis before the litigation reaches the courtroom. A Part 36 offer will set out the amount that the party making the offer is willing to pay (or accept if the offer is made by the claimant) to settle the claim. Such an offer can be made by way of a simple letter to the other side stating the terms of the offer, so long as the letter complies with the regulations laid down by Pt 36 of the CPR. A Part 36 offer can be made by either the defendant or the claimant.

Under r.36.5 a letter setting out a Part 36 offer must:

(a) be in writing;
(b) state on its face that it is intended to have the consequences of Section I Part 36;
(c) specify a period of not less than 21 days within which the defendant will be liable for the claimant's costs in accordance with rule 36.10 if the offer is accepted;
(d) state whether it relates to the whole of the claim or to part of it or to an issue that arises in it and if so to which part or issue; and
(e) state whether it takes into account any counterclaim.

Once a Part 36 offer has been made, it may not be withdrawn or amended until the expiration of 21 days from the date that the offer is first made. Once the 21 days have expired, the offeror can remove the offer from the table and either proceed to trial or make a further, often less favourable offer. 8–039

An important point to note with the making of a Part 36 offer is that the making of such an offer by the defendant is not an admission of liability by the defendant; nor does it necessarily indicate that the party making the offer believes they have a weak defence/claim, but rather it is a show of willingness to deal with the claim and move on. Often a defendant to a claim would rather pay out a set sum at an early stage in the proceedings to conclude the claim rather than continue to a full hearing of the matter, or the claimant would rather receive a set amount they are happy with than go through the stress of a trial. The reasons for a defendant making such an offer can be numerous and varied, but normally it comes down to factors such as the defendant wishing to control the amount of money they ultimately pay to the claimant, or that the defendant wishes to avoid any bad publicity that may arise if the case were to progress to a full trial.

The clever thing about Part 36 offers is that they are made in secret, and if the case progresses to a full hearing then the judge in the case will not know the amount offered under Part 36 until after the case has finished, after all issues of liability are decided, and after the judge has dealt with quantum (this being the amount of damages to be paid by the losing party to the winner). Only upon all of these matters being decided will the amount put forward in the Part 36 offer be revealed to the judge, and it is at this point that the amount set out in the offer may have an impact on one of the parties in the case. The effects of a Part 36 offer revealed after a trial are listed below.

1. If the claimant is awarded by the court a sum greater than the amount put forward by the defendant in the offer, then they have beaten the offer. The consequence of this is that the claimant will have their costs in the case paid by the defendant, which is standard practice in a claim.
2. If the claimant is awarded by the court a sum equal to or less than the amount set out in the offer then the court will make what is known as a split order to costs. What this means is that the defendant will pay the claimant's costs from date of the cause of action until the expiration of the 21 days after the making of the offer (as detailed in r.36.2 above). From this point on the claimant is then responsible for paying the defendant's costs until the date on which the trial has concluded. The claimant is effectively penalised for not being reasonable and accepting the original offer made by the defendant.
3. If the defendant is successful at trial then the Part 36 offer is of no consequence, as the claimant will be ordered to pay the defendant's full costs in the matter.

Over to you

Jessica bought a homemade cake from her local bakery. She alleges that, after taking a few mouthfuls of the cake, she found half a cockroach in it. Jessica then decides to sue Louise (the owner of the bakery) for the mental anguish she has

suffered from eating the cake. Louise has only recently opened the bakery and wants to avoid any bad publicity, as she is worried that her business will fail if she has no customers. Louise offers, by way of a Part 36 offer, to pay Jessica £2,000 in full and final settlement of the claim. Jessica decides to refuse the offer and press on to a full trial. At the trial the judge accepts Jessica's allegations and finds against Louise, but the judge only awards Jessica £1,500 in damages.

What does this decision mean for Jessica?

The result of this is that Louise has to pay Jessica £1,500 in damages and Jessica's costs up until the expiration of the Part 36 offer (the offer expires 21 days after it is put on the table). After this date Jessica is then liable to pay all of Louise's costs until the date of the conclusion of the trial. This may not sound such a bad deal, especially if the trial takes place in relative succession to the making of the offer, but, if the trial does not proceed for another five months then the costs accrued by Louise in this time may significantly exceed the £1,500 paid to Jessica in damages, which would have the effect of making her case completely pointless and disproportionately expensive. **8-040**

When it is the defendant who refuses to accept a Part 36 offer made by the claimant then they will be subject to further financial sanctions, as imposed by s.55 Legal Aid, Sentencing and Punishment of Offenders Act 2012. Under s.55 if a defendant does not accept the claimant's offer and the court gives at least as advantageous settlement to the claimant as put forward by the claimant, then the defendant will be required to pay an additional amount. The additional sanction is 10 per cent of the total damages awarded, or 10 per cent of the costs in respect of non-damages claims. The maximum sanction that can be imposed in this way is £75,000.

Part 36 offers are a useful tool for the party (normally the defendant) relying upon them. It could be argued that this style of offer actually forces or bullies the claimant into conceding to the offer made by the defendant due to the fear that if they do not "beat the offer" at trial they will then be faced with a large bill for the defendant's costs (and vice versa where is it the claimant who has made the offer). The main problem that a party has when making such an offer, especially if it is the defendant who is making it, will be to consider what amount of money the offer should be. If the claim relates to a set figure (so X amount of pounds owed for goods supplied to the claimant) then the figure to put forward should be simple to calculate, but where the claim is for an unspecified amount (take, for instance, the cockroach scenario above) then the level of offer put forward will not be any more than an educated guess. The defendant will always want to try and pay out the minimum amount possible and therefore it is likely that the Part 36 offer will reflect this fact. A defendant in a case of unspecified damages needs to be wary, though, as their educated guess, even if advised by experienced counsel, will still only be a guess, and this guess may backfire if the claimant refuses to accept the offer and the amount later awarded in court exceeds that offer. The defendant also needs to calculate as **8-041** part of their figure any interest that the court may award the claimant if they are successful at trial. It would be extremely bad luck for a defendant to beat the offer on the basic sum awarded (so, a Part 36 offer was made of £5,000 and the claimant was only awarded £4,500 at court) but then to have this small victory stripped away when the court adds £750 of interest to the total, bringing the total to £5,250 and meaning that the claimant has beaten the claim and the defendant is then liable to pay the claimant's full costs as well as their own costs in the case.

As mentioned above, although it is a procedure usually instigated by the defendant, Part 36 offers are not just confined to use by a defendant in a case, but can also be used as a tactical manoeuvre by the claimant to a claim. The claimant may put forward an offer that they are willing to accept in settlement of the claim in an effort to make the defendant accept the offer and, therefore, liability in the matter.

The final point to mention in respect of Part 36 offers is that they do not just apply to monetary claims and they can be used to great effect in cases where the claimant is claiming another remedy, such as an injunction. If a claimant is claiming for a nuisance, for example, a smell produced from a process undertaken by a working factory, the defendant may put forward an offer setting out that they will only undertake that process on two days of the week, as opposed to five days. If the claimant refuses the offer, the matter goes to court and the judge holds that the process can occur for three days a week, then the claimant will not have beaten the offer and will be liable for the defendant's costs as set out above.

Settling a Claim

8–042 There are a number of ways in which a civil claim can be concluded, and the most appropriate resolution will depend upon what the case is about. The most obvious method is that the claimant is awarded their desired remedy by the judge at the conclusion of the trial, or that the claimant has not managed to satisfy the burden of proof and the claim is dismissed. However, the other methods by which a claim can be concluded are detailed below.

Default Judgment

8–043 One of the simplest ways in which a claim can be concluded is detailed under Pt 12 of the CPR, and is known as default judgment. Default judgment can be utilised when the defendant to a claim fails to respond in any way to the claim made against them, either by not acknowledging service of the claim or not filing a defence to the claim in the prescribed time.

Rule 12.4 sets out the procedures for obtaining default judgment and the relevant procedure will differ depending on whether the claim is one for a specified amount of money or if the claim is for any other type of remedy (e.g. an injunction). If the claim involves a specified amount, such as a defined debt, or for unspecified damages, for example, as in a personal injury claim, then the procedure is a rather simple one. In such instances the claimant to the claim is required to fill out the prescribed form for requesting a judgment in default in the matter. If the claim is for a specified amount, e.g. B is alleged to owe A £3,000, then, if B fails to acknowledge service of the claim or file a defence in time, A can achieve default judgment in respect of the claim and will be awarded by the court the £3,000 as claimed.

Where the claim is for an unspecified amount of damages (so A is suing B for personal injuries but these injuries have not yet been quantified by the courts) then the claimant will again fill in the relevant court form and the court, if satisfied with the request, will pass judgment on liability (so B is liable for the damages incurred by A) but will hold off deciding on the level of damages at this point. Once the judgment for liability is confirmed, then the court will direct that a hearing be arranged so that an accurate assessment of the damages to be paid by B to A can be ascertained. This is a sensible method of dealing with such cases as, if the defendant fails to respond to the claim they effectively accept liability and responsibility for the damages claimed, but the courts cannot simply pluck a number from the air in respect of what would be an appropriate level of damages. A later hearing in respect of the amount of damages is necessary so that the court can hear evidence on the damages and receive relevant evidence, such as an expert's report, etc. so that the appropriate figure can be determined.

Where the claim is for a remedy besides damages, then the claimant is required to make a **8–044** formal application for default judgment. This formal application is necessary so that the court has the opportunity to assess to the claim and make an appropriate judgment based on the claimant's claim. This formal hearing is necessary to ensure that claimants, such as vexatious ones, are not afforded the opportunity of sneakily succeeding in achieving remedies that would be deemed as inappropriate if the situation were fully explored. To determine whether the requested remedy is appropriate or not the court will consider the merits of the claim and the effect of the remedy claimed (e.g. does the injunction need to be permanent or would one lasting for six months suffice?).

The delivery of default judgment is a serious step for the courts to take; it basically imposes liability upon a party without the court having had the benefit of hearing directly from that party. It would be a cruel and unfair justice system if a defendant who was faced with default judgment could not seek to remedy such matters. It may be the case that the defendant was unaware of the proceedings (even if service was correctly carried out) or that they did not comprehend the meaning or seriousness of the proceedings until after the default judgment was delivered. In such circumstances the defendant is allowed the opportunity to apply for the default judgment to be set aside or varied. If the court decides that the judgment should be set aside or varied then this does not automatically mean that it is the end of the matter. Rather, it means that the claim is put back to the position where the defendant is able to enter a defence to the allegations. The judgment is simply removed and the case will progress as if the judgment had never been made in the first place.

Judgment on Admission

8–045 The most satisfactory conclusion to a claim for the claimant is for the defendant to simply admit the truth of the whole claim and to accept liability for the matters set out in the claim form. This is a scenario that does not occur frequently within the civil justice system, but it is not completely unheard of, and therefore the CPR makes provisions for such situations under Pt 14.

Part 14 sets out that a defendant can conclude a claim at any time by making an admission. This means that the defendant can aim to conclude matters quickly by making the admission before the commencement of the proceedings, or at a later point after the formal proceedings have commenced. The defendant is also not obliged always to admit to the whole of the claim, as there is the ability to make admissions to certain parts of the claim and deny other elements of the claim.

If the defendant makes a partial admission to the claim then the defendant may hope that the claimant will accept this partial admission as full and final settlement of the claim. A defendant may try and use this method of settlement as a way to avoid liability for the full amount allegedly owed, and this may be viewed as acceptable by the claimant; for instance, if the claimant alleges that the defendant owes them £700, but the defendant only admits to owing them £550, then, if the partial admission is accepted by the claimant, the defendant may get away without paying £150 of the alleged debt, whilst the claimant at least recoups a large portion, if not all, of their money. The claimant does not have to accept the partial admission by the defendant if it is felt that it is unreasonable, and can still proceed against the defendant for the full amount claimed. If, however, the claimant does accept the partial admission then they are precluded from returning to the claim at a later date to try and recoup the remainder of the money allegedly owed (in the illustration above this would be the £150 difference between the amount claimed and the amount admitted).

Summary Judgment

8–046 Summary judgment under Pt 24 of the CPR is an incredibly important and often-used method of concluding a civil claim. Summary judgment can be used by *either* the claimant *or* the defendant and it will be allowed where either the claim is a spurious one and has no real prospect of success (here the *defendant* would be relying upon summary judgment), or the defence offers very little in the way of substance in that there is no real prospect of successfully defending the claim (here the *claimant* would be making an application for summary judgment). The parties to a case can make an application of their own volition, or the court can decide to make such a judgment of its own initiative after consideration of the claim and/or defence.

The court, when determining whether summary judgment is appropriate, must also take into consideration whether there is any other compelling reason why the case should not be disposed of in such a manner. The courts' approach can be illustrated by the case of **Swain v Hillman** [2001] C.P. Rep. 16 where Lord Woolf MR stated:

> **The court now has a very salutary power, both to be exercised in a claimant's favour or, where appropriate, in a defendant's favour. It enables the court to dispose summarily of both claims or defences which have no real prospect of being successful. The words "no real prospect of being successful or succeeding" do not need any amplification, they speak for themselves. The word "real" distinguishes fanciful prospects of success or, [...] they direct the court to the need to see whether there is a "realistic" as opposed to a "fanciful" prospect of success.**

It can be taken from the Court's view of such proceedings that a summary judgment should only be used where appropriate. This is to be taken as where the issues do not need to be fully investigated at trial. If there is a likelihood that the summary judgment hearing will turn into a mini-trial of the issues then a summary judgment hearing will not be appropriate in the circumstances. However, the test is not so restrictive that there needs to be a substantial prospect of success, simply a realistic one. **8–047**

The idea of summary judgment is for the court to be able to deal effectively and expeditiously with unmeritorious and weak claims, and unsubstantiated and ill-fated defences. This method of case disposal goes towards furthering the Overriding Objective and helps to ensure that the court system is not overrun by worthless cases.

Enforcement of Judgments

Civil cases differ dramatically from criminal cases in a number of ways. One of these differences occurs with respect to the enforcement of a decision. Under the criminal system, if a defendant fails to comply with the sanction imposed by the court (e.g. imprisonment or the service of a community order) then the defendant will often be found to have committed a further offence by way of non-compliance. Ensuring that a party to a civil action complies with the decision of the court (or the agreement between the parties if formal proceedings were not commenced or concluded) is not quite as easy to achieve due to the fact that the matters are between private individuals and there are not the persuasive sanctions available as there are in the criminal arena. Another problem with ensuring the enforcement of civil judgments is that the CPR does not directly govern the issue of enforcement, and the relevant rules are found in the Rules of the Supreme Court (RSC) and the County Court Rules (CCR) (which are preserved under Schs 1 and 2 of the CPR, respectively). **8–048**

The first point to note in relation to civil judgments is that the court (be that the High Court or the county court) does not automatically enforce its decisions. Refusal to comply with a court order is contempt of court, but the party who wishes to enforce the order has to apply to the court for action to be taken against the party who is in contempt. The way in which an order can be enforced will mainly depend on what the focus of the order is (e.g. an order for payment of monies or an injunction, etc.), and the court that made the order will also have a bearing on the action that can be taken by the party wishing to enforce the order.

Writ/Warrants of Execution

8-049 It is not unusual for a judgment debtor (the party who has lost a case and owes the winning party money) to refuse to pay what is owed. To enable the creditor (the person owed the money) to be able to reclaim the money from the debtor, a procedure, known as "execution", has been developed by the civil law. Execution means that the goods of the debtor will be seized and then sold at auction to pay the monies owed to the winning party, as well as covering any legal costs and costs of enforcement incurred via the process. This method of enforcement is often known to the public as it involves the employment of bailiffs, who most people have at least heard of even if they have not dealt with them personally.

If the High Court has issued the order, then to execute the order the person who wishes to enforce it will have to obtain a High Court "writ of execution" as prescribed under Orders 45 and 46 of the RSC, as set out in Sch.1 to the CPR. If the county court made the original judgment, then the enforcement will be conducted under a "warrant of execution" under Order 26 of the CCR, as set out in Sch.2 to the CPR. Once the writ or warrant has been issued, the enforcement (or execution) of it will be carried out by a relevant individual. These individuals are not employees of the court but rather private persons or companies who hold themselves out as suitable for such work and are otherwise known as enforcement officers or bailiffs. The bailiffs are allowed, upon the receipt of such a writ, to attend the debtor's premises and seize any goods owned by the debtor that can be sold at auction to satisfy the debt. However, the bailiffs cannot simply break into the debtor's property and must gain lawful entrance so as to be able to exercise their rights to seize the debtors' goods.

Over to you

Imagine you are a bailiff collecting a large debt. The debtor has the following items in their possession:

- **widescreen HD television;**
- **DVD player;**
- **a white van;**
- **power tools;**
- **an expensive bed;**
- **an expensive fridge freezer (one that makes ice cubes, etc.); and**
- **a designer bag.**

Which items, if any, would you take?

The civil law puts restrictions on the type of property that can be seized to satisfy a debt. As the dispute involves matters between private individuals, the law has to take into account the balancing of the different parties' interests in the case, as it would be unjust to make one person suffer exceptionally just so that the other party can prove a point. All decisions must be proportionate and reasonable to all the parties involved. Goods that cannot be seized include such tools, books, vehicles and other items of equipment as are necessary to the debtor for use personally by them in their employment, business or vocation, and such clothing, bedding, furniture, household equipment and provisions as are necessary for satisfying the basic domestic needs of the debtor and their family. The goods must also belong to the debtor and not be on hire-purchase or belong to another member of the debtor's family, etc.

Third Party Debt Orders

Another option available to a person owed money under a judgment is known as a third party debt order. This method of enforcing judgment can be used where the debtor is owed monies from a third party and the person who is owed the money (and who is making the application) can intervene between the debtor and the third person, freeze the relevant assets and seize this owed money to satisfy their own debt. Situations where such a method can be employed can be such as where the debtor is in business and is owed money by customers, or if the debtor simply has a bank balance in credit (as this is viewed as the bank owing a debt to the debtor). By using a third party debt order the person owed the money bypasses the debtor so as to realise the judgment by access to these assets. 8-050

Charging Orders

Charging orders are a rather heavy-handed method of enforcing judgment that can result in serious consequences for the judgment debtor. A charging order itself is not actually a method of securing payment of the judgment, but it allows the judgment creditor to secure the payment of the debt by placing a charge on the property of the judgment debtor. Thereby, if the judgment debtor owns any land (normally this will be their residential house) then the creditor can have an interest in this property registered, which can be later realised so as to satisfy the debt owed. A charge of this nature can be placed upon the judgment debtor's property even if they own the property jointly with a person who is not involved in the proceedings. 8-051

A charge over a property is quite an easy order to achieve, especially since the recent changes in the way that the Land Registry stores its property details. As all the Land Registry details are now stored electronically, a judgment creditor can have virtually instant access to the Charges Register and Title Plan of any property for a nominal fee of £8. This means that it is very simple for an interested party to discover whether a judgment debtor has any beneficial interest in a property and, if they do, then they can provide substantive evidence of this to the court by the simple click of the mouse on a computer.

A party who obtains a charging order over the property is granted a pretty large axe to wield in respect of achieving payment of the debt. The court may, upon a claim by a person who has obtained a charging order over an interest in property, order the sale of the property so as to enforce the charging order. The property of the debtor can literally be sold out from under them so as to pay off the debt.

The court does have the discretion to refuse to make an order for an enforced sale and, in considering whether to make one or not, it will take into account the position of both the creditor and the debtor as it will try to avoid any disproportionate hardship being caused to either party. If an order of sale is granted, then it is likely that the court will also order the judgment debtor and any other person living at the property to vacate the premises prior to the house being marketed for sale so that the sale can be achieved quickly and with the minimum of fuss.

Attachment of Earnings

8-052 An attachment to the earnings of the judgment debtor can be a highly effective method of recouping monies owed to the creditor, but such an order will only be made in very specific instances. Where the judgment debtor owes the creditor money and the debtor is in long-term gainful employment with no other substantial assets or any dependents, an attachment of earnings order may be the most appropriate method to achieve enforcement.

The term "earnings" does not just mean the judgment debtor's weekly or monthly take-home pay but can be expanded to encompass many forms of income including wages, salary, fees, bonuses, commission, overtime pay, pensions (although not a state pension) and statutory sick pay. Forms of income that cannot be subject to an attachment of earnings order include sums paid by an authority outside the UK (including those from Northern Ireland, state benefits or allowances, or self-employed income).

An attachment of earnings order is obtained via a relatively straightforward procedure. The applicant makes an application to the court by way of the prescribed form; the judgment debtor is notified of the hearing date at least 21 days prior to the scheduled hearing and, on notification of the hearing, provided with a means questionnaire to complete. Once the judgment debtor has completed and returned the means questionnaire to the court, then an administrative officer of the court will assess the information provided and make an order if they believe there to be sufficient information and that the order is appropriate. The only time that an attachment of earnings order will be reviewed by a judge is when a party to the proceedings disputes the application or the decision by the court officer. Upon the granting of such an order, the court will notify the judgment debtor's employer, who will then deduct the required sum from the judgment debtor's earnings and pay this to the court so that it can be passed on to the judgment creditor.

Non-Money Judgments

In cases where the judgment relates to a non-money solution (i.e. an injunction), the sanction for non-compliance is that the offending party is held to be in contempt of court, so that when a person refuses or neglects to do something set out in an order (a mandatory injunction) or does not restrain from doing whatever is set out in an order (a prohibitory injunction), then an application can be made for a committal order against that person. The order must contain the penal notice, which sets out that by refusing to obey the order they are placing themselves in contempt of court and, if the individual continues to defy the order, then a hearing will be held to determine whether the individual needs to be remanded into custody as a sanction for non-compliance. **8–053**

An individual can be committed for up to two years for contempt of court under the CCA 1981. As the committal proceedings have originated from a civil action, the courts are generally reluctant to impose custody upon an individual and will only really turn to it as a last resort when the individual in question has flagrantly disregarded the order and there is no other alternative but to commit the offender into custody for a suitable amount of time.

Alternative Dispute Resolution

Bringing litigation to court may not always be the most appropriate or desirable course of action and, as such, alternative ways in which to resolve disputes have developed. These methods of alternative dispute resolution (ADR) have become formalised over recent years and there are now four recognised methods of ADR. **8–054**

- Negotiation.
- Mediation.
- Conciliation.
- Arbitration.

There are a number of different factors why parties to a dispute may wish to resolve the matter without recourse to the formal litigation process, such as the cost of litigation, as once court costs and lawyers' fees are factored into the equation what seemed like a small and inexpensive claim to defend may become very expensive, to the point of the costs being disproportionate to the amount of the claim. The uncertainty of outcome may have a bearing on the decision to turn to ADR as, once the claim has entered the formal court process, the parties to the dispute have no real power or influence over the decision, by using ADR parties are able to steer matters to a degree so that they receive a more favourable outcome. The potential delay that may be incurred before the dispute is resolved is another factor that might be taken into account by those considering litigation as, even after the Woolf reforms; it may still take many months for a case to come to court, whereas ADR may help to resolve the situation quickly. Litigation through the court process is a stressful procedure that can take its toll on those involved and **8–055** the trauma of waiting for a case to reach court and the potential for massive legal bills can have an adverse effect on all the parties and their families. Often, the use of ADR will help alleviate some of this stress. Also, cases that go through the formal court process are often likely to attract some level of publicity and, depending on the parties in the case, such publicity may be undesirable as, if a party is, for example, a businessman, then any bad publicity may have a negative effect on their livelihood. Using ADR as a method to resolve the dispute may avoid any unwanted media attention and may help to ensure that the reputations of those involved are preserved. Finally, the fact that the atmosphere of a court is often intimidating in nature may be off-putting to a large number of potential litigants, and the fact that ADR is a more informal and relaxed process may make it a more attractive one to undertake.

Negotiation

8–056 Negotiation between parties often occurs naturally at the beginning of any form of dispute and it is the quickest and easiest method to try and resolve the issues in an informal manner. Parties will try and attain an outcome that is mutually acceptable to all, and it is often the case that parties will try and achieve a settlement by way of negotiation before moving on to more formal and structured forms of ADR. Negotiation can take place privately between the individuals of the claim and it will involve them discussing the issues and putting forward a solution that they feel may be acceptable to all. It may be that one party will put forward an amount that they are prepared to settle the matter for and then the responding party will decide whether they are happy with the figure proposed; if not, then they may put forward a counter-offer so as to resolve the case. Negotiation can involve a lot of to-ing and fro-ing between the parties until a happy resolution is realised.

If the parties to a claim cannot negotiate successfully between themselves, then they may decide to appoint a trained negotiator to act in the matter. Solicitors often act as negotiators between the parties and they will endeavour to find a solution before the matter reaches the court. It is by way of the solicitors negotiating between themselves and the parties that out-of-court settlements are often achieved.

Mediation

8–057 With mediation, an appointed person will act as a conduit through which the two disputing parties can communicate and negotiate in an attempt to resolve the problem. The individual who acts as a mediator is normally trained and experienced in such matters (although qualification is not a prerequisite for acting as a mediator); they may be lawyers who have undergone specialist training, or individuals whose main work is mediation. The main aim of a mediator is to be an impartial facilitator in the resolution of the dispute.

Unlike negotiation, where each party has their own representative, mediation will only involve the use of one mediator. The mediator's role is to discuss the issues with both parties so as to discover where the common ground lies and then to try and facilitate a satisfactory outcome.

Often, a mediator will undertake an evaluative role in the proceedings by offering their opinion on the merits or disadvantages of a proposed solution, but they will not suggest what they believe to be the best way in which to conclude the matter, as that is for the parties only to decide. Mediation is based on the principles of helping the parties involved in the dispute to take an active role in collaborative problem-solving in order to achieve a mutually agreeable and acceptable outcome; and that there is a focus on rebuilding or ensuring continuing relationships between the parties in the future, with an emphasis upon solution, as opposed to apportionment of blame. The process may also be viewed as cathartic for those involved, in that they can express their feelings, have them acknowledged, and then move on from them with a positive solution.

Mediation will normally take place over the course of a single morning or afternoon, or possibly even taking up a full day where the issues are particularly complex. The parties will attend a neutral venue (often the court) where each party will be provided with a private room. To begin with the parties will take part in a joint meeting where the ground rules are agreed and the main issues are identified. After this each party may retire to their own room and the mediator will go between the parties, gathering information and building up a picture of the disagreement so that a solution can be explored. The mediator will gain and maintain the trust of the parties and will not disclose any information that was disclosed in confidence to them. It is hoped that, by way of mediation, the parties are able to come to an amicable conclusion to the problem that will allow the matter to be resolved and the parties to move on. If a consensus can be achieved, then this will be drawn up into a binding agreement between the parties and ratified by the court. If the parties are unable to agree upon a course of action, then the court will become involved and set dates for a court hearing for the matter.

Mediation is often attempted where the dispute revolves around matters of the family, as the **8–058** court system is not viewed as the best forum in which to attempt to resolve issues arising from divorce and the care of children and, from April 2011, divorcing couples were encouraged to use mediation first before they are allowed to access the court system. If the parties can come to a mutual, autonomous agreement over such matters, then there is a higher chance that the decisions will be respected and adhered to, thereby causing less stress and trauma in the future; this expectation of initial recourse to mediation in family matters then became a legal requirement through the enactment of the Children and Families Act 2014.

Conciliation

Conciliation is very similar in nature to mediation in that there is a neutral third party involved **8–059** in the discussion of a resolution but, whereas with mediation the mediator is mainly facilitative, with conciliation the third party is more interventionist and involved in the decision-making process. With conciliation the third party will make suggestions as to the most suitable method for resolution (so, more evaluative than facilitative) and try and move the parties forward towards settlement. A party to conciliation is not obliged to accept the proposals suggested by the third party and they can request that the case goes forward to a formal hearing if they do not find the proposals acceptable. Even where a dispute does go forward to a formal hearing following conciliation, it does not mean that the conciliation was pointless, as it will have helped to identify and narrow the issues in the case so that the matter can then be dealt with by the courts quickly and efficiently.

Arbitration

8-060 Arbitration could be described as a halfway house between informal and formal dispute resolution. By agreeing to use arbitration as a method of resolution the parties agree to the matter being adjudicated by a third party (who is not a judge). The process of arbitration is governed by statute, namely the Arbitration Act 1996, and s.1 of the Act sets out that:

> (a) the object of arbitration is to obtain the fair resolution of disputes by an impartial tribunal without unnecessary delay or expense;
> (b) the parties should be free to agree how their disputes are resolved, subject only to such safeguards as are necessary in the public interest;

The agreement to undergo arbitration as opposed to more formal court procedures is one that is taken voluntarily by the parties involved in a dispute. The agreement to use arbitration is normally made well in advance of any dispute arising and is often written into the initial contract as a precautionary measure, but it can be selected as the most appropriate method of resolution upon a dispute occurring. Many trade associations, such as the Association of British Travel Agents (ABTA), automatically turn to arbitration as the primary method of resolution (for example, in dealing with customer complaints) and the decision to use arbitration will be set out in the paperwork that customers sign (i.e. when arranging their holidays).

Where the agreement to undertake arbitration is made in writing, then the Arbitration Act 1996 will be applicable (however, this Act does not apply to verbal agreements, although the spirit of it should be followed wherever possible). The 1996 Act sets out (under s.33) the duty of the arbitrator, this being to act fairly and impartially between the parties, and to give each party a reasonable opportunity of putting their case and dealing with that of their opponent, but how this should be achieved is left to the discretion of the individual arbitrator.

8-061 Any person can be an arbitrator and there is no requirement that an arbitrator has to be specially trained in arbitration, although an arbitrator will generally be an expert in the area under consideration. Quite often, an arbitrator will be a legally qualified person who acts as an arbitrator in professional capacity as a lawyer, or they will be a person who is a member of the Chartered Institute of Arbitrators. The number of arbitrators appointed to resolve a dispute and who the arbitrators are will be dependent upon the individual parties to a case. The contract may have set out that in the case of a dispute the parties will abide by the findings of a single arbitrator who is appointed by the Charted Institute of Arbitrators, or the contract may have not set out any more specifics than the fact that arbitration will be used. If it is the latter situation, then the parties can decide between themselves as to who will be the arbitrator, or if they cannot do so then the court will appoint an arbitrator on their behalf.

So as to ensure that the general principles as detailed under s.1, above are satisfied, the arbitrator will schedule an oral hearing. Both parties will be notified well in advance of the date so that they are given reasonable opportunity to prepare for, attend and present their case at the hearing. The objective of avoiding unnecessary expense is kept firmly in mind when arbitration is undertaken and, as such, disproportionate, lengthy hearings are not acceptable. If appropriate, an arbitrator may attempt to resolve the dispute by only considering a paper-based case.

Upon making a finding in a case; an arbitrator is normally required to give an explanation of the reasons for the decision (unless the parties have specifically excluded this requirement in their agreement) and, once made, the decision becomes legally binding and therefore enforceable in the courts. The parties to the case may agree on costs between themselves. However, if they are not able to agree on this, then the issue of costs will be at arbitrator's discretion. If a party to the case disagrees with the final outcome of the arbitration, then they are afforded the possibility of appealing to the High Court, but only where there is either a serious irregularity affecting the proceedings or the award, or where they are appealing on a point of law. To bring an appeal then either all parties must consent to the appeal or the court must grant leave to appeal (s.69 of the Arbitration Act 1996). The court will generally only grant leave following arbitration where the question of law could substantially affect the rights of the parties involved in the case, or the decision of the arbitrator is obviously wrong, or the issue is one of general public importance and the decision is open to serious doubt.

FIGURE 29 **Alternative dispute resolution**

Tribunals

8–062 Functioning alongside the courts are a number of tribunals, each specialising in their own area, such as employment law or asylum and immigration. The public are aware of the existence of the most prominent tribunals, as the work they carry out features regularly in the media and headlines such as "Employment Tribunal award an employee dismissed due to her pregnancy £2.3 million in compensation" or "Immigration and Asylum Tribunal refuse to allow a mother of five children to stay in the UK" can often be found in the daily newspapers.

The tribunal system arose out of the need for members of the public to have recourse to a panel of impartial persons who had the power to review administrative decisions taken by either governmental departments or by private bodies, where they did not have the grounds for the commencement of traditional legal action. Tribunals are essentially administrative in nature and they are an important element of the justice system as they help to ensure that any perceived unjustness is fairly assessed and remedied where appropriate. There are also a number of domestic tribunals (such as the General Medical Council and the Football Association) that regulate professional conduct in different professions. Overall, tribunals are invaluable as they help to redirect a high volume of potential cases away from the courts and provide justice and fairness where otherwise there might be none.

History

In May 2000, a review of the effectiveness and work of the tribunal service was commis- **8-063** sioned by the Government. The review was headed by Sir Andrew Leggatt, a former Lord Justice of Appeal, and the review reported its findings in March 2001 by the Department for Constitutional Affairs under the title Tribunals for Users: One System, One Service. The Leggatt Report recommended that the Lord Chancellor should assume responsibility for the fragmented tribunal service (at that time there were over 70 separate tribunals) and that there should be a single, overarching structure that would give an individual access to all of the tribunals. To provide effective and independent administration of the individual tribunals, the Report further recommended that a Tribunals Service should be set up so that the individual tribunals were easy to access and navigate, and the service and approach offered was of the highest quality whilst being responsive to the user. To achieve this, the Report proposed that the Tribunal Service should be grouped into nine separate divisions, the first eight divisions dealing with disputes between the citizen and the State, and the ninth to deal with disputes between parties. The suggested nine divisions were:

- immigration;
- social security and pensions;
- land and valuation;
- financial;
- transport;
- health and social services;
- education;
- regulatory matters; and
- employment (disputes between parties).

The Government then produced the White Paper *Transforming Public Services: Complaints, Redress and Tribunals* in July 2004 (Department for Constitutional Affairs, Cm 6243), which set out the proposals for implementing the recommendations of the Leggatt Report. The result of the White Paper and the catalytic Leggatt Report was that, in April 2006, the Tribunals

Service came into force under the Tribunals, Courts and Enforcement Act 2007 (TCEA 2007). The Tribunals Service was a government executive agency of the Ministry of Justice with the purpose of providing administrative support to the main central government tribunals. In April 2011 HM Courts Service and the Tribunals Service was combined into one integrated agency and became HM Courts and Tribunals Service, which is now responsible for the administration of the criminal, civil and family courts and tribunals in England and Wales.

8-064 The TCEA 2007 also put into action a new two-tier framework for tribunals. There is now a First-tier Tribunal and an Upper-tier Tribunal, both of which are split into distinct Chambers, and these Chambers consider similar jurisdictions. The First-tier hears first instance cases within the relevant jurisdiction; the Upper-tier has a predominately appellate capacity in respect of appeals arising from the First-tier Tribunal decisions. The Court of Appeal hears decisions that are appealed from the Upper-tier, but the appeal must be based on a point of law, and the decision of a tribunal is also open to judicial review in the High Court if it is believed that the tribunal has acted ultra vires.

There are now seven Chambers of the First-tier Tribunal dealing with different jurisdictions.

- Social Entitlement Chamber, dealing with the following areas:
  - asylum support;
  - social security and child support; and
  - criminal injuries compensation.
- Health, Education and Social Care Chamber, dealing with:
  - care standards;
  - mental health issues;
  - special educational needs and disability; and
  - primary health lists;
  - War Pensions and Armed Forces Compensation.
- The Property Chamber, dealing with:
  - Land Registration;
  - Agricultural Land & Drainage; and
  - Residential Property Tribunal.
- The General Regulatory Chamber, dealing with:
  - alternative business structures;
  - charity;
  - claims management services;
  - consumer credit;
  - environment;
  - estate agents;
  - gambling appeals;
  - immigration services;
  - information rights;

- local government standards in England; and
- transport;

- Immigration and Asylum Chamber, dealing with:
  - immigration and asylum decisions.
- Tax Chamber; dealing with:
  - First-tier Tribunal (Tax); and
  - MPs expenses.

The Upper-tier Tribunal is split into four separate jurisdictions, these being:

- Administrative Appeals;
- Tax and Chancery;
- Lands; and
- Immigration and Asylum.

Over to you

Where would an appeal from the Immigration and Asylum Chamber go? Or where would an appeal from the General Regulatory Chamber be heard?

The Employment Tribunal has not come under the new framework but, rather, remains an independent tribunal, with its own appeals process (Employment Appeal Tribunal).

Tribunal Hearings

Tribunals are normally either headed by a single judge or by a panel of two or three (of whom the chair will be legally qualified and the others will be experts in the respective field). For example, in the Immigration and Asylum Chamber it is usual to find a solo judge sitting; whilst hearings in the Care Standards Chamber will normally be conducted by a panel of three, consisting of a judge and either two mental health experts, or one mental health expert and one layperson. Each Chamber has its own set composition appropriate to the matter it deals with and there is no uniformity within the tribunal service as a whole. 8–065

Hearings held within the Tribunal Service are an informal and rather relaxed affair with there being no formal rules on the production of evidence or the course of the case. Tribunal judges wear business dress and not robes or wigs. The primary focus of a tribunal is to ensure that justice is done and, therefore, it will allow both parties to present their cases in the most appropriate manner for this to be achieved. The only real exception to this rule is that the Employment Tribunal is more formal than most tribunals in nature and the proceedings within this tribunal closely resemble those found within the traditional court system.

In the majority of cases the parties themselves will present their own cases and it is unusual to find legal representation present at a tribunal. The main reason behind this is that it is difficult to secure legal aid for a tribunal hearing, with the only exception to this rule really being found where there is an issue concerning the applicant's liberty or human rights (i.e. within the Immigration and Asylum Chamber).

FIGURE 30 **Advantages and disadvantages of tribunals**

Advantages	Disadvantages
Specialist knowledge of the bench or panel	**Mistakes may be made due to the speed of the hearings**
Informal nature of hearings	**Lacks impartiality (due to being overseen by the Ministry of Justice and the wider government)**
Inexpensive (compared to traditional legal proceedings)	**Lack of case precedent at First-tier level**
Cases are dealt with quickly and efficiently	**Often full reasoning for a decision is not provided**
Majority of hearings are in private and therefore receive little publicity	**Lack of legal aid**

Summary

1. The parties to a civil claim are normally known as the claimant (the person bringing the claim) and the defendant (the person defending the claim). The names can change depending on the focus of the proceedings, as in an appeal the party appealing would be named the appellant or, if making an application, the applicant.
2. The burden and standard of proof in a civil claim is that the case must be proven by the party bringing the claim on the balance of probabilities. This means that they must show that it is more likely than not that the facts are as they assert them to be.
3. In 1996 Lord Woolf completed an extensive review of the civil justice system, *Access to Justice*. The conclusion and recommendations of the Woolf Report led to an overhaul of the civil justice system by the introduction of the Civil Procedure Rules (CPR). The main objective of the CPR is found in the Overriding Objective and this is to ensure that all cases are dealt with justly. The CPR also introduced extended case management powers for the judiciary so that they can achieve the Overriding Objective.

4. The Woolf reforms introduced a "track system" into the civil courts. Claims under £10,000 are now dealt with by way of the small claims track. The fast-track deals with claims between the value of £10,000 and £25,000 (or over £50,000 in a personal injury case, and the multi-track deals with claims over £25,000 (or £50,000 for personal injury) and the more complex claims.

5. To further aid the Overriding Objective, the Woolf Report introduced the concept of pre-action protocols, which aim to identify the main issues in a case prior to the commencement of formal action and to potentially aid early settlement wherever possible. There are a number of template protocols for different causes of action (i.e. personal injury and judicial review) but where the cause of action does not fall under one of the set protocols then the parties are still expected to follow the spirit of the pre-action protocols.

6. Part 36 offers are a method of trying to achieve an early settlement in a case. A party may put forward what they are prepared to settle the claim for (or what they are prepared to accept in settlement) and if this offer is not accepted and is then matched or beaten in the courts, then there may be cost implications. Part 36 offers can be used tactically to force a settlement.

7. There are a number of ways to settle a claim besides the judge in the case deciding the outcome. Settlement can occur by way of default judgment (where the defendant fails to respond to or defend the claim), summary judgment (where there is no realistic prospect of success or no valid claim), or judgment on admission, where the defendant accepts liability for at least part of the claim in full and final settlement of the whole claim.

8. Judgments can be enforced in a number of ways by the court. A writ or warrant of execution can be issued where outside agents (bailiffs) will be requested to attend the debtor's premises and recover property to the value of the outstanding judgment. A third party debt order can be imposed so that the judgment value is recouped directly from a third party who owes the debtor money. A charge can be placed over a debtor's property in lieu of the debt and then sale of the property can be forced to realise the debt, or an attachment of earnings order can be made whereby the value of the judgment is directly claimed from the debtor's earnings.

9. There are a number of other ways to resolve a dispute that do not include resorting to the traditional court system—these are known as alternative dispute resolution or ADR. ADR can occur by way of negotiation (between the two parties), mediation (with the help of a facilitator), conciliation (whereby a third party actively encourages settlement) and arbitration (where the parties agree to a third party adjudicating the issues). Each method has its own advantages (cost, speed, privacy, etc.) but they also carry with them a number of disadvantages (non-binding, potential for no settlement, etc.).

10. Tribunals work alongside and complement the main court system. Tribunals are mainly administrative in nature and they provide a forum for a party to pursue a challenge to a decision taken that they would not be able to pursue in the courts.

Further Reading

J. Baldwin and R. Cunnington, "The crisis in enforcement of civil judgments in England and Wales" [2004] P.L. Sum. 305–328.

Discusses how default judgments can be enforced and whether there is an art.6 ECHR consideration to be considered.

V.R. Handley, "Changing the burden of proof" [2007] 1 J.P.I. Law 35–48.

Considers pre-action protocols relating to personal injury.

M. Partington, "Alternative dispute resolution: recent developments, future challenges" [2004] 23(Apr) C.J.Q. 99–106.

Considers how ADR sits with the rest of the civil justice system.

S. Prince, "Mediating small claims: are we on the right track?" [2007] 26(Jul) C.J.Q. 328–340.

Looks at the use of the small claims system with reference to the pilot study at Exeter County Court.

A.A.S. Zuckerman, "CPR 36 offers" [2005] 24(Apr) C.J.Q. 167–184.

Discuss the judicial approach to Part 36 offers with reference to case examples as illustration.

Self Test Questions

1. The party name of a person appealing against a judicial decision is the:
- **(a)** claimant
- **(b)** plaintiff
- **(c)** appellant
- **(d)** applicant

2. The Overriding Objective of the Civil Procedure Rules is that cases should be dealt with:
- **(a)** justly
- **(b)** efficiently
- **(c)** inexpensively
- **(d)** proportionately

3. A case involving a claim for the sum of £13,500 will be heard on/in the:
   (a) small claims track
   (b) fast-track
   (c) multi-track
   (d) magistrates' court
4. The passing down of summary judgment means:
   (a) that the case had no realistic prospect of success
   (b) that the defendant admitted the claim
   (c) that the claimant withdrew their case
   (d) that the claim was settled out of court
5. Conciliation means that:
   (a) the parties decide the matters between themselves
   (b) the parties are aided in their decision-making by a third party
   (c) the matter is decided for the parties by a third party
   (d) a judge determines the outcome prior to trial

The Criminal Justice System

9

CHAPTER OVERVIEW

In this chapter we will:

- **Set out the criminal court hierarchy.**
- **Consider the function of the Criminal Procedure Rules 2013.**
- **Discover the ways in which a prosecution can be commenced and the factors that must be considered in determining whether or not prosecution is appropriate.**
- **Explain the alternatives to prosecution.**
- **Explain the different offence classifications.**
- **Consider the complexities of an either-way offence.**
- **Evaluate practices such as plea-bargaining and advanced indication of sentence.**
- **Discuss the issue of bail.**
- **Learn about the criminal trial process.**

Introduction

9–001 The chapter title of "The Criminal Justice System" is a broad title that does not really denote a specific focus. The reason for this is that the criminal justice system itself is a wide and varied structure that has many different facets. There is no better title to encompass the various areas that are found within this area of law as the criminal justice system requires detailed consideration of myriad issues, such as how the decision to prosecute is made and how criminal offences are classified, through to what, if any, bargains the defendant can make in respect of their sentence. This chapter will now consider the more salient pre-trial issues, as well as the common trial procedures.

FIGURE 31 **The progression of a criminal case**

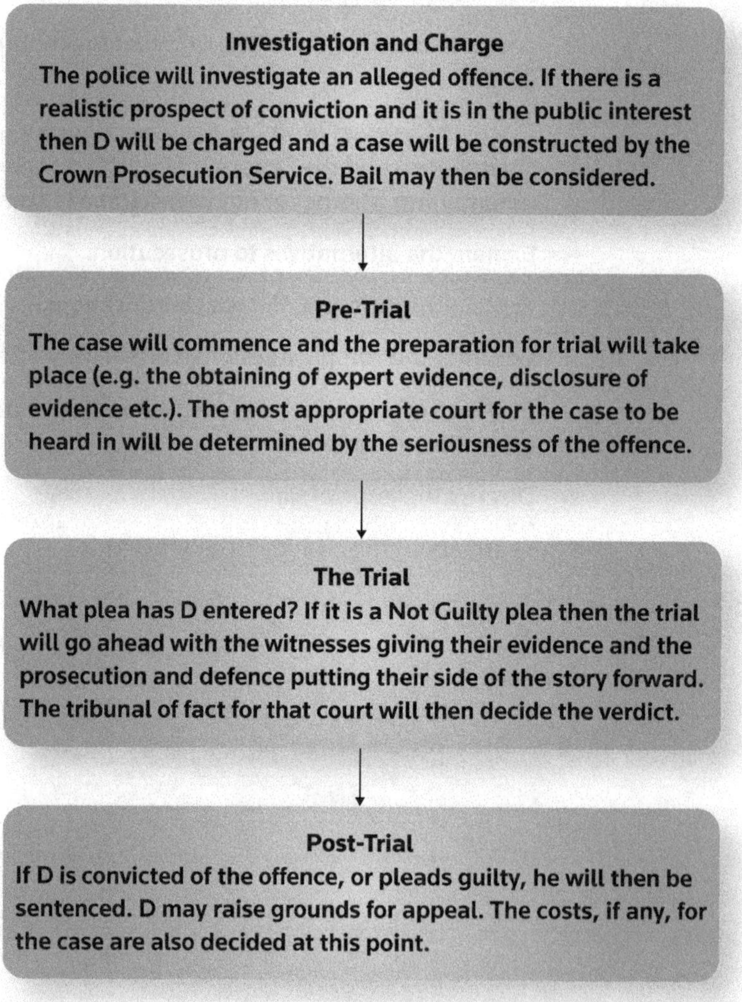

The Criminal Court Hierarchy

There are two main functions of the courts within the criminal jurisdiction; these are either as courts of first instance or appellate courts. The structure of the court system is such that there is not really a clear distinction between those courts that are first instance courts and those that have an appellate jurisdiction. **9–002**

Courts of first instance are those courts that hear and decide the original case; they have evidence adduced and witnesses called. In criminal matters, they determine the guilt or innocence of the defendant. Appellate courts are those courts that hear cases on appeal. This means that a court of first instance has already determined the case but that one party to the case is then disputing the decision made by that court. The issue of appeals is dealt with in detail in Ch.12 and therefore it is only intended at this point to give an overview of the courts and their respective jurisdictions.

Magistrates' Court

The magistrates' court is a court of first instance and it is often viewed as being at the bottom of the court hierarchy. The magistrates' court can hear a number of civil matters (certain family proceedings, and often issues concerning licensing applications, etc.) but its main jurisdiction is criminal matters. The magistrates' court hears the majority (approx. 98 per cent) of criminal trials at first instance, although all cases will pass through the magistrates' court, albeit very briefly. The magistrates' court has the power to hear cases involving summary offences; these offences being the least serious criminal offences. However, the more serious cases also briefly pass through the magistrates' court. Either-way offences (explained below at "Either-way Offences", at **9–033**) have a preliminary hearing in the magistrates' court to determine the venue of the trial (this is known as an allocation procedure hearing, about which greater detail can be found later in this chapter), and the most serious (indictable) offences, such as murder and rape, are presented at the magistrates' court so as to be formally sent to the Crown Court for trial. **9–003**

The magistrates' court is presided over either by magistrates or district judges. Magistrates are laypeople who have volunteered their time to come and sit at the court in a judicial capacity. In general, they are not legally qualified and they hold the official title of justices of the peace, although they are commonly referred to as magistrates (see Ch.5). District judges are legally qualified, appointed members of the judiciary, and they were known until recently as stipendiary judges (see Ch.6).

Crown Court

The Crown Court is both a court of first instance and an appellate court. In its role as a first instance court it hears trials on indictment (and those either-way offences deemed too serious **9–004** for the magistrates' court, or where the defendant has elected trial by jury (see "Allocation Hearings", at **9–037**)) and will, in some cases, sentence on either-way cases sent up from the magistrates' court. The Court, when sitting as a court of first instance is comprised of a judge and a jury. The function of the judge is to direct upon the law, whereas the jury is the tribunal of fact that will determine the guilt or innocence of the person being tried. When the Court is acting in its appellate function, the Crown will hear matters on appeal from the magistrates' court. The judicial personnel who preside over the Crown Court can vary from case to case, as all High Court judges, recorders and circuit judges have jurisdiction to sit in the Crown Court. Occasionally, magistrates will also sit in the Crown Court alongside a judge when a matter is being heard on appeal from the magistrates' court.

Administrative Court, King's Bench Division of the High Court

9–005 The Administrative Court within the King's Bench Division of the High Court, also known as the Divisional Court of the King's Bench Division when hearing appeals, is a court that has both civil and criminal jurisdiction. In respect of its criminal remit it has the power to hear cases on appeal from the magistrates' court by way of case stated. This form of appeal can be made by either the prosecution or the defence and is explained in further detail in Ch.12 ("Appeal by way of case stated"). The High Court can also hear judicial review of the decisions of magistrates, however this is a civil claim and it is used less frequently in criminal matters but can be used when there is some allegation of unfairness in the trial.

Court of Appeal (Criminal Division)

9–006 The Court of Appeal is a court of appellate function and it has the power to hear and determine cases on appeal in respect of either the conviction or the sentence from the Crown Court, references made by the Attorney-General, and referrals by the Criminal Cases Review Commission. The Court also has civil jurisdiction under the Court of Appeal (Civil Division). The Civil Division is headed by the Master of the Rolls, and the Criminal Division by the Lord Chief Justice and the judges of the court are known as Lord or Lady Chief Justices of Appeal. The Court of Appeal (Criminal Division) originally started out life in 1848 as the Court for Crown Cases Reserved, this then changed to the Court of Criminal Appeal in 1907, and, finally, the Court became the Court of Appeal (Criminal Division) in 1966.

Supreme Court

9–007 The Supreme Court is the final court of appeal for England and Wales. It is the highest judicial court in the land and it mainly hears appeals from both the Court of Appeal and the High Court. To appeal to the Supreme Court, leave to appeal (or permission) must be obtained from either the court being appealed from, or from the Supreme Court itself and the appeal must be based on a point of law of general public importance. In recent years, few criminal matters have reached the Supreme Court, as the bulk of their work has been civil matters. The judges who sit in the Supreme Court are known as Justices.

FIGURE 32 **Criminal court hierarchy**

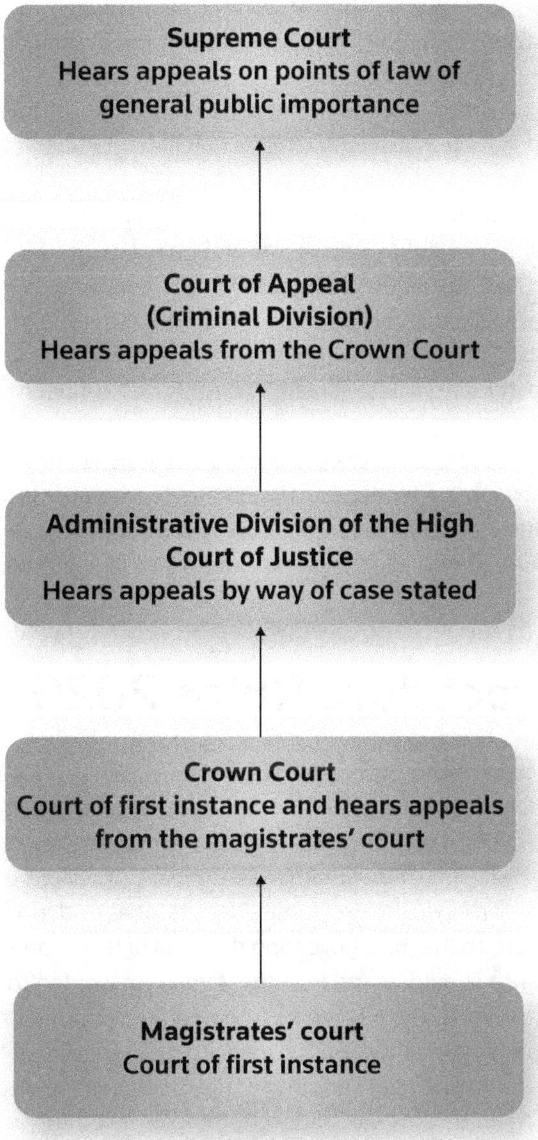

Privy Council

9–008 The Privy Council, or the Judicial Committee of the Privy Council if using the full title of the court, is the final appeal court for several Commonwealth countries, the British Overseas Territories and the Crown Dependencies (such as Jersey and Guernsey). The court is composed of the Supreme Court Justices but it does not deal directly with domestic cases. Examples of the Commonwealth countries that have the right of appeal to the Privy Council include Antigua, Trinidad and Tobago, Jamaica and Mauritius. It used to be that all Commonwealth countries had the right of appeal to the Privy Council but, over time, a large number of the countries have established their own courts of final appeal, which has reduced the reliance upon the Privy Council.

In 1875, Canada established its own Supreme Court and abolished appeals to the Privy Council, in 1978 Sri Lanka abolished its right of appeal to the Privy Council for criminal cases, in 1997 Hong Kong established its Court of Final Appeal, thereby removing its need for reference, and in 2003 New Zealand abolished its right to appeal to the Court. The nations of the Caribbean community are currently pushing for the right of appeal to the Supreme Court to be abolished in favour of the Caribbean Court of Justice, but so far this has not been successful.

Decisions of the Board, as they are called, from other jurisdictions are persuasive only in England and Wales. They are, generally, highly persuasive when the law is relatively the same and the very fact that Justices of the Supreme Court sat on those appeals. Privy Council decisions tend to feature more in English criminal law than civil law, but both are equally valid as persuasive authorities.

Criminal Procedure Rules 2020

9–009 Rules and procedures govern how every case within the criminal justice system is dealt with. These rules are fundamentally intertwined with the substantive and evidential areas of the law and give guidance to all of the parties involved in a case, in respect of nearly every aspect of their case. The law of evidence will determine whether a defendant's previous convictions are admissible into court as evidence of propensity to commit offences, or as evidence of guilt; but the parties to the case will need to turn to the rules governing this area of law to determine how an application to admit such evidence should be made. If the defendant wanted to contest the admission of such evidence the procedures required to be followed are set out in the relevant rules, such as the forms needing completion and the time limits in which they need to be completed. Such rules are entirely sensible in trying to ensure that a trial is conducted fairly and justly. If the rules did not exist then there could be the possibility, for example, that the prosecution enter evidence at the last minute, not giving the defendant a chance to oppose its admission.

On 4 April 2005 the Criminal Procedure Rules (CrimPRs) were introduced into the criminal justice system of England and Wales by way of statutory instrument: Criminal Procedure Rules (now updated in SI 2020/759). This was the beginning of a massive step towards the consolidation of all the different criminal procedure rules and codes that existed under English law. The intention behind the CrimPRs was to bring together, under a single umbrella, all of the existing codes and rules, so that they were easy to access, well structured, and in a format and language that was understandable by criminal practitioners and laypeople alike.

Prior to the enactment of the CrimPRs in 2005, there were almost 50 separate sets of rules containing a total of nearly 500 individual rules. This meant that finding the right source or sources could be a time-consuming and often very confusing job for both criminal-practitioners and judges. Even if they managed to identify the right source, then actually understanding what it said could be difficult and add further to the mounting confusion; particularly as a rule for one court (for example the Crown Court) could completely contradict its parallel rule in another court (the magistrates' court).

Lord Justice Auld, in the Auld Review, identified the underlying problems with the system and gave the recommendation that what was needed was:

> **A concise and simply expressed statement of the current statutory and common law procedural rules [...]. It should be in a single instrument and laid out in such a form that it, the Code, can be readily amended without constant recourse to primary legislation.**

By creating such an instrument he envisaged that the result would be a fair, efficient and effective criminal justice system that would have simple procedures that were accessible and, so far as practicable, the same for every level and type of criminal jurisdiction.

To facilitate the development of such a Code, Auld LJ also recommended that a dedicated committee should be commissioned to undertake the work required to create it. In response to Auld's recommendations the Government, in the White Paper *Justice for All* (published July 2002), confirmed its commitment to modernising the criminal justice system. Parliament then passed primary legislation, by way of the Courts Act 2003, to facilitate the achievement of a consolidated criminal code and the Criminal Procedure Rule Committee was established in June 2004 with its main objective being to devise the rules of procedure for all criminal courts in England and Wales, up to and including the Court of Appeal (Criminal Division). The Committee then created the CrimPRs, which came into force in April 2005 and have been updated regularly since their inception. **9–010**

The CrimPRs 2020, as most recently amended in 2022, can be conveniently divided into 11 sets of "parts" that chronologically follow the progression of a case through the criminal courts. Under each of these 11 sets of parts are a number of sections; there are found the individual rules, and groups of rules, that are relevant to that particular stage of the case. The 11 sections are broken down as follows:

1. **General matters** (Parts 1–6)
   This section contains the Overriding Objective, a glossary of commonly used terms and provisions for case management, service of documents, forms and court records.
2. **Preliminary proceedings** (Parts 7–12)
   Here are set out the rules for the commencement of proceedings, pre-trial hearings, committal, transfer and sending for trial, the indictment, dismissal of charges and objections to discontinuance, restrictions in reporting, public access and extradition.
3. **Custody and bail** (Parts 13–14)
   Deals with warrants, bail and custody time limits.
4. **Disclosure** (Part 15)
   This section contains the rules on advance information, disclosure by the prosecution, the defence and prior disclosure of expert evidence, public interest immunity and confidential information.
5. **Evidence** (Parts 16–23)
   Here are found the rules governing witness statements and summonses, special measures directions, restrictions on cross-examination by a defendant acting in person, international co-operation, expert evidence, hearsay evidence, evidence on bad character and a complainant's previous sexual behaviour.
6. **Trial** (Parts 24–27)
   Contains the rules for trial and sentence in a magistrates' court, trial on indictment, trial of children and young persons, tainted acquittals and retrials.
7. **Sentencing** (Parts 28–32)
   Contains the rules on sentencing in special cases, breach, revocation and amendment of community and other orders, civil behaviour orders after verdict or finding, enforcement of fines or other orders for payment and road traffic penalties.
8. **Confiscation proceedings** (Part 33)
   This section takes into account the application of the Proceeds of Crime Act 2002.
9. **Appeal** (Parts 34–44)
   Deals with the various types of appeals that can be made to the Crown Court, High Court, Court of Appeal, Supreme Court and the European courts.
10. **Costs** (Part 45)
    Contains the rules on costs.
11. **Other proceedings** (Parts 46–50)
    Contains the rules on representatives, investigation orders and warrants, contempt of court, international cooperation, and extradition.

Not all the parts of the CrimPRs are simply a consolidation of existing rules and procedures though. Part 1 contains what is termed as the Overriding Objective and Pt 3 contains the rules pertaining to case management. These two areas had not previously existed in any rule or Practice Direction within the criminal justice system, though they are an expression and solidification of the practices found at common law within the criminal courts of first instance and the appellate courts, and they are essentially a criminal law counterpart to the civil Overriding Objective and case management rules (see Ch.8).

Commencing a Prosecution

The criminal justice system really comes into play upon a suspect being charged by the police for the alleged commission of an offence. How and why the police decide to charge that particular suspect is outside the remit of this textbook, so the analysis of the process will begin with consideration of the commencement of a prosecution. 9–011

Historically, there were two ways in which a prosecution against a suspect could be commenced. A single way of commencing criminal proceedings was introduced when s.29 of the CJA 2003 came into force, however this section is still not full in force, with outstanding amendments yet to be commenced. Before this, a police officer with the authority of a senior officer had the authority to lay information before a magistrate which contains details of the alleged offence and the suspect's alleged involvement in it. The Criminal Justice Act 2003 moved the decision to charge away from the police to the Crown Prosecution Service (the CPS) in order to promote a more efficient relationship between the police (who investigate) and the CPS (who ultimately would conduct the trial).

Charging a suspect is a process that can only be undertaken by the CPS. The police will initially review the evidence that they have against the suspect to determine whether there is enough evidence to initiate proceedings. If there is then the police, under s.37 of the Police and Criminal Evidence Act 1984 (PACE 1984) (as amended by the CJA 2003), will refer the case to the CPS to make the decision as to whether or not to charge the suspect. 9–012

The Crown Prosecution Service

As can be surmised from above, the CPS is the primary agency responsible for deciding whether to charge an individual with a criminal offence. The CPS was created by way of the Prosecution of Offences Act 1985 (POA 1985) and, under s.3(2)(a) of the POA 1985, it is charged with the responsibility of taking over the conduct and control of nearly all cases instituted by the police. The CPS was established following concerns that the police (who at that time conducted all prosecutions "in house") were not independent of the process. Therefore, it appeared that many cases were going to court with little or no hope of a conviction; not a satisfactory state of affairs. 9–013

The decision to prosecute an individual for a criminal offence is a serious step to take, as even the least serious offence can still have implications for all involved. To enable the CPS to make informed judgements as to when it is appropriate or not to initiate proceedings, s.10 of the POA 1985 required that the Director of Public Prosecutions (DPP) (who is the head of the CPS) provide the CPS with a code that contained guidance on the general principles it should apply when making such decisions; this is known as *The Code for Crown Prosecutors*. If the police are to charge the suspect they will also refer to this Code to determine whether prosecution is appropriate or not.

THE CODE

9–014 In determining whether or not to prosecute an individual, prosecutors will apply what is known as The Full Code Test, which is found at para.4 of the Code. The Full Code test is split into two distinct stages. The first part is known as the evidential stage and the second part is the public interest test. Essentially, the CPS is required to ask two main questions: is there enough evidence against the defendant? And is it in the public interest for the CPS to bring the case to court?

The evidential stage

9–015 To satisfy this first stage the CPS must be sure that there is a "realistic prospect of conviction". This test is an objective one and it concerns looking at the available evidence and deciding whether the trier of fact (the jury, judge or magistrates) would be *more likely than not* to convict the defendant of the alleged offence. This, however, is not the same test employed by the criminal courts (the test of beyond reasonable doubt) when deciding whether or not the defendant is guilty of the offence.

For prosecutors to determine whether there is a realistic prospect of conviction, they must ask themselves two questions, these being:

- can the evidence be used in court?
- is the evidence reliable?

The first question relates to the admissibility of the evidence against the defendant. If the evidence is not allowed to be used in court, maybe due to the way in which it was obtained (for example, the arrest of the suspect was unlawful, or the confession relied upon was beaten out of the suspect), then there may be no admissible evidence against the defendant and therefore any prosecution will be futile. If the evidence is usable and admissible in court then the second consideration to be determined is how reliable the evidence is. The Code lists five points that prosecutors may take into account when deciding this question, and this may involve taking into account the defendant's age or mental ability, the credibility of defendant's explanation, or a witness' background, etc. For example, if the defendant gives an innocent explanation of events and the evidence supports this explanation then there is little likelihood that there will be a realistic prospect of conviction.

If there is no admissible or reliable evidence then the intended prosecution must stop here and the charges against the defendant should be dropped. Only if the evidential test is positively satisfied should a prosecutor then go on to consider the public interest test.

The public interest stage

In 1951, Lord Shawcross, who was the then Attorney-General, made what has since become a classic statement on public interest: 9–016

> **It has never been the rule in this country—I hope it never will be—that suspected criminal offences must automatically be the subject of prosecution.**
> ***Hansard*, HC Vol.483, col.681 (29 January 1951)**

If the evidential test is satisfied, it still does not mean that a prosecution will automatically follow. For a prosecution to continue, the prosecutor must determine whether it would be in the public interest for the individual to be prosecuted for the alleged offence. To decide this, the prosecutor must look at the factors for and against prosecution, and then balance these carefully and fairly. To help prosecutors with this decision the Code lists a number of common factors both for and against prosecution; these factors are not an exhaustive list and which, if any, factors should be taken into account will be dependent upon the individual facts of each case.

For example, prosecution in respect of the more serious offences will be likely to be needed in the public interest if:

- a conviction is likely to result in a significant sentence;
- a conviction is likely to result in a confiscation or any other order;
- a weapon was used or violence was threatened during the commission of the offence;
- the offence was committed against a person serving the public (for example, a police or prison officer, or a nurse);
- the defendant was in a position of authority or trust;
- the evidence shows that the defendant was a ringleader or an organiser of the offence;
- there is evidence that the offence was premeditated;
- there is evidence that the offence was carried out by a group;
- the victim of the offence was vulnerable, has been put in considerable fear, or suffered personal attack, damage or disturbance;
- the offence was committed in the presence of, or in close proximity to, a child;
- the offence was motivated by any form of discrimination against the victim's ethnic or national origin, disability, sex, religious beliefs, political views or sexual orientation, or the suspect demonstrated hostility towards the victim based on any of those characteristics;
- there is a marked difference between the actual or mental ages of the defendant and the victim, or if there is any element of corruption;
- the defendant's previous convictions or cautions are relevant to the present offence;
- the defendant is alleged to have committed the offence while under an order of the court;

- there are grounds for believing that the offence is likely to be continued or repeated, for example, a history of recurring conduct;
- the offence, although not serious in itself, is widespread in the area where it was committed; or
- a prosecution would have a significant positive impact on maintaining community confidence.

9–017 Whereas, the factors where prosecution would be less likely to be needed include:

- the court is likely to impose a nominal penalty;
- the defendant has already been made the subject of a sentence and any further conviction would be unlikely to result in the imposition of an additional sentence or order, unless the nature of the particular offence requires a prosecution or the defendant withdraws consent to have an offence taken into consideration during sentencing;
- the offence was committed as a result of a genuine mistake or misunderstanding (these factors must be balanced against the seriousness of the offence);
- the loss or harm can be described as minor and was the result of a single incident, particularly if it was caused by a misjudgement;
- there has been a long delay between the offence taking place and the date of the trial, unless the offence is serious, the delay has been caused in part by the defendant, the offence has only recently come to light, or the complexity of the offence has meant that there has been a long investigation;
- a prosecution is likely to have a bad effect on the victim's physical or mental health, always bearing in mind the seriousness of the offence;
- the defendant is elderly or is, or was at the time of the offence, suffering from significant mental or physical ill health, unless the offence is serious or there is a real possibility that it may be repeated;
- the defendant has put right the loss or harm that was caused (but defendants must not avoid prosecution or diversion solely because they pay compensation); and
- details may be made public that could harm sources of information, international relations or national security.

Over to you

You are a CPS prosecutor.

The police have presented to you for consideration the case of a 79-year-old man who has allegedly stolen a bottle of milk from his local corner shop.

With reference to the Full Code Test, do you prosecute?

In such a case the CPS, after trawling through the common public interest factors for and against prosecution, might be likely to reach the conclusion that very little public interest would be served by prosecuting such an individual for the theft of a bottle of milk; the court would be likely to impose a nominal sentence, there was no weapon or violence used and the defendant is elderly, etc. However, this decision might change if the facts were that the man was a persistent offender and this was the fifteenth time he had been arrested for shoplifting in the past four months. The factors for prosecution here would be that there are grounds for believing that the offence is likely to be continued or repeated (for example, by a history of recurring conduct, the defendant's previous convictions or cautions are relevant to the present offence), and a prosecution would have a significant positive impact on maintaining community confidence. Therefore, the factors for prosecution would probably outweigh the factors against prosecution. **9–018**

Whether to prosecute or not is determined by balancing the facts and factors of the individual case. However, just because there are more ticks next to the list of factors against prosecution does not necessarily mean the prosecution should not go ahead. It could be that the balance lay more in the public's interest to prosecute, and then any potentially mitigating factors would be raised at sentencing if the defendant were convicted.

As well as deciding initially whether an alleged offender should be prosecuted, the CPS is also responsible for continuously reviewing the case right up until the point of trial. The evidence and the facts of a case are not always static and new evidence may come to light at any time. The CPS should regularly review each case by reference to the Full Code Test, to ensure that the prosecution is still appropriate. By undertaking such review the CPS will also be able to identify any areas in the case where the evidence is weak and, by doing so, it may be able to advise the police as to where to focus their investigations.

Charge Selection

The CPS is, in most cases, responsible for determining which is/are the most appropriate charge(s) to be levied against the alleged offender. To ensure this is done properly, the CPS is required, under para.6 of the Code, to select charges that: **9–019**

- reflect the seriousness and extent of the offending;
- give the court adequate powers to sentence and impose appropriate post-conviction orders; and
- enable the case to be presented in a clear and simple way.

This means that an offender is not always charged with the most serious offence, but rather with the offence that is most suitable in the circumstances. An example of this could be that, following a drunken Friday night street brawl where a number of people sustained injuries, the police wish to charge participants in the fight with a s.18 (OAPA 1861) grievous bodily harm with intent (the most serious non-fatal offence against a person which can result in a term of life imprisonment), whereas after consideration of the evidence the CPS lawyer feels that a s.47 (OAPA 1861) actual bodily harm charge (which is much less serious and can be dealt with by a magistrates' court) would be more appropriate. The CPS have the choice to charge the offender with the more serious offence but it may decide that, when taking into consideration the Full Code Test and the factors set out in para.7 of the Code (above), that the lesser charge is more appropriate and that there will be a more realistic prospect of conviction with it. The CPS is also responsible for reviewing, and possibly amending, the offence charged if new evidence comes to light.

FIGURE 33 **Commencing a prosecution**

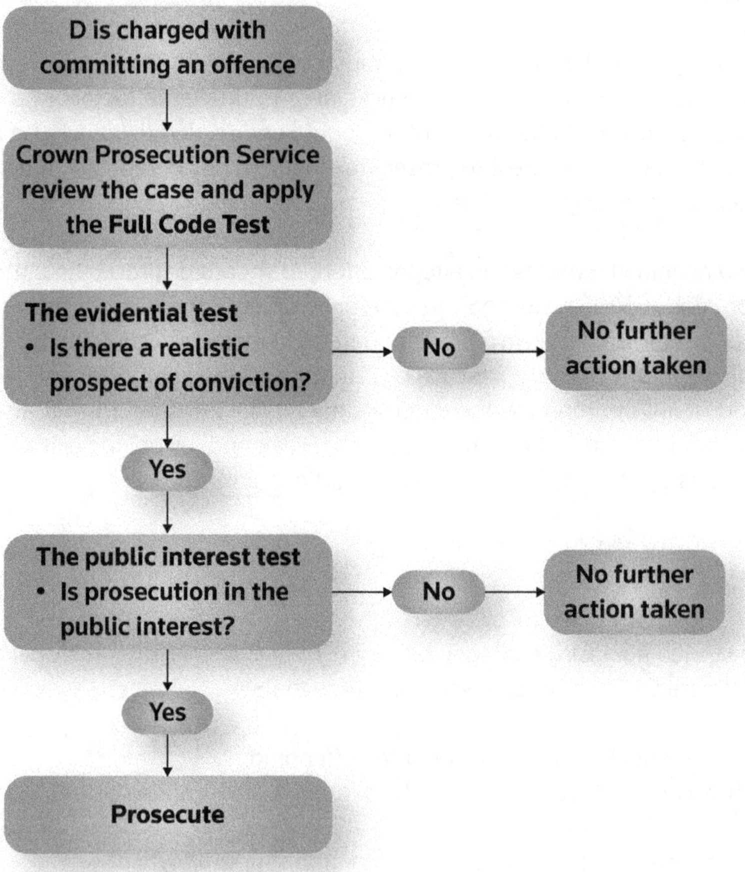

Alternatives to Prosecution

Returning to the scenario above of the 79-year-old man and the theft of a bottle of milk, if the CPS decides that prosecuting is not in the public interest then it does not mean that he will necessarily get away with the offence as the CPS has available to it a number of alternatives to formal prosecution, known as out-of-court disposals. If there were not these alternatives then many offences would go unpunished and this could result in more individuals being tempted to commit crime due to the lack of sanctions and, as a result, there could be a further potential loss in public confidence in the criminal justice system as a whole. So, what are these alternatives to prosecution? 9-020

The available out-of-court disposals are:

- cautions (adults);
- youth cautions (juveniles);
- community resolutions;
- adult cannabis or khat warnings; and
- fixed penalty notices.

Cautions (Adult)

Cautions come in two different forms, either a simple caution or a conditional caution. 9-021

SIMPLE CAUTIONS

Simple cautions are governed by Simple Caution for Adult Offender Guidance (MoJ Guidance, 13 April 2015) and are a non-statutory means of disposal. The aims behind a simple caution are to deal quickly and simply with less serious offences, to offer a proportionate response to low level offending, to divert offenders from criminal courts, and to reduce the likelihood of reoffending. The main questions to ask are whether a simple caution is appropriate on consideration of the facts of the case and, if so, whether a simple caution will be effective when taking into account the aims behind this form of caution. A simple caution cannot, at present, be given in respect of an indictable only offence unless the CPS agree (s.17(2) of the Criminal Justice and Courts Act 2015). This restriction is to be repealed by the Police, Sentencing and Courts Act 2022 and replaced with diversionary and community cautions, but this has not yet entered into force at the time of writing. 9-022

A simple caution may be viewed as appropriate if the offender is over the age of 18, they have made an admission of guilt in relation to the offence, there is sufficient evidence to warrant a prosecution and it is in the public interest to dispose of the matter by such a caution.

Simple cautions will generally be administered at a police station and the person receiving the caution must consent to it. A caution must be entered onto the Police National Computer and may be cited in any subsequent criminal proceedings and must be disclosed to potential employers if requested. There is also the potential for a person to still be prosecuted for the offence after receiving a caution, although this is unlikely. This form of disposal would be the most appropriate for our 79-year-old shoplifter.

CONDITIONAL CAUTIONS

9-023 A conditional caution is a method of statutory disposal and is at present dealt with by ss.22–27 of the CJA 2003. Section 22(2) defines a conditional caution as:

> **a caution which is given in respect of an offence committed by the offender and which has conditions attached to it with which the offender must comply.**

The conditions are required to fall into one or more of three categories:

- rehabilitation (treatment for drug or alcohol dependency, anger management classes, restorative justice, etc.);
- reparation (making good any damage caused, restoring stolen goods, paying modest financial compensation, etc.); or
- punishment (financial penalty conditions which punish the offender for their unlawful conduct).

The conditions must, however, be appropriate, achievable and proportionate. The key to determining whether a conditional caution should be given is whether the imposition of specified conditions will be an appropriate and effective means of addressing the offending behaviour or making reparation for the effects of the offence on the victim or the community. The police are generally responsible for the administering of a conditional caution but they have no discretion as to the decision to use a conditional caution as a method of disposal, under s.23 of the CJA 2003 this responsibility falls on the CPS.

For a conditional caution to be viewed as appropriate, the defendant must first have attained the age of 18. If this is the case then the five requirements under s.23 must be satisfied. These five requirements are:

- there is evidence that the offender committed the offence (a realistic prospect of conviction);
- the offender has admitted the offence;
- the prosecutor has decided that a conditional caution is appropriate;
- the offender must have the effect of the conditional caution explained to them; and
- the offender must consent to the conditional caution.

Over to you

Can you think of an example when a conditional caution might be appropriate and what type of conditions may be relevant to your example?

The whole idea behind the use of a conditional caution is that prosecution may not be in the best interest of the public, whereas the imposition of a condition may be. 9-024

If the defendant is a drug user who has just started stealing to fund his habit then the journey through the criminal justice system may be very detrimental to his wellbeing, this could result in further reliance upon drugs, which, in turn, could mean that he commits more crime to sustain his habit; in other words, it could become a vicious circle. However, if that defendant is given a conditional caution with the condition of attending treatment for drug dependency, it may break his drug habit, prevent the defendant committing further crime and allow the defendant to become a positive member of society. If a defendant subsequently breaches the conditional caution they can then be prosecuted for the original offence and therefore justice will be done. Defendants must always consent to the caution, and by agreeing to a caution they are formally admitting guilt to the offence charged. If a defendant disputes involvement in any way with an alleged offence then a caution is not be appropriate and the CPS would have to consider whether prosecution was a viable option, by reference to the Code, as discussed above.

Youth Cautions

So far the simple and conditional cautions considered above can only be administered to adult offenders but sadly, in this world, there are also a high number of young offenders, so appropriate sanctions for them also need to be available. The Crime and Disorder Act 1998 introduced, under s.65, a young person's equivalent to cautions, reprimands and warnings, which applied to those aged 17 and under; these were replaced by Youth Cautions under s.135 of the Legal Aid, Sentencing and Punishment of Offenders Act 2012. Youth cautions are a formal out-of-court disposal that can be used as an alternative to prosecution for young offenders between the ages of 10 and 17 years where: 9-025

- there is sufficient evidence against the defendant;
- they make admissions as to the offence; or
- it would not be in the public interest to prosecute.

A conditional caution may be given to a young person aged between 10 and 17 years and the same factors that are taken into account in respect of adult conditional cautions are applicable to youth ones. Factors such as the young person's age, maturity, and personal circumstances should also be taken into account when considering what the appropriate conditions to impose are.

Fixed Penalty Notices

9–026 The final alternative to prosecution is the issue of a fixed penalty notice. Fixed penalty notices are generally thought of as synonymous with road traffic offences, such as speeding, etc. Offenders are issued with a penalty notice that requires a set monetary amount to be paid in order to discharge any liability to be convicted of the offence that the notice relates to, as set by primary or secondary legislation. Fines can range from about £50 up to £300 depending on the offence in question. Most people only equate fixed penalty notices with motoring offences but they can, in fact, be issued for a number of different offences such as being drunk in a public place, trespassing on a railway, criminal damage, selling alcohol to children and knowingly giving a false alarm of fire. Persons who receive a notice can request being tried for the offence instead of making an admission of guilt by payment. However, if a fixed penalty notice is ignored, then, after a set time (normally 21 days from issue of the notice), a further fine, which is a sum equal to one and a half times the original fine, will then be issued. By way of example, Penalty Notice for Disorder is a statutory disposal introduced by the Criminal Justice and Police Act 2001 (ss.1–11) whereby penalty offences are divided into lower and upper tier offences depending on seriousness and attract penalties of £60 and £90 respectively.

Adult Cannabis or Khat Warning

9–027 An Adult Cannabis Warning is an informal verbal warning administered by a police officer either on the street or at a police station. It will be given when an adult (aged 18 years or over) is found in possession of a small amount of cannabis or khat consistent with personal use. The Warning is a three-stage process and is only available to first-time offenders under the Penalty Notice for Disorder scheme as described above. The intended effects are to deter the misuse of khat amongst the UK public, curb availability by removing the khat trade from the UK and remove opportunities for the onward trafficking of khat.

Before issuing a Warning an officer will consider the quantity of cannabis or khat involved, whether there is sufficient evidence against the offender, if the offender has made an admission to the possession, the age of the offender, whether there is any victim, and the fact that it will be recorded on the offender's record. The drug is confiscated, but the warning is not a conviction and should not be regarded as an aggravating factor when sentencing for any subsequent offences.

Community Resolutions

9–028 A Community Resolution is a form of restorative justice that encourages the offender to face up to the impact of their offending and to take responsibility for the consequences of their actions. It is thought that requiring an offender to make good on the harm they have caused will make it less likely that they will reoffend in the future. Again, there must be sufficient evidence against the offender and the offender must have admitted the offence and have explicitly consented to taking part in the restorative justice process. A Community Resolution may involve the offender apologising to the victim of their actions, or putting right the harm or damage they have caused.

Part 6 of the Police, Crime, Sentencing and Courts (PCSC) Act 2022 introduced a two-tier framework of out of court disposals for adults; Community Caution (Lower tier) and Diversionary Caution (Upper tier). Despite not appearing in the PCSCA 2022, community resolutions can continue to be used as an out of court disposal option by Police. As community resolutions are non-statutory, such interventions agreed cannot be legally enforced or escalated to a higher disposal. The available options (in ascending order of severity) are;

- Community Resolution;
- Community Caution (Adult) or Youth caution;
- Diversionary Caution (Adult) or Youth conditional caution; and
- Charge/Postal Requisition.

Offence Classification

In England and Wales there are two forms that a trial in criminal proceedings may take; trial on indictment or summary trial. Summary trials are heard by a magistrates' court, and, will be presided over by either a Bench of three lay justices of the peace (magistrates) (see Ch.5 for further details as to who magistrates are) or a single district judge. Trials on indictment are heard in the Crown Court before a judge and jury. **9–029**

One of the main determining factors as to whether the case will be tried on indictment or heard summarily will be the actual offence that the defendant has been charged with. Each offence falls into a specific offence classification and this classification will then establish which method of trial will be used, this also subsequently dictates the necessary pre-trial procedures that need to be undertaken or considered in relation to the case.

There are three different offence classifications, and these are:

- summary;
- either-way; and
- indictable.

The Interpretation Act 1978 (IA 1978) sets out what these classifications mean. Paragraph 1 of Sch.1 to the IA 1978 provides that: **9–030**

(a) "indictable offence" means an offence which, if committed by an adult, is triable on indictment, whether it is exclusively so triable or triable either-way;
(b) "summary offence" means an offence which, if committed by an adult, is triable only summarily;
(c) "offence triable either-way" means an offence, other than an offence triable on indictment only by virtue of the Criminal Justice Act 1988 which, if committed by an adult, is triable either on indictment or summarily;
and the terms "indictable", "summary" and "triable either-way", in their application to offences, are to be construed accordingly.

Section 5 of the IA 1978 states that when the words "summary", "either-way" and "indictable" are used in a statute then they must be construed as meaning the above definitions, unless their intention is contrary to these meanings. This, however, does not really provide enough detail to determine which specific offence falls into which specific classification. To discover the offence, classification of an individual offence regard first needs to be given to whether the offence has been created by statute (and if so what the statute says about it) or whether the offence is one found at common law.

Summary Offences

9–031 Summary offences are generally the least serious of all of the criminal offences. A summary offence, as stated above, will normally only be tried in a magistrates' court and the level of the seriousness of a summary offence is reflected by the magistrates' sentencing powers. The maximum penalty that can be imposed by a magistrates' court was increased from a six-month term of imprisonment to 12 months maximum under the Sentencing Act 2020 (Magistrates' Court Sentencing Powers) (Amendment) Regulations 2024 (SI 2024/1067) or a £5,000 fine. This recent change should drive down the remand population in jail awaiting a Crown Court trial and save time in that trial court for more serious and complex matters. Summary offences are created by statute and the Act and offence in question will provide details of the maximum penalty that can be imposed upon conviction for that offence. If the statute sets out that the maximum penalty is either 12 months' imprisonment or a £5,000 fine then the offence can be taken to be summary. Some examples of summary offences are:

- common assault;
- driving whilst disqualified; and
- taking a motor vehicle without the owner's consent.

Indictable Offences

9–032 Indictable only offences are seen as being the most serious types of criminal offence that can be committed. They are so serious that they can only be heard in the Crown Court in front of a judge and a jury and they have the potential to carry heavy sentences, such as life imprisonment. All common law offences, such as murder, are generally only triable on indictment, unless they are specifically listed in Sch.1 to the Magistrates' Courts Act 1980 (MCA 1980). If it is an offence created by way of statute, then, if the maximum penalty is beyond the powers of a magistrates' court, then it is an indictable offence.

Indictable only offences are further split down into four different categories called classes. In Class 1 the most serious indictable only offences are listed, and these include murder, treason, genocide and torture, etc. Class 2 indictable only offences include manslaughter, rape, infanticide, sex with a girl under the age of 13, piracy and mutiny. Classes 3 and 4 contain the remaining indictable only offences such as wounding with intent or robbery or assault with intent to rob.

The alleged commission of indictable only offences and the subsequent trials on indictment are regularly reported by the media, and therefore the public can be forgiven for thinking that most of the crimes dealt with by the criminal justice system are in fact very serious indictable ones. In reality, though, only a small number of crimes committed are indictable only, and the approximate figure of cases involving offences charged on indictment is 2 per cent of all criminal cases, with approximately only 0.5 per cent of these actually making it to trial; meaning that the remaining 98 per cent are charged and tried summarily. This can be looked at in one of two ways and the way in which an individual will choose to view it will depend upon their perception of society and the media. The first approach to interpreting these figures could be to decide that the media over-report and over-sensationalise the most serious offences committed and therefore, as a result, the public have a distorted perception of the crime levels and the nature of the crimes committed in the UK. The flip side of this, and the second way in which these figures can be viewed, is that there are in fact a substantial amount of indictable only offences committed and, if this is the case, then consequently there must be a phenomenal amount of less serious and petty crimes occurring within this country on a very regular basis.

Either-way Offences

Either-way offences are generally viewed as hybrid offences and they do not have a set home as summary offences and indictable only offences do (magistrates' courts and the Crown Court, respectively). They can either be tried summarily or on indictment and this decision will be dependent on the facts of the individual case and the seriousness of the offence committed. It appears that they are in fact a derivative of the indictable only offence classification, because when (according to s.5 of the IA 1978) a statute speaks of an indictable offence but does not provide further detail, then it must be taken to be referring to an indictable only *or* an either-way offence because both can be tried on indictment. 9–033

Whether an offence is an either-way offence or not can be discovered in one of two ways. The first is by reference to the statute if the offence is one created statutorily. If the statute sets out that the maximum penalty is *either* punishable by a penalty for summary conviction *or* by a penalty for an indictable conviction, then the offence is triable either way. If the offence is not one created by statute (a common law offence), then reference should be made to Sch.1 to the MCA 1980, as this Schedule contains a list of offences which are triable either-way.

9–034 The more commonly known offences that appear in the Schedule are offences such as assault occasioning actual bodily harm under s.47 of the OAPA 1861, or the offence of theft under the Theft Act 1968 (TA 1968), but the Schedule also contains a number of more obscure offences, such as the offence of making false representations, etc. with a view to procuring the burning of any human remains, or the offence of damaging submarine cables. The majority of the offences listed under Sch.1 are old offences (some are very old) ranging from 1751, and there are no offences listed later than 1971. The reason behind this is not that no new either-way offences have been created since this date, but rather that, when such an offence is created, the penalties for the offence are drafted directly into the statute and therefore the offence does not need to be added to the Schedule.

Obviously, there are only two forms of trial, summary (magistrates' courts) and on indictment (Crown Court), so when dealing with an either-way offence a decision needs to be made as to which court the case will be heard in. The procedure and realities of this process are discussed below.

PLEA BEFORE VENUE

9–035 As discussed, all cases initially pass through magistrates' court, even if it is only briefly whilst on the way to the Crown Court. With an either-way offence, the first court hearing to take place in the matter is known as a plea before venue hearing, and this is what is heard at the magistrates' court. This hearing is the earliest point at which defendants' pleas can be formally taken and it is effectively a preliminary hearing where no matters of substantive law will be heard.

To illustrate the procedure involved in determining the trial location of an either-way offence the below case study will be referred to.

CASE STUDY

Bertie Bunting is a 26-year-old drug addict. He has been charged with burglary under s.9 of the TA 1968. It is alleged that he entered 73 North Road, a residential property, at approximately 3.10am and stole a number of items of jewellery, including a Rolex watch valued at £7,000 and a diamond ring worth £4,000. Bertie already has one previous conviction for burglary.

Section 17A of the MCA 1980 contains the procedure on how a plea before venue hearing should be conducted. At the hearing, the charges will be put before the defendant, so in the above case Bertie would have the charge and particulars of the offence of burglary put to him. The form of words used would be something along the lines of:

Clerk: "Are you Bertie Bunting of 1A Main Street, Nonchester?"

Bertie: "Yes."

Clerk: "Bertie Bunting, you are charged with burglary contrary to s.9 of the Theft Act 1968. The particulars of the offence are that on the 2nd February 2007 at 3.10am you entered 73 North Road and stole a diamond ring and a Rolex watch. How do you plead to this indictment, guilty or not guilty?"

It would then be explained to him (as the defendant) that if he pleads guilty at this point then he will be dealt with summarily and the magistrates may pass sentence without hearing any evidence. If, however, the magistrates' court felt that its sentencing powers were insufficient (see Ch.5, "Sentencing Powers", for details as to magistrates' sentencing powers) for the case then Bertie could still be sent to the Crown Court for sentence under s.14 of the Sentencing Act 2020 (SA 2020) and then be sentenced as if tried on indictment (so the full range of sentences which could be imposed at the Crown Court for the offence would be available to the court in respect of him). After this has all been explained to him in language that he can understand, he would then be asked to indicate his plea of either guilty or not guilty. If the defendant refused to enter a plea, or the plea was equivocal, then a not guilty plea would be entered on his behalf by the court (s.17A(8) of the MCA 1980). 9–036

ALLOCATION HEARINGS

If defendants choose to enter a not guilty plea then the next step is for an "allocation hearing" to be conducted in order to determine which court (magistrates' or Crown Court) will hear the case. The CJA 2003 changed the title of these proceedings from "mode of trial" hearing to "allocation hearing", but many practitioners still refer to them as "mode of trial" hearings. 9–037

The procedure for the determining the court allocation of a case is set out extensively in ss.17A–21 of the MCA 1980. Section 19 provides the basis that the magistrates are responsible for determining whether the case should remain in magistrates' court or be committed to the Crown Court for trial. Section 19(3) sets out that when considering whether the offence is more suitable for summary trial or for trial on indictment, the court should have regard to:

> (a) whether the sentence which a magistrates' court would have power to impose for the offence would be adequate; and
> (b) any representations made by the prosecution or the accused under subsection (2)(b) above,
> and shall have regard to any allocation guidelines (or revised allocation guidelines) issued as definitive guidelines under section 122 of the Coroners and Justice Act 2009.

9–038 The court will also have regard to the Sentencing Council Allocation guidelines, which stipulates that all cases should be tried at the appropriate level and that, in general, all either-way cases should be tried summarily unless it is likely that the court's sentencing powers will be insufficient. These guidelines set out that, in ascertaining the likely sentence to be imposed, the court must assess it in light of the facts alleged by the prosecution and by any defence put forward by the defendant; and the Magistrates' Court Sentencing Guidelines drawn up by the Sentencing Guidelines Council in determining whether or not to send the case to be tried on indictment or for it to remain as a summary hearing. These guidelines provide sentencing information on the most commonly encountered offences in the magistrates' court; they also detail the aggravating and mitigating factors frequently raised, and provide a starting point for sentencing for each offence.

If the court reaches the decision that the case is suitable to be dealt with summarily then the procedure as set out under s.20 of the MCA 1980 must be followed. This section requires the court to inform the defendant of the fact that the case is deemed appropriate in seriousness to be dealt with by magistrates' court; at that point the defendant can either consent to a summary trial or refuse this and elect to be tried by the Crown Court. This procedure is often described as the "right to elect trial by jury" and it is quite a controversial and heavily criticised "right" of the criminal justice system, the criticisms of which we will consider in a moment.

9–039 Either-way offences are offences that are allocated to the appropriate court depending on the nature and circumstances of the offence, the other factors noted in s.19 of the MCA 1980, and the allocation and sentencing guidelines. Offences such as theft or assault occasioning actual bodily harm are either-way offences and there can be a vast difference in the levels of seriousness of these offences. For example, take the offence of theft; theft can be the stealing of two chocolate bars from a local corner shop with a value to the tune of £1, but the same offence can also be committed by the stealing of £200,000 from an employer. It is the same offence, charged under the same statutory provision, but with greatly varying degrees of seriousness. Another example can be seen with the offence of actual bodily harm under s.47 of the OAPA 1861; this may be committed by occasioning a bruise to someone's arm, or it could be that the victim sustains a broken nose; again, varying degrees of seriousness in the same offence. In the more serious cases, the magistrates' court will hand jurisdiction over to the Crown Court for trial on indictment, but in the less serious matters, where magistrates feel that they are capable of dealing with the case, defendants can still elect to have the case heard before a jury in the Crown Court. There are two sides to the argument in relation to the right to elect a trial by jury. The first is that everyone has the fundamental right to a fair trial (as stated in art.6 of the ECHR) and, if defendants wish to have their case heard before 12 peers then they should be allowed to exercise this right. The alternative side to the argument, and the reason why this provision attracts such criticism is that a jury trial for a low level theft, such the £1 worth of chocolate above, is completely disproportionate (in time, expense and resources) to the seriousness of the actual offence committed. Allowing defendants to elect trial by jury in these kinds of cases, it can be argued, amounts to an abuse of the system, which could ultimately lead to the criminal justice system becoming increasingly overloaded and ineffective.

Under s.20 of the MCA 1980 defendants also have the right to ask for an indication of sentence before deciding whether to consent to a summary trial or elect for a Crown Court trial. The only indication that the court is permitted to give in these circumstances is as to whether the sentence will be custodial or non-custodial. The court is not obliged to give such an indication if they feel it would be inappropriate to do so and the indication given may have an impact on how the defendant decides to proceed.

Burglary and criminal damage

There are special rules relating to the either-way offences of burglary and criminal damage in relation to allocation hearings. If the burglary is the third burglary committed by the defendant since November 1999 then under s.314 of the SA 2020 a custodial sentence of three years will be imposed. If the case is viewed as being beyond the scope of the magistrates' sentencing powers then the defendant must be sent to the Crown Court for trial on indictment by way of s.51 of the Crime and Disorder Act 1998 (CDA 1998). Section 51 formally sets out the fact that any defendant charged with an offence triable only on indictment will be sent to the Crown Court for trial, but this also applies to either-way offences. Sending for trial is a simple administrative process. 9-040

In respect of the offence of criminal damage contrary to s.1 of the Criminal Damage Act 1971, if the value of the item damaged is less than £5,000 then the case must be tried summarily and defendants cannot elect trial in the Crown Court. If the damage was however caused by fire, or the damage inflicted is worth over £5,000 then normal allocation hearing proceedings must be undertaken.

Over to you

Refer back to the case study of Bertie (above).

If you were a magistrate hearing this case, do you think you would decide that the case was suitable for summary trial or would you commit to the Crown Court?

If we relate the allocation hearings provisions to the case study of Bertie then, as this is only the second burglary that Bertie has been charged with, the magistrates would not need to consider the provisions under s.314 of the SA 2020. They would therefore need to consider the statutory factors found in s.19 of the MCA 1980; these being the nature of the offence, the circumstances of the offence, their sentencing powers and any other relevant circumstances, and they must also refer to the allocation and sentencing guidelines. The burglary was of a domestic nature and it occurred during the night when the homeowners were likely to be 9-041 asleep in bed, plus the items stolen were also of a high value. So, should the case be sent to the Crown Court or can the magistrates retain jurisdiction?

If the magistrates in Bertie's case decide the case is suitable for trial on indictment and intend to commit him to the Crown Court, Bertie loses all power to elect a summary trial in the magistrates' court. Once the magistrates have decided that the case is not suitable for summary trial, due to the fact that they have insufficient sentencing powers, the case must be sent to the Crown Court under s.51 CDA 1998 (the complicated committal procedure for either-way offences was abolished under the CJA 2003) and the defendant no longer has any say in the matter. To allow him to then elect a summary trial would be perverse as, if this were allowed and he was then convicted after a trial, the magistrates would not be able to impose a just and appropriate sentence.

9-042 The final point to make is that if a defendant has been charged with an either-way offence *and* a summary offence, and either elects trial at the Crown Court or is sent to the Crown Court, then the linked summary offence will, under s.51 of the Crime and Disorder Act 1998 (CDA (1998)), also be heard in the Crown Court. However, if a guilty plea is then entered or guilt is proven in relation to the summary offence, after trial the Crown Court can only sentence in respect of it as if it were a summary offence.

MAGISTRATES' COURT v CROWN COURT

9-043 If the magistrates feel that they have sufficient sentencing powers to deal with a matter summarily the defendant will then need to make a choice as to whether to remain in the magistrates' court or elect trial on indictment, but what are the factors that the defendant will need to take into account when making this decision?

- **Conviction rates**
  Magistrates' courts are believed to have a higher conviction rate, convicting in approximately 90 per cent of cases, whereas there is believed to be a higher chance of acquittal in a trial by jury. This difference may be due to the composition of the triers of fact in each forum; the selection process for magistrates tries to ensure that the Bench is representative of society but the number and type of people who volunteer to become magistrates limits this; a jury is randomly selected from the electoral roll which offers a greater chance that the composition will be reflective of society.
- **Delay**
  Cases proceed with more speed through magistrates' courts. Defendants may have to wait up to nine months before their case can be heard in the Crown Court, whereas, in a magistrates' the case may only be waiting a few weeks or months. A lengthy delay in a case coming to court will often be very stressful to those involved, such as defendants, victims, witnesses and the families. Summary trial will resolve the matter more quickly. However, from a defendant's point of

view, a delay may be advantageous as witnesses are less likely to appear for the trial, and the reliability of their evidence will be undermined by the passage of time.

- **Publicity**
  Generally cases that are heard in the Crown Court will command more media attention than those heard in magistrates' courts and this public scrutiny can cause even more stress for the parties involved. The publicity may have a detrimental effect on a defendant's quality of life both personally and professionally.
- **Legally qualified**
  The Crown Court has the advantage that the case is overseen by an experienced criminal judge who should be able to deal with any evidential issues as they arise. The jury will also generally be excluded from the hearing when points of law are raised so that such matters do not prejudice it. In a magistrates' court the Bench is not legally qualified, although a legal adviser advises it. Also, if points of law are raised then the Bench is (at times) required to deal with them and this may inadvertently have a prejudicial effect on its decision.
- **Sentencing powers**
  Although magistrates' courts are believed to have a higher conviction rate they also have lesser sentencing powers than the Crown Court. By electing to have a case heard by a jury a defendant is running the risk of receiving a much harsher sentence if eventually convicted. Since the increase in maximum sentences of imprisonment for magistrates' courts from six to 12 months in 2024, this is a weaker, but still valid, point.

FIGURE 34 **Either-way offences**

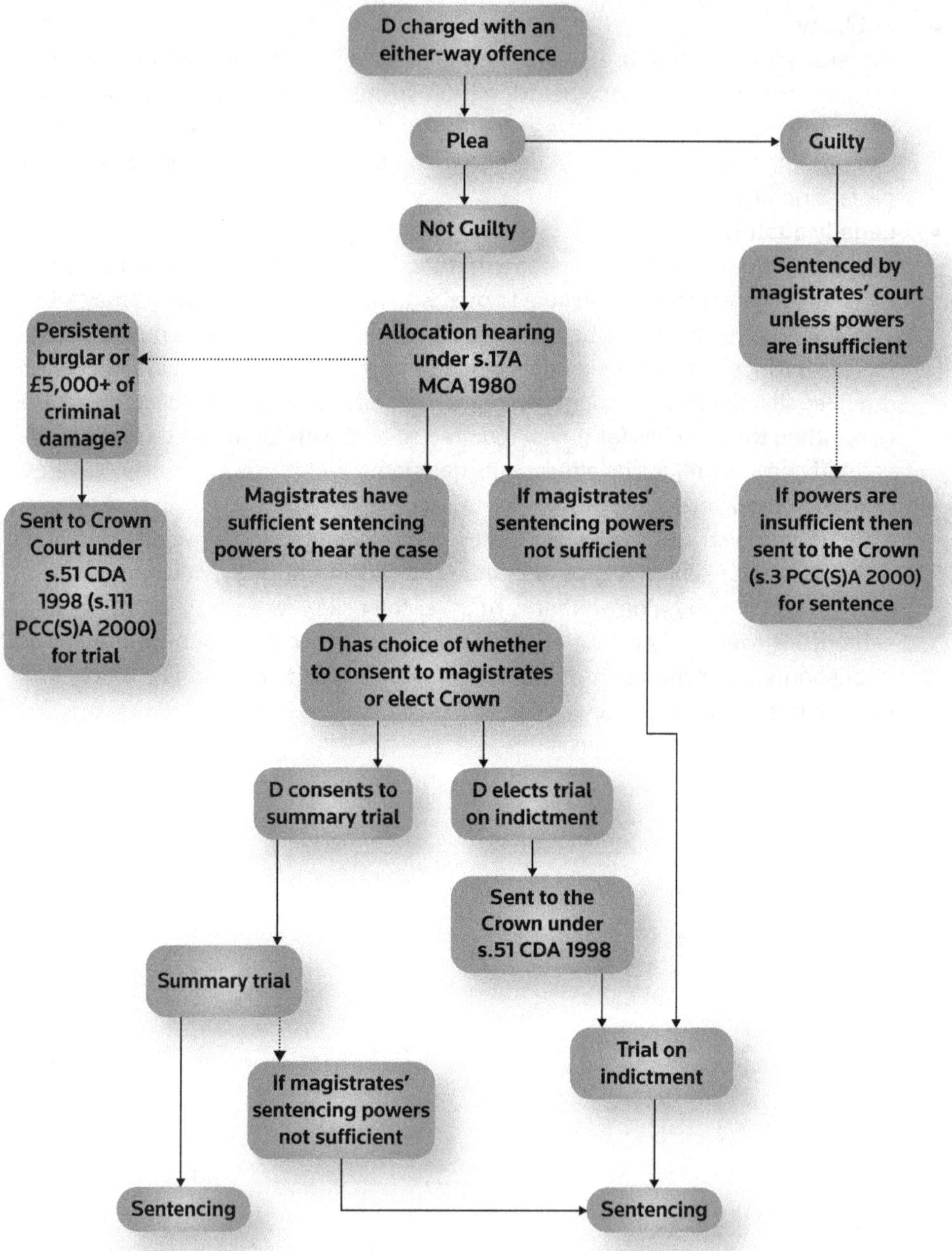

Pleas

There are two common types of plea that defendants may give in a criminal case, either "guilty" or "not guilty". However, the subject of pleas is not as straightforward as it first seems and there is a whole grey area in between the pleas of guilty or not guilty. 9–044

Guilty Pleas

Defendants will enter a guilty plea when they admit that they committed the offence. It is essentially a full and frank admission of guilt and an agreement as to the facts of the offence put forward by the prosecution. 9–045

There are a number of reasons why defendants decide to plead guilty to an alleged offence. There may be overwhelming evidence against a defendant, such as a number of credible eye-witnesses to the offence, or that there may be undisputable forensic evidence. Alternatively, defendants may simply know and admit they did wrong, be full of remorse and willing to accept the inevitable consequences of their actions. The law, however, also provides some incentives for guilty pleas from defendants. Section 73 of the SA 2020 sets out that a reduction in sentence as a result of a guilty plea can be considered by the court if it feels that it is appropriate in the circumstances. To determine this, the court is directed (under s.73(2)) to look at:

(a) the stage in the proceedings for the offence at which the offender indicated the intention to plead guilty, and
(b) the circumstances in which the indication was given.

The general rule has been that if a defendant enters a guilty plea at the earliest opportunity (normally at the first court hearing) then a reduction in sentence will be afforded to reflect this fact. However, the closer a case draws to trial before a guilty plea is entered, the lesser the reduction in sentence will be, to the point that if a defendant pleads guilty on the day of the trial it may be unlikely any sentence reduction at all is received; the chance of redemption via the entering of such a plea will be viewed as having long passed. Essentially, there is a progressive loss of mitigation. The court, under s.73(2)(b), is also required to consider the circumstances in which the indication was given. If it appears that a defendant has refused to plead guilty until an irrefutable case against him is made out by the prosecution then he may be viewed as having been simply backed into a corner with no other option but to plead guilty. In these circumstances the courts are less likely to look upon the guilty plea in a sympathetic light and a defendant may not receive the full sentence reduction that could be granted in the circumstances.

Traditionally, the maximum percentage reduction was about 33 per cent (one-third of the sentence), this percentage then decreasing to 10 per cent depending (amongst other things) on the timing of the guilty plea in relation to the start of the trial.The Sentencing Council and 9–046 the Sentencing Code (chapter 2 of the SA 2020) are now effective in all cases where sentencing occurs on or after 1 December 2020 to help make sure that judges and magistrates take a consistent approach to sentencing.

9–047 The court is firstly required to decide the sentence for an offence by taking into account any aggravating or mitigating factors, as well as any other offences that have been formally admitted so as to be taken into consideration in respect of sentencing (Chapter 3 Part 4 of the SA 2020). The court, once having decided the full sentence, must then apply a sliding scale to determine the appropriate level of reduction. The sliding scale ranges from one-third where the guilty plea was entered at the first reasonable opportunity (as was the case prior to the review); reducing to a recommended one-quarter when the trial date has been set; and then down to a recommended one-tenth for a guilty plea entered just prior to or after the commencement of the trial.

9–048 The guidelines also consider what was is meant by the term "first reasonable opportunity" and it concluded that it may be considered to be the first time that a defendant appears in court, but it could also be (especially in relation to indictable offences) that it was reasonable to have expected an indication of willingness to admit guilt at an earlier opportunity, such as during interview at the police station. The Court of Appeal considered this point in the case of **R. v Caley** [2013] 2 Cr. App. R. (S.) 47, where it held that the "first reasonable opportunity" would not normally include an admission by the defendant in police interview, although such an admission may be viewed as a mitigating factor. The court in **Caley** also identified the numerous advantages to providing defendants with a reduction in sentence in return for a guilty plea, such as the fact that it removes the need for a trial, shortens the whole criminal process between charge and sentence, helps to preserve and save on resources and costs, and prevents victims and witnesses having to go through the ordeal of a trial. In being able to provide such an incentive to plead guilty, the courts are able to help in alleviating the burden upon the criminal justice system, which, in turn, allows the time and resources to deal with other cases in a more efficient and expeditious manner.

However, one of the criticisms that can be made against the policy of sentence reductions for guilty pleas is the argument that this system potentially places unfair pressure on defendants to plead guilty to offences, even when they may not be guilty (see discussion on plea-bargaining and advanced indication of sentence at **9–054**).

NEWTON HEARINGS

9–049 Occasionally, situations may arise where defendants admit commission of the offence, but that the circumstances were not as the prosecution alleges. To illustrate what this means let us look at the facts of the case study below.

CASE STUDY

Alfie is 20 years old and has never been in trouble with the police before. He has been charged with the offence of assaulting a constable in the execution of his duty under s.89 of the Police Act 1996 following a night out on the town. It is alleged that PC Short was attempting to arrest Alfie's friend, Frank, for urinating in the street when Alfie tried to stop him from carrying out the arrest by pushing PC Short, spitting in his face and calling him a "pig".

Alfie has been charged with the summary offence of assaulting a police officer in the execution of his duty contrary to s.89 of the Police Act 1996.

Alfie has decided to plead guilty to the offence of assaulting a police officer in the execution of his duty. Alfie admits that he pushed PC Short and called him a pig, but the prosecution are also alleging that Alfie spat in the officer's face. Alfie denies this element of the facts. The issue as to whether Alfie spat in the police officer's face or not will have an effect on the sentence that he receives following his guilty plea (as it aggravates the offence), therefore this is an issue that needs to be decided. To determine the facts that he should be sentenced upon the court is required to hold what is known as a **Newton** hearing, following the principles set out by Lord Lane CJ in the case of **R. v Newton** (1983) 77 Cr. App. R. 13. **9–050**

A **Newton** hearing involves the judges or magistrates listening to the evidence called by both parties, and then making a decision as to the facts upon this evidence. This may involve calling witnesses for either side, such as other police officers or other people present at the scene of the incident. The prosecution is required to prove its version of the events beyond reasonable doubt and any element of doubt will be afforded to the defendant (unless the defendant's version is completely implausible, **R. v Hawkins** (1985) 7 Cr. App. R. (S) 351). **Newton** hearings are not just confined to summary offences and may be used in relation to both either-way and indictable offences. They are an important part of the judicial process in ensuring that justice is administered effectively and that the sentence imposed is representative and relative to the crime that has been committed.

EQUIVOCAL PLEAS

Guilty pleas by defendants must be unequivocal to be accepted by the court. This means that the plea cannot be ambiguous, in that it raises a possible defence such as self-defence or provocation, or the defendant does not understand the charges or case. **9–051**

Over to you

Can you give an example of what would be an equivocal plea?

A few examples of what could be classed as an equivocal plea are:

- "Yeah, I'm guilty, I punched her three times in the face, but it was only cos she wouldn't leave me alone. I'd told her to get off but she wouldn't, she just kept coming back at me again and again" (possible defence of self-defence);
- "I pleaded guilty to the murder of my daughter. I wasn't thinking straight at the time because I had post-natal depression and I thought social services were coming to get her. I really thought she was better off dead than in care. Now I have recovered from this illness and I realise what I did was wrong so, yes, I'm guilty" (possible defence of diminished responsibility); and
- "I admit that I went into the house and stole old Mrs Brown's savings from her teapot in the kitchen but I wouldn't have normally done something like this, I'm not a bad person really; it's just because they said they'd kill my little brother if I didn't" (possible defence of duress).

9-052 If a plea is equivocal then judges are duty bound to raise the issue of what may be a potential defence and request the case to be adjourned so discussions can take place with the defendant and so that a new plea of not guilty can possibly be entered into the court. If it becomes apparent that a defendant does not understand what he is pleading guilty to then the court must also enter a not guilty plea on his behalf.

If a defendant refuses to enter any plea at all then, under s.6 of the Criminal Law Act 1967 (CLA 1967) the court must enter a plea of not guilty on the defendant's behalf. This was the situation that arose in the 2006 trial of Saddam Hussein for crimes against humanity, genocide and war crimes. Saddam Hussein challenged the legitimacy of the court that was trying him and refused to enter a plea to the charges against him, as a result the court was obliged to enter a plea of not guilty on his behalf. Even though this was at international level the principle is still exactly the same. If a person does not unequivocally plead guilty then they are entitled to have the case against them proved to the requisite standard of proof.

Not Guilty Pleas

9-053 If a defendant pleads not guilty to the charges brought against him then the case will proceed to trial. This means that the prosecution is required to prove the case (meaning each element of the actus reus and mens rea) to the requisite criminal standard, as well as disproving any defence that a defendant may raise (also to the same standard). In a criminal trial the required standard is that the prosecution must prove the case against a defendant beyond reasonable doubt (see "Burden of Proof", at 9-075).

Plea-bargaining

Entrenched in the fundamental principles of English law is the common thread that defendants are "innocent until proven guilty" and that the prosecution is required to *prove* that defendants are guilty of the offence charged and *not* that defendants are required to prove innocence. This principle is one of great importance to a large proportion of the modern civilised world and many jurisdictions have adopted this paradigm, often terming it "due process". It can be, and often is, argued that the reduction in sentence policy and other forms of plea-bargaining, such as advanced indication of sentence, go against the grain of this principle of due process in a number of ways. 9–054

Over to you

Consider the following scenario:

A career criminal, who has a long list of previous convictions for both petty theft and minor violent offences, has been arrested on a charge of causing grievous bodily harm with intent (maximum sentence of life imprisonment). The CPS has just approached him before the start of the trial saying that it will accept a plea of guilty to the lesser offence of assault occasioning actual bodily harm (maximum sentence of five years custodial). The defendant did not commit the offence.

What do you think he would do?

Plea-bargaining can be described as where defendants plead guilty in return for sentence reductions (see "Guilty Pleas", at **9–045**), or defendants being offered the opportunity to plead guilty to a lesser offence than the one charged; both of which have inherent problems. 9–055

Many defendants in this position would be inclined to accepted the offer of a lesser charge and plead guilty to it. They would face a much lower sentence (grievous bodily harm with intent carries a maximum life imprisonment) and would potentially still receive a 10 per cent reduction in the sentence imposed due to pleading guilty just before the start of the trial; couple this with a previous history of violent offences and it may begin to start looking like an attractive offer. But, if innocent defendants were to agree to these offers then have they not been pressurised by the CPS (and the criminal justice system) into making admissions of guilt to crimes they did not commit?

In this scenario the offence of grievous bodily harm with intent (the most serious non-fatal offence) being dropped to the *much* lesser offence of assault occasioning actual bodily harm was purposely used to illustrate the fact that the offer of a guilty plea to a lesser offence may seem like an attractive proposition, even when it is actually a cover for the fact that the prosecution does not have enough evidence to reach the required standard of proof necessary for the more serious offence. A criticism that can be made of plea-bargaining is that the offer of a plea to a lesser offence may simply be a way for the CPS to attain its conviction targets, particularly in weak cases. It could be quite easy to spot this motive when the two offences are considerably different in respect of severity, but what if the offered offence was only slightly less serious (so, in the above scenario, maybe grievous bodily harm under s.20 of the OAPA 1861 (s.18 without the offence requirement of intent)), would such a motive be so easy to spot?

This tactic of the CPS is sometimes described as over-charging. Over-charging can be described as the CPS deciding to press ahead with a charge of a more serious nature than the facts of the case warrant, such as charging an individual with the offence of grievous bodily harm with intent under s.18 of the OAPA 1861 in a case that warrants, at the very most, a charge of assault occasioning actual bodily harm under s.47 of the OAPA 1861 (as in the scenario above). By over-charging a defendant and then offering a plea to a lesser offence the CPS manages to secure a conviction and fulfil target goals.

9–056 Obviously the CPS and the police do not work in a vacuum and there are other arms to the criminal justice system that will to some degree, have an effect or some input into the issue of plea-bargaining; the main one being the judiciary.

The case of **R. v Turner** [1970] 2 Q.B. 321 was one of the first cases to deal directly with the issue of plea-bargaining and judicial involvement. Following the judgment in this case the judiciary were only allowed a very limited involvement in the process of plea-bargaining. In this case the appellant was told by his counsel that the judge had indicated the imposition of a custodial sentence should he be convicted following a not guilty plea. However, if he pleaded guilty, a non-custodial punishment would ensue. Turner changed his plea from not guilty to guilty. On appeal Lord Parker CJ stated, in relation to the issue of plea-bargaining, that:

> **... counsel on both sides may wish to discuss with the judge whether it would be proper, in a particular case, for the prosecution to accept a plea to a lesser offence.**
>
> **It is of course imperative that so far as possible justice must be administered in open court. Counsel should, therefore, only ask to see the judge when it is felt to be really necessary and the judge must be careful only to treat such communications as private where, in fairness to the accused person, this is necessary. The Judge should, subject to the one exception referred to hereafter, never indicate the sentence, which he is minded to impose. A statement that on a plea of Guilty he would impose one sentence but that on a conviction following a plea of Not Guilty he would impose a severer sentence is one that should never be made. This could be taken to be undue pressure on the accused, thus depriving him of that complete freedom of choice which is essential.**

In essence he was saying that the judiciary should not become involved in any questions concerning plea-bargaining, especially in relation to the issue of sentencing, because if they were to do so it could be seen as undue pressure being exerted over the defendant. The only exception to this rule was that judges could indicate the type of sentence they were minded to impose if the type of sentence would be the same regardless of whether the conviction resulted from a guilty plea or upon conviction after trial. 9–057

Even after the clear guidelines laid down in **Turner** a number of legal and academic professionals were still of the opinion that the judiciary should be more actively involved in the concept of plea-bargaining. One of the strongest arguments for greater judicial involvement was that the more active the judiciary were in this area of law, the less opportunity there would be for abuse of the fundamental principle of due process. This state of affairs, however, continued on as settled principle for 25 years until the 2005 case of **R. v Goodyear** [2005] 1 W.L.R. 2532, where the issue of judicial involvement in the concept of plea-bargaining was revisited.

ADVANCED INDICATION OF SENTENCE

In the case of **Goodyear** Lord Woolf CJ concluded that the principles set down by **Turner** in respect of plea-bargaining were no longer satisfactory in today's legal culture. He gave consideration to the fact that counsel were entitled to give opinion and advice (the basis of which was drawn from their own experience and court knowledge) to defendants upon the possible sentence that they may receive, but that judges, who would ultimately have a much more certain and clear idea as to the likely sentence, could not intimate such, even if requested to do so by a defendant. In his deliberations over this point Lord Woolf CJ stated: 9–058

> **Therefore, a somewhat strange situation developed that although the defendant's decision about his plea could properly be informed by the views of counsel about the sentence the judge would be likely to pass (provided always that he, counsel, had not participated in any discussions with the judge) it had simultaneously to be made ignorant of the judge's own views, even if the defendant wanted to know them. That position requires examination. In any event, the further question remains whether it continues to be appropriate to proceed on the basis that clear, and if necessary strong, but inevitably incompletely informed advice from counsel, about the advantages which would accrue from and the consequences which would follow an early guilty plea is permissible, while an intimation of these matters initiated by the judge should always, without more, be deemed to constitute improper pressure on the defendant, and therefore prohibited.**

In our judgment, there is a significant distinction between a sentence indication given to a defendant who has deliberately chosen to seek it from the judge, and an unsolicited indication directed at him from the judge, and conveyed to him by his counsel. We do not see why a judicial response to a request for information from the defendant should automatically be deemed to constitute improper pressure on him. The judge is simply acceding to the defendant's wish to be fully informed before making his own decision whether to plead guilty or not guilty, by having the judge's views about sentence available to him rather than the advice counsel may give him about what counsel believes the judge's views would be likely to be. [. . .] Accordingly it would not constitute inappropriate judicial pressure on the defendant for the judge to respond to such a request if one were made.

Following the guidelines laid down in **Goodyear**, judges in a case can now, in prescribed circumstances, give an *advanced indication of sentence*. This is only available in the Crown Court. An advanced indication of sentence is not the same as plea-bargaining and the latter is prohibited under English law.

The circumstances in which an advanced indication of sentence can be given are:

1. the defendant must have voluntarily requested such an indication from the judge;
2. the judge must give an indication of the maximum sentence if a plea of guilty were tendered *at the stage at which the indication is sought* [emphasis added];
3. the factual basis of the plea must be agreed between the two parties; and
4. once an indication has been given it is binding upon the court.

9–059 Judges, of course, retain an unfettered discretion to refuse to give an advanced indication of sentence, if they are of the opinion that it would not be appropriate to do so under the circumstances. A judge's decision to refuse to give such an indication may be for a variety of reasons, such as a defendant already being under pressure or a defendant not having fully appreciated that the plea should be not guilty unless actually guilty. Judges may also choose to reserve indications until they feel that it is appropriate to give one. For example, if the prosecution and defence have not agreed the factual basis of the case (for the purposes of sentence indication) then a judge would be likely to reserve comment until this was decided between the parties, as this is obviously likely to have an effect on the maximum sentence a judge is minded to impose.

Despite the clear guidelines and safeguards laid down in **Goodyear** there is still a wealth of legal and public opinion that is strongly opposed to the idea of plea-bargaining. It can be argued that by allowing an advanced indication of sentence there is the potential for it to undermine the judicial function of the criminal justice system. By allowing defendants to plead guilty to receive a reduced/lesser sentence it could be argued that defendants are avoiding the full consequences of their actions, which, in turn, is unfair on the victims of the crime; potentially, justice is not being seen to be done, in either the eyes of victims or the eyes of the public. Nor can innocent persons pleading guilty to crimes they have not committed, still a realistic possibility even despite the safeguards laid down in **Goodyear**, be said to be the sign of a completely effective and healthy criminal justice system.

FRAUD TRIALS

A formalised concept of plea-bargaining, or rather "plea-negotiation" has been proposed **9–060**
for fraud cases. The Attorney General's Guidelines on Plea Discussions in Cases of Serious or Complex Fraud set out a process by which a prosecutor may enter into discussions with a suspect before charge in cases of serious or complex fraud. It is intended that plea discussions should happen at the earliest possible stage. The earlier in the case they start, the more advantageous they are likely to be. A joint submission on the appropriate sentence is an integral part of the final plea agreement; a large part of the incentive for the defendant to enter into plea discussions will be to clarify and (if possible) limit the eventual sentence. The submission must not set out a proposal for a specific sentence and the submission on sentence is limited to setting out the applicable sentencing range and starting point in accordance with any relevant sentencing guidelines.

FIGURE 35 **Pleas**

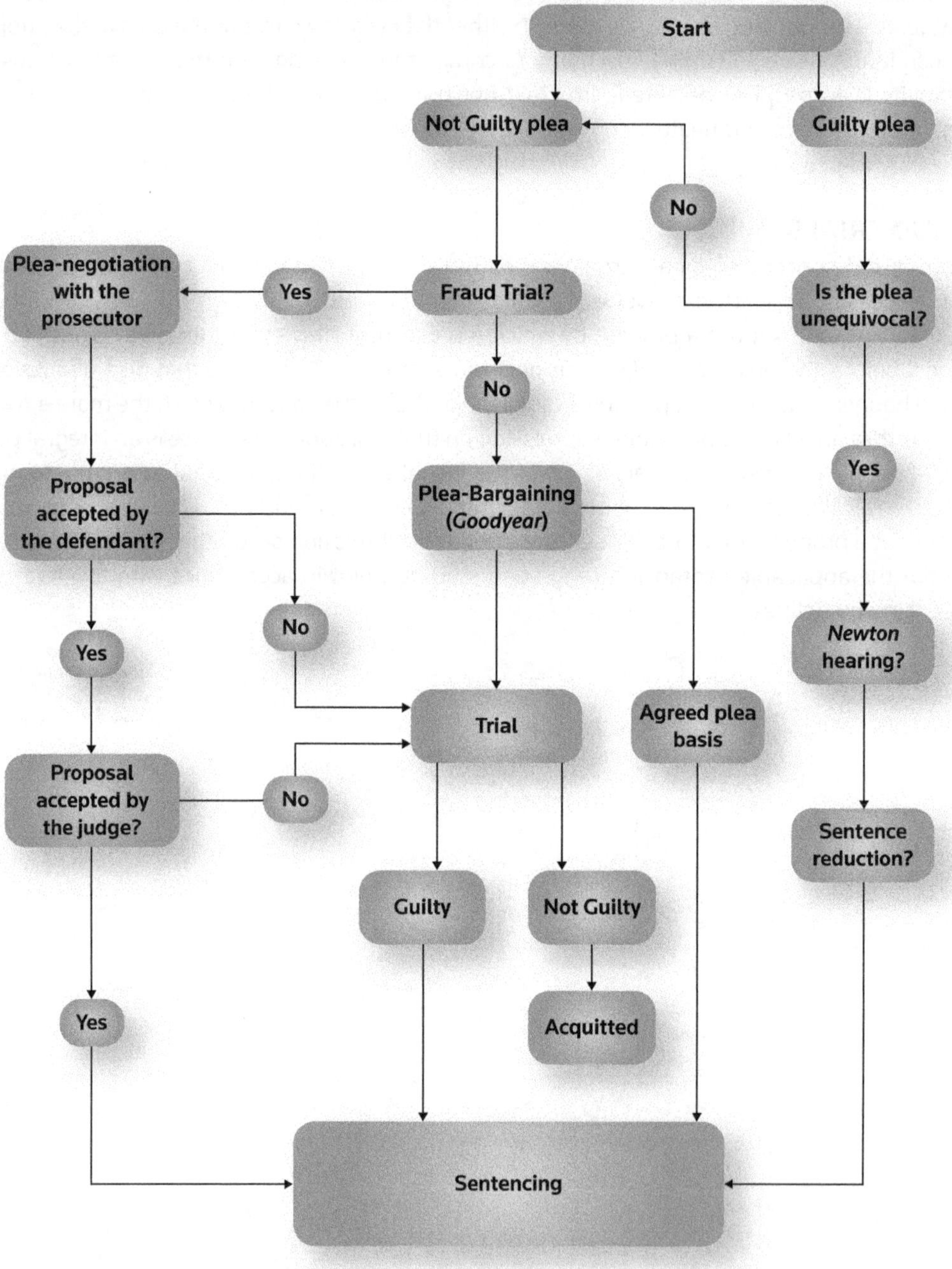

Bail

Bail can be granted by both the police (s.47 PACE 1984) and by the courts. This text will only focus on court bail, but be assured that police bail is very similar, so the understanding of court bail will automatically bring with it the ability to understand police bail. **9–061**

What is Bail?

The phrase "being on remand" is often bandied about in everyday conversation and in the media, but what does it mean? Most people make the assumption that if defendants are "on remand" then they are locked up in a prison cell for 23 hours a day, but it does not just mean this, as "being on remand" can also mean being released from custody on bail. Bail is where defendants are released from the custody of the court (or the police), so that they can go home, sleep in their own beds, go to work, etc. but they are under a requirement to surrender to the custody of the court at a future date. Essentially, bail is a promise by the bailee to return to the court when told to do so, and not to commit further offences whilst on bail. **9–062**

Bail can be granted for the time between pre-trial hearings (so the time between a preliminary hearing and a plea and case management hearing (PCMH), or between a PCMH and the trial) and it can also be granted post-conviction if a pre-sentence report is pending so as to enable the court to sentence appropriately. A bail hearing pre-trial is generally heard by a magistrates' court and this court can deal with any bail issues relating to all offence classifications at first instance. A point to note is that, in summary offence cases where the defendant has been brought to the court by way of a summons and has not previously been remanded in custody, bail does not necessarily need to be considered. The Crown Court can hold bail hearings and grant bail in cases where defendants have been committed or sent for trial or sentence in the Crown Court, or where defendants have been remanded into custody pending trial on a summary offence or upon conviction pending an appeal. The High Court has very limited powers in relation to granting bail and can only grant it where defendants are appealing a conviction by way of case stated. The Court of Appeal can also grant bail, but this is extremely rare and only really occurs in relation to retrials, such as in the case of Sion Jenkins who was retried twice for the alleged murder of his stepdaughter, Billie-Jo (see Ch.12, "Appeals against conviction" at **12–027**, for further details of this case).

The Presumption of Bail

The granting of bail is governed by the Bail Act 1976 (BA 1976) and s.4 sets out that defendants are afforded a statutory presumption in favour of being granted bail under subs.(1). This presumption, though, only applies to defendants who appear before either magistrates' court or the Crown Court (so it not applicable to police bail) and it only applies prior to conviction. After conviction (whilst awaiting sentence), the court has the discretion to grant bail but there is no automatic presumption of it being granted. This presumption of bail has been statutorily **9–063** removed in certain circumstances, such as where defendants have been charged with murder, attempted murder, manslaughter, rape or other specified sexual offences and they have previously been convicted of such an offence (s.25 of the CJPOA 1994), although the court does retain a discretionary right to grant bail in these cases where it is satisfied that there are exceptional circumstances to justify the granting of bail.

There are a number of issues for consideration that are raised by the statutory presumption under s.4. The statutory presumption to bail means that prolific offenders, like a repeat burglar, for example, are always to be granted bail, regardless of how many times they have offended. Another issue that needs to be considered is whether alleged murderers or rapists, who have not previously been convicted of such an offence should automatically get bail. It would seem unjust that alleged rapists, against whom there is overwhelming evidence, should then be allowed back into society whilst their cases are pending due to a statutory presumption. However, simply denying bail outright because a heinous crime may have been committed could, conversely, breach human rights such as being innocent until proven guilty. So how does the court deal with issues such as these?

The exceptions to the general presumptions of bail are set out in para.2 of Sch.1 to the BA 1976. There are three reasons set out in para.2 as to why the granting of bail can be refused. These are, if the court is satisfied that there are substantial grounds for believing that, if released, the defendant on bail would:

(a) fail to surrender to custody, or
(b) commit an offence whilst on bail, or
(c) interfere with witnesses or otherwise obstruct the course of justice, whether in relation to himself or any other person.

9–064 When considering these grounds in relation to the refusal of bail, the court must take into account: the seriousness of the offence that the defendant has been charged with; the defendant's character; any antecedents (this means previous convictions) the defendant may have, if the defendant has been through the court process before what the previous bail record is like; the strength of the evidence against the defendant; the defendant's associations and ties with the community; and any other relevant considerations. The court must have *substantial grounds* for believing a defendant falls into one of these exceptions. A hunch, based on little or no evidence, that a defendant might disappear whilst on bail will be insufficient to rebut the presumption to bail, there must be a justifiable reason as to why bail should be withheld and this reason must stand up to scrutiny as the right to liberty is a fundamental right under the ECHR—refusal could be seen to breach this right.

The paragraph also sets out that only one of the conditions must be satisfied for the presumption of bail to be withdrawn, however, in practice, the courts often require two of the conditions to be fulfilled in the case before it refuses to grant bail. One of the reasons behind this seems to be that if all defendants who were at risk of committing an offence whilst on bail were simply remanded into custody then the prison system would become even more overloaded than it is at the minute (about 40 per cent of offenders arrested are already on bail at the time of arrest), and the prison system would simply not be able to cope if they were all refused bail.

Schedule 1 also includes other situations in which the courts are allowed to refuse bail. These include circumstances such as where the court is satisfied: that the defendant should be kept in custody for their own protection; that they are a child or young person; that it is for their own welfare; of the fact that they are already serving a custodial order; that the court does not at that time have enough information to make an informed decision. The right to bail will also be removed if defendants have already been released on bail for an offence and have either subsequently breached the bail conditions, attempted to abscond, or committed further offences. **9–065**

The CJA 2003 amended the BA 1976 and introduced a new provision in an attempt to tackle the growing drug-related crime culture that is currently prevalent within our society. This new provision can be found under para.6B of Sch.1 to the BA 1976, which states that defendants may be declined bail if they:

- are over 18 years of age;
- have tested positive for Class A drugs;
- have been charged with a drug offence or the crime was completely motivated by drugs; and
- decline to take up the offer of a "relevant assessment" in respect of their drug-taking.

The purpose of this newly added exception is to try and address the problems caused by drugs and drug-taking as, by agreeing to treatment, defendants retain their liberty and receive help and support to address their drug habits, which, in turn, will hopefully reduce the drug-related crime rate.

Bail Conditions

It is not always the case that when a defendant receives bail they can then just disappear off and do what they like until the next court appearance. Bail can come in two forms, either unconditional or conditional. Unconditional bail is exactly as it sounds—without any conditions attached—so, in this instance, a defendant will be allowed to go and live their life as normal until the next court date, with the only provisos being that they turn up on time for their next court hearing and do not commit any further offences. **9–066**

Conditional bail is where the court imposes conditions upon a defendant, which the defendant is then obliged to keep. Conditions may involve reporting to a police station weekly, twice weekly or even daily; requiring defendants to be under house arrest (not leaving the house at all); imposing a curfew between, say, the hours of 11pm and 7am; electronic tagging; staying away from a particular geographical location; specifying where a defendant must live, which could be a defendant's own house, a parent's house or even a bail hostel, depending on the circumstances. Only conditions that are suitable for the individual facts of the case will be imposed and the purpose of the conditions imposed is to prevent defendants reoffending or absconding whilst on bail.

9–067 It was argued in the case of **R. v Mansfield Justices Ex p. Sharkey** [1985] Q.B. 613 that conditions to bail should only be imposed where there were substantial grounds for believing that an offence would be committed whilst a defendant was on bail if the conditions were not imposed, in effect mirroring the reasoning behind the refusal of bail found in Sch.1 to the BA 1976. The case of **Sharkey** arose in relation to the miners' strikes in the mid 1980s. The majority of miners were on strike and the nine applicants had been involved in the picketing of collieries in the East Midlands. The nine applicants were arrested whilst picketing and were charged with threatening behaviour. The justices, when considering granting bail to each applicant, took into account the numerous outbreaks of disorder that were occurring on the picket lines and, in order to prevent the commission of further offences by the applicants whilst on bail, decided to act in this case as they had acted in the case of other miners, by imposing the condition that each applicant did not visit any premises or place for the purpose of picketing or demonstrating. On the miners' application for judicial review, Lord Lane CJ stated:

> **In the present circumstances the question the justices should ask themselves is a simple one: "Is this condition necessary for the prevention of the commission of an offence by the defendant when on bail?" They are not obliged to have substantial grounds. It is enough if they perceive a real and not a fanciful risk of an offence being committed.**

9–068 Thereby, the Court set out that a substantial risk of an offence being committed, or the defendant absconding is not required in respect of imposing bail conditions. All that is required is an affirmative response to the fact that the conditions are "necessary". The reasons for necessity are (s.3 of the BA 1976):

> (a) to secure that he surrenders to custody,
> (b) to secure that he does not commit an offence while on bail,
> (c) to secure that he does not interfere with witnesses or otherwise obstruct the course of justice whether in relation to himself or any other person,
> (ca) for his own protection or, if he is a child or young person, for his own welfare or in his own interests,
> (d) to secure that he makes himself available for the purpose of enabling inquiries or a report to be made to assist the court in dealing with him for the offence,

(e) to secure that before the time appointed for him to surrender to custody, he attends an interview with a person who, for the purposes of the Legal Services Act 2007, is an authorised person in relation to an activity which constitutes the exercise of a right of audience or the conduct of litigation (within the meaning of that Act).

Under s.5 of the BA 1976 an application can be made to vary the conditions imposed.

If a defendant moves address from the one to which they are bailed they will need to apply to have the living address condition changed. Defendants may change jobs whilst on bail and this may mean they are unable to report to the relevant police station at the scheduled times, or they may need to enter a banned geographical location for work purposes, etc. and so their bail terms will need to be varied to take account of this. An application can also be made (under s.5B of the BA 1976) by the prosecution to impose conditions on what was originally unconditional bail.

Sureties

The BA 1976 abolished the need for defendants to provide recognisance (money or security) in an effort to secure release on bail, but this concept still exists today in relation to "sureties", although in practice it is rarely used. Sureties effectively act as sponsors for defendants. A surety agrees to put up a certain amount of money or an item of security (such as a house) to ensure that a defendant is released from custody. This act is called standing bail and the courts take it very seriously, as if a defendant breaches bail and fails to attend the next court date, the surety may end up forfeiting his recognisance. 9–069

The courts may decide to fix a set amount for bail, and this could range from a few hundred pounds to £100,000 depending on the seriousness of the case and the level of flight risk defendants are perceived to be. The court, before agreeing to sureties standing bail, must be convinced that a proposed surety understands the commitment to be undertaken and is fully aware of the consequences if the defendant breaches bail. The court will also investigate a surety's character, financial resources, previous convictions and relationship with the defendant before agreeing to the surety standing bail.

If a surety stands bail but the defendant does not attend court at the next court date, the court may waive the forfeiture if the surety can show that he tried to ensure that the defendant attended court. If the defendant breaches bail and the surety the refuses to pay the forfeit, the surety can be held in contempt of court and could receive a maximum of a 12-month custodial sentence.

Sureties only feature occasionally in bail hearings and are not a prerequisite of being granted bail. A surety should only be required if there is a risk that the defendant might fail to surrender to custody. In **R. (on the application of Shea) v Winchester Crown Court** [2013] EWHC 1050 (Admin) it was confirmed that there was no power under the BA 1976 to grant conditional bail with a surety to ensure no further offending.

Refusal of Bail

9–070 If magistrates refuse to grant a defendant bail then they are required to produce a certificate stating so. Initially, defendants are allowed two attempts to secure bail; if refused on first application then a further application at a subsequent hearing can be made. However, once two bail applications have been refused, the court is not obliged to hear any further applications; it will generally only do so when it appears that there has been a change in circumstances in respect of a defendant or case. These changes in circumstances need not be substantial, something as simple as a defendant now having a suitable address to be bailed to, or a change in the strength of the prosecution's case may be sufficient to persuade the court to rehear the application and, potentially, grant bail.

Another option open to defendants upon refusal of bail by the magistrates' court is to make an application to the Crown Court under s.81 of the Senior Courts Act 1981 (SCA 1981). Under such an application, the Crown Court will hold a full bail hearing within 48 hours of the refusal by the magistrates.

The prosecution is also entitled to appeal against the granting of bail by the magistrates where the offence a defendant is charged with is an imprisonable one. The prosecution is required to notify the court of its intention to appeal bail at the end of the initial bail hearing and, again, this appeal will be heard within 48 hours of the bail being granted.

Breach of Bail

9–071 So what happens if a defendant breaches bail? Perhaps they failed to report to the police station at the scheduled time, or perhaps they were spotted in a pub they had been banned from going into.

If a defendant breaches their bail conditions then they can be rearrested and brought before the court. Breaching a bail condition is not seen as the commission of an offence so there will be no separate penalty for the breach. However, the court may view the breach as a sign that the defendant has no regard or respect for the court and therefore, under s.7 of the BA 1976, it may revoke bail and remand the defendant in custody for the remainder of the time before the case comes to trial.

If a defendant breaches their bail by failing to appear at court at the allotted time then this carries with it a much more serious consequence. Failure to appear is an offence under s.6(1) of the BA 1976, however, failing to appear will not be classed as a criminal offence if defendants have a reasonable excuse as to why they did not surrender into custody at the required time.

The onus is upon defendants to show reasonable excuse. If a defendant does have a reasonable excuse then they must still surrender themselves to the court as soon as is practicable under s.6(2) of the BA 1976, and explain this excuse to the court.

A normal part of the working day in the criminal courts is dealing with cases where defendants have breached their bail conditions by failing to attend court. A surprisingly large number of defendants fail to appear at court and lawyers will often find themselves taking phone calls from clients where clients proceed to tell them that they are not at court for such reasons as "my taxi did not turn up", "I haven't got enough money to travel to court", "I'm ill" or that they simply got their court dates muddled up. Often the court will accept these reasons (it will require proof such as a doctor's note) and it will either grant an extension to the bail until the next court hearing, or, alternatively, it may issue a "warrant backed for bail", which means that the defendant will be arrested and then, if the reason for non-appearance is accepted, re-bailed. Occasionally, when the offence does not carry with it a custodial sentence, the court may decide to continue on and try a defendant in their absence. **9–072**

When a defendant fails to attend and no explanation is provided then the court will issue a "warrant not backed for bail". This means that the defendant will be arrested and brought before the court at the earliest opportunity. Once this has occurred it is likely that further bail will be refused and that the defendant will be remanded into custody. If the defendant is then prosecuted for a BA 1976 offence, then, under s.6, they may receive a maximum of a three-month prison sentence or a £5,000 fine from a magistrates' court, or a maximum of a 12-month prison sentence or an unlimited fine if bailed from the Crown Court. The court guidelines advise that offenders should generally be given a custodial sentence for this offence.

Bail and Human Rights

It could be argued that bail breaches a fundamental human right under art.5 of the ECHR. Article 5 states that: **9–073**

> **Everyone has the right to liberty and security of person.**

Obviously, being remanded in custody is an encroachment upon this right to liberty and freedom. However, art.5 is not an absolute right as there are qualifications to it in certain circumstances.

Article 5(1) sets out the qualifications that can result in the setting aside of this right. These qualifications include lawful detention after conviction and after non-compliance with a court order, and bringing a person before a court on reasonable suspicion of having committed an offence. Subsections (b) and (c) are particularly relevant to the issue of bail and if the right is abrogated under subs.(c) then art.5(3) must be complied with, which states:

Everyone arrested or detained in accordance with the provisions of paragraph 1.c of this article shall be brought promptly before a judge or other officer authorised by law to exercise judicial power and shall be entitled to trial within a reasonable time or to release pending trial. Release may be conditioned by guarantees to appear for trial.

9–074 The main two factors that must be balanced when considering bail in relation to the rights under the Convention are the issue of public interest and the issue of the presumption of innocence. Everyone is presumed innocent until found guilty so how can the detention of an innocent person be justified? The only ground upon which such detention can be justified is that the defendant needs to be detained in an effort to protect the public. This detention does have limits and a person cannot be detained indefinitely, as was decided in the case of **A v Secretary of State for the Home Department (A); X v Secretary of State for the Home Department** [2004] UKHL 56; [2005] 3 All E.R. 169. In **A** the appellants were all foreign nationals who had been certified by the Secretary of State as suspected international terrorists. They could not be deported since that would, in the circumstances, have involved a breach of their human rights, so they were detained without charge or trial in accordance with the derogation from art.5 of the ECHR as permitted by the Human Rights Act 1998 (Designated Derogation) Order (SI 2001/3644); the Order having been enacted to deal with the perceived terrorist threat from Al-Qaeda after the terrorist attacks in the US on 11 September 2001. The suspected terrorists successfully appealed to the House of Lords, which stated that their detention was unlawful, and a breach of their human rights, and the Order was quashed.

FIGURE 36 The bail process

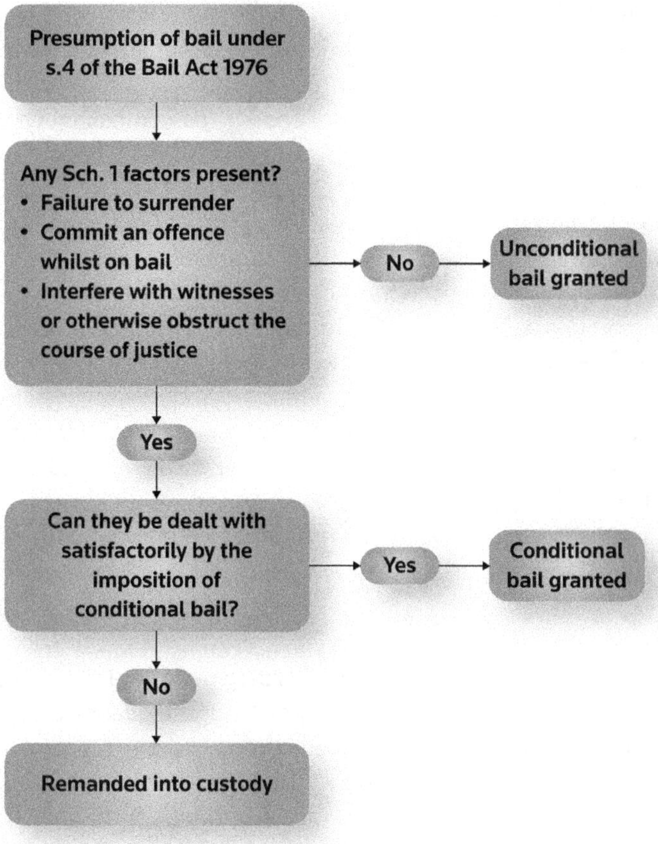

Course of Trial

Burden of Proof

One of the fundamental principles of English law is that a defendant is innocent until proven guilty. This is known as the "presumption of innocence" and it is defined within art.6 of the ECHR: 9–075

> (1) In the determination of his civil rights and obligations or of any criminal charge against him, everyone is entitled to a fair and public hearing within a reasonable time by an independent and impartial tribunal established by law. Judgement shall be pronounced publicly by the press and public may be excluded from

all or part of the trial in the interest of morals, public order or national security in a democratic society, where the interests of juveniles or the protection of the private life of the parties so require, or the extent strictly necessary in the opinion of the court in special circumstances where publicity would prejudice the interests of justice.

(2) Everyone charged with a criminal offence shall be presumed innocent until proved guilty according to law.

(3) Everyone charged with a criminal offence has the following minimum rights:

(a) to be informed promptly, in a language which he understands and in detail, of the nature and cause of the accusation against him;

(b) to have adequate time and the facilities for the preparation of his defence;

(c) to defend himself in person or through legal assistance of his own choosing or, if he has not sufficient means to pay for legal assistance, to be given it free when the interests of justice so require;

(d) to examine or have examined witnesses against him and to obtain the attendance and examination of witnesses on his behalf under the same conditions as witnesses against him;

(e) to have the free assistance of an interpreter if he cannot understand or speak the language used in court.

9–076 It is at art.6(2) that the presumption of innocence is set out. What this means is that defendants in a criminal case will not be viewed as being guilty of the offence charged until this fact has been determined by a court of law. This overall burden of proof in a criminal case rests with the prosecution and the prosecution must prove that a defendant is guilty of the offence; as the Latin maxim states, *necessitas probandi incumbit ei qui agit*, which, when translated, means "the necessity of proof lies with he who complains". Lord Sankey VC confirmed the existence of the doctrine of the presumption of innocence at common law in the case of **Woolmington v DPP** [1935] A.C. 462, where he famously stated:

Throughout the web of the English criminal law one golden thread is always to be seen, that it is the duty of the prosecution to prove the prisoner's guilt subject to what I have already said as to the defence of insanity and subject also to any statutory exception. If, at the end of and on the whole of the case, there is a reasonable doubt, created by the evidence given by either the prosecution or the prisoner, as to whether the prisoner [committed the offence], the prosecution has not made out the case and the prisoner is entitled to an acquittal. No matter what the charge or where the trial, the principle that the prosecution must prove the guilt of the prisoner is part of the common law of England and no attempt to whittle it down can be entertained.

The standard of proof to be evidenced by the prosecution in a criminal case is that a defendant is guilty "beyond reasonable doubt". What this means is that the prosecution must prove its case to the point that the jury is "sure" that the defendant committed the alleged offence. Any element of doubt in the minds of the triers of fact must be afforded to the defendant. The Judicial Studies Board provides the judiciary with specimen directions for directing a jury, and the specimen direction in relation to the burden and standard of proof reads as follows: 9–077

The prosecution must prove the defendant's guilt. He does not have to prove that he is innocent. The prosecution must prove that the defendant is guilty beyond reasonable doubt. Proof beyond reasonable doubt is proof that leaves you firmly convinced of the defendant's guilt. There are very few things in this world that we know with absolute certainty, and in criminal cases the law does not require proof that overcomes every possible doubt. If, based upon your consideration of the evidence, you are firmly convinced that the defendant is guilty of the crime charged, you must find him guilty. If on the other hand you think that there is a real possibility that he is not guilty, you must give him the benefit of the doubt and find him not guilty.

If defendants rely on a specific statutory defence or the common law defence of insanity then they will hold the burden of proof in respect of that one issue (the prosecution will still retain the burden to prove the case overall against a defendant). Where defendants do bear the burden of proof in relation to a specific issue then the standard required to be met is "on the balance of probabilities"; what this means is that defendants must show that it is more likely that what the defence alleges is true than not. Quite often this lower standard of proof is quantified in numerical form and is set out as "greater than 50 per cent" (there is no equivalent way to quantify "beyond reasonable doubt"). In all civil matters the standard of proof is at this lower level of "on the balance of probabilities". 9–078

The rationale for the burden of proof—for it being placed on the prosecution and it being set at such a high standard—is set out by Paul Roberts in his article "Taking the burden of proof seriously" [1995] Crim. L.R. 783–798, where he states:

The burden of proof checks and constrains the power of the state to intervene in the lives of individuals and their families in the far-reaching and sometimes catastrophic ways sanctioned by the machinery of criminal justice.

The reason that the overall burden of proof is placed upon the prosecution and not the defence really comes down to the issue of fairness. In many cases a defendant's liberty is at stake and it would be unjust to require that the defendant prove innocence of the offence especially when the prosecution has infinite resources available to prove guilt, whereas the defendant may have very limited resources available to prove innocence, and the resources available will undoubtedly be controlled by finances.

Criminal Trial Process

9–079 The majority of criminal trials will be held in open court, this means that persons who are not involved directly with the case, i.e. members of the public, can enter the court at any time and watch the proceedings. Actually, going along to court for a morning and watching part of a criminal case is excellent experience and is well worth considering as some of the cases are fascinating (though be warned some proceedings can be just the opposite), and the knowledge that can be gained by watching experts at work is often invaluable. Sometimes the courtroom will be closed to the public and the hearing will be *in camera*, this means that the proceedings are private and that only those with a direct interest in the case will be permitted to be present in court. Hearings are normally *in camera* in family proceedings (for obvious reasons), in the youth court, and an adult criminal case will occasionally be heard *in camera* where there is sensitive material being heard.

Prosecution Case

9–080 The prosecution will always open the case as it is bringing the proceedings against the defendant and therefore must show that there is a case for the defendant to answer. The prosecution will begin its case with an "opening speech"; this is a speech setting out the allegations against the defendant, and it will provide a summary of the evidence that the prosecution intends to present, the details of the relevant law relied upon (although this should be qualified with an acknowledgment that the judge in the case will direct them further on the law), and a brief conclusion of what the prosecution will (hopefully) have proven by the end of the case.

The prosecution will then call its first witness, who will be its main witness. Counsel for the prosecution will ask the witness a number of questions by way of examination-in-chief, so as to elicit the witness's version of events. There are rules and regulations regarding the types of questions that a party can ask of his own witness. When a party is conducting examination-in-chief, it means that that party can only ask the witness non-leading questions; questions which do not put words into the mouth of the witness, but are intended to enable the witness to tell the story in the witness's own words.

Over to you

Can you think of some examples of non-leading questions?

9–081 The whole purpose of non-leading questions is for witnesses to tell what they actually witnessed. Counsel calling the witness will lead him through his evidence, often stopping and asking him to expand on points if he feels that something has been missed or has not been given enough attention. If however, the witness fails to mention crucial evidence and does not "come up to proof" then there is little that counsel can do to remedy the situation. Even if the witness provided damning evidence in their police statement, if repeated in court it will not become part of the evidence in the case.

Examples of non-leading questions are:

- "Tell me where you were on the night in question"
- "What did you see?"
- "What happened next?"

Once the prosecution has finished its examination-in-chief then the defence is given the opportunity to question the same witness. The style of questioning employed by the defence here will be entirely different to that of the prosecution. In questioning the prosecution's witness, the defence uses a method of questioning known as cross-examination. Cross-examination involves defence counsel challenging the witness's testimony and putting the defence case to them. Examples of questions/statements used within cross-examination are:

- "Do you like a drink, Mrs X? Did you have a couple too many on the night in question? Isn't it really the case that you were upstairs throwing up in the bathroom at the time of the alleged offence and that you never even saw what happened?"
- "You have poor eyesight and wear glasses, don't you? Isn't it entirely possible that you are mistaken in your identification of the defendant due to your poor eyesight?"
- "I put it to you that you are lying and that you never saw the defendant at the time that you say you did"

Cross-examining witnesses, as can be seen by the examples given above, is not really **9–082** about allowing the witness to tell the court what happened (this has already been done via examination-in-chief), but, it is, rather, about picking holes in the testimony of the witness and trying to find the weak points so that the witness's credibility is lowered (or even destroyed) in the eyes of the triers of fact.

Once the defence has cross-examined the witness, the witness may then be re-examined by the prosecution so that the prosecution can effectively undertake a method of damage limitation; clarifying the points that came out during cross-examination and getting the witness to expand further on any new information that has come to light. The prosecution is not obliged to re-examine a witness, and may be of the opinion, when taking all things into consideration, that there is either no need to re-examine, or that re-examination will only compound an already bad situation. At the conclusion of the witness's evidence, the judge or magistrates may wish to ask a number of further questions, possibly in an effort to seek further clarification on a matter, and, occasionally, a jury may wish to ask a question. When the jury does ask a question, it does not do so orally, it hands a note to the judge (by way of the court clerk) that sets out the question. The judge will then consider whether the question is allowable and, if so, will ask the witness the question on behalf of the jury. This sequence of questioning will then be repeated for all of the prosecution witnesses.

Defence Case

SUBMISSION OF NO CASE TO ANSWER

9–083 After the prosecution has set out its case and has presented all its evidence, the trial then arrives at a point informally known as half time or, more formally, as the close of the case for the prosecution. It is at this point that the defence has the opportunity to make a submission to the court that the prosecution has not established a prima facie case against the defendant. This submission is called a submission of no case to answer and it is a request to the judge that the case be stopped at this point and the defendant be acquitted as, if the prosecution has not established a case against the defendant, then there is no need to defend the case. The test that the court must consider when deliberating on a submission of no case to answer is contained in the case of **R. v Galbraith** [1981] 1 W.L.R. 1039 and can be found at 1042 where Lord Lane CJ states:

> **How then should the judge approach a submission of "no case"?**
>
> **(1) If there is no evidence that the crime alleged has been committed by the defendant, there is no difficulty. The judge will of course stop the case.**
> **(2) The difficulty arises where there is some evidence but it is of a tenuous character, for example because of inherent weakness or vagueness or because it is inconsistent with other evidence. Where the judge comes to the conclusion that the prosecution evidence, taken at its highest, is such that a jury properly directed could not properly convict upon it, it is his duty, upon a submission being made, to stop the case.**

A submission for no case to answer must be made in the absence of any jury in the case, because, if the jury was aware of it and the submission was not accepted, then it may become prejudiced by the knowledge of such a submission and, consequently, may find it difficult to place the correct amount of weight on the prosecution evidence. If the court accepts the submission then that is the end of the case and the defendant will be formally acquitted of the charges made against him. If the submission is not accepted then the case will move onto the second half where the defence presents its case.

THE DEFENDANT'S TESTIMONY

The first point to mention in relation to the presentation of the defence case is that the defendant does not have to give evidence if they do not want to. All persons are deemed as competent to give evidence in criminal proceedings (s.53(1) of Youth Justice and Criminal Evidence Act 1999 (YJCEA 1999)) but defendants cannot be compelled (forced) to give evidence as s.1(1) of the Criminal Evidence Act 1898 states: 9-084

> **A person charged in criminal proceedings shall not be called as a witness in the proceedings except upon his own application.**

This means that if the defendant wishes to sit in the dock and simply watch and listen to the proceedings they are completely entitled to do so. There may be a variety of reasons why the defendant does not wish to give evidence; however, the main one is usually that, once they are on the witness stand, they will not only give their side of the story, they will also be cross-examined by the prosecution. This is something that the defendant may wish to avoid as cross-examination could potentially result in them incriminating themselves or, if they have numerous previous convictions then by putting themselves on the stand these convictions may become admissible in court; which could have disastrous consequences for the case. However, if the defendant decides refrain from giving evidence, this can have a negative effect as, under s.35 of the CJPOA 1994, the court or the jury, in determining the defendant's guilt, may draw adverse inferences from their failure to testify. The defendant must be warned that such inferences may be drawn if they refuse to give evidence or answer any questions asked of them.

If the defendant does decide to give evidence then, under s.79 of the PACE 1984, they should give evidence before any other defence witness as s.79 provides: 9-085

> **If at the trial of any person for an offence—**
>
> **(a) the defence intends to call two or more witnesses to the facts of the case; and**
> **(b) those witnesses include the accused,**
> **the accused shall be called before the other witness or witnesses unless the court in its discretion otherwise directs.**

The rationale behind this provision is to prevent defendants tailoring their evidence to that of the other defence witnesses. By giving evidence first it is believed that defendants will be as truthful in evidence as possible and not amend evidence to fit other witnesses in the case.

OTHER DEFENCE WITNESSES

9–086 The questioning of the remaining defence witnesses (if there are any) will take the same format and style as that of the prosecution witnesses, but simply in reverse, so counsel for the defence will undertake the examination-in-chief and the prosecution will conduct the cross-examination. After all the defence witnesses have been called, both sides, the prosecution and the defence, will deliver closing speeches to the jury. The prosecution will go first, summing up its evidence and setting out its case; the defence is then afforded the last word on the matter, this is again a summary of the evidence but often with the added edge of an emotive speech as to the defendant's innocence.

Judicial Summing Up

9–087 Finally, the judge will sum up the evidence and provide guidance and direction on the law to the jury (guidance on the law is provided by the legal adviser in the magistrates' court (see Ch.5, "Legal Advisers" at **5–030**)). The judge's role in the case is an objective one; no extra weight must be given to either side's case, but comment can be made on the credibility of the evidence where appropriate to do so. The judge's role is to guide the jury through the minefield that is the criminal law and to direct it so that it can make sense of the law and relate it to the case being tried.

The JSB Specimen Directions on judicial summing up suggests that the following format should be followed:

1. the functions of the judge and jury;
2. basic directions of law (including the burden of proof and the offence particulars);
3. other relevant directions (those arising out of specific issues in the case, e.g. joint enterprise or self-defence);
4. a summary of the evidence for the prosecution and defence; then
5. directions regarding verdicts.

Once the judge has summed up the evidence and given any necessary specific directions, the jury is then required to retire and consider the evidence in detail before returning its verdict on the case (for further discussion on juries and jury deliberation see Ch.7).

FIGURE 37 **Pre-trial process**

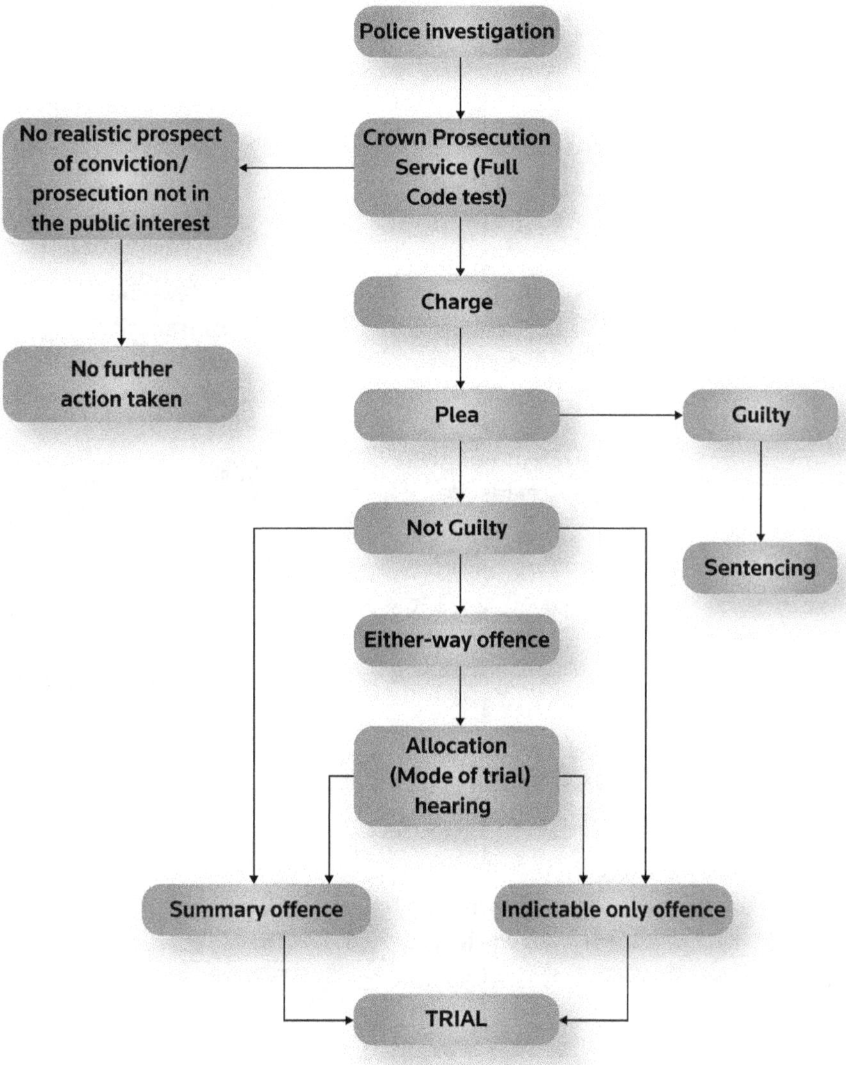

FIGURE 38 **Trial process**

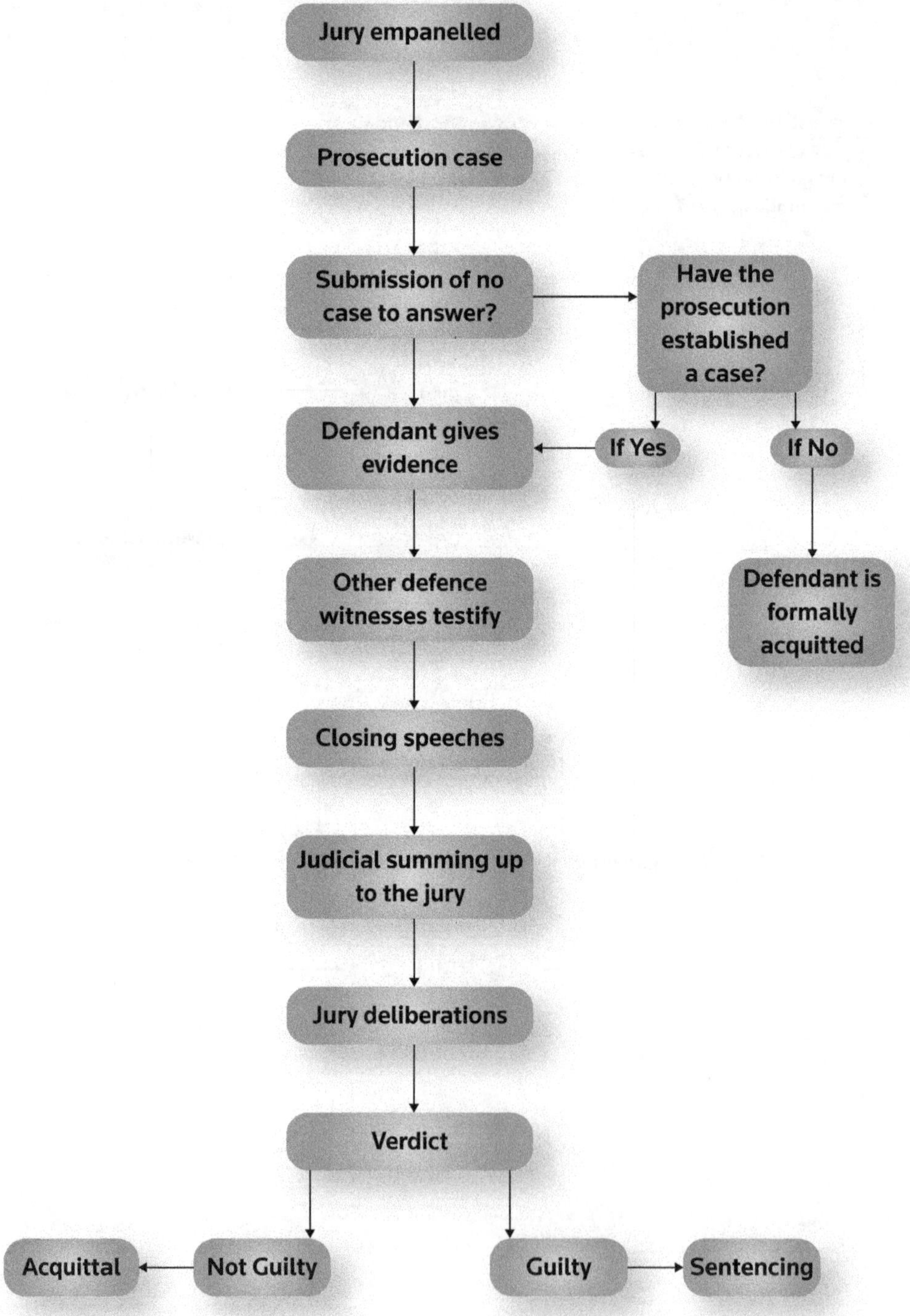

FIGURE 39 **Order of witness examination**

Prosecution witness		Defence witness	
Type of question	Asked by	Type of question	Asked by
Examination-in-chief	**Prosecution**	**Examination-in-chief**	**Defence**
Cross examination	**Defence**	**Cross examination**	**Prosecution**
Re-examination	**Prosecution**	**Re-examination**	**Defence**

Summary

1. Criminal courts can either be a court of first instance, an appellate court or both. The criminal court hierarchy spans from the magistrates' courts as the lowest courts, to the Supreme Court as the final court of appeal.
2. The Criminal Procedure Rules 2020 (CrimPRs 2020) contain a consolidation of all of the 500 or so individual rules on criminal procedure that existed under English law. They are the first step towards the creation of a comprehensive criminal code. As well as consolidating the previously existing rules on procedure, the CrimPRs have codified a number of common law principles, such as the Overriding Objective (an overarching principle the courts and all parties to a case must adhere to), and judicial powers of case management.
3. The Crown Prosecution Service (CPS) is the primary agency concerned with charging and prosecuting offenders. In most cases the CPS will determine the appropriate charge, although the police may decide this in certain minor cases. To determine whether prosecution is appropriate, prosecutors must refer to the Full Code Test to decide whether there is a realistic prospect of conviction and whether prosecution would be in the public interest.
4. The alternatives to prosecuting an offender are to issue them with a caution (either simple or conditional), a community resolution, a cannabis warning, or a fixed penalty notice.
5. How and where an offence is tried will be dependent upon the offence classification. Offences are categorised as either summary, triable either-way or indictable. Summary offences include the less serious offences and are tried in the magistrates' court. Either-way offences are triable summarily or upon indictment following an allocation hearing. Indictable offences include the most serious criminal offences and are tried upon indictment in the Crown Court.

6. To determine the appropriate venue for an either-way offence, a magistrates' court will hold an allocation hearing (otherwise known as a mode of trial hearing). If it has sufficient powers to sentence the defendant then it may decide that it can hear the case, if it does not have sufficient sentencing powers then it will send the case to the Crown Court for trial. If a magistrates' court feels that it can keep jurisdiction of the case then the defendant must agree to this. Otherwise the defendant can elect for their case to be heard in the Crown Court before a judge and jury.

7. A defendant can either plead guilty or not guilty to charges alleged against them. If they plead guilty then the plea must be unequivocal, if the plea is determined as equivocal then a not guilty plea will be entered into court on the defendant's behalf. Where the defendant pleads guilty to an offence but the facts of the case are not agreed between the prosecution and the defence the court can order a **Newton** hearing to determine the facts upon which to sentence.

8. If a defendant considers pleading guilty to an offence then they are permitted to ask the judge to indicate the maximum sentence the judge would be minded to impose at that time. The defendant must request such an indication voluntarily so as to avoid any improper pressure being applied.

9. Court bail may be granted at any point pending trial, as well as post-trial pending sentencing and there is a presumption in favour of the defendant being granted bail. Bail may either be unconditional or conditional. The granting of bail may be refused where it is believed that the defendant is likely to fail to surrender, may interfere with witnesses or commit an offence whilst on bail.

10. In a criminal case the defendant is afforded a presumption of innocence (art.6 of the ECHR) in that the prosecution must prove the defendant's guilt as opposed to the defence having to prove the defendant's innocence. The standard of proof in a criminal trial is "beyond reasonable doubt".

11. The prosecution opens the case and calls its witnesses first. It must succeed in establishing a prima facie case against the defendant. At the close of the prosecution case the defence can make a "submission of no case to answer", which, if accepted by the judge, will mean that the defendant is formally acquitted of all charges. If not accepted, the defence will then present its case. If the defendant is to be called as a witness they will be called before any other defence witness. The defendant does not have to give evidence but if they does not then an adverse inference may be drawn from his silence. The judge will then sum up the evidence for the jury and direct on the law before the jury retires to consider its verdict.

Key Cases

Case	Court	Salient point
R. v Newton [1983]	Court of Appeal	Where there is a dispute to the evidence at a sentencing hearing the court is entitled to hold a hearing to determine which version of the facts it should sentence upon.
R. v Goodyear [2005]	Court of Appeal	Overruled the previous case of R. v Turner [1970] on the issue of plea bargaining. The Court of Appeal laid down guidelines for a judge when giving an advance indication of sentence.
R. v Mansfield Justices Ex p. Sharkey [1985]	Queen's Bench Division	When considering whether or not to impose conditions in relation to bail the court only need to determine that the conditions are necessary; they do not need to conclude that there would be a substantial risk if the conditions were not imposed.
A v Secretary of State for the Home Department [2004]	House of Lords	The only ground upon which a suspect can be detained is on ground of public protection but that the powers to detain is limited in that a person cannot be held indefinitely; to do so would be unlawful and would violate their ECHR rights.
R. v Galbraith [1981]	Court of Appeal	A submission of no case to answer will be accepted where there is no evidence submitted that the defendant in question committed the alleged offence, or where the evidence is of tenuous character that a jury properly directed could not properly convict upon it.

Further Reading

J. Morton, "If I ran the criminal justice system" [2006] 70(2) J. Crim. L. 93–96.

Considers the changes to the criminal justice system that have been implemented over the past 40 years.

J. Morton, "Pleas please me" [2005] 69(4) J. Crim. L. 277–279.

Considers the decision of **R. v Goodyear** and the precedent it has set in respect of advance indication of sentence and plea bargaining.

P. Roberts, "Taking the burden of proof seriously" [1995] Crim. L.R. 783.
Discusses the principles governing the burden of proof in criminal trials.

P.W. Tague, "Tactical reasons for recommending trials rather than guilty pleas in Crown Court" [2006] Crim. L.R. 23–37.
Examines why defence counsel may advise their clients to elect a Crown Court trial instead of pleading guilty to an either-way offence dealt summarily.

Self Test Questions

1. The Crown Prosecution Service will commence a prosecution where:
   (a) it is in the public interest to do so
   (b) there is a realistic prospect of conviction
   (c) it is in the public interest to do so and there is a realistic prospect of conviction
   (d) the prosecutor believes that the defendant is guilty
2. The term "realistic prospect of conviction" means:
   (a) that the trier of fact would find the defendant guilty
   (b) that the trier of fact might find the defendant guilty
   (c) that the trier of fact would be more likely than not to convict the defendant
   (d) that the trier of fact will find the defendant guilty beyond reasonable doubt
3. A **Newton** hearing is used to determine:
   (a) the guilt of the defendant
   (b) the facts that the defendant will be sentenced upon
   (c) the defendant's sentence
   (d) the facts of the case
4. An either-way offence can be tried in:
   (a) the Crown Court
   (b) the magistrates' court
   (c) either the magistrates' court or Crown Court, depending on the seriousness of the offence
   (d) the county court
5. An equivocal plea is where the defendant:
   (a) provides an ambiguous guilty plea
   (b) provides an ambiguous not guilty plea
   (c) provides an unambiguous guilty plea
   (d) provides an unambiguous not guilty plea

Funding

10

CHAPTER OVERVIEW

In this chapter we will:

- Consider whether there is equality of access in respect of the justice system.
- Discover the history of the legal aid system.
- Explain the agencies involved in the administration of public funding for litigation.
- Discuss the eligibility criteria used to determine whether an individual can be awarded public funding.
- Discuss how conditional fee agreements and damages-based agreements work.

Summary

Further Reading

Self Test Questions

Introduction

10-001 The funding of legal services has been in an almost constant state of flux for the past 70 years. Just as everyone must abide by the laws of the land, there is also the ideal that everyone should be able to access the justice system when they need to do so. In fact, the right to a fair trial is a fundamental human right under art.6 of the ECHR. However, access to legal services can be costly, as all of those involved in the case (the solicitors, barristers, administrative staff, judges, and the court, to name but a few) must be paid for their services, therefore the cost implications of a case can be huge. The Woolf Report found that costs for an average personal injury claim could amount to £20,413. This chapter will not consider the issues of funding in minute detail, as an entire book could be written on this subject alone, but it will consider the development of the funding system for legal services within England and Wales and the main issues that have arisen in respect of it, and set out the state of the funding system at present.

The Unmet Legal Need

10-002 The legal system of England and Wales prides itself on that the fact that it provides access to justice for all. However, just as the fact that everyone has the right to buy an expensive racing car or go on a round-the-world trip does not mean that everyone is actually able to treat themselves to these items; the same can be said in respect of the equality of access to justice. Not every person that requires legal services is able to access them, and this sector of society has become known as the unmet legal need.

There may be many reasons why an individual who needs to access the legal system is not able to do so. Research commissioned by the Legal Services Commission and undertaken by Pascoe Pleasence (Pascoe Pleasence, *Causes of Action: Civil Law and Social Justice*, 2nd edn, LSRC Research Paper No.14 (LSRC, 2006)) identified a number of reasons why this unmet legal need exists. The main findings of the research were that:

- people thought that nothing could be done to resolve the situation and therefore did not attempt to access legal services;
- people thought that taking action would make no difference to the situation, often due to lack of knowledge as to the help, advice and potential remedies available;
- people thought that there was no need to take any action for a variety of reasons, such as that no wrong had been committed or that the wrong was not serious enough to warrant legal action;
- there was uncertainty as to individuals' rights—due to a lack of knowledge and education, potential claimants were not aware of what they were entitled to bring an action for;
- there was uncertainty as to where to get help—even though many people lived within a few miles of legal representation (solicitors, Citizen's Advice Bureaux, etc.) they did not know where to begin looking in order to access such advice;

- concerns were present as to the psychological, economic or social consequences of resolving the situation;
- concerns as to the potential cost of any action were apparent—there was a general view that all litigation is very expensive and therefore out of the normal person's reach; and
- a number of people were frightened to take action, either due to the potential repercussions of commencing legal proceedings or due to the fact that many people viewed legal professionals as personally unapproachable.

Public Funding

Prior to 1949, there was virtually no public funding for people who were involved in or wished to bring litigation. If persons wanted to bring a claim, they had to find the money themselves to pay for its costs, and only limited representation was provided for those charged with a criminal offence under the Poor Prisoners' Defence Acts 1903 and 1930. This was obviously an unsatisfactory state of affairs, as many people were denied justice purely due to the fact that they were not rich enough to undertake litigation. In 1945, a Government review undertaken by the Rushcliffe Committee was the catalyst that began to change and shape the public funding of legal services as the concept of the "Welfare State" in general was introduced (access to medical services, educational facilities, etc. for all) and this was to also encompass the introduction of public funding for legal services. The Rushcliffe Report ((1946) 13(2), *University of Chicago Law Review*, 131–144) recommended that the funding system (or its nonexistence) for legal expenses needed a radical overhaul as access to justice was just as important as access to medical services, etc. The Report recommended that: **10–003**

- legal aid be made available in all courts;
- legal aid should not just be limited to the poor but should also be available to those of more moderate means;
- the level of legal aid available to an individual should be assessed by way of a means test;
- a merits test should also be employed to assess the appropriateness of the litigation and funding;
- the legal aid costs should be borne by the State but administered by the legal profession; and
- all lawyers providing legal aid services should be adequately rewarded for their services.

The essence of the Rushcliffe Report was that public funding for legal services should be "demand led and never cash limited". The Government broadly accepted these proposals and, in 1949, under the Legal Aid and Advice Act 1949, the first legal aid services were established. Legal aid as a concept quickly became an entrenched and fundamental right within the justice system and by the 1980s the system had developed into six clearly defined limbs under the **10–004** enactment of the Legal Aid Act 1988 (this Act also established the Legal Aid Board which was charged with managing the scheme and maintaining a legal aid fund). The distinct limbs of the legal aid system, as they were, are below.

- **Legal advice and assistance scheme**
  This form of legal aid was otherwise known as the Green Form scheme and was applicable to both criminal and civil matters alike. Persons entitled to aid under this scheme would receive up to two hours' worth of work and this work could involve the provision of advice and the drafting of documents, but not representation at court.
- **Assistance by way of representation**
  This limb of the legal aid provided cover for the conduct of and representation in proceedings in either the courts or the tribunal system. It was essentially an extension of the legal advice and assistance scheme but its application was limited in use (it could not be used in defamation cases) and eligibility was subject to a means test.
- **Civil legal aid**
  This scheme allowed the cost of legal advice and representation in court to be covered regardless of whether individuals were defending or bringing the claim. Eligibility for this limb of the legal aid scheme was subject to means testing.
- **Criminal legal aid**
  Again, this covered the cost of legal advice and representation in court and was subject to a means test.
- **Duty solicitor scheme (police stations)**
  This scheme provided free access to legal representation for persons detained by the police regardless of whether they had been arrested or not. Solicitors worked on a rota so that access to a solicitor would always be available. The provision of this service was not subject to any form of means or merit testing and was essentially free for all. This scheme is still available under the new public funding scheme (discussed below).
- **Duty solicitor scheme (magistrates' courts)**
  Similar to the police station duty solicitor scheme above, solicitors were available at the magistrates' court to provide legal services to unrepresented defendants. Again, there was no means or merit testing for the provision of this service and the scheme is still available under the new public funding scheme.

FIGURE 40 **The six limbs of legal aid under the Legal Aid Act 1988**

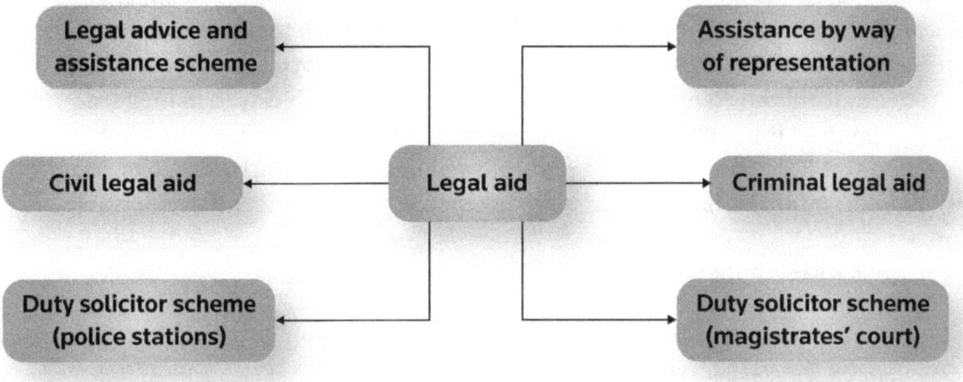

The legal aid scheme worked extremely well for a considerable length of time but, as litigation became more common and the crime rates began to increase, the strain placed upon the legal aid system became untenable. The Government attempted to stem the amount of money that was being ploughed into the legal aid system as, despite the fact that each individual scheme had its own terms and conditions of eligibility, the annual legal aid bill was still amounting to millions of pounds (in 1997 the legal aid bill totalled £1,477 million). The Government introduced severe cuts in the funding available and tightened up the eligibility criteria but these moves provoked the widespread criticism that the Government was reducing the equality of access to justice, as only those who were very poor or very rich were able to access the justice system. In 1997, Sir Peter Middleton, on the invitation of the Lord Chancellor, undertook a review of the system in his report *Review of Civil Justice and Legal Aid: A report to the Lord Chancellor* (Lord Chancellor's Department, 1997). The report considered the state of the legal aid system as it was then and made recommendations as to how it should be reformed. The three main problems identified by the review were: 10–005

- the rapidly growing costs of the scheme and the lack of satisfactory mechanisms for controlling that growth;
- the inability to target resources in priority areas and thereby address areas of unmet legal need with existing resources; and
- poor value for money.

The main principles proposed by the review were that: 10–006

Legal aid should be the servant of civil justice, not its master. In particular, legal aid should work with the grain of the justice system and be organised in a way that reinforces its objectives. It should contribute to ensuring that disputes are settled in the best forum, and to the efficiency with which they are handled [...] It is reasonable and legitimate for the Government to reach a decision on how much legal aid the country can afford, and to put a legal aid system in place which enables it to adhere to that decision. The issue is not whether to limit expenditure, but how to devise a legal aid scheme under which decisions about resources, priorities and targeting are taken in a transparent and accountable way.

Essentially, the report recommended a change to the philosophical theory that underpinned the whole legal aid system. The proposed change involved a move away from a demand-led system and the establishment of a finite funding service that was more cash limited. Following the publication of the Middleton Report, the Government drafted the White Paper, *Modernising Justice*, Cm.4155 (Lord Chancellor Department, 1998), which largely embraced the reforms suggested by the earlier report. The end result of this was the enactment of the Access to Justice Act 1999 (AJA 1999).

Access to Justice Act 1999

10–007 The introduction of the AJA 1999 resulted in a radical overhaul of the legal aid system. Under s.1(1) the Legal Services Commission (LSC) was established and the old Legal Aid Board abolished. The LSC was charged with the responsibility of administering the legal aid system in England and Wales and it had a budget of over £2.1 billion to do so. The LSC governed legal aid by the provision of two separate schemes:

- **Community Legal Services (CLS)**—providing advice and legal representation for people involved in civil cases; and
- **Criminal Defence Service (CDS)**—providing advice and legal representation for people facing criminal charges.

Under the old legal aid scheme, legal representatives would simply make an application to the Legal Aid Board for funding on an individual client basis. The LSC replaced this system and if a defendant or litigant in a matter wished to receive public funding then they must approach a firm of solicitors that held a contract (was franchised) with the LSC for the provision of civil or criminal work.

Funding Review

10–008 The legal aid system came under intense scrutiny by way of the Coalition Government's Spending Review. One of the Structural Reform Plans (which were a key tool of the Coalition

Government to ensure that all departments were accountable for the implementation of the reforms set out in the Coalition Agreement) was to make the reform of the courts and legal aid system a departmental priority, with the aim of reforming the legal aid system so as to make it work more efficiently, whilst still protecting the most vulnerable members of society.

In November 2010 the Ministry of Justice published its Green Paper on legal aid (*Proposals for the Reform of Legal Aid in England and Wales, CP12/10* (HMSO, 2010)), in which it detailed its aim to cut £350 million of funding by 2014 from the £2.1 billion the legal aid system received. In order to achieve this level of funding cuts the paper proposed removing entire areas of law from the remit of public funding, such as private family law (unless it involved issues of domestic violence or forced marriage), clinical negligence, debt (unless it involved the potential loss of the home), certain housing issues (again, unless there was a risk of homelessness), consumer issues, immigration (where the client was not detained) and welfare benefits. The paper also set out the intention to redraw the lines on financial eligibility for receiving legal aid so that individuals with more than £1,000 of capital would be required to contribute to their legal costs (at present individuals with less than £8,000 are not required to contribute).

In its Green Paper the Ministry of Justice set out the reasoning behind the decision to make drastic cuts to the legal aid system: **10–009**

> **Since the modern scheme was established in 1949 its scope has been widened far beyond what was originally intended. By 1999 legal aid was available for very wide range of issues, including some which should not require any legal expertise to resolve. We believe that this has encouraged people to bring their problems before the courts too readily, even sometimes when the courts are not well placed to provide the best solutions. This has led to the viability of taxpayer funding for unnecessary litigation. There is a compelling case for going back to first principles in reforming legal aid.**

It was argued that these cuts would result in more than just a simple return to the first principles of the legal aid system and that the result would be a much reduced level of access to justice, especially for those individuals in the more vulnerable sectors of society. However, the Ministry of Justice was adamant that this would not be the case but rather that the aims were to:

> **[f]orm part of a wider radical programme to move towards a simpler justice system; one which is more responsive to public needs, which allows people to resolve their issues out of court, using simpler, more informal remedies where they are appropriate, and which encourages more efficient resolution of contested cases where necessary.**

Legal Aid Reforms

10-010 The provision of legal aid was dramatically altered again when the Legal Aid, Sentencing and Punishment of Offenders Act 2012 took effect on 1 April 2013 (LASPO 2012). The Act was a culmination of a funding review aimed at saving £350 million per year on the legal aid bill. As a result of the funding reforms, cases involving matters such as divorce, welfare benefits, employment, child contact, clinical negligence and housing law, are no longer eligible to receive public funding. Legal aid is now only accessible to those involved in cases where there is a risk to life or liberty, or where serious harm would result if legal aid were not provided. Even those involved in cases where recourse to public funding is still permissible may find their way blocked due to strict eligibility criteria rules in respect of means testing. There has been widespread public outcry at the perceived effects and injustice of the cuts; lawyers have gone on strike and courts have ground to a halt as a result. Those who oppose the cuts, such as the Law Society, argue that it has undermined the justice system by denying access to justice for some of the most vulnerable members of society.

LASPO 2012 abolished the Legal Services Commission (and with it the Community Legal Service and Criminal Defence Service), replacing it with the Legal Aid Agency. The Legal Aid Agency is a government organisation administered by the Ministry of Justice. It oversees, commissions and procures the provision of legal aid throughout both the civil and criminal justice system, and it states that its work is essential to the fair, effective and efficient operation of both of these systems. The organisation states that its strategic priorities are to:

- improve legal aid casework, for example by speeding up payments and eligibility assessments
- grow the capability of the Legal Aid Agency by investing in staff development and improving our working environment
- work with our partners to deliver changes to legal aid, including informing policy development and increasing online working

10-011 Whether it is achieving these aims is matter for debate, as in March 2014, Bellamy J, a family court judge sitting in the High Court, said that the Legal Aid Agency was "wasteful and inefficient" with an "almost impenetrable" level of bureaucracy following a refusal by the Agency to fund an expert's report requested by the court; the refusal of the Legal Aid Agency directly contradicted, and essential overrode, the judicial case management direction, thereby impacting upon the delivery of justice.

Legal aid will now only be provided in respect of private law services, such as divorce and financial disputes, if there is evidence of domestic violence and the client can produce "trigger evidence" to back it up. Regulation 33 of the Civil Legal Aid (Procedure) Regulations 2012 sets out how the "trigger evidence" must be provided; some examples of how a client could achieve this are by them producing evidence of an unspent conviction for domestic violence, or of a relevant police caution for domestic violence in the preceding 24 months, or by providing evidence of relevant criminal proceedings not yet concluded, or by giving evidence of a protective injunction, or letters from a health care professional or multi-agency risk assessment conference. Due to the very nature of domestic violence the accepted ways in which the evidence must be produced may simply not be achievable for those wanting to rely upon them, thereby denying them recourse to both public funding and access to justice.

One of the initiatives introduced by LASPO 2012 was the Civil Legal Advice Service (CLAS), which is a telephone and website service for providing free legal advice on matters involving housing, social security, debt, special education needs, or discrimination. Those seeking legal advice on matters which fall within the last three listed areas must go through the CLAS and will only get to speak to an advisor face-to-face if their case is assessed as being too complex to be dealt with via the telephone. **10–012**

Those seeking legal advice can check whether or not they are eligible for legal aid through the CLAS, as it is a nationwide service funded by the Legal Aid Agency. The service will provide free and confidential legal advice to those eligible for legal aid and there is a simple legal aid eligibility questionnaire on their website (*https://www.gov.uk/check-legal-aid* [accessed 1 May 2025]).

It is not just the civil justice system that has been hit hard by the funding cuts; the criminal justice system has been hit equally hard, if not more so. The government aim was to cut the criminal legal aid budget by £220 million, a reduction of almost a quarter. In bringing about the changes the Ministry of Justice argued that the legal aid bill had historically cost taxpayers £1 billion per year and that public confidence in the system was undermined by wealthy defendants routinely receiving legal aid in criminal matters, and the existence of a small number of very high cost cases. It claimed that the changes would result in public confidence being boosted, the system becoming more streamlined and a more accurate reflection of the recent reduction in crime levels. However, senior lawyers, judges and the bodies responsible for governing the provision of legal services nationally were concerned that the proposals would have a detrimental impact upon our justice system, with the potential to destroy access to justice for some of the most vulnerable people in society.

The proposals initially included price-competitive tendering, whereby firms would be required to bid for a legal aid contract, and fixed fees were also to be introduced where there was to be one set fee, regardless of case length or amount of work undertaken. Concerns were raised that this would end in defendants being provided with inadequate legal representation and that some defendants might even be encouraged to plead guilty so as to conclude the case as quickly as possible as the representative would still receive the full fee despite the fact that they carried out little actual work. Perhaps the most controversial proposal though was that a suspect receiving funding under the legal aid scheme would no longer be permitted to choose his own lawyer, but would be allocated one instead. No consideration was to be given to the suspect's wishes or previous relationships, either good or bad, with a particular law firm. This would have resulted in the total elimination of choice and the most vulnerable potentially **10–013** being allocated a lawyer who is not versed in, or even aware of, their individual needs. The overwhelming reaction of the legal world to these proposals was that they would ultimately end up undermining Britain's international reputation for upholding justice. The Bar Council, the governing body of barristers, stated that by introducing the scheme the government risked "damaging the British justice system, which is renowned worldwide for fairness and impartiality".

Fortunately, the Ministry of Justice took on board the concerns raised with the proposed system, and consequently what was implemented was a slightly different creature to what was first suggested, although certain elements still remained. The criminal legal aid system now consists of two types of funding contracts. The first is the Duty Provider contract; this contract is awarded to specific geographical areas and is obtained through competitive tendering; under this process defendants do not have the choice as to their representing firm. The second is the Own Client Crime contracts, which are not geographically restricted and which permit the defendant to select their own legal representative.

10–014 Whether or not a defendant will be eligible to receive public funding is determined by a two-stage test means and the merits tests (prior to 2010 a defendant in the Crown Court had to satisfy the merits test only). If the defendant is successful in his application for legal aid, then the order will cover all of the proceedings, from the preparation for trial to the end of the appeal process.

A means test is used to assess whether defendants have the means to pay for a defence privately or whether a representation order should be granted. The means test is comprised of two elements:

- an initial assessment; and
- a full means test.

The initial assessment will consider a defendant's weighted gross annual income and is undertaken to determine whether a defendant is either automatically eligible or ineligible for public funding, or to determine whether a full means test will be required. For a magistrates' court trial, if a defendant's gross annual income is below £12,475 then qualification for a representation order is automatic; if the defendant's gross annual income is above £22,325, then a defendant fails the means test and will be required to fund the proceedings privately. If a defendant's income falls in between these two figures then a full means test will need to be undertaken so as to decide upon eligibility. A defendant's income from all sources (minus State benefits) will be taken into account in this initial assessment and this may then be weighted by taking into account a partner's income if a partner exists (unless there is a contrary interest such as the partner being the victim, prosecution witness, or joint defendant) and any dependants. In the Crown Court there is a financial eligibility threshold of an annual disposable household income of over £37,500 and once this has been reached a client will not be eligible for legal aid.

The full means test for both courts will calculate a defendant's disposable income and will take into account a defendant's housing costs, maintenance payments, childcare fees, income tax and national insurance contributions, as well as annual living allowance. If, after calculating all of above, a defendant is shown to have a disposable income exceeding the specified amount, then the defendant will be deemed ineligible for public funding. **10–015**

Even if a defendant passes the means test, this does not automatically secure a representation order, the merits test will still need to be satisfied and proof shown that it is in the interests of justice to grant a legal aid.

Section 17(2) LASPOA 2012 sets out the circumstances in which the merits test will be deemed to have been satisfied, mirroring the previous provisions within para 5 of Sch. 3 to the AJA 1999. It states that it will be in the interests of justice to grant a representation order where:

- the individual would, if any matter arising in the proceedings is decided against them, be likely to lose their liberty or livelihood or suffer serious damage to their reputation;
- the determination of any matter arising in the proceedings may involve consideration of a substantial question of law;
- the individual may be unable to understand the proceedings or to state their own case;
- the proceedings may involve the tracing, interviewing, or expert cross-examination of witnesses on behalf of the individual; and
- it is in the interests of another person that the individual be represented.

This list is not exhaustive and there may be other factors in a case that mean it is in the interests of justice to warrant the issuing of a representation order. If a defendant fails the means test, there is no right to appeal this decision. However, if such a situation were to occur, a defendant could request that a hardship review be undertaken, especially if a high level of outgoings was not factored into the initial calculations or if the cost of defending the case is likely to be beyond the average level for such a case. Also, if, after initially being refused public funding, a defendant's personal circumstances change then they are entitled to request that their means be reassessed based on the new circumstances. If a defendant fails the merits test, then they are permitted to appeal to the court on this point and request that the decision be reconsidered. **10–016**

The final point to note in respect of public funding of criminal justice is the existence of the Public Defender Service (PDS) and the Criminal Defence Direct (CDD) service. The PDS is a department of the Legal Aid Agency that operates alongside private providers to deliver legal services relating to criminal law matters. The department consists of a number of legal professionals ranging from KCs to solicitors and police station representatives, all of whom can be appointed by an individual who is in receipt of legal aid to provide legal advice and representation in court. The PDS also offers its expertise to other lawyers, and solicitors can approach the department to act for them in complex cases. The PDS currently has four offices—Cheltenham,

Darlington, Pontypridd and Swansea. The CDD is a free telephone advice service which can be accessed by people detained at a police station for a non-imprisonable offence.

Despite the significant changes already made to legal aid funding the provision of it is constantly under review and the next few years may bring with it further change that could well impact further upon the ability of the lawyers to provide the high standards of legal services expected from our legal system, and which will potentially reduce even further the accessibility of the legal system to the more vulnerable members of society.

Conditional Fee Agreements

10-017 When individuals wish or need to bring litigation but are not eligible for public funding, and cannot afford to pay the costs privately, they may be able to enter into a conditional fee agreement (CFA) with a solicitor so that the legal costs in the case are covered. A CFA is often described as a "no-win, no-fee" agreement and these agreements have become more popular in recent times due to the frequent daytime TV adverts offering this service to help people litigate for "any slip, trip or fall in the past five years".

CFAs were first introduced by s.58 of the CLSA 1990. Section 58(2) sets out that a CFA is:

(a) [...] an agreement with a person providing advocacy or litigation services which provides for his fees and expenses, or any part of them, to be payable only in specified circumstances; and
(b) a conditional fee agreement provides for a success fee if it provides for the amount of any fees to which it applies to be increased, in specified circumstances, above the amount which would be payable if it were not payable only in specified circumstances.

10-018 Under a CFA a solicitor will agree to provide legal services on the premise that if the client does not win the case, then he will not be liable to pay any of the solicitors' costs. If the client does win, then he will be liable to pay the solicitors' costs as well as a pre-agreed success fee (which must be written into the CFA contract). The success fee (sometimes called the "uplift" fee) is calculated as a percentage of the solicitor's fee for the work. So, for example, if a solicitor charged £1,000 for his work in a case and the success fee was set at 50 per cent, then the total the client must pay the solicitor would be £1,500. The solicitor will calculate the percentage of the success fee to be set on the risks involved in the case; if the likelihood of success in a case was very low then the success fee would be set as a high percentage, whereas if success in the case was almost a sure thing then the success fee percentage would be quite low. The maximum percentage that can be set as a success fee is 100 per cent of the solicitor's fee (so, in the above example, if the success fee was 100 per cent then the client would be required to pay the solicitor £2,000 if the case was won), however, the Law Society has recommended that the average success fee (obviously depending on the individual facts of the case) should be between 20–25 per cent. Persons wishing to undertake litigation covered by a CFA can enter into such an agreement and that person's personal means will not be taken into account. Even the multi-millionaire supermodel, Naomi Campbell, was allowed to enter into a CFA regardless of the fact that she had more than enough money to pay for the litigation privately (**Campbell v MGN Ltd** [2005] UKHL 61).

When CFAs were first introduced by the CLSA 1990, they could only be used in a limited number of cases, these being personal injury claims, insolvency claims, and claims involving human rights issues. However, this limited usage was widened in 1998 when the Government allowed them to be employed in most civil matters involving money claims (minus family law issues), and the AJA 1999 widened their use even further when it amended the CLSA 1990 by inserting s.58A. Section 58A of the CLSA 1990 now sets out that CFAs can be used to fund any legal proceedings except those involving criminal proceedings or family proceedings.

On the face of it, CFAs appear to be a very simple and attractive way of solving the funding issue as individuals are not dependent on receipt of public funding so as to gain access to the justice system; if they lose they pay nothing and if they win they are only obliged to pay solicitors a little extra so as to thank them for a case well done. However, if the CFA system is investigated further then this simplistic view is not a true representation of it. Issues as to costs arise when a client loses a case. The traditional stance taken by the courts is that a losing party is liable to pay a winning party's costs in the case. Therefore, even if a losing party is not liable to pay their own legal costs, they will be responsible for paying the other side's legal costs, which could amount to a hefty sum of money. Also, when preparing a case, solicitors will often incur extra costs that are outside own fees. These are known as disbursements, and a common disbursement that can be incurred in a claim is the preparation of an expert's report. If an expert (say, a doctor) is required to write a report on the injuries suffered by a claimant in the case, then they will expect to be paid a fair fee for doing so. The solicitor does not factor such expenses into their own fee agreed with the client, and therefore the client is liable to pay this disbursement regardless of whether they win or lose the case. So as to avoid having to pay out personally for all of these extra costs, individuals who agree to fund litigation by way of a CFA would be advised to take out insurance (known as after-the-event (ATE) insurance) to cover any further expenses incurred. After-the-event insurance is similar to any other insurance premium (car, buildings, or contents) and the underwriter of the insurance will assess the risks involved in the claim to determine the premium that is required to be paid. If an insured person is then unsuccessful in their claim, the insurance company will pay for any of the costs for which they are liable. **10–019**

A further issue that initially arose in respect of CFAs was that the winning party was liable to pay the solicitor's success fee and after-the-event insurance premium out of their own money (the solicitor's basic costs being paid by the losing party as per the norm). This seemed to be an unsatisfactory state of affairs, as a winning party would normally have to use part of (or even all of) the damages awarded in the case to pay these costs. This was argued to be unjust, as the damages awarded were to compensate the party for losses incurred due to the cause of action and not for funding litigation. The House of Lords considered this issue in the case of **Callery v Gray** [2002] UKHL 28.

10–020 In **Callery**, the claimant suffered minor injuries in a road traffic accident and, on first instructing solicitors to claim damages from the defendant, entered into a CFA with an agreed success fee of 60 per cent. Shortly thereafter, and before the defendant's response to the claim was known, the claimant also paid a premium of £350 for ATE insurance to cover the risk of any liability for costs they might incur if the claim failed. The claim settled quickly without the issue of proceedings, and the defendant agreed to pay the claimant damages and reasonable costs. The district judge ruled that a success fee of 40 per cent was reasonable and could be recovered as part of the claimant's costs, and that the cost of the insurance premium was also recoverable. The defendant appealed to the Court of Appeal, which upheld the district judge's decision. The Court stated that in modest and straightforward claims following road traffic accidents it would normally be reasonable for a claimant to enter into a CFA and take out ATE insurance when they first instructed their solicitor and that, where a reasonable premium and a reasonable success fee were agreed, each was recoverable from the defendant if the claim succeeded or was settled on terms in which the defendant had to pay the claimant's costs. The Court also concluded that the maximum reasonable success fee in such a case was 20 per cent.

On further appeal to the House of Lords, the House held, whilst dismissing the appeal, that it was pre-eminently the responsibility of the Court of Appeal, not the House of Lords, to supervise the developing practice of the use of CFAs and ATE insurance, as the House could not respond to changes in practice with the speed and sensitivity of the Court of Appeal and, accordingly, it was inappropriate for the House to interfere with the rulings which that Court had given in the instant case.

The principle that was developed by this case was that the losing party (or rather his insurance company if they have taken out ATE insurance) was liable to pay all reasonable costs incurred by the winning party and that these reasonable costs can include the winning party's solicitor fees, any success fee agreed (so long as it is a reasonable amount) and any premium paid out for ATE insurance obtained. Considering the potential level of costs for which the losing party could have been liable for, remembering to take out ATE insurance at the earliest point possible seems to be a rather prudent step.

10–021 However, the judiciary became increasingly concerned about the cost of litigation and so, in 2008, the Master of the Rolls asked Lord Justice Jackson to undertake a review into civil litigation costs. Lord Jackson published his final report in 2010, which became known as the Jackson Review, and made a number of recommendations that have impacted upon the way in which cost related issues are dealt with by the civil justice system.

Lord Jackson recommended that the principle of qualified one-way cost-shifting be implemented. Traditionally, in the civil courts the losing party would be responsible for paying the legal costs of the winning party; this meant that if a claimant brought a case and won that the defendant would have to cover any financial award imposed by the courts *and* the cost of any legal fees incurred by the claimant. However, the converse of this rule was that often if the claimant lost their claim, they would be liable to cover any legal costs incurred by the defendant—this was viewed as potentially unjust and that it acted as a deterrent to individuals bringing legitimate claims. Having a qualified one-way cost-shifting policy in place would mean that a claimant would not be required to pay the defendant's costs if unsuccessful in their claim, but that the defendant would still remain liable to pay the claimant's costs if the claimant were successful.

Another recommendation made by Lord Jackson was that the success fee and any ATE insurance premium should cease to be recoverable. This helps to rebalance the positions between the parties. Before the reforms a defendant to a claim was at risk of having to pay out a large sum of money if the claimant's claim were successful; often the success fee and ATE premium could amount to a figure similar, or even greater to, the cost of the legal fees. In **Campbell** [2005] the success fee and ATE premium alone amounted to almost £1 million. Under the new rules a losing defendant will now not be faced with the prospect of enormous costs being incurred in various ways, but rather will just be responsible for the true legal costs of the case.

The other main recommendation made by Lord Jackson related to the introduction of contingency fee agreements in to the civil justice system, and these have now been introduced under LASPO as "damage-based agreements".

Damage-based agreements

An important point to note in relation to CFAs is that they are different to the American system of funding litigation known as a contingency fee agreement. Contingency fee agreements, or "damage-based agreements" (DBAs) as they are now known in our domestic justice system, work on the same basic "no-win, no-fee" premise, but with a DBA the success fee claimed by the lawyer upon winning the case is based on a percentage of the damages awarded (as opposed to a percentage of the basic legal fees as with CFAs). DBAs were, for a long time, illegal in the UK as it is thought that they provided the lawyer with a far greater financial interest in the case than was healthy. If solicitors were to be paid a percentage of the damages awarded, it was thought that there would be the possibility that unethical lawyers could exaggerate the facts of the claim so as to increase the damages payable, or that they would only take those cases in which the return was likely to be lucrative, which would then have the effect of denying parties with a minor claim the ability to secure legal representation and gain access to justice. **10–022**

However, research undertaken by the Civil Justice Council suggested that these fears were unfounded and DBAs were introduced into the Employment Tribunal without issue. Lord Justice Jackson, in his review, commented that the arguments in favour of contingency fees outweighed the arguments against them. Under LASPO 2012 DBAs have been introduced widely into the civil justice system, and it is thought that they will eventually become a primary method of funding litigation and replace CFAs. A number of safeguards have been put in place (on the recommendations of Lord Justice Jackson) to avoid any negative impact through the introduction of DBAs. Strict upper limit caps apply to the percentage amount a lawyer can take from their client's damages; for personal injury cases the maximum permitted success fee is 25 per cent of the awarded damages; in employment law cases that percentage increases to 35 per cent; and, in all other cases the maximum permitted percentage is 50 per cent. There has also been a change on the way that costs are dealt with, as instead of the losing party being required to pay the winning party's costs, as is the norm in civil litigation, the defendant is required to pay the claimant's costs if they are successful in their claim but they cannot claim the costs from the claimant if their claim is unsuccessful. Also, if successful, the claimants are now responsible for paying the success fee and this cannot be recovered from the defendant. It seems that this American-style funding system will become common place within the English civil courts and as it becomes more accepted it will hopefully help to expand access to justice to those who would otherwise not be able to afford to bring their claims to court.

Pro Bono Work

10–023 The Latin term "*pro bono publico*" (shortened to *pro bono*) translates as "for the public good". The term is used to describe legal work that is conducted for free. There are a number of organisations that will conduct litigation on behalf of an individual without charge where the individual cannot secure any form of funding to otherwise undertake the work. The Free Representation Unit (FRU) is one of the largest *pro bono* providers in England and Wales. It was set up in 1972 and is now a registered charity, and it provides free representation in cases heard in employment tribunals, social security appeals and some immigration and criminal injury compensation cases. The volunteers who undertake the cases for the FRU are law students and legal professionals in the early stages of their careers, and, currently, there are approximately 270 volunteers registered with the FRU as willing to undertake such work. As well as registered charities, such as the FRU, there are many other organisations that offer *pro bono* work. The Citizen's Advice Bureau and many law schools at universities up and down the country also offer free legal advice clinics (although they do not usually provide legal representation for formal hearings), and these are excellent and worthwhile forums for potential lawyers to gain experience in advising real clients in real cases.

Summary

1. Within the English legal system there is an unmet legal need where members of the public, for a variety of reasons, are not accessing the legal services available to them. These reasons vary from a lack of awareness that any wrong has been committed to concerns regarding the cost implications of litigation and the fact that the legal profession is viewed as unapproachable.

2. Public funding for legal proceedings began in 1949 with the introduction of the Welfare State. Legal aid was available for a number of different legal services (such as advice or representation in court). Eligibility for public funding was determined in most cases by way of a means and/or merits test.

3. The AJA 1999 abolished the old-style legal aid and introduced the LSC, which is now charged with overseeing and administrating the provision of funding for both civil and criminal matters.

4. The wide-scale reform of the public funding system has seen the public legal aid bill cut drastically. The Legal Aid Agency is now responsible for managing the legal aid provisions. Public funding in civil matters is only available for very specific cases where there is a risk of loss of life or liberty, and criminal justice matters in both the magistrates' and the Crown court are subject to means testing.

5. A conditional fee agreement (CFA) is a private method for paying for legal costs. A "no-win no-fee" agreement is made between the solicitor and the client on the understanding that, if the case is successful, the client will be liable to pay the solicitor's costs and a further success fee, which is calculated as a percentage of the basic legal fee.

6. After-the-event insurance should be obtained when entering into a CFA, as this will cover an individual for any extra costs incurred or pay the other side's costs if the individual loses the case.

7. Damage-based agreements (DBAs) have been introduced into the civil justice system following the Jackson Review recommendation. With DBAs the lawyers are entitled to claim a success fee based on a percentage of the damages awarded. The percentage claimable is capped between 25 per cent and 50 per cent, depending on the type of claim.

8. Pro bono work is free legal work carried out by a number of organisations on a voluntary basis.

Further Reading

K. Ashby and C. Glasser, "The legality of conditional fee uplifts" [2005] 24(Jan) C.J.Q. 130–135.
Considers the development of the use of CFAs within the civil justice system and whether their introduction breaches the ECHR.

Lord Justice Jackson, "Review of Civil Litigation Costs: Final Report", (The Stationery Office, 2010).
A review of the civil costs situation in England and Wales, with recommendations.

Ministry of Justice, "Transforming Legal Aid: Delivering a more credible and efficient system", (2013) Consultation Paper CP14/2013.
Consultation paper on the proposed reforms to the legal aid provisions.

Self Test Questions

1. Public funding was originally:
   (a) cash limited
   (b) demand fed
   (c) demand limited
   (d) cash fed

2. The Access to Justice Act 1999 introduced the:
   (a) Legal Services Committee
   (b) Legal Funding Committee
   (c) Legal Services Commission
   (d) Legal Funding Commission

3. A defendant who wishes to receive public funding for a trial in the Crown Court will have to satisfy:
   (a) a means test
   (b) a merits test
   (c) a means and merits test
   (d) nothing, as criminal representation is always publicly funded

4. The success fee in a Conditional Fee Agreement is a calculated percentage of:
   (a) the damages awarded in the case
   (b) the public funding granted for the case
   (c) other side's costs
   (d) the solicitor's costs

5. The success fee in a Damage-Based Agreement is a calculated percentage of:
   (a) the damages awarded in the case
   (b) the public funding granted for the case
   (c) other side's costs
   (d) the solicitor's costs

Sentencing

11

CHAPTER OVERVIEW

In this chapter we will:

- Consider the different types of sentences available to the courts, such as custody, community sentences and fines.
- Evaluate the aims of sentencing.
- Discuss how the courts achieve consistency in the sentences they impose.
- Consider the factors taken into account when sentencing.

Introduction

11–001 Throughout the various chapters of this book we have worked our way through almost the entire criminal trial process. What we come to consider now is the point in time where a defendant has been either convicted or acquitted and the witnesses and the viewers in the public gallery have gone home either satisfied that the criminal justice system seems to work or, alternatively, horrified that justice has not (in their eyes) been done. However, the verdict delivered by the jury is not the final instalment in the case as there are still a few final issues to be determined, namely sentence (if the defendant has either pleaded guilty or been found guilty) and the possibility of an appeal (after either conviction or acquittal).

It is important to be aware of the various penalties and punishments that can be imposed by the courts as the legal process does not just stop at the verdict. This penultimate chapter will explore the sentences that may be imposed in the criminal courts, as well as the issues that commonly arise in respect of sentencing. This may not seem as exciting or glamorous as the actual trial process but it is an issue of equal importance; especially to a defendant, who will undoubtedly want to know whether he will be sentenced to a term in prison or if he will simply be sentenced a number of hours of unpaid work as a means to pay penance.

Types of Sentence

11–002 The sentencing options available to the court, i.e. the types of sentence that could be imposed, were originally governed by the Power of Criminal Courts (Sentencing) Act 2000 and then the Criminal Justice Act 2003. However, the introduction of the Sentencing Act 2020 has since taken over on these matters and sentencing now falls mainly under the proviso of this statute.

Over to you

What different types of sentence do you think are available to the courts?

There are a number of different types of sentence available to the court, but the first sentence that most people would think of if asked to write a list of available sentences would be imprisonment or a custodial sentence (it matters not how it is termed, unless it is a younger offender who would serve a term of "detention" as opposed to "imprisonment"), as this is often seen as the most serious sentencing option available to the courts. Custody is the type of sentence that is often reported in the media in relation to criminal trials, and so most laypeople are familiar with, at the very least, the concept of it; custody is also the form of sentence that the majority of defendants will want to try and avoid at all costs. Other sentencing options that may have been considered include non-custodial sentences such as unpaid work, drug rehabilitation orders and fines, etc. There are, in fact, four general categories of sentence that can be split down further to cover the numerous more specific forms of sentencing. These four general categories are:

- custody;
- community sentences;
- financial penalties;
  - fines,
  - compensation, etc;
- other (including bind overs and deferred sentences):
  - absolute discharges,
  - conditional discharges, etc.

And yes, discharges, even absolute ones, as surprising as it may seem, are forms of sentence, as will be explained later in this chapter. 11–003

Each type of sentence, and each specific sentence within a type, has various rules governing whether it will be an appropriate and allowable sentence for the individual case in question. Obviously, a life sentence cannot be imposed for a crime of petty theft, nor can a cold-blooded contract killer be given an absolute discharge after a conviction for murder. What will now be considered is how an appropriate and commensurate sentence is decided upon, as well as what the rules are preventing judges from handing out life sentences arbitrarily, perhaps because they do not like the look of a defendant or because a defendant is a prolific repeat offender of petty crimes. However, before we move on to consider the individual sentences and their application, it is useful here to take a moment to stop and consider the aims of sentencing to discover whether there is more to the idea of sentencing individuals than simply punishing them.

Aims of Sentencing

Over to you

What do you think the main aims of sentencing are?

It is guessed that most lists would include the main aim of sentencing being to punish the proverbial "bad man", or to make offenders pay for their crimes and to repay society and victims for whatever offence they have been subjected to. If the list were to include any of the above then it would have certainly pinpointed one of the aims of sentencing, that being punishment of offenders; but if the list had included similar words or phrases to those above, such as "pay for their crimes" or "repay society and the victim", etc. then it would have actually identified more than one aim of sentencing. There are, in fact, a number of aims of sentencing and the aim that 11–004 will be focused upon (the *priori*) will depend very much on the type of offence, the defendant, the circumstances of the crime and the parties involved in the crime. As a general rule, the aims of sentencing can be listed as:

- punishment of offenders;
- reduction of crime (including its reduction by deterrence);
- reform and rehabilitation of offenders;
- protection of the public; and
- reparation by offenders to persons affected by their offences.

These aims are set out in s.57 of the SA 2020 in relation to adult offenders, and in s.58 in relation to young offenders, which are those offenders who are aged under 18. These general aims do not apply when a mandatory sentence requirement applies or the making of various hospital orders or directions.

Over to you

Consider the following short examples and attempt to state the main aim(s) of the sentences imposed.

1. **Eric (aged 16) has been convicted of 10 separate counts of indecently assaulting young children. He has been sentenced to detention at His Majesty's pleasure (an indefinite term of imprisonment).**

2. **Frank has been convicted of spraying malicious graffiti on an elderly lady's house. He has been sentenced (by the imposition of a referral order) to clean off the graffiti and make a formal apology to the victim.**

3. **Gary has been convicted of possession of a Class A drug and an imitation firearm. He has been sentenced to two years in a Young Offenders Institution, where there are the facilities for him to possibly receive drug and alcohol dependency treatment.**

11-005 Whilst working through these short illustrative examples it is hopefully understood that there does not just have to be one aim behind the chosen sentencing option. An individual sentence, depending on the type of sentence imposed, can actually cover two or even more of these aims depending on the circumstances.

In example 1, Eric has been sentenced to detention at His Majesty's pleasure; the aims of this sentence could be said to be both punishment (Eric has been deprived of his liberty for the foreseeable future) and protection of the public (as he is detained indefinitely he will not be able to assault any more young children). In fact, if Eric were to have access to appropriate treatment whilst he was in custody, then the sentence could possibly even be said to have the aim of reforming and rehabilitating him.

In example 2, Frank has been requested to clean off the graffiti and apologise to the victim. By undertaking these two actions Frank will be making two acts of reparation (firstly, making amends to the victim by putting right the damage he has caused and secondly by making the apology), and there will also be an element or aim of reform behind the sentence as well. By having to apologise to the victim of his actions and therefore seeing first-hand the effect his actions have had upon another, it is hoped this will have the effect of reforming his character so that he does not commit a similar offence again. This method of sentencing by way of a referral order has been quite popular with the courts in recent years when sentencing young offenders because, as stated above, it is hoped that the young offenders, by carrying out such acts of reparation, will then be turned away from travelling further down the route of a criminal life.

Finally, in example 3, Gary being sentenced to a Young Offenders Institution which has drug and alcohol treatment facilities has more than one aim. The first could be said to be the rehabilitation of the offender; placing Gary into a unit where he will be able to access appropriate treatment will mean that he can potentially overcome any drug or alcohol dependency issues that he may have. In the short term the aim of the sentence could also be to reduce the amount of crime being committed in the locality by the removal of an individual who is involved with both drugs and firearms. Considering the current climate in the UK in respect of violent and drug-related crime, this may be a factor that is taken into account by the judiciary whilst determining sentences in similar cases. 11–006

Each of the sentences above had aims behind them, but, as can be seen, it is not just a matter of course that the outright punishment of the offender will be the principal aim. An individual's ideas about the aims behind each sentence may have differed slightly or even completely to those set out above and there probably is no definitive correct answer to which aims are the most predominant in each scenario. The aims act as a form of guidance for the courts when they are required to determine the appropriate sentence in an individual case.

Sentencing Guidelines

As well as considering the aims of the sentence, one of the fundamental principles behind determining an appropriate sentence is that the sentence should never be more severe than the seriousness of the offence warrants. How, then, do the courts determine the seriousness of the offence in such a way as to assess the severity of the sentence? How do they determine whether Gary, in the example above, should be given two years' detention or two months' detention? Consistency of sentence for similar crimes is an important issue to both the courts and all of those involved in the criminal justice system. The system would become unworkable 11–007 if the judiciary were allowed to make arbitrary decisions as to type and length of sentence; the necessary certainty that the public requires and relies upon in the criminal justice system would disappear. Imagine how the layperson would react if, upon conviction for the offence of drunk driving, they were told that their sentence (whether custodial or a fine) would depend on whether the judge had had his lunchtime glass of port or not. Society would be in uproar and any remaining confidence in the criminal justice system would crumble.

To help determine the appropriate sentence the courts will look to a number of sources. The first step (as stated above) is to establish the seriousness of the offence, and the authority that deals with this element is ss.57–63 of the SA 2020. Under these sections there are a number of factors that the court is required to have in mind when deciding on the seriousness of the offence for sentencing purposes. Under s.63, the court must consider an offender's culpability in committing the offence and any harm that the offence caused, may have caused or could foreseeably have caused. It is also permitted to take into account, as an aggravating factor, any previous conviction that an offender may have (whether the conviction arises from a UK court or from another jurisdiction). If the offence was committed whilst on bail then this fact will also be treated as an aggravating factor. Further, if the offence was motivated by any religious or racial bias or had an element of hostility relating to either sexual orientation or disability then, the presence of this factor requires the court to increase the sentence imposed to a level that it feels appropriately reflects the seriousness of the offender's actions.

11–008 The statutory provisions under the SA 2020 do go some way to assisting the court when determining sentence, but they do not provide the in-depth guidance that a normal everyday working court would require. If magistrates faced with a case of assault had to determine what would be a suitable sentence on the facts of the case in front of them, based only upon the provisions in the legislation they would immediately run into difficulty. How would they know what the starting point of the sentence should be? Three months' custody? Six months? Would a community sentence be more appropriate? It may be thought that experience would guide the Bench as to where it should begin in its considerations, and this assumption would not be wrong, but, for the sake of consistency and certainty, more than experience alone must be employed when identifying the starting point for the sentencing of specific offences.

Historically, the CJA 2003 provided for the creation of the Sentencing Guidelines Council (SGC). The SGC was established with the primary aim of providing sentencing guidelines for all criminal offences. This organisation has now been replaced (under Pt 4 of the Coroners and Justice Act 2009 (CJA 2009)) with the Sentencing Council, which began work in April 2010. The Sentencing Council has taken over the work of the SGC in an effort to promote greater transparency and consistency in sentencing, whilst maintaining the independence of the judiciary. It is an independent, non-departmental public body of the Ministry of Justice and although it replaces the SGC it has the aim of building on what the SGC had started to achieve. Lord Justice Leveson, the Chairman of the Sentencing Council and a Court of Appeal judge, upon appointment stated that:

The job of the Sentencing Council is to build on what has already been achieved – evolution not revolution.

The functions of the Sentencing Council, as detailed under the CJA 2009, are to: 11–009

- prepare sentencing guidelines;
- publish the resource implications in respect of the guidelines it drafts and issues;
- monitor the operation and effect of its sentencing guidelines and draw conclusions;
- prepare resource assessments to accompany new guidelines;
- promote awareness of sentencing and sentencing practice; and
- publish an annual report that includes the effect of sentencing and non-sentencing practices.

It is envisaged that the Sentencing Council will eventually set out a sentence range for each offence, and then detail any aggravating and mitigating factors that the court must take into account, along with the general provisions of the SA 2020, when deciding where in the sentence range a specific case should fall. The Sentencing Council has produced a number of definitive guidelines covering a variety of offences and sentencing issues, such as the sentencing of young persons and children. However, until the Sentencing Council has produced a guideline for every offence then the courts also remain reliant on the methods of determining appropriate sentence that were used prior to the creation of the Sentencing Council.

Traditionally, if an offender has been convicted of a statutory offence then the relevant statutory provision may provide some assistance in determining the sentence. However, statutes invariably only set out the maximum sentence that can be imposed by the court for the offence in question; Acts do not normally set out the minimum or recommended sentence. Consequently, the statute will only go so far in providing assistance to the court in this matter and, of course, consideration must also be given to the fact that not all offences are laid down in statute. Currently, there are two methods employed by the courts to determine this difficult and very important issue of appropriate sentence, and which of these two methods will be used will depend on the level of the court (magistrates' or Crown Court) dealing with the case.

The Magistrates' Court

When the issue of determining the appropriate sentence arises in magistrates' courts the Bench will turn to the guidance provided in the Magistrates' Court Sentencing Guidelines (MCSG) provided by the Sentencing Council (as previously discussed in Ch.9). The MCSG set out the offences that the magistrates will deal with frequently in the adult criminal court. The guidelines provide a sentencing structure which details how to establish the seriousness of each case and determine the most appropriate way of dealing with it. The guideline 11–010 sentences are based on a first-time offender being convicted after pleading not guilty. The guidelines speak of reaffirming the principle of "just desserts" so that any penalty must reflect the seriousness of the offence for which it is imposed and may take into account the personal circumstances of offenders. The magistrates must always start the sentencing process by taking full account of all the circumstances of the offence (such as any relevant aggravating and mitigating factors) and make a judicial assessment as to which category of seriousness the offence falls into. The magistrates are required to consider in every case whether:

- a discharge or a fine is appropriate;
- the offence is serious enough for a community penalty; or
- it is so serious that only custody is appropriate.

11–011 To fully understand how the MCSG work in practice we will now return to the case study of Alfie, which you first encountered in Ch.9. We will work on the assumption that he was convicted of assault of a police officer contrary to s.89 of the Police Act 1996 after trial in a magistrates' court and it was determined at trial that Alfie had spat at the police officer in question. The maximum sentence that can be imposed is a Level 5 fine and/or 26 weeks' custody. The first step for the court to take in deciding on an appropriate sentence is to determine the offence category.

Over to you

Refer to Figure 41, which is a copy of the MCSG factors to be taken into account when determining the offence category for the offence of assaulting a police officer. Use the guidelines to determine what you believe is the appropriate offence category for the offence facts.

FIGURE 41 Determining the offence category

STEP ONE
Determining the offence category

The court should determine the offence category using the table below.

Category 1	Greater harm **and** higher culpability
Category 2	Greater harm **and** lower culpability; **or** lesser harm **and** higher culpability
Category 3	Lesser harm **and** lower culpability

The court should determine the offender's culpability and the harm caused, or intended, by reference **only** to the factors below (as demonstrated by the presence of one or more). These factors comprise the principal factual elements of the offence and should determine the category.

Factors indicating greater harm
Sustained or repeated assault on the same victim
Factors indicating lesser harm
Injury which is less serious in the context of the offence

Factors indicating higher culpability
Statutory aggravating factors:
Offence racially or religiously aggravated
Offence motivated by, or demonstrating, hostility to the victim based on his or her sexual orientation (or presumed sexual orientation)
Offence motivated by, or demonstrating, hostility to the victim based on the victim's disability (or presumed disability)
Other aggravating factors:
A significant degree of premeditation
Use of weapon or weapon equivalent (for example, shod foot, headbutting, use of acid, use of animal)
Intention to commit more serious harm than actually resulted from the offence
Deliberately causes more harm than is necessary for commission of offence
Leading role in group or gang
Offence motivated by, or demonstrating, hostility based on the victim's age, sex, gender identity (or presumed gender identity)
Factors indicating lower culpability
Subordinate role in group or gang
Lack of premeditation
Mental disorder or learning disability, where linked to commission of the offence

Source: Magistrates' Court Sentencing Guidelines, p.210

Looking at the factors that the court must take into account it would appear that Alfie had committed a Category 3 level offence as there are factors indicating lesser harm (no serious injury) and lower culpability (no premeditation).

Once the offence category has been established the court is then required to reach an appropriate sentence within the category range.

Over to you

Refer to Figure 42, which is a copy of the MCSG factors to be taken into account when determining the appropriate sentence. Use the guidelines to determine what you believe is the appropriate sentence to impose on Alfie.

FIGURE 42 **Starting point and category range**

STEP TWO
Starting point and category range

Having determined the category, the court should use the corresponding starting points to reach a sentence within the category range below. The starting point applies to all offenders irrespective of plea or previous convictions. A case of particular gravity, reflected by multiple features of culpability in step one, could merit upward adjustment from the starting point before further adjustment for aggravating or mitigating features, set out below.

Offence Category	Starting Point *(Applicable to all offenders)*	Category Range *(Applicable to all offenders)*
Category 1	12 weeks' custody	Low level community order – 26 weeks' custody
Category 2	Medium level community order	Low level community order – High level community order
Category 3	Band B fine	Band A fine – Band C fine

The table below contains a **non-exhaustive** list of additional factual elements providing the context of the offence and factors relating to the offender. Identify whether any combination of these, or other relevant factors, should result in an upward or downward adjustment from the starting point. In some cases, having considered these factors, it may be appropriate to move outside the identified category range.

When sentencing **category 1** offences, the court should also consider the custody threshold as follows:

- has the custody threshold been passed?
- if so, is it unavoidable that a custodial sentence be imposed?
- if so, can that sentence be suspended?

Factors increasing seriousness
Statutory aggravating factors:
Previous convictions, having regard to a) the nature of the offence to which the conviction relates and its relevance to the current offence; and b) the time that has elapsed since the conviction
Offence committed whilst on bail
Other aggravating factors include:
Location of the offence
Timing of the offence
Ongoing effect upon the victim
Gratuitous degradation of victim
Failure to comply with current court orders
Offence committed whilst on licence
An attempt to conceal or dispose of evidence
Failure to respond to warnings or concerns expressed by others about the offender's behaviour
Commission of offence whilst under the influence of alcohol or drugs
Established evidence of community impact
Any steps taken to prevent the victim reporting an incident, obtaining assistance and/or from assisting or supporting the prosecution
Offences taken into consideration (TICs)

Factors reducing seriousness or reflecting personal mitigation
No previous convictions **or** no relevant/recent convictions
Single blow
Remorse
Good character and/or exemplary conduct
Determination and/or demonstration of steps taken to address addiction or offending behaviour
Serious medical conditions requiring urgent, intensive or long-term treatment
Isolated incident
Age and/or lack of maturity where it affects the responsibility of the offender
Lapse of time since the offence where this is not the fault of the offender
Mental disorder or learning disability, where **not** linked to the commission of the offence
Sole or primary carer for dependent relatives

Source: Magistrates' Court Sentencing Guidelines, p.211

The guidelines require the court to consider every possible sentence from a discharge up to custody depending on how serious they deem the offence to be after taking into account the facts of the case, including aggravating and mitigating factors. It appears from the facts that there are two of the aggravating factors present, those being that Alfie spat at the officer and showed gross disregard for police authority by calling the officer a "pig". There is also a potential mitigating factor present in the case as Alfie's behaviour could be termed as impulsive action (so lack of premeditation), and the magistrates could also consider other points, such as the fact that Alfie is still quite young, and he may have shown remorse for his actions (although he has not pleaded guilty so could not be described as overly remorseful). Looking at the guidelines a Category 3 offence has a starting point as a Band B fine, which is 100 per cent of the defendant's relevant weekly income, but depending on the impact of the aggravating and mitigating factors, the full range available is between a Band A fine (50 per cent of relevant weekly income) and a Band C fine (150 per cent of the relevant weekly income). It is likely that Alfie would find himself facing sentence in the mid-range for this offence, and so a Band B fine may be imposed. 11–012

The court would have to explain why it imposed the sentence is did as whenever the court hands down a sentence it is required, under s.52 of the SA 2020, to provide its reasoning for the sentence imposed in addition to the aims of such a sentence. This is to ensure that the sentence is commensurate to the seriousness of the offence and to ensure that the magistrates have taken all relevant and necessary factors into account in their deliberations. As is explained in the final substantive chapter on Appeals, this requirement to provide full reasoning for the sentence imposed can be crucial in determining whether the sentence was appropriate and, if not, the reasoning will provide the grounds for any subsequent appeal.

The Crown Court

11–013 The Crown Court, at present, does not have its sentencing guidelines contained in any one text but instead relies upon Court of Appeal (Criminal Division) decisions to guide it in determining appropriate sentence, as well as advice from the Sentencing Council in respect of certain offences. Judgments that contain sentencing guidance are normally reported in the Criminal Appeal Sentencing Reports, and an edited version of useful judgments can also be found in criminal law practitioner texts, such as *Archbold* and *Blackstones*, as well as a number of other specialised sentencing texts.

To illustrate exactly how the Court of Appeal sets out such guidelines it is useful to look at judgments produced by the Court. The case of **R. v Millberry** [2003] 1 W.L.R. 546, for example, in response to the Sentencing Advisory Panel's advice on the revision of the current sentencing practice for offences of rape, sets out some very clear guidelines as to how an appropriate sentence should be determined in rape cases.

The Court indicated that rape almost invariably called for an immediate custodial sentence. It broadly agreed with the principal suggestions of the Panel that the guidelines should deal explicitly with the question of sentencing levels for relationship rape and acquaintance rape, as well as stranger rape. It also agreed that the same guidelines should apply equally to male and female rape, and that anal rape should be treated similarly to vaginal rape. The Court also considered that the offender's culpability, especially in relation to the victim's behaviour, or historic cases, where the event was reported many years after it occurred, would be relevant.

11–014 In general, the Court laid down guidelines that the normal starting point of five years should apply where there were no aggravating features. If there were certain aggravating factors, such as the rape of a child, a vulnerable victim, if the rape was racially aggravated or due to the victim's membership of a vulnerable minority, or if the rape was committed by a man who was knowingly suffering from a life-threatening and sexually transmittable disease, then the starting point to be adopted would be eight years' imprisonment. Fifteen years' imprisonment was thought to be a suitable starting point where the case involved a campaign of rape on either the same or multiple victims and, finally, an automatic life sentence would be appropriate where the offender already had a conviction for a serious offence (under s.273 of the SA 2020).

The case of **Millberry**, therefore, is a very useful tool for a court to turn to when required to determine the seriousness of the offence and decide the appropriate sentence in rape cases.

In respect of other offences there are many Court of Appeal judgments dealing with specific offences and setting out relevant guidelines. If you were to use one of the online legal databases and search the term "sentencing" with a specific offence then it would undoubtedly return a suitable and contemporary case to use as guidance.

For example, inputting the search terms "sentencing" and "supply of Class A drugs with intent" returns the case **Re Attorney General's Reference No.20 of 2002** [2003] 1 Cr. App. R. (S) 58. Here, the Court provided guidelines on the appropriate sentence for offenders who have committed the offence of possessing a Class A drug with a street value of between £6,000 and £12,000, with intent to supply. The Court in this case held that the usual range of sentence for an offence of this kind was three to four years' imprisonment and that only in the most exceptional cases could such a case result in a non-custodial sentence. **11–015**

If the terms "sentencing" and "aggravated burglary" are searched then the case **Re Attorney General's Reference (No.101 of 2001)** [2002] EWCA Crim 86 is displayed. This case involved the offences of grievous bodily harm, robbery and aggravated burglary. The defendant had stabbed an 83-year-old man in his own home and then demanded money following a forced entry. He also slashed a married couple, who were in their sixties, with a razorblade while demanding money after having called at their home. The Attorney-General stated that when the violent attacks were on elderly victims in their own homes then the deserved sentence would be one in double figures (a commensurate sentence being one of 10 years' imprisonment), and if the case involved issues of public protection then a longer commensurate term of 14 years' imprisonment would be more appropriate.

As stated above, it is intended that the Sentencing Council will eventually produce guidelines for all criminal offences, but until that occurs the Crown Court will continue to rely upon the many Court of Appeal decisions to help it determine the seriousness of the offence and the appropriate sentence to impose. As each case will have its own individual facts therein does lay a certain danger that the courts will not always sentence consistently. Every year there are a number of appeals based on the grounds that the sentence is either too lenient or too harsh (depending, of course, on the party bringing the appeal (see Ch.12 for further detail on appeals)). However, as the law stands at present, reference to previous sentencing precedent is the most effective method for the Crown Court to determine the appropriate level of sentence, and if the Sentencing Council does manage to eventually produce guidelines then these guidelines will still carry with them an inherent possibility of inconsistency as they will only ever be guidelines—the courts will likely never be faced with two offences with an identical set of circumstances. **11–016**

Other Factors Affecting Sentence

11–017 In addition to the sentencing guidelines discussed above there are also a number of other factors that the courts regularly take into account when deciding upon sentence—these include things such as pre-sentence reports, victim impact statements, personal offender mitigation and other offences that are to be taken into consideration.

Pre-sentence Reports

11–018 Pre-sentence reports, commonly known as PSRs, are reports compiled by the Probation Service after consultation with the offender. They are primarily aimed at assisting the court in its quest to determine the most appropriate sentence for the offender in question. To help the court with this deliberation, the PSR focuses on a number of different elements, such as the offence itself, an offender's culpability, an offender's attitude (i.e. whether remorseful or unconcerned), an offender's personal circumstances (such as history, education, employment, health, previous convictions, risk of reoffending), and any other relevant matters that probation officers feel are pertinent. Often the PSR will also contain a recommendation that the offender be sent for psychiatric or medical reports. The report will not usually specify an exact sentence but will detail those sentences that the probation officer feels the offender is most suitable for. For example, it would not recommend a community order with the requirement of attending a drug and alcohol treatment programme for an offender who is teetotal, but it may consider that this would be a suitable and appropriate sentence for a drug addict who has expressed a desire to undergo rehabilitation.

The governing statutory provision for the obtaining of PSRs is s.30 of the SA 2020. Under s.30, the court is obliged to obtain a PSR, whenever minded to:

- impose a custodial sentence; or
- impose a community order with requirements.

Under subs.(2) the court is not required to obtain a PSR in situations where it is of the opinion that it is not necessary, such as if the offence carries with it a mandatory life sentence (although a PSR may be helpful in identifying the minimum term to be served), or if the offence can only be dealt with by way of a fine, etc. In essence, a PSR will not be necessary when the sentence is already predetermined, irrespective of an offender's personal circumstances and, consequently, the PSR would not have any effect on the proceedings. It is normal practice, however, to order a PSR, and they are a rather routine request within the criminal court system. A full PSR (allowing the sentencer all options) will take approximately three weeks to compile, however, a fast delivery report or oral PSR (allowing the sentencer to impose a community penalty and below) is normally done either on the day of, or within a day of, conviction. An offender's sentencing hearing will be adjourned until the expected date of the report.

Victim Personal Statements

Victim personal statements (VPSs) are a relatively new addition to the criminal justice system and as such do not appear within criminal proceedings with the same regularity as PSRs. A VPS allows the victim of the offence to voice their thoughts and feelings about the offence to the court as a way of ensuring that the sentencing court would consider the harm caused. They also identified any need for support or protection (see **R. v Perkins (Robert)** [2013] EWCA Crim 323). Victims will detail how the offence has affected their lives and how they view the particular offender. This statement could have one of two effects when considered in relation to offence seriousness and appropriate sentence, in that, depending on its contents, it may constitute an aggravating or mitigating factor. An impact statement for business (ISB) provides a similar opportunity for businesses to set out the impact that crime has upon their financial loss, operational disruption or reputational damage. **11–019**

A VPS could be taken into account as an aggravating factor if the victim of the offence sets out the negative ways in which the offence has affected, and is possibly still affecting, their life. If a victim, after being subjected to the offence of rape or a violent street robbery, states that they are terrified to leave the house or walk to the shops alone, that they still have nightmares and have to take medication to cope with life on a day-to-day basis, then the court will take this into account as an aggravating factor when considering the appropriate sentence. If, however, the victim to the offence states that they forgive the offender, that they are not suffering any long-lasting detriment as a result of the offence, and that they wish the offender to be dealt with leniently, then the court may take this into account when considering any mitigating points in relation to the offence. A VPS can also be made to the parole board, when the offender has a parole board review, to explain what the impact of release will be.

One point to question here is really how much input the victim should have into the offender's sentencing. It is submitted that, in the majority of cases, a VPS will be quite helpful to the court as it will be able to assess the level of the harm caused by the offender, but if the prosecution and conviction of an offender was more malicious in nature (imagine a jilted ex-partner alleging rape in an effort to seek revenge) then a VPS could further compound a rather bad situation and possibly increase a sentence that maybe should not have been imposed in the first place.

Personal Offender Mitigation

Personal offender mitigation (POM) has some common elements to a PSR, in that the court considers the offender's personal circumstances and situation when coming to the conclusion as to what is an appropriate sentence. POM is generally raised at the point of oral advocacy in the case known as the plea-in-mitigation. A plea-in-mitigation will be presented to the court by defence counsel during the sentencing hearing proceedings. The aim of a plea-in-mitigation is to minimise the severity of the sentence that an offender receives by putting forward personal circumstances and feelings (i.e. remorse as to involvement in the offence). By submitting a plea-in-mitigation, it is hoped that the court will, to a degree, empathise or sympathise with **11–020** the defendant and therefore impose a less onerous sentence. POM will focus on the individual concerned in the instant case. So, for example, if, at the age of 45, the offender has been convicted of the offence of fraud then the court will not be interested, in respect of considering sentence, to learn that the defendant came from a broken home and spent three years in foster care; this would be likely to be viewed as an irrelevant sob story. However, if the offender has been convicted of an offence, such as theft, and the court learns, through the POM, that she is a single mother with four young dependent children and no family support system to care for the children if she is imprisoned, then the court may be more minded, if possible, to impose a non-custodial sentence to avoid the children being taken into care. Nevertheless, the court is not obliged to take into consideration any personal mitigation submitted to the court by the defence counsel, but is duty bound, however, to consider all the aggravating and mitigating circumstances of the offence itself as required by ss.73–75 of the SA 2020.

Offences Taken into Consideration

11–021 In the English court system, the general rule is that an offender is only sentenced on the basis of the offences for which he has been convicted. However, there is one exception to this rule. This exception only occurs when the offender in question requests that the court, when it comes to the point of considering sentence, takes into account other offences that the offender has committed, but for which they have not been formally convicted. These offences are termed as "offences taken into consideration", or TICs. This may seem to be quite a strange concept to understand when first introduced to it, but there is logic behind the principle.

TICs can be beneficial to both the prosecution and the offender in a case. The principle behind TICs is that an offender requests the court take into account any other offences committed and confessed to when determining sentence. It may be the case that the offender has been convicted of four dwelling-house burglaries but also asks the court to take into account a further 12 burglaries when deciding sentence. By doing so, the prosecution (and police) benefit as it has the result that another 12 burglaries are "solved" and so can be struck from the unsolved crime statistics. The offender also benefits as it means that, although the sentence may be increased in the immediate instance so as to take into account the other offences, the offender will not subsequently be prosecuted and convicted separately of the offences that have been the basis of the offences considered.

11–022 For an offence (or offences) to be taken into consideration an offender must first admit to the offences and then the detail of the offence must be set down in a schedule, which is signed by the offender and then entered into court. Once in court the offender will then be asked to confirm and consent to the schedule so that the offences can be formally considered. Guidance on how the court should then deal with the TICs in relation to sentence (particularly in relation to weight) is provided in the case of **R. v Miles** [2006] EWCA Crim 256, by Sir Igor Judge:

In relation to offences taken into consideration, we have these observations: the sentence is intended to reflect a defendant's overall criminality. Offences cannot be taken into consideration without the express agreement of the offender. That is an essential prerequisite. The offender is pleading guilty to the offences. If they are to be taken into account (and the court is not obliged to take them into account) they have relevance to the overall criminality. When assessing the significance of TICs, as they are called, of course the court is likely to attach weight to the demonstrable fact that the offender has assisted the police, particularly if they are then able to clear up offences that might not otherwise be brought to justice. It is also true that cooperative behaviour of that kind will often provide its own very early indication of guilt, and usually means that no further proceedings at all need be started. They may also serve to demonstrate a genuine determination by the offender (and we deliberately use the colloquialism) to wipe the slate clean, so that when he emerges from whatever sentence is imposed on him, he can put his past completely behind him, without having worry or concern that offences may be revealed as that he is then returned to court.

As in so many aspects of sentencing, of course, the way in which the court deals with offences to be taken into consideration depends on context. In some cases the offences taken into consideration will end up adding nothing or very little to the sentence which the court would otherwise impose. On the other hand, offences taken into consideration may aggravate the sentence and lead to a substantial increase in it. For example, the offences may show a pattern of criminal activity that suggests careful planning or deliberate rather than casual involvement in a crime. They may show an offence or offences committed on bail, after an earlier arrest. They may show a return to crime immediately after the offender has been before the court and given a chance that, by committing the crime, he has immediately rejected. There are many situations where similar issues may arise. One advantage to the defendant, of course, is that once an offence is taken into consideration, there is no likely risk of any further prosecution for it. If, on the other hand, it is not, that risk remains. In short, offences taken into consideration are indeed taken into consideration. They are not ignored or expunged or disregarded.

TICs do not fit into the normal English legal system pattern of an offender having to be formally convicted of an offence to be sentenced upon it, but they are a very useful and often productive procedure when employed by the courts.

Custodial Sentences

11–023 Custodial sentences are the most severe form of sentence that a court can impose. The pronouncement of a term of imprisonment means that an offender will be deprived of liberty and (fundamental) right to freedom for a set period of time. Not only does a custodial sentence affect an offender detrimentally in a physical sense, it can also have a substantial impact on them and their wider family in an emotional, financial and social sense. It may well be the case that the offender is the only person in gainful employment within the family and that his removal for a period of time could have significant consequences upon the financial wellbeing of the rest of the family. Alternatively, if the offender has children then absence may result in emotional hardship for the children who have temporarily lost their parent. Society in general also looks unkindly upon those who have been imprisoned for a criminal offence, and an offender and his family could be faced with the stigma that a spell in custody can often carry. Therefore, the imposition of a custodial sentence is an action only taken by the courts where it is felt that, on the facts of the case, it is an absolutely necessary sentence.

To determine when it is appropriate to impose a custodial sentence, the courts will refer to the guidance laid down in s.230 of the SA 2020. Section 230(2) provides the details of the test that the court must apply when deciding whether or not to impose custody. Section 230(2) states that:

The court must not pass a custodial sentence unless it is of the opinion that the offence, or the combination of the offence and one or more offences associated with it, was so serious that neither a fine alone nor a community sentence can be justified for the offence.

Simply because a custodial sentence can be imposed for a certain type of offence does not then mean that it will always be imposed in every case. So how does the court determine whether custody is necessary, or if a fine or community order could be justified instead? How does the court reach such a decision, especially in those cases where there is a very fine line between the possible imposition of custody and the choice of another, less serious sanction. The statute itself is silent on this matter but the courts have laid down valuable advice on how to determine this question in the case of **R. v Howells** [1999] 1 W.L.R. 307.

11–024 The Court, by way of the judgment given by Lord Bingham CJ, sets out that there are five points that should be taken into account when considering custody in a borderline case:

In deciding whether to impose a custodial sentence in borderline cases the sentencing court will ordinarily take account of matters relating to the offender.

(a) The court will have regard to an offender's admission of responsibility for the offence, particularly if reflected in a plea of guilty tendered at the earliest opportunity and accompanied by hard evidence of genuine remorse, as shown (for example) by an expression of regret to the victim and an offer of compensation.

(b) Where offending has been fuelled by addiction to drink or drugs, the court will be inclined to look more favourably on an offender who has already demonstrated (by taking practical steps to that end) a genuine, self-motivated determination to address his addiction.

(c) Youth and immaturity, while affording no defence, will often justify a less rigorous penalty than would be appropriate for an adult.

(d) Some measure of leniency will ordinarily be extended to offenders of previous good character, the more so if there is evidence of positive good character (such as a solid employment record or faithful discharge of family duties) as opposed to a mere absence of previous convictions. It will sometimes be appropriate to take account of family responsibilities, or physical or mental disability.

(e) While the court will never impose a custodial sentence unless satisfied that it is necessary to do so, there will be even greater reluctance to impose a custodial sentence on an offender who has never before served such a sentence.

The guidance from this case then is that the handing down of a custodial sentence should only be done where it is *absolutely necessary* and can be *justified*. Further, the sentence imposed should not be any longer than is required to satisfy the penal purpose of the sentence. So what forms of custodial sentences can be given and in what circumstances?

Life Imprisonment

This is probably the best-known custodial sentence and is often viewed by the media and the public as the most controversial in its application, as it is often quoted that "'life' does not actually mean 'life'". Essentially, there are two types of life sentence: discretionary and mandatory. Discretionary life can be imposed by a court for common law offences, and where the maximum specified in the statute pertaining to the offence is life. 11–025

However, when an offender has been convicted of the offence of murder the courts are statutorily obliged, under s.275 of the SA 2020, to impose the penalty of life imprisonment. This sentence means that judges in these cases have no discretion to impose any other type or length of sentence. Life imprisonment is the only penalty that can be imposed on offenders aged 21 years or over who are convicted of murder. Although judges have no discretion as to the *type* of sentence in these cases they do, however, have a certain element of discretion as to the *minimum term* that the offender must serve (the starting point) before being eligible for release on licence. Being released on licence means that a defendant will serve the remainder of the custodial term out of prison, with the looming possibility of return to custody to serve the remainder of the full term if further offences are committed whilst on licence.

Section 275 and the relevant Sch.21 to the SA 2020 set out the starting point that must be imposed in relation to a mandatory life sentence depending on the circumstances of the offence; these starting points range from the whole life sentence down to one of 12 years depending on the individual facts of the case. Conveniently, Sch. 21 largely duplicates its predecessor, Sch. 21 to the CJA 2003, but with some amendments.

11–026 A whole life term should be imposed (under para.2 of Sch.21) where the offence falls into one of the following categories:

(a) the murder of two or more persons, where each murder involves any of the following—
   (i) a substantial degree of premeditation or planning,
   (ii) the abduction of the victim, or
   (iii) sexual or sadistic conduct;
(b) the murder of a child if involving the abduction of the child or sexual or sadistic motivation;
(ba) the murder of a child involving a substantial degree of premeditation or planning;
(c) the murder of a police officer or prison officer in the course of his or her duty;
(d) a murder done for the purpose of advancing a political, religious or ideological cause; or
(e) a murder by an offender previously convicted of murder.

A number of high-profile murderers such as Myra Hindley, Rosemary West, Roy Whiting and Levi Bellfield have received "whole life" sentences (or their pre-2003 equivalent), which means that they were to stay in prison for the entirety of their lives. In 2013 Mark Bridger was sentenced to a whole life for the sexually motivated abduction and murder of 5 year-old April Jones. Only a very limited number (approximately 30) of these whole life sentences have been imposed since their introduction. The legality of a whole life sentence and the potential resulting breach of the European Convention on Human Rights (ECHR) was considered by the European Court of Human Rights in **Vinter v UK** (9 July 2013). The Court held that the imposition of such a sentence was a breach of art.3 because leaving a prisoner with no prospect of release was inhuman and degrading. However, the Court later overruled this decision in **Hutchinson v UK** (3 February 2015) and determined that a whole life sentence was compatible with the Convention because the Secretary of State can release a prisoner from such a sentence in exceptional circumstances.

A starting point of 30 years will be imposed (under para.3 of Sch.21), where the offence involved:

(a) the murder of a police officer or prison officer in the course of his duty (if committed before 13 April 2015);
(b) a murder involving the use of a firearm or explosive;

(c) a murder done for gain (such as a murder done in the course or furtherance of robbery or burglary, done for payment or done in the expectation of gain as a result of the death);
(d) a murder intended to obstruct or interfere with the course of justice;
(e) a murder involving sexual or sadistic conduct;
(f) the murder of two or more persons;
(g) a murder that is aggravated by racial or religious hostility or by hostility related to sexual orientation;
(h) a murder that is aggravated by hostility related to disability or transgender identity
(i) a murder falling within paragraph 2(2) committed by an offender who was aged under 21 when the offence was committed.

The notorious Soham murderer, Ian Huntley, received a sentence with the recommendation that he should serve at least 40 years before being considered for parole. He was convicted prior to the CJA 2003, however, his appeal joined a backlog of cases waiting for the decision on the role of the Home Secretary in relation to mandatory life sentences (see below), and therefore the appeal judge was able to increase his tariff to one of 40 years. **11–027**

If the offence does not fall into any of the above categories then the minimum starting point is 25 years if the offender took a knife or other weapon to the scene and used it to commit murder, under para.4; or 15 years, under para.5 if no weapon is present. If the offender is under the age of 18 at the time of the offence, then the starting point under para.6 varies according to age and severity, ranging from a minimum of 8 years' imprisonment to a minimum of 27 years. Previously, the starting point for offenders aged under 18 was simply 12 years under the CJA 2003.

A quick point to note regarding the minimum starting point before release is that it is only a starting point. Judges can then take into account any case-specific mitigating or aggravating factors and adjust the starting point accordingly. The imposition of a minimum time that an offender must serve before being considered for release on licence does not also mean that they will be automatically released when they have served this time; the fact of their release will be determined by the Parole Board who will decide if the offender is suitable to serve the remainder of the time in the community, although remaining "on licence for life".

The whole "life" does not mean "life" discussion has been very much in the public eye over recent years. Historically, the Home Secretary had the power to impose a minimum tariff for those convicted of an offence carrying with it a life sentence. This power came very much to the attention of the media in the case of the two child killers, Robert Thompson and Jon Venables, who had been convicted of murdering toddler James Bulger in 1993, as the former Home Secretary, Michael Howard, set the minimum tariff that they should serve at 15 years. Thompson and Venables appealed against the decision to set a minimum tariff, submitting **11–028** that this was beyond the powers of the Home Secretary. Upon hearing the case (**R. v Secretary of State for the Home Department Ex p. Venables** [1998] A.C. 407), the House of Lords held that the actions of the Home Secretary had been unlawful and that he was not permitted to impose minimum sentences in respect of juvenile offenders; this decision was then later confirmed by the ECtHR (**V v United Kingdom** (1999) 30 E.H.R.R. 121). This was the start of erosion of the Government's powers in being able to determine sentence in life imprisonment cases.

In 2002, the powers to determine minimum sentence in respect of adults convicted of offences carrying with them a life sentence was also stripped from political control, following the challenge made by Anthony Anderson. Anderson had been convicted in 1988 of two murders; at the time of sentencing the judge in the trial recommended that he should serve at least 15 years. Six years later the former Home Secretary, Michael Howard, increased the minimum term that Anderson would have to serve before being considered for release to 20 years. Anderson appealed the decision to the House of Lords (**R. (on the application of Anderson) v Secretary of State for the Home Department** [2002] UKHL 46), which allowed his appeal, holding that it was unlawful for a politician to set a minimum tariff to be served, Lord Bingham of Cornhill commenting:

> **The conclusion that the Home Secretary should play no part in the fixing of convicted murderers' tariffs makes for much greater uniformity of treatment than now exists. The tariff term to be served by a discretionary life sentence prisoner is already determined by the trial judge in open court [...] and the Parole Board decide whether it is safe to release the prisoner at the end of that tariff term. The Home Secretary has no role.**

11–029 The fact that certain murderers, in fact the majority of murderers, including those who are as notorious as Ian Huntley and Mark Goldstraw (who killed his 16-year-old ex-girlfriend and her family in a premeditated arson attack and was recommended a minimum tariff of 35 years), do not receive full life sentences has been the subject of much debate and outrage by both the media and the public alike. The fact that politicians can no longer interfere with these sentences does seem to mean that such offenders are free from being used as political pawns for personal or party gain which, it is submitted, can only be a good thing for the interests of justice. However, there is the other side of the coin to consider, this being that the law cannot make any exceptions for those convicted of murder who have mitigating circumstances (e.g. a parent who kills his severely disabled child in a "mercy killing"). If such offenders cannot have their convictions reduced to manslaughter then they will face a life sentence regardless of the circumstances. They will be convicted as murderers and serve their prison sentences as murderers. When the two extremes, and all the shades of grey in between, in respect of cases of murder are compared, the question that begs to be asked is just how fit for purpose such a "rigid" sentencing structure is.

Schedule 21 of the CJA 2003 was subject to criticism by the Government in the consultation paper "Breaking the cycle: effective punishment, rehabilitation and sentencing of offenders" (Dec 2010), where it was said to be based on "ill-thought out and overly prescriptive policy" (p.50) resulting in it going into too much detail and therefore being unnecessarily complex, and that the implementation of a clearer sentencing framework was required. Judges can depart from the sentencing structure as now set out in Sch.21 of the SA 2020, but they must provide cogent reasons for doing so.

Section 283 of SA 2020 allows for a "life sentence for a second listed offence" to be imposed. This sentence is applicable where the defendant is convicted of a specified offence (a violent or sex offence) for which the court would impose a determinant sentence of 10 years or more, and where the offender has a previous conviction for a specified offence, for which they received a custodial sentence of 10 years or more. It is a "two strikes and you're out approach"; although the court can avoid this if it would be unjust to impose such a sentence in the circumstances.

EXTENDED SENTENCE

Section 254 of SA 2020 governs the imposition of an extended sentence for adults. This **11–030** extended sentence replaced the previous indeterminate sentence that was available under CJA 2003 s.225. An extended sentence can only be imposed where the defendant has been convicted of a specified offence (a sexual, violent or terrorist offence that merits a determinant sentence of at least four years), the court is of the opinion that the defendant presents a substantial risk of causing harm though reoffending by committing a further specified offence, and the imposition of such a sentence is necessary for the purpose of protecting members of the public from serious harm. The defendant will be sentenced to the appropriate sentence for the offence committed and then, upon having served that initial sentence, they will serve a further extended sentence period of at least one additional year. The maximum extended sentence is five years for a violent offence and eight years for a sexual offence or a specified terrorist offence; s.16 of the Counter-Terrorism and Sentencing Act 2021 has since added a maximum extended sentence of 10 years for serious terrorism offences. The sum of the total sentence imposed (initial and extended) must not exceed the maximum available penalty for the offence.

Fixed Term Sentences

Certain offences carry with them a mandatory minimum sentence as fixed by statute. Examples **11–031** of such sentences can be found on the statute books under s.313 of the SA 2020, which imposes a minimum sentence of seven years' imprisonment upon a third conviction of Class A drug trafficking; or under s.314, which imposes a minimum sentence of three years' imprisonment upon the third conviction of domestic burglary. Such fixed term sentences are clearly laid out in statute and the courts must follow the recommendations unless of the opinion that upon the circumstances of the offence it would be unjust to do so. In **R. v Giff (Derek)** [2023] EWCA Crim

594 the trial judge had overlooked SA 2020 s.73 which dealt with a reduction in sentence for guilty pleas. This provision allows a trial judge to reduce a minimum sentence imposed under s.314 but only to a lesser sentence which is not less than 80 per cent of the required minimum sentence.

Suspended Sentences

11–032 Under s.277 of the SA 2020 the court can, in certain circumstances, impose a suspended sentence. This means that the offender will remain out of custody but will have the suspended sentence hanging over their head, which, it is hoped, will work as a deterrent to committing further offences during the foreseeable future. To impose a suspended sentence the custodial sentence must be at least 14 days and not more than 2 years and it can then be suspended for between six months and two years.

The SA 2020 also requires offenders to comply with set requirements whilst they are "serving" the suspended sentence. These requirements are the same as for community orders (see below). If an offender refuses or fails to comply with the requirements imposed then the suspended sentence is activated under s.286(3) and the offender can be required to serve the remainder of his prison term actually in custody.

Detention at His Majesty's Pleasure

11–033 The term "detention at His Majesty's pleasure" is effectively the equivalent of a life sentence for a juvenile offender (this is what Thompson and Venables, discussed above, were sentenced to). Offenders are detained at His Majesty's pleasure when they are aged between 10 and 17 and have committed the offence of murder, under s.259 of the SA 2020. The judge must impose a minimum term to be served before parole can be considered and the young person will be kept under supervision for the rest of their life following their release.

Home Detention Curfews

11–034 Under s.246 of the CJA 2003 offenders can be released early from prison to serve a maximum of the 180 remaining days of their sentences in their own homes. This is expected to increase to 365 days on 3 June 2025 as the successful completion rate of HDCs is 90% and there have been over 80,000 participants since its inception in 1999 (when release was only 135 days early). This concept is different to that of being on licence (see below) as the offender is still very much seen as serving a custodial sentence. The offender will be required to comply with curfew requirements and be electronically tagged at all times until the sentence expires. The creation of this novel way to serve out a sentence has resulted from the need to alleviate the severe overcrowding that has occurred in prisons over the past few years. Not all prisoners are eligible for release under the HDC scheme. Those ineligibles include prisoners serving one of the sentences applicable to dangerous offenders, and prisoners who are liable to deportation. Also, prisoners who have less than 14 days to serve of their required custodial period following sentence (e.g. due to remand time being deducted from the required custodial period) are not eligible for HDC.

Release Upon Licence

Under s.244 of the CJA 2003, offenders can be released upon licence to serve out the remainder of their sentences in the community. An offender is normally released on licence after serving half of a full sentence. If serving two or more concurrent or consecutive sentences, the offender must be eligible for release for all of the sentences which have been passed before being released on licence. If an offender reoffends whilst on licence then they will be returned to custody to serve the remainder of the original sentence as well as any subsequent sentence for the latter offence. 11–035

Consecutive and Concurrent Sentences

If an offender has been convicted and sentenced to a custodial term in respect of more than one offence then the court can decide whether to run the sentences concurrently, which means that they run at the same time as each other, or whether to run them consecutively, which means that an offender will serve the sentences one after another. To determine whether to run the sentences consecutively or concurrently the court must take into consideration the totality of the sentences imposed. Section 231(2) of the SA 2020 sets out that: 11–036

> **The custodial sentence must be for the shortest term (not exceeding the permitted maximum) that in the opinion of the court is commensurate with the seriousness of the offence, or the combination of the offence and one or more offences associated with it.**

Over to you

A defendant has been convicted of 10 counts of theft and has been sentenced to six months for each respective count.

If you were the judge would you order that the sentences run consecutively or concurrently?

If these sentences were to run consecutively the defendant would be facing a custodial sentence that totalled five years. It is likely that this totality would be completely disproportionate to the seriousness of the offences. If they ran concurrently so that he only served six months in prison, this is likely to be far more proportionate to the seriousness of the offence; this is the "totality principle".

Is it Serious Enough for Custody?

11–037 To help the courts determine whether an offence is of such a serious nature that custody should be imposed, the Sentencing Council has, in the guidelines entitled "Overarching Principles: Seriousness" (originally published by the SGC), set out the approach that the courts should now adopt under the SA 2020. The flowchart below (Figure 43) details the considerations the courts should undertake.

FIGURE 43 **Considerations to be undertaken by the court when considering custody**

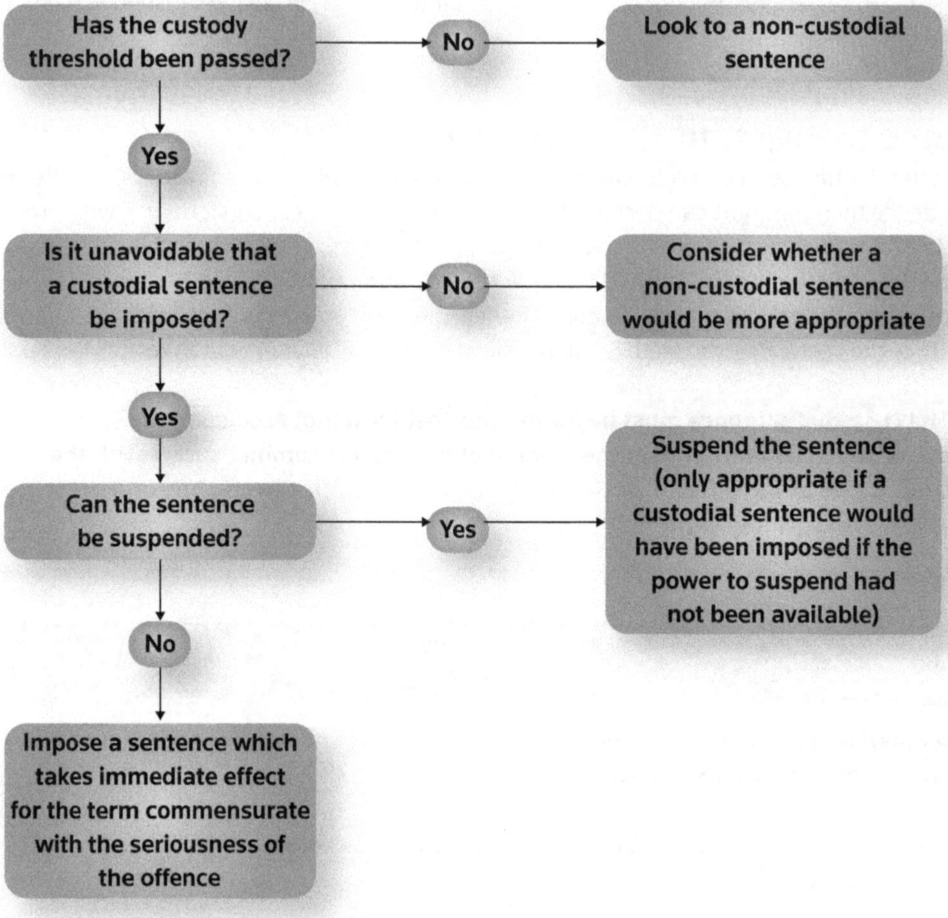

Non-Custodial Sentences

If the custody threshold has not been passed in the case then the court is required to consider which non-custodial sentence would be appropriate to impose. 11–038

The non-custodial sentences currently available to the courts are:

- community sentences;
- financial penalties; and
- discharges and other disposals.

Community Sentences

Under the SA 2020 the courts have the power to impose a single generic community order with certain requirements added on that are appropriate for the individual circumstances of the offender. This community order allows the court to have access to the whole range of orders available so that the sentence can really be tailored to the offender. 11–039

Section 201 of the SA 2020 sets out 16 different types of order that may be imposed upon persons aged 18 or over at the time they have been convicted of an offence. The court has the option to impose any one or more of the following types of order:

- an unpaid work requirement;
- a rehabilitation activity requirement;
- a programme requirement;
- a prohibited activity requirement;
- a curfew requirement;
- an exclusion requirement;
- a residence requirement;
- a foreign travel prohibition requirement;
- a mental health treatment requirement;
- a drug rehabilitation requirement;
- a drug testing requirement;
- an alcohol treatment requirement;
- an alcohol abstinence and monitoring requirement;
- an attendance centre requirement;
- an electronic compliance monitoring requirement; and
- an electronic whereabouts monitoring requirement.

Section 204 sets out that a community sentence should only be passed if the court is of the opinion that the offence is serious enough to warrant such a sentence; again, it must be proportionate and commensurate to the crime committed (how this is decided will be considered below). In addition to this, s.208 states:

(3) The particular community order requirement or community order requirements imposed by the order must, in the opinion of the court, be the most suitable for the offender.

THE REQUIREMENTS

Unpaid work/Community payback

11–040 This requirement is defined by Sch.9 Pt 1 of the SA 2020. A probation officer will organise for the offender to work on a suitable project within the local community for between 40 and 300 hours (the exact amount of time to be fixed by the court) and for that work to be completed within 12 months of the sentence being passed. The work will normally take place during the week but can occasionally take place at weekends (so as to allow for people in full time employment) and the type of work undertaken (gardening, painting, litter collecting, etc.) will depend upon the schemes that the probation office have running at that time. This form of community sentence is now referred to as "Community Payback" and those undertaking it are required to wear high visibility orange vest whilst working so that the local community are aware that the offender is paying back the taxpayer for the wrongs they have committed.

Rehabilitation activity requirement

11–041 Under a rehabilitation activity requirement the offender must (as directed by Sch.9 Pt 2 of the SA 2020) participate in the activities specified in the order. The number of days that the offender is required to participate in a certain activity must be specified and the types of activities required have behind them the purpose of reparation and may take the form of day centre attendance, education or contact between the offender and the victim of the crime.

Programme requirement

11–042 Schedule 9 Pt 3 of the SA 2020 requires the offender to attend a specified place and take part in a programme accredited by the Secretary of State. For example, an offender who has been convicted of drink driving may be required to attend a Drink Impairment drivers programme to address the behaviour and prevent reoffending.

Prohibited activity requirement

11–043 This order (under Sch.9 Pt 4 of the SA 2020) requires an offender to refrain from a specified activity on specified days or during a specified period. So, if an offender has a history of committing violent offences whilst drunk the order may prevent him drinking alcohol for a set period of time, or if an offender was involved with football hooliganism then the requirement may prohibit him from attending certain football matches.

Curfew requirement

11–044 A curfew order under Sch.9 Pt 5 of the SA 2020 requires an offender to remain in a specified place (normally the home address) for between two hours in any day and not more than 116 hours in any period of seven days. To ensure that the offender remains at the set address they will wear an electronic tag, which sends out signals to the central monitoring service via a telephone line. If the offender leaves the address within the curfew hours then the monitoring service will alert the police so that they can check on the offender's whereabouts. Curfew requirements are normally imposed to stop the offender re-offending; if the offender is in the habit of committing burglaries at night then being under curfew will hopefully curtail criminal activities. However, this is not a failsafe method as occasionally there are technical problems with the electronic tag, which result in the tags not properly transmitting to the tracking system and offenders then being arrested for breaking curfew even though they were actually within the specified premises during the curfew hours.

Exclusion requirement

Under Sch.9 Pt 6 of the SA 2020 an offender is barred from entering a specified place or locality for a specified period of no more than two years. This, again, is monitored electronically with an offender wearing a tag, and the places could include premises such as football stadiums (e.g. for the football hooligan above), or public houses (e.g. for the offender who becomes violent when drunk). As with curfew requirements there can occasionally be problems with the electronic tagging equipment. 11–045

Residence requirement

An offender (under Sch.9 Pt 7 of the SA 2020) may be required to reside at a certain address. However, the court cannot specify a hostel or other institution unless it has been recommended by the probation office as a suitable address. 11–046

Foreign travel prohibition requirement

A foreign travel prohibition requirement is governed by Sch.9 Pt 8 of the SA 2020 and it prevents an offender from travelling to specified countries for a period of up to 12 months. 11–047

Mental health treatment requirement

This order is aimed at rehabilitating an offender who is suffering from a mental illness. The offender (Sch.9 Pt 9 of the SA 2020) must submit, during a specified period, to treatment by or under the direction of a registered medical practitioner or a chartered psychologist (or both, for different periods) with a view to the improvement of the offender's mental condition. For this requirement to be imposed by the courts the offender must consent to the treatment and the court must believe that the offender requires and will be susceptible to the treatment. 11–048

Drug rehabilitation requirement

Under Sch.9 Pt 10 of the SA 2020 the offender must submit to treatment that has the aim of reducing or eliminating dependency on, or propensity to misuse, drugs. The offender will normally be required, at specified points during the order, to provide bodily samples so that it can be ascertained if he has been taking drugs. The court may only impose a drug rehabilitation requirement if it is satisfied that the offender is dependent on or has a propensity to misuse drugs, and that this dependency or propensity is at such a level that he requires and will be 11–049 susceptible to treatment. The order must include provision for review if the order is to last more than 12 months.

Drug testing requirement

11–050 This order is very similar to the drug rehabilitation requirement, as described above. Under Sch.9 Pt 10A of the SA 2020 the offender is required, at specified points during the order, to provide bodily samples so that it can be ascertained if he has been taking drugs. The court may only impose a drug testing order if it is satisfied that the offender is dependent on or has a propensity to misuse drugs.

Alcohol treatment requirement

11–051 This order is also very similar to the drug rehabilitation requirement above but for persons dependent on alcohol as opposed to drugs. The order (under Sch.9 Pt 11 of the SA 2020) has the aim of reducing or eliminating an offender's dependency on alcohol. The court must be certain that an offender is dependent on alcohol to the point that they require treatment, and that they will be susceptible to treatment.

Alcohol abstinence and monitoring requirement

11–052 This requirement, under Sch.9 Pt 12 of the SA 2020, imposes a total abstinence for a period of not more than 120 days. The requirement cannot run in tandem with an alcohol treatment requirement and the court must be satisfied that the offender is not dependent on alcohol, but that consumption of alcohol was a factor that contributed towards the commission of the offence.

Attendance centre requirement

11–053 This requirement is what was known as a probation or community rehabilitation order prior to the introduction of the CJA 2003. Under this requirement an offender is required to attend an attendance centre for a particular number of hours, not less than 12 and not more than 36. The offender must then attend set meetings fixed by the officer in charge of the centre, in an attempt to achieve their rehabilitation. The requirement is governed by Sch.9 Pt 13 of the SA 2020.

Electronic compliance monitoring requirement

11–054 This requirement, under Sch.9 Pt 14 of the SA 2020, means a requirement for securing the electronic monitoring of the offender's compliance with other requirements imposed, such as those described above, aside from the alcohol abstinence and monitoring requirement, which has its own monitoring provisions.

Electronic whereabouts monitoring requirement

11–055 Additionally, under Pt.14 of Sch.9 of the SA 2020, the offender's whereabouts, otherwise than for the purposes of compliance, is monitored over a specified period.

HOW TO DETERMINE THE APPROPRIATE REQUIREMENT

Deciding on which order is the most appropriate for a particular individual may be very easy to do on the facts of the case (i.e. a drug addict who has been convicted of possession of drugs would probably benefit from a drug treatment order). However, not all cases are as easy to pinpoint, and just because an order is an obvious choice it does not necessarily mean that it is the right one to impose. 11-056

To decide on the appropriate community sentence the courts may look to a number of sources. Section 57 of the SA 2020 sets out the main purposes behind sentencing and s.208 gives the courts the guidance that a community order should not be imposed unless it is both suitable for the offender in question and that the recommended order is commensurate with the seriousness of the offence.

The Sentencing Council (in material published originally by the SGC) also provides the courts with valuable advice in relation to how to determine the appropriate sentence and requirements by way of the guidelines, "Imposition of Community and Custodial Sentences Definitive Guideline". The Sentencing Council states that when deciding which requirements to include, the court must be satisfied that the restriction on liberty is commensurate with the seriousness of the offence and that the requirements are the most suitable for the offender. Also, at least one requirement must be imposed for the purpose of punishment and/or a fine be imposed in addition to the community order.

In determining what requirements to impose the court should firmly keep in mind the possibility of breach of the sanctions when it passes sentence for the original offence. To reflect the seriousness of an offence, it is required to ensure that the requirements selected are demanding enough for the offender, but equally are not so demanding that they "set an offender up to fail" and therefore end in an inevitable breach of the sentence. The guiding principles of selecting the appropriate requirements for a community sentences are proportionality and suitability. 11-057

As can be seen, the imposition of a community sentence is to be considered with the same degree of seriousness and responsibility that the imposition of a custodial sentence demands. Just because this type of sentence is below custody in the sentencing hierarchy it does not mean that it is a lesser sentence in any way and therefore the courts are required to give it the same amount of consideration as they do to other sentences.

ENFORCEMENT

Before the introduction of the new range of sentences under the SA 2020, and even before the CJA 2003, the old community sentence was often seen as the "soft option" by the media and the public as enforcement was lax and little was done to punish the offender for a breach. Under the CJA 2003 and now, under Sch.10 to the SA 2020 the enforcement and breach 11-058 of a community sentence is taken very seriously, and the court must take action against the offender if the breach is admitted or proven.

There are two ways in which a community sentence can be breached. The first is an offender failing to comply with the requirements of the order(s); the second is by way of an offender committing further offences whilst the subject of a community sentence. If an offender breaches the sentence then the courts have the power to deal with the breach in a number of different ways. The courts can:

- impose further requirements upon the offender;
- revoke the order(s) and re-sentence the offender for the original offence(s).

The Probation Service will issue a first and final warning, as a means of encouraging the offender to comply with the requirements before the offender is brought back before the court. When the court is faced with a breach of a community sentence it will take into account the efforts that the offender has made in attempting to fulfil the requirements imposed, so as to check that the original order was suitable for the offender in question and to see what further options are available. The imposition of custody for the breach of a community sentence should only be used as a last resort. However, often it is found that a vicious circle begins to occur with repeat offenders, as each time they fail to comply with the sentencing requirements they are brought back before the court where the court is likely to impose further requirements for the offender to comply with. As the offender was not able to comply with the original requirements then it is unlikely that they will do any better with the new requirements and will end up failing to comply with all of the requirements, which will result in their being brought back to court, and so on.

Financial Penalties

Fines

11-059 Both magistrates' courts and the Crown Court have the ability to impose a fine upon an individual convicted of an offence; in fact, the imposition of a fine is one of the most common methods of disposal in magistrates' courts. A fine can be imposed for any offence except those specified by law (i.e. murder). The court will look at imposing a fine as punishment where it is felt that the offence is not serious enough to warrant the imposition of a custodial or community sentence. Section 125(1) of the SA 2020 requires that the fine is fixed to reflect the seriousness of the offence and the court (under subs.(2)) must enquire into the financial circumstances of the offender before fixing the fine amount; obviously ordering an offender who lives on benefits to pay £75,000 in fines would be a completely pointless exercise.

The magistrates' court was historically limited to imposing a maximum fine of £5,000 but this cap was removed on offences committed on or after 12 March 2015 and now the court is able to impose any level of fine that it feels is appropriate in the circumstances—even a fine exceeding a million pounds can be given as long as the court believes that it reflects the seriousness of the crime committed and is proportionate. The Crown Court has always been able to impose an unlimited fine.

The magistrates' court can find guidance on how to assess the level of fine to impose in a way that reflects the seriousness of the offence in the MCSG. Fines in the magistrates' court are set by way of certain levels. The level is the maximum fine that can be imposed in respect of the individual offence. If reference is made back to the guidance given by the MCSG on the offence of assaulting a police officer it can be seen that the maximum fine that can be imposed is one that is level 5 on the scale; the offence of criminal damage, when tried summarily, carries with it a maximum fine of level 4; whereas the offence of trying to enter a football ground whilst drunk only carries with it the maximum statutory fine of level 2. Each offence that can be dealt with by way of a fine will carry with it a maximum fine that can be imposed in respect of it. So how do these fine levels equate to monetary figures? The fine scales in the magistrates' court are shown below in Figure 44, which shows the current fine levels.

FIGURE 44 **Magistrates' court fine scale**

Level of fine	Maximum amount of fine
Level 1	£200
Level 2	£500
Level 3	£1,000
Level 4	£2,500
Level 5	Unlimited

Over to you

What do you think this reasoning is?

The reasoning being that the most suitable level of fine will depend upon the circumstances of the offence and the offender.

To determine the exact fine amount the magistrates will consider the seriousness of the offence by taking into account any aggravating or mitigating factors and then assign it a level of seriousness on the scale of A to C (C being the most serious and A the least serious). This level of seriousness combined with the court's knowledge of an offender's financial circumstances, 11-060 following the enquiry under s.125 of the SA 2020, will then determine the level of fine to be imposed. Levels A to C have the following meanings:

FIGURE 45 Level of fine to be imposed

Level of seriousness	Level of fine to be imposed
Level A	**50% of the defendant's weekly income**
Level B	**100% of the defendant's weekly income**
Level C	**150% of the defendant's weekly income**

In some cases fine bands D–F may be used even where the community or custody threshold have been passed, when the maximum range can extend to 700% of relevant weekly income.

Obviously, not all defendants will have the spare cash to be able to pay the fine to the court outright, so if a defendant is not able to pay the fine as one lump sum the court can direct that the fine be paid by way of instalments. A Fines Collection Order will be made at the same time as fixing the fine, which delegates certain powers to administrative staff to collect the fine. If a defendant then defaults on a payment, the court can enforce the fine by way of making an Attachment of Earnings Order (or a Deduction of Benefits Order if a defendant is on certain benefits). The court also has the option of increasing the fine on default of payment or enforcing the sale of an offender's vehicle to meet the payment of the fine. The court can also issue a distress warrant, allowing bailiffs to enter an offender's home and remove goods to the value of the outstanding amount. As a last resort, the court can impose detention within the court building or, in more serious circumstances, custody, in respect of an unpaid fine. A fine defaulter should only be committed to prison as a last resort and custodial terms are imposed in accordance with a scale of the following maximum periods:

Up to £200 7 days;
£200.01–£500 14 days;
£500.01–£1,000 28 days;
£1,000.01–£2,500 45 days;
£2,500.01–£5,000 3 months;
£5,000.01–£10,000 6 months; or
Over £10,000 12 months.

Compensation

Under ss.133–146 of the SA 2020 the court is under a duty to consider compensation in every case where loss, damage or injury has resulted from the offence. The purpose of compensation in the criminal courts is to compensate victims for loss or injury. There are two types of compensation that the court must consider for loss. The first is known as special damages, and includes compensation for any financial loss sustained as a result of the offence, such as the cost of repairing the damage or any loss of earnings incurred. The second type of loss is known as general damages. These general damages include compensation for the pain and suffering of the injury itself and for any loss of facility that has occurred as a result of the offence. 11–061

When calculating the compensation to be awarded the court will again take into account the circumstances of the offender (their means and ability to pay any compensation together with any offer of compensation they may have already made). If an offender does not have sufficient means to pay both a fine and compensation order then the compensation will take precedence. The MCSG gives guidance on the level of fines that should be imposed for certain types of personal injury. If the court is minded to not award a compensation order then it is required to state its reason.

Discharges

Discharges are at the bottom of the sentencing hierarchy in respect of seriousness and are the final form of sentence to be considered in this chapter. Discharges come in two forms: conditional and absolute (as governed by Pt 5 of the SA 2020). 11–062

Conditional Discharge

Apart from fines, a conditional discharge is the most common form of disposal within magistrates' courts. A conditional discharge made under s.80 of the SA 2020 is where an offender is discharged on the condition that no further offence will be committed within the time set by the court (up to a maximum of three years). When an offender is given a conditional discharge the court will explain that, as long as they do not reoffend within the period of the conditional discharge then no further action will be taken in relation to the matter. If, however, the offender does reoffend and is convicted within the period of the conditional discharge then they will be brought back to court and the discharge will be revoked under s.81 SA 2020. This then means that the court will not only sentence them for the new conviction but that it will also revisit the previous offence and re-sentence on that matter as well. Conditional discharges are often passed down in magistrates' courts for those offenders who are first-time offenders and have committed a minor offence. The aim behind this type of discharge is to deter the offender from committing another offence in the future. 11–063

Absolute Discharge

11–064 An absolute discharge under s.79 of the SA 2020 is where an offender is formally convicted of the offence but then no punishment is imposed and so is discharged from the court without further action. This type of discharge is only really used when the offence is one of a trivial nature and the offender, although technically guilty, was found to be morally blameless, or where the court is showing its displeasure with the police and/or the CPS for their handling of the case. They are quite a rare occurrence in the courts as it is not often in today's society that the court finds stood before it defendants who are not morally responsible for their own actions and the resulting consequences, or that the law enforcement agencies have acted reprehensibly.

BIND OVERS

11–065 If offenders receive a "bind over" then they are formally "bound over to keep the peace". This, essentially, means that if they were to reoffend within a set time then they would be punished for breaking the bind over, as well as for the new offence committed. Again, this is another method of trying to ensure that an offender does not reoffend. The power of the magistrates' court to do so is contained within s.115 of the MCA 1980.

Summary

1. There are four broad categories of sentence that can be imposed upon a criminal conviction: custody, community sentence, financial penalty and other (including discharge). The most appropriate sentence for the offence and offender in question should be the one that is ultimately imposed.
2. The aims of sentencing can be seen to be punishment, deterrence, reparation, reform and rehabilitation, protection of the public and reduction of crime. Any sentence imposed upon an offender will have one or more of these aims.
3. The sentence that is imposed must reflect the seriousness of the offence. It must be proportionate and appropriate in the circumstances.
4. To determine the seriousness of the offence, the courts can turn to guidelines issued by the Sentencing Council, the Magistrates' Court Sentencing Guidelines and appellate court decisions. The courts will also take into consideration other factors such as pre-sentence reports and victim impact statements when assessing the seriousness of the offence.
5. Custodial sentences should only be imposed where the custody threshold has been passed. There are a number of different types of custodial sentences ranging from life imprisonment down to a suspended sentence.

6. The court can impose a community sentence when the community threshold of "serious enough" has been passed, but the offence is too serious for disposal by a lesser sentence. Community sentences have "add on" requirements, such as unpaid work or a prohibited activity order, so that the sentence can be tailored to suit the offender's circumstances.

7. Financial penalties (such as fines or compensation) and discharges (either absolute or conditional) can be imposed by the courts in situations where a custodial or a community sentence would not be not appropriate.

Key Cases

Case	Court	Salient point
R. v Millberry [2003]	**Court of Appeal**	**Sets out clear guidance on how sentencing courts should determine an appropriate sentence in rape cases.**
R. v Miles [2006]	**Court of Appeal**	**Sets out guidelines as to how sentencing courts should approach the issue of TICs and their impact upon sentence.**
R. v Secretary of State for the Home Department Ex p. Venables [1998]	**House of Lords**	**The House held that the actions of the Home Secretary in setting a minimum tariff went beyond his powers and was therefore unlawful. This decision was later confirmed by the ECtHR.**

Further Reading

J. Cooper, "The Sentencing Guidelines Council—a practical perspective" [2008] 4 Crim. L.R. 277–286.

Considers the role of the Sentencing Guidelines Council and questions whether or not it has achieved its purpose in increasing public confidence in the criminal justice system.

J.V. Roberts, "Aggravating and mitigating factors at sentencing: towards greater consistency of application" [2008] 4 Crim. L.R. 264–276.

Considers whether the Sentencing Guidelines Council's failure to provide more than minimal direction on how to approach aggravating and mitigating factors in relation to sentencing is impacting upon consistency of approach.

J. Roberts, and A. Rafferty, "Sentencing Guidelines in England and Wales: exploring the new format" [2011] 9 Crim. L.R. 681–689.

Considers the revised guidelines of the Sentencing Council using the example of the offence of assault occasioning actual bodily harm.

M. Wasik, "Going around in circles? Reflections on fifty years of change in sentencing" [2004] Crim. L.R. 253–265.

Reviews the way in which sentencing has changed over the past 50 years, with consideration of common themes that have arisen during this time and the differing approached taken to remedy them.

Self Test Questions

1. The main aim of sentencing is:
   (a) to punish
   (b) to reform
   (c) to protect the public
   (d) all of the above
2. The magistrates' court, when considering sentence, will:
   (a) always start by considering whether a custodial sentence is appropriate
   (b) always start by considering whether a community sentence is appropriate
   (c) always start by considering whether a fine or a discharge is appropriate
   (d) always start by imposing a custodial sentence
3. The Crown Court is guided in its sentencing by:
   (a) House of Lords/Supreme Court decisions
   (b) Court of Appeal decisions
   (c) Privy Council decisions
   (d) other Crown Court cases
4. Adherence to the totality principle means that a sentencer should:
   (a) impose the maximum sentence possible for the offences in question
   (b) impose the minimum sentence possible for the offences in question
   (c) take into account the overall level of seriousness of the offences and sentence proportionally to this
   (d) impose whatever level of sentence they feel like based upon their personal opinions
5. The maximum fine that can be imposed by the magistrates' court is to be:
   (a) £10,000
   (b) unlimited
   (c) £1,000
   (d) £5,000

Appeals

12

CHAPTER OVERVIEW

In this chapter we will:

- **Consider the different methods by which the prosecution can appeal a decision.**
- **Discuss the different routes to appeal open to defendants in a criminal case.**
- **Explain the function of the Criminal Cases Review Commission.**
- **Consider the different civil appeal routes and how they differ to the criminal ones.**
- **Discuss the concept of judicial review.**

Introduction

12-001 In his report *Access to Justice* (1996), Lord Woolf wrote that there are two main purposes of appeals. The first is the private one of doing justice in individual cases by correcting wrong decisions. The second is the public one of engendering public confidence in the administration of justice by making corrections, and clarifying and developing the law. Although the report was focused on the civil law jurisdiction, this comment is also applicable to the criminal forum. When Lord Justice Auld conducted his *Review of the Criminal Courts* (2001), he referred to Lord Woolf's comments and added that the main criteria of a good criminal appellate system are that:

- it should do justice to individual defendants and to the public as represented principally by the prosecution;
- it should bring finality to the criminal process, subject to the need to safeguard either side from clear and serious injustice and such as would damage the integrity of the criminal justice system;
- it should be readily accessible, consistently with a proper balance of the interest of individual defendants and that of the public;
- it should be clear and simple in its structure and procedures;
- it should be efficient and effective in its use of judges and other resources in righting injustice and in declaring and applying the law; and
- it should be speedy.

If, in a criminal case, a defendant has been convicted of an offence, or, in a civil claim a finding has been made against a defendant, then the possibility of an appeal will be of extreme importance. It is with these points in mind that this final substantive chapter will now explore the routes of appealing within the criminal and civil systems where the case originated and which court will hear the appeal, the procedures that need to be followed, as well as the issues that can be appealed upon. Whilst progressing through this chapter, bear in mind the criteria set out by Lord Justice Auld and consider whether these criteria have been successfully achieved by the present appeal system.

Criminal Appeals

12-002 Criminal appeals can be a complicated matter depending on a variety of factors such as the court the decision is being appealed from, the party bringing the appeal and the ground(s) for the appeal.

Prosecution Appeals

The issue of appeals, especially in relation to the criminal courts, has, over recent years, been the subject of much discussion and debate. This is especially true following recent changes in the law such as the fact that the prosecution is now, in certain circumstances, permitted to appeal against acquittal since the abolition of the long-standing principle of autrefois acquit, more commonly known as the rule against double jeopardy. The prosecution has the limited ability to appeal a decision by the routes set out below and can also use the process of appealing known as appeal by way of "case stated", which is also explained at **12–017**. 12–003

ATTORNEY GENERAL'S REFERENCES

Issues of precedent

An appeal by the prosecution by way of an Attorney General's reference (the Attorney General is the chief law officer of the Crown in England and Wales and in this context acts to represent the public interest) can occur in one of two ways. The first of these is when the prosecution, after the acquittal of a defendant following a trial on indictment, refers a point of law to the Court of Appeal for it to give its opinion. The power for the prosecution to appeal in this manner is governed by s.36 of the Criminal Justice Act 1972 (CJA 1972). No matter what the outcome of the appeal, even if the Court of Appeal holds that the trial court applied the law incorrectly, the defendant in the case will remain acquitted. The purpose of an Attorney General's reference is simply to clarify the law in anticipation of future cases, or, in other words, so that binding precedent can be set down. 12–004

Unduly lenient sentence

The second way in which an Attorney General's reference can be made is under ss.35 and 36 of the Criminal Justice Act 1988 (CJA 1988). Section 36 applies where the prosecution wishes to appeal against an "unduly lenient sentence" set by the Crown Court. Section 35 sets out that the provisions to appeal against an unduly lenient sentence can be activated where a sentence is passed upon a person for an offence triable only on indictment, or for an offence of a description specified in an order under that section. Upon review of the sentence, the Court of Appeal has the power to affirm the sentence imposed by the Crown Court or quash the original sentence and substitute a new one that it feels is more appropriate. If the Court of Appeal is minded to quash the original sentence in these circumstances, then it is likely that it will then impose a heavier sentence. 12–005

So what then is meant by the term "unduly lenient sentence"? Surely most victims to a case will view the sentence imposed as "unduly lenient"? The phrase "they should have locked him up and thrown away the key" is often voiced in general conversation; should the victim's or the victim's family's view be taken into account here? What about the prosecution or the police who investigated the crime? They will often be displeased with the sentence handed down. Is it their views that will be taken into account when deciding if a sentence is too lenient?

Over to you

What do you think is meant by the term "unduly lenient sentence"?

What do you think an unduly lenient sentence would be in respect of the offence of murder or of rape?

12–006 Obviously the prosecution will be disputing the length of the sentence imposed, as it has made the reference, but its views will not be the driving force behind the court's ultimate decision. The Court of Appeal in **Attorney General's Reference (No.4 of 1989)** [1990] 1 W.L.R. 41 set out what it viewed as the correct approach to take when considering whether a sentence imposed was in fact too lenient. Lord Lane CJ stated, at 46, that:

> **A sentence is unduly lenient, we would hold, where it falls outside the range of sentences which the judge, applying his mind to all the relevant factors, could reasonably consider appropriate.**

What sentence should be handed down is not a decision that should be made based on emotion or simply on the facts of the case, but rather it should be made with regard to reported cases and to the guidance given by the Court in guideline cases. What one person views as unduly lenient could well be viewed by another as unduly harsh; a rounded and objective view of all the factors should be taken into account in deciding whether a sentence is really too lenient.

Although the prosecution is afforded this method of appeal, it will not be able to revert to it in every case where it feels slightly aggrieved by the sentence. Leave to appeal (permission to appeal) must be obtained, and even where the prosecution is granted leave to appeal it does not necessarily follow that the sentence will be increased upon appeal. The Court is generally reluctant to interfere with a trial judge's decision because, if it were to constantly interfere with lower court rulings, it would be highly likely that the public would begin to lose confidence in the whole justice system. In the case of **Attorney General's Reference (Nos 3 and 5 of 1989)** (1990) 90 Cr. App. R. 358 the Court of Appeal, by way of judgment delivered by the Lord Chief Justice, stated that the Court would only interfere in a sentencing decision where there was an error of principle in the case and public confidence in the judicial system would be damaged if the original sentence were to stand.

12–007 An issue that does arise with an appeal brought this way is that it is possible for offenders to feel as though they have been sentenced twice for the same offence. Court proceedings, even after the offender has been found guilty, will still be a nerve-wracking experience, and the court is aware of the potential effects that a further review of sentence may have upon the offender, especially when there is a high chance that the sentence will be increased. In many instances the Court will mitigate the increased sentence to recognise the detrimental effect the further proceedings have had upon an offender. For example, in the case of **Attorney General's Reference (No.1 of 1991)** [1991] Crim. L.R. 725, the Court increased the sentence from five years to seven. Whilst giving judgment, the Court indicated that it felt a minimum sentence of eight years would have been appropriate on the case facts, but to allow for the offender's added anxiety caused by the appeal, it would mitigate this by reducing the sentence by a year. In murder cases, however, the court is barred from mitigating the new sentence in this way under s.272 of the CJA 2003.

Any increase in sentence can also mean that the offender is remanded into custody from an original non-custodial sentence. This is what happened in the case of **Attorney General's Reference (Nos 3 and 5 of 1989)** at **12–006**. The defendants in both these matters had caused death by reckless driving. S **(No.3)** had been originally convicted and the defendant was sentenced to 15 months imprisonment. H **(No.5)** had originally been sentenced to a fine of £2,500 and disqualified from driving for three years. The court held this was an error of principle, that public confidence in the judicial system could not properly be met with a fine. The fine was quashed and replaced with a sentence of 21 months custody in a young offender institution, the disqualification order remained.

TERMINATING RULINGS

Under s.58 of the CJA 2003 the prosecution may appeal against a judicial decision that has **12–008**
had the effect of terminating the proceedings against the defendant. The ruling that is being appealed can have occurred at any point in the trial up to the point at which the judge begins to sum up the case. Examples of rulings that may effectively terminate proceedings are a ruling that there is no case to answer, or a judge's refusal to allow the admission of crucial evidence against the defendant.

There are two possible procedures for an appeal on this point; one is the expedited route and the other is the non-expedited route. Under s.59, if a judge decides to follow the expedited route he can order an adjournment in the case whilst waiting on the outcome of the appeal, whereas under the non-expedited route the judge (again under s.59) has the option to either order an adjournment or discharge the jury whilst waiting on the outcome of the appeal. The route taken will be dependent on the action he feels to be more appropriate in the circumstances.

In respect of such an appeal, the Court of Appeal has three possible options to consider: it may confirm, reverse, or vary any ruling to which the appeal relates. If the Court decides to reverse or vary the ruling, then this must be because either the ruling was wrong in law, wrong in principle, or unreasonable. If it does decide that the decision was incorrect then there are three possible outcomes that may occur in respect of the trial. The Court may order, on a decision to reverse or vary a terminating ruling, that:

- proceedings for that offence be resumed in the Crown Court;
- a fresh trial take place in the Crown Court for that offence; or
- the defendant be acquitted of that offence.

If the Court confirms the Crown Court judge's decision in respect of the ruling, then the defendant will be acquitted of the offence in question.

ABOLITION OF THE RULE AGAINST DOUBLE JEOPARDY

12–009 The abolition of the rule against double jeopardy (more formally known as the common law doctrine of autrefois acquit) has proved controversial in recent years. The old rule of law was that if a defendant was acquitted of an offence then he could not be retried for the same offence at a later point. The reason behind this was one of due process; a defendant did not have to worry about constantly being chased by the law and there was finality to the proceedings, which reduced the potential for abuse of process and safeguarded the liberty of individuals. This meant that if a defendant was lucky enough to be tried for a crime he had committed and be acquitted, he could then boast about his exploits or even write a book about them (as some individuals have actually chosen to do), as there was no fear of further prosecution. The rule against double jeopardy was a doctrine stretching back into the roots of the common law, and was firmly entrenched in not just the UK legal system, but in many other legal systems around the world such as those of France, Germany and even Japan.

The racially motivated murder of Stephen Lawrence in April 1993 began the wheels of change to this long-standing doctrine of the common law. Stephen Lawrence was stabbed to death whilst waiting for a bus home and five suspects were arrested but no conviction ever resulted from these arrests. Stephen's family brought a private prosecution, but the case against two of the suspects was dropped before trial due to lack of evidence, and the other three men were acquitted after trial, again due to lack of sufficient evidence (the judge ruled that evidence identifying the suspects was inadmissible). The family of Stephen Lawrence then made a complaint to the Police Complaints Authority, alleging that the investigation into their son's death had been conducted incompetently due to the alleged racism of the investigating police officers. The Police Complaints Authority exonerated the officers involved but a public inquiry was ordered. The result of the public inquiry was the Macpherson Report: The Stephen Lawrence Inquiry (HMSO, 1999 Cm.4262–1), which alleged that the initial investigation into Stephen's murder had involved fundamental errors and that the police were institutionally racist. The report made a number of recommendations, one of these (recommendation no.38) being that consideration should be given to allowing the Court of Appeal to prosecute after an acquittal where fresh and viable evidence is presented.

12–010 The Law Commission, in its report *Double Jeopardy and Prosecution Appeals* (Law Com No.267, Cm.5048 (2001)), which followed on from the recommendation made in the *Macpherson Report*, put forward the proposition that the rule against double jeopardy should be abrogated in the case of acquittals in murder cases, and Lord Justice Auld in his *Review of the Criminal Courts* took this point further, stating that where:

> **a guilty man has probably been wrongly acquitted [...] that the public interest requires the matter to be re-opened.**

The Government heeded this recommendation for reform, and the introduction of the CJA 2003 dramatically changed this area of law by abolishing the rule against double jeopardy for certain crimes. If a defendant is acquitted of an offence the prosecution can now, in certain circumstances, appeal against the acquittal under ss.75 and 76 of the CJA 2003, and a retrial can be ordered. Such an appeal will be entertained if there is:

- new (not adduced in the original trial) *and* compelling evidence of the acquitted person's guilt; and
- it is in the public interest to retry the accused.

There are currently over 50 qualifying offences in which the rule against double jeopardy has been abolished—these, as listed in Sch.5, include murder, rape, manslaughter, kidnapping, certain drug and sexual offences, war crimes and terrorism offences. The former Director of Public Prosecutions, Sir Ken McDonald KC, stated (BBC News, 3 April 2005) that only a handful of cases per year are likely to be retried under the new rule, and only a few cases had been brought before the courts so far.

The first case to be brought under the new rules was the prosecution of Billy Dunlop for the murder of Julie Hogg. In November 1989 Julie was attacked in her own home, murdered, and then hidden behind the bath panel in her flat, where her mother found her body three months later. On 12 September 2006, Dunlop was rearraigned for the murder of Julie Hogg. Dunlop had already been tried twice for the offence, but each time the jury could not decide on a verdict and so he was formally acquitted. Later, he confessed the murder to a prison officer whilst he was serving a seven-year sentence for an unrelated attack. He was subsequently charged with perjury, as at the time retrying him for murder was not an option due the rules against double jeopardy. After the abolition of the rule against double jeopardy for murder cases, fresh charges were laid against Dunlop for the murder of Julie Hogg, to which he pleaded guilty (**R. v D** [2006] EWCA Crim 1354). **12–011**

The second case, and the first one to go through a new trial process under the change in the law, was the trial of Mark Weston for the murder of Vikki Thompson. Vikki Thompson, a mother of two young children, was battered to death in 1995 whilst walking her dog. Mark Weston, an odd-job man who lived in the same village as Vikki, was tried a year later for her murder but was acquitted. The jury deliberated on the case for only 50 minutes and the foreman of the jury, after the trial, wrote to Weston to wish him all the best for the future and to say that he hoped Weston would receive a large compensation payout as the police had "no evidence of any sort whatsoever" against him. The case was reopened and Weston's boots (which had been retained) were re-examined by forensic scientists who found two drops of Vikki's blood on them. Weston was retried for the murder following the 2005 change in the law, and was convicted of the murder on 13 December 2010, receiving a minimum term of 13 years (**R. v Weston (Mark)** [2010] EWCA Crim 1576).

Perhaps the most satisfying case tried under the new rules was the prosecution and conviction of Gary Dobson for the murder of Stephen Lawrence. Dobson was one of the men originally tried and acquitted of the murder in 1996. He and David Norris, who was identified as a prime suspect but was not at that time charged, were both found guilty after trial in 2011—19 years after Stephen's death (**R. v Dobson (Gary)** [2011] EWCA Crim 1255).

FIGURE 46 **Prosecution appeals**

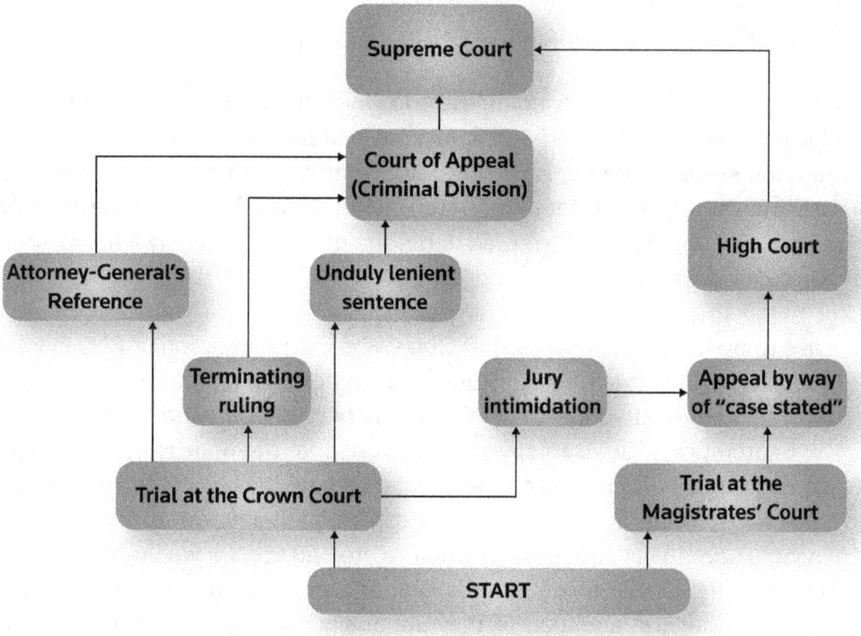

ACQUITTALS TAINTED BY INTIMIDATION

12–012 The final way in which the prosecution can appeal is under s.54 of the CPIA 1996. Here, the prosecution can appeal against an acquittal where a person has been convicted of intimidating a juror in order to effect an acquittal. The appeal is made to the High Court, which will allow such an appeal if it appears to the court that, but for the interference or intimidation, the defendant would not have been acquitted. So far this provision has not been used in practice.

Defence Appeals

There are a number of ways in which the defence can appeal, and the court from which the defendant is appealing as well as the reasoning behind the appeal will determine the most appropriate method. 12–013

APPEALS FROM THE MAGISTRATES' COURT

Reopening a case

Following a conviction in a magistrates' court by way of either a conviction after trial or a guilty plea, the defence may be presented with the ability to appeal under s.142 of the MCA 1980. Section 142 involves the defence requesting that the case be reopened in order to rectify a mistake made in the original proceedings. The case will be heard by a differently constituted Bench from that which heard the original trial; obviously, if there is an allegation of an error in the original trial, the same Bench cannot be seen as objective enough to deal with the matter. By hearing the appeal in this manner, the magistrates' court has the option of varying or rescinding the sentence imposed in the original trial. The court is permitted to allow the appeal when it appears that it would be in the interests of justice to do so. This type of appeal can often be a quicker route than appealing to the Crown Court (see **12–015**) and is mainly used where a defendant has been convicted of an offence in his absence or if the original court made an obvious error in the case. 12–014

Appeals to the Crown Court

After conviction, a defendant can also appeal to the Crown Court by way of s.108 of the MCA 1980. When using this route, the appeal must be based upon either a question of law or a question of fact. When convicted after trial, the appeal can be against conviction *or* sentence. However, where a guilty plea was entered, the appeal may only be against sentence. 12–015

A defendant does not need to obtain leave (otherwise known as permission) to appeal from magistrates' court to the Crown Court under s.108, as the right to appeal truly exists as a "right", and a defendant is afforded the benefit of an automatic appeal if he wishes to go this route. The Crown Court will rehear the case under a procedure known as a trial *de novo* (new trial). The evidence in the case will be reheard, and the witnesses who appeared at the original trial will be recalled. Even though the case is reheard in the Crown Court, there will not be a jury present to deliberate on the matter. The Bench that will hear the appeal consists of a judge, who is normally either a circuit judge or a recorder, and two magistrates, neither of whom will have sat in the original trial. The judge will direct and rule on the law, but the overall decision as to the issue on appeal will be decided by way of a majority decision.

The Crown Court will have the option of confirming, varying, or reversing the original decision (or any part of it) of the magistrates' court, or of remitting the case back to the magistrates' court with an opinion as to how the matter should be disposed of. If a defendant chooses to proceed with this form of appeal, then he needs to be warned that the Crown Court has the power to increase the original sentence given by the magistrates, though it cannot exceed the maximum sentencing powers allowed by the magistrates' court for the offence in question.

12–016 This process of allowing a defendant a complete rehearing of the case, or having a "second bite of the cherry", was criticised by Lord Justice Auld in his 2001 *Review of the Criminal Courts*. Lord Justice Auld stated that this right of appeal had its origins in the general lack of confidence in the impartiality and competence of the old "police courts", and that, due to the development in the abilities and knowledge of magistrates' courts over recent times by way of training and the provision of legal advisers in the court, etc. these courts' new standing and function bore little resemblance to the courts of old. He concluded (Ch.10, para.17):

> **it is hard to see what is left of the original justification for permitting another tribunal, even one presided over by a judge, to re-hear the case.**

It can be argued that this conclusion is erroneous as a magistrates' court, although a highly respectable and worthwhile tribunal, is still only composed of laypeople who have volunteered to help in the distribution of justice and who are only aided by a legal adviser whose advice they can decide to ignore if they wish. It would be unfair for a defendant to be denied the opportunity for his case to be reheard by a legally qualified tribunal where it is felt that the original decision was made in error. To deny this, it could be argued, would be to breach a defendant's right to a fair trial under art.6 of the ECHR. The very low number of appeals brought in this manner is also an argument for the retention and continuation of such a process. Even Lord Justice Auld acknowledged this point, commenting that less than 1 per cent of magistrates' court decisions are appealed in this way. Surely, then, this very limited use of the procedure indicates that it is a process that is only used when appropriate and therefore only when it is necessary for justice to be done.

Once a defendant's case has been reheard and decided upon by the Crown Court, no further form of appeal is afforded except by way of "case stated" under s.28 of the SCA 1981. For an appeal to be made by way of case stated from the Crown Court, the basis of the appeal must be that an error in law was made by the court. If the appeal by way of "case stated" is allowed to progress, then it will be treated as any other appeal by way of "case stated" from the magistrates' court, as described at **12–017**.

Appeal by way of case stated

12–017 An appeal by way of case stated can be made under s.111 of the MCA 1980, and it is unusual in that *both* the prosecution and the defence can appeal by way of it (s.111(1)). This means that defendants who have been acquitted may then find themselves subject to an appeal, even though they have been found innocent by a court of law. In such a situation, the purpose of the appeal by the prosecution is not to try and have the defendant convicted of the offence, but rather to try and have the law settled so that it is clear for future cases. An appeal under this process is from the magistrates' court direct to the Administrative Court of the King's Bench Division of the High Court (previously known as the Queen's Bench Divisional Court). Once an appeal is made in this manner, then all grounds for appealing to the Crown Court in the case are lost (s.111(4)); often it is better to begin by appealing to the Crown Court, and then, if that proves unsuccessful, to appeal by way of this method (as stated above).

The grounds of an appeal by way of case stated can be either that the magistrates were:

- wrong in law; or
- exceeded their jurisdiction.

The court from which the appeal originates (normally a magistrates' court but possibly the Crown Court) is then required to "state its case" to the High Court, which effectively means that it must set out to the KBD court its reasoning for the decision. The High Court will then decide whether the court did in fact exceed its jurisdiction or if the decision was made in error of the law. This method of appeal only works in relation to cases heard in the magistrates' court (or from the Crown Court after appeal from the magistrates' court), as it is the only court of first instance that is required to set out the reasoning behind its decision when it delivers its verdict. A jury in the Crown Court is not required to provide details of its deliberations, but is simply required to hand down the verdict of either guilty or not guilty. Therefore, the Crown Court would not be able to "state its case" to a High Court as neither the court nor the party appealing would have the details necessary to do so.

The appeal must be lodged within 21 days of the decision being delivered (s.111(2)). This form of appeal does not carry with it an automatic right to appeal, and therefore the party wishing to bring the appeal must request leave to do so. This leave will normally be requested from the court that made the decision and that is to be the subject of the appeal (s.111(1)).

Over to you

What, if any, potential problems can you see with leave to appeal being requested from the court that made the decision being appealed?

There is a potential difficulty with this process in that, by requesting that the court state the matter to a higher court, and then by its doing so, it may appear that the court is being asked to admit that it was (or at least might have been) wrong in its original decision. Nobody likes to be wrong, and so is there not the danger that leave to appeal in this way will always be refused? Under s.111(5) of the MCA 1980 the justices (magistrates) can refuse to state a case if they believe that the application is "frivolous". What is meant by the term "frivolous" was explored by the Court of Appeal in the case of **R. v North West Suffolk (Mildenhall) Magistrates' Court Ex p. Forest Heath DC** [1998] Env.L.R. 9, where the Court held that it meant an application 12–018 was "futile, misconceived, hopeless or academic". If the justices do refuse the application on the basis that it is frivolous, then they must give full reasoning as to why they have found in this way.

If leave to appeal is granted, then the High Court will consider a written "statement of the case". This written statement will include a number of questions upon which the party appealing wishes the court to decide; normally these questions have been agreed in advance between the appellant (the party appealing) and the respondent (the party responding to the appeal). No evidence is called, as the appeal is not a rehearing of the case but rather more a paper-based exercise in legal argument; the case will be heard by at least two High Court judges. There are a number of options open to the court in respect of the determination of such an appeal; it can affirm, reverse, or amend the magistrates' original decision, or it can remit the case back to the lower court with an opinion that the court should acquit, convict, or rehear the case against the defendant. There is a further option of appeal from the High Court directly to the Supreme Court in these matters (under s.1 of the Administration of Justice Act 1960), but only if the point of law is one of general public importance and leave to appeal is granted by the Supreme Court.

Judicial review

12–019 The issue of judicial review is governed by Pt 54 of the CPR, which is applicable even when the content of the review is criminal in nature as it is an administrative matter. Judicial review can occur when the jurisdiction of the court is called into question due to the fact that the court acted illegally in respect of its powers (ultra vires), failed to follow the correct procedure, or acted unreasonably.

A useful example is **R. v Bow Street Metropolitan Stipendiary Magistrate Ex p. Pinochet Ugarte (No.2)** [2000] 1 A.C. 119 in which the impartiality of the judiciary was challenged. Judicial review is considered in further detail later in this chapter at **12–036**.

APPEALS FROM THE CROWN COURT

12–020 Under s.1 of the Criminal Appeal Act 1968 (CAA 1968) and Pt 36 of the CrimPRs, a defendant can appeal from the Crown Court to the Court of Appeal against conviction or sentence after trial, or upon sentence only where he pleaded guilty to the offence. The first hurdle that needs to be dealt with in an appeal of this nature is the securing of leave to appeal. Either the original trial court or the Court of Appeal can grant this; although the preferred court from which to seek leave is the Court of Appeal. The application for leave to appeal is made by way of written application, and whether the leave is to be granted is then decided by way of a review by one judge. If the leave is granted and the appeal proceeds to court, the case will be heard by a panel of appeal court judges. Normally the panel will consist of three judges, but occasionally, for the more notable cases, a "full" court of five judges may sit.

Appeals against conviction

An appeal against conviction will be brought where a defendant believes that he should not have been convicted in the original trial. Many (if not most) defendants will probably say that they should not have been convicted and will still be protesting their innocence long after the end of the trial. If a defendant is convicted, then one of his first comments may well be "can we appeal?" So, for what reasons can a defendant appeal, and on what grounds can an appeal against a conviction be allowed? Why are the appellate courts not swamped with appeals from every disgruntled defendant who has been convicted? 12-021

Over to you

Can you think of what the legal ground(s) of appeal could be?

Section 2 of the CAA 1968 states that the Court of Appeal shall:

> **allow an appeal against a conviction if they think that the conviction is unsafe; and ... shall dismiss the appeal in any other case.**

The Court of Appeal is therefore only permitted to allow an appeal if it believes that the conviction is "unsafe", and in all other instances the appeal must be dismissed. Therefore, leave to appeal will only be granted where it seems there is a question as to the reliability of the conviction; the concern as to whether the conviction is safe or not will arise from the facts of the original trial. Common grounds for appeal against conviction are that the trial judge misdirected the jury, that evidence was wrongly admitted or excluded, or that there were errors in either counsel's or the judge's conduct. Whatever the reason, there must be the possibility that the ground for appeal has led to the conviction potentially being unsafe; the one thing that the appeal will not focus on is the guilt or innocence of the defendant in question. 12-022

To determine whether a conviction is unsafe or not the judges will consider the question of whether they *personally* believe that the conviction is unsafe. It is a subjective test and each individual judge in the court must consider it. To help the Court determine whether the appeal should be allowed on this ground or whether it should be dismissed, the Court will hear arguments from counsel on both sides, and, if relevant, it also has the discretion to hear new evidence under s.23 of the CAA 1968. Section 23(2) sets out that the court should decide to hear fresh evidence in an appeal by considering:

> **(a) whether the evidence appears to the Court to be capable of belief;**
> **(b) whether it appears to the Court that the evidence may afford any ground for allowing the appeal;**

> **(c) whether the evidence would have been admissible in the proceedings from which the appeal lies on an issue which is the subject of the appeal; and**
> **(d) whether there is a reasonable explanation for the failure to adduce the evidence in those proceedings.**

12–023 The provisions under s.23 have been under scrutiny in numerous appeals, raising the question in what circumstances new evidence should really be allowed to be adduced. In the case of **R. v TS** [2008] EWCA Crim 6, the Court of Appeal was faced with a request to adduce new evidence of a recently diagnosed medical condition. In TS the appellant had been charged and convicted of the rape of his estranged wife. At trial, the judge, when directing the jury, stated that in the case of a rape there might be room for misunderstanding on the defendant's part in a situation where a woman did not make clear that she was not consenting, but in the instant case there was no room for doubt or misunderstanding. The appellant was later diagnosed with Asperger's syndrome, which had the effect of him being liable to misunderstand even the straightforward indications and body language of those with whom he came into contact. At appeal, the Court viewed the doctor's evidence as being capable of belief and considered that it would have been admissible at trial and that it was covered by a reasonable explanation for the failure to adduce it at trial. On balance, it came to the conclusion that the appellant's conviction was unsafe and therefore the appeal should be allowed.

However, just because there is new evidence that was not adduced at trial does not mean that the evidence will automatically be adduced in appeal. In the case of **R. v Hill** [2008] EWCA Crim 76 the appellant had been convicted of murder. The facts of the case were that Hill had been out drinking with the victim, a known homosexual, on the day of the murder. He returned to the victim's flat, where he fell asleep in a chair. Hill awoke to find the victim undoing his trousers with the intention of sexual activity. Hill lashed out and killed the victim by way of strangulation. After the conviction, Hill appealed on the basis that he had been sexually abused as a child and that it was a flashback to this that caused him to kill the victim. No evidence of the sexual abuse had been raised during the original trial. The evidence *may* have been capable of belief, and therefore it *may* have afforded a ground for allowing the appeal as it would have been relevant to the defence of provocation and the evidence would have been admissible at the original trial. However, the evidence was held not to be admissible by the appeal court.

Over to you

Re-read s.23 of the CAA 1968. Why do you think the evidence was not held to be admissible in Hill's case?

12–024 The evidence was not held to be admissible as there was no reasonable explanation for Hill having failed to advance evidence of this abuse at the original trial. Lord Justice Hughes stated that:

It is of central importance to the law that a person charged should advance whatever material is available to him at trial. This court will not ordinarily so exercise its powers to admit fresh evidence as to permit a defendant to change his account after trial in order to run a different defence on appeal, in the absence of the witnesses and of the jury.

The Court therefore took the view that fresh evidence should only be adduced in an appeal where it is relevant and pertinent to the issues under review and where it really could not have been adduced at the earlier hearing. The principle to be taken away is that an appeal should not be used by the appellant as a method to try and raise another defence in an effort to be afforded a second chance of acquittal.

One problem that arises out of the use of the word "unsafe" in s.2 of the CAA 1968 is that of what should be done where there is a procedural irregularity in the case but the defendant *is* guilty of the offence in question. The appellate courts have had to consider this issue on more than one occasion, and their approach to this dilemma can be seen in the case of **R. v Mullen (No.2)** [1999] 2 Cr. App. R. 143. In **Mullen**, the Court held that the meaning of "unsafe" in s.2 of the CAA 1968 was broad enough to permit the quashing of a conviction on the sole ground that it was unsafe because of an abuse of process prior to the trial. In this case, British authorities, by unlawful means, had obtained the appellant's deportation from Zimbabwe for the purposes of putting him on trial. In so doing they had encouraged unlawful conduct in Zimbabwe and had acted in breach of public international law. The certainty of guilt could not displace the essential feature of this type of abuse of process, namely the degradation of the lawful administration of justice. The Court, in making this decision, had to take into account the gravity of the offence and balance it against the failure to adhere to the rule of law. It stated that for a conviction to be safe it must be lawful, and where it resulted from a trial which should never have taken place it could not be regarded as safe. It allowed the appeal against conviction despite the fact that the defendant was guilty of the offence. The conclusion that can be drawn from this decision is that the Court was of the opinion that it is more satisfactory for a guilty person to be released due to a procedural irregularity than for the conviction to be upheld regardless of the person's guilt.

The Court's own opinion of how the case should have been decided at trial should also not be **12–025** a considered factor in the deliberations of whether a conviction is unsafe or not. In the case of **R. v Pendleton** [2001] UKHL 66 the appellant had been convicted of a murder committed 14 years previously. The appellant had made admissions to the police during interview but had not given evidence in the original trial due to his counsel's view concerning the strength of these admissions in the jury's eyes. On referral by the Criminal Cases Review Commission (explained below), the Court of Appeal dismissed the appellant's appeal against conviction, even though it heard fresh evidence from a psychologist that raised serious doubts about the reliability of the statements the appellant had made to the police. The Court was of the opinion that the new evidence did not put a "flavour of falsity" on the admissions made and it found it inconceivable that the accounts given by the appellant were imagined or invented. The House of Lords then granted leave to appeal and it considered the actions of the Court of Appeal in the case, holding that the conviction was unsafe and that:

> **In holding otherwise the Court of Appeal strayed beyond its true function of review and made findings which were not open to it in all the circumstances. Indeed, it came perilously close to considering whether the appellant, in its judgment, was guilty.**

The Court of Appeal had acted outside of its remit by considering the facts of the case and the defendant's guilt as opposed to considering the safeness of the conviction by undertaking a review of the case. What it should have considered was whether the psychological evidence, if presented at trial, would have affected the decision of the jury to convict, and if it was of the opinion that it would have then it should have allowed the appeal. This principle has been confirmed in later cases such as **R. v Newcombe** [2007] EWCA Crim 2554.

12–026 An issue that has arisen a number of times within the courts is the relationship between the words "unsafe" in s.2 and "unfair" in art.6(1) of the ECHR. On first sight it would be logical to assume that if a case breaches the right to a fair trial under art.6 then it must also be "unsafe" under the test employed by s.2. Unfortunately, case law would seem to indicate otherwise. In **R. v Togher (Appeal against Conviction)** [2001] 3 All E.R. 463 the Court of Appeal followed the logical thought process that if there was a breach of art.6 then the result would be that the conviction was also unsafe. The ECtHR confirmed this approach in the case of **Condron v UK** (35718/97) (2001) 31 E.H.R.R. 1, where it implied that where there was an unfair trial the conviction should always be quashed. However, the domestic courts in **R. v Davis, Rowe and Johnson** [2001] 1 Cr. App. R. 8 and **R. v Williams** [2001] EWCA Crim. 932 came to the conclusion that a breach of art.6 would not automatically lead to a finding that the conviction was unsafe, but rather would require the court to consider the fairness of the trial as a whole. The approach taken in **Togher** would seem to be the most sensible decision, because if the defendant has been denied the right to a fair trial, how can the resulting conviction be safe? However, the issue will need to arise before the courts again before it can be said with complete certainty which is the correct approach to adopt.

If the Court of Appeal finds that the defendant's conviction is unsafe, then it has a number of options open to it. It may quash the conviction and acquit the defendant, quash the conviction and order a retrial, find the defendant guilty of an alternative offence (e.g. allow the appeal against conviction for murder but then find the defendant guilty of the offence of manslaughter instead), allow part of the appeal, or dismiss the appeal completely. One thing that it cannot do, however, is increase the original sentence imposed by the court of first instance.

The Court of Appeal's powers to order a retrial in a case have been expanded over recent years. Prior to 1989, the Court only had the statutory power to order a retrial in one specific instance, this being that the appeal had been allowed due to fresh evidence being received by the Court. In all other cases, the appellant who successfully managed to demonstrate the unsafeness of his conviction was acquitted completely, irrespective of whether there was overwhelming evidence as to guilt. In 1989, the CJA 1988 amended the law under the CAA 1968. Section 7(1) of the CAA 1968 now provides that the Court of Appeal has a general discretion to order a retrial whenever it allows an appeal against conviction under s.2(1) of the CAA 1968 and the interests of justice require the appellant to be retried. The new trial must not be for a completely different offence but only for (a) the offence of which the defendant was convicted in the original trial and in respect of which the appeal is allowed, (b) an offence for which the defendant could have been convicted in the original trial on an indictment for the first mentioned offence, or (c) an offence charged in an alternative count of the indictment in respect of which the jury was discharged from giving a verdict in consequence of the defendant being convicted of the first mentioned offence.

A well-reported retrial that gained considerable media attention was that of Sion Jenkins (**R. v Jenkins** [2004] EWCA Crim. 2047), where the Court of Appeal allowed Jenkins' second appeal in respect of his conviction for the murder of his 13-year-old foster daughter, Billie-Jo Jenkins. The Court ordered that Jenkins stand trial for her murder again after new evidence came to light that cast doubt on the safety of his first conviction. Jenkins then underwent two more trials for the alleged murder. In both trials the jury could not agree on a majority verdict, and eventually, in February 2006, Jenkins was formally acquitted of the murder. 12-027

The point to remember in respect of the Court of Appeal's power to order a retrial is that it is not under a *duty* to order a retrial, this is a discretionary power and it may choose simply to quash the conviction instead. The decision not to retry an appellant may be taken for a number of different reasons, and these could include factors such as that the alleged crime took place many years ago and the recalling of witnesses and evidence would be difficult or even impossible, or that the case was heavily covered in the press and consequently there would be a real risk that the appellant would not receive a fair trial (imagine if Ian Huntley were to be retried for the Soham murders—there would be little chance that any jury convened would not be prejudiced in one way or another).

Appeal against sentence

A defendant can appeal against the sentence imposed by a court on the grounds that the sentence is either: 12-028

- wrong in law;
- wrong in principle; or
- manifestly excessive.

The Court of Appeal has the option of dismissing the appeal, quashing the sentence, or imposing a new sentence in substitution of the one in question. If the Court is minded to impose a new sentence, then it is permitted to impose any sentence that could be imposed by the Crown Court in the matter.

APPEAL TO THE SUPREME COURT

12-029 Appeals can be made directly to the Supreme Court from both the Divisional Court (under s.1 of the Administration of Justice Act 1960) and the Court of Appeal (under s.33 of the CAA 1968). Leave to appeal is required in both circumstances and the appeal will only be heard if a point of law of general public importance is certified.

CRIMINAL CASES REVIEW COMMISSION

12-030 There are strict time limits in which an appeal can be brought (generally 21 days after the decision that the appeal relates to has been handed down). Once these time limits have expired, then the case is out of the court system (unless leave out of time is granted) and this then leaves the possibility of defendants remaining in custody despite the fact that their convictions may be unsafe and that miscarriages of justice may have occurred. The Criminal Cases Review Commission (CCRC) was created by Pt.2 of the Criminal Appeal Act 1995 (CAA 1995) as an independent body with the primary purpose of reviewing such cases. The CCRC does not decide the appeal but simply refers the case to the appropriate court for review. The CCRC can review and investigate any case where there is a suspected wrongful conviction and/or sentence, whether the case was tried summarily or on indictment, or where there has been a finding of not guilty by reason of insanity. Most of the cases that the CCRC deals with are the more serious cases that have been tried on indictment as due to the low sentencing powers of the magistrates' court it is very rare for a person who has been convicted of a summary offence to be detained long enough for the CCRC to become involved.

The CCRC will refer a case to the Court of Appeal where, in the case of a conviction, it considers that there is a real possibility that the conviction would not be upheld because of an argument or evidence not raised at the trial or on appeal; or, in the case of a sentence, it considers that there is a real possibility that the sentence would not be upheld because of an argument on a point of law, or information not raised at the trial or on appeal (s.7(2) of the CAA 1968).

Over to you

Why do you think miscarriages of justice occur? Give some examples of how they might arise during (or even prior to) the trial process.

12-031 The Commission is really there as a safeguard against miscarriages of justice since no matter how many provisions and procedures are put in place miscarriages of justice will occur. These miscarriages of justice can arise due to reasons such as unfairly obtained confessions and abuse of police powers, the wrongful identification of the defendant, witnesses perjuring themselves in court and bad trial tactics. The decision to review a case can be made on the Commission's own initiative, or the case could be referred to it by an application from the convicted person. The Commission has a large caseload of referred cases to work through. To date, there have been 33,020 applications made to the Commission; there are currently 207 cases waiting for review, and 953 cases under review. The Court of Appeal has heard 841 cases referred by the CCRC, out of which 592 appeals were allowed. In total so far, the CCRC has completed 31,860 cases since its inception in 1997 (figures correct as of February 2025; Criminal Cases Review Commission, *https://ccrc*.gov.uk/*facts-figures/* [accessed 1 May 2025]).

FIGURE 47 **Defence appeals**

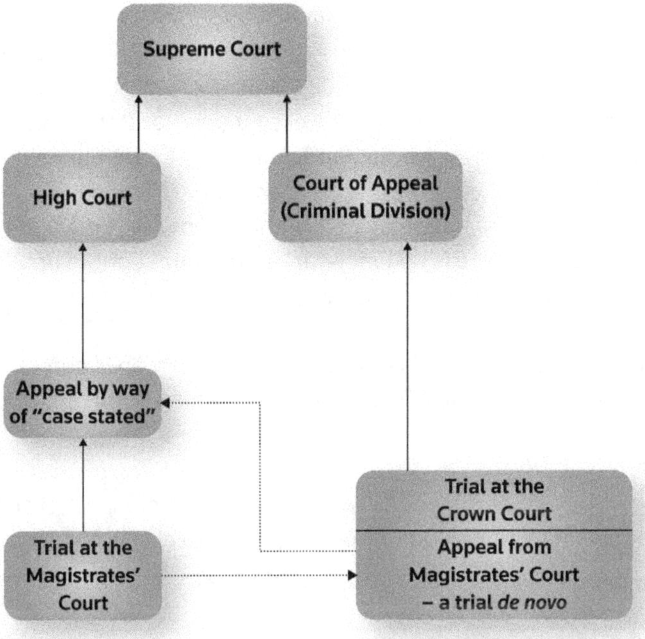

Civil Appeals

The appeals system within the civil jurisdiction of the courts is a far simpler affair than that found within the criminal court system. Prior to the introduction of the AJA 1999 and the CPR, there were two common forms of appeal; the first was a complete rehearing of the case, where the parties would again present their full cases to the court, with evidence and witnesses, etc. and where new evidence and issues could also be presented; the second was a review of the previous case decision, where the appeal court would examine the decision and 12–032 decision-making process of the lower court. Under the old system the "right to appeal" was mainly an automatic right, which meant that parties could lodge an appeal to a decision without having to prove the merits of the proposed appeal.

The right to an automatic appeal, although generally viewed as a positive for those using the appeal system (especially those who lost a case), certainly led to a large number of unmeritorious appeals. The effect of such a right was that cases were not dealt with effectively or expeditiously; a claimant who was successful in a claim would have the threat of the decision being appealed by the disgruntled defendant. Alternatively, a defendant who was vindicated at first instance would often have to face the possibility of being chased through the courts once more as the claimant appealed the decision, hoping to be more successful the second time around. Parties to a claim would face further months of uncertainty, and the courts became overrun with numerous appeal cases, which created delays and unnecessary costs for all involved.

One of the main aims of the introduction of the CPR was to ensure that justice was done and that cases were dealt with fairly, effectively and expeditiously. Civil appeals are now governed mainly by Pt 52 of the CPR (although the AJA 1999 contains statutory provisions on the matter as well), which provides comprehensive guidance on what can be appealed, under what circumstances an appeal will be allowed to progress, and how an appeal will go forward. Two of the main differences between civil appeals before the inception of the CPR and civil appeals governed by the CPR are that there is no longer an "automatic" right to appeal, and that there is no longer the option for the rehearing of a case, except in very limited circumstances.

12-033 Permission to appeal in a civil matter will only be granted in certain circumstances (as provided for under r.52.6 of the CPR). Rule 52.6(1) sets out that permission to appeal will only be given where:

> (a) the court considers that the appeal would have a real prospect of success; or
> (b) there is some other compelling reason why the appeal should be heard.

The introduction of such a limitation on the possibility of appealing was an effort to stop vexatious litigants continuing with a claim or appealing a decision where the case itself did not merit such actions. The main focus of the courts when deciding whether or not to grant permission to appeal is generally subs.(a), and the court has to be convinced that there is a good reason for allowing a person to continue on to an appeal (such as that the judge erred in law, etc.) and that the case really does have the merit to continue. The courts can grant permission for a general appeal against the overall decision in a case, or they could also decide, when granting the permission to appeal, that the appeal should be limited to certain issues in the case as opposed to the overall decision.

As permission is now required in all but the most unusual cases, the normal procedure is for the party seeking permission to appeal to apply to the court whose decision is being appealed (known as the lower court) for permission. This may seem a rather strange concept, as it could be thought unlikely for a judge to grant a party permission to appeal against his own decision, but this does seem to be the most sensible approach for the courts and the system overall to take. The majority of judges do not take an application to appeal as a personal slight and will grant permission if the benchmark found in r.52.6(1) is, in their opinion, satisfied. It is logical for the court that has heard the case to consider whether an appeal is appropriate, since it will be in full possession of the facts of the case and will have the adequate in-depth knowledge required to make such a decision quickly and appropriately, without the need for further recourse to precious court resources. However, if permission to appeal is refused by the lower court and the party making the application is of the opinion that the court was wrong in its refusal, then a further application to the court to which the appeal would be made (known as the appeal court) can be made. This application must, however, be made within 21 days of the initial refusal (again so that the case is dealt with both expeditiously and fairly, as required by the Overriding Objective).

As stated above, if permission to appeal is granted, then the appeal will normally take the form of a review of the lower court's decision. This review will generally be a legally based exercise, where submissions are made to the court on the relative merits or flaws of the appeal, and it will not involve the hearing of any oral or new evidence. **12–034**

An appeal in a civil case will only be allowed in two situations, these being where the earlier decision was either:

- wrong; or
- unjust.

A decision will be seen to be wrong where the appeal court, after having reviewed the previous hearing, reaches the conclusion that it would have decided the appeal differently. A decision will be viewed as being unjust when the appeal court considers that there was a serious procedural or other irregularity in the previous proceedings. If this is its conclusion, then the court is not criticising the overall decision of the deciding court, it is simply saying that, due to the irregularity, etc. the decision cannot stand in the interests of justice.

When considering a case on appeal, the appeal court is afforded a variety of powers. These powers are provided so that the court can deal with the case at hand in the most appropriate and effective way, dependent on the individual case facts and requirements. The court can:

(a) affirm, set aside or vary any order or judgment made or given by the lower court;
(b) refer any claim or issue for determination by the lower court;
(c) order a new trial or hearing;
(d) make orders for the payment of interest;
(e) make a costs order.

Civil appeals are generally straightforward affairs, but there is one interesting distinction that really separates the workings of a civil appeal from that of a criminal appeal; this is that civil appeals do not go to the next *court* in the hierarchy but to the next *judge* in the hierarchy. This is an individual foible of the civil appeal system and it can be quite confusing to work out where an appeal will actually lie, so below is a brief chart to aid understanding of the civil appeal routes.

FIGURE 48 **Routes of appeal (civil)**

Appeal from	Appeal to
District judge in the county court	Circuit judge
District judge in the High Court	High Court judge
District judge on the small claims/fast track	Circuit judge
Circuit judge on the fast track	High Court judge
High Court judge	Court of Appeal
Multi-track cases (when a final decision)	Court of Appeal

12–035 Occasionally, an appeal from a High Court judge will not be heard by the Court of Appeal but will "leap frog" up to the Supreme Court by virtue of the provisions set out in s.12 of the Administration of Justice Act 1969 (AJA 1969). The provisions under this Act allow the Court of Appeal to be bypassed in situations where there is a point of law of general public importance that relates to the construction of an Act or statutory instrument, or the judge in the case is bound by a previous court decision and all the parties to the case agree to the appeal proceeding to the Supreme Court. This is a rarely-used statutory provision but a useful and recent example is **R. (on the application of Miller) v Secretary of State for Exiting the European Union** [2017] UKSC 5.

There is one more point to note about civil appeals that sets them apart from the criminal system, this being that there is generally only one appeal per case. The idea is that once an appeal has been determined, that is the end of the matter, unless one of the criteria under r.52.30) is satisfied. Rule 52.30 sets out that a further appeal will only be allowed if the court considers that reopening a final determination would be necessary to do so in order to avoid real injustice; the circumstances are exceptional and make it appropriate to reopen the appeal; and, there is no alternative effective remedy.

Again, the introduction of this restriction on the ability to appeal was focused on stemming the number of unmeritorious appeals that were present in the civil courts before the introduction of the new rules under the CPR and the AJA 1999. The introduction of such restrictions does not mean that a further appeal is impossible, but rather that such a further appeal will only be allowed where it is truly required.

Judicial Review

As briefly mentioned above, there is another form of "appeal" open to the parties of a case, which is known as judicial review. The term "appeal" is set in quotes as judicial review is not so much a traditional form of appeal but rather a supervisory function, as it allows the decisions and actions of a court to be reviewed. The process of judicial review will only be given a brief mention here, as it can be found detailed in great depth in other law texts that focus more on the administrative aspects of the legal system. **12-036**

Part 54 of the CPR governs the process of judicial review and r.54.1(2) sets out that a claim for judicial review is

> . . . a claim to review the lawfulness of
>
> **(i)** an enactment; or
> **(ii)** a decision, action or failure to act in relation to the exercise of a public function.

An application for judicial review is made to the Administrative Court situated within the King's Bench Division of the High Court, and the application is for the court to determine whether the public body in question has acted ultra vires, or beyond its powers. Section 6 of the HRA 1998 sets out what is classed as a public body and includes any court or tribunal and any persons whose functions are of a public nature. This may then include bodies such as the police, the prison service, healthcare trusts, and even universities.

Who Can Make an Application for Judicial Review?

For a person to be eligible to bring a claim for judicial review, they must have what is known as locus standi in that they have a "sufficient interest in the matter to which the application relates" (s.31(3) of the SCA 1981). What, then, is a sufficient interest in a claim? **12-037**

Over to you

Do you think you have to be a party to the case to bring a claim for judicial review?

In the case of **R. v Secretary of State for the Environment Ex p. Rose Theatre Trust Co (No.2)** [1990] 2 W.L.R. 186 during the development of a building site in London there was discovered what was believed to be the remains of the Rose Theatre, which had seen the first performances of works by William Shakespeare and Christopher Marlowe. A group of archaeologists and actors joined together to form the Rose Theatre Trust Company, which had the main aim of preserving the remains and making them accessible to the public. The Trust applied to the Secretary of State for the Environment for the theatre to be listed in the Schedule of Monuments but the Secretary of State, whilst acknowledging the remains were of national importance, declined to list them and in his decision letter gave his reasons for doing so, one being that, in his view, the site was not under threat. The Trust applied to the High Court for judicial review of the decision but the High Court dismissed the application, as it was believed that the Trust did not have a sufficient interest in the claim. Schiemann J, whilst addressing the issue of locus standi, stated that, for an applicant to be successful in an application for judicial review:

> **The challenger must show that he "has a sufficient interest in the matter to which the application relates." The court will look at the matter to which the application relates—in this case the non-scheduling of a monument of national importance—and the statute under which the decision was taken (in this case the Act of 1979) and decide whether that statute gives that individual expressly or impliedly a greater right or expectation than any other citizen of this country to have that decision taken lawfully. We all expect our decision makers to act lawfully. We are not all given by Parliament the right to apply for judicial review.**

The Trust, although interested in the case, simply could not show a sufficient enough interest in the matter to be granted leave (as judicial review is a form of appeal, leave has to be granted in the normal way) to proceed with a judicial review of the Secretary of State's decision.

Grounds for Judicial Review

12–038 There are three possible grounds for bringing an appeal for judicial review, as set out by Lord Diplock in the case of **Council of Civil Service Unions v Minister for the Civil Service** [1985] A.C. 374 at 410. Lord Diplock stated that:

> **Judicial review has I think developed to a stage today when without reiterating any analysis of the steps by which the development has come about, one can conveniently classify under three heads the grounds upon which administrative action is subject to control by judicial review. The first ground I would call "illegality", the second "irrationality" and the third "procedural impropriety".**

By illegality it is meant that the body in question has no right or power to make the decision; it has effectively acted ultra vires. An example of this would be a local council deciding that everyone who lived in the locality must dress in black at all times or face a £70 penalty—it would have no power to make such a decision and would be acting unlawfully if it started fining people.

The second ground of irrationality is commonly referred to as "**Wednesbury** unreasonableness" following the case of **Associated Provincial Picture Houses Ltd v Wednesbury Corp** [1948] 1 K.B. 223. **Wednesbury** unreasonableness is said to occur where the decision made is:

> **so outrageous in its defiance of logic or of accepted moral standards that no sensible person [...] could have arrived at it.**
>
> **(per Lord Diplock in Council of Civil Service Unions v Minister for the Civil Service).**

The standard of the test employed under **Wednesbury** reasonableness has been criticised for being too strict, in that if the decision is not *completely* outrageous, but just a little outrageous, then the decision will be deemed legal. In the case of **Smith v UK** (33985/96) (2000) 29 E.H.R.R. 493, the ECtHR criticised the use of **Wednesbury** unreasonableness by the UK court. The case involved four applicants who had all been discharged from the armed forces for being homosexual. They had applied for judicial review of the Ministry of Defence's decision, and their appeals were dismissed. They appealed to the House of Lords and then to the ECtHR on the basis that their discharge constituted an infringement of their right to respect for their private lives and discrimination under art.8 and art.14 of the ECHR. They also contended that an application for judicial review in the UK did not afford them an effective domestic remedy as required under art.13. The ECtHR held that their art.8 rights had been infringed and that the applicants did not have access to an effective domestic remedy as required by art.13. It further commented that the test of irrationality (or **Wednesbury** unreasonableness) formulated by the domestic courts had been set at such a level that the UK courts were precluded from even considering whether the alleged interference with private lives could be justified on the basis of social need, national security or public order. These were matters that constituted the very essence of the Court's considerations under art.8, and the test under English law had been set at such a high level, the Court was precluded from considering such issues. It may be that the best route for the courts to take would be to move away from the strict irrationality test and look towards consideration of proportionality, which is now commonly referred to by the courts in areas outside judicial review when they were considering the balancing of domestic law with European law. **12–039**

Remedies

Under an application for judicial review, the courts have available to them three prerogative orders: **12–040**

- quashing order—this order annuls the original order and returns events to the situation prior to the making of the decision that has been annulled;
- mandatory order—this order sets out what the public body *must* do to rectify matters; and

- prohibiting order—this order prevents the public body from taking a certain course of action.

The Court also has available to it the full range of other remedies, such as injunctions (although the same effect can be achieved by way of a prohibiting or mandatory order) and, in extremely rare cases, the award of damages. The final point to note in relation to judicial review is that the prerogative remedies are discretional and the Court need only impose them where it feels they are appropriate in the circumstances.

Summary

1. Both the prosecution and the defence may have the opportunity to appeal a decision in a case. The prosecution has the power to appeal against acquittals, by way of an Attorney General's reference, in cases of a terminating ruling or an acquittal due to juror intimidation, and, since the abolition of the rule against double jeopardy in 2003, the prosecution can now retry an acquitted defendant for certain specified offences.

2. The defence has a number of routes to appeal open to it depending on the court of first instance. If appealing from the magistrates' court the defence may request that the case be reopened, it may appeal to the Crown Court, or, by way of "case stated", to the Divisional Court, and it can bring a judicial review if challenging the jurisdiction of the magistrates' court.

3. From the Crown Court the defence can appeal against conviction and/or sentence after trial or just against sentence after a guilty plea. An appeal against conviction will be allowed where the original conviction is felt by the court to be unsafe. If the route to appeal is barred due to time limitations, then the Criminal Cases Review Commission may investigate the case and refer it back to the courts.

4. There is limited scope to appeal in a civil case. The right to appeal is no longer automatic, and there is only to be one appeal per case. Permission to appeal must be granted, and the next judge in the hierarchy, as opposed to the next court, normally hears a civil appeal.

5. Judicial review is more a supervisory function than an appellate function of the High Court. An interested party can make an application for judicial review of a public body where the party believes that the body has acted ultra vires. The Court may then use its prerogative powers to remedy the situation.

Key Cases

Case	Court	Salient point
Attorney General's Reference (Nos 3 and 5 of 1989) (1990)	Court of Appeal	An appeal court will only interfere with the trial judge's sentencing decision where there had been an error of principle and public confidence would be damaged if the original sentence were to stand.
R. v Mullen (No. 2) [1999]	Court of Appeal	The meaning of "unsafe" in s.2 CAA 1968 is broad enough to permit the quashing of a conviction on the sole ground that it was unsafe because of an abuse of process prior to the trial.
R. v Togher [2001]	Court of Appeal	If there is a breach of art.6 ECHR then any resulting conviction must be unsafe.
R. v Davis, Rowe and Johnson [2001]	Court of Appeal	A breach of art.6 ECHR does not lead to an automatic finding that a conviction is unsafe, but rather the court must consider the fairness of the trial as a whole.
Smith v UK (2000)	European Court of Human Rights	The ECtHR criticised the use of Wednesbury reasonableness by the domestic courts

Further Reading

K. Kerrigan, "Miscarriage of justice in the Magistrates' court: the forgotten power of the Criminal Cases Review Commission" [2006] Crim. L.R. 124–139.

Reflects on the power of the Criminal Cases Review Commission (CCRC) to refer convictions in magistrates' courts to the Crown Court.

L.H. Leigh, "Lurking doubt and the safety of convictions" [2006] Crim. L.R. 809–816.

Considers the significance of the phrase "lurking doubt" in appeals against conviction.

D. Ormerod, A. Waterman and R. Forston, "Prosecution appeals — too much of a good thing?" [2010] Crim. L.R. 169–194.

Considers the ability of the prosecution to appeal under the Criminal Justice Act 2003 provisions.

J.R. Spencer, "Does our present criminal appeal system make sense?" [2006] Crim. L.R. 677–694.

Considers the historical development of the appeal system with particular focus on the different systems found within the magistrates' court and the Crown Court.

Self Test Questions

1. A prosecution appeal against an unduly lenient sentence goes to the:
   (a) Supreme Court
   (b) Court of Appeal
   (c) High Court
   (d) Privy Council
2. A prosecution appeal against an acquittal tainted by intimidation goes to the:
   (a) Supreme Court
   (b) Court of Appeal
   (c) High Court
   (d) Privy Council
3. If, after an appeal from the magistrates' court to the Crown Court for a trial *de novo*, the defendant still wishes to appeal, he can do so by:
   (a) appealing to the Court of Appeal
   (b) appealing to the Court of Appeal by way of case stated
   (c) appealing to the High Court
   (d) appealing to the High Court by way of case stated
4. In a civil claim, an appeal from the decision of a district judge in the High Court would go to:
   (a) a circuit judge
   (b) a High Court judge
   (c) the Court of Appeal
   (d) the Supreme Court
5. The term "Wednesbury unreasonableness" means that:
   (a) the judge was unreasonable on a Wednesday
   (b) the judge who was unreasonable was called Wednesbury
   (c) the judge made a decision with which the appealing party disagreed
   (d) the judge made a decision that was completely outrageous

Appendix
Answers to Self Test Questions

Chapter 1: Introduction to the English Legal System

1. The "English legal system" encompasses:
   (a) England
   (b) England and Scotland
   (c) England and Wales
   (d) England, Scotland and Wales

The correct answer is (c)

2. Parliamentary sovereignty means that Parliament is:
   (a) supreme to any other law-making body in the UK
   (b) supreme to any other law-making body in Europe
   (c) supreme to any other law-making body in the world
   (d) supreme to any other law-making body in the universe

The correct answer is (a)

3. Equity developed due to failings in:
   (a) the civil law system
   (b) legislation
   (c) the European Union
   (d) the common law

The correct answer is (d)

4. If the House of Lords rejects a Bill on two successive occasions, then:
   (a) the Bill is dropped
   (b) the Bill returns for a third passing through the House of Commons
   (c) the Bill bypasses the need for House of Lords' approval and receives Royal Assent
   (d) the Bill has to be redrafted entirely

The correct answer is (c)

5. Delegated legislation is:
   (a) superior to primary legislation
   (b) inferior to primary legislation
   (c) equal to primary legislation
   (d) subordinate to primary legislation

The correct answer is (c)

Chapter 2: Judicial Reasoning

1. Persuasive precedent can come from:
   (a) the Privy Council
   (b) academic commentary
   (c) lower courts
   (d) all of the above

The correct answer is (d)

2. The Court of Appeal can depart from one of its own previous decisions when:
   (a) it does not agree with the decision
   (b) the decision is made per incuriam
   (c) the decision is res judicata
   (d) it wants to develop the law

The correct answer is (b)

3. The term "reversing" means:
   (a) the facts of the case are different
   (b) the court declares a previous case as bad law
   (c) the court changes the outcome of the instant case
   (d) the court changes its own mind

The correct answer is (c)

4. To avoid an absurd result a judge will employ which technique of statutory interpretation:
   (a) the literal rule
   (b) the golden rule
   (c) the mischief rule
   (d) the purposive approach

The correct answer is (b)

5. Which source below is not an extrinsic aid to interpretation:
   - **(a)** case law
   - **(b)** *Hansard*
   - **(c)** another Act of Parliament
   - **(d)** the *Noscitur a Sociis* rule

The correct answer is (d)

Chapter 3: How to Find the Law and Use It

1. Authoritative case law can be found:
   - **(a)** online
   - **(b)** in the library
   - **(c)** in a journal
   - **(d)** all of the above

The correct answer is (d)

2. The case name *Charleston v DPP* means that:
   - **(a)** Charleston is appealing and the DPP is the defendant
   - **(b)** the DPP is appealing and Charleston is the defendant
   - **(c)** Charleston is being prosecuted by the DPP
   - **(d)** the Attorney General is clarifying a point of law upon Charleston's conviction

The correct answer is (a)

3. The citation [2000] 5 Q.B. 202 means:
   - **(a)** the case was the fifth case reported for the Queen's Bench Division for 2000
   - **(b)** the case was the 202nd case reported for the Queen's Bench Division for 2000
   - **(c)** the case was reported in the fifth volume of the Queen's Bench Reports for 2000 at page 202
   - **(d)** the case was the 202nd case reported in the fifth volume of the Queen's Bench Reports for 2000

The correct answer is (c)

4. The All E.R. reports are:
   - **(a)** the most authoritative law reporting series
   - **(b)** the least authoritative law reporting series
   - **(c)** published by the ICLR
   - **(d)** commercially published

The correct answer is (d)

5. The most commonly used title for legislation is the:
   (a) chapter number
   (b) short title
   (c) long title
   (d) preamble

The correct answer is (b)

Chapter 4: The Legal Profession

1. The body that represents solicitors in England and Wales is the:
   (a) Legal Services Commission
   (b) Law Society
   (c) Solicitors Regulation Authority
   (d) Legal Complaints Service

The correct answer is (b)

2. Barristers are called to the:
   (a) Bar
   (b) Bench
   (c) Cloth
   (d) Inn

The correct answer is (a)

3. King's Counsel are otherwise known as:
   (a) satins
   (b) velvets
   (c) silks
   (d) God

The correct answer is (c)

4. Barristers can refuse to take a case because:
   (a) they do not like the client
   (b) they are disgusted by the nature of the case
   (c) they suspect the defendant to be guilty
   (d) they are inexperienced in the area of law involved

The correct answer is (d)

5. The higher rights of audience for solicitors were introduced by the:
   (a) Administration of Justice Act 1985
   (b) Courts and Legal Services Act 1990
   (c) Access to Justice Act 1999
   (d) Legal Services Act 2007

The correct answer is (b)

Chapter 5: Magistrates

1. The maximum length of time that a magistrates' court can impose a custodial sentence for a single offence is:
   (a) 6 months
   (b) 12 months
   (c) 24 months
   (d) a magistrates' court cannot impose custodial sentences

The correct answer is (a)

2. Magistrates can sit in the:
   (a) youth court
   (b) family court
   (c) Crown Court
   (d) all of the above

The correct answer is (d)

3. Magistrates are appointed on their:
   (a) political views
   (b) sentencing policies
   (c) personal qualities
   (d) physical appearance

The correct answer is (c)

4. Once trained, magistrates are appraised:
   (a) annually
   (b) every three years
   (c) every five years
   (d) never

The correct answer is (b)

5. Magistrates are expected to sit in court for a minimum of:
   (a) 10 days per year
   (b) 26 half-days per year
   (c) 52 half-days per year
   (d) 100 days per year

The correct answer is (b)

Chapter 6: The Judiciary

1. The most superior type of judge in England and Wales is:
   (a) the Lord Chancellor
   (b) a circuit judge
   (c) a Lord Justice of Appeal
   (d) a Justice of the Supreme Court

The correct answer is (d)

2. The Lord Chancellor is now:
   (a) the head of the judiciary
   (b) the head of the Ministry for Justice
   (c) Speaker in the House of Lords
   (d) a member of the judiciary

The correct answer is (b)

3. Judges used to be appointed by way of:
   (a) secret soundings
   (b) secret ballots
   (c) open competition
   (d) automatic promotion

The correct answer is (a)

4. Judges are now appointed by:
   (a) the Commissioner for Judicial Appointments
   (b) the Judicial Appointments Commission
   (c) an election process
   (d) the Judicial Appointments Committee

The correct answer is (b)

5. The Supreme Court incorporates the:
   (a) Court of Appeal and House of Lords
   (b) Court of Appeal and Privy Council
   (c) House of Lords and Privy Council
   (d) House of Lords

The correct answer is (c)

Chapter 7: Juries

1. To be eligible to sit as a juror a person must be:
   (a) registered on the electoral roll
   (b) between the ages of 18 and 65
   (c) have lived in the UK for at least three years
   (d) own their own property

The correct answer is (a)

2. A person is disqualified from serving as a juror for 10 years if they have:
   (a) been cautioned by the police
   (b) received a speeding ticket
   (c) received a community sentence
   (d) been declared bankrupt

The correct answer is (c)

3. Routine jury vetting involves checking a juror's:
   (a) credit score
   (b) employment history
   (c) professional qualifications
   (d) criminal record

The correct answer is (d)

4. An individual's right to sit on a jury can be challenged on the grounds that:
   (a) he looks like he will convict the defendant
   (b) a witness in the case knows him
   (c) the defendant lives in the same town as him
   (d) the jury is unrepresentative

The correct answer is (b)

5. Section 20D of the Juries Act 1974 applies to:
   (a) the court
   (b) the defendant
   (c) the prosecutor
   (d) any person who discloses details of the jury room deliberations

The correct answer is (d)

Chapter 8: The Civil Justice System

1. The party name of a person appealing against a judicial decision is the:
   (a) claimant
   (b) plaintiff
   (c) appellant
   (d) applicant

The correct answer is (c)

2. The Overriding Objective of the Civil Procedure Rules is that cases should be dealt with:
   (a) justly
   (b) efficiently
   (c) inexpensively
   (d) proportionately

The correct answer is (a) (although the answers of (b), (c) and (d) are ways in which this can be achieved)

3. A case involving a claim for the sum of £13,500 will be heard on/in the:
   (a) small claims track
   (b) fast-track
   (c) multi-track
   (d) magistrates' court

The correct answer is (b)

4. The passing down of summary judgment means:
   (a) that the case had no realistic prospect of success
   (b) that the defendant admitted the claim
   (c) that the claimant withdrew their case
   (d) that the claim was settled out of court

The correct answer is (a)

5. Conciliation means that:
   (a) the parties decide the matters between themselves
   (b) the parties are aided in their decision-making by a third party
   (c) the matter is decided for the parties by a third party
   (d) a judge determines the outcome prior to trial

The correct answer is (b)

Chapter 9: The Criminal Justice System

1. The Crown Prosecution Service will commence a prosecution where:
   (a) it is in the public interest to do so
   (b) there is a realistic prospect of conviction
   (c) it is in the public interest to do so and there is a realistic prospect of conviction
   (d) the prosecutor believes that the defendant is guilty

The correct answer is (c)

2. The term a "realistic prospect of conviction" means:
   (a) that the trier of fact would find the defendant guilty
   (b) that the trier of fact might find the defendant guilty
   (c) that the trier of fact would be more likely than not to convict the defendant
   (d) that the trier of fact will find the defendant guilty beyond reasonable doubt

The correct answer is (c)

3. A *Newton* hearing is used to determine:
   (a) the guilt of the defendant
   (b) the facts that the defendant will be sentenced upon
   (c) the defendant's sentence
   (d) the facts of the case

The correct answer is (b)

4. An either-way offence can be tried in:
   (a) the Crown Court
   (b) the magistrates' court
   (c) either the magistrates' court or Crown Court, depending on the seriousness of the offence
   (d) the county court

The correct answer is (c)

5. An equivocal plea is where the defendant:
   (a) provides an ambiguous guilty plea
   (b) provides an ambiguous not guilty plea
   (c) provides an unambiguous guilty plea
   (d) provides an unambiguous not guilty plea

The correct answer is (a)

Chapter 10: Funding

1. Public funding was originally:
   (a) cash limited
   (b) demand fed
   (c) demand limited
   (d) cash fed

The correct answer is (b)

2. The Access to Justice Act 1999 introduced the:
   (a) Legal Services Committee
   (b) Legal Funding Committee
   (c) Legal Services Commission
   (d) Legal Funding Commission

The correct answer is (c)

3. A defendant who wishes to receive public funding for a trial in the Crown Court will have to satisfy:
   (a) a means test
   (b) a merits test
   (c) a means and merits test
   (d) nothing, as criminal representation is always publicly funded

The correct answer is (b)

4. The success fee in a Conditional Fee Agreement is a calculated percentage of:
   (a) the damages awarded in the case
   (b) the public funding granted for the case
   (c) the other side's costs
   (d) the solicitors' costs

The correct answer is (d)

5. The success fee in a Damage-Based Agreement is a calculated percentage of:
   (a) the damages awarded in the case
   (b) the public funding granted for the case
   (c) other side's costs
   (d) the solicitor's costs

The correct answer is (a)

Chapter 11: Sentencing

1. The main aim of sentencing is:
   (a) to punish
   (b) to reform
   (c) to protect the public
   (d) all of the above

The correct answer is (d)

2. The magistrates' court, when considering sentence, will:
   (a) always start by considering whether a custodial sentence is appropriate
   (b) always start by considering whether a community sentence is appropriate
   (c) always start by considering whether a fine or a discharge is appropriate
   (d) always start by imposing a custodial sentence

The correct answer is (c)

3. The Crown Court is guided in its sentencing by:
   (a) House of Lords/Supreme Court decisions
   (b) Court of Appeal decisions
   (c) Privy Council decisions
   (d) other Crown Court cases

The correct answer is (b)

4. Adherence to the totality principle means that a sentencer should:
   (a) impose the maximum sentence possible for the offences in question
   (b) impose the minimum sentence possible for the offences in question
   (c) take into account the overall level of seriousness of the offences and sentence proportionally to this
   (d) impose whatever level of sentence they feel like based upon their personal opinions

The correct answer is (c)

5. The maximum fine that can be imposed by the magistrates' court is to be:
   (a) £10,000
   (b) unlimited
   (c) £1,000
   (d) £5,000

The correct answer is (b)

Chapter 12: Appeals

1. A prosecution appeal against an unduly lenient sentence goes to the:
   (a) Supreme Court
   (b) Court of Appeal
   (c) High Court
   (d) Privy Council

The correct answer is (b)

2. A prosecution appeal against an acquittal tainted by intimidation goes to the:
   (a) Supreme Court
   (b) Court of Appeal
   (c) High Court
   (d) Privy Council

The correct answer is (c)

3. If, after an appeal from the magistrates' court to the Crown Court for a trial de novo, the defendant still wishes to appeal, he can do so by:
   (a) appealing to the Court of Appeal
   (b) appealing to the Court of Appeal by way of case stated
   (c) appealing to the High Court
   (d) appealing to the High Court by way of case stated

The correct answer is (d)

4. In a civil claim, an appeal from the decision of a district judge in the High Court would go to:
   (a) a circuit judge
   (b) a High Court judge
   (c) the Court of Appeal
   (d) the Supreme Court

The correct answer is (b)

5. The term "Wednesbury unreasonableness" means that:

(a) the judge was unreasonable on a Wednesday

(b) the judge who was unreasonable was called Wednesbury

(c) the judge made a decision with which the appealing party disagreed

(d) the judge made a decision that was completely outrageous

The correct answer is (d)

Index

This index has been prepared using Sweet and Maxwell's Legal Taxonomy. Main index entries conform to keywords provided by the Legal Taxonomy except where references to specific documents or non-standard terms (denoted by quotation marks) have been included. These keywords provide a means of identifying similar concepts in other Sweet & Maxwell publications and online services to which keywords from the Legal Taxonomy have been applied. Readers may find some minor differences between terms used in the text and those which appear in the index.

Suggestions to **sweetandmaxwell.taxonomy@tr.com**

(All references are to paragraph number)

The 11th edition has been fully revised to incorporate the many developments in the field. Features of the new edition include:

- Reflection of the changing patterns in the English rules of the conflict of laws as the courts continue to deal with the new position following the departure of the United Kingdom from the European Union.
- Extensive changes in the material on jurisdiction (following the rejection of the UK's application to rejoin the Lugano Convention), including the Hague Choice of Court Convention and the further development of the English rules as to service out of the jurisdiction.
- New material on the recognition of foreign judgments with the coming into effect in the United Kingdom of the Hague Judgments Convention.
- Much rewriting in the field of international family law where the Hague Child Protection Convention has become a central feature of English practice; and continued attention to developments relating to the Rome Regulations, the assimilated EU legislation central to many aspects of international commercial law.
- In many parts of the book, a greater emphasis on the work of the Hague Conference on Private International Law; many of its conventions now being reflected in English law, and its work having assumed greater importance as the influence of EU law has declined.
- Inclusion of new case-law, including no fewer than 13 decisions of the UK Supreme Court, reflecting the growing practical importance of the subject.
- Rewritten and reordered material (including on such varied topics as the act of state doctrine and parentage) designed to help the reader to a critical understanding of the subject.